Inside
Adobe Photoshop
for Windows

Gary Bouton
Barbara Bouton

NRP
NEW RIDERS
PUBLISHING

New Riders Publishing, Indianapolis, Indiana

Inside Adobe Photoshop for Windows

By Gary David Bouton
   Barbara Mancuso Bouton

Published by:
New Riders Publishing
201 West 103rd Street
Indianapolis, Indiana 46290
317-581-3871

Copyright © 1994 by New Riders Publishing

Printed in the United States of America 2 3 4 5 6 7 8 9 0

Library of Congress Cataloging-in-Publication Data

```
Bouton, Gary David, 1955-
    Inside Adobe Photoshop for Windows / Barbara Mancuso
  Bouton, Gary David Bouton.
      p.        cm.
    Includes index.
    ISBN 1-56205-259-4  :  $42.00
    1. Computer graphics.   2. Adobe Photoshop for Windows.
  I. Bouton, Gary David, 1953-       .   II. Title.
  T385.B682    1993
  006.6'869--dc20
                                        93-39366
                                        CIP
```

Warning and Disclaimer

Publisher	**Lloyd J. Short**
Associate Publisher	**Tim Huddleston**
Acquisitions Manager	**Cheri Robinson**
Managing Editor	**Matthew Morrill**
Marketing Manager	**Ray Robinson**

Acquisitions Editor

Alicia Krakovitz

Product Director

Cheri Robinson

Production Editor

Rob Lawson

Editors

Gail S. Burlakoff
Patrice Hartmann
Andy Saff
Cliff Shubs
Suzanne Snyder
Steve Weiss

Technical Editors

Kathy Hanley
Jason Kuffer

Acquisitions Coordinator

Stacey Beheler

Publisher's Assistant

Melissa Lynch

Editorial Assistant

Karen Opal

Imprint Manager

Juli Cook

Production Analyst

Mary Beth Wakefield

Book Design

Roger Morgan

Production Team

Nick Anderson
Lisa Daugherty
Rich Evers
Dennis Clay Hager
Stephanie McComb
Rochelle Palma
Kim Scott
Amy Shatz
Elaine Webber
Alyssa Yesh

Proofreaders

Ayrika Bryant
Terri Edwards
George Bloom
Kim Hannel
Jenny Kucera
Jamie Milazzo
Ryan Rader
Tonya R. Simpson
SA Springer
Kris Simmons
Suzanne Tully
Dennis Wesner

Indexer

Jennifer Eberhardt

About the Authors

Gary David Bouton has been an illustrator, designer, and art director for almost 20 years, and presently uses computer technology to give complex visual ideas shape and exposure in the real world. Now an author, Gary hopes to help others with similar backgrounds in the traditional communications arts, to make the cross-over between conventional, physical tools, and their digital equivalents through books like *Inside Adobe Photoshop*. As Gary puts it, "Every artist's tool has its binary alter-ego in PC applications, with the possible exception of a virtual screwdriver to pry the top off a virtual paint can."

He and his wife are owners of Exclamat!ons, a company "that polishes rough ideas" for clients whose needs vary from electronic presentations to desktop publishing. Gary is more than a believer in the personal computer's capability to magnify productivity and to lend incredible precision to a craft—the work, the exercises, and the techniques developed through practice all prove it throughout this book.

Inside Adobe Photoshop is Gary's second New Riders book, and the first one he has collaborated on with his wife, Barbara. A winner in CorelDRAW!'s International Design Contest for two years in a row, Gary also is involved with the Central New York PC Users Group. As Editor of the group's newsletter, Gary received the Intergalactic Newsletter Competition's award for best publication in its category in 1993, which was sponsored by InfoWorld and Lotus.

Barbara's technical and artistic contributions to *Inside Adobe Photoshop* stem from a rich background in the IBM-PC platform. She is also a consultant, a WordPerfect Certified Resource, a contributing author to NRP's *Inside WordPerfect 6 for Windows,* and a Director of CNYPCUG. Barbara's personal commitments to education and communication are only equaled by her desire to learn about cutting-edge technology.

"We experimented with a lot of techniques before designing the *Inside Adobe Photoshop* exercises," says the coauthor. "Digital photography is very new to the public, yet it has a charm and fascination that is as timeless as the first hand-drawn picture." Trying something new, and approaching the conventional with a sense of freshness is a challenge for any author, and is especially demanding in the computer publication field. It is the wish of the authors that the reader can have as much fun trying and doing the exercises prepared for *Inside Adobe Photoshop* as the authors have.

The Boutons can be reached at: 7300 Cedar Post Road, No. A31, Liverpool, New York, U.S. 13088-4843. Pizza Hut deliveries are always welcome, even if the order was placed by someone else, and you rang the wrong doorbell.

Acknowledgments

The list of people we need to thank, for their words, deeds, and gracious contributions to *Inside Adobe Photoshop* is so massive, we wish we could present it to you in JPEG format! You've already read the "set up" for acknowledgments in other books, so imagine a similar one here, so we can give more room on these pages for those who deserve it!

We want to thank:

- ✔ Cheri Robinson, Acquisitions Manager at New Riders Publishing, for allowing us the leeway to tell the Photoshop Story in a way that gives the person interested in computer graphics a running start. She understands that authoring is an art, and let us practice the trade the way we know best.

- ✔ Lead Editor Rob Lawson, for patiently sticking this out with us through the flu season and the holidays, so we could get the book out on schedule. Even up to our "drop dead" date on IAPSFW, you let us tune, refine, and verify our information, so we'd have the most accurate, freshest book of its kind to share with our readers. Rob, you have a spirit and dedication that's hard to match, you went the extra kilometer, and we forgive you for liking Gary Larson's cartoons better than Gary Bouton's!

- ✔ Stacey Beheler at NRP, whom authors don't thank enough. Stacey contacted the hardware and software vendors that put the gas in the tank of this book. Stacey, all our efforts would have come to a grinding halt were it not for your magnificent ability to provide for us at all the right times.

- ✔ Editor Gail Burlakoff for reeling us back in when the plot got too deep. A program as rich as Photoshop makes you lose sight of little things, like actually communicating (!), and you contributed to making this book more accessible to readers of all skill levels.

- ✔ Matthew Morrill, Managing Editor at NRP, and the folks in PHPD (Prentice Hall Production Department), for their valuable efforts in making this book look handsome and easy to read. Production was accomodating to a fault with last-minute changes and should be especially acknowledged for the after-hour and weekend work most authors don't get the privelege of tapping into. Who you gonna call? "Schedule Busters!" Thanks, PHPD!

- ✔ Greg Phillips at Diversified Graphics, who compiled the many TIFF images, shareware, freeware, and miscellaneousware on the companion CD that accompanies this book.

- ✔ John Niestemski of Graphic Masters, a good friend whom we went to for his exhaustive knowledge of file formats, imaging, and color theory. His willingness to share that knowledge (and his film recorder!) was an invaluable contribution to the authors' education, and in turn, for our readers.

- ✔ Adobe Senior Technical Support Person Fred Barling, who kept us straight arrows on the finer points of Photoshop. Fred, we thank you for your patience, and the artist's angle in your explanations.

✔ Mike Groh, who helped get the work back and forth from Syracuse to Indy during an all-time record snowstorm, which shut down our airport. No airport, no FedEx, but Mike was able to modem us everything we needed to complete the very last chapters. Thanks, Mike, and we promise to get a faster modem real soon. :)

✔ Corel Corporation's Jeff Johnson, Mike Bellefeuille, Bill Cullen, and Kerry Williams, for CorelSCSI! and other support items we needed. You folks were just as gracious and responsive to our requests concerning this book, as you were when we wrote *CorelDRAW! for Non-Nerds*. We wish every company could get behind a concept with the generosity and enthusiasm you've displayed.

✔ Jan Sandford at Pixar, who provided us with their software to create a lot of the wonderful figures in this book. Jan, you people are tops, and we hope Pixar decides to let other Mac and graphic workstation apps port to the IBM-PC.

✔ Pam Hogarth and Douglas Richard, CEO of Visual Software, for lending their Renderize for Windows program to the cause of state-of-the-art designs in this book.

✔ Carol DiSalvo at CM DiSalvo Photography, for allowing us to use the beautiful photo of Lauriellen in one of our chapter exercises.

✔ Lauriellen Murphy, for permitting us to use Carol's picture of her in our book. Laur, you didn't even ask me for a decent explanation when I made the request! Friendship of this order can only hope to be repaid in kind. Say 'hi' to pussycats for us.

✔ Don Leclair of Toggle Booleans, for graciously allowing us to put a lot of his nutty, nutty "Non-Productivity" tools on the companion CD. Don, you're a man of diverse interests and skills. Who else could have invented something as necessary and useful as a Resource Monitor for Windows, then in the same shareware bundle feature a desktop Elvis Detector? Don't be cruel, Don. And thanks again!

✔ Robyn Jenkins at Logitech, for extended use of their Color ScanMan and FotoMan digital camera.

✔ Lou Misenti, for allowing us to poke the Logitech FotoMan digital camera in his face all too early on a Sunday morning.

✔ The folks at Procom Technology, for the use of their PhotoCD disk drive.

✔ Andy Chang and Yvonne Knott at UMAX, for the use of their model 840 flatbed color scanner.

✔ Burt Holmes at the Wacom Company.

✔ Daryl Wise at Fractal Design Corporation.

✔ JASC, Inc, Niko-Mak, and Phil Katz at PKWARE, Inc for making great shareware.

✔ Cindy Smith and Chuck Richburg at Capitol Filmworks.

✔ Alan Reed at ImageTects, for the use of some of the texture images on the companion CD.

✔ Richard Bloom at Slide Systems, Inc., for getting the ball rolling for this book with some knockout chromes of our work.

vii

- ✔ Mike Stewart at Kodak PhotoCD Hotline Technical Services for his insight into this new technology both as a technical support person and as an experienced photographer. Also Cindy Traino and Paul McAfee at Kodak.

- ✔ David Bouton, for acting as our professional model in four chapters in this book, and never complaining once about the circumstances we put him through, the hours, or the pay. Dave, you're everything a brother should be about. Thank you.

- ✔ The folks at Federal Express, whose bonded couriers delivered our manuscripts to NRP in Indiana with unswaying dedication and great alacrity. FedEx employees saw us more than our parents did while this book was being written. We've come to really like purple and orange, and we may have our car painted in this scheme in hopes it'll make it run faster.

- ✔ Sweetheart Diary, just up the road a piece, for the coffee and doughnuts that magically inspired the ink to flow at all odd hours.

Trademark Acknowledgments

Adobe, Adobe Type Manager, ATM, PostScript, Adobe Illustrator are registered trademarks, and Adobe Photoshop is a trademark of Adobe Systems, Incorporated.

Aldus FreeHand and PageMaker are registered trademarks and Aldus Gallery Effects is a trademark of Aldus Corporation.

Amiga is a registered trademark of Commodore-Amiga, Inc.

Bernoulli and Iomega are registered trademarks of the Iomega Corporation.

Central Point PC Tools and PC Tools are trademarks of Central Point Software, Inc.

CompuServe is a registered trademark, GIF is a service mark, and Graphic Interchange Format is a copyright by CompuServe Incorporated.

Corel, Corel Professional Photos, Corel ArtView, CorelMosaic, Corel PhotoCD Lab, Corel Wallpaper Flipper, CorelSCSI!, and CorelDRAW! are trademarks of Corel Systems Corporation.

Digix is a service mark of Digix Imaging.

Fractal Design Painter is a registered trademark of Fractal Design Corporation.

Lotus and Freelance Graphics are registered trademarks of Lotus Development Corp.

Harvard Graphics is a registered trademark of Software Publishing Corporation.

Helvetica, Times, and Times Roman are registered trademarks of Linotype Ag and/or its subsidiaries.

HP and LaserJet are registered trademarks of Hewlett Packard Company.

IBM is a registered trademark of International Business Machines Corporation.

ImageCELs is a registered trademark and IMAGETECTS is a trademark of IMAGETECTS.

Kodak, Kodak PhotoCD, Kodak PhotoCD Access, Kodak Acquire Module for Photoshop, Kodak Shoebox are trademark and/or copyrighted materials of the Eastman Kodak Company.

Dedication

To Wilma, John, Eileen, and Jack, our parents, who, as all understanding parents do, dismissed us from attending family functions with only .7 percent guilt while we assembled images, words, and equipment to do our part in creating this book. Your love and devotion through the years has made us want to pass *our* passion on to our readers. And we know you're excited for us about that. Because this stuff *is* exciting!

New Riders Publishing

The staff of New Riders Publishing is committed to bringing you the very best in computer reference material. Each New Riders book is the result of months of work by authors and staff, who research and refine the information contained within its covers.

As part of this commitment to you, the NRP reader, New Riders invites your input. Please let us know if you enjoy this book, if you have trouble with the information and examples presented, or if you have a suggestion for the next edition.

If you have a comment or question about any New Riders book, please contact NRP at the following address:

New Riders Publishing
Attn: Associate Publisher
201 W. 103rd Street
Indianapolis, Indiana 46290
Fax: (317) 581-4670

New Riders Publishing also maintains a CompuServe forum. We welcome your participation in this forum (**GO NEWRIDERS**). Please feel free to post a public message there if you have a question or comment about this or any other New Riders product. If you prefer, however, you can send a private message directly to this book's product director at (73164,2773).

We will respond to as many readers as we can. Your name, address, phone number, or electronic mail ID will never become a part of a mailing list or be used for any purpose other than to help us continue to bring you the best books possible.

Please note that the New Riders staff cannot serve as a technical resource for Adobe Photoshop-related questions, including hardware- or software-related problems. Refer to the documentation that accompanies your hardware or software package for help with specific problems.

Thank you for selecting *Inside Adobe Photoshop for Windows*!

Contents at a Glance

Table of Contents

Imaging with Photoshop

A dobe Photoshop is acknowledged in professional fields as *the* cutting-edge program, the final word in image editing. It has been used for years to edit and create images as diverse as cosmetic ads, news photos, motion picture footage, animation cells, and fine artwork. Yet when John Warnock, Adobe's CEO, was asked in an interview about where his company stood technologically, he replied with a laugh, "Oh, we're always at the beginning!" And this is where we'll begin our adventures with Adobe Photoshop.

As a new Adobe Photoshop user, you've just leapt into the big league. Photoshop is the image editing software of choice for photographers, retouchers, graphic artists, and designers. Hollywood and Madison Avenue use Photoshop to make images come alive and to add magic to images that lack that certain "something." Photoshop is a professional tool to be sure. But you *don't* have to own a Fortune 500 company to find lots of uses for it, or have a pair of hands like DaVinci to use it. *Inside Adobe Photoshop for Windows* will show you how to make the best use of the program, and the best use of your skills. It can be a challenge starting something new, but where we begin exploring Photoshop is on the ground floor, the most basic element people have to work with — the graphic *image*.

There are 1,001 ways a picture can go bad on its way from the designer's eye to the finished product. It is rare indeed to find a picture or image that couldn't use help; specifically,

Photoshop's help. Photoshop contains all the tools for retouching, compensating, correcting, enhancing, and manipulating images at all stages of their creation.

Although most people use Photoshop to retouch photographs, Photoshop is more than this. It is a *digital imaging* program. It can work with a wide spectrum of source material—still photos, video and film frames, paintings that have been digitized . . . even computer graphics that have no roots in the physical world!

All of this is possible because computers handle visual material as *digital data*—lots of little ones and zeros. Our adventure in the "digital darkroom" with Photoshop, and the manipulation of what we see, is called *imaging*, not "photography," and not "painting." Here's why . . .

The All-Encompassing "Imaging"

To a computer, the information that makes up a photograph, drawing, or spreadsheet is the same—it's a lot of mathematics that can be *manipulated*. You recognize a digitized photo on your monitor as a photo, a cartoon as a cartoon, and so on, and never the twain shall meet. The computer, from the other side of the cathode tube, sees it all the same way—it's data that describes an image that can be changed by the user.

Our PC's ignorance about image types, then, is our gain. The possibilities for spectacular melding and modifying of images are *endless*! It means you can put drawings in your photos, and photos in your drawings, because to the computer they are the same thing.

Hand retouching photographs is hard work and expensive to have done. Adding type to a drawing is not easy and requires a separate discipline. Creating photo or multimedia collages is painstaking, exacting work that often requires razor-sharp tools and noxious fumes. But *imaging* with Photoshop is done in a common workspace where anything that's visual can be worked on with an integrated set of tools.

In this book, we'll show you how to take images and make the most of them, regardless of their physical origin. Even if you have an idea in your head that *cannot be photographed* in the real world, we'll show you how Photoshop, and some programs that work with Photoshop, can make your ideas a reality.

So, is our adventure in Photoshop about drawing, painting, photography, typography, or pure imagination? The answer is "Yes." Imaging encompasses all these things, and it's all because you're simply doing one thing with your computer—you're handling data.

Where *Inside Adobe Photoshop* Fits In

We've mentioned a little about imaging and Photoshop here, but not very much about this book. *Inside Adobe Photoshop* is not a rehash of the *Owner's Manual* to the program. *Inside Adobe Photoshop* is a hands-on book full of exercises that directly relate to your own work.

The *Inside Photoshop* exercises, along with the images we provide you with on the companion CD, will show you methods to overcome many of the most common obstacles you find separating you from an excellent, finished, commercially viable image. Through the course of this book, you'll learn that previously insurmountable tasks are actually the "easy stuff" when Photoshop and your PC are used. Then, we'll take you beyond to a plateau of the seemingly impossible, where your imagination, unencumbered by chemical photography and framed canvas, can breathe and express itself freely. Imaging begins with imagination, and this book and Photoshop will be your guides.

David Oglivy, owner of one of New York's most prestigious advertising agencies, once commented about the creative role of people in his trade, "It's a lot easier to take a great idea and tone it down, than to try to make a dull idea great." If this strikes a chord in you, if you feel a profound need for that "I don't know what" to get your work off the pavement and give it wings, you're starting in the right place! Let's talk about the approach to this book before your approach to Adobe Photoshop.

Preparing for Photoshop

Photoshop lives up to its reputation, and yields better and more sophisticated results than the average computer program. But to do so, it requires a computer *setup* with higher than average capabilities. The hardware requirements that Adobe puts on the outside of the box—a 386 or better processor, 4M of RAM, a VGA display adapter and monitor, and a mouse—are the bare minimums. The adage, "You get what you pay for" holds true here. Getting results with the minimums will be tedious, and you will be limited in what you achieve. Trust us. We're talking out of class. You will *not* be happy with the minimum configuration.

System Configurations

We recommend at *least* a 486 processor, 8 to 12M of RAM, a display adapter and monitor able to display 24-bit, 16.7 million colors, and 60M of free space on a 200M hard disk. That's to learn Photoshop through this book, with no extracurricular activities. If you're serious about imaging, as a profession or even as a hobby, a PhotoCD-capable, XA-standard CD-ROM disk drive, and a color scanner should be additions to your base-system configuration as soon as your wallet heals! PhotoCDs and scanners are vital links to your computer to bring image samples from the physical world to your Photoshop workspace.

The exercises in this book were created using systems that are not all that exotic when compared to industry preferences and budgets for imaging. We don't believe them to be out of the reach of a serious creative type. We used 486DX2 66MHz processors, 20M of RAM, a 24-bit display adapter (Diamond Stealth with 1M of Video Ram), and compatible monitors.

...In Addition to the Photoshop Software

On the software side, you must have *Adobe Photoshop 2.5 for Windows* (this is a fairly obvious one), *Microsoft Windows 3.1*, and DOS 5 or 6. We strongly recommend that you use an upper-memory manager like Helix's *Netroom 3.0* or Quarterdeck's *QEMM*. You should also have a disk compression program like Stac's *Stacker 3.x* to expand your hard disk's storage capacity further than you imagine because high-quality digital images are typically more than 1 or 2M *each*. A hard disk optimizing program, like Symantecs' *Norton Speed Disk* can also speed your work up by defragmenting disk information, so it can be read by your PC more quickly. And you'll want to use a backup program regularly, too, because the only way to completely insure your imaging work is to keep a copy separate from your hard disk.

We describe in greater detail the hows and whys of the hardware and software that we recommend in Chapters 1 and 2.

We are also assuming that in addition to having all the "right" hardware and software installed and running that you are familiar with Windows 3.1 and that you know how to copy, save, and delete files; make directories; back up your work; and are fairly comfortable navigating a 101 PC keyboard and a mouse.

Syntax: How To Read the "Shorthands" in Our Exercises

Each *Inside Adobe Photoshop* exercise is laid out step-by-step. If you follow along, your screen should look exactly like our book's figures (except yours will be in color)! Each exercise is set up in a two-column format—in the left column is what you should do, and in the right column is what will happen when you do it or an explanation of why we asked you to do a particular step.

Most of Photoshop's tools have different, or enhanced functions when you hold down the Shift, Alt, or Ctrl keys while you mouse click, or press other keyboard keys. These commands appear in exercises as Ctrl+plus key, Alt+click, Ctrl+D, and so on. Function keys appear as F1, F2, F3, and up.

Special Note to Southpaws

This book was written a little chauvinistically, in that we assume you are right-handed, and haven't reset the mouse in Windows Control Panel to be a "right-click" mouse. If you have, use the right button instead of the left one in the following situations. *Dragging* in this book refers to holding down the *left* mouse button and moving the mouse. *Click* means to press and release the left mouse button once, *double-click* means to quickly press the left mouse button twice, and directions like *Shift+Click* means that you should hold down the Shift key while you click with the left mouse button.

Here's a short exercise to help you get familiar with our exercise format.

Creating a Minimalist Painting

Choose **F**ile, **N**ew (or press Ctrl+N)	Calls up Photoshop's New options box.
Type **640** in the Image Size **W**idth box, and select pixels from the drop-down list	Establishes the width of the image window you are creating.
Type **480** in the Image Size H**ei**ght box, and select pixels from the drop-down list	Establishes the height of the image window you are creating.
Type **72** in the **R**esolution box, and select pixels/inch from the drop-down list	Specifies how many pixels per inch your new image will be created at.
Choose **RGB Color** from the Mode drop-down list	Tells Photoshop you want to work in 16.7 million colors.
Click on **OK**	Confirms your selections, and you are returned to Photoshop's workspace, with a new image window, Untitlcd-1.
Choose the Paintbrush tool from the toolbox	This is the tool for applying foreground color to an image.
Click on a medium tip on the Brushes palette	Sets the characteristics for how the Paintbrush tool applies foreground color.
Click and drag the cursor diagonally across UNTITLED-1	Applies foreground color to the new image.

There are more commands in store, for sure, and we reference "key" operations with figures along the way, but this is how you'll find all the exercises set up.

Other Conventions Used in This Book

Throughout this book, conventions are used to help you distinguish various elements of Windows, DOS, their system files, and sample data. These conventions include the following:

Special Text

✔ **Shortcut keys.** These accelerator keys sometimes appear in the text, but normally appear in the exercises to indicate a keyboard technique for achieving several steps with a couple of keystrokes. For example, (Ctrl+N) is the shortcut key for calling up Photoshop's **N**ew options dialog box.

✔ **Key1+Key2.** When you see a plus sign (+) between key names, hold down the first key while you press the second key. Then release both keys. If, for example, you see "Press Ctrl+F2," hold down the Ctrl key and press the F2 function key, then release both keys.

✔ **Hot Keys.** On-screen, Windows underlines the letters on some menu names, file names, and option names. The File menu name, for example, is displayed on-screen as **F**ile. This underlined letter is the letter you type to choose that menu, command, or option. In this book, such letters are displayed in bold, underlined type: **F**ile.

✔ Information you type is in **boldface**. This rule applies to individual letters, numbers, and text strings. The convention, however, does not apply to special keys, such as Enter, Delete, Tab, Esc, or Ctrl.

✔ New terms appear in *italic*.

✔ Text that is displayed on-screen but is not part of Windows or a Windows application—such as DOS prompts and messages—appear in a `special monospace typeface`.

✔ In the text, function keys are identified as F1, F2, F3, and so on.

Mouse Notes

This book repeatedly uses terms that refer to mouse techniques: *click, double-click, Shift-click, drag,* and *Marquee-zoom. Clicking* on an object or menu item selects the object or item. *Double-clicking* usually performs a function, without the need to click an OK button in a dialog box. With Photoshop's selection tools (identified in upcoming chapters), you use *Shift-clicking* to select more than one object. By holding down Shift, you add objects to the already selected objects. *Dragging* means to hold the mouse button and move the mouse and on-screen pointer to a new location, usually taking the selected area to the new position. *Marquee-dragging* is performed by clicking, then diagonally dragging, which produces different results depending on which Photoshop tool you have chosen. You Marquee-zoom into a view of an image when you click and diagonally drag using the Zoom tool, whereas you Marquee-select an image area when you have the Rectangular marquee tool chosen. In the latter instance, using the mouse pointer, you click and drag a rectangle around the objects to be selected.

The program Adobe Photoshop for Windows is commonly referred to in this book by its nickname, Photoshop.

Reader Icon Aides

This book also has margin icons that provide added information, including notes, tips, and stops that help you use the book and the program. You can find these margin icons easily and refer to them in the future. Examples of each are included on this page.

A *note* includes "extra" information that you should find useful but that complements the discussion at hand instead of being a direct part of it.

A *tip* provides quick instructions for getting the most from Photoshop. A tip might show you ways to conserve memory or speed up a procedure, or provide ideas for creating specific types of artwork.

A *Stop* is a signpost that tells you to proceed with caution before executing an upcoming step. No one likes to make a mistake that costs time, particularly when it's over a paying assignment, so the text points out potential areas to watch out for when working with Photoshop.

The Six Parts to *Inside Adobe Photoshop*

Inside Adobe Photoshop is divided into six parts, and five of these are broken down into chapters. The exercises are goal-oriented, and have a clear beginning and end, so you can put this book down once in a while without losing where you left off! Each part addresses a different aspect of imaging with Photoshop. Part One begins with working definitions of different computer graphics types, explains how to optimize Photoshop to work in it comfortably and speedily, and gives you a road test of all the tools you'll be using in future exercises.

Part I: From the Source to the Sample

Part One starts with some information that makes using Photoshop with digital images more meaningful. If you've had experience in a traditional, chemical darkroom, you'll want to check out Chapter 1, which defines image types and relates how each one is equivalent to physical images you may have experience with.

Chapter 2 is all about *acquisition techniques*, and how to best use a scanner to make a copy of a physical image you can modify as a datastream inside your PC.

Chapter 3 shows you the hows and whys of gamma correction, and how to set yourself up for Kodak's PhotoCD technology, perhaps the most exciting new way you can work with digital images in Photoshop.

Chapters 4 and 5 give you hands-on, trial-size helpings of Photoshop's workspace, to give you a feel for the power and integration of the tools. And we'll show you how to set defaults (which Photoshop has tons of), to make working with the program easier. We also get into the tuning of your monitor and PC, to give you the most accurate look at images you will learn to edit.

Part II: Steak 'n Potatoes Assignments

This is where we put some of Photoshop's tools, filters, and effects to the test in everyday situations. You'll quickly learn how to overcome workaday photo errors and learn simple methods for making a common photograph sparkle.

Chapters 6 and 7 are an in-depth two-parter on the fine points of restoring a photograph that's been aged and damaged.

Chapter 8 teaches you how to handle text in a graphical image. Adobe's other claim to fame is Adobe Type Manager, so you'd better believe that Photoshop can do some pretty sophisticated stuff in integrating type within a digital image.

Chapter 9 is devoted to all the wonderful retouching work you can do with a single tool, Photoshop's Rubber Stamp. It's only part of Photoshop's complete set of tools, but its robustness in its capability to do incredible retouching work deserves the complete coverage all its own.

Chapter 10 is our "integrating" chapter, which explores how new tools work in combination with the ones you've become familiar with. *Technique* is emphasized throughout this book, and learning how to select and use the right tools for an assignment is a rite of passing the imaging-type person needs in order to work at a professional level.

Part III: Gourmet Assignments

As you quickly grow comfortable with imaging, Photoshop-style, you'll become hungrier for more sophisticated imaging challenges. We move from the workaday to very special assignments in this part. These chapters contain exercises that take your skills and work from great to a certain level of recognition in professional business circles.

Chapter 11 shows you the ins and outs of retouching an image of a house to postcard perfection. If you do industrial or commercial photography for a living, this chapter is for you.

Chapter 12 gets a model off the grass in the suburbs and onto the beach in sunny Florida. Find the secrets for seamless photographic combinations right here.

Chapter 13 has an exercise demonstrating how to create a dream scene out of two lifeless images. You'll learn how to create reflections in an image that weren't originally photographed, and how to color balance a cold, harsh landscape into a warm, breathtaking landscape.

Chapter 14 graduates the Photoshop user from creating pleasing scenes to impossible ones. "Special Effects with Ordinary Photos" gives the user a feel for accomplishing surreal, original, provoking images using only a golf course and a couple of plastic chess pieces!

Chapter 15 shows you how to create a photo-collage with impact. Using different poses of the same model, we create a "group" photo that contains all the reality people typically see in a physical photo. Learn how to manipulate people in this chapter. *Digitally*, of course!

Chapter 16 is devoted to the black-and-white, or Grayscale, image. The world still publishes in black and white, and this chapter shows you how to create powerful, striking photographs in this Photoshop mode.

Part IV: Fantastic Assignments

This is the part a lot of imaging people will buy into the heaviest. For all the PC world has been told about the powers of Photoshop, it's only been available for Windows since January of 1993. Creating Virtual Reality via Photoshop is our destination in Part IV's chapters.

Chapter 17 shows how applications other than Photoshop can be used to create a spectacular, high-end graphic. Photoshop is our home-base as we go shopping in CorelDRAW! and Typestry for the raw elements we integrate using the program.

Chapter 18 uses Fractal Design Painter along with Photoshop to create a photorealistic graphic out of nothing but a few fractal textures, an EPS file or two, and your own skills.

Chapter 19 goes one step beyond reality, as we show you how to build an image for a science-fiction book cover. It's not hyper, or even ultra-reality. *Virtual* reality and Photoshop go hand in hand as we explore the how-tos of fantastic imagery.

Part V: Inking Up and Doing Yourself a Service

Becoming a master at imaging through Photoshop doesn't do much good unless you can show your work to the world on hard copy. The final part of our book helps you get a handle on the fine points of mapping digital images to a physical medium instead of to your monitor.

Chapter 20 is all about questions, answers, and little-known math that play a very direct role in your printed image's quality. How many shades of gray can your laser printer produce? What's a halftone cell? Even if you've never asked yourself these, or dozens more questions, you will eventually. And Chapter 20 is where some of the answers lie.

Chapter 21 is a guide to possibly the best resource an imaging-type person could have. The imaging center, or service bureau, has lots of expensive hardware, and trained professionals whose responsibility is to make incredible slides and prints out of your image files. No, it's not too good to be true, but the service bureau is definitely a stop on your road to wonderful computer graphics, and we knock on their door for you here.

By the time you've done all the exercises in this book, you'll have more questions than answers about your new imaging skills and Photoshop. A good one that every successful artist asks himself is, "How good am I?" And it's all relative. We figure, hey, we don't know each and every one of our readers, so we can assist in a pretty objective fashion with the pressing questions you may have about the whole process of creating images out of light. Chapter 22 is a peer-to-peer reflection on your new skills, ambitions, and the possibilities that are out in the real world once you shut the PC off.

Part VI: Appendixes

Don't you hate getting to the end of a good book, and then find out the authors skimped on the research work they put into it?! Everyone who works with a PC has a natural curiosity about where they can learn more, where the best sources are for more tools, and what stuff means when they read it out of context.

Inside Adobe Photoshop's Appendix A is a complete resource guide where suppliers of software, hardware, and support services are located. And a lot of the listings are for companies that helped in the creation of this book, so think of this as sort of a "private stock" for a privileged few!

Back of the Book

Our Super-Glossary is here to *honestly* help you, when it comes to the obscure terminology that Photoshop and the field of digital imaging use. Our listing is more in-depth than typical glossary entries, and it offers helpful asides that actually tell you where you can *find* a function under a menu in Photoshop.

A good judge of a book is its index. *Inside Adobe Photoshop* has been diligently, thoroughly, exhaustively indexed.

Folks Just Like You

Our equipment and resources for getting the images we've included on the companion CD, and used in this book, are middle of the road. We used available lighting most of the time, a 35mm SLR camera, and the patience of a lot of family and friends as subjects. We believe that business professionals will see where these examples can lead with their own work, and novices won't be put off by the loftiness of an image outside of their grasp.

We kept in mind while designing *Inside Adobe Photoshop*'s exercises that techniques you'll learn can be tailored and patterned toward *your own* work. For the artist in us all, we've devoted some space to art for art's sake. We've also tried to be as commercial as possible because we understand the appeal of Photoshop to commerce, and we'd like you to enjoy both the personal and business rewards of using Photoshop.

Electronic imaging is such a wonderful, magical thing that it's impossible to keep the child in us quiet, and for that reason, some of our exercises are a little "larger than life." We want to show you some of the fun we've had with a very serious product, and perhaps that will kindle or fan the flame of the creative spark in you, as well.

From both ends of the spectrum, Photoshop and this book are within easy reach. But the proof is in the learning.

So let's get started!

Part I

From the Source to the Sample

Chapter Snapshot

In this chapter, you learn how to:

✔ Recognize the unique
   properties of different types of images

✔ Manipulate image qualities
   to display a digital image in its best light

✔ Identify the different kinds of file
   formats that can be saved as a digital image

CHAPTER

Understanding Image Types, Formats, and Resolutions

As an artist, understanding the technical workings of your tools, like a camera, has led you to gain more control over a finished piece. And whenever you add a new tool to your trade, like the PC and Adobe Photoshop, you broaden your scope as an artist, but the ante is necessarily upped in the technical-understanding area. Creating art out of a digital image is not a totally automated process, but it can be more fun and rewarding if you first learn the basics about the medium. Then you can move into the fun stuff more quickly. As you might expect, the correlations between a traditional, chemical photograph and a digital image are not direct ones. Each has its own peculiarities, advantages, and stumbling blocks.

Although conventional photography has produced beautiful keepsakes for almost two centuries, traditional chemical photography does have its limitations. Time fades even the best of photographic emulsions, and depending on the format of a film negative, a photo may appear smooth or extremely grainy when enlarged.

Conversely, you can easily enlarge a digital image, but the resulting computer file is preposterously large. Also, you may find it hard to sell a convincing, life-like scene expressed digitally because some people balk at the concept of a digital image.

The main difference between a photographic image and a digital image is the means by which an image is produced. But the grains in photographic film or the pixels in a data stream are simply two paths to a common goal: to communicate an image to the viewer.

What You Get Is What You See

Digital imaging and traditional chemical photography share a closeness, as different mediums used to express ideas, as you'll see throughout this book. Don't think of electronic images as a compartmentalized technology set apart from the chemical photo, because both media depend on one another at this time in history and can actually benefit from their "alter ego's" strong points. Chemical photography is a static medium in which the image is actually fixed on a coated surface and cannot be changed within a session; however, an experienced user can enhance a photographic image by running it through a nonchemical Photoshop "bath." Digital imaging, nevertheless, would be an impoverished medium without a camera lens to capture the original image that Photoshop manipulates.

Microsoft Windows *WYSIWYG* (what you see is what you get) capability ensures that the files you acquire, view, and build are mapped the same way to the monitor as they are output to the printer. Usually, for spreadsheets and word processing, you can trust WYSIWYG and perform your work without considering *how* WYSIWYG works.

Photoshop, being a Windows program, obeys the WYSIWYG rule. However, if you're going to do extraordinary things with images, you need to understand why *the images* behave as they do in various circumstances.

From the time that you capture a digital image, until it is converted to the binary soup that resides on your hard drive, the image goes through three phases in which it is viewed:

✔ The *acquisition phase*, during which a scanner (or an application software if you're *creating* an image) looks at the image

✔ The *viewing phase*, during which the image is displayed on-screen as the image is loaded in system RAM

✔ The *saving phase*, during which the computer looks at the image while saving it to your hard drive in the format of your choice

Because each image that you use may have different data properties, you must learn to evaluate each digital image and make different determinations during each phase—for example, how faithfully the image is reproduced, or how closely the digital data matches the original image.

To make these determinations, you need a basic understanding of different graphical natures of computer images. *Vector-based* images, for example, are strongly suited for technical illustrations, but leave much to be desired in attempting to portray a soft landscape with a gentle haze about it. And a line art, bitmapped-type computer image can never be scaled properly, if you ever have the occasion to need a smaller or larger, precisely readjusted image for different purposes.

A good way to see the similarities and discern the differences is in a tree-shaped diagram that illustrates the relationships that different computer images bear to one another. To see these relationships, let's start at the root of the tree and work our way up toward the branches.

The PC Graphics Tree

At the root or ground level of the computer graphics tree is a single image or collection of images. Computer animation, for example, consists of a series of still digital images. Throughout this book, you work with stills rather than animated graphics images. However, what you learn will help you to eventually use Photoshop to create animation.

At the first branch in the graphics tree, the still digital image can either exist as a vector or bitmapped (raster) image.

Vector images are not scanned; you *create* them with design software such as CorelDRAW! and Adobe Illustrator. Such software defines angles, circles, squares, and various other shapes as calculations. Vector images consist of only outlines and fills, which are created by mathematical equations when you draw a vector image. A vector graphic is also called an object-oriented drawing because an image file of this type contains discrete, separate image elements that are free to be rearranged ad infinitum. Vector graphics are also resolution-independent— you can scale a peanut as large as a Winnebago— and the image still has the same amount of visual detail, clarity, and smooth edges when printed. This resolution independence is achieved because no actual rendering (or rastering) is involved when the vector graphic is saved to a file format. It exists as *mathematical equations,* that are only rasterized to a printer after you've specified the image dimensions and resolution.

Figure 1.1 is an example of a vector graphic created in a "draw-type" program. Smooth edges and precisely placed lines in a computer graphic often point toward a vector-based application as the artist's tool.

Figure 1.2 was designed in a "bitmap-type" program. In contrast to figure 1.1, the bitmapped image evokes a warmer, softer feeling to the viewer, and is the best graphics type to portray a photographic image.

Bitmapped images are not created or saved as pure mathematical equations. Bitmapped images require your input as to the resolution and image dimensions the moment you decide to create this type of graphic. The most common way imaging-type people can create a bitmapped image is by scanning a photograph. You can also create a bitmapped image by filling an imaginary grid with colored dots, or *pixels*, using a paint-type program (rather than a vector draw-type program). Later in this chapter, you'll learn more about pixels. A bitmapped image can convey wonderful nuances and subtleties about the image it represents, mostly because it doesn't depend on line and fill math equations as vector art does.

Figure 1.3 shows the graphics tree in full bloom. As you can see, it branches out into four distinct categories of bitmapped images.

During the acquisition phase, a typical color scanner has settings that enable you to control how the scanner samples, or looks, at a physical image. Note that specifying an inappropriate setting during the acquisition phase can result in a digital image that doesn't contain enough information. Without enough information about the physical, *source* image, it's hard to do satisfying work in Photoshop.

Photoshop sees an image, after it's been digitally acquired with a scanner, as having a Mode of color-capability. Bitmap, Grayscale, and RGB modes are all examples of modes, and each refers to how thoroughly the scanner sampled visual information about the physical original. Scanners can sample a full-color image as a grayscale mode, but it deprives the acquired image of important visual content. A color image scanned at a grayscale setting can't spring back to color in Photoshop because the scanner sampled inadequate visual information.

Figure 1.1
Vector art draw-ing programs are capable of precise geometric designs.

Figure 1.2
Bit-mapped images have a different "mood" to them, compared to vector graphics.

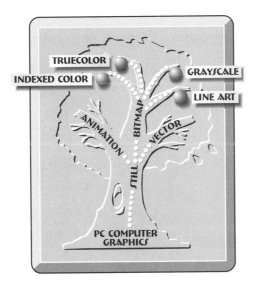

Figure 1.3
Four distinct "fruits" grow on the bitmap branch of the graphics tree.

The Line Art Graphic

Of the four "fruits" of the graphics tree, the closest to the ground is line art. Let's take a look at how meaningful line art is to your work in Photoshop.

When a pen-and-ink drawing is scanned into your computer, you can specify a scanner setting that usually is called Line Art. Software developers and artists also call this setting black and white art, bitmap art, and art that has a one-bit depth. (A *bit*, or binary digit, is the smallest amount of information that people deal with on their PC.)

When set to Line Art, the scanner looks at your source image with a one-bit color model. The scanner sees a turned-off pixel if the sample is of a black area, and a turned-on pixel if the sample is a white portion of a pen and ink drawing. Pixels, fortunately, can handle more than one bit of digital sampling information. Otherwise, color images would not be possible.

When you have an image that consists of black and white only (with no shades of gray), the Line Art scanner setting is proper and prudent. The scanning goes quickly and results in a small, manageable file with which you can work because you have perfectly captured the very limited amount of information of the original.

However, don't scan a color photo or illustration while your scanner is set to Line Art. This assigns all the glorious color information to either a black slot or a white one. (This is called letting a machine run your life and decide things for you.) The picture will look solarized or something, and you may find yourself resorting to harsh, antisocial language when this happens.

A line art scan, when acquired from a line art source image, produces a digital image similar to figure 1.4.

Figure 1.4
One-bit graphical images are small because they contain information about black and white only.

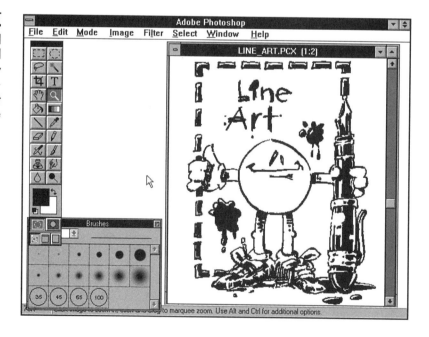

The Half-Breed Halftone

A fairly esoteric offshoot of the line art scan is the *halftone*, which is a one-bit-per-pixel sample of any sort of source material (color or not). Chapter 20 covers how *halftone screens* are important to a commercial printer's livelihood. Commercial printers use scanners in their work as well as do artists, and many printers use Photoshop for pre-press work. *Halftones* are dots that form a line on a printed page. Each halftone dot represents a density value that corresponds to a certain value of gray in an original image, since shades of gray aren't really possible to be commercially reproduced. Halftone dots are arranged in lines, and these lines fill a page with what is called a *halftone screen.*

Whether a sepia-tone antiquity or a glorious Kodachrome snapshot, a traditional photograph has *continuous tones.* A continuous-tone source image has gentle graduations from light to dark, with no "stair-steppy" increments of solid color values along the course. However, because laser printers and commercial print presses use only tonal ink dots on white paper, they cannot accurately reproduce a continuous-tone image. Therefore, when printing to anything other than photographic media, you must rely on the use of halftones.

A continuous-tone source image can be rendered as a halftone image while it is acquired with the scanner, or you can later use Photoshop to render a color scan as a halftone.

A halftone image is the digital equivalent of a continuous-tone photograph that has been screened for commercial print presses. Print presses cannot produce a continuous-tone image. Whenever an image is printed commercially (such as in a newspaper, magazine, or an FBI Wanted poster), it must be screened to create a halftone.

If you run a commercial printing press for a living, you might want to scan a continuous-tone image with a halftone setting that's optimal to print from to create press plates. You'd know what line frequency and screen angle work best with your printing press and the types of ink you use. But you'd also have to forgo any of Photoshop's wonderful image enhancement powers, too, because a scanner that essentially converts a continuous-tone image to camera-ready halftone art deprives Photoshop of information to work with found in the original image.

Whereas a halftone scanner setting can make quick work of prepping a photo for press, sampling a continuous-tone image at a halftone scanner setting with hopes of modifying it later with Photoshop is a big mistake.

Figure 1.5 shows an image scanned with a halftone setting of 53 lines per inch and a screen angle of 45 degrees.

Think of halftones as a "post-production" image rather than a true digital image. Scanners, like Photoshop, handle the halftoning of continuous-tone images because halftone representations of photographic tonal values are the final conversions press people make before an image can be put on paper as ink. It's the final step to getting a digital image in a physical format, not your first step through the doors of creative image manipulation. Even though your scanner may support a halftone option, *don't* use it. Chapter 20 discusses halftones in more detail.

Figure 1.5
A halftone set-
ting changes a
continuous-tone
image into one
consisting of dots.

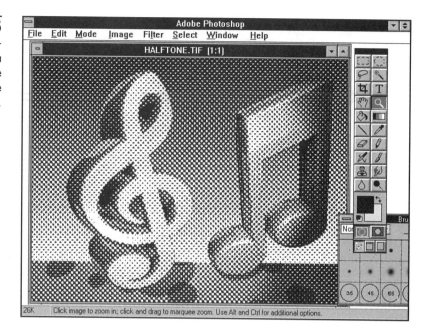

The Grayscale Image

The expression of a captured image in a one-bit line art sampling is pretty low on the bitmapped-image totem pole. If you need to retouch an 8 by 10 glossy, you may want to consider how the grayscale mode found on most scanners "fits into the picture."

Turning pixels on or off to express black or white isn't a good way to capture a source image that contains shades of color, even if the colors within the source image are only shades of gray. Taking a quantum leap here in bit-depth, you arrive at the eight-bit-per-pixel grayscale scan. A color scanner can recognize a wealth of color information, as you'll see in later sections of this chapter. For now, let's see what happens in the acquisition phase when you scan eight bits per pixel.

Binary machines express everything as 2 to a certain power. For the on/off pixel quality, when eight bits are assigned to each pixel, 2 to the 8th power results in 256 distinct combinations. The number 256 is an important one to remember because that's typically how many shades of gray can be rendered when grayscale is specified as your scanner mode. Photoshop recognizes a grayscale digital image as having a one-color (*monochrome*) channel of information consisting of 256 different levels of densities. When you save a grayscale image in a proper format, the resulting file contains a 256-shade, eight-bit digital image.

As well-adjusted, normal people, we usually refer to the snapshots taken with black and white film as being "black and white." However, they should actually be called "black and white, and a whole lotta shades in between" photos. Technically, these are monochrome images whose values run a 256-density gamut from black to white. *Gamut* is a fancy term for the range of available values within a setting on your scanner, monitor, or stored image file. To capture a monochrome photo properly, use the grayscale setting on your scanner.

Sometimes you may want to scan an aged monochrome photo in the scanner's color mode. Even though the photo was taken with black and white film years ago, some of the grayscale information has turned to brown (as with sepia tones). To capture all the available information in this photo, you must scan not only for the grayscale information, but also include information about the brown that once was part of the rest of the shades in the continuous-tone, black and white photo. Scanning such a photo with a grayscale scanner setting limits the scanner's view during the acquisition phase to only 256 levels of monochrome density. The aged brown areas need to be included as well. Think of it this way—grayscale will get you 256 shades of gray. In order to accurately capture all the tonal information in an aging photo, you need a capture setting on your scanner of 256 *and then* a few shades of brown. This puts the estimated number of colors in the image at greater than 256, which an eight-bit grayscale scan can't faithfully acquire.

An image like the one we've just described should be saved in RGB color mode, then restored using Photoshop's tools. Chapter 16 has details about working between color and black and white imaging, and Chapter 6 has the how-tos on image restoration.

Figure 1.6 shows an eight-bit-depth rendering of a grayscale image. Note the difference between this type of image and the line art image shown in figure 1.4. Although both figures are scans of artwork, figure 1.6 has much more warmth and realism than one-bit scanning can capture.

Indexed Color

As you've ascended the graphics tree so far, you've focused on the wonderful world of black and white for so long that you're probably beginning to feel like a character trapped in a Humphrey Bogart, black and white, eight-bit, grayscale movie. But as you climb still farther up the graphics tree, you find that vibrant color is blossoming from each branch.

Color information, as gathered by a scanner, seen by Photoshop, and then rendered to a file format, is fairly complex. Chapter 2 discusses the best way to view a color digital file. But before going out on a limb with color graphics types, you need to understand how Photoshop and your PC handle color.

The vast majority of color scanners currently on the market sample a color source image in a 24-bit mode. This gives you the ability to sample 16.7 million different colors in a scan of a source image. Although a source image may consist of only a handful of colors, a color scanner nevertheless acquires data and presents it in a mode *capable* of showing 16.7 million colors.

Photoshop, and many technical folks at service bureaus, call this *RGB* (red, green, and blue) color. Red, green, and blue are the building blocks of color for your system (your monitor uses RGB as a color model).

Figure 1.6
A gray-*scale* image (get it?).

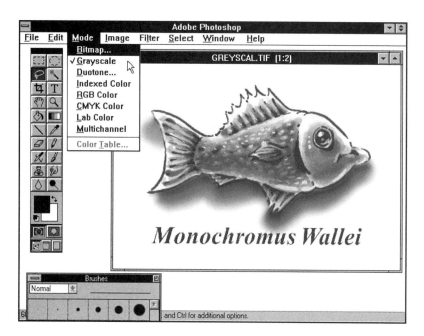

A TrueColor Story about Indexing

TrueColor images with a 24-bit-per-pixel depth are the highest order of color information that you currently can acquire, view, and store digitally. TrueColor is the name computer publications and manufacturers have adopted to indicate that a scanner or monitor is capable of expressing color the human eye finds the most real or "true." It is spelled several different ways, and it's the name for a type of image, not a trademarked technology.

However, computer graphics started some time ago, and the pioneers in this field didn't always have 24 bits per pixel to play around with. For this reason, indexed color was created before the technology or the scheme for formatting a 24-bit image.

Indexed color is often called *mapped* color. In this mode, colors are predefined, like color crayons, and you are provided only a limited set of them to do your coloring. (If this seems unsophisticated, think about how revolutionary a Sony Walkman was 20 years ago.)

Figure 1.7 illustrates how your computer views an indexed color image. Each color is defined in the image's computer file. When you open the file, an index of the specific colors that make up the image is read into a program like Photoshop.

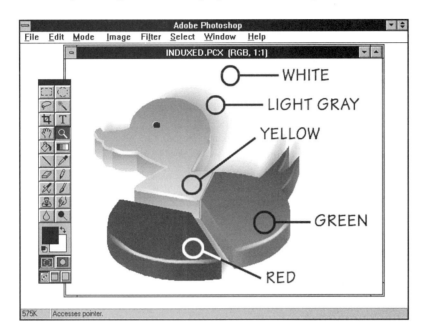

Figure 1.7
When you create or save an indexed color image, it's "color by number" time.

Conversely, TrueColor (24-bit RGB color) is *unmapped.* (After all, unless you own a paint store, why would you want to index 16.7 million colors?) Both mapped and unmapped color image types serve their purposes in business today, and for that reason, indexed color is still used.

However, Photoshop needs a full range of color, the type found in an RGB, TrueColor, 24-bit sample, in order to do its interpolation work when you edit a digital image. Interpolation is the heart of Photoshop's power when it comes to twisting, recoloring, and modifying a digital image. *Interpolation* is the averaging of two neighboring pixels' color values to come up with a pixel that appears to fit smoothly between the two when you command Photoshop to stretch or recolor a bitmapped image. Anti-Aliasing, soft-tip brushes, and effects filters in Photoshop need to avail themselves of a full, 16.7 million color range of expression to do the sophisticated sort of bitmap manipulation they do. You cannot take full advantage of these sophisticated features when using indexed color images, whose range of expression is limited to displaying only 256 unique colors. In fact, some Photoshop options are unavailable in an indexed color mode.

Soon you'll see how to switch color modes in Photoshop. First, though, you need to understand how a mode gets to be a mode. This depends largely on the bit-depth of image types.

How Deep the Pixel; How Wide the Index

Earlier you learned that a grayscale image contains eight bits per pixel, to provide 256 shades in which an image can be rendered. The eight-bits-per-pixel indexed color image is quite common, and just happens to play by the same rules as a grayscale image. Like a grayscale image, the mode of indexed color allows 256 possible colors to be supported within this image type. The difference between the two types of images is that a grayscale image is "complete" in expressing itself in 256 shades of gray—you simply cannot create any other pure combinations of black and white at any bit-depth without adding a third color.

However, a grayscale image is an image *type* recognized as being different than Indexed color in Photoshop. This is because pixels in a grayscale image are modeled (represented) as having only a brightness value, ranging from 0 to 255. The color components pixels use to display grayscale tonal values are equal, for example R=200, G=200, B=200, in order to come up with a very light shade of gray in an image area. For this reason, software developers decided not to reference an equal amount of colors when representing each of the 256 possible tonal values in grayscale images, but to adopt a single channel, a non-color channel, if you will, for the grayscale mode, where brightness values are expressed ranging from 0 (black) to 255 (white).

To express color, which requires *un*equal RGB values to create different colors in a single color channel, the colors have to be Indexed in order to keep track of the 256 possible, single-channel shades. There *are* no other brightness values, or shades of gray a Photoshop user can add to a grayscale image because the mode expresses all the tones the software engineers believe the human eye can see in this format. In reality, the human eye can only distinguish 10 or 11 different gray shades in an image simultaneously. But our eyes move around in an image, and there are other reasons why grayscale was designed to occupy eight bits.

But color adds a new dimension to image-file creation. And the simple reality that an Indexed color image can hold only 256 unique shades makes it unsuitable for sophisticated Photoshop editing. The moment you want to paint in a color to an indexed image, you need to expand the image's color capability to greater than 256. This is why Photoshop can switch color modes for an image—to allow the designer to add color to both a grayscale and an Indexed color image. In both cases, the way to do this is to change either type image to RGB mode. You gain color capability in a specific image this way. Photoshop won't spring your grayscale to living color, and it won't make an Indexed color image look more refined than the way it was saved to file, but you're changing the image Mode, the type of image it is, to accept more colors than were originally specified in its native type.

Indexed color, on the other hand, depends totally on the image's bit-depth, unlike grayscale, which represents all the information about a black and white image type in eight bits. For example, when an eight-bit indexed color image is forced to portray a 24-bit color image, you know it will look somewhat like a caricature of the original; there are simply too many intermediate-level shades to produce faithfully.

The bits-per-pixel unit of measurement indicates how many colors the image type can contain. A simple way to determine how many colors can exist in a color image by image type, or mode, is to calculate 2 to the power of the bit-depth. An even *simpler* method is to refer to table 1.1.

Table 1.1
Color Counts

Bit-Depth (Bits/Pixel)	Underlying Math	Maximum Number of Different Colors
1	2 to the 1st	2
4	2 to the 4th	16
8	2 to the 8th	256
16	2 to the 16th	65,536
24	2 to the 24th	1,667,216

Photoshop handles an indexed color image up to eight bits per pixel. Grayscale and line art images are always mapped to an eight-bits-per-pixel index because they fit comfortably within a larger index scheme that many other indexed images use.

When an image expresses more colors than can be saved at eight bits per pixel, Photoshop, by default, assigns this image a straight, unmapped RGB image type, or mode. This is because otherwise there are too many different color possibilities to index, and the indexed color information must be written to the same file as the format, header, and other information.

You have some control over how an indexed color image turns out, even if the image uses only a few different colors. Keep in mind that many scanned color photographs contain only a few thousand unique colors within their RGB color mode, even though 16.7 million are possible within this mode. Soon you'll see how to fine-tune an indexed color image made from an RGB file. But first, let's take a look at how you build the palette for indexing.

The Lookup Table

A *lookup table* is the part of a graphics image file that contains the information about how color is supposed to be mapped. In Photoshop, the lookup table is called an *indexed color palette*. A lookup table's task is to map the colors to an indexed image according to how the user specifies the mapping. Photoshop plays a very active role in the Indexing process. After you select how many color "opportunities" can exist in an indexed image by specifying a bit-depth, select how many color "opportunities" can exist in an indexed image by specifying a bit-depth, Photoshop then identifies for the lookup table the closest matches to the original image. Then the lookup table fills the indexed color image's registers with the colors that you and Photoshop select.

Here's an example of the decisions and processing that go on when you want to do some color-mapping of an RGB image to create an indexed color image out of it.

Suppose you want to design some Windows wallpaper. You have a 24-bit, RGB, TrueColor image that looks promising for this wallpaper. You decide to make it four bits deep because that's the color resolution (bit-depth) of most of the wallpaper that ships with Microsoft Windows v3.1.

In figure 1.8, you can see the Indexed Color dialog box that pops into Photoshop when you select <u>I</u>ndexed Color as the <u>M</u>ode you want to change an RGB image to for this task.

Figure 1.8
The Indexed Color dialog box is used to set specifications for reducing an RGB image to Indexed.

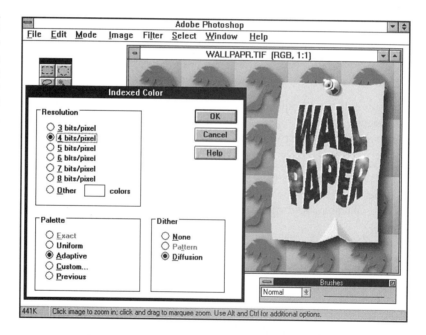

Four bits give Photoshop a maximum of 16 different colors to portray your RGB original. You can't, however, use an Exact palette because your RGB image consists of 30,576 unique colors, and Photoshop obviously cannot fit this many colors into 16, so the Exact palette radio button is grayed out.

Instead, you consider using a Uniform palette. A System palette isn't an option when you want to go from 16.7 million colors to just 16. When you want to *dither* an RGB color image down to eight bits, 256 colors, however, the Uniform radio button turns to a System button. *Uniform*

palette means that all the visible colors in the spectrum are represented in 16 colors, each of the 16 being given equal preference in an image.

Microsoft Windows offers *System palette* to represent images in 256 colors. However, the System palette contains no user-definable colors, and a uniform palette is a pretty pathetic method of describing 30,576 colors, when some shades in the WALLPAPR image are *weighted* more heavily toward the orange part of the spectrum, and therefore not distributed uniformly across the visible spectrum in the image.

In either case, Photoshop cannot tap into its wealth of 16.7 million possible shades to pick its 16 best ones to create this wallpaper. For tough assignments such as this one, Photoshop's default is the Adaptive palette.

The *Adaptive palette* enables Photoshop to calculate the mean difference between certain ranges of the same hues and then do *averaging*—estimating how these calculations portray the overall image scheme. Photoshop then can determine the 16 different colors that convey the original RGB image with the least degree of error.

Figure 1.9 is a somewhat liberal depiction of how Photoshop handles this indexing problem.

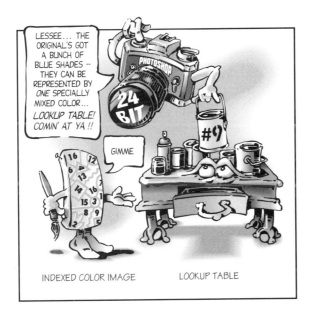

Figure 1.9
The process by which an indexed image gets its color, the liberal interpretation version.

Now that you understand what indexing accomplishes and how it accomplishes it, you're ready for your first exercise:

Creating a Decent Indexed Color Image from an RGB Image

Open ALAMODES.TIF from the companion CD.

Click on the Rectangular Marquee tool	Selects a square portion of an active image.
Click and drag the area in ALAMODES.TIF where you can pick up some blue, white, brown, and pink all in one selection	Tells Photoshop to refer to this area when indexing, as shown in figure 1.10. The upper-left button on the toolbox is the Rectangular Marquee tool.
Choose **M**ode	Creates types of images different from your present one.

In the **M**ode menu, Photoshop places a check mark to the left of the **R**GB Color option, indicating that it has identified this image type as the active image.

Choose **I**ndexed Color	Displays the Indexed Color dialog box, in which you specify the type of indexed image.
Choose 8 bits per pixel	Specifies 256 as the maximum number of different colors that can be displayed.
Choose **A**daptive Palette	Tells Photoshop to build a lookup table with a weighted consideration for the colors within the area you selected with the Rectangle tool.
Click on **D**iffusion from Dither	Causes pixels in the image with the highest degree of error compared to the original to "fan out," so an obvious color error is thinned and spread over a greater area.
Click on OK	Accepts your choices and returns you to Photoshop's workspace.
Choose **F**ile, **S**ave, name the image, and save it to a directory on your hard disk	Saves your work to hard disk. You may not care to save this work, though, so you may ignore this step, and you haven't hurt our feelings.

Figure 1.11 shows the results of your indexing. As you can see, you didn't fare too badly. Some values are missing, certainly, but most of the visual integrity from the RGB original remains.

The whole point to learning about the best settings for converting images is so that your images can be used for other purposes; presentation packages and desktop-publishing applications sometimes insist on using a BMP or PCX indexed color image as import criteria. After rendering ALAMODES.TIF as an eight-bit image, you can now save disk space by saving the file in BMP or PCX format. A TIF image is inherently burdened with substantial data overhead because it can hold up to 16.7 million colors. Some currently available presentation packages don't even accept TIF images.

Before moving on to the ripest images available from the graphics tree, let's examine a few of the finer points of indexing images.

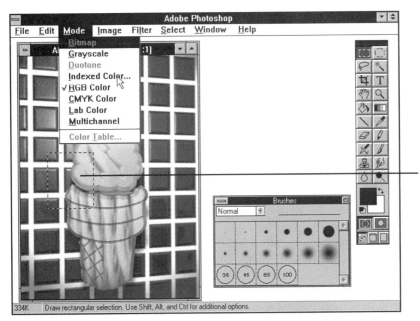

Figure 1.10
Marquee-selecting an area in an active image lets Photoshop concentrate on optimizing an Adaptive lookup table.

Rectangular Marquee tool

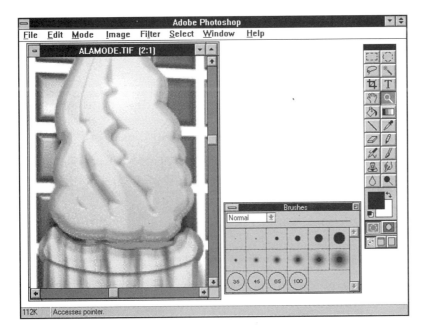

Figure 1.11
Smaller file sizes and more common file formats are the advantages of indexed color images.

The Adaptive Palette

The Adaptive palette performed wonders in rendering a 30,756-color image in only 256 indexed colors. (Later in this chapter you learn how to determine exactly how many unique colors a photo has.) But you should use an Adaptive lookup table only on a case-by-case basis. Different photos have different areas that need Photoshop's attention most during the indexing process. With the ALAMODE image, selecting an area that represented the prime color values was easy because there weren't that many of them. Photoshop gave preference to the pinks and blues that you selected, and didn't give much consideration to the murky gray shadows toward the bottom of the image. If you have an image of a sunset over the ocean at dusk, the Adaptive lookup table weights the palette toward warm reds and golden shades, and places no emphasis on displaying purple or green.

But consider a photo of a peacock holding a PANTONE swatch book and throwing confetti against a rainbow background. Besides being weird, such an image might well include hundreds of thousands of unique colors, with each unique color requiring Photoshop's attention as much as the next. For fair indexing, you would choose not the Adaptive palette, but rather the Uniform palette from the Indexed Color dialog box. A Uniform palette is *unweighted*; that is, the visible spectrum of colors is segmented, with each segment equally represented in the lookup table.

To see how to calculate the number of unique colors in the ALAMODE.TIF file, unload the shareware utility PaintShop Pro, found in the companion CD's SHAREWAR subdirectory. Like all shareware, PaintShop Pro allows you a period of free evaluation—no strings attached for 30 days, during which you can try out its features. Then you decide whether to register it with the creator. The program includes an order form as well as the documentation and the executable file.

After you install PaintShop Pro, load an image by selecting the **O**pen command from the **F**ile menu. When your image is displayed, select the **C**ount Colors Used command from the **C**olors menu. PaintShop Pro then tells you how many unique colors an image has. The number may surprise you!

PaintShop Pro can help you determine the best bit-depth (bits per pixel) to use when converting an RGB image to an indexed image. It's a handy little sidekick to Photoshop, and it costs as much to register the product as a piano lesson—and piano lessons usually aren't as much fun.

Diffusion Dithering

Chapter 2 covers dithering as it applies to your monitor. *Dithering* on your monitor is an attempt by your video card to display more colors than it is set to, like viewing a 24-bit RGB image with a 16-color video driver. It doesn't affect the RGB *image*; it just causes the *display* to look a little funky. Indexed-color dithering (like the dithering you did to the ice cream cone in the preceding exercise) differs from monitor dithering only in that it *is permanent* and actually *changes* the file.

Diffusion dithering, as you saw in the previous indexing adventure, attempts to "soften the blow" when an image gets important color information knocked out of it during indexing. Diffusion dithering bumps a color pixel into an adjacent pixel's place when Photoshop determines that the pixel falls out of the range of available colors you established in the index. The bumped pixel in turn bumps another adjacent one, and this "musical chairs" routine continues until the last pixel is deemed close enough to a color in the Index to hold a place.

Diffusion dithering creates subtle currents and eddies in an image, as though you were viewing the image through ground glass. When reducing the available color of an RGB image to Indexed, diffusion dithering is one possible solution to reduce harshness and image areas displayed as flat colors. The next section describes another.

Pattern Dithering

Unlike diffusion dithering, *pattern dithering* uses two adjacent pixels of available indexed colors to approximate a third, unavailable color. Consider, for example, an Adaptive color table that includes deep red and mustard, but no brown. If you specify a pattern dither when you index, Photoshop "weaves" red and mustard pixels together to create brown.

It is mostly a question of aesthetics as to whether or not this is your dithering preference. If you stand far enough away from your monitor, your eyes meld the two colors together and the image appears more full-bodied. If you sit in front of a 21-inch monitor all day while imaging, however, this sort of dithering can be distracting, and your mind may wander off to thoughts of knitting a sweater.

Why You'd Want To Index an RGB Image

Both types of dithering can help you create a decent, viewable image within the confines of a limited Indexed color palette. But as stated earlier, the indexed color image type is inherently inferior to 24-bit color. Why, then, have you just spent so much time learning so much about indexed color?

The PC enables you, for the first time in the history of art, to make exact duplicates of your work. Because you can generate digital copies, you can experiment with an effect and still keep the original somewhere on disk. More importantly, you can make an image, then specify different modes for your copies, creating each image file for a different application or use. An RGB image prints lousy if you send it directly to a laser printer. Too much data information slows you down, and you'd want to do a little "tweaking" to a color image expressed as black and white before printing it anyway (see Chapter 16 for more info on the Black and White image). But you'd definitely want to create a grayscale out of an RGB image if you knew it was destined to become an image for the front page of a black and white newsletter.

I

From the Source to the Sample

The same holds true on occasions when you need an Indexed color copy of your original RGB masterpiece. Wallpaper is only one instance where using the right Index commands will give you pleasing results from a less color-capable file type. Video screen shows, word-processing programs, and other applications need a graphical helping hand on occasion, and they don't always have the capability to display or import an RGB-mode image saved in a TIF file format.

When you installed Photoshop, you took a big step toward professional imaging. But the level of perfection you can achieve won't matter much if your client runs a presentation package in DOS on an XT that can display only 16 colors. For such an assignment, you gain more control by decreasing the image's resolution and the number of colors available for the image. You still have the 24-bit original, and you will overwhelm the client with the clarity and graphical sumptuousness in your art that you bring to the client's system.

Try using 256-color wallpaper in Windows. Before you boot into the Windows session, though, specify the Windows default VGA video driver. You'll be appalled by how awful the image looks, and this reaction is analogous to how your client would respond to your work if you fail to fine-tune it with indexed color that suits its modest monitor capabilities.

You broaden your knowledge, and then your abilities, by knowing how to swing from limb to limb on the graphics tree.

The TrueColor Image

Earlier, when you learned about indexed color, you also learned something about 24-bit TrueColor. This type of image is the pinnacle of pixel-rendering capability—and also eats up hard drive space like so many salted peanuts. When you want to edit a superb color picture into an award-winner, this is definitely the image type you want to use. TrueColor should also be your preferred image mode for working in Photoshop, and you'll soon see why.

TrueColor and RGB Color

TrueColor is the popular name for what color experts in the computer field have called RGB color since its inception. Technically, *TrueColor* refers to an image type that has been written to disk, and *RGB color* refers to the monitor's mode of display. However, the terms are used synonymously, and the results are the same—the capability to display 16.7 million different colors simultaneously. RGB images are unmapped and freely draw from the "color well" of your system because the file type's capacity matches the technological capability to display color on a PC. This lack of mapping constraints leads to another unique quality of the RGB file—its use of channels.

Using Channels

Photoshop sees a 24-bit RGB image as having three channels of color information: one for red, one for green, and one for blue. Each channel works with eight bits of color information, which translates to a gamut of brightness values from 0 to 255. The three channels, when combined, can hold 256 by 256 by 256, or 16.7 million, possible colors.

Grayscale and indexed color, on the other hand, have a maximum of 256 values, and Photoshop sees them as having only one channel. The three channels of 24-bit TrueColor files give you a lot of room for experimentation. Figure 1.12 shows the channels of a 24-bit scanned image, which were split using Photoshop's Channels palette (which is something you should never do unless you're a commercial printer, a computer imaging guru, or an author trying to illustrate a concept!). Notice the different densities in each component image. The "fourth channel," the RGB composite, is actually the normal view of an image as you'd see it in Photoshop. The default view of an image is always the RGB composite "channel," and the individual color-component channels can be seen by clicking on the title bar of the Channels palette.

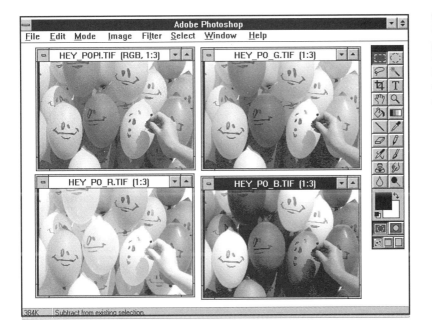

Figure 1.12
An RGB image has three separate Photoshop channels that you can work with.

In Photoshop, an RGB image can have up to 16 *extra* channels of information assigned to it, as later chapters will explain. The important thing to note here is that because you can work with an RGB image in many different channels, you have ample opportunity to fine-tune parts of an image to enhance it overall.

Vector images are called *object-oriented images* because each piece you build in this sort of design program always remains a separate object that you can change later. By using channels in an RGB-type bitmapped image, you can achieve close to the same advantage. TrueColor image quality, combined with the flexibility of saving selections in special information Alpha Channels, provides the Photoshop user with advantages found on both branches of the computer graphics tree.

Using Photoshop Tools and Filters with RGB Color Images

As mentioned earlier, some of Photoshop's tools and filters don't really work with an indexed, line art, or grayscale image unless you convert the image to RGB color using the **M**odes menu. (This is like wearing an oversized shoe; there's room inside to grow, even though you're already fully grown.) The reason you want to convert these images to RGB color is to apply color to a grayscale image, to color in line art, or to refine an indexed color image.

You can define Photoshop's Brush tips (found on the Brushes palette) as having a certain degree of hardness, or amount of "spread." This enables you to create a very soft edge wherever you paint, and can be useful when you retouch photographic images. For example, you can make the ice cream cone shown in figure 1.11 look a little more "drippy" by painting an area at the bottom of the ice cream. In figure 1.13, the left side of the screen shows the ice cream cone as an RGB image, and the right side as an indexed color image. As you can see, the RGB image is more successful because Photoshop enables you to use a Brush tip hardness feature when applying color.

Figure 1.13
You cannot use all of Photoshop's powers with an indexed color image.

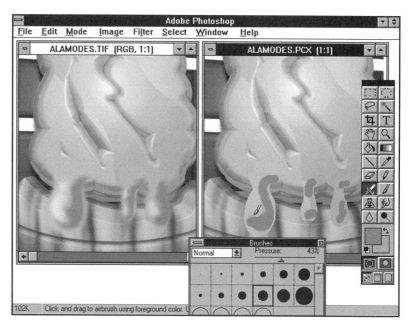

Many other Photoshop features—including Gradient Fills, soft edges for the editing and painting tools, and stretching or skewing an image—cannot be used with an indexed color image. Other Photoshop techniques simply do not work as well with indexed color images because they cannot use the gamut of 16.7 million colors available to RGB images. For example, with an RGB image, Photoshop can use the gamut of 16.7 million colors to simulate

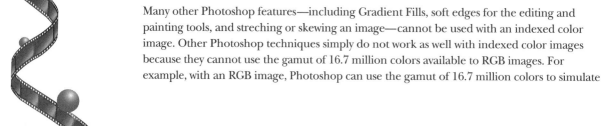

ink or paint "bleed" left on a canvas by a physical brush, by lightening adjacent pixels ever so slightly. Figure 1.14 zooms in on an RGB image (shown on the left side) and an indexed color image (shown on the right) to demonstrate Photoshop's soft-edge capability.

This is the secret to soft and smooth edges in Photoshop. Even when you use the Type tool to caption an image, the Type tool's Anti-Aliasing feature requires that you use an RGB image mode to create clean type.

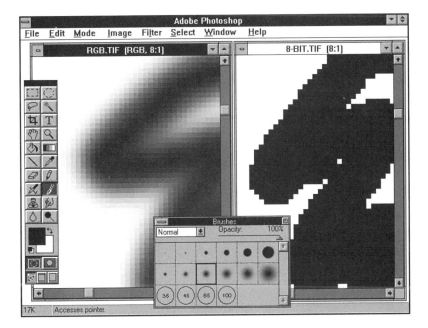

Figure 1.14
You can soften edges in Photoshop by gradating adjacent pixels.

Pixels, Dots, and Samples

Although these digital image types differ substantially, they also have much in common. The common heritage all bitmapped image types share is in their fabrication from pixels. *Pixels* are a unit of measurement, like inches or gallons, but refer to a quantity that is specific to computer graphics.

Occasionally you also see and hear references to *dots* and *samples*. Pixels, dots, and samples are used to measure work at various stages of its completion on a PC. A common misconception is that they are the same thing, especially because professionals tend to use the terms interchangeably. In this section you learn the difference between pixels, dots, and samples.

Samples versus Dots

When scanning an image, you set the scanner to a certain *resolution*. This resolution determines how many digital *samples per inch* the scanner creates from a source image. At the acquisition phase, the scanner views the image through an imaginary grid, and then assigns each space in this grid a color value based on an equal area the scanner samples.

However, most documentation that accompanies scanner hardware refers to samples per inch as *dpi*, or *dots per inch.* Therefore, you can call your scanner settings 150 dpi, 75 dpi, and so on. However, don't confuse different kinds of dots per inch. A laser printer's dpi is not the same as the dots (samples) per inch that a scanner produces. In fact, a scanned image at 150 dpi (*samples* per inch!) is actually best represented by a laser print generated at 1200 dpi.

Throughout this book, resolutions for scanned images are measured in dpi, to follow convention. For now, simply be prepared for Chapter 20's discussion of commercial print presses, in which the term *dot* is redefined.

Pixels and Resolution

For acquired (sampled) images in Photoshop, different measurements are used. A *pixel* is a unit of light as displayed on your monitor, which is where you usually do most of your actual imaging work. *Pixels per inch* is also called a measurement of *resolution* when you work on an acquired image.

Figure 1.15 shows two images in Photoshop that measure the same inches high and wide, but are expressed in different pixels per inch. The left side shows a 50-pixel-per-inch image, and the right side shows the same image at 150 pixels per inch. When you acquire an image at a low sampling rate, like 50 dpi, Photoshop is forced to display the image information using fewer pixels per inch. To do that, Photoshop makes the pixels larger. A pixel is not an absolute measurement the way a gram or an inch is.

Figure 1.15
Examples of a
low-resolution and
high-resolution
image.

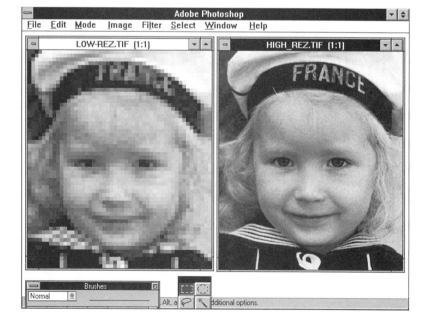

To do precision work on an image, you depend on pixel resolution. Chapter 2 explains the relationship between resolution and image dimensions, but your basic working knowledge starts here: Sample your work at a resolution and image size that are a comfortable fit for your work. If you want to enlarge an image, you must lower the pixel-per-inch ratio. The image then tends to get fuzzy and "computery" looking. This effect is similar to what happens when you blow up a film negative too much and begin to see the film's grain. Pixels are the digital image's equivalent to film grain.

If you need to produce wallpaper or a computer slide show, using pixels per inch as the standard of measurement in Photoshop is very helpful. To switch to pixels, first select **I**mage Size from the **I**mage menu. This displays the Image Size dialog box shown in figure 1.16. Then in the New Size window, click the buttons adjacent to the scroll boxes to the right of the **W**idth, H**e**ight, and **R**esolution text boxes until the scroll boxes display pixels as the new unit of measurement, as shown in figure 1.16. Photoshop then tells you that the drippy ice cream cone measures 330 by 314, at 150 pixels per inch.

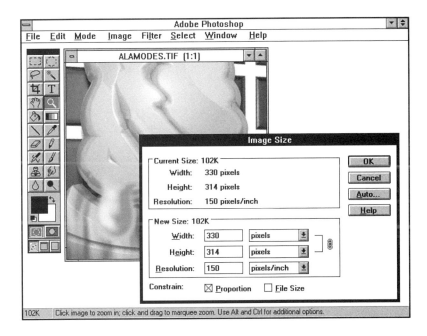

Figure 1.16
Pixels are the unit of measurement you use when measuring digital image sizes on your monitor.

If you want to fill the screen from border to border, the image size would have to be 640 by 480 pixels, 600 by 800, or 1024 by 768 pixels, depending on the monitor mode you are using with your video card.

Regardless of monitor mode, 72 to 96 pixels per inch is the maximum a monitor will display, so if your slide show consists of the drippy ice cream cone, it contains twice as many pixels as are necessary to display it. In this case, your system simply ignores the excess information when displaying it, it takes longer to read the image into system RAM, and the file size is needlessly large for your purpose.

Understanding File Formats

No chapter on digital images would be complete if it didn't make some recommendations as to how to store your acquired image in an ideal file format, so the next few sections focus on file formats.

Digital images are like ideas; they literally live as information stored from one nanosecond to the next as electrical impulses temporarily stored in RAM as the "thought is being held." These digital ideas eventually have to be given a shape, a format written to disk. What the proper format is that can hold your digital image/idea should be considered. The image may not look the same the next time it's read into RAM if the form—the file format you give it— isn't capable of holding the visual information you want it to hold.

The right format for a specific image type sustains the quality of the image you slaved over in Photoshop, but the wrong one can turn the image into a cartoon. The following sections cover the most popular file formats in which you can save your image. If you have a special application you use with your imaging, it may require a special file format, in which case it's best to check the application's documentation for file-format preferences. In any case, this chapter briefly covers some of the more exotic formats in addition to the most common ones.

Formats for RGB Images

The TIF (Tagged Image File) format was created as the most versatile format for 24-bit images. One of the advantages of saving images in this format is *portability*. A TIF image saved on a PC can be read by a Macintosh, a host of UNIX platforms, and other proprietary platforms. An image saved in the TIF format, unlike formats associated only with indexed color, can have special information (Alpha) channels within it.

You can save line art and indexed images in the TIF format. Before you do, however, you should consider whether a larger file size is okay because TIF images have a format-specific header that is larger than other those of other formats. The TIF format enables you to access all of Photoshop's sophisticated tools and filters, so you should save your grayscale scanning in this format.

The TrueVision Company developed the Targa file format (which uses the file extension TGA) to work with its proprietary video boards. Since the format's inception, many other companies have adopted it, and Photoshop currently supports the TGA format. A Targa image ports nicely to the Macintosh. Like the TIF format, TGA handles high-quality, 24-bit images. Photoshop v2.5, however, only recognizes a total bit-depth of 32 in images saved to this format, so a *.TGA image file can only retain one extra information channel in addition to the Red, Green and Blue ones.

PSD is Photoshop's default file format. It supports all image types, from line art to TrueColor. The only problem with saving a file to the PSD format is that few other graphics programs can read this proprietary format. You should save an image in PSD format only if you haven't decided the final format you want for the image.

PSD and TIF files both support up to 16 channels and vector-based paths you can create in Photoshop. Later in this book you'll become familiar with the virtues and dangers associated with saving an image with extra channels and paths.

PCX Images

The ZSoft Corporation created the PCX file format quite some time ago as a proprietary format that many software companies have since adopted. The PCX format is excellent for indexed and line art images because its file format is not as complex as the TIF format. The downside of PCX images, besides featuring only one channel of color information, is that so many versions of the format exist. Because the PCX standard was openly published so that independent developers could tinker with it, this format is continually being upgraded.

Photoshop supports version 5 of PCX, but you may encounter an image saved in an earlier version. If so, the image may not look very good. You're safe in saving an indexed, grayscale, or line art image as a PCX file as long as you remember that you must convert it to RGB mode in Photoshop to take advantage of soft brushes, gradient fills, and other useful features.

BMP

The BMP file extension indicates that Microsoft technology was used to create the file's image. Like PCX, the BMP file format uses Indexed color. BMP is also a platform-independent format, so you can view it on a PC running DOS, Windows on DOS, Windows NT, or OS/2. However, you cannot use BMP files with the Macintosh, so if your service bureau, boss, or friends use Macs, save your images as TIFs rather than BMPs.

GIFs

H&R Block's CompuServe information service created the file format *GIF* (Graphics Interchange Format) to shorten downloading time for its subscribers. GIF files are small, and support Indexed color image types (as well as line art and grayscale images). Different types of computers can read this format, but only if your software will read the GIF format. Photoshop reads GIF files just fine, whereas other, less capable programs may display a less-than-perfect GIF image on their workspace.

Beware of different versions of GIF. GIF files can be read in a DOS environment, and they're created as both *interlaced* and *noninterlaced* varieties, to allow a person reading a GIF image online on a BBS a low-resolution preview to help decide whether or not to download the image. Interlaced versions of GIF files cannot be read by some programs. Use a GIF file format for an indexed image only after you know what the specific program's GIF format requirements are.

Less Frequently Used File Formats

The following formats are not used as frequently as those you'll be using in this book's Photoshop exercises. However, Photoshop is a very complete imaging program designed to accommodate every need and file format. The following sections cover some of the lesser-known Photoshop Save As capabilities you may want to use for special situations.

JPEG

JPEG is a file format and compression scheme that Photoshop supports. Chapter 2 discusses this scheme in detail. File compression is always a useful capability to have when dealing with images that are more than a megabyte in file size, but don't save your original as a JPG file until you read about JPEG in Chapter 2.

IFF for the Amiga

If you're sending an image to an Amiga Commodore computer system, use an IFF file format on a copy of your work.

RAW

If you need to work on an image for a different application on a different platform with which you're unfamiliar, you might try using the RAW file format. Photoshop takes an image saved as a RAW format and creates several channels of color information, each having levels of color in a gamut from 0 (black) to 255 (white). RAW saves unmapped images, writing the color information as a stream of bytes rather than using the lookup table method of Indexed color images.

Still *Other* File Formats!

You can also write Scitex CT, MacPaint, PIXAR, EPS, and a few other really exotic file formats from Photoshop. However, if you are new to computer graphics for Windows, you are unlikely to encounter the need. For further information, check the Photoshop documentation, Photoshop Help, or the service bureau that does your imaging work.

The Long and Short of the Data Byte Stream

Usually you want to acquire an image in 24 bits, view it as an RGB image, and save it as a TIF file. This chapter has provided ample examples to justify this preference. Photoshop can make the most out of an image that is sampled at higher than 100 dpi to yield an image that's at least 72 pixels per inch in resolution.

You probably will want to do your work in at least a 5 by 7 image because at a view of 100 percent (1:1) such an image fills the screen in Photoshop's workspace. To work with tiny

images, you must zoom in on the image. If a small image has been inadequately sampled, the more you zoom in the more conspicuous the pixels—the image's color building blocks—become.

PCX and BMP are the most common file formats for storing line art and Indexed images. To work with such formats with Photoshop's full complement of features, you must convert them to RGB mode. To see the wonderful ways that you can enhance grayscale images in Photoshop, you should store them in TIF format, not as Indexed images.

Summary

Now that you've seen some of the possible color formats and file types of an acquired image, you have a better idea of the importance in correctly acquiring, viewing, and saving a digital sample of a physical image. You've just taken a big step that will let you have more creative freedom in your Photoshop adventures. Remember to always look at the sample source to understand how many colors it's made of and how you'd like these colors expressed. A color image can be captured so that it looks magnificent on your monitor, and it can be saved in a format that will let it look that way time after time when you open the file.

Chapter 2 covers the scanning process in more detail so that you have plenty of independent work with which you can experiment. You'll also see how important it is to run your monitor in a mode that's in sync with your image type. You'll also discover how monitor dithering may not affect your image, but still mess up your work.

Chapter Snapshot

In this chapter, you learn how to:

CHAPTER

The Digital Image

The last chapter mentioned that there are several ways you can get a digital image into Photoshop. One way is to originate a piece of work in a computer program that can create a file that Photoshop recognizes. Another is to let Kodak digitize your camera film onto a PhotoCD. PhotoCDs will be explored in the next chapter, but for now let's devote some time to the most versatile tool for acquiring digitized images—the scanner.

Scanning is almost an art in itself. A well-executed scan can immediately be used as a digital sample for enhancing and editing with Photoshop, whereas a hastily done scan can delay your creative endeavors, requiring time and effort just to get the image into a workable state. Whether it's artwork, a photo, or a simple cartoon, different scanner options are available for bringing different image types into Photoshop. Your monitor's settings also play heavily in the scheme of scanning because it's difficult to tell how well an image was sampled if you can't see it! If your work deals more with acquired images than original computer graphics, this chapter shows you how to get the best information from the source material, so you can refine it with Photoshop later.

Accurately Viewing an Acquired Image

Before you capture an image to work on in Photoshop, it's vital that your monitor can display the *bit-depth* or *bits-per-pixel ratio* of your capture. Have you ever looked at a high-quality image in Windows while you were using a standard VGA video driver? The image looks posterized, hard on the eyes, and generally crummy, right?

That's because the number of bits per pixel contained in a lot of TIFF and Targa image file formats is TrueColor, which is greater than the 4-bits per pixel standard VGA mode can handle. When you use a standard VGA video driver, you can only display 16 colors. This is good enough to work on most spreadsheets, but it's an inadequate number of colors when it comes to realistically viewing or working with high-quality digital images. Before you begin to scan (and certainly before you begin to edit!) a high quality *color* image, make sure that your video card will support *at least* 16-bit (32,768 colors, or HiColor) or better yet, a 24-bit, TrueColor (16.7 million colors) video mode.

An important practice to adopt before scanning is to make sure you are running a video mode that's in synch with the bit-depth of the scanner setting. If, for example, you're scanning an original image with a 24-bit scanner setting, your monitor should be capable of displaying 24 bits/pixel. When Photoshop is forced to display a 24-bit image with an inadequate number of display colors, it'll perform something called *dithering*.

Dithering is a method of arranging adjacent colored pixels on your screen to "fake" a color that's in your work, but not available in the current video mode. Monitor display dithering is something that happens only on your screen; it doesn't change the information in your image file. If you're viewing a 24-bit, 16.7 million color digital image with an 8-bit video driver loaded, you'll see a dithered display of this image, yet when you then switch to the appropriate 24-bit video driver, you'll then see the true image colors without any dithering.

In figure 2.1, a TrueColor, 24-bit depth image is displayed in Photoshop's workspace while using an 8-bit depth video mode. By default, Photoshop represents the 16.7 million possible colors by *dithering* all the image's color information into *patterns* using only 256 colors to crudely represent the image. This "look" is similar to the patterns Windows uses to simulate different colors in its Paintbrush program while working with a 4-bit video driver.

Diffusion dithering is another way Photoshop displays different colors of an image that has a limited amount of display colors available (see fig. 2.2). It's not as obvious or visually distracting as pattern dithering, but is still inaccurate for proofing your captured images. Diffusion dithering the display of a TrueColor, RGB digital image looks the same as when dithering is *actually applied* to an image file, as you saw in Chapter 1 when an RGB image was dithered down to an Indexed color image type. This type of dithering is also called *error diffusion* because it's an imprecise view of the color data in an image file.

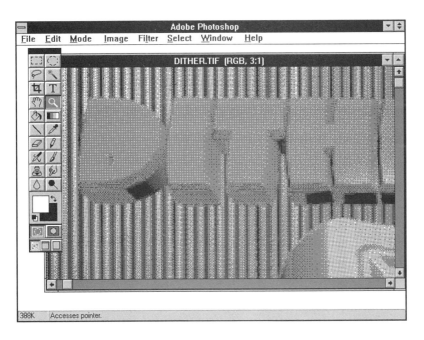

Figure 2.1
Dithered patterns are an attempt to approximate colors in an image that a particular video mode won't handle.

From the Source to the Sample

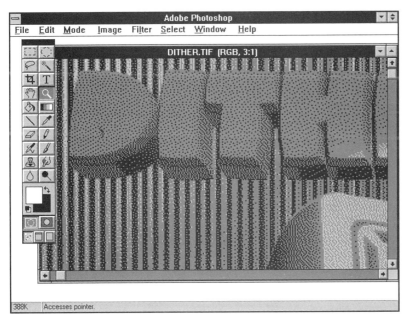

Figure 2.2
Diffusion dithering approximates the full range of colors using a limited palette.

Whether you choose to use **D**iffusion dither (from **F**ile, General Preferences), or leave this box unchecked to accept Photoshop's default of pattern dither, you'll be operating with inherent inaccuracy when you view and edit an image displayed with dithering. Whenever possible, use a video display driver that matches the color depth of your digital image. Figure 2.3 shows how a TrueColor image should look while running an appropriate video driver. If you'd like to actually see what this image displays like with diffusion and pattern dithering, and with no dithering, load the file NO_DITH!.TIF from the *Inside Adobe Photoshop* companion CD into Photoshop, and then choose different video drivers from Windows Setup (use SETUP.EXE in your Windows subdirectory).

Figure 2.3
An image captured at 16.7 million colors displayed with a 16.7 million color video driver.

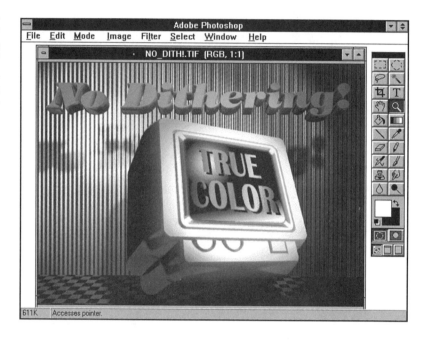

If you don't see the video driver listed in Windows Setup that you think you need, check the box your video card came in. Most manufacturers ship additional drivers on disk that you can usually load from Windows Setup by clicking **O**ptions, **C**hange System Settings, and choosing Other display (requires OEM disks) from the **D**isplay drop-down list. Look in the documentation that came with the video card for any special installation instructions specific to your video card. You may want to call the manufacturer's technical support number or their electronic bulletin board (BBS) for your card's newest video drivers. Manufacturers frequently update these drivers to make them work better and to add new features.

You don't need an expensive SVGA video board to use Photoshop; the important thing is to have a video display that matches the type of digital images you acquire so you may view them accurately. Most 1M video cards today will support 16.7 million colors at a 640 by 480 pixel screen resolution. This is the resolution (24 bit, TrueColor) at which you can do your most satisfying and accurate color image editing. However, if most of your work involves grayscale art and photos, an 8-bit video card and driver will display a grayscale scan of a source image with perfect fidelity.

Even though a grayscale image can be accurately displayed while being scanned and saved using a 256-color video driver, *editing* a grayscale image in Photoshop will be a frustrating experience unless you first switch to a driver capable of supporting 16 or 24 bits.

Although an 8-bit, 256-color video driver can display all the possible 256 shades of gray in a grayscale image, Photoshop has special features which require *more* information to be displayed than 256 shades. For instance, Photoshop's Quick Mask feature makes easy work of defining a selection area in an image by displaying a selected or masked image area in a tinted color. This additional color needs to be mapped to the display *in addition to* the other 256 shades, and a 256-color video driver then becomes inadequate for showing you 257 colors! What Photoshop does in this instance, is to dither your display when Quick Mask mode is active, and then return you to the accurate representation of a grayscale image when Quick Mask is turned off.

Having Photoshop re-map your display back and forth between dithered and non-dithered presents a confusing way to image edit, and it taxes your computer's video subsystem needlessly. 8-bit, 256 color is fine for viewing and acquiring a grayscale image, but when it comes time to edit your captured image, use at least a 16-bit, 32,768 color video display mode.

Accuracy is a prime element in the successful manipulation of delicate digitized images in the PC world. Your image goes through many convolutions in the acquiring, modifying, enhancing, and reproducing phases. It is best, then, to get an honest look at an acquired image from the very beginning. This means not bothering with dithering.

A trip through the scanning process is next, starting from a pre-purchase point of view. Many different kinds of scanners can sample 24-bit color that you can display on your monitor in 24-bit, RGB, non-dithered color. We'll narrow the field down as we take a look at each type of scanning hardware.

Before Getting into Scanning...

Scanning hardware can be classified into three basic types: sheet-fed scanners, hand-held scanners, and flatbed scanners. Each type has advantages and disadvantages. The type of scanner you choose depends on the type of work you want to do.

All scanning devices bounce light off a physical sample source onto a photo-sensitive grid. The grid is composed of lots of cells; each cell passes along the unit of light information it receives. A single light information unit (pixel) becomes a part of a collective tapestry that winds up on your PC as a digital image.

Where this photo-sensitive grid is located in the scanner, how well the hardware is designed, and the method of transporting the source image across the photo-sensitive grid are what distinguishes the types of different scanners.

The Sheet-Fed Scanner

The sheet-fed scanner is an economical approach to scanning. You can get one for under $300 if you shop smart. The reason for a sheet-fed scanner's economy is that it uses rollers to pass the source image across the scanner's photo-sensitive cells. Rollers are a very economical transport mechanism used in every sort of electronic and household device, like photo copiers and fax machines.

Many sheet-fed scanners support color, but before you're sold on this scanner type, consider how they work—you are obliged to affix a 4 by 6 color photo to a sheet of copier paper to feed it through! This sometimes jams the scanner, and the photo is going to look the worse for wear after it passes through! Sheet-feeder scanners are inexpensive and ideal for capturing the printed word on paper, but are just *not* suited for serious image acquisition.

Hand-Held Scanners

The hand scanner is inexpensive, fast, small, and presently comes in grayscale as well as 24-bit color versions. Hand-helds are very compact because there's no transport mechanism to pass source material across the photo-sensitive cells. Instead, the transport mechanism is your hand! Figure 2.4 is the Logitech Color ScanMan used to digitize some of the exercise images you'll find on the companion CD.

The downside to all hand-scanners is that they work best with source material that is less than 4 inches wide. You also need a very steady hand to evenly guide the scanner across your source material. A cough or a wiggle on your part will produce a noticeable defect in the digital image that's almost impossible to correct later. But all things considered, hand scanners are good entry-level hardware for the budding imagist.

Figure 2.4
The Logitech Color
ScanMan.

Flatbed Scanners

Although flatbed scanners are more expensive, physically the size of a photocopier, and take longer to digitize sources than hand-held scanners, they produce more professional results. They handle larger and bulkier source material, and you don't need a steady hand to operate them because the scanner controls the speed and motion of the sampling pass.

Flatbed scanners also offer an array of options. The UMAX scanner as shown in figure 2.5, for example, offers a wide range of resolutions, can produce halftones, and handles up to 8 1/2-by-14 inch source material.

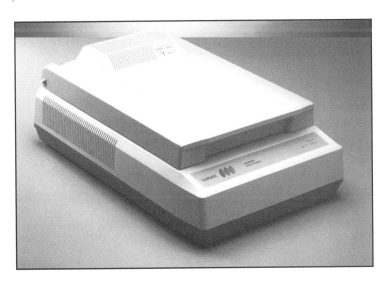

Figure 2.5
The UMAX flatbed
scanner.

Scanner Selection

Flatbed and hand-held scanners are good choices for Photoshop work. A UMAX UC80 Color flatbed was also used to scan source images for figures in this book, and to acquire sample images for the companion CD. If you plan to use Photoshop professionally, purchase a flatbed scanner that'll give you the features like those described and explained next. The imaging hobbyist can get terrific results with a color hand-held, or even a grayscale, but professional work demands professional tools, from the source image straight through to Photoshop.

The *digital camera* is yet another source for digital images. It's the odd man in this world of digitizing devices. It captures images much the same way as a scanner, but you would choose to use it under different circumstances. Digital cameras are presently a young technology, offering varying degrees of quality and a typically steep price, but they are becoming more capable, affordable, and important in the digital imaging world. Digital cameras are covered later in this chapter.

Developing Scanner Standards

Scanning on the PC platform was not the easiest thing to do before the development of a standard in late 1990. You usually had to scan with the proprietary software supplied by your scanner manufacturer, save your file, start your imaging application, and then view the image. Every scanner's software worked differently. Sometimes you couldn't even see the resulting image as you scanned! This process worked for many professionals, but it was primitive, clumsy, and limited.

The development and popularity of Windows 3.0 encouraged a consortium of companies to create a standard that worked in Windows, making scanning easier and more flexible for the user. The consortium, made up of representatives from Aldus, Logitech, Hewlett-Packard, Caere, and Eastman Kodak, developed and promoted the TWAIN standard. Any scanner that supports TWAIN will work with any software that also supports the TWAIN standard. Installing and using a TWAIN-compliant scanner is a breeze.

Aldus Corporation dubbed TWAIN the **T**oolkit **W**ithout **A**n **I**nteresting **N**ame. However, Logitech's explanation is a tad less whimsical and more descriptive: "We selected this name to describe this unique interface that brings together two entities—applications and input devices—in a meeting of the 'twain.'"

If you bought a scanner recently, it probably supports TWAIN. If you are not sure, check your documentation, or call your scanner manufacturer. Additionally, you may be able to get a TWAIN upgrade for an existing, non-TWAIN scanner. Because Photoshop is TWAIN compliant you can scan an image directly into the Photoshop workspace and have it immediately available for use—if your scanner is also TWAIN compliant.

Photoshop additionally supports some common scanners that do not use TWAIN. When you install Photoshop, pick your scanner from the list that the installation program offers (or one that your scanner can emulate), and you should be in business in terms of Photoshop imaging. The procedures for starting a scanner and operating its controls vary from manufacturer to manufacturer, but from within an imaging application, the TWAIN interface is almost always found under the Acquire command, usually under the File menu. Check your scanner documentation for more details.

If You Go Color Scanning, Go Full Color

Some monetary considerations inevitable go hand-in-hand with investing in a digital darkroom. If you're coming from a chemical photography background, you already appreciate the order of magnitude difference between outfitting your darkroom with color versus black-and-white developing and printing goods. New hardware and software add-ons to your equipment, as well as to your wish list, crop up almost daily. And for this reason, it's difficult to recommend a specific scanner that suits your individual taste and budget.

The authors do have a personal preference, as to the type (not brand) of scanning device, that through experience, has proved to be of the most worth for digitally capturing images. Buy either a 24-bit color scanner, or buy a 256 grayscale model. Don't try to hedge with one of the 16-bit (also called HiColor, *not* TrueColor) models available for less money because if you do this, you'll be cheating your own vision. Grayscale and 24-bit color are the standards most high-end image editing programs prefer to work with, and they're also the same color modes that correspond to real world photography.

An 8-bit grayscale scanner captures all the available tonal information in a black-and-white photo. Computer images of the Grayscale type are built around 256 possible shades, and an 8-bit capable scanner captures them all. And TrueColor, 24-bit sampling accurately captures all the color information that's contained in an RGB type image; 8 bits for the red channel, 8 for green, and 8 for blue. A 16-bit scanner simply can't fill the maximum 8 bits per color channel your PC is capable of handling. An RGB, 24-bit scanner is the closest you can afford to capture color the way the human eye sees it.

24 bits is not the upper threshold of scanning capability, just a sampling rate non-millionaires use to produce fine work. 32-bit scanning is commonly done to original color photographs for direct output to commercial printing of high-quality magazine work. In this instance Cyan, Magenta, Yellow, and Black (CMYK) are scanned for in the original, each color channel being 8 bits deep. By basing the scan of the original color photo around a CMYK model instead of RGB, the image retains more of its faithfulness when transferred to the four process plates used to create an image on the printed page.

But for most intents and purposes in your Photoshop adventures, 24-bit sampling captures original image information with perfect fidelity for practically all professional output needs.

How Does TWAIN Work?

For all of its intricacies, TWAIN is simple to understand and easy to use. The application software, such as Photoshop, calls for the source interface supplied by the scanner manufacturer. A *source interface* is an option/dialog box that appears on your screen and offers the controls for the scanner. The exact arrangement of options, and the extent of options available to you depend on how many features your scanner has, and how the scanner manufacturer decided to arrange the items on the screen.

The following example shows how the UMAX version of the TWAIN source interface is called up from Photoshop. If you have a different scanner, your source interface will look a little different, but will work in a similar fashion.

Connecting a Scanner to Photoshop through TWAIN

Turn on your scanner and put something in it to scan, then from within Photoshop, do the following:

Choose **F**ile, Acq**u**ire	This command makes it possible to select a scanning source.
Choose TWAIN source	Lists the available source interfaces on your machine to connect Photoshop with the desired TWAIN device, as shown in figure 2.6.
Choose your scanner from the list	The UMAX Scanner v1.01 was selected in this example. You'll see other selections depending on your own scanner.
Click on the OK button	The source interface has now been chosen. You shouldn't have to set this option again unless you install a different TWAIN-compliant scanner.
Choose **F**ile, **A**cquire TWAIN	Calls the source interface (see fig. 2.7).
Click on the Preview button	This tells the UMAX scanner to run a low-resolution pass over the entire sampling area so the photo's position and orientation can be checked.

In figure 2.7, you see what the layout of a UMAX interface looks like with a photo in place.

Because a fair amount of time is involved when a flatbed scanner digitizes a photo, many scanners of this type offer a preview. It's important to be certain about the image you'll be acquiring *before* you press the Scan button because otherwise you'll waste valuable time waiting for the flatbed scanner to make its passes over an unwanted, poor, or crooked image.

Hand-held scanner owners don't have this preview luxury, or need it, because they have immediate feedback as to whether an image is crooked or upside-down, by simply looking down at the scanner as they guide it across the source image.

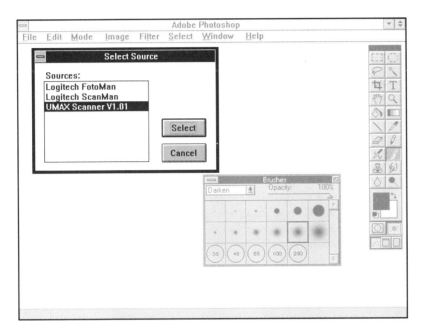

Figure 2.6
Different TWAIN devices require different source interfaces.

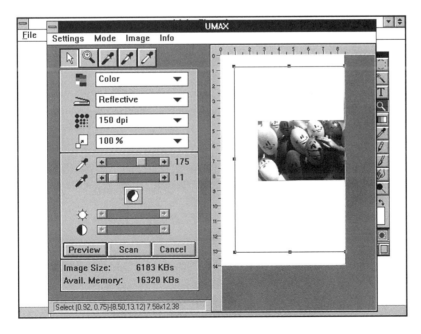

Figure 2.7
The source interface for a TWAIN-compliant scanner appears on top of the Photoshop workspace.

Preparing To Scan

Before you press the Scan button, consider the *type* of image you want to acquire. Color-capable scanners also have settings for grayscale and line art images. Is your source image a black-and-white photo? Is it a line art drawing? Through the TWAIN interface, set your scanner to a mode that matches the type of color information to that of the source image.

We are using a color photo in this example. The mode choices the UMAX source interface offers are Line Art, Halftone, Grayscale, and Color. We chose Color, to capture the full-color image as a 24-bit, 16.7 million possible color, RGB color data stream. This is also the *only* color option the UMAX scanner offers, so it wasn't a tough decision to capture the color photo in a color mode!

If you want to turn a color photo into a grayscale digitized image, let Photoshop do the converting. In a traditional setting, *luminosity*, the brightness found in colors, is not evenly distributed within the RGB channels that make up a TrueColor digital image. To get a natural-looking grayscale image from a color picture, the relationship of the relative luminosities must be preserved when the color is removed from the original. Most scanners don't automatically compensate for the weighted average of Red, Green, and Blue luminosities when you capture a full color image using a grayscale setting. But *Photoshop* does compensate for this when it makes a conversion.

Photoshop has the right tools for transforming a color image to grayscale, so scan a color image *as a color image* when acquiring it digitally. You'll learn all about how Photoshop sees and transforms colors to grayscale in Chapter 16.

Resolution versus Image Dimensions

Before you scan, you should consider what image resolution you want to wind up with. *Resolution* is the frequency of digital samples per inch the scanner creates from a source image. *Image dimensions* (the height and width) are dependent on your scanner's resolution. Both play a role in determining the size and quality of an image you edit and then send to a printer.

If your scanner can change the size as well as the resolution of a scanned image, let it do the math for you. If you don't, you'll have to use the relationship between image dimension and resolution to calculate the ideal scan for a specific assignment.

Digital images are made up of pixels, which in turn have a relative size depending on how many per inch you decide to scan from an original image. Without altering the structure of a digital image file, you can take advantage of a digital Truth: image dimensions increase as image resolution decreases. Try scanning a 1" by 1" image at a 300 dpi setting, then use the **I**mage, Image **S**ize command within Photoshop to decrease the image's resolution. If you check the Constrain: **F**ile Size box item and then enter **150** in the pixels/inch box, the image's

dimensions will increase to 2" by 2". By constraining the file size, you change the size of the pixels, not the number or placement of the pixels. This process doesn't require any interpolation on Photoshop's part, so you don't lose any image quality. What you end up with is a good image size and resolution for printing to a medium-quality publication. When you're given a photo to work with that is destined to appear in print at a size *other* than its original width and height, the benefit of understanding the interrelationship of file size, image dimensions, and image resolution becomes immediately apparent.

On the other hand, you may want to underscan an 8 by 10 photo at 75 dpi, if you know it's going to press as a 4 by 5 image at 150 dpi. It's also important that a scanned image is easy to see when you use Photoshop's tools to modify it. The smaller the pixel/inch sample, the larger the pixels will appear onscreen, each pixel representing a coarser view of the corresponding area in the original that was scanned. You can retouch an image area more easily if the pixels that make up the image aren't visible at your chosen viewing resolution. It's the same as traditional chemical retouching; it's much easier to restore a photo that has fine film grain, than muddling through a mass of grain the size of golf balls.

Before you scan an image, ask yourself the following questions:

✔ What dimensions are you comfortable working with when editing a particular image?

A 6 by 4 snapshot, for example, when sampled at more than 100 dpi will fill your Photoshop workspace at a 100-percent view. When you scan a larger photograph that will be used at a smaller size, you can set your scanner sampling rate anywhere from 100–150 dpi. You'll get a good image that you can zoom in on to do your work, and a small image file size, so your system's RAM isn't deluged with unwanted digital information.

✔ How big is the final print from your Photoshop work going to be?

In this example, a 4 by 6 photo would make a good accompanying graphic in an article within a publication. If you're targeting a publication for your work, and you want your digital image to be the same size as your original photo, the question then becomes one of resolution.

Chapter 20 covers printing, but as a simple rule of thumb, use table 2.1 to approximate the resolution of the digitized image for the best printing type.

Table 2.1
Sampling Resolutions (Approximate)

Type of Printer	Printer Lines/Inch	Ideal Scanning
2540 dpi image setter	133–150 lpi	300 dpi
1200 dpi laser printer or imagesetter	85 lpi	150 dpi
300 dpi laser printer	43–50 dpi	75–100 dpi

Remember that these figures are approximations—a mixture of math combined with experience. Commercial printers' line screens vary, but you can estimate the ideal sampling rate for your scanner by multiplying a printer's lines-per-inch value by two.

Ask your commercial printer how many lines per inch are the best for his presses. He'll be able to tell you what line screen will be used on your piece to produce the best printed results, and this in turn should play a deciding factor before scanning any image destined for publication.

The hard and fast rule for computer screen presentations, however, is entirely different. A monitor displays graphical images at 72 to 96 pixels per inch. A commercial printers' ink dots are *not* the same size as a monitor's pixels. If you're scanning an image at a 100 percent, one-to-one ratio that will end up in a computer slide show (like Lotus Freelance Graphics or Microsoft PowerPoint, for example), you don't need to sample (scan) an original image any higher than 96 dpi.

Determining the Best Sampling Rate

Determining the best sampling rate for an image can be a little tricky. Too low a sampling rate, and you have an image composed of fewer pixels per inch, a coarser image, and much less information to work with. You'll get a nice small file size, but you can't refine the image or do detail work in Photoshop on the image because "the dots are too big."

More is not necessarily better, though. If you over-sample an image, you end up with a large file size and more information in the file than you need for editing and/or printing purposes. Large files are a burden on your system's memory resources and hard drive space. Printing a file that has more information in it than a printer can handle will take an eternity to output, and will undoubtedly irritate any commercial printer or service bureau you engage. Time is money to them, just as it is to you. And even if you're not professionally printing an image, an image file whose resolution exceeds a laser printer's capability to reproduce is bound to bottleneck the printer cue in an office environment, and not win you a lot of thanks from your coworkers!

For example, one of a Linotronic imagesetter's output resolutions is 2540 dots per inch on film. It typically uses a line screen value of 133 lines per inch at this resolution. If you send the Linotronic an image file that was scanned at 600 dpi (twice the ideal scanning resolution for the imagesetter, as shown in table 2.1), the data in the image file will be read into memory, spooled to the imagesetter, and then half of it will be discarded in the printing process as unnecessary and unusable information.

Always keep an image's final printed dimensions and resolution in mind before you scan an image. It's very easy to get carried away with "ambitious" scanning without a clue as to the consequences or what the resulting file sizes for these digital captures will be.

Use the information in table 2.2 as a guide to the file size you can expect when scanning 24-bit color images.

Table 2.2
Typical Graphic File Sizes

At a sample of	A photo that's (in inches)	Becomes
75 dpi	4 × 6	400K
150 dpi	4 × 6	1.5M
300 dpi	4 × 6	6.2M
75 dpi	5 × 7	578K
150 dpi	5 × 7	2.2M
300 dpi	5 × 7	9M
75 dpi	8 × 10	1.3M
150 dpi	8 × 10	5.1M
300 dpi	8 × 10	20.6M

Controlling File Size

As you can see in the preceding table, there's a need to select an ideal resolution for your digital samples, and the need for extra RAM, hard drive space, and a file compression utility if you're going to be working with even a handful of high-quality images.

But if you have an assignment that's due tomorrow, you don't have the luxury of mulling the numbers over, we've provided some ballpark guesstimates as to the dpi settings for scanning for different kinds of output:

If you're printing an image at a 1:1 size for an in-house newsletter using a 300 to 600 dpi PostScript laser printer, scan black-and-white photos at a grayscale setting of no more than 125 dpi. If you're scanning a 1-to-1 image that will be shown only on a monitor, scan no higher (in color or B&W) than 96 dpi. If you're going for the cover of *Vogue* magazine, scan at 300 dpi, color, 1-to-1, and we'd like to talk with you about future business collaborations!

A good first step in economizing file sizes is to watch out for white space. *White space* is the empty, uncropped area surrounding an image. It contributes nothing, and needlessly creates large digital image files. In figure 2.7, notice the 8 1/2 by 13 cropping box in the active window of the UMAX source interface. Most of the contents of the box is the white of the scanner's cover and not the photo. If the white space isn't cropped out before scanning it will be captured along with the balloons. With the scanner set at 100% at 150 dpi, the file size will be a whopping 6.18M file! In figure 2.8, the cropping box was dragged to fit the photo. The file size has decreased to a comfortable 1.6M after most of the white space was cropped from the active window. If you have a scanner with a similar interface, pay attention to what is inside the cropping box.

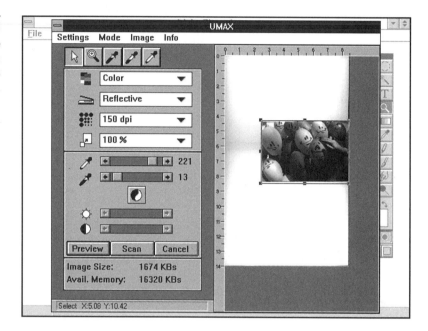

The UMAX Source Interface has an onscreen button that when clicked, auto-adjusts the *density range* for the source image. Some source images may lack contrast, may appear too dark to register good detail in certain areas, or may be faded and not contain enough visual information to produce a good scan at default density settings.

Density ranges can be compensated for to a certain degree with an automatic feature found in several scanning software packages, or with the physical on-board adjustments many scanners have. The non-fancy name for density adjustment controls on some less expensive scanners is the Brightness and Contrast control.

Is adjusting density ranges the same thing as adjusting the Brightness and Contrast? Not quite. It's analogous to having a graphic equalizer on your stereo, or simple bass and treble controls. But in any case, if the scanner you're considering for purchase doesn't have *any* sort of pre-scanning adjustments, keep shopping. It's important to be able to compensate for source deficiencies at the earliest possible stage of the digitizing process. Otherwise, it's a time-consuming pain to have to use Photoshop to make these corrections when they are so easily made *before* scanning.

Out of a possible 256 density values in a picture, the UMAX interface indicates that the balloon photo (fig. 2.8) has a density range from 13, our darkest value, to 221, our "whitest white." These figures and experienced eyes indicate that this is a pretty good photo and will make a good scan. There won't be any areas blocking in or blowing out because we have a wide range of values, and with lots of in-between values expressed.

When an image has most of its density values toward the center, the gray point, the image (information-wise) is low in contrast, muddy looking, and *blocked in*. Conversely, an image with no gray values near the center of the density range, with only absolute blacks and whites, is very contrasty and is said to be *blown out*.

 When any one particular density range from 0 to 255 is packed—absolutely saturated—with image information, the scanner's photo-sensitive cells will *clip* that range, and your scan will feature an ugly spot in that image area. *Clipping* in an image area can be corrected in Photoshop, and it also can be *created* in Photoshop. Read Chapter 6 on color-correcting an heirloom image for more information about saturating and clipping.

Getting the Information Straight

Make sure that your image is parallel to the scanner's edge when you scan. In English—don't scan crookedly, unless you're trying to achieve this effect. A lot of folks get careless when they scan, figuring that imaging *software* can cope with ham-handed scanning practices. After a breeze through Photoshop's (or another imaging program's) feature set, they discover that it's possible to *rotate* a sloppy scan to get the telephone poles vertical in an image. *Rotating* is the spinning of the image around an imaginary center spoke, and Photoshop does this very well. But Photoshop's ability to rotate isn't the point.

The Rotate effect in Photoshop is intended for creating artistic effects, not to compensate for poor scanning procedures. The rotate effect requires processing power (RAM) proportional to the file size of the image. It is conceivable, and even possible, to rotate an image to straighten it out, but if the image exceeds 3M or so, you will force your PC's processor to gnash and churn for minutes on end. And then your system may crash because you ran out of memory or scratch disk space on your drive.

There's another disadvantage to correcting an image's angle with software. Photoshop has to perform *interpolation* in order to rotate an image, which involves reassigning each pixel in the image a new color and tonal value. Sometimes this comes out looking fine, sometimes not. When you Skew, Rotate, or otherwise distort an image, you're actually creating an *effect*, and this requires "translating" the data that makes up the image. Something is always lost in the translation. Save translations for creating a new effect, not to compensate for a bad scan.

There's one exception to the rule. You *do* want to scan an image crooked when you're scanning a screened photo from a magazine or other printed source. The trick is to scan it at precisely the exact amount of crookedness necessary to eliminate moire patterns (those zigzags or rosette patterns that disrupt an image's visual content. This happens when the angle of a pattern is laid on top on another pattern whose angle is neither complementary, nor exactly opposing). Photos that have been printed on a press are made up of ink dots that were produced using the line screens and frequencies mentioned in table 2.1. For black-and-white printing, the screen is usually applied at a 45 degree angle. Screens used in process color printing are set at varying angles to each other.

Experiment with scanning a printed image at various angles until you get the results you want. Don't scan at a rate of more than 100 dpi. An image printed using dots of ink only has a limited, fixed amount of information you can capture, unlike a continuous tone photographic print.

But before you dive into scanning printed material, check out the *copyright* on the source material first. Many budding desktop publishers have been nipped because of using another professional's work without consent or paying royalties. Scanning your own original art yields better quality, it's more rewarding, and less costly than getting hauled into court for appropriating someone else's craft.

Now that important considerations have been covered about how image placement, resolution, image dimensions, and tonal balance fit into optimizing the scan of an image, it's time to resume the actual process. All the theory and explanations are put into practice in the following exercise.

Scanning the Right Image at the Right Settings

Choose an appropriate image type (Color/24-bit was chosen in this example)

Determines the type of image created.

Change your image dimensions or percentage if necessary

In the balloon example, nothing was changed. It was set to 100% or 1:1 ratio.

Set your sampling rate (resolution) to 150 dpi

This will produce a digital image that's easy to edit, moderate in file size, and will print well to a high-resolution output device.

Position your cropping box loosely around your Preview image

Sets the area the scanner will scan and turn into a file.

Use your scanner hardware or software controls to adjust the lightness/darkness of the scan	The UMAX Auto adjust button was used, and the results were double-checked by eye. In this case, the setting was okay.
Press the Scan button	The image is scanned.
Exit the scanner source interface, by choosing **S**ettings, **E**xit (or press Alt+F4)	You are returned to the Photoshop workspace with your newly acquired image in a window ready for editing, naming, and saving.

Try to leave a *little* bit of white space or room around your photo when scanning. *Rough* cropping should be done in the scanning process, with final cropping performed in Photoshop, where you get a better view of the image than in a source interface preview.

Transferring all of the information generated from a 4 by 6 photo captured at 24-bits per pixel, and 150 samples per inch into your PC's memory is a time-consuming one. (The authors calculated it to be 0.7 coffee breaks.) But it was worth the wait. The image scanned appears in Photoshop's workspace as seen in figure 2.9.

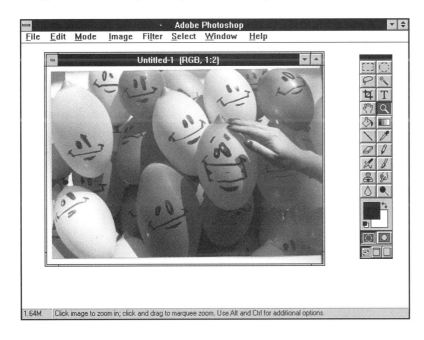

Figure 2.9
Photoshop displays the scanned image that's in your PC's RAM.

From the Source to the Sample

A Histogram of the Scan

Now that the scanned image is displayed in Photoshop, think about the density level setting
that was used for the scan. The scanner evaluated the photo's white point as 221 and the black
point as 13. It then based all the other in-between values densities on this initial information
about absolute white and black points.

We may never have *total* control over how color densities are arranged in a digital image to
create the "perfect" picture. But Photoshop's powerful mapping options can go a long way
toward making a dull picture sparkle, and a good picture great. One such mapping function
has to do with seeing (and changing!) the actual levels of densities from where they originally
were mapped by the scanner. You can snap up a dull picture, or retrieve parts of an image you
thought had faded away through time, by redistributing the amount of pixels in a given area
in the density range.

Redistributing the tonal densities in an image is accomplished through using one of the
Adjust commands in Photoshop's Image menu. Several of Photoshop's commands have the
capability to redistribute densities, and they vary in their level of sophistication and ease of
use. The easiest and second most robust command is Photoshop's Levels. With an image open
and active in the Photoshop workspace, choosing Image, Adjust, then Levels (or pressing
Ctrl+L) brings the Levels command dialog box to the screen.

The Levels command dialog box sports a graph, called a histogram, of the active image. As
you'll see in Chapter 3, a *histogram* is a map that represents graphical data plotted against a set
of parameters. The Levels histogram shows you where all the pixels that make up the active
image are located with respect to how bright a pixel appears (the X axis) versus how many
pixels in the image occupy a specific brightness value (the Y axis). Color and Grayscale images
alike are portrayed in the Levels histogram according to one set of criteria—tonal density, or
brightness, measured between absolute white (255), and the darkest point (0).

A histogram of a digital image is unique to that image; you'd rarely find two identical brightness maps for different pictures. One picture may have wild fluctuations in neighboring
brightness values between 0 and 255, whereas another might have a flat curve, as you'd find in
a dim, low-contrast picture.

You'll be using the image of the balloons in this chapter's exercises soon. The file is named
THEBUNCH.TIF on the companion CD. Now's a good time to open this file, so you can see
for yourself how the Levels command maps brightness ranges for an image, and how this
information can be modified to produce a clearer, more dynamic digital photograph. In
figure 2.10, we've called the Levels command to the screen to see the "landscape" of brightness values in the image as it was just scanned.

As you can see in figure 2.10., the scanner did a good job of separating neighboring pixel
brightness values to create a digital image with a lot of detail and contrast. Note that there are
numerous spikes in the histogram, followed by "dropouts"—tonal points on the brightness
scale where there are no pixels occupying them. The extreme, narrow differences in the tonal,
brightness scheme of this image are visually represented in the picture as slightly harsh

contrasts in areas across the balloons. What we'd *expect* to see should be an even gradation of tones on the main subjects, the balloons, as sunlight gently cascades across their surfaces from light to shadow. The sunlight illuminating the scene obviously was too intense on the surface of the balloons, and although the scanner faithfully captured the visual information, it's presently aesthetically wrong.

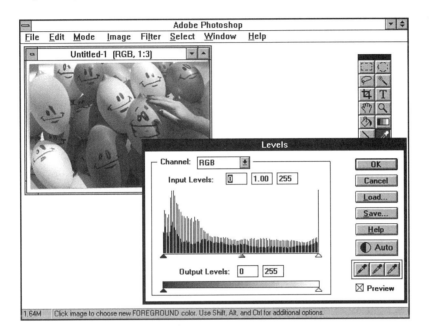

Figure 2.10
A "comb" effect in a histogram is saying that graduations from dark to light are uneven; there are missing components to an even tonal transition from light to dark.

Fortunately, post-processing work can be performed on a captured image in Photoshop before an image is saved to hard disk. The Auto range button in the Levels dialog box can be used to automatically "clip" the bottom and topmost ranges from the brightness scale for the image. In effect, the Auto range option redefines the Black Point and White Point in an image, allowing Photoshop to recalculate and redistribute tonal values along the image's brightness scale proportionately. Typically, this creates vacancies in the midtone range of an image, where pixels may "fill in" and smooth the flow of the image's tones from light to dark.

In figure 2.11, we've clicked on the Auto range button, and the histogram in the Levels dialog box now reflects the proposed changes Photoshop will execute if OK is clicked on. After you press the Auto button, or make any other changes to an active image with the Levels command, the resulting histogram *does not* represent the future distribution of pixels on the brightness scale, but rather represents the delta, the *change* from the original histogram of the image. If Photoshop could speak, it would say, "these are the changes I propose to make when you allow me to Auto-adjust the range of tonal densities in this image."

Figure 2.11
In general, the Auto Levels adjustment will enhance the scanner's capture of an original photograph.

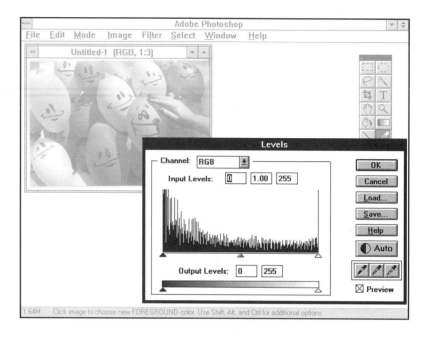

But Photoshop doesn't speak (at least the authors' copy doesn't), and the changes Photoshop proposes as reflected in the histogram aren't easily understood at a casual glance. That's why you should look at the digital image with your own eyes, with the Preview box in the Levels dialog box checked, so you can see the *visual* effect of the proposed changes *before* clicking OK in the Levels command.

Our observation was that Photoshop's Auto range option did indeed smooth out the distribution of pixels in the image and created a more eye-pleasing digital capture from the scan of the original. In your own experiences with particular images, though, you may not want to do any adjusting before saving an image to your hard disk.

The important observation here though, is that although you have several means available for precisely viewing and adjusting an image according to detailed information Photoshop can provide, never forfeit the years of experience you may have with your own trained eyes. There are several artificial means for whipping an image into mathematical perfection, but your vision and judgment are the best tools you have when scanning.

The Photoshop Levels dialog box can be moved around your workspace, but you can't move your photo if the Levels box covers it up. Tuck your photo up into a corner of Photoshop's workspace *before* you issue the Levels command. This way you'll be able to preview any changes you may make. This also holds true for any number of Photoshop dialog boxes, so it's always a prudent move to keep images positioned away from the center of Photoshop's workspace.

How a histogram should be "read" and manual changes should be affected based on these readings is discussed in detail in Chapter 3.

Now that the image has been acquired and adjusted, it's time to save this digital image data to your hard drive. It's a good idea to save a scanned image to hard disk as soon as you are happy with the tonal balance and basic look of the scan. Scanned images continue to reside in system RAM after acquisition, and naming and saving the image to disk assures you that a sudden power outage or other unscheduled event doesn't wipe out your work!

A scanned image, regardless of color content, can be saved in any number of graphical file formats, and this is the topic covered in the next section.

Saving Your Scanned Image

Now, this balloon picture is a good one, but not a great one. The Photoshop status bar says in the bottom left corner that it'll cost you 1.63M of hard disk space to save it, as is, in an uncompressed format. What the authors usually do with images created for examples or to experiment with is to JPEG (jay-peg) them. It sounds violent, but for the most part, it simply reduces the stored file size of an image to about a 10 to 1 ratio. When you open a JPEGged file (when Photoshop loads the file into system RAM), the file expands in size once more. It's pretty useful, but it's also "lossey compression," a scheme that discards almost undetectable color information within the image in the process.

JPEG file compression is covered in the next section. But one or two things need to be done with this image first, and audience participation is required now so you can actually evaluate the JPEG format. If you don't already have the THEBUNCH.TIF image found on the companion CD active in Photoshop right now, now's an ideal time to open it.

Saving an Image, JPEG-Style

If you have not already done so, click on the Auto button in the Levels dialog box	Changes the distribution of intermediate density levels as previously discussed.
Choose OK to accept the changes and return to the workspace	
From the toolbox, choose the Rectangular marquee tool (the icon on the first row left) and click and drag it from the upper-left hand corner to the lower-right hand corner of the photo	You want to select only the photo and none of the surrounding white space.
From the **E**dit menu choose C**r**op	You have cropped the picture so that no white border shows, and you have reduced the image's file size.

continues

From the Source to the Sample

continued

Choose **F**ile, **S**ave	Brings up a dialog box where you can name the file and choose a file format from the drop-down box in the lower-left hand corner of the screen.
From the Save File as Format **T**ype drop-down box in the lower-left hand corner, choose JPEG (*.JPG)	
In the File **N**ame box, highlight the asterisk and type an eight letter (or less) name for the file; using the Dri**v**es and **D**irectories fields, choose a suitable subdirectory location on your own hard disk; be sure the file has the JPG extension	
Click on OK to save the file	The JPEG Options box appears.
Choose Save to accept the Photoshop default of Good for the JPEG quality level	The scan is saved to your hard disk as THEBUNCH.JPG.

Figure 2.12 shows the result of your work.

Figure 2.12
When stored as a JPEG compression format, this image is 52K. When loaded into memory, it expands back to 1.46M!

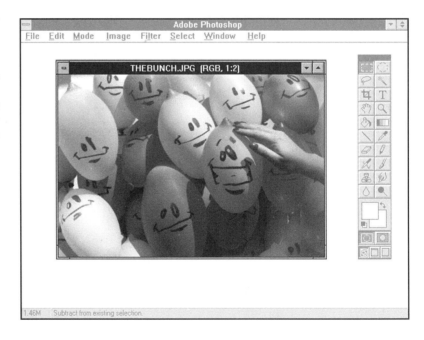

An image has to ultimately become a saved file. It can't stay in your system's RAM indefinitely unless you have a weird arrangement with your local power company. The preceding discussion has outlined a solid working path from source image to Photoshop here. Now it's time to talk about *file compression* for digital images.

Squeezing the Most out of an Image

If you're really into image enhancing, you'll quickly amass an entire hard drive full of images. At the tune of 1 to 12M each, you'll have no elbow-room for other programs, files, or games! But you can *compress* images so they take less disk space, and compression schemes come in two categories; *lossless* compression and *lossey*. These terms mean exactly what you think they mean. With one method, you don't lose any information when you do it; the other loses some information when you compress, like when using JPEG.

Lossless Compression

Photoshop supports LZW lossless compression of TIFF formatted files. Figure 2.13 shows an uncompressed file on the right (taken from HANDBAG.TIF on the companion CD) and a LZW-compressed file on the left. When the file on the left was saved to a different name—HANDBAGZ.TIF—IBM type and LZW Compression were checked in the TIFF Options box. This dialog box pops up whenever you save a *.TIF format image.

A side-by-side comparison of the two files shows no difference between the two. That's because the image on the left, the LZW, *losslessly* compressed file, contains identical information to the image on the right in the figure. HANDBAGZ.TIF expands back to its original size of 1.13M when it's called up in Photoshop and it's loaded into system RAM.

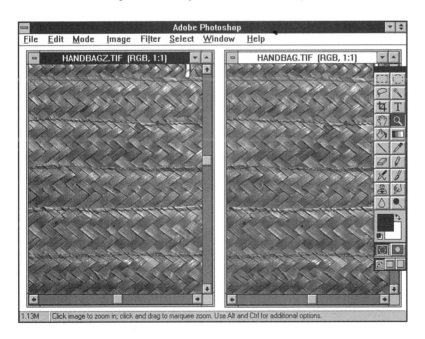

Figure 2.13

Lossless compression only shrinks the image's file size while it's inactive, being stored on your hard disk.

Lempel and Ziv, two mathematicians who wrote a treatise in the late 1960s on algorithmic compression, are responsible for the many types of lossless compression available today in programs like Photoshop. They understood the eventual need for condensing, or compressing mathematical data in a secure way that didn't lose any of the data's information.

The LZW compression scheme recognizes repetitive streams of data within a file and "shorthands" them. Imagine a file that contained a 1, followed by 100 zeros, then another 1 on the end. Then try writing it! It's much simpler to write 1, then 100 zeros, then 1, isn't it? This is the basic theory of lossless compression based on Lempel and Ziv's postulate. Photoshop's particular flavor of Lempel-Ziv's lossless compression is called LZW (for Lempel, Ziv, and Welch, a third contributor), and it's available for the TIF file format type.

Before anyone goes running off saying, "Oh, yes, lossless compression is for me! The handbags are identical! Total integrity and fidelity using LZW compression!", take a look at how well (how much) you compressed the handbag. Windows File Manager shows where the two handbags are stored and what their file sizes are. Check out HANDBAG.TIF and then HANBAGZ.TIF at the bottom of the directory tree (see fig. 2.14). It's apparent that the handbag would be better stored in your *closet,* than on your hard drive with LZW compression.

Figure 2.14
HANDBAGZ.TIF,
over
HANDBAG.TIF,
shows about a 3.5
percent overall
compression.

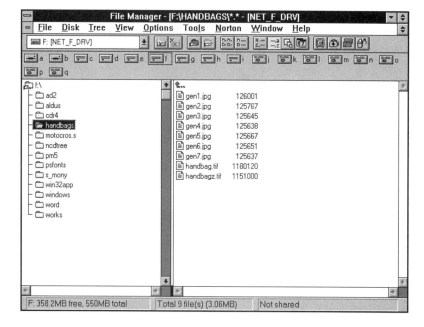

Don't get the idea that LZW, lossless compression will always squash an image file 3 percent. This number varies on a case-by-case incidence. The handbag has a repeating pattern in it, but the weave does not repeat *exactly* from border to border, and this slight variation may be why LZW compression couldn't condense the information very well. If you took a picture of a Japanese flag, a red circle on a field of white, LZW compression would probably compress the image substantially, due to its simple design, and a lot of repeated information about the white background.

The role LZW compression can play in the struggle to keep file sizes small is a minor one, yet it offers absolute visual integrity. If you deal with a lot of images in your work, there's a clear need for a more substantial compression scheme, though, and this is where JPEG enters the scene.

Taking a Hint from the Experts

JPEG stands for the Joint Photographer's Experts Group, and it is both a file format and a compression technology. It's a special sort of compression that's intended to be used with photographic images. During this compression, some information about the image is discarded, or lost.

Is a JPEG image a flagrantly inaccurate one, then? Not at all. A group of professional photographers took great care in deciding exactly which component of visual information in an image can be discarded without the human eye really perceiving it.

A color component in a digital image has Hue, Saturation, and Brightness (sometimes also called Intensity or Value). Saturation is the presence of color, and the absence of all color in a photo creates a monochrome photo (which we often call a black-and-white photo). Saturation expresses the relationship of color component to grayscale in an image. Although color is an important component in an image, the grayscale component is responsible for setting the tone in an image—whether the image displays a little, or a lot of contrast. The human eye is very sensitive to changes in contrast. Contrast is affected when grayscale values are altered.

JPEG doesn't touch the grayscale components, but instead does some averaging of the *hues* within a photo. This is a fairly safe thing to do because in reality the human eye only sends a limited amount of different hue information to the brain at one time. By reducing the overall amount of different hues, JPEG can create a file similar to the original, but with greater economy.

Because the screen captures in this book don't reflect the subtleties and nuances in color photography, you may want to follow along with both the HANDBAG and the MOTOCROS files found on the companion CD, as you examine the lossey, JPEG method of compression.

In figure 2.15, the HANDBAG.TIF file was saved as GEN1.JPG. Good compression, as offered in Photoshop's JPEG Options, was chosen for the quality of the JPEG image. If you look at both images side by side on your own screen, you probably won't notice any difference in photographic quality.

Figure 2.15
A picture that's been JPEGged once, compared to the original.

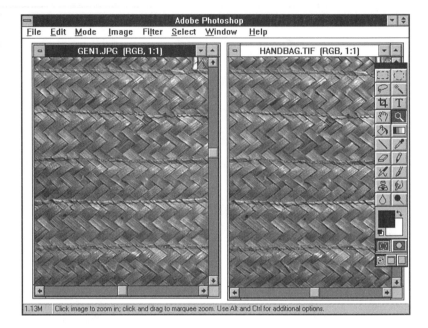

The Good compression ratio (which is Photoshop's default setting) yielded about a 10 to 1 compression ratio. The range of compression that may be set is from Fair Quality to Excellent quality. The faithfulness with which JPEG compression renders a file is based on the compression ratio (the higher the quality, the less compression), *and* the nature of the photo.

The handbag photo may be described as a *low-frequency* picture. It has only a few different hues in it. It has large areas of similar color and the overall variation in the brown hue of the handbag is slight. The actual number of colors used in this 16.7 million, 24-bit file is 9,111.

Surprising, isn't it? The human eye finds more visual information in the *weave* of the handbag (the variations in contrast, the grayscale components) than the 9,111 different shades of color. It's simple for JPEG to average out the hue differences with little *perceivable* alteration to the overall image quality.

By using JPEG compression to store this image, you now have a lot more hard drive space. Look back at the file sizes as shown in figure 2.11. If you delete the original TIF file and keep only the GEN1.JPG, you'll recover more than a megabyte of precious drive space!

If you have a once-in-a-lifetime, you're-never-going-to-see-it-again photo you've digitized, you may not want to use a lossey compression scheme like JPEG on it at all. In the examples that follow, you'll learn exactly what part of the original image JPEG discards. You are the best judge of how to treat your images.

It would be unfair to suggest *all* your valuable images should be compressed in a lossey format. Most of the time you'll be satisfied with a JPEG, and you can delete the original, uncompressed file, but there may be exceptional circumstances and times you won't want to do this.

It was mentioned earlier that the handbag image is a low-frequency image with a small "palette" of colors. What happens when you JPEG a *high*-frequency image, with a wider color range? To perform a little experiment in Photoshop with an image to see what is actually lost when you do lossey compression, open the MOTOCROS.TIF file from the companion CD, and follow these steps.

Putting the Squeeze on Some Bikers

Open the MOTOCROS.TIF file

Choose **F**ile, Save **A**s	Lets you rename the file.
Choose *.JPG from the available File Formats	Specifies the JPEG compression scheme as your new file format.
Type **MOTOGEN1.JPG** in the File **N**ame box; click on OK to save the file	Indicates that this file is the first generation of lossey compression done on the image.
Open the MOTOCROS.TIF file from the companion CD once again	This is the original image that will be used for comparison.
Choose **I**mage, **C**alculate, and then Difference	Maps the difference between two different images that have the same size and resolution.
Choose MOTOCROS.TIF and RGB Channel as the Source **1** selections, choose MOTOGEN1.JPG and RGB Channel as the Source **2** selections, choose New Document and RGB Channel in the **D**estination field, and then click on OK	Creates a new image made up of the differences between the TIF and the JPG images.

continues

I

From the Source to the Sample

continued

Choose **I**mage, **M**ap, and then Threshold (or press Ctrl+T)	The new UNTITLED-1 image contains information too subtle to see clearly. The Threshold command casts all visual data into a white category or a black one, super-contrasting any and all visual data.
Enter **9** in the Threshold Level box	This is an arbitrary value, which revealed file discrepancies in this instance. Other levels of Thresholding may work better depending on the image.
Click on OK	Returns you to Photoshop's workspace.

In figure 2.16, a Threshold command has been used with the image Untitled-1, which was created out of the differences between the lossey, JPEGged file, and the original image.

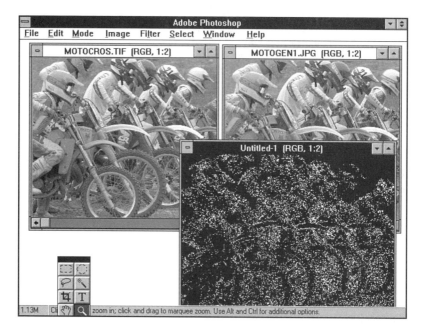

Figure 2.16
Use the Difference menu option to see the differences between two images of the same subject.

The motocross bikers and their bikes create a high-frequency scheme within the image because the colors vary drastically from neighboring pixel to pixel. The way JPEG handled the averaging of these color differences is obvious in Untitled-1; there's practically no difference in the dirt background, but when red graduates quickly to white, and so on, JPEG had to round off a lot of color values in order to reduce the file size.

How Far Can You Go Before I Notice?

A very natural question people ask about JPEG compression is whether you lose some of the original material with every *successive* opening and closing of the file. This is a fair question; in theory it's analogous to what a 10th generation photocopy looks like compared to the original.

You are not going to be asked to perform compression 10 more times on the motocross image in order to witness the net effect. After all, *Inside Adobe Photoshop* is supposed to make your work easier! The authors' own curiosity was piqued, however, and the following examples may shed some light.

Whatever discernible loss performed on MOTOCROSS.TIF occurred on the *first* instance of JPEGging it. Figure 2.17 demonstrates the difference between the first JPEG and one done seven times later. As you can see, the difference is nominal.

From the Source to the Sample

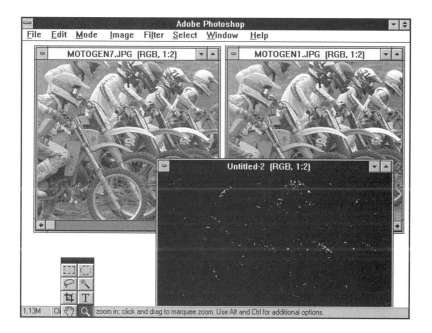

Figure 2.17
The difference between the two images has been exaggerated using the Threshold command so you can see if there is a difference.

Figure 2.14 bears out the observation that once you've used lossey compression on an image, no more significant compression takes place whether you've re-squashed the file once, or a half a dozen times. The file size difference between a first generation JPEG and a 7th are in the bytes-range, which is very small. Part of the reason for this is that certain pixels that have been questionable candidates for averaging in the first generation may have been sitting exactly on the "halfway point" of JPEG's compression criteria. Successive generations of JPEGging simply "tipped the scales" in favor of including them in the lossey process.

But most of the reason for the nominal discrepancies between generation 1 through 7 is due to the authors' use of *Stacker*, and not with JPEG or Photoshop. *Stacker* is a hard drive compression utility, like MS-DOS 6.0's *DoubleSpace*, that actively optimizes a PC's available hard drive space.

Therefore, our numbers for the JPEG files are not hard-and-fast data, but rather reflect Stacker's reportage of the file sizes at the time of compression. Use JPEG with the same image on different days, and a hard disk outfitted with "on the fly" compression like Stacker will report different, yet similar numbers.

So Should I Use JPEG or Not?

Sorry, the ball's in your court on this one. The authors' personal practice is not only to JPEG images on their hard disks but also to archive an uncompressed original on floppy and tape backups.

The Joint Photographer's Experts Group gave a lot of mathematical and aesthetic consideration to imaging when they cooked up JPEG. It was designed to accommodate the professional photographer's need to relieve their hard drives from a suffocating sea of visual information. JPEG is more subtle than you imagine when it comes to lossey compression, and the authors suggest that the real world difference between a JPEG image and an uncompressed image is very close to *none*.

Toss the hard-core, empirical data you've been shown out the window for a moment. Skip the Difference menu option and look at the two images side by side with your own eyes.

Seeing Is Disbelieving

Perceived differences are not always *actual* differences. Perceived differences are skewed by other information we are given that doesn't relate to the absolute evaluation we have before us. Remember the coffee commercials where folks are asked to taste the difference between fresh-brewed and freeze-dried crystals? They were blindfolded to remove the extra visual information about the two coffees, so they could concentrate on true differences. We all know that Coffee #2 tastes just fine with the blindfold on, but the moment you see the freeze-dry jar, this coffee doesn't taste as good! That's a false perceived difference that had nothing to do with the *actual* difference in coffees.

The same holds true with a JPEGged file when compared to the original. There is a difference between the two, but it's virtually imperceptible. Any perceived difference is really in your head because we've shown you the Difference Experiment. The bottom line is that you can save lots of hard disk space by JPEGging your work. Period. Use your eyes to honestly evaluate the images when you choose a storage method. And understand too, that the way you store a digital image is as important as the effort you put into creating it.

Computer hardware and software enhance your productivity as an imaging-type of person. But PCs take instructions from you; they can't evaluate your specific needs on a particular

assignment. Simply know your tools, and have the confidence in your eyes and your own judgment. The next section has a perfect example of how to select the right tool, and decide the best use for it in your work.

The Digital Camera

As mentioned earlier, a digital image can be generated in several ways. Aside from generating an image within a PC design program, this chapter has mostly dealt with using a scanner to bring a real world photo, or piece of art into the Land of Binary Files. A recent invention however, the digital camera, needs to be discussed. Instead of using film, the digital camera uses a photo-sensitive grid consisting of thousands of cells that respond to reflected light as it's passed though the lens. Its importance to the field of imaging will become more prevalent in the coming years.

The advantages a digital camera presents are ones of convenience, ecology, and timeliness. Since the data a digital camera captures is piped directly into the PC, there is no developing time, no intermediate stage of a film negative, no running to the store for film, and no chemical waste that calls for proper environmental disposal methods.

Digital cameras currently range in price from $600 to $10,000. The wide variation in price reflects both the newness of the technology and the wide range in capability that these camaras have. Logitech's FotoMan, a modestly priced digital camera, was used for the following experiment.

Downloading a Captured Image

Like a modem, a digital camera downloads the captured information to the PC through an umbilical cable. The FotoMan camera only needs to be attached to the cable during a download, so a PC wasn't needed on site during our field excursion.

FotoMan is a monochrome (black and white) camera, capable of capturing a 3 by 4.133 image at 8-bits/pixel, and 120 digital samples (dots) per inch. Depending on the complexity of the subject, this averages out to about 150K per image. When you consider that you can take 32 images before downloading the visual information, it's a well designed little camera. FotoMan is also TWAIN-compliant, so you're able to do your downloading directly from Photoshop's workspace. In figure 2.18, File-Acquire-TWAIN Source has been chosen from the Photoshop menu.

All you do is double-click on the thumbnail picture of the image you want from FotoMan, then click Done in its source interface, and you'll have the selected image in Photoshop within seconds. In figure 2.19, notice that the image is sideways! This is because the camera was turned sideways in order to take a portrait view of the building. You can remedy this by choosing **I**mage, **R**otate, and then selecting 90CW from the submenu list. The image is then turned in a 90 degree clockwise direction.

From the Source to the Sample

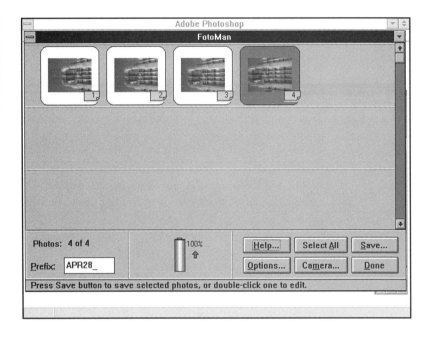

Figure 2.18
The source interface for the TWAIN-compliant FotoMan digital camera.

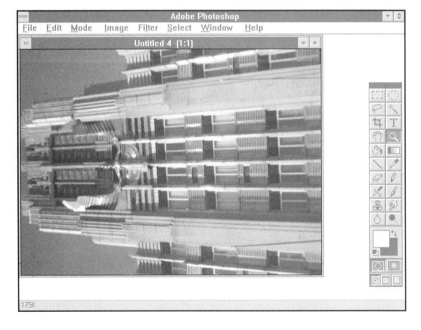

Figure 2.19
Employees at Niagara Mohawk complain about vertigo and papers falling off their desks a lot.

A digital camera is very much like a video camcorder, in that *hot spots*—intense highlights like the reflections from chrome—will cause undesired effects in the captured image, often seen as streaking. Although this image was taken on a brilliant day, the highlights on the building aren't really noticeable. So what *is* noticeable?

The intention in photographing the building was to do a study in geometry. We wanted the art-deco figure that graces the building's fourth floor to be the central point of the composition. So the artist's eye and judgment were correct in selecting and framing the subject, *but the selection of the best tool was wrong.*

FotoMan's standard 64 mm lens was used, which permitted a fixed view of the building. The problem was with FotoMan's fixed resolution of 120 samples/inch. After blowing the image up to twice its original size, both the fixed resolution and the camera's lens design became painfully obvious.

For comparison's sake, figure 2.20 shows the digital camera's capture of the building on the left and a conventional chemical print on the right, captured on film with a Minolta 35mm, SLR camera. A similar length lens (53 mm) was used, and the print was scanned at 150 dpi, a little better than FotoMan's 120 dpi fixed rate.

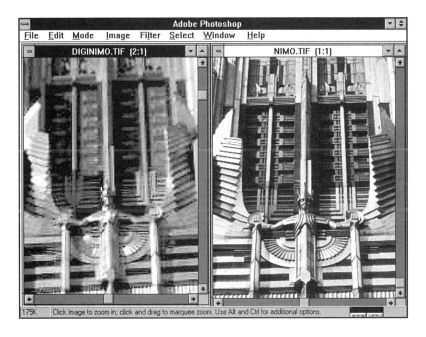

Figure 2.20
The digital camera's fixed resolution "pixellated" the image when it was enlarged.

Any sort of digital imaging, scanner, digital camera, whatever, will reveal its "building blocks" to the naked eye when an image is enlarged. A *pixellated* image is similar to the undesired effect of film grain when a small film negative is used to reproduce a wall-sized poster. If you go back to the observation that the correct tool is part of the key to successful imaging, you learn that in this instance, a scanned chemical photograph is better suited to capture the art-deco winged figure four stories away, than the inexpensive digital camera.

Resolution was the problem, and the right tools for this situation were a regular photo print, and a scanner whose resolution could be varied. The lessons here are to use the right tool for the assignment, and sample stuff with a resolution that will hold up if you intend to enlarge it.

The Proper Tool for the Right Occasion

But don't dismiss the digital camera by any means (see fig 2.21). First of all, you can purchase separate lenses for digital cameras, you can buy more expensive, full-featured models, and you can even equip a lot of present, conventional cameras with a digital film replacement part. The digital camera is quick, candid, and unobtrusive. And if people *do* by chance catch you using it on them, they're fascinated with its design and the technological wonder of it. Both qualities made it an excellent tool for capturing Lou—a friend who *hates* having his picture taken!

Figure 2.21
The FotoMan
digital camera.

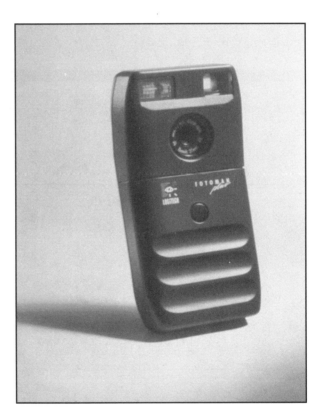

Lou agreed to pose for the picture in figure 2.22 basically because he wanted to see this gizmo work. The authors impressed upon him the immediate gratification of seeing himself on screen in Photoshop, and his camera-shyness abated. So, quick as a Polaroid, his picture was snapped, the information downloaded to Photoshop's workspace, and the Levels command was called up for a fast Auto range adjustment. In about four mouse clicks, here's a before and an after photo that's suitable for placing in a 1200 dpi publication at its original size.

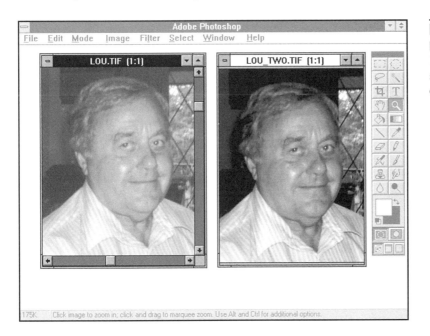

Figure 2.22
It's not the cover of *Time*, but it's a solid, workable, everyday image.

Digital photography, like the digital image enhancing covered later in this book, is an exciting medium. In fact, the two go hand-in-hand. You can compensate for the digital camera's lack of maturity at this time with the techniques covered in this book.

Scanning, the digital camera, and original PC artwork can all be combined to create original imaging work. Photoshop accepts them all, and lets you take advantage of the wonderful plastic quality of working with images seen as electronic data by your PC.

Summary

This chapter covered the phases of the proper setup, the capturing of an image, and the options for saving the digital image, but there's another kind of digital image left to explore that's sort of a "hybrid." Chapter 3 will introduce the PhotoCD, a file format that exists because of a little chemical photography, a little scanning, and more than just a passing nod to file storage. The image quality is superb, and the only requirement is adding the proper CD player to your system. The PhotoCD can be the best of all digital "worlds" to work with in Photoshop.

Chapter Snapshot

In this chapter, you learn how to:

CHAPTER

The PhotoCD

After you have captured and saved an image to a file format, it contains color qualities that form the image. In Photoshop, you can modify several properties of color within an image, but the most basic property is image *gamma*. Although gamma is a very technical attribute, you can easily change it if you understand how digital color components interact with and affect one another.

Now is a good time to explore how dramatically you can change a digital image through *gamma adjustment* because shortly you will be introduced to an exciting new technology that can benefit from your gamma wisdom. PhotoCDs improve the quality of images, free precious hard drive space, provide instant cataloging of scores of images, and offer an economical alternative to scanning—*if* you understand a few things about PhotoCD images and gamma correction.

This chapter provides an actual sample of PhotoCD technology and shows you how to acquire, correct, and work with the PhotoCD format. Even if you're "just looking" at Kodak's latest innovation, you will still want to master the Photoshop features that give you total control over the brightness, contrast, and gamma of an image.

Pixels, Gamma, and Ranges

A *pixel* is the smallest unit of light displayed on a monitor and the smallest element in a digital image. Everything that happens in the digital world—the things that you create, modify, and work with—aren't physical in the sense that they are things you can touch. Pixels are light when you see them on your monitor, but the *qualities* of that light are based on information about color that is *associated* with the pixel. How light behaves, and how color is defined and expressed, is done through *models*: virtual representations of a phenomenon.

Models are concepts that are plotted out in wheel, circles, or other types of *maps*. A color wheel is a *model* of the visible spectrum of light. Models allow you to work with phenomena that can't be (easily) physically manipulated. A model of a color pixel can be expressed as having a gray component, mixed with a color component, then the amalgam that models the pixel is finished by assigning an attribute of how light reflects, or passes through the model. Figure 3.1 is a model of color pixels. The gray and color components of them are struck by light, coming from the left, so we can see the model. It is through models that you can virtually grasp, delete, and arrange pixels with Photoshop.

Figure 3.1
A light unit, or *pixel*, consists of gray and color components.

Although a model of a pixel is useful for describing and controlling aspects of pixel behavior, we commonly don't use this model for most Photoshop functions. A pixel is only the most basic of image building blocks. Another model, the Hue, Saturation, Brightness model, is used instead for specifying color in part, or in all, of a digital image's pixels.

When using Photoshop, you can control many image qualities, but precise editing of individual pixels is a time-consuming and self-effacing ambition. Instead, Photoshop offers options so that you can edit *ranges* of pixels within an image based on similar characteristics. You are indirectly affecting changes to pixels when you edit an image's tonal ranges. The two most common ranges that cause the most dramatic enhancement of an image's realistic qualities are brightness and gamma. *Brightness* is the degree of intensity that you perceive as a color is reflected by (or passed through) an object. *Gamma* is a measurement of contrast—how much different pixels vary in their brightens values—in a specific brightness range: the image's midtones. It's a very important quality to be able to adjust in an image because the midtones represent a lot of the visual content in most images.

Photoshop gives you control over each of the three components of color: hue, saturation, and brightness.

Hue, Saturation, and Brightness: Partners in Color

You can use Photoshop to modify the brightness of an image. This is a particularly powerful capability that can make changes to an image without affecting the overall hue and saturation of the picture. *Hue* and *saturation* are the two other members of the triumvirate that make up an image's color. Before seeing how Photoshop can adjust the pixels within the range of brightness in a digital image to make it picture-perfect, you need to understand how these three components work together.

Hue

The first thing that the human eye uses to distinguish different colors is *hue*. Hue is often called color, but it's wrong to adopt this slang when discussing color as it relates to work in Photoshop. A hue is a particular wavelength of light, and is termed a *pure color* only when saturation and brightness are both at 100 percent. Pure colors are used by Photoshop when you use the Defringe command, but pure colors don't often serve a direct purpose or use in most of your image work. Unlike pure colors, which get their color characteristic purely from Hue, most digital simulations of conventional colors aren't totally saturated, and aren't totally brilliant. You correct color-casting (undesired bluish, greenish, or reddish tinting) in an image by adjusting the hue.

The saturation and brightness components of color lend shading to a hue.

Saturation

Saturation, as modeled (represented) digitally, is the result of mixing gray with a pure color. Gray (also called neutral density) steals from the saturation of a color; an object with highly saturated color (such as a bright, colorful detergent package or bubble gum wrapper) includes almost no gray component. Conversely, color with *no* saturation contains all gray component and displays as a monochrome part of a picture.

For example, an image consisting of rocks, such as that shown in figure 3.2, does not feature highly saturated colors. As figure 3.2 shows, Photoshop's Info palette provides a direct reading of saturation on the spot over which you place the cursor. A reading of 3 percent saturation indicates that the rocks have more gray component than color. Oversaturation, on the other hand, causes clipping in a video image. You learn how to recognize and correct oversaturation in Chapter 6.

Figure 3.2
This photograph lacks color saturation.

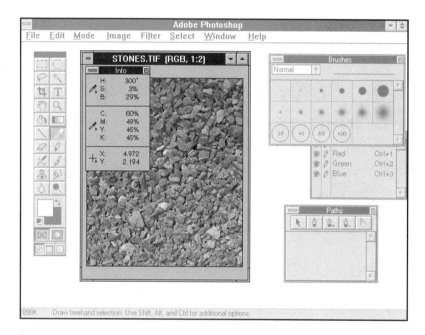

Brightness

The brightness component shapes, bends, and drags the most out of a picture, using the *color content* of the pixels in the digital image to control the image's *visual content*.

Brightness is the only component in the color model that has nothing to do with a color value (referring instead to the *tonal* quality of an image), and yet destroys a picture when it is featured too little or too much in image areas. When mismanaged, this component can wipe out a subject's facial features, turn a sunset into a "blobset," and generally make a photo look like an artist's overused palette.

Managing an Image's Brightness through Mapping

You can express an image's overall brightness as a map. A computer map is just like a physical map; it has an axis and stuff is plotted on it. However, computers display mapping of different image aspects in a very simplified format. Massive number-crunching is performed behind the scenes when you make what *seems* to be the simplest adjustment to a map.

Most computer programs and tools can map one object to another, which means that you can use your PC's innate capability to make swift calculations to help with your imaging work, if you have *coordinates* to plot on a brightness map.

Photoshop provides several types of maps, including one for the brightness component. Before you begin experimenting with the PhotoCD images on the companion CD, you need to understand a brightness mapping feature, which is the Levels command from the **I**mage, **A**djust menu. Once you understand the principle behind this option, you can use it to make educated evaluations of what you need to modify in both PhotoCD format and regular digital images.

Figure 3.3 is a highly stylized illustration of the Levels histogram you'll find when you open an image in Photoshop and select **A**djust from the **I**mage menu and then choose the Levels option. A *histogram* is a graph that represents the range of brightness in an image measured against the number of pixels in a particular value in the range. Each pixel contains color information, which is used with that of the other pixels to weave an image. Unless you change an image's size or resolution, the number of pixels is a constant within an image.

The histogram shown in figure 3.3 represents an incredibly small, 19-pixel digital image, but nonetheless you can make some observations from the graph. The Levels command lets you define a black point, a white point, and a midpoint value other than that which was used to create the original histogram of the image. This histogram was created on the scale of 0 (no brightness) to 255 (absolute brilliance). The result of changing an image's original histogram is the *redistribution* or *reassignment* of the image's color pixels.

Using the Levels dialog box, you can specify an input and output range. When you open the Levels dialog box, the figures and the histogram report the current condition of the image. Changing the input black-and-white point level values invariably increases the contrast in the image. Conversely, the output values decrease the contrast in the image. You change the output by typing in new numbers or moving the sliders on the bar at the bottom of the Levels dialog box.

There is a difference between *points* and *ranges*. Although the Levels command lets you adjust points along the ranges (and enhance an image significantly by doing so), the command doesn't give you full control over ranges of tonal values. See Chapter 6's discussion of the Curves command for more information on making total tonal control work for you in Photoshop.

Figure 3.3
A Photoshop
histogram plots
brightness against
pixel population at
each brightness
value in an image.

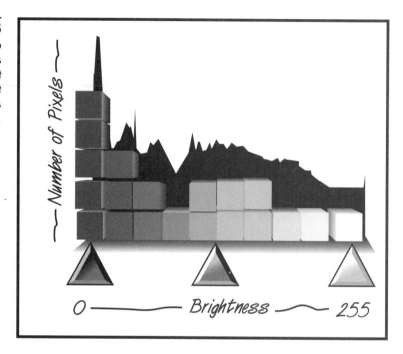

Remapping a Histogram

To remap a histogram, you start by specifying the ideal darkest and lightest shades in the brightness range. By moving the black point up within an image, you eliminate some shades of brightness, thereby *increasing* the contrast in part of the image. You don't destroy pixels by increasing the black point, you simply reassign a higher brightness value to the pixels existing at that point.

The same holds true when you decrease the white point in an image; you don't change the hue or saturation of any pixels, but simply squeeze out part of the brightness range. This forces a sharper shift in brightness values between neighboring pixels to create more contrast.

Controlling Midpoints and Midtones

Photoshop goes a step beyond the simple brightness and contrast controls that you find on even the least expensive TV set. Within the range of brightness on the histogram is a slider that controls where an image's *midtones* lie. In the center of the midtones is a *midpoint,* represented by the middle slider on the Levels histogram.

As mentioned before, the middle of the brightness scale is a vital information range for many snapshots. Fleshtones, nature colors, and even the texture of clouds require much visual information in the pixels that sit in the middle of the histogram. These midtones must express enough contrast within this range so that you can clearly see, for example, the ridges in a piece of wood. To correct the midtones of your image's brightness range, you should move the middle Input Levels slider to the right or left while the Preview checkbox is marked so you can see how these changes affect the midtones in your image.

Adjusting an Image's Gamma

If the shadows in the midtones are mottled rather than crisp, and the highlights are faded and provide little contrast between brightness values, the gamma of the image is too high for your PC. Image *gamma* is a measurement of contrast in the midtones of an image. If you calibrate this midtone part of an image too high, you get a dull, yet brilliant, overall image. The "perfect" picture has sharp blacks, crisp whites, and much variation (contrast) between the midtones. If the whites in your image seem whiter than possible and the darkest shadows have too much visual information, you can't fix these gamma problems by adjusting brightness and contrast. Photoshop can adjust the levels in the midtones right down to the quartertones to reduce the brilliance overkill in specific ranges of the image.

Photoshop offers three tiers of sophistication in adjusting the brightness map this way: the Curves command provides the most complex map, the Levels command is the next most complex, and the Brightness/Contrast command results in the roughest tuning. The next exercise, which introduces the PhotoCD image with all its super-luminescent virtues, uses the Levels command.

PhotoCDs—Optimized for TV, Not PC

PhotoCDs were developed to hold high-quality photographic images in a digital format. Although the images look and behave like your average RGB TrueColor file, Kodak has given the PhotoCDs some extraordinary qualities.

An image from a PhotoCD is scanned from the original negative at several different resolutions to offer the user many different sizes of the same image from which to work. All these views, which Kodak calls *BASES*, are contained in one image file, which is done using a proprietary technology of Kodak's.

With the proper playback equipment, you can also view a PhotoCD on a television set. This was a wise move on Kodak's part because currently far more people own television sets than computers.

Unfortunately, Kodak, seeking to corner the broader market, optimized PhotoCD playback for the gamma of an analog television receiver, not the digitally fed PC monitor. As a result, PhotoCD images suffer from luminescence—a brighter-than-white phenomenon—which is unappealing to look at in an image unless you take certain steps to correct it in a copy of the image. Color theory becomes color *practice* when you follow the exercise we have in the next exercise.

Adjusting a PhotoCD's Tonal Levels

So if the gamma is off on PhotoCDs, why bother with PhotoCD images? Why not just scan all your Photoshop work? The answers become clear in the next exercise.

The companion CD includes the image file IMG0003.PCD, which is in Kodak's compressed, proprietary PCD image format, exactly as you would get the image back from Kodak on a PhotoCD disk. Soon you'll see exactly how to open this image, and then how to perform a little gamma correction that results in the image blossoming into unbelievable color that you could never achieve by scanning a color print.

Bear in mind two things in this first exercise:

✔ You can't save any changes you make to a CD image, PhotoCD format, or otherwise. CD-ROMs are all read-only memory (ROM) media. If you want to save changes, you must do so to a floppy disk, a hard drive, a Bernoulli cartridge, or other rewritable media.

✔ Changes that you make to the brightness, contrast, and gamma of an image are *relative* changes, not absolute ones that are based on the original image's values. Therefore, every time you use the Levels command, modify the graph, and then click OK, you cause changes *in addition* to previous changes; you change the *distribution* of pixels along the Levels graph, not the graph itself or the number of pixels in an image. For example, the histogram always represents the brightness scale from 0 to 255, so the second time that you display the Level dialog box to make additional changes, a black point that you reset to 10 is still shown as set to 0.

You're now ready to begin the next exercise, which provides a unique visual demonstration of how you can use tonal controls to bring out an image's visual information.

Opening a PhotoCD Image

Choose **File**, **O**pen, and then choose IMG0003.PCD from the companion CD	The PhotoCD Options dialog box appears as shown in figure 3.4.
Click on OK	Accepts the defaults of RGB Color and BASE (512 × 768).

This opens the file in RGB color and at the standard (BASE) resolution of the photo.

Choose the Zoom tool (magnifying glass) on the toolbox, and then click once on the image	Zooms you into the image by a power of resolution.
Pull the sides of the window to the right and down until the scroll bars are no longer visible, as shown in figure 3.5	Provides a better view (at 2:1 resolution) of the image, and moves you into position for the next exercise.

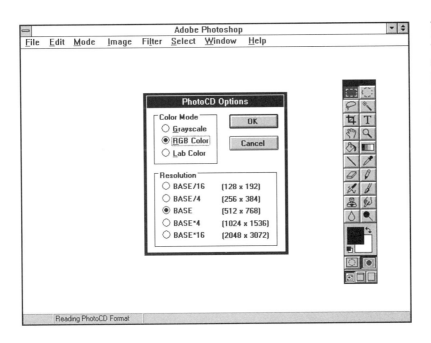

Figure 3.4
The PhotoCD Options dialog box appears whenever you open a PhotoCD file.

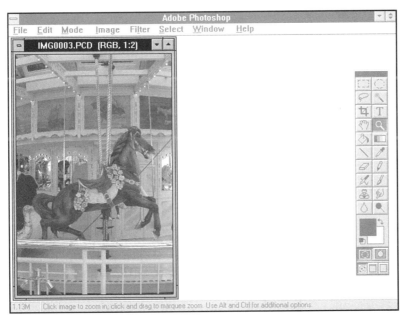

Figure 3.5
PhotoCDs look washed out when you open them; to enhance their appearance, you have to adjust them.

As shown in figure 3.5, the image is pretty, but washed out. Television, the medium for which Kodak developed PCD files, has a gamma display setting of 2.2, but the monitor on which you're viewing this image has a gamma of about 1.8. Before you can take full advantage of a

PhotoCD's quality in Photoshop, you have to adjust the image to bring out the detail that is lost due to the high gamma of the image.

Typically, PhotoCDs do not have a true black point, and extend the white point beyond 100 percent white to include the whiter-than-white information commonly found in natural highlights, such as direct reflections over water. The combination of high gamma and the extension of the white point produces a low-contrast image, with midtones that are higher than an ideal image's midpoint. In plain English, the image doesn't look so hot.

Fortunately, Photoshop can bring the heightened brightness values back to a range that results in spectacular color. In the following exercise, you use Photoshop's Levels command to create a dramatic change in the PhotoCD image's quality:

Finding the Right Levels

Choose **I**mage, **A**djust, and then choose Levels (or press Ctrl+L)	Displays the Levels dialog box as shown in figure 3.6.

Enter the following values in the Input Levels boxes: **49**, **1.14**, and **201**

The corresponding black point, gray midpoint, and white point sliders move in. Notice how the photo changes as you enter each value.

You determine the correct values by moving the sliders until the results look good. You have to trust your eye to find the right values.

Click on OK	Applies the corrections and closes the Levels dialog box.
Press Ctrl+L	Displays the Levels dialog box again, which now looks like figure 3.7.

The histogram in the Levels dialog box has changed dramatically to reflect the changes you made in the previous steps.

Click on the Cancel button	Closes the Levels dialog box without making any changes.

The PhotoCD image has much more punch, and its detail is restored by reducing the image's gamma. As you can see in figure 3.7, altering the histogram can result in a better distribution of color pixels. Although your own eyes are your best tool in this process, you should learn to rely on them *in addition* to all the visual information that Photoshop can map for you.

The first histogram that you saw in this exercise showed no pixels at the black point and almost none in the upper-white range. Everything was bunched together in a small range of color values that differed very little.

The second histogram shows color values across the entire range, with more values in the mid to upper ranges than in the first histogram. This distribution is good for this particular photo, because with the exception of the horse and the love seat upholstery, the image consists of whites and pastels.

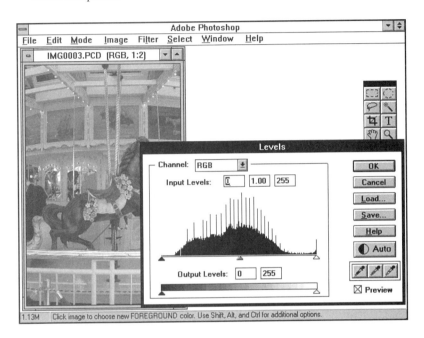

Figure 3.6
The Levels dialog box.

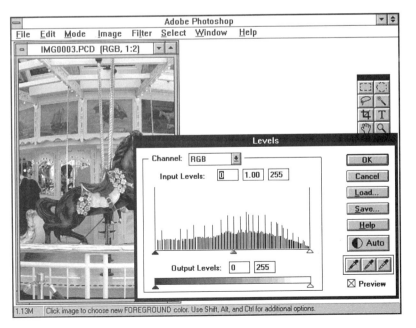

Figure 3.7
As you input values in the Levels dialog box, the quality of the photo changes.

Histograms for Doing, Histograms for Viewing

Earlier you learned that the brightness curve on the Levels histogram has no effect on the hue and saturation components in an image, just the brightness, the intensity with which light appears to be cast from a color object. The Histogram command from the Image menu keeps you updated as to the *current* status of the tonal distribution and by default presents a Gray channel view that shows how the brightness of the pixels affects their position in the histogram.

As you continue with this book's Photoshop exercises, the concept of a Gray channel may seem odd because an RGB image does not include a Gray channel. Remember that a histogram is a view of properties in a color model, and this is simply a different view. Photoshop's Histogram represents pixel frequency on a scale that disregards the hue and saturation of an image. You cannot change it directly, but the Levels command, which corresponds to the Histogram command, can.

When a graph shows only tonal differences, Photoshop offers a Gray channel that's a tonal composite of the Red, Green, and Blue color information channels.

Telling a Good Histogram from a Bad One

Histograms are like fingerprints: no two are identical. Therefore, there is no such thing as "the best histogram for all pictures." But like fingerprints, there are always tell-tale signs at the scene of the crime that reveal where a histogram may have gone amiss.

Take a look at the FALL.TIF image, which is shown in figure 3.8 and is included on the companion CD. The gamma for this PhotoCD image has been corrected, so it looks pretty good.

Now let's walk through the areas in this image as they correspond to the Gray channel view, the view that shows how bright each pixel is and where each is located within this image.

From the Bottom Up

FALL.TIF shows a sunny, cloudless view over a cornfield into some trees that are changing their seasonal colors. Although some dark areas emerge from shadows cast between the trees and the corn stalks, absolute black rarely occurs in this picture. Therefore, a histogram view of the overall brightness in this image should indicate some density near the low end of the midtones and even some toward the black point, but not much.

Figure 3.8
A gamma-corrected PhotoCD image.

The Midtones of Fall

For this image, you shouldn't expect a high frequency of color pixels with a brilliance factor on the high end of the midtones. Earth colors, like leaves and the dried, sandy-colored cornstalks, should occupy the lower end of the midtones and contribute little brightness to the high end of the midtone map. This makes sense if you consider that a grouping of leaves creates a texture that consists of great variation in brightness between neighboring values, all within a moderate range of tones.

The Sky's the Limit

You see the greatest contrast in this image where the treeline reaches the blue sky. The sky in FALL.TIF accounts for about a quarter of the visual information in this image and, therefore, many of its pixels. You should expect, then, to find a high occurrence of color pixels in an upper range on the histogram map. Whatever highlights this image contains will be represented in the same brightness range as the sky because the histogram plots brightness, not color.

Because the image content doesn't include any physical objects that are highly reflective, you shouldn't expect an appreciable amount of white points in FALL.TIF. Still, there should be some, if not many, 255-value pixels because some of the hues in this image are almost pure colors (a hue plus 100-percent saturation).

Figure 3.9 shows a histogram of FALL.TIF after undergoing some gamma- and contrast-correcting of the image, using the same steps in the last Levels exercise. The figure includes some notes along the Brightness map, and you should see the points described in the last section as Photoshop plotted them.

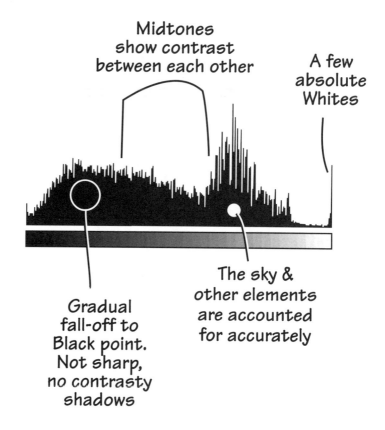

Figure 3.9
A histogram of
FALL.TIF after
some intelligent
tonal adjustments.

Midtones
show contrast
between each other

A few
absolute
Whites

Gradual
fall-off to
Black point.
Not sharp,
no contrasty
shadows

The sky &
other elements
are accounted
for accurately

Figure 3.10 shows what can happen in a histogram if some of the visual information in FALL.TIF is *destroyed.* In this case, deliberate misuse of Photoshop's tools incorrectly changed the image's gamma. (Trust me; you don't want to see the image.) Compare this histogram to that in figure 3.9, noting which areas lack brightness and which are filled in.

Looking Back on Brightness

In this chapter, you have spent quite a bit of time learning about how brightness affects pixels in an image, particularly those in PhotoCD images. This time is well spent, though, because any image that was scanned, either by you or by the Kodak PhotoCD process, usually needs this kind of correction.

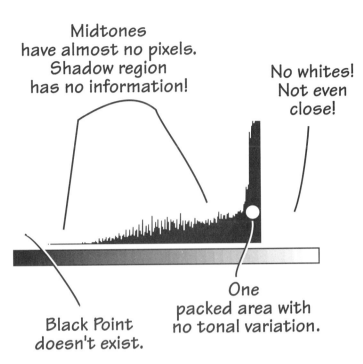

I

From the Source to the Sample

Figure 3.10
A FALL.TIF histogram after the image was tonally maladjusted.

Call it a challenge or a hurdle, but brightness is one of the first components that you should adjust before you retouch an image. But brightness is only one component of the overall information that the digital image contains. You'll use the Levels and Curves commands and several other global modifying features in the exercises, and you should learn how to use a combination of Photoshop features to enhance digital images.

Whenever you make an important change to an image in Photoshop, remember to use your own judgment to evaluate how the work is going. Although Photoshop helps you plot an image's contrast and gamma, your eyes will always tell you far more about eye-pleasing qualities. When something is drastically wrong with the display of visual content in an image, remember to use the tone controls that you have learned about as a resource or a guide to remapping. Then, after these controls have improved the image's overall quality, rely on your own judgment as you apply the finishing touches.

Kodak has released a plug-in module for Photoshop on the Macintosh platform that "automatically" corrects many of the contrast and gamma problems that must be corrected after you load a PhotoCD image. The manufacturer may also release the module for Windows users, but until then, you'll have to follow the

continues

procedures described in this chapter to make PhotoCD work well in the Windows environment.

The module is "automatic," so it does a good job with most (but not all) images. But even with the module you have to use your understanding of how to fine-tune an image's tonal values in Photoshop.

The Basis of BASES

Before you even begin adjusting the gamma of a PhotoCD image, you should consider how large a file you want to load in your system RAM while you work with the image in Photoshop. The file extension PSD indicates that not one but five different resolutions of the same image are tucked away in that Kodak box. Let's explore what the PSD format is, what it does, and how it affects your imaging work.

When you open a PhotoCD image in Photoshop, you are immediately presented with the PhotoCD Options dialog box (see fig. 3.4), which you used earlier in this chapter's exercise for making color corrections. In the dialog box, you choose one of the five BASE resolutions (measured in pixel height and width) with which to open the image. For the color-correcting exercise, you accepted the default, but that's not always the best choice. This section and the next series of exercises will help you make the right choice from a not-so-intuitive dialog box.

Five Ways To Cover Your BASES

Which resolution you should use when loading an image into Photoshop is a good question, and the dialog box is pretty oblique on the subject. Images are stored in PhotoCD format as one highly compressed file that ranges from about 2.5M to 6M. This file contains five different versions of the image that reflect five different resolutions at which the original, physical negative was scanned.

The PhotoCD Options dialog box essentially asks, "If you had scanned this image, how much information would you have captured?" The five different base sizes correspond to five different (and arbitrary) scanner settings that you could have chosen. They range from a very low resolution scan to a very high one.

When you choose a file resolution from the PhotoCD Options dialog box, the image file component that has the resolution you requested is opened and expanded to its original size in your computer's RAM (memory). PhotoCD lingo refers to these five file components as BASES.

PhotoCDs are always set at a 72-pixel-per-inch setting because that is the optimal setting for viewing an image at 1:1 resolution on a TV set or a monitor. This resolution is far too low to produce good results from a commercial printing press. Fortunately, in Photoshop's Image Size dialog box, you can reduce the size of a large-dimensioned, low-resolution image so that it has a higher pixel-per-inch value. As you'll recall from Chapter 2, image resolution is inversely related to image dimension: the smaller the dimension, the higher the pixel-per-inch value. An image's quality is unchanged this way.

When choosing the BASE at which to open a file, you must consider both dimension and resolution:

✔ The image must be the same height and width as you intend to print.

✔ The resolution must be in synch with the commercial printer's line-screen frequency.

The default of BASE (512×768) is the most common, convenient size for general usage in Photoshop. Such a BASE image loads into Photoshop as a file that is 512 pixels wide (7.11 inches) and 768 pixels high (10.66 inches) and has a pixel-per-inch resolution of 72. The file will occupy 1.13M of memory, and if you save it to disk as a TIFF file, it will occupy 1.18M of hard disk space.

Opening an image at the default BASE size, you can print a high-quality image using a 133-lpi line screen (magazine quality) at a maximum size of 2.56-inches wide by 3.84-inches high. A medium-quality image printed with a 85-lpi line screen (newsletter quality) has a maximum size of 4-inches wide by 6-inches tall using the default BASE image.

If you need a larger image, you can choose either the BASE*4 or the BASE*16 and then increase the resolution (and thus decrease the image dimensions) to get a correctly sized image for a specific printer's line screen. Conversely, if you need your finished image to be smaller, you can choose either the BASE/4 or the BASE/16 size.

Putting Resolutions To Work

Although all the BASEs that Kodak offers for the PhotoCD are a wonder of modern technology, making use of them in different situations requires that you plan carefully before loading the image. In the next section, you get an opportunity to experiment with an image that's "larger than life," in more ways than one.

Like traditional photography, digital imaging often involves cropping. In many of the assignments for which you use Photoshop, you need to use only part of a photographic image, and a cropped section often winds up with a resolution that is lower than you want. In chemical photography, an excessively enlarged image displays grain, marring the quality of the image, but there isn't much you can do about it.

However, if you're using Photoshop, and especially if you're using a PhotoCD image, you *can* do something about this problem: open a *higher resolution* version of the image. The higher the resolution of the image (and consequently the larger the *file dimensions*), the more information you have to work with. If you have enough information to work with after you crop and resize the image, you can achieve a final image that looks good when printed.

The following exercise uses Photoshop's Cropping tool to select only the day lily flower in the photo shown in figure 3.11. In this exercise, your imaginary assignment is to come up with a flower image for the cover of a three-fold brochure. The layout calls for the photo to be about 2-inches square and the printer wants the image at a resolution of 150 ppi.

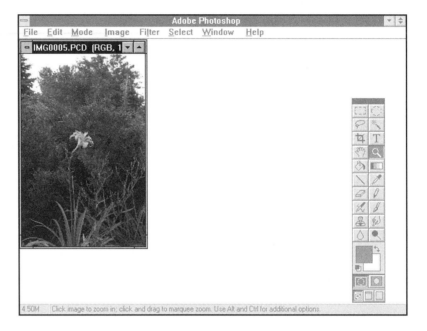

To meet the assignment's specifications, you need a high-resolution version of the image, BASE*4, so that the small, cropped portion of the image will end up the right size and resolution. The image is in PhotoCD format, so you can choose your resolution sizes, which Kodak calls BASES. Part of the convenience of using the Kodak PCD format is that it eliminates the need to rescan an image each time you use it for a different purpose. Recall that PhotoCDs presents you with five BASES of the image scanned at different resolutions, and not one megabyte of image information has to reside on your hard drive.

Before you start this exercise, be aware of the PC processing demands in opening a BASE*4 image. On a fast 486 machine with 20M of RAM, this action may take as long as 15 minutes.

Now that you know the downside of the following exercise, you can choose to pass it up and still not suffer from the lack of experience. Be aware, however, that the problems of cropping and maintaining resolution in an image may come up in your own imaging assignments, and that this exercise shows the only way that you can handle such problems with a PhotoCD image.

So, while your PC loads this image, you may want to take a coffee break or read ahead for an overview of the next steps in this exercise. Rest assured that the purpose of this exercise is not to tie up your machine as a mean-spirited practical joke played by the authors.

Picking a Flower

Choose **F**ile, **O**pen, then choose IMG0005.PCD from the companion CD	Opens the PhotoCD and displays the PhotoCD Options dialog box.
Leave the Color Mode set to **R**GB Color and change the Resolution setting to BASE*4, then click on OK	Specifies the image resolution of the file that you're opening.

Don't panic if the results aren't immediate; you're opening a 4.5M file.

Click on the up-arrow box in the upper-right corner of the screen	Maximizes your view in the active imge window.
Click on the Zoom tool on the toolbox, and then click on the resolution flower twice with the Zoom tool	Displays a full-screen, 1:2 view of the area that you need.
Click on the Cropping tool on the toolbar	Use the Cropping tool to eliminate image areas outside of the marquee border that you define.
Place the cursor to the upper left of the flower; then, while holding down the Shift key, click and drag down and to the right to create a square around the flower; then release the mouse button and the Shift key	Creates a special selection border around the flower as shown in figure 3.12 and discards everything outside the border.

If you're dissatisfied with the marquee cropping border, click outside the border area. Your cursor turns into a small international "no" symbol and the marquee border disappears. Then retry the last few steps.

Click inside the marquee when you're satisfied with the Cropping tool selection	Turns your cursor into a small pair of scissors, and crops the outside of the marquee selection as shown in figure 3.13.

Notice that on Photoshop's status bar the file size has decreased significantly, from 4.5 to 200 or 300K, depending on where you made the Cropping selection.

The trick to the technique demonstrated in the last exercise is to be patient
while loading the oversized BASE file and then to crop to the dimensions that
you want as quickly as you can.

Resizing a PhotoCD Selection

PhotoCD images are always brought into your computer at a 72 ppi resolution, which is too low for high-quality commercial printing. So now that you have cropped your flower, you need to adjust the size and resolution by using the Image Size dialog box.

Keeping Things in Proportion

You want your final image to maintain its aspect ratio—the proportional ratio of width to height—and the file size in bytes. If you uncheck the **P**roportion and the **F**ile Size check boxes and then increase the resolution, the file size increases as Photoshop adds information, but the height and width remain the same. In this instance Photoshop *interpolates* pixels in the image to create "in-between" pixels that are calculated on an average of the neighboring pixels' color values. The result is a loss of image fidelity because Photoshop *changes the image information*. You might not be able to see the degradation of image quality on your screen, but it becomes evident when you print the image. A nonproportionately resized image becomes *pixellated*—that is, it looks like a chemical photograph that was enlarged excessively and became grainy.

You can solve this problem by using a higher resolution scan (in this case, a BASE*4 image) so that more native information is used. In the next exercise, when you change the resolution from 72 to 150, the height and width change, but the file size does not. The resulting image then has enough information to print correctly. Let's see how this is done:

Sizing Up an Image

Display the cropped image of the lily from the last exercise

Choose **I**mage, **I**mage Size

Displays the Image Size dialog box, as shown in figure 3.14.

Your file dimensions and file size may differ slightly from those shown in figure 3.14.

Choose the **P**roportion and **F**ile Size check boxes, and change the **R**esolution setting to 150

Changes the **W**idth and H**e**ight from about 4 inches to about 2 inches; the file size remains the same.

Choose **F**ile, Sa**v**e, type **LILY.TIF** in the File **N**ame box, and then click on OK

Saves the adjusted image with the file name LILY.TIF, as shown in figure 3.15.

Choosing the right resolution when you start a project is an intelligent, informed move. Table 3.1, which shows the relationship between the PhotoCD BASES and the image and file sizes, can help you choose the right BASE for your project.

From the Source to the Sample

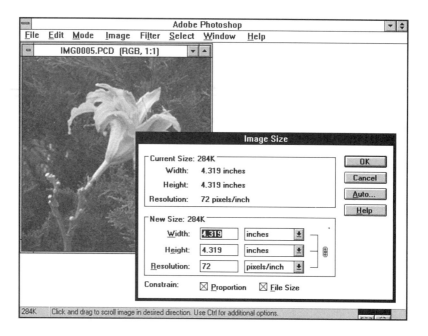

Table 3.1
PhotoCD Options in Real Terms

BASE	Dimensions (Width × Height) in Pixels	Dimensions (Width × Height) in Inches	Size in Memory W × H	Size When Saved to Disk as a TIFF
BASE/16	128 × 192	1.8 × 2.7	72K	74.2K
BASE/4	256 × 384	3.6 × 5.3	288K	295K
BASE	512 × 768	7.11 × 10.7	1.13M	1.2M
BASE*4	1024 × 1536	14.2 × 21.3	4.5M	4.7M
BASE*16	2048 × 3072	28.4 × 42.7	18M	18.8M

Here's quick rule of thumb for picking the right BASE size. This rule works if you are going to use the whole image and your printer uses an 85-lpi screen (a common screen size for medium-quality brochures, reports, and newsletters).

Double the width and height at which you will print the finished image, and then open a BASE for which the width and height is greater than or equal to the doubled dimensions.

For example, if you want to print a 1.5 inch by 2 inch image, double those dimensions to get 3 inches by 4 inches. As table 3.1 shows, BASE/4 has a dimension of 3.6 by 5.3, so for this job you would pick that BASE size.

Understanding PhotoCD Technology

These PhotoCD images are included on the companion CD to give you a taste of the technology in action. But it would be unfair to give you this taste without explaining how the technology works and the equipment that you need to take advantage of it while you work in Photoshop.

Probably the most exciting thing about PhotoCDs is that they can contain *your own photos*. You can take your undeveloped 35mm film, negatives, or slides to just about any photo finisher and tell them "PhotoCD it!" You can also take existing 35mm negatives you may already own and have a PhotoCD copy made from them. In about a week you'll get a PhotoCD back with your pictures in the same PCD format that you've been working with throughout this chapter. The cost for developing 24 PhotoCD images is only about $20. In contrast, to transfer your images to a conventional CD would cost at least $250.00.

Unlike a conventional CD-ROM disk, a PhotoCD disk is *multisession*. This means that you can return your PhotoCD to the photo finisher and have them put more images on the same PhotoCD. You can do this as many times as you want, until you fill the 550M PhotoCD (which takes about 100 images). You cannot add more photos to a conventional CD; instead, you would have to buy a new CD, which again costs over $250.

 How can Kodak and photo finishers produce PhotoCDs at such a reasonable price? Hoping that many consumers are interested in displaying their vacation snapshots on their TV screen, Kodak has tried to price its services competitively enough to encourage a large volume of consumer business, which in turn will support the considerable equipment investment required to produce PhotoCDs.

The PCD Format

The Kodak PhotoCD process scans a 35mm film negative or slide five times at different resolutions, or BASES. If stored as TIFF images on your hard disk, the five scans would occupy more than 25M of hard drive space. However, the PhotoCD process uses a proprietary image format, PCD, to store these five scans in one large, highly compressed file. This file typically is about 4.5M, but file sizes for color images can range from about 3.5M to 8M.

If you scanned the images without using the PCD format, it would take 2 gigabytes of hard disk space to store the uncompressed images that one PhotoCD can hold!

The PCD files are then written to a special kind of compact disk, the Photographic Quality Kodak PhotoCD Master, which can hold up to 100 24-bit TrueColor images. You can also put black-and-white images on the same PhotoCD.

A CD-ROM Player Isn't a PhotoCD-ROM Player

All this may sound too good to be true, but there is a catch. Not all computer CD-ROM drives can read a PhotoCD disk from a photo finisher. If you want to use PhotoCDs to archive your own photographs, you need a CD-ROM drive that is PhotoCD-compatible. A PhotoCD-compatible drive (which includes most drives manufactured after 1992) can also read conventional CD-ROMs, so you can use it with any conventional CDs you already have.

Any CD-ROM drive can read the PhotoCD images on the companion CD because the PCD image files were copied from a PhotoCD disk to a conventional, single-session CD-ROM disk. Some companies that sell stock photos in PhotoCD file format also transfer the PhotoCD images to conventional CD-ROM disks, so that everyone can use the photos, regardless of the kind of CD-ROM drive he or she has.

This is the key to taking advantage of PhotoCD technology: you can buy PhotoCD stock photography from a vendor who sells images in the Kodak PSD format. Commercial photographers have spent many years taking exquisite photos of scenes you'll never be able to travel to photograph. Further, many companies now include volumes of work categorized by topic, at very low fees. If the such-a-disk says that it's a *regular* CD-ROM disk, you can display this photography collection on a regular CD-ROM player. But whenever you send a roll to the photo finisher to get your images back on PhotoCD, you can read the disk only on a PhotoCD player.

You can also copy from a PhotoCD disk to a hard drive, to tape, or to other removable media. Third-party stock photo companies often do this as an intermediate step between writing the images to regular CD-ROM standards. A copied PCD file can be opened and used just as if it were still on the original CD. This is useful if you need to transfer the file to someone who wants to choose among BASES but lacks a PhotoCD player.

So the catch is, if you want to transfer your photos to a PhotoCD, you need a PhotoCD-compatible CD-ROM drive to read them. The drive you are using for the companion CD may be PhotoCD-compatible if it is a newer drive. Later in this chapter you learn how to determine whether your drive is PhotoCD-compatible and what to look for in a CD-ROM drive if you need to buy a new one.

PhotoCDs can also be read by CD-I players, which are designed for CD-based interactive books and games. However, these players don't hook up to a PC properly. So, although you cannot do any Photoshop work with a CD-I player, you can preview your PhotoCD images with this Nintendo-like unit.

The Types of PhotoCDs

There is more than one kind of PhotoCD. The type of PhotoCD discussed in this chapter, the Photographic Quality Kodak PhotoCD Master, is the simplest, least expensive, and most universal format that Kodak has introduced. This is the consumer version, and for most Photoshop work, this format will suit your needs quite nicely.

The Professional Photographic Quality format, called the Kodak Pro PhotoCD Master, can hold film formats other than 35mm. You can transfer 35mm, 70mm, 120mm, and 4 by 5 inch negatives and chromes to this PhotoCD format. With this format, you can adjust the color balance of the film scans to emulate the different "looks" produced by different types of film (such as Ektar, Kodachrome, Plus-X, and so on). With this format, you can also request a higher resolution scan, BASE*64 (which yields a whopping 72M file), and to include a professional copyright notice within the PhotoCD.

These PhotoCDs can be quite expensive, but are still a bargain compared to buying an expensive ($10,000 and up) drum scanner and then scanning negatives yourself. A service bureau charges as much as $150 to do a high-resolution scan of a 4 by 5 inch negative or positive. You can have the same image transferred to a Pro Photo CD for about $50.

Working Smarter with PhotoCD Technology

After you start using PhotoCDs and Photoshop, you start to collect images and need a convenient way to view them. Photoshop opens PhotoCD image files the same as other file formats that it supports, but you still must open image files one at a time. This is definitely a handicap when working with a collection of PhotoCD images. According to the PhotoCD file-naming convention, every PhotoCD starts with IMG0001.PCD, then IMG002.PCD, and so on—and such titles aren't very helpful when you're scrambling to find an image. When you have 24 images on a PhotoCD, searching for the one that you want is a tedious process; with a hundred images, you *definitely* will want an overview of the PhotoCD's contents.

However, inexpensive image display and management programs are available that catalog the entire contents of a PhotoCD. Some even let you enter keyword descriptions of each image so that you can find it faster. Let's take a look at how these programs work.

The Interfaces for Viewing a PhotoCD

There are two ways that you can get an overview of what is on a PhotoCD. One is to use the paper index sheet that's attached to the PhotoCD's plastic cover. The other is to use a computer-image browsing program, like Kodak Access, or Corel Corporation's CD-ROM Utilities.

The Index Sheet

Your PhotoCD images return to you with a small piece of photographic paper that has 5/8 by 3/4 inch miniature thumbnails (or reproductions) of all the images contained on the disk. This index sheet is like a traditional contact sheet, with each thumbnail sequentially numbered starting with number 1.

Because all PhotoCDs look alike and use the same file names, the index sheet is the only physical directory to the files on the PhotoCD, so it's important not to misplace it. Number 1 on the index sheet corresponds to the file IMG0001.PCD on the PhotoCD.

The index sheet is helpful for figuring out which PhotoCD you need to insert in your drive. The thumbnails on the index sheet are tiny reproductions (about the size of a gnat), so using them to evaluate the quality of the images can be frustrating—after much squinting, you usually find that you've wasted time loading the wrong, huge, resource-intensive image. You can avoid this frustration, however, by using a software browsing program.

Image-Browsing Software

Many companies offer software for viewing and managing images, including PhotoCD images. These programs come in two basic types: those that work only with PhotoCDs, and those that work with PhotoCDs in addition to file formats like TIF, PCX, and BMP.

When working with PhotoCDs, both types of overview software read and display OVERVIEW.PCD, which is the contact sheet file written on each PhotoCD. Some browsing software also lets you load and display a single image.

Programs that provide overviews of *any* graphical file type typically build a catalog of images that you select, and display the images in groups. An overview of a group of files is extremely helpful for Photoshop work. As you continue using Photoshop, you save to your hard drive copies of the same image that you've enhanced in several different ways. Viewing thumbnails of files side by side on screen beats trying to figure out which file name corresponds to which variation.

Image-browsing programs usually provide simple editing tools and file-conversion capabilities. As a Photoshop user, you have no need for such utilities; a good cataloging feature is all you seek from them. While writing this book, I found Corel Corporation's Corel CD-ROM Utilities and Kodak's PhotoCD Access to be the two most helpful.

Kodak's PhotoCD Access software shows you a contact sheet of all the photos on the PhotoCD, or you can choose a single photo to view, as shown in figures 3.16 and 3.17. You can specify how large to display the images and how many colors to display. Included on Access package's CD is an assortment of 24 full-color photographs that you can use royalty-free. Access offers a basic suite of editing tools—cut, copy, paste, rotate, flip, and crop—and lets you save a PhotoCD format image to a variety of more common formats, such as TIF.

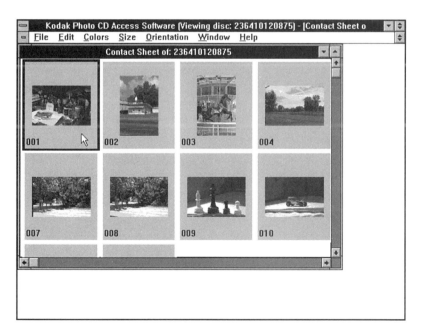

Figure 3.16

A PhotoCD contact sheet displayed by the Kodak Photo CD Access program.

Figure 3.17
A single PhotoCD
image displayed
by the Kodak
Photo CD Access
program.

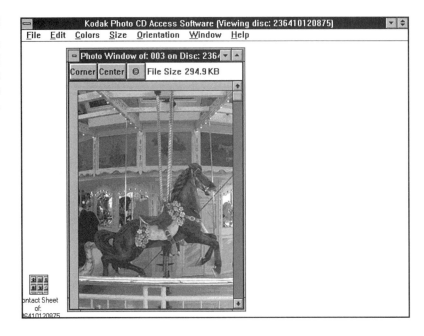

Currently Access does not work across a network or with Windows for Workgroups. You can access Access only by using a PhotoCD drive attached directly to the PC on which you're working. The Access program file takes up about 1M on your hard disk.

Corel doesn't sell you utilities that come with sample images; instead, you can purchase sample images and the utilities are included for free as part of the bundle! The Corel Professional Photos CD-ROM series disks each contain over 100 photos that you can use royalty-free, and the Corel CD-ROM Utilities are free with each collection. Thus, you can choose a collection of photos and get some useful software to boot, taking advantage of a marketing approach that is the opposite of that used by Kodak.

The utilities included with the Corel Professional Photos are CorelMosaic Visual File Manager, Corel PhotoCD Lab, Corel Screen Saver, Corel Wallpaper Flipper, and Corel CD-Audio. Two of these utilities—CorelMosaic and Corel PhotoLab—are of special interest to the Photoshop user.

With CorelMosaic, you can display a PhotoCD "contact sheet" or build an equivalent to this contact sheet (also called a catalog) of the images as shown in figure 3.18. CorelMosaic also can build catalogs from images belonging to other graphics formats. If you build a catalog consisting of other types of images, or consisting of both PhotoCD images and other types of images, you can assign keywords to each image. This speeds up your image-hunting process later.

Corel PhotoLab works only with PhotoCD images. This utility quickly loads and displays your PhotoCD images in either an automatic or manual slide show on your screen, as shown in figure 3.19. PhotoLab also contains all the editing and conversion features of Access, except that you cannot use PhotoLab to crop an image.

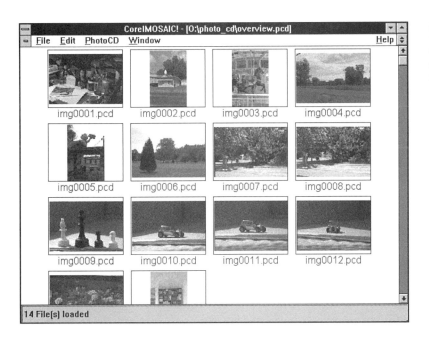

Figure 3.18
A PhotoCD contact sheet shown in CorelMosaic.

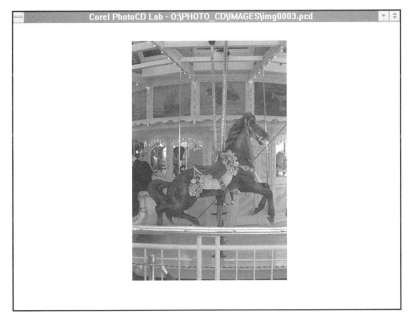

Figure 3.19
A Corel PhotoLab slide show is good for viewing a PhotoCD quickly at a large size.

Corel CD-ROM Utilities work with Windows for Workgroups and with networked PhotoCD drives. If you install all the utilities, they take approximately 4.5M of hard disk space.

No matter which browsing software you eventually decide to use, such a program is necessary to make cataloging your Photoshop-bound images a breeze.

The PhotoCD Drive

Making PhotoCD technology part of your Photoshop tools is not a decision to make over-night. Adding a PhotoCD drive *complements* your current hardware, but doesn't replace your need for a scanner or a large hard disk. However, with it you can bring your photos into Photoshop in a higher-quality digital format than is privately affordable. Also, it's one way of keeping a mountain of source images off of your hard drive.

If you already own a CD-ROM drive that isn't PhotoCD-compatible and want to take advantage of all the PhotoCD format, you must invest in a PhotoCD drive. This section will help you thread your way through technical specifications a little more easily.

Choosing the Right CD-ROM Drive

If you currently own a CD-ROM drive that was manufactured before 1992, you probably cannot use it to play a PhotoCD. A PhotoCD drive and a regular, older CD-ROM drive look identical. Only the technology inside is new, and just like everything else in the PC world, you have to reinvest regularly to keep up with better, faster technology.

The key words that you should look for in a PhotoCD drive's documentation are the following: *PhotoCD-ready* or *-compatible, XA* or *XA Mode 2,* or *multisession.* When purchasing a CD-ROM drive, be sure to look for one that is a *multisession, PhotoCD-compatible* drive. Some drive manufacturers also certify their drives with Kodak and display a PhotoCD logo on their packaging and literature.

When shopping for a PhotoCD drive, beware of CD-ROM drives that advertise that they are PhotoCD-compatible but seem much less expensive than their competitors. Some early drives could read PhotoCDs, but only if they were recorded in a single session. You don't want one of these drives, because they have already fallen behind in the technology—buying one would be like buying a 286-class computer at a really good price. Insist on a multisession drive, to protect the investment you'll be making accumulating PhotoCD disks.

Choosing a Fast Drive

In addition to demanding a multisession drive, you also want to buy as fast a PhotoCD-compatible drive as you can afford. Fast drives are more expensive, but the amount of visual information held on a PhotoCD is immense. You'll come to appreciate a fast drive, particularly if you have several Photoshop image assignments going on at once.

The speed of a CD-ROM drive is primarily measured by its sustained data-transfer rate, its average access time, and the size of its onboard cache. You should look for these three technical specifications when comparing the speed of one drive to another.

While writing this book, I used the Procom Technology Model MCD-DS drive, which is one of the fastest drives currently on the market. It has a 330K-per-second sustained data transfer rate, which is how much data the drive can read from the disk in one second. This measurement is important when reading large image files. The higher the number, the better.

The Procom also has an average access time of 200ms, which means that the drive takes 200ms on average to find what you want to read and to prepare to read it. The lower the access time, the better. To a PhotoCD user working with images, this specification is not as critical as the transfer rate. However, it is important when you use the drive for other types of CDs, like encyclopedias or multimedia hypertext.

The Procom drive also has a 256K onboard cache. Caches usually range from 64K to 256K, and the larger the cache the better. Onboard cache is the amount of memory on the drive that's dedicated only to storing data that it "thinks" you may want to use next.

Drives get faster and cheaper all the time. The rates that define a fast PhotoCD drive will certainly change. But a high data-transfer rate, a low average access time, and a large cache will always define a fast drive.

Summary

Besides explaining the technical aspects of the PhotoCD, this chapter has shown you how useful the PCD file format can be in your Photoshop imaging. A digital image file is just like any computer file, except that it's usually much, much larger. Imaging people collect image files the same way that spreadsheet people collect spreadsheets, and both types of files do the same thing to your hard drive—they fill it up!

But if storage were the only perk of owning a PhotoCD player and a collection of PhotoCD disks, you would be as well served buying a removable media player, like a Bernoulli or a SyQuest. But of course, PhotoCD technology offers many other advantages.

Quite simply, you can't beat PhotoCD technology for the cost-efficient negative scanning it provides. Without PhotoCD technology, we couldn't have brought you the high quality original images found on the companion CD. The technology gave us the freedom to crop images and maintain a high resolution for each TIF file. And yes, we had to open a BASE*16 image or two in the process! You'll have to do this too, from time to time, when you work with high-quality images—the kind you can do the most with in Photoshop.

In Chapter 4, you'll see how gamma affects your monitor, and even your images. Additionally, the next chapter will show you where to find the many bells and whistles of Photoshop before you launch into full-fledged image editing. Chapter 4 is all about setting defaults and options. If it doesn't sound like a fun chapter, do *not* pass this one by because we *make* it fun!

Chapter Snapshot

In this chapter, you learn how to:

4

CHAPTER

Setting Photoshop's Defaults and Options

O nce you understand how and why to use the techniques demonstrated throughout this book, you will find that working with images in Photoshop is a tremendously rewarding personal experience.

When designing Photoshop, Adobe Systems had no idea who you, the *person* in "personal," might be—your preferences, work habits, or the type of PC that you own. However, Adobe Systems compensated for this by providing in Photoshop's workspace a wealth of user-definable options and customizable features.

Optimizing Photoshop's workspace for your personal use is no more difficult than adding an icon or wallpaper to the Windows Program Manager. All you need to know is where the little buttons are and what they do.

Fine-Tuning Your Monitor

Calibrating (adjusting) your monitor's settings may sound like a funny, nit-picky thing to most PC users; an action reserved for hi-tech nerds who wear white lab smocks while they work. But calibrating your monitor helps ensure that the images you see will appear the same on *other* computers, and print with the same color values. The right calibration is critical to creating work in Photoshop that is reproduced accurately. But even if you calibrate your monitor perfectly, your finished image may not look so great when processed by a service bureau or when viewed on another monitor.

Every computer monitor, printer, scanner, and film recorder has its own inherent range of colors it can express, and its own calibration settings. And in this sense, monitor calibration is relative. If you find through experience that when you send your file to a specific output source (printer, film recorder) that everything prints too dark, or too light, or that blues turn into purples, you may want to calibrate your monitor to match that device more closely. Fortunately, Adobe has made calibrating your monitor easy, and you can save and recall different sets of custom calibration information that match different situations. When calibrating your monitor, you want to make relative adjustments that suit your own needs while trying to maintaining consistency with the world of clients and suppliers that you send your files to.

The method that Photoshop provides to calibrate your monitor is not the most scientifically precise method available. Photoshop's method relies on the user trying to match things by eye. The most precise and objective way to calibrate a monitor or other output device requires expensive special equipment that actually reads the wavelengths of light produced, or measures the density and color values of printed output. These physical calibration systems are often used with color management software that helps ensure that the settings for all de-vices—your scanner, your monitor and your output device—are tuned to match each other.

If you have a physical color calibration system, you should use it instead of Photoshop's "eyeball" method. If you don't, you shouldn't let this deter you from calibrating your monitor using Photoshop's features. Any kind of calibration is better than no calibration at all! If your clients also use Photoshop, you can adjust their monitors' settings, if necessary, so that they can accurately view your work. Chapter 21 contains some additional tips on how to doublecheck that the color your monitor shows matches different custom color matching systems for specifying color like PANTONE or TRUEMATCH.

Installing a Video Driver

The first step to providing a precise view of all 16.7 million colors starts with your own monitor. Be sure to load your video card's 16.7-million-color video driver before you do any of the following steps; otherwise you won't fine-tune your monitor for the video mode you'll want to use most frequently in Photoshop.

Before you do anything, though, warm up your monitor for at least a half hour. (Calibration and cold monitors don't mix!)

Figure 4.1 shows the Change System Settings dialog box that is displayed when you call Windows Setup. This program has nothing to do with Photoshop; you summon it from Program Manager by selecting **R**un from the **F**ile menu, and then selecting the SETUP.EXE file. SETUP.EXE was placed in your WINDOWS subdirectory when you installed Windows 3.1 on your PC. In this dialog box, you can scroll down the list of video drivers that are currently installed on your computer and pick one to use, or you can install different ones from floppy disks provided by your video card's manufacturer. In any event, make sure you choose a video driver that will display as many colors as your video card is capable of displaying. Using a 16.7-million-color driver provides the only way to view a TrueColor TIF file without monitor dithering, and it's the only way to work accurately and productively in Photoshop.

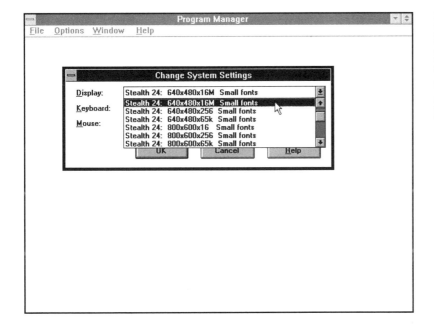

Figure 4.1
Before adjusting your monitor, select the video driver that you will use with Photoshop.

I

From the Source to the Sample

Setting Up the Monitor

After loading the proper video driver, you next need to refer to your monitor's documentation, which should include important information you need for Photoshop's Monitor Setup. In particular, you need to know the brand of your monitor and the type of phosphors that were used to construct it. If your monitor is an OEM (Original Equipment Manufacturer) unit that you bought as part of a system package, you may not have access to these details. However, there is a workaround that you can use to get the right settings.

Do the following steps to tell Photoshop what kind of monitor you have, and make only those changes that apply to your monitor:

Photoshop's Monitor Setup

Double-click on the Photoshop icon in Program Manager	Starts the Photoshop program.
Choose File, Preferences, and then choose Monitor Setup	Displays the Monitor Setup dialog box, as shown in figure 4.2.
Choose the Monitor drop-down list	Displays a short list of setup arrangements that ship with Photoshop.
Choose the monitor you are using, or choose Default, or Other	Sets the parameters listed in the Monitor Parameters window to match your monitor.

If you choose Default, the monitor parameters don't change. If you choose Other, you must set the parameters manually by choosing one of the options from the drop-down boxes next to each parameter. Be sure to read the following tip and section on Monitor Parameters before you make these changes.

Figure 4.2
The Monitor Setup dialog box.

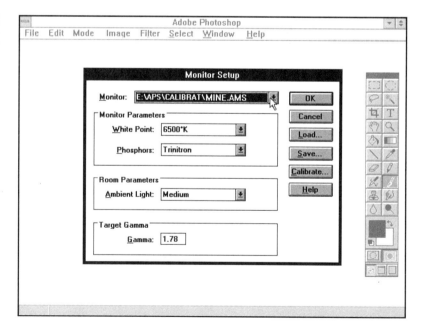

You don't harm your PC, your monitor, or Photoshop by selecting a monitor from the Monitor drop-down list a monitor other than that which you use. Monitor Setup and the following calibrations simply specify the range with which Photoshop displays contrast, colors, and values.

For example, the specification sheet for my Philips 17-inch monitor, which is not listed in the **M**onitor drop-down list, is almost identical to a Nanao monitor, which *is* listed. Including the Nanao as part of the setup that follows resulted in a dramatic difference in my personal viewing and editing of images in Photoshop.

The gamma of the display was lowered, and the colors on the monitor more closely matched the original source material I work with. In addition, work imported into other programs (like Aldus *PageMaker*) looked closer in tone and color values to the images I'd worked with in Photoshop.

None of the changes you make with your monitor settings in Photoshop affect Windows or other programs. Although you can save any changes to the Photoshop environment indefinitely, you also can reset them at any time.

Monitor Parameters

If your monitor isn't listed in the **M**onitor drop-down list, you can adjust the Monitor Parameter settings by choosing Other. In such cases, Adobe recommends that you choose a **W**hite Point of 6500 degrees Kelvin. This setting complies with most newer displays.

If your whites don't look as white as you think they should with this setting, try the following *before* you change it:

✔ Wipe your monitor's screen with a damp cloth. Your screen attracts dust and other airborne matter, which accumulates and dims your view quicker than you realize.

✔ Adjust your monitor's brightness and contrast. These dials are usually located on the monitor in a place where it's easy to nudge them out position accidentally. A little tweak sometimes can restore brighter whites.

When you select different setup settings, you actually *change* how Photoshop responds to your image editing, so make certain a less-than-ideal monitor view is due to the wrong **W**hite Point color temperature, and not dust nor a misadjusted knob on your set *before* you change the setting.

Usually you can leave the **P**hosphors setting alone. Many modern monitor tubes are Trinitrons. However, if your monitor uses red, green, and blue phosphors that were not manufactured according to Sony's Trinitron standards, this setting lets Photoshop compensate. If the drop-down menu lists the specific kind of phosphors your monitor uses, then select it. Otherwise, stick with Trinitron, even if you're guessing. You *do* have to be a rocket scientist to give Photoshop Custom phosphor information.

Room Parameters

Adobe included the Room Parameters window in this dialog box with the most finicky folks in mind. In theory, the high, medium, and low options can compensate for bright, dim, or average lighting in your work environment. The setting doesn't make much difference, though, so you may as well accept Medium as the **A**mbient Light setting. (It's better to ask yourself a question at this point: Why would a serious imaging person want bright lights bouncing off his or her monitor? Unless your boss is a tyrant, *you* can do something about harsh or dim lighting conditions yourself, and not fuss with this Photoshop setting, the functionality of which is more of a psychological stroke than an actual benefit.)

Target Gamma

In the Target Gamma window you specify the setting that may make the most difference for viewing your Photoshop work. *Gamma* is the measure of the breadth of midtone values (grayscale) as an image is displayed. But what does this rather complex definition actually mean?

When your monitor displays an image with a narrow midtone range, the image's contrast seems excessive because little image information is retained for showing variations in skin tones, a view of the sky, and other features that require this range of values to adequately describe detail in an image. In the **G**amma setting, midtone ranges that are narrow and display a lot of contrast are expressed as a low number. To display images consisting of dramatic black and brilliant white, many imaging software products set this point low, to 1.0. Conversely, television gamma is around 2.2. Although such images appear light and color-filled, they lack a certain dynamic quality in the gray, midrange color component and sometimes appear washed-out.

Try setting your Photoshop gamma to 1.8, the default, and then refine it as necessary. You can evaluate the best gamma for your monitor display honestly only after spending some time working with different images. The perfect gamma is not realized with one image in five minutes.

The gamma on your display *will* affect your finished work in two situations.

First, if you're editing a file that originated from a Macintosh machine, you *must* match the gamma of that particular Mac to get consistent results in your imaging.

Second, if you're editing a file to be used on an imagesetter, film recorder, or video output device, you must also set your monitor's gamma to match the gamma of that particular device.

Saving Your Settings

Even before you're certain that the settings you entered in the Monitor Setup dialog box are final, you can save them to an AMS file. AMS is the file extension Photoshop gives to files that contain monitor settings. Photoshop will not recognize the file as a monitor settings file if it has any other extension. The next exercise shows you how to save your monitor settings.

Saving a Photoshop Setting

Click on the **S**ave button of the Monitor Setup dialog box	Displays the Save As dialog box for monitor settings.
Find the PHOTOSHOP directory, and then the CALIBRAT subdirectory	Use the Drive and Directory fields in the dialog box to locate the CALIBRAT subdirectory.

The CALIBRAT subdirectory, which Photoshop installed when you ran the installation program is a good place to store all your Photoshop calibrations.

In the File **N**ame text box, enter an eight-letter or less name for you custom setting, and use AMS as the file extension	Specifies the name of the file.

Choose a name that you will easily remember, such as MONSET1.AMS.

Click on OK	Returns you to the Monitor Settings dialog box.

Now every time you experiment with your monitor settings, you can return to any setting you previously made and saved by clicking **L**oad from the Monitor Setup dialog box and then clicking the AMS file of your choice.

The Save and Load options are available in several of Photoshop's dialog boxes, not just the Monitor Setup dialog box. As you'll see throughout this book, you can save Calibration, Levels adjustment, Variations, and other global changes to Photoshop and your images, and then load them at any time.

Saved settings are very useful in Photoshop work, and the saved file sizes are very small, typically 50 to 200 bytes. You should take advantage of this Photoshop feature when it's available because it often enables you to backtrack when you make a mistake.

Monitor Calibration

Calibrating your monitor is another important step you need to take to set up your monitor so that it faithfully represents your image. You set it up so that its display capability is optimized when you edit images.

From the Monitor Setup dialog box, click the **C**alibrate button to display the Calibrate dialog box. This section explains how the settings in this dialog box affect your imaging.

At the top of the dialog box is the Gamma Adjustment window, which consists of a pattern of stripes with a slider beneath it. This setting enables you to manually adjust the gamma value in the Target Gamma window of the Monitor Setup dialog box. If you fine-tune the gamma for your monitor, people who view your images from other workstations will see color values that are closer to those that you intended. Although this isn't the perfect solution, it is the best available short of buying a monitor calibration package. So, let's learn how to use this feature of the Calibrate dialog box.

The stripes above the slider are something like an eye test. In this eye test, you try to blend the stripes together by moving the slider in either direction. First, check the Balance radio button, as shown in figure 4.3. This button controls the balance between the black point and white point. In figure 4.3, the stripes are pretty well blended together with a value of 16 showing beneath the stripes in the Gamma Adjustment window. The value 16 is an arbitrary point on the scale, and doesn't correspond to the absolute value of the gamma. The scale setting *you* see when the bands blend together may be different than ours, since you may not own the same monitor as the authors.

Figure 4.3
To set the best gamma balance for your monitor, click on the Balance radio button and adjust the slider until the stripes go away.

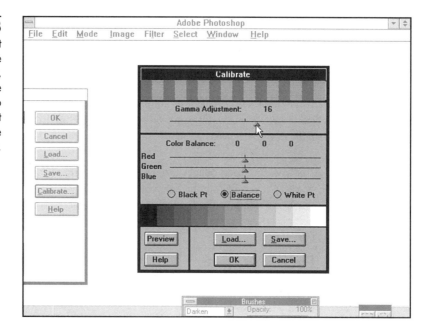

Do the same for the black point and the white point. First you click on their radio buttons and then adjust the slider so that the stripes at the top invisibly blend. Finally, click on the Balance radio button again and readjust the balance if necessary to blend the bands together.

Your settings in the Calibrate dialog box affect Photoshop differently than your settings in the Monitor Setup dialog box. Whereas the Monitor Setup settings—Monitor type, Phosphors, and the like—change your view of the image, the Calibrate settings change an image file's color properties.

Monitor calibration has a direct impact on how Photoshop translates the RGB color model (the model your monitor uses to display color) into the CMYK color model used when creating color separations for four color process printing. The CMYK color model has four channels (Cyan, Magenta, Yellow, and Black) compared to RGB's three channels. Any time Photoshop has to translate information about color into a different color model format, the accuracy of that translation depends largely on having accurate RGB information to start with. Calibration is designed to help ensure that the RGB information is correctly displayed.

Calibration is not critical for displaying an RGB image in its native RGB monitor mode, but a badly calibrated monitor will affect the color information generated and written to a file for an image that has been translated into a CMYK or other Photoshop Modes format. Files in the CMYK image format will also not display with any degree of accuracy if the original RGB display/ information was not accurate.

Whenever image data is "translated," it adheres to the old computer adage "GIGO," or "garbage in, garbage out"; don't expect to get great results if you don't feed your computer great information.

Additionally, if your monitor setup is not optimized, the result will be less than perfect when you try to blend a selection area into a background image. The brightness of the overall image is affected as well.

Keep all these concerns in mind if you ever doubt that fine-tuning your monitor is worth the hassle.

On Color Balance

Some early models of monitors shipped with a bluish color cast to them. This is obviously a problem if you try to do precise retouching to a color image. To compensate for a color cast from your monitor, Photoshop offers a color correction feature. This feature enables you to achieve color balance in the same way that you correct gamma, except that you use Red, Green, and Blue sliders instead of the Gamma slider to make the stripes match.

Unless your monitor was manufactured before 1991, or you've recently dropped it or suspended it in liquid nitrogen, you probably won't need to reset the color balance for Photoshop. Try sliding the little triangles from the zero point; if this causes the stripes at the top of the dialog box to blend better, your monitor needs calibration. If the stripes' contrast increases, you should leave the settings alone.

I

From the Source to the Sample

The "test strip" near the bottom of the dialog box should ideally have nice, sharp, even graduations of black. This provides another visual clue as to how you can get the best display in Photoshop. When you move a calibration slider, this strip's shades of black change. This, in addition to matching the stripes at the top of the dialog box, are a means of visually adjusting your monitor calibration to work more accurately in Photoshop sessions. For additional details about calibration, see Photoshop's documentation.

Again, when you have the best settings for gamma calibration, select the <u>S</u>ave button to save them; then you can always recall them, as you can with the monitor settings.

Fine-Tuning Your Photoshop Environment

Now that your monitor is fine-tuned, it's time to address the way you want Photoshop to perform functions that affect your work discipline, and sometimes your work itself. For instance, Photoshop includes a wonderful Color Picker model that lets you choose a specific color to paint with. But if you prefer the familiar sight of Windows' color selection dialog box, press Ctrl+K, *or* select Pre<u>f</u>erences from the <u>F</u>ile menu, and then choose General.

You should get familiar with this keystroke combination. When working an assignment there will be occasions when you'll need to quickly alter settings that affect various Photoshop options. The next exercise uses the Photoshop Color Picker option.

Picking Photoshop Colors

Choose <u>F</u>ile, <u>P</u>references, and then choose General (or press Ctrl+K)	Displays the General Preferences dialog box (see fig. 4.4) where you select settings that affect the way that Photoshop offers different features.
Choose <u>C</u>olor Picker, and then choose Photoshop from the picker drop-down list	Sets the type of color you get when choosing a color.
Click on OK, then click the foreground color selection box on the toolbox	Displays Photoshop's Color Picker (see on fig. 4.5), which you selected in the General Preferences dialog box.
Click and drag the circle in the Color Picker model around	Sets the foreground color to whatever color the circle is over when you click on OK.
Enter the following values in the respective boxes: H **241**, S **100**, and B **100**	Sets the foreground color to the brilliant blue these values specify, if you choose OK at this point. But don't press OK yet.

Enter the following values in the respective boxes (as shown in fig. 4.5): R 0, G 255, and B 186

Would set the foreground color to the misty sea green specified if you clicked on OK now. Don't click on OK now.

The little ! button that appears after the last step is a "flag" that appears when you select a color in Photoshop that commercial printers can't reproduce with ink.

Click on the ! button

Automatically readjusts the misty green color to a similar one that commercial printers *can* reproduce, and in the dialog box, changes the numbers displayed for affected values.

Choose OK

Sets foreground color to printable misty green and returns you to the workspace.

Press Ctrl+K

Opens the General Preferences dialog box.

Choose Color Picker, and then choose Windows from the drop-down list

Sets the type of color model to that which ships with Windows version 3.1.

Click on OK, and then click on the foreground color selection box on the toolbox

Displays Windows Color dialog box, as shown in figure 4.6.

This is the same Color dialog box that you see when you click on the Colors icon in the Windows Control Panel.

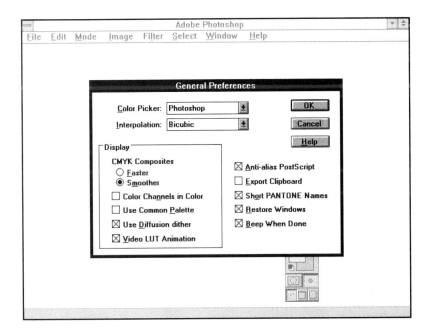

Figure 4.4
The General Preferences dialog box.

Figure 4.5
Photoshop's
Color Picker.

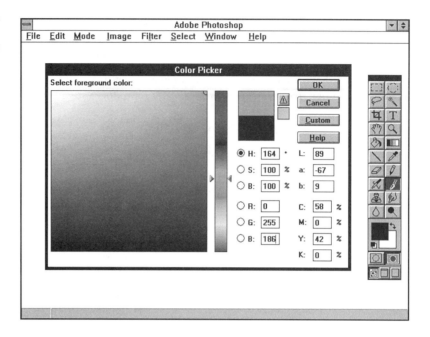

Figure 4.6
You can use
Windows' Color
dialog box in
Photoshop.

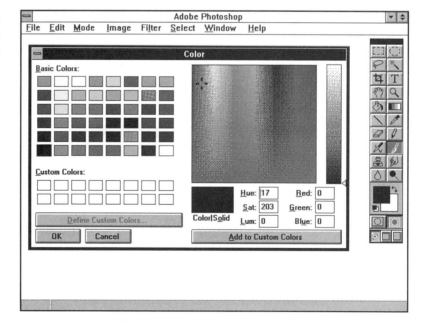

Although less familiar to a Windows user than the Windows Color dialog box, Photoshop's Color Picker is more feature-rich and easier to learn.

One feature that the Windows Color dialog box lacks is the exclamation point that Photoshop displays when you select a color unavailable for painting. This omission is significant when you send out your Photoshop work for four-color separations. Printing color is not the same as monitor/computer color, and because of impurities in commercial inks, certain shades cannot be reproduced. Therefore, you should learn to use Photoshop's Color Picker. If you followed the last exercise, press Ctrl+K to display the General Preferences dialog box, and then reset the **C**olor Picker option to Photoshop.

Interpolation

As Chapters 1 and 2 discussed, Photoshop uses interpolation rather than diffusion to build and display editing work and images while you edit them in the RGB, TrueColor mode. Interpolation may seem to rearrange color pixels in an image, but it actually adds and deletes them to complete an action or edit. The quality of Photoshop's interpolation calculations depends on the speed with which you choose to accomplish them. Speed is the trade-off for accuracy, and you have three choices as to how Photoshop interpolates your editing work:

✔ The *Bicubic* option is the most accurate method of rearranging pixels. It takes the longest for Photoshop to calculate, but on a 486 machine, the wait is nominal, and the result is the highest quality image. Usually this is the option you should choose.

✔ The *Bilinear* option is the middle ground between quality and speed of interpolation. If you have deadlines to meet, and a 386 machine, the results are good, and your work will go quickly.

✔ The nearest *Neighbor* method of interpolation is Photoshop's on-the-fly estimate of what an altered pixel in your image should look like. It's fast, but not terribly precise. You should reserve this option for the night when you need 100 images retouched the next morning and your client has no taste in Art.

CMYK Composites

If you're new to commercial printing or electronic imaging, CMYK may be a buzz word that means nothing to you. So before you learn how to use the CMYK Composites radio buttons of the General Preferences dialog box, you need to understand what CMYK (or "See-Mac") is.

Color models serve a very real purpose in the imaging world, and different models were invented for different reasons. Many artists like to describe color using the Hue, Saturation, and Brightness (HSB) model, as was classically taught before the advent of computer technology. The Red, Green, Blue (RGB) color model serves a very useful purpose, enabling artists to communicate clearly with electronics folks by describing color output to a monitor's red, green, and blue phosphors.

The Cyan, Magenta, Yellow, and Black (CMYK) model is used for color separation printing. The mixture of these colors as ink, not light, makes up the color images you see in magazines and books. Also known as *process color,* CMYK is a subtractive color-building process. As you'll recall from school, pigments are subtractive colors and light is additive.

To make an RGB image printable on a commercial print press which uses the standard four process colors for printing, the image must be converted to the CMYK standard. This is the reason that you must calibrate your monitor. Photoshop does the conversions very adeptly. A CMYK color file has four channels, as opposed to an RGB image's three, and they can be stored as TIF images. TIF images get to be CMYK mode images either by acquiring a color image with a 48-bit scanner or by having a program like Photoshop convert the image from RGB.

You probably won't often encounter a CMYK TIF file unless it's been converted from an RGB image as part of the pre-press process. *Pre-press* is the work and the procedures a commercial printer or service bureau goes through to take the elements (digital or otherwise) that comprise a finished piece and make printing plates out of them.

The file-format change from RGB to CMYK, which is part of the pre-press process, should take place *after* you've finished creating and enhancing your image in Photoshop. Each time you change the mode, Photoshop must interpolate the information to change from a three channel color model (RGB) to a four channel model (CMYK). Interpolation always causes some reduction in the quality of the image.

Do all your work in RGB mode, and when you finish your editing and enhancing, save the RGB mode file. Then save a copy of the RGB file to a new name. Use the Mode menu command to then change the copy from RGB to CMYK mode.

If you need to, make any minor corrections in the CMYK mode file and then print your separations, or save the file for your service bureau. If you must make major adjustments, discard the CMYK file, make your changes in the original RGB copy. Repeat the previous procedure for saving the RGB file to a new name and converting the copy to CMYK.

Figure 4.7 shows an RGB image as it is normally displayed in Photoshop.

Figures 4.8 and 4.9 were split from their composite image, using the Split Channels command found on the command button menu on the Channels palette (F6). The RGB components in figure 4.8 are based on an entirely different color model than the CMYK image components. In figure 4.9, a CMYK TIF file of the same subject is split.

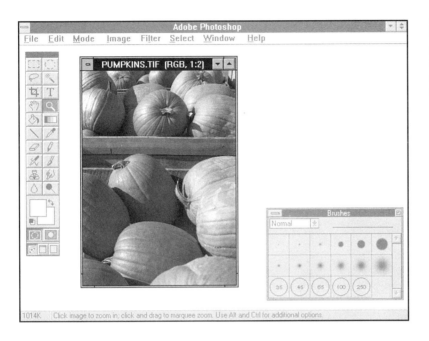

Figure 4.7
An RGB image consists of three channels: Red, Green, and Blue.

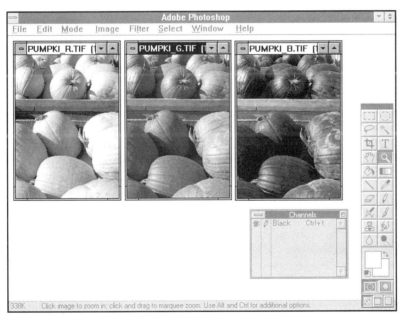

Figure 4.8
Each of these image channels is identical in composition but carries different color information.

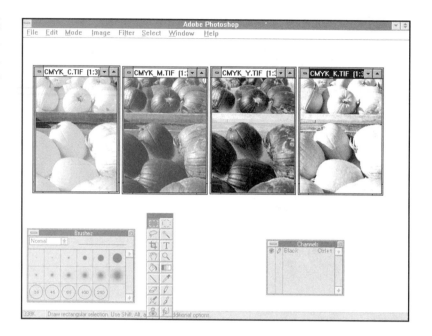

When Photoshop reads a CMYK image, it must convert the image to an RGB mode before it can be displayed on your monitor, which doesn't have any cyan or magenta phosphors. The conversion for display purposes doesn't affect the information stored in a CMYK *file* unless you change the Mode setting by means of the menu bar and save the file as an RGB-type image, or if you paint or otherwise edit the file.

The option regarding how you want to display CMYK composites is made from the General Preferences dialog box. There you can select either the Faster or Smoother options by pushing the appropriate radio button. This choice is another speed/accuracy trade-off. When you select Faster, Photoshop will use interpolation and a lookup table to assign the CMYK color values in the file to approximately comparable RGB color model values. This method is quick, but not very accurate. When you select Smoother, Photoshop then takes its time to translate and assign the CMYK color values to the RGB model. This last method is slower but more accurate.

If you work in the production department of a magazine or other publication, you want to render CMYK files to the screen using the Smoother option. The Smoother option will show you potential problems that may occur when you use Photoshop to generate the color separations. If you want to view a CMYK file that you intend to convert to RGB image mode with the Mode menu command, select the faster display option in the General Preferences dialog box. This option determines the methodology Photoshop uses to generate the *display* of the image; not how it *converts* the image type when you change image modes from CMYK to RGB using the Modes menu commands.

Show Channels in Color

As previously noted, Photoshop can display the color channels that your image contains. You can edit the channels, copy them, and treat them as parts of a composite image. You can also choose to display them in color as you view the component channels. To do this, you check the Color Channels in Color option in the General Preferences dialog box.

All channels are actually based on an eight-bit grayscale color model, and as such, don't actually contain any color information to display. By default, each channel, except the RGB composite channel, appears the same (grayscale) when you view it. Checking this option tells Photoshop to "fake it" and show you the channel in shades of the color that corresponds to the channel being viewed. If you leave Color Channels in Color option unchecked, it's easy to become confused while editing channels or when creating new ones.

You can assign up to 16 extra Alpha (information) channels to a single image, and unless you keep a sharp eye on the title bar of the active image window, you may make unwanted changes to the wrong channel. Thus, checking the Color Channels in Color option gives you a visual reminder that you're editing in a color channel and not an Alpha channel.

If you're just beginning to get into electronic imaging, you may want to display channels in color. If you're more familiar with image editing, however, you might find the "candy-coating" that Photoshop puts on the channels a distraction to precise editing, and that it serves no purpose. It *is* harder to edit with this feature selected. Try both ways and decide for yourself.

Use Common Palette

Virtually no modern software program uses the Windows Common palette, so there's no reason that *you* should have to, either. The Use Common Palette option of the General Preferences dialog box activates a programming hook that enables software programmers to take advantage of the graphical support designed into Microsoft's Windows engine.

Programmers often can't wait for Windows to support the kinds of things that they want to accomplish. When this happens, they develop their own, proprietary ways of doing things instead of relying on Windows. The Adaptive palette is a case in point. It is far more sophisticated than the system palette Windows provides for handling color information. Is it unorthodox? Sure it is! Certain video drivers may not be able to handle Photoshop's Adaptive or its other custom palettes. If your video driver objects, you may have to check the Use Common Palette option. This option will instruct Photoshop to use the Windows Common Palette that offers only the most basic level of color-handling capability, but which is supported by most of the software and hardware that is currently available.

But if you want the cleanest view of full-color images, leave this option unchecked and let Photoshop provide the palette. Then when you exit Photoshop, you are returned to the Windows way of providing colors.

From the Source to the Sample

Use Diffusion Dither

The first two chapters discussed dithering. Now here's your big chance to have a say in how you prefer images to be displayed when you're running less than a 16.7-million-color video driver. You should check the Use Diffusion Dither option. If you do, the next time you run a 256-color driver while viewing a TrueColor image, the color errors from the resolution mismatch will be diffused across the image. Although it's a tedious way to work with an image, it beats using a patterned dither, which is Photoshop's default when you leave this option unchecked. Chapter 1 provides good examples of patterned and diffusion dithers.

Video LUT Animation

This option speeds up Photoshop screen redraws when you make editing changes. It animates the color lookup table for each of the RGB image components, and this only works in a 16-bit or higher display mode. Leave Video LUT Animation checked. It asks more of your processor, but will speed up your work.

Anti-Alias PostScript

You should definitely leave the Anti-Alias PostScript option of the General Preferences dialog box *checked*. Although Photoshop is a bitmap-type design program, it accepts material from sources that are not. All of this makes sense when you import an image from the clipboard. For example, figure 4.10 is a zoomed-in view of a part of a graphic that was generated by copying a vector graphic of type from a vector drawing program to the clipboard with Anti-Alias PostScript option checked, and then pasting the object into a new file in Photoshop. With the Anti-Alias PostScript checkbox marked, the hard edges of the vector art "wave" that are *rasterized* (that is, mapped to the screen as a bitmap) have shades of gray mixed in to smooth the display of the image.

If you turn off the Anti-Alias PostScript option, the same object looks like figure 4.11.

Photoshop's Anti-Aliasing feature works with its native Text tool, also. Anti-Aliasing works with black and white image types only when they are in grayscale mode, or with color images only when they are in RGB mode.

Export Clipboard

You probably should leave the **E**xport Clipboard option turned off because what you see *isn't* always what you get if you use the Windows clipboard to export a much-loved design piece from Photoshop into another application. People often use the clipboard to export a selected object quickly, but unless you're copying and pasting within Photoshop documents, Photoshop automatically converts clipboard images to a bitmapped format so that other applications can use them, and thus the quality of your beautifully enhanced clipboard item will diminish. Therefore, you should use another application's import filter to bring a finished TIF or PCX Photoshop piece into it.

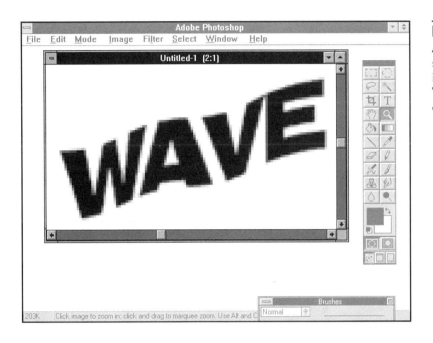

Figure 4.10
Anti-Aliasing helps smooth objects imported from the Windows clipboard.

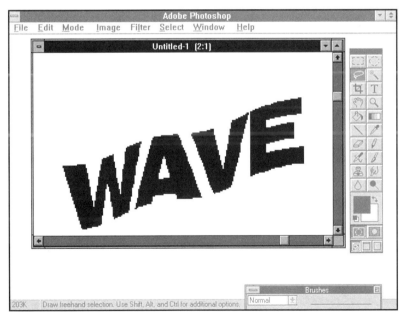

Figure 4.11
Sharp, jagged edges are a mark of an object that has no Anti-Aliasing.

Additionally, Photoshop images, like all non-vector images, can get quite large, and Windows clipboard works best when it doesn't have to hold massive amounts of information. The result of copying (and holding) a Photoshop image on the clipboard is slower system performance.

Copied items are held in system RAM, along with all your other changes to an image. So, to let your system work faster, don't check **E**xport Clipboard.

Short PANTONE Names

You can paint with colors that approximate PANTONE colors in Photoshop. PANTONE colors (like those you find in the fanning swatch books) are color specifications for paints and inks. If your assignment calls for using a specific PANTONE color for corporate colors, for example, Photoshop is very good at approximating paint and ink values to the screen.

When you use a pure PANTONE color in a design, it is reproduced at press time as a combination of ink colors that are mixed to exacting standards. The worth of the whole PANTONE color matching system is to ensure a design's faithful reproduction off a printing press that may be a thousand miles away from the designer. Or if someone another thousand miles away wants you to design a graphic when they have an exact shade of color in mind. If you check the Sh**o**rt PANTONE Names option of the General Preferences dialog box, the PANTONE colors you then select can be matched when you export an image to other programs.

For example, figure 4.12 features a TropicAir logo that uses two PANTONE colors. Photoshop represents these by using colors that closely approximate those that will be reproduced on coated stock paper. You can specify different color books from Photoshop by clicking on the foreground color selection box on the toolbox and then selecting **C**ustom. *Color books* are Photoshop's euphemism for different color measurement standards several manufacturers, like PANTONE and TRUEMATCH offer in real life, in bound book form, for expressing different color values. You don't access Photoshop's special color books directly; after you click on the foreground or background toolbox color selection boxes, you must always use the Color Picker options to access the color books.

This option is not user-definable. If you checked the Windows **C**olor Picker option before, you get nothing when you specify PANTONE colors because Windows doesn't support them.

After you finish the TropicAir logo, export it to Aldus PageMaker, a desktop publishing program that also acknowledges and uses the PANTONE short-naming convention for producing spot colors in work. Figure 4.13 shows the finishing touches being put on a small announcement incorporating the Photoshop logo, along with highlighted text and a headline that uses the same PANTONE color specifications. The match in PANTONE colors between PageMaker text and Photoshop paint colors is as close as possible for a computer image, and the Photoshop Sh**o**rt PANTONE Names option makes it easy to choose PageMaker color matches.

Restore Windows

You should leave the Restore Windows option checked in the General Preferences dialog box. You will soon learn about the Photoshop palettes. You use these palettes in combination with tools and effects, and your work will often call for completing a specific task in more than one Photoshop session. By checking this option, Photoshop remembers the settings, location, and position of the palettes and keeps them the way that you leave them when you exit the program. If you leave Restore Windows checked, you will find that the exercises in this book are easier to follow after you take breaks.

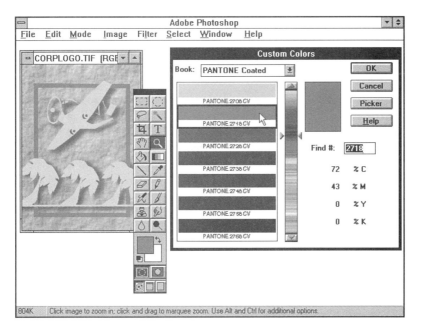

Figure 4.12
A design incorporating PANTONE spot colors.

Figure 4.13
Photoshop enables you to select short PANTONE names, which other applications then adopt identically in their naming conventions.

Beep When Done

Photoshop may take a while to complete a task such as opening a large TIF file or applying an effect. Sometimes you ask Photoshop to do something barely perceptible, like subtly sharpening an image. When you check the Beep When Done option of the General Preferences dialog box, you tell Photoshop to beep whenever you can proceed with your next step. While Photoshop is processing a command, you can't continue working on an image, so leave this option checked so you can get some feedback on Photoshop's progress.

If you leave the Beep When Done option checked and have a sound card or the PC Speaker for Windows file installed on your machine, you can define the "beep" that Photoshop uses. For example, you could have Photoshop play a loud siren WAV file after completing a task. You select Default Sound from the Windows Control Panel, Sound dialog box, then assign it a sound from a directory you have sound files stored in. Then, if you scoot down the hall for coffee while waiting for Photoshop to "thunk," you can hear the alert—and so can your co-workers!

Specifying Photoshop's Memory Settings

The settings that you specify in Photoshop's Monitor Setup and General Preferences dialog boxes become invaluable when you use Photoshop extensively in imaging work. Now that you are familiar with these settings, it's time to see how you can get more from your PC system so that Photoshop practices its magic more quickly and smoothly.

By choosing Pre**f**erences from the **F**ile menu, and then choosing Memory From the resulting Memory Preferences dialog box, you can set the best configuration of memory for your PC. The following sections provide examples that show you how to do so.

Virtual Memory

When you work on an image, Photoshop needs to store multiple copies of the image in your system RAM. To reside in RAM, a 1M image may require only 1M of RAM, but to do fancy stuff like performing an Undo, Photoshop needs memory more than two to three times that of the file size, depending on the effects or tools that you're using. But having several images open on the Photoshop workspace at the same time is also a serious drain on your system RAM. Photoshop's memory requirements can easily exceed the amount of RAM you have in your machine.

Even though you may have set up a permanent swap file in Windows, that file is a buffer that most programs use to swap *themselves* in and out of when you have insufficient RAM.

Photoshop won't use the Windows swap file. Instead, Photoshop offers you a proprietary scratch disk on which you can temporarily store image information when your system RAM is full.

Photoshop can locate the scratch disk on any drive, and you can even specify two different drives to use if you don't have much space on one drive. When you end your Photoshop session, all the temporary files in the scratch disk are deleted. The next time you start Photoshop, it creates a new scratch disk on the drive or drives that you specify in the Primary and Secondary field boxes of this dialog box. This is a particularly nice way to handle the need for temporary storage because it doesn't lock you out of precious hard drive space when you're not running Photoshop.

Figure 4.14 shows how I set up the memory preferences for my machine. As this section continues, I'll explain why I made these choices and how I came to them on my particular setup. Your settings may vary, and you should apply the settings in the Memory Preferences dialog box based on the specifications of your system.

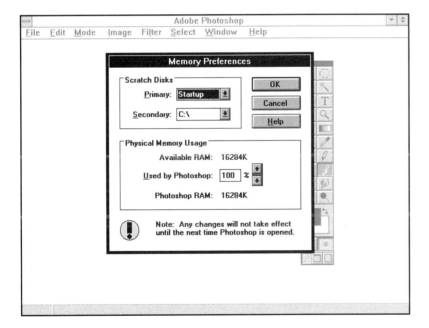

Figure 4.14

The Memory Preferences dialog box.

From the Source to the Sample

The Primary selection box specifies the location at which Photoshop sets up a scratch disk (a *virtual* memory file) where it will store data if it runs out of available system RAM. By default, Photoshop specifies your Startup directory because many systems have only one, non-partitioned hard disk. By defaulting to the Startup directory, Photoshop ensures that it will always find some space. But if you have more than one hard disk, or your hard disk *is* partitioned, you may want to select a different physical or logical hard disk location. To do so, click the down arrow next to the Primary selection box and then choose from the list of drive options.

If drive A or B are your floppy drives, don't specify them as your primary scratch disk locations. Otherwise, your performance will suffer terribly because you would tell Photoshop to use a space no larger than 1.44M, with a seek time of about 150 ms, rather than the 8–20ms range that a hard drive has.

Unlike Windows, Photoshop can set up virtual memory on a hard drive that uses on-the-fly compression, like Stacker. You don't need to specify an uncompressed hard drive partition for your Photoshop scratch disk locations.

Secondary Considerations

In the Secondary selection box, you can specify a secondary scratch disk location or simply select None from the drop-down list. Usually you should give Photoshop everything it needs to do its work, so you should specify both a primary and secondary place to swap data in and out of when it has used all available system RAM.

Try to free as much space as possible on your hard drives for your Photoshop work. If one of your drives is faster than the other, try to use it as your primary drive. Keep images on a PhotoCD, and save them on floppy disks (or other removable media) when you aren't using them. Use your own judgment to balance hard drive space for use as both storage *and* virtual memory.

Maximizing Physical Memory

The bottom part of the Memory Preferences dialog box is the Physical Memory Usage window. This memory doesn't refer to the scratch disk virtual memory at all, but rather the collective talents of the little SIMM chips you have installed that provide system RAM.

In figure 4.14 you'll notice that, in the Used by Photoshop option, 100 percent of all system RAM has been specified—that is, 100 percent of what Windows allows an application to use for its session is devoted to Photoshop work. (Actually, my machine has 20M RAM installed, but Windows has earmarked 4M for environment housekeeping, so Photoshop can hook into only 16M while it operates.)

Again, you should give Photoshop everything it needs to work its magic. Windows is not the true multitasking environment it's touted to be (although Windows NT is), so don't run other applications while you're in Photoshop. If you try downloading a modem file, or recalculating a spreadsheet in the background while Photoshop is running, your system will crash, or at very least your performance will bog down.

If you have 12M RAM or more installed on your system, dedicate 100 percent in the Used by Photoshop box. If you have only 8M RAM or less, seriously consider buying more. Photoshop is a "power" application in every sense of the word, virtual *and* physical.

When you change a Memory Preferences option, remember to restart Photoshop so that the changes take effect.

Specifying Units of Measurement

As you'll see in upcoming exercises, Photoshop can express measurements in different kinds of units to help you size up your work. In two instances you want to specify the unit of your choice: when you check the **I**mage Size and Canvas **S**ize settings (both under the **I**mage menu), and when you select the Show **R**ulers option (by pressing Ctrl+R) around an active image window.

Figure 4.15 shows the Unit Preferences dialog box, which you access by selecting Pre**f**erence from the **F**ile menu and then choosing Units.

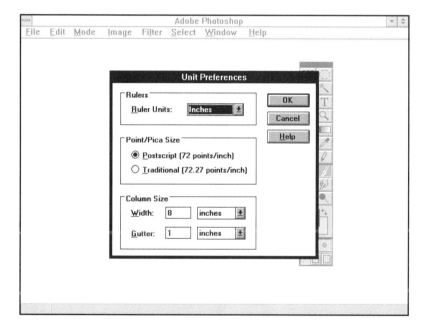

Figure 4.15

You can set Photoshop's rulers and other measurements to your desired specifications in the Unit Preferences dialog box.

The Rulers window at the top of the Unit Preferences dialog box controls the unit of measurement that the rulers use in an active image. You probably should keep Inches as the default. However, occasionally you'll need to measure an area for placing text, in which case you will need to specify Points as the unit of measurement for rulers. Additionally, you may be assigned work that is measured in picas or centimeters, and Photoshop enables you to measure an image according to these specifications as well.

When measuring how well conventional type sets into an image, click the Traditional radio button in the Point/Pica Size area of the Units Preferences dialog box. As you can see in figure 14.15, the difference between Traditional and PostScript point measurements is nominal (72 and 72.27 points per inch). I leave this setting to PostScript because I usually add typography to an image with Photoshop's Type tool, which can use the TrueType and PostScript Type 1 fonts I have on my PC, and proofs are printed from Photoshop to a PostScript printer.

In the Column Size window, the Width and Gutter options show you how an image fits into a page layout of another application, such as a desktop publishing application. When set to inches, this unit of measurement is also used in the Image Size and Canvas Size options of the Image menu. You should set this option to inches, unless your work calls for European or typographic standards.

From Preferences to Workspace Options

You are now pretty well familiar with Photoshop's preference settings (except for those that affect printing inks and separations, which Chapter 20 gets into). You can now move more quickly and efficiently because, if you followed along to this point, you have completed some customizing of the Photoshop workspace.

Taking Control of Photoshop's Mask/Selection/ Channel Features

You're now ready to take a look at some of the features that are available from within the Photoshop workspace. These functions are used extensively in future exercises. The following are the most commonly used of these functions:

✔ A *mask* is an area that you define in an image to protect either the surrounding area or the selected area from changes that you make with tools, filters, and effects in Photoshop. Everything that is *not* masked in an image is the inverse, or *selection*. A *Quick Mask* is a temporary mask that you usually don't save when you finish some editing work. A Quick Mask has a color and opacity so that you can see the underlying image and how precisely you're defining the selection area while using painting and editing tools. When you save a selection created by a mask (by choosing **S**ave Selection), it becomes a selection in a *channel*, which you can recall later.

✔ A *selection* is an active area in an image that's subject to paints, filters, and so on. There are two types of selections: floating and non-floating. Chapter 5 distinguishes between them. You can edit selections independently of the image it's hovering over. When you deselect an area, it becomes part of the image over which it was selected (that is, it becomes *composited*).

You can save a selection area as the geometry (shape) of a border that you defined. Saving a selection enables you to recall the border later and use it for masking or selecting part of an image. A selection area can also contain grayscale information so that it partially masks an image area. You can manipulate the selection area inside the selection border independently of the image area surrounding the selection border. A

Saved Selection area is retained in a channel, where it is represented by areas of black, white, and sometimes shades in between that you can modify using the painting and editing tools. The exercises in this book frequently use selection areas.

✔ A *channel* can either be part of a composite image (for example, an RGB image is a composite of a Red, Green, and Blue channel) or an additional eight-bit grayscale channel that the user creates by either defining or by saving selection areas composed in the RGB view of an image. Extra user-created channels are called *Alpha* channels. You create an Alpha channel each time you perform the New Channel command from the Channels palette (see future exercises for demonstrations) or you save a selection (by choosing the **S**ave Selection from Photoshop's **S**elect menu).

Masks and selections are opposite sides of the same coin, and it's often confusing to the budding imagist because Photoshop offers so many ways to create them, and sometimes a different function serves the same purpose.

The next couple of exercises will help you get up and running before the you encounter the Photoshop test drive in Chapter 5. First, open the PUMPKINS.TIF image from the companion CD, and then follow along as the exercises describe how you can use the various Photoshop options to select and mask areas of an image.

Selections, Masks, and Saving

Open PUMPKIN.TIF from the companion CD

Double-click on the Quick Mask Mode button on the toolbox	Displays the Mask Options dialog box (see fig. 4.16).
Click on the Color Indicates Marked Areas radio button	Tells Photoshop that areas displayed as Quick Mask color are to be marked as masked areas, not selected ones when you return to Standard mode.
Click on the Color box at the bottom of the Mask Options dialog box	Displays Photoshop's Color Picker.
Click and drag the Color Picker slider to a green hue, then click and drag the selection circle in the main color model down to the right, and then click on OK	Green has been defined as the color of the Quick Mask.

Stop when you have a dark green color selected. A value of R 3, G 150, and B 3 is good, but you don't need this exact color. See the tip that follows.

continues

continued

Type **75%** in the Opacity box, and then click on OK

Specifies a very opaque, dark green mask, which will be displayed over nonselected areas of the PUMPKIN.TIF image. You are returned to the image, and you are in Quick Mask mode.

Click on the Standard mode button

Returns you to a normal editing view of the active image.

Click on the Lasso tool on the toolbox

Selects a freehand selection tool that enables you to draw selection borders with free, unconstrained mouse movements.

Click and drag a rough outline around a pumpkin image in PUMPKIN.TIF, and then release the mouse button

Draws a selection border around a pumpkin image, as shown in figure 4.17.

Click on the Right Quick Mask button

Displays inactive areas in the image with a dark green mask over them, while leaving your rough pumpkin selection area without this color.

Figure 4.16
Using the Mask Options dialog box, you can display a mask in any color or degree of transparency.

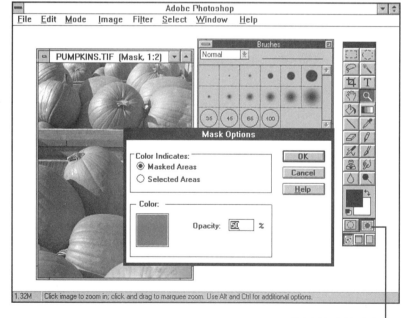

Quick Mask Mode button

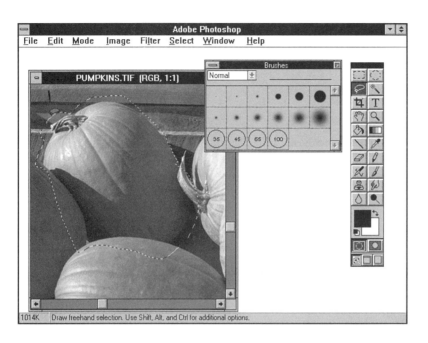

Figure 4.17
The Lasso tool draws a selection area that you can view in quick mask mode.

The reason for changing the quick mask color and opacity is to address the colors in the PUMPKIN.TIF image. This image sports a great deal of orange, so a 50 percent opaque, red-colored quick mask would be difficult to see over all the orange. For most images, you may find the less dense default of 50 percent red to be better.

The little exclamation triangle that popped up when you chose this particular shade of green should not concern you. This flag warns you that you selected a color that print presses cannot reproduce. However, in this case you are specifying a color for a mask that you intend to display only on the monitor, and not to be printed.

The Quick Mask mode is an inactive state for your selection area. You can't move, copy, or paste it and the underlying image can't be edited at all. You can, however, edit the Quick Mask by tracing more closely around the selection area, and then switch to Standard mode (the button to the left of the Quick Mask Mode button) to continue your work with the area.

To edit a Quick Mask, you can use several Photoshop tools, which are covered more extensively in Chapter 5. For the following exercise, you use Photoshop's Pencil tool to refine the Quick Mask that you create.

The Brushes palette should be on your workspace by default. If the palette is currently hidden, press F5 before you begin the following exercise.

Cleaning Up a Mask

Click on the Pencil tool on the toolbox	Selects a tool that enables you to stroke in areas with a clean, no-spread color.

Choose a medium-size tip
from the Brushes palette

I used the tip in the middle of the top row in the Brushes palette, but you don't have to select the same one. Just choose a medium- to small-size tip and maintain Photoshop's default settings of 100% opacity and Normal mode. (If you have been experimenting independently, change the settings back now!)

Use short strokes to color areas outside the
pumpkin image that you failed to include
in the rough Lasso selection

These strokes will color the mask green, even though your toolbox color selection boxes are black and white. Don't be alarmed; this is the way that editing a mask with a painting tool is *supposed* to work. Figure 4.18 shows what your screen should look like.

Click on the inverse colors icon (two-headed arrow) at the top-right of the toolbox foreground/background color selection boxes	Reverses the colors that you use with the Pencil tool to edit the quick mask.
Click and drag the Pencil tool around an area that you don't want to mask	Erases the specified masked area.

With the color selection box reversed, the white foreground selection now erases the green masked areas that you don't want to mask.

Click on the inverse colors icon on the toolbox again	Sets the Pencil tool to apply masking color once more.
Click and drag around the mask border using short strokes	Completely refines the mask border so that the pumpkin border is defined as well as possible.

As you may have already guessed, the Quick Mask, which represents your selection area, doesn't have to be a contiguous piece of image area. Selection borders don't have to be linked, so you can paint any area in the active image that you want to add to or subtract from a selection.

You still can't *do* anything with the selection area. However, in the next exercise, you use the Normal mode to return editable qualities to the pumpkin selection area. Then you'll see a way that you can use the selection area as the basis for a *path*, which has its own unique properties and can be modified with great precision.

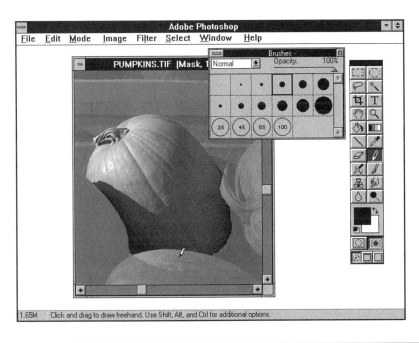

Figure 4.18
You can use the Pencil tool to paint on an unmasked area to refine the selection you made with the Lasso tool.

Changing a Selection to a Path

Click on the Standard Mode View button, which is to the left of the Quick Mask Mode button	Turns the green Quick Mask into a fully operational masked area outside the image. The marquee border now selects only the pumpkin area that displayed no green mask color before.
Press Ctrl+plus key	Magnifies the image to a 2:1 viewing resolution for better editing in Photoshop.

Ctrl+plus key is a shortcut key for the Zoom tool. Chapter 5 discusses this tool in more detail.

Choose **W**indow, Show **P**aths, or press F9	Displays the Paths palette.
Click on the command button on the Paths palette, and then select Make Path	Displays the Make Path dialog box.
Type **0.5** in the **T**olerance (measured in pixels) field, and then click on OK	Instructs Photoshop to do the least possible amount of averaging when it translates the selection area to Path information.
Click on the Arrow Pointer tool on the Paths palette	

continues

continued

The Arrow Pointer tool moves only *Anchor points* (the little nodes on the path) and *direction points* (the little handles on direction lines that change a path's direction at each anchor point).

Click and drag an Anchor on the path and then a a direction point	Moves the Anchor point and readjusts the direction of the path.

Play with this feature a while, as shown in figure 4.19. Try to move the path closer to the border of the pumpkin image.

Figure 4.19
The tools of the Paths palette enable you to manipulate a selection converted to a path.

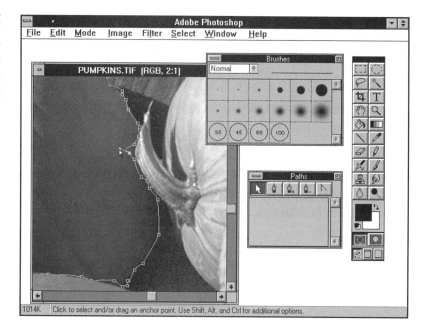

The Paths palette tools are an independent set of tools from the toolbox tools in Photoshop. You'll see how to use these tools in Chapter 12, but don't be afraid to experiment with them for a while between exercises. Paths are much like outlines you may have used in drawing packages like Adobe Illustrator, MicroGrafx Designer, and CorelDRAW!. Although Photoshop belongs to the bitmap family of computer graphics design software, it uses vector-type paths to define areas that can be acted on later as a selection. Paths are inert as far as the effect they have on bitmap images—they are sort of a blueprint that Photoshop uses for defining geometric areas that will be changed later using tools suited for bitmap image work.

After you achieve a pretty tight fit around the pumpkin image area with your path, it's time to create a selection area based on its shape so that we can move on to see how the Channels palette in this program offers you yet another "view" of selection and masked image areas.

Retrieving and Saving a Selection

Choose Make Selection from the Paths palette drop-down list	Displays the Make Selection dialog box, which enables you to specify how faithfully a selection is created from the path.
Choose Feather Radius **0** pixels in the Rendering area, and make sure that **A**nti-Aliased is checked	Creates a smooth selection border, with no imprecise feathering. (Chapter 5 explains feathering.)
Click on OK	Returns you to the Photoshop workspace, with both a selection border and a path around the pumpkin image area.
Press the Backspace key twice	Deletes the path, but keeps the marquee selection border. (See the following tip.)
Choose **S**elect, **S**ave Selection	Saves the selection area—the geometric outline, and not the contents (the pumpkin image area)—to a channel.
Choose **W**indow, Show C**h**annels or press F6	Displays the Channels palette, which lists the color and Alpha channels.
Click the Channel #4 title area, or press Ctrl+4	Displays a visible and editable view of the new selection as it's held in an Alpha channel.

This view is shown in figure 4.20. Note in the Channels palette the Eye and Pencil icons in the two rows to the left of the channel 4 title. These icons indicate that the view is visible and editable, respectively.

When you edit a path as you did in the preceding exercise, paths that previously were converted to selections still exist *in addition to* the new selection area. You can save paths as often as you want, but in the last exercise, you don't *want* to save a path. When a path still exists after you make it a selection area, delete it by pressing the Backspace key twice. Otherwise, if you use the Copy command, you'll copy the path rather than the selection area. Only when you haven't changed the Path created from a selection with the Arrow, Pen, or Corner tool, will a path automatically go away after a selection has been created from it.

Palettes are great. Click the **W**indow menu, and you find many Photoshop palettes. Each of them augments your options as they relate to different selection and paint application tools. You will use the palettes in exercises throughout this book, so don't feel cheated because you didn't get to explore the full potential of each palette in this chapter.

Figure 4.20
The selection area is now saved to a channel.

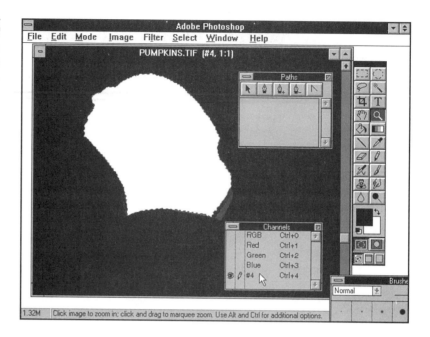

You now should have a pretty precise selection area saved to a channel. How do you call it back onto the RGB image? First, go back to the editable view of the RGB channel by clicking on the RGB title on the Channels palette. Then double-click the Control button on the Channels palette to remove it from view. (Keeping all the palettes in Photoshop open is unwise because your workspace sometimes gets so crowded that you can't see the image!) Then select **L**oad Selection from the **S**elect menu, and your near-perfect selection area is displayed as a marquee-selection border around the image area that you defined.

You will have plenty more chances to work with selections and use Alpha channels, so close PUMPKIN.TIF now and respond **N**o when you are prompted to save changes. Alpha channels increase image file sizes dramatically, and you really don't want a bunch of digitally plumped-up pumpkins on your hard drive.

Brushes Palette Options

Your final stop on your tour of the options that you can set in Photoshop involves the Brushes palette. This is the palette, you will use most in image editing.

Photoshop ships with three Brushes palettes—Default (DEFAULT.ABR), Shadows (SHADOW.ABR), and Custom (CUSTOM.ABR). The files for these palettes are all located in the BRUSHES subdirectory of Photoshop. Although the Shadow and Custom palettes are not loaded by default, they can be very useful in special situations if you know how to load them. Additionally, you can create a brush or a collection of them as an entire palette that you can work from in Photoshop. The last two exercises in this chapter show you how to make the Brushes palette work the way that you want while you do your imaging work.

Load LOOK!.TIF into your Photoshop workspace from the companion CD. You need this file to do the next exercise, which shows you how Photoshop redefines the traditional concept of a brush tip. In this exercise, you work with a special Alpha channel to mask part of the image area. I created this channel using the same steps that you followed in the last few exercises.

Making a Large, Angled Brush Tip

Choose **W**indow, Show C**h**annels, or press F6

Choose **S**elect, **L**oad Selection	Displays a selection border around the LOOK! image area shown that the authors created using the techniques covered earlier. See figure 4.21.

The area inside the LOOK! lettering is selected, and the rest of the image is not affected by painting or effects.

Click on the channel #4 title on the Channels palette	Displays a view of the selection as it exists in the Alpha channel, as shown in figure 4.22.
Click on the RGB title on the Channels	Returns you to the full-color, editable view palette of the LOOK!.TIF image.
Click on the control button on the Brushes palette, and then select New Brush	Displays the New Brush dialog box, as shown in figure 4.23.
Enter **200** pixels for the Diameter, **45** degrees for the Angle, and **25**% for the Roundness	Specifies a flat, angled brush tip that is larger than any of Photoshop's defaults.
Click on OK	Confirms your selection and returns you to the Photoshop workspace with a new brush tip at the bottom of your Brushes palette.

You can modify a brush by double-clicking an existing brush tip space on the Brushes palette, or create a new brush by double-clicking a vacant area on the palette.

Figure 4.21
Selecting the Load
Selection
command from the
Select menu
displays any
selection border
that you have
saved to an Alpha
channel.

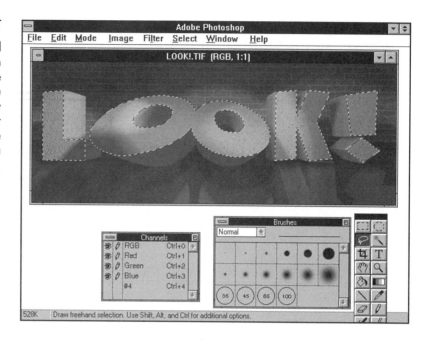

Figure 4.22
A saved selection
area appears
around a mask
that you create
with selection or
paint application
tools.

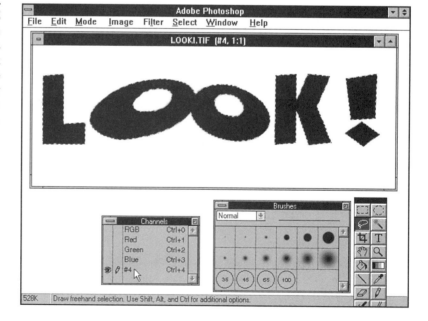

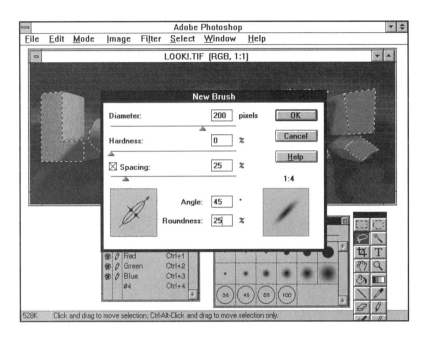

Figure 4.23
The Command button on the Brushes palette enables you to modify or create a brush tip.

Your new brush tip has some interesting characteristics, being huge and operating at an angle. Having a huge brush tip can be useful when using Photoshop, particularly when you need to cover a large area quickly. However, unless you save the Brushes palette *configuration* now—by clicking the Command button, selecting Save Brushes, and entering a file name—this huge brush tip will disappear when you load a different Brushes palette, then recall the default palette. You can save a single new Brushes tip within a collection when you do the Save Brushes command, but not a single Brushes tip under a unique file name.

In the next exercise you use your new 200-point brush tip to create a little lighting effect in LOOK!.TIF in a single stroke. As a taste of the creative applications you'll get into in future chapters, the exercise also shows you how to create your first realistic-looking shadow.

LOOKing for Some Shade

Click on the Paint Brush tool in the toolbox

Click on the default colors icon in the lower corner of the toolbox	Sets the default Photoshop paint colors to a black foreground and a white background.
Click and drag the Opacity on the Brushes palette to 45%	Restricts the slider application of the foreground color to partial coverage, allowing some of the background to show through.

continues

continued

| Click and drag the cursor across the selection area in the image | Creates a shadow effect only within the selected area. |

Figure 4.24 indicates a good location for heightening the moody lighting in the cartoon piece.

| Choose **E**dit, **U**ndo Brush, (or press Ctrl+Z) | Undoes your last stroke, in case you find the result aesthetically displeasing. |

Figure 4.24
If you decrease the opacity, your paint strokes will not completely color in a selected image area.

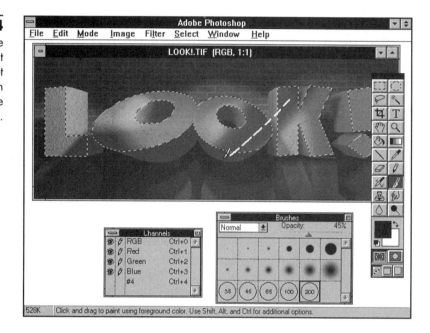

The Custom Brushes palette is the neatest, weirdest collection of brush tips that you would ever want to see in a paint-oriented application. The Custom Brushes are Adobe's gesture to complement your painting with some design elements usually found in drawing, vector-type programs.

Using the Custom Brushes, the technique you're likely to prefer isn't to stroke the image "canvas," but rather to *click* an area, much as you would stamp a check CANCELED.

When you change Brushes palettes in the next exercise, you will lose the 200-pixel custom brush you built and used in the previous exercises, if you didn't save the modified palette as described earlier.

Using Photoshop's Custom Brushes

Click on the command button on the Brushes palette, and then select Load Brushes	Displays the Load dialog box.
Click on CUSTOM.ABR, which is in the BRUSHES subdirectory of the PHOTOSHOP directory, and then click on OK	Selects the Custom Brushes palette you need for this exercise, and then exits the Load dialog box.
Say "Oh, wow!" two or three times	Expresses your awe at all the strange Custom Brushes tips, which look more like little icons than brush tips.
Click on the Eye brush tip in the Brushes palette	Selects a tip design that makes painting strokes look like eyes.
Click repeatedly inside the selection border	"Stamps" an eye image wherever you click, leaving the area outside the border unaffected, as shown in figure 5.25.
Click on the command button on the Brushes palette, and then select Load Brushes	Displays the Load dialog box.
Choose DEFAULT.ABR, and then click on OK	Returns the Brushes palette to a more workable default set of tips, so that you don't mess up your exercises in the rest of the book!

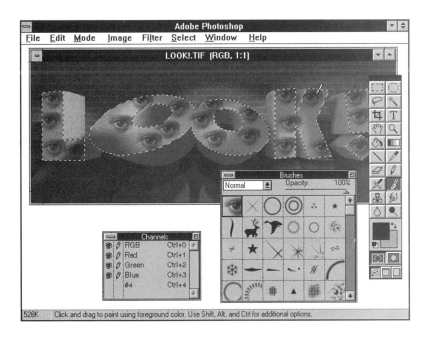

Figure 4.25

You can apply a design by clicking a selection area with a Custom Brushes tip.

To create a Custom Brushes tip, you use the Rectangle Marquee tool (which is covered in the next chapter) to select an area on an image that contains a desired design element. You can select any image area, but you'll have more fun with a simple black and white bitmap-type image. Try a character from a typeface symbol set, for example. Although you can choose any area you want, you can define the tip only as an eight-bit, grayscale-type image. Then you can apply any color using this grayscale Brushes tip by accessing a foreground color through the Color Picker or the Colors palette.

After selecting the image area with the Rectangle Marquee tool, click the Command button on the Brushes palette, then select Define Brush, and the area is defined as a Brushes tip.

Summary

If you have now managed to customize your Photoshop workspace to work the way you want it, then this chapter has been time well spent. During and after future exercises, feel free to flip back to Chapters 4 and 5, the "up and running" parts of this book. That's another perk of having this information printed on pages. Although these last two chapters are not a complete reference guide by any measure (points, millimeters, or inches), you now have learned about half of the basics of Photoshop, and Chapter 5 provides more information that will make the exercises throughout this book more meaningful and rewarding.

Photoshop's tools and functions are integrated, but you may have to travel to several places in the workspace to accomplish a full task. Keep this in mind and develop a working set of techniques that accommodate Photoshop's circuitous tools and menus. What Photoshop lacks in organization, it more than makes up for in functionality.

There's one last thing you should try every time you start up Photoshop. Although it won't enhance your tool skills, it may provide a little visual relief. Double-click the Photoshop title bar *after* the program is launched. It seems like every program—*except* Photoshop—maximizes its window on startup automatically, or at least gives you a crack at setting this startup mode from a Windows shell manager such as Norton Desktop. Why Photoshop won't maximize is one of the great mysteries in Life.

I think it's a Mac convention.

Chapter Snapshot

In this chapter, you learn how to:

A Photoshop Test Drive

Photoshop offers quite an arsenal of features that are analogous to the tools used in a conventional darkroom, and it offers several effects that photographers have only *wished* for. This chapter surveys the tools that you use constantly in Photoshop and demonstrates how they work. However, this chapter isn't a complete guide to Photoshop's tools, but only a "test drive," intended to familiarize you with the basics so that you can forge ahead more quickly into the sophisticated stuff!

One of the wonders of electronic imaging is that your mistakes are never irrevocable—if you get into the habit of opening *copies* of your digitized images before you work with them. A digital copy is an exact duplicate of its source and practically invites experimentation. There is no right or wrong way to enhance an image. You might mistakenly use the "wrong" tool to create an effect, but if the result proves to be pleasing to the eye, then you've just added an effect to Photoshop's and your own repertoire!

The companion CD, for example, includes a graphics file, MY_DESK.TIF, that shows the top of my desk. Although you'll use this image in several of this chapter's exercises, there's no "right" or "wrong" way for you to handle it. In fact, you should play with the file and discover ways to modify the image in addition to the ones suggested in this chapter. Play time is learning time, and experimenting on your own is definitely the order of the day.

Families of Tools

Life in Photoshop's digital darkroom is much easier to understand if you remember that Photoshop provides three different function sets, and that you can combine these sets to enjoy fantastic imaging capabilities:

✔ The *selection* functions consist of the toolbox's selection tools, and the options in menus and dialog boxes for refining the selections.

✔ The *paint application* functions also provide dialog boxes and tools, as well as menu selections, that offer still greater control over how you apply "digital paint" to an image.

✔ The *modifying* functions are the filters, menu options, and editing tools that change image areas without the use of paint. These functions include Photoshop's digital equivalents to the techniques that photographers use when they retouch their film images: color-correction, brightness and contrast, and sharpening and blurring. Throughout this book, sound, working examples of modifying functions are highlighted, and you'll see a small sample of them shortly.

As varied as each of these sets of functions may seem, their interrelationship in Photoshop work is vital to enable you to make passable images look outstanding. Unfortunately, these group functions are organized about as logically as my sock drawer. They are scattered and hidden under buttons and behind menus, and you activate them by keyboard and mouse contortions. Fortunately, all the work it takes to access these functions inevitably leads you to stumble on new tricks and tools along the way.

Adjusting Your View

Navigating Photoshop's workspace is an important skill to develop early in the game. You'll want to be able to zoom in and out effortlessly and scroll around an image to retouch different areas. Photoshop provides several ways that you can get to different viewing resolutions and areas of an image.

The first exercise in this chapter gives you some experience finding the controls you need to access to view an image. After you finish this brief exercise, you'll be able to move around the digital image easily. You'll be able to concentrate on discovering how to use and apply Photoshop's painting, selecting, and editing tools.

Just Looking

Select **F**ile, **O**pen, then choose MY_DESK.TIF from the companion CD, and then click on OK

This opens the exercise image you'll use for the next steps.

Double-click on the Hand tool on the toolbox	Increases the image to a full-image viewing resolution, with no scroll bars around the active image.
Click on the Zoom tool	Selects the tool, but does not enlarge the view of the image.
Click and drag the Zoom tool diagonally in the image area	Draws a small marquee as you drag the tool diagonally and zooms into the area within the marquee box.

This technique is called *marquee-zooming*. The smaller the area you marquee-zoom, the closer you get.

Press Alt and click with the Zoom tool	Zooms you out of a picture, to a view that's half the current image size.
Press Ctrl+plus key	Increases the image window to full size on the workspace, and zooms into a view 1 power greater than the previous one (for example, 2:1, then 3:1, and then 4:1).
Press Ctrl+minus key	Performs the opposite action of Ctrl+plus key combination—you zoom *out* one viewing resolution increment.
Choose the Hand tool and then click and drag this tool in the image area	Moves your view within the active image window.

The Hand tool, which works only when an image is greater than its window size, is an alternative to using window scroll bars.

Click the bottom-center button on the toolbox	Displays the image at the same viewing resolution as the left, Standard Mode display (Photoshop's default), except without scroll bars.

Because this display has no scroll bars, you must use the Hand tool to move within the image.

Click on the Display Mode button on the bottom right of the toolbox	Displays the image in a mode that does not include scroll bars or a menu bar around an active image.

This Photoshop display mode is useful for presentations, but uncomfortable to work in.

Click on the Standard Display Mode button on the bottom left of the toolbox	Returns you to a normal display mode in the workspace.

Refer to the Adobe toolbox and palette button display in the inside front cover of this book.

Double-click on the Hand tool	Returns you to a full-frame view of MY_DESK.TIF that doesn't include scroll bars.

From the Source to the Sample

Photoshop offers you so many different ways to zoom in and out from an image because you need each of them at one time or another to work on specific areas in your assignments. The Hand tool is, well, *handy*, because it always returns you to a full-frame view of a piece when you double-click it. If you get caught up on working in a specific area of an image, you should double-click the Hand tool periodically to gain a perspective on how the whole image is coming together.

You can show off a finished piece to a client or to yourself in the windowless, menuless display mode that Photoshop uses when you click on the right Display Mode button. The primary function of the mode is to remove distracting Windows operating environment controls from a view of your artwork.

Your palettes, however, are usually open and hovering about your finished piece after several hours of work, and this puts a damper on an otherwise magic moment. Palettes may be closed individually, but Photoshop's toolbox never closes. If you notice, it's the only on-screen element without a command button in the upper right corner. So how do you make it disappear for a while?

You can press the Tab key once to hide the toolbox no matter what display mode you are using. This also removes the status bar and any open palettes from the screen. To display the toolbox and status bar again, press the Tab key a second time. This is called *toggling* a function, and you'll see this term used to describe other Photoshop features that turn on and off.

Understanding Resolution

The last exercise used the term *resolution* to refer to the various fields of view as a result of zooming. Resolution, as described in Chapters 1 and 2, relates to how many pixels per inch are used to build an image. The same unit of measurement is used when you display an image on your monitor, particularly if you zoom in or out. Photoshop must *interpolate* pixel size when you zoom in to an image. Interpolation, when used in this context, means that Photoshop is placing color pixels in between adjacent pixels in order to convey a smooth tonal transition when the image is viewed as a whole. Therefore, when you zoom in to an image, a single pixel is *displayed* at 4, 16, 256, and more pixels. This is where the term *pixel* gets a little confusing. When you zoom into an image, although you may be viewing a single pixel in a file, Photoshop gives you this view by interpolating the image and using several *screen* pixels on your display to represent it.

This effect is called *pixelation* when taken to its extreme. The square sample areas (the pixels) become obvious, and the eye can't integrate them as part of a whole image. You can see the same effect by viewing a chemical photograph under a magnifying glass; you'll see more film grain than actual image.

This is why zooming to a 1:1 viewing resolution is so important in your work. This viewing resolution presents the image as it will print. If the image is too small for a layout, for example, increasing the file dimensions degrades (lessens) the image resolution. In other words, enlarging a picture results in the same effect as zooming in on an image: pixelation. Figure 5.1 shows an 8:1 zoom resolution of a detail from MY_DESK.TIF—the tiny, framed reproduction of Frans Halz's *Laughing Cavalier*. Because this file does not include much image information, Photoshop had to create "giant" pixels to display this close-up.

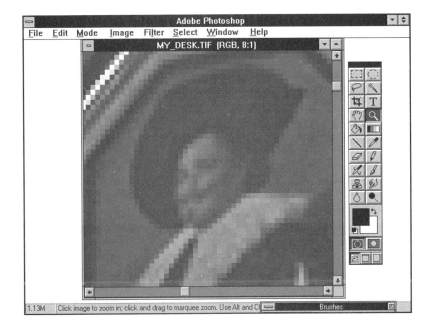

Figure 5.1

Frans Halz's *Laughing Cavalier*, as displayed here, contains much fewer pixels than in the original.

None of this makes zooming into an image "bad." In fact, to do retouching work that the observer will not perceive at a 1:1 resolution, you *need* to zoom into a pixellated view of an image. Understand that the image information sent to a printer is a 1:1, 100-percent view of the image.

Defining a Selection Area

Using the selection tools, you can pick a portion of your image and change it without affecting the other parts of image. Some of the tools let you define the *shape* of the area on which you want to work. These are the Lasso, the Rectangular Marquee, and Elliptical Marquee tools, which are located on the top of Photoshop's toolbox. The Magic Wand tool, however, is an *automatic* tool that selects an area based on *color values*, not shape. You don't need incredible eye-hand coordination to define selected areas when using the Magic Wand. But to do outstanding Photoshop work, you will find both types of selection tools, sometimes used in combination, necessary.

Soon you will learn how to refine selection areas. But first, let's see what happens when you use different selection tools on an area of the MY_DESK.TIF image.

Choosing the Right Selection Tool

You don't try to jam a round peg in a square hole, unless you want to fail an aptitude test; you also shouldn't try to use an inappropriate Photoshop selection tool and expect accurate results when creating a selection border around part of an image.

Selecting Squares and Circles

Both the Rectangular Marquee and Elliptical Marquee selection tools are great for selecting symmetrical areas. After the next exercise introduces you to the properties of the Rectangular Marquee tool, you'll also understand how to use the Elliptical Marquee tool. You use the same key combinations and mouse moves to manipulate both tools. The only difference is that one draws squares and the other doesn't.

You may not find an area in MY_DESK.TIF that these tools can precisely select, but that's okay. You don't lose points here; you only gain familiarity with the way basic selection tools operate in Photoshop. Double-click the Hand tool now, to zoom out on MY_DESK.TIF so that your screen looks like figure 5.2.

Figure 5.2
My desk usually doesn't look this tidy.

There's No Angles Like Rectangles

Marquee-zoom to a 1:1 resolution on the sticky notes area of MY_DESK.TIF.

Select the Rectangular Marquee tool from the toolbox	Your cursor turns into a crosshair cursor when positioned over an active image.
Click and drag diagonally over the sticky note image	You are marquee-selecting the image area.

Marquee-selecting is performed exactly the same as marquee-zooming, except the result is a *selection area* within an image, not a closer view of it.

Press Shift while clicking and dragging over the same area	Constrains the Rectangular Marquee selection to a perfect square.
Choose **S**elect, **N**one (or press Ctrl+D), and then press Alt while clicking and dragging in the same area	Starts a new Rectangular Marquee selection from the center of where you first click.
Press Ctrl while marquee-selecting the corner of the last selection area	Subtracts a rectangular portion from the selection area that you selected in the preceding step.
Press Shift while clicking and dragging over another corner of the selection area	Adds another rectangular area to the area that you selected in the previous steps, as shown in figure 5.3.
Click outside of the selection area	Deselects the selection border, and removes the marquee from the screen.

If you've tinkered with shareware or low-end image-editing software, you'll immediately appreciate how frustrating it is to be limited by your selection tools' capabilities. You'll also be delighted to know that the Rectangular Marquee and Elliptical Marquee selection tools are Photoshop's most *basic* selection tools!

When subtracting a rectangular selection, you don't have to use the Rectangular Marquee selection tool. As you learn more about selecting, you'll see that you can change selection tools to modify an original selection. This gives you virtually unlimited freedom to define a border that contains an area that you can modify without affecting the overall image.

Selecting with the Lasso Tool

This section broadens your repertoire of selection tools with the one that you'll probably use most frequently—the Lasso selection tool.

Several image-editing programs besides Photoshop feature a tool similar to the Lasso, and each works pretty much the same way. What is unique, however, is the tremendous versatility and power of Photoshop's *other* tools and filters, which you can use to enhance your Lasso selection.

Figure 5.3
The Rectangular Marquee selection tool is best suited for areas that are parallel to an active image border.

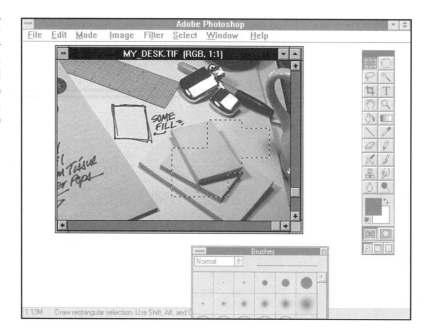

Photoshop's Lasso tool enables you to trace a freehand selection area. You can subtract from or add to the selection area with any of the other selection tools. Although you can use the Alt, Ctrl, and Shift keys to augment the Lasso tool's selecting prowess just as you can with the Rectangular Marquee and Elliptical Marquee tools, the Lasso tool adds a twist to this process, as you'll soon discover.

If you want to access other features of the currently selected tool, the status bar offers context-sensitive hints on how to do so. And don't forget to double-click just about anything that moves in Photoshop. Double-clicking a tool button reveals other tool options and settings that you can make in a dialog box.

Selection borders aren't particularly interesting unless you *do* something with them, which is the purpose of the next exercise. Remember to choose <u>U</u>ndo from the <u>E</u>dit menu when you finish this exercise. The changes you'll be making are a tad destructive, and you'll need to return MY_DESK.TIF to its pristine state.

Taking a Sticky Note from the Top

Marquee-zoom (as you learned earlier in this chapter) into the image area with the pads of sticky notes

Click on the Lasso selection tool

A 1:1 viewing resolution is good for this exercise.

Click and drag around the top of the sticky pad, and then release the mouse button	Draws a marquee-selection border around the pad that is as precise as your eye-hand coordination allows.
Press Shift while clicking and dragging around an area of the sticky pad that you missed in the last step	Adds to the first Lasso selection border.
Press Ctrl while clicking and dragging around part of the selection border	Removes part of the total selection area.
Click outside the selected selection border	The selection area disappears.
Choose **E**dit, **U**ndo Deselect	Restores the selection border, but only if you did no other Photoshop action between the last two steps.
Choose **S**elect, **N**one (or press Ctrl+D)	Deselects all the active selection borders in the active image, including the one you just drew.
Press Alt while clicking the lower-left corner of the top sticky pad	Sets a point for the Lasso tool.
Press Alt while clicking the lower-right corner of the top sticky pad	Sets a second point and draws a selection border edge between both points.
Press Alt while clicking the top-right corner of the top sticky pad	Sets the third point for the Lasso selection, with a second selection edge created between the current point and the second one you defined.
Press Alt while clicking the top-left corner of top sticky pad	Sets the fourth point for the Lasso selection, with a third selection edge created between the current point and the third one you defined.
Release the left mouse button and the Alt key	Completes the selection area's last side automatically.

You should now have a marquee-selection border like that shown in figure 5.4.

Click on the Paint Bucket tool on the toolbox

The Paint Bucket is one of Photoshop's paint-type tools.

Click within the marquee-selection area with the Paint Bucket tool	Fills the marquee-selection area with Photoshop's foreground color.
Choose **E**dit, **U**ndo	Undoes the Paint Bucket flood fill.

Figure 5.4
Marquee selection areas invite changes to be made within them; areas outside the selection are unaffected by filters, paints, or effects.

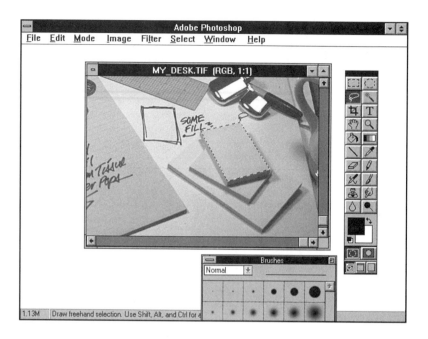

If the little marquee running around your selection irritates you and interferes with your viewing of how two image areas come together, select Hide **E**dges from the **S**elect menu or press Ctrl+H. Pressing Ctrl+H a second time toggles the marquee border back to visibility. Note that this key combination simply removes the marquee from view, and does *not* deselect anything. It's also an example of a Photoshop *toggling* function, so you press Ctrl+H a second time to Show **E**dges.

The marquee lines automatically reappear as soon as you select something else or paste a selection to an image.

Part of the wonder of using Photoshop's sophisticated selection tools is that you can create complex selection borders that contain an area that you want to change without affecting the rest of the image. By pressing the Alt key while clicking, you change the Lasso tool into an almost entirely different tool, that is ideally suited for selecting sticky notes, pieces of architecture, or any other image area that has straight but nonparallel geometry.

Think of the last Paint Bucket maneuver as a simple payoff for the selecting exercise you've just gone through. The paint that you apply to your selection is discussed in more detail shortly. First, though, let's address a type of selecting you can do in Photoshop that has nothing to do with squares, circles, or freehand selections.

The Magic Wand Tool

You often need to select an area of an image that has a fuzzy outline. You can't find the edge of it, so clicking and dragging around it with the Lasso is out of the question. In other instances, perhaps the border is too complex and the time for the assignment too short. In either case, when an image area is composed of mostly the same color, the Magic Wand tool enables you to select it based on its *color value* rather than its geometry.

The next exercise will familiarize you with the Magic Wand tool. The Magic Wand creates a marquee-selection border around an area, which you can then modify with the Lasso, Rectangular Marquee, or Elliptical Marquee selection tools. This tool also lets you use the Ctrl and Shift keys to subtract from and add to an original selection area.

Chapter 4 discussed Photoshop's default settings, which make your work in the program more rewarding. As you'll see in the next exercise, you'll also often want to reset the settings in the Magic Wand Options dialog box before you use the tool.

Let's continue selecting the sticky note pad, but use the selection tool that you can calibrate for the range of color you want to select.

The Wonder of the Wand

Marquee-zoom to a 2:1 viewing resolution of the sticky notes	You need a closer view than 1:1 to see what you will be selecting in this exercise.
Double-click on the Magic Wand tool	Displays the Magic Wand Options dialog box.
Type **10** pixels for the **T**olerance option, choose the **A**nti-Aliased check box, and then click on OK	Makes the Magic Wand select a narrow range of similarly colored pixels in an image that are adjacent, and Anti-Aliasing creates a smooth selection border.
Click on the top sticky note with the Magic Wand tool	Creates a selection area based on the parameters that you typed previously in the Magic Wand Options dialog box, as shown in figure 5.5.
Press Ctrl+D (or Choose **S**elect, **N**one)	Deselects the area that you previously selected with the Magic Wand.
Double-click on the Magic Wand tool to display the Magic Wand Options dialog box, reset **T**olerance for **60** pixels, and then click OK	Broadens the range of color values that the tool will select after you click a specific area.

continues

continued

Click the same sticky note area	Includes in the selection area the sticky notes and parts of the surrounding areas, as shown in figure 5.6, because the **T**olerance option of the Magic Wands Options dialog box is set too high.
Press Ctrl+D (or Choose **S**elect, **N**one)	Deselects the selection area.
Double-click on the Magic Wand tool to display the Magic Wand Options dialog box, set **T**olerance to **32** pixels, and then click OK	Specifies a moderate value that narrows the range in color values that are selected.
Click on the top of the sticky notes area again	Selects only the top leaf of the sticky pad, with a little roughness around the border of it, as shown in figure 5.7.

Figure 5.5
An example of the Magic Wand tool selection, with the Tolerance option set too low.

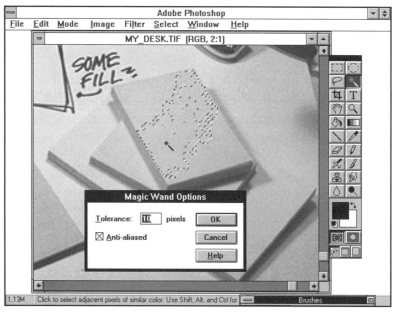

Think of the Magic Wand Options dialog box's **T**olerance setting as the number of qualifying candidates for a position based on a single criterion. For example, suppose that you click with the Magic Wand tool directly above a blue pixel in an image; with a tolerance of 5, the Magic Wand selection area picks the blue pixel and adjacent pixels that are no more than five shades off from the blue pixel that you selected. A *shade* is a color range, measured by the Magic Wand **T**olerance setting from 0 to 255.

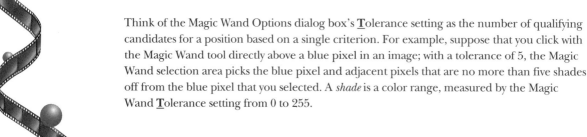

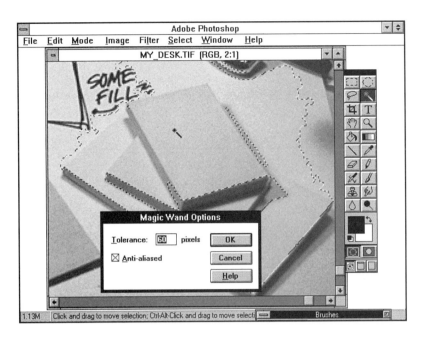

Figure 5.6
The Magic Wand tool is set too high to select only the sticky note.

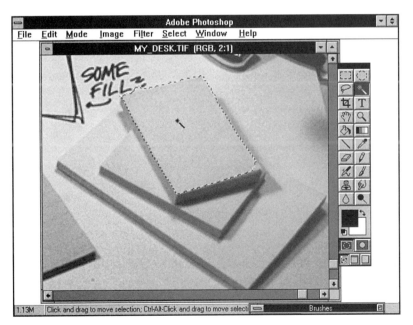

Figure 5.7
Through trial and error, you can set the Magic Wand's Tolerance option to select an image area with precision.

In the previous exercise, a <u>T</u>olerance setting of 10 was too narrow to include all the different shades that make up the top sticky note image area, and a <u>T</u>olerance of 60 lets the selection area run all over the area. With practice, you'll be able to "guesstimate" the best color tolerance to use with the Magic Wand tool to select a color area with some accuracy. But even if the area isn't perfect, such as with the top edge of the sticky pad in figure 5.7, you can use the Lasso tool to refine the selection border by subtracting from or adding to it, as described earlier in this chapter.

To find out whether you should use the Magic Wand tool to select an image area, use Photoshop's Info palette to see what the Hue, Saturation, and Brightness color values are in an area. To display the palette, press F8. Then move your cursor over an area, regardless of which tool is selected.

If you move the cursor over the top of the sticky note pad, from edge to edge, the Info palette displays HSB color values that vary no more than 4%. This indicates that the sticky note area is a good candidate for the Magic Wand selection tool. But try running the cursor over an image of an argyle sock sometime. If you needed to select the entire sock in one fell swoop, the Magic Wand tool would most likely be an unsuitable candidate for the task.

The Anti-Aliased Option

The <u>A</u>nti-Aliased check box appears in many places in Photoshop's workspace. But what is Anti-Aliasing? When you are selecting things, Anti-Aliasing adds semi-transparent, gray pixels to the image pixels on the inside edge of the selection border which produces a subtle color transition. Selections made with Anti-Aliasing turned on, that are then copied and pasted into a new image area, are usually less noticeable to the eye because of the semi-transparent gray values.

At least that is the quasi-scientific explanation for how Anti-Aliasing works. For the imaging artist, what really matters is the *result* of Anti-Aliasing. Anti-Aliasing visually smoothes rough edges in a selection border. When you want to fill a selection with a color, or copy and paste the selection, Anti-Aliasing makes the inside edge of the selection border semitransparent, so that the modified selection area blends softly into the rest of an image.

The magic of Anti-Aliasing a Photoshop selection area requires the color capabilities of an RGB, 24-bit image. With 16.7 million possible colors available, Photoshop can create subtle variations in the gray content of neighboring pixels that fall on the edge of a selection border. However, Photoshop doesn't support the Anti-Aliasing feature for indexed color images, which contain a fixed number of colors and shades of color, defined from a lookup table.

The Feathering Radius Option

A feathering option is available for the Rectangular Marquee, Elliptical Marquee, and Lasso tools, and can also be applied to any shaped selection area with the command from the Select menu. To set this option for a tool's use, double-click on the tool on the toolbox and set Feather Radius before you use it to select an area. Feathering yields an effect similar to Anti-Aliasing, but produces a less subtle blending of selection edges and is, in principle, different than Anti-Aliasing.

Anti-aliasing adds a gray component to the edge pixels inside the selection border to smooth the transition between them and the background image. Feathering, however, *replaces* color values in bordering selection and background pixels. A Feather Radius of three pixels creates transition colors between three rows of pixels inside and three pixels outside a selection edge. These transition colors are a mixture of what Photoshop determines is the predominant color for the three pixels inside and the three pixels outside the selection border.

To blend a copied selection smoothly into a background area, try both features. You usually should use Anti-Aliasing, because it keeps the edges of a selection area soft enough to blend into a background, but sharp enough not to blur the *content* of the selection.

Floating Selections

There is a solar system full of things you can do with a selection in Photoshop! Besides flooding a selection with color, you can copy, move, save, and filter a selection. You can even separate a selection border from its contents. You'll have plenty of opportunities to access each of the selection features in your work to accomplish some wonderful effects. The concept of a selection is more intricate than a casual glance first suggests. This is because selections also have properties.

Before moving on to the next exercise, you need to understand the different properties that *floating* and *non-floating* selections have. The fundamental properties of a selection determine what happens when you edit the *contents* of the selection.

Photoshop views a selection area in an image as being part of the *foreground* of an image. When you cut or move a *non-floating* selection area, you expose the image's *background color.* (And no, you can't look behind the image of a tree in a picture by moving it with a selection border.) By default, Photoshop's background color is white, so when you move a selection, you end up with a plain white area where the selection was.

A *floating selection* is a different breed of digital image, however. Floating selections can hover over an active image. You can move a floating selection and apply effects to it while leaving the underlying image untouched. The floating selection doesn't become a part of the image until you deselect the floating selection, by clicking outside its border with a selection tool, or deselect it by using the **S**elect, **N**one command.

You can produce floating selections in three different ways. The most common way is to copy a selection and then paste it back to the source image or into a different image file altogether.

The second way is to select an area and then choose **F**loat from the **S**elect menu. This command generates a duplicate of the selection, which can float freely and be edited independently of the rest of the picture. The third way is the easiest, and provides perhaps the most dramatic results. It's featured in the next exercise, where you'll gain a working knowledge of the different kinds of selections and a digital way to make your money grow.

The Floating Coin Trick

Click on the Hand tool, and then click and drag the center of the image window to the right	Moves your view to the left in the active image window.
Click and drag down and right until you see the coins on the legal pad	
Pick the Elliptical Marquee tool	This round selection tool is ideally suited for selecting elliptical coins.
Position the cursor in the center of the top-right coin	This is the starting point of the selection.
Press Alt while clicking and dragging down and to the right	Creates an elliptical marquee from the center outward around the coin.

You may have to try more than once to select the coin perfectly. If so, click outside your first marquee to deselect it and start again.

Press Alt while clicking and dragging from the center of the selection border down and to the right, and then release the mouse button	Turns the cursor into a small arrow, and moves a copy of the selection area's contents away from the original image, as shown in figure 5.8.
Press Ctrl+Alt while clicking and dragging inside the selection border, and then drag downward	Moves the selection marquee itself, *not* its contents, and deselects your duplicated coin.
Choose **E**dit, **U**ndo Duplicate (or press Ctrl-Z)	Places the selection border back around the duplicate coin, and makes it a floating selection again.
Click on and drag the duplicated coin	Exposes a white background.

Note that if you don't press Ctrl+Alt, the selection becomes an ordinary selection.

Select **E**dit, **U**ndo Move (or press Ctrl+Z)	Returns the duplicate coin to its previous location.

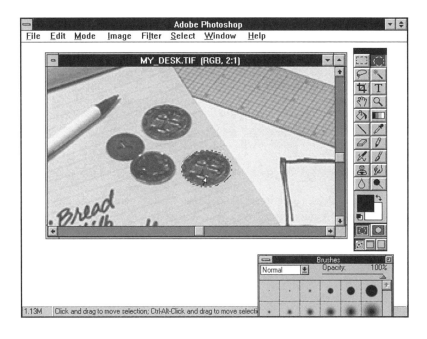

Figure 5.8
Did Bill Gates start his fortune this way with Photoshop?

Moving just a selection border is an invaluable feature if you need to cover up something that is surrounded by a regular pattern. Because you can move the selection border, you can use it as "cookie cutter" that selects an area of pattern exactly the right size and shape to patch an area without ruining the pattern. You use this technique of selecting and pasting in Chapter 11 to make some repairs on a house's roof.

Moving a selection border can also save you time if you need to modify several objects that are shaped almost identically. Create the selection border once, then drag it from item to item and do your work. If the border doesn't fit precisely, you need to take only a nip here or a tuck there, and don't have to recreate the whole selection border.

The Eraser Tool and Saved Images

Periodically choosing **S**ave from the **F**ile menu or pressing Ctrl+S ensures that the intermediate phases of your work are written to disk. You won't have to start from square one again if an unexpected Windows event turns your screen black. But Photoshop's Eraser tool can perform a little magic *between* saves, by bringing information from the last saved version of the image into the current version of your image. When you decide to save your work, you have to balance the risk of power outages and the like against what artistic information is in the file that you may want to work with later. Before you discover the magic that the Eraser tool is capable of when working with saved images, let's take a brief look at two *non*-magical ways the Eraser tool can work.

Double-clicking on the Eraser tool will remove the entire active image, not just the contents of any selection area. This is a handy feature if you are experimenting with color, effects in a scrap file, or an Alpha channel and feel it's time to clear the slate. A confirmation box asks whether you want to `Erase entire image?`, which is a welcome precaution if you've been experimenting with the program or if you've accidentally clicked more than once.

A normal erasure, which is performed by clicking and dragging over an area, removes the foreground image to reveal the background color. The Eraser's size is fixed, so the viewing resolution that you specify before working with the image determines the size of the physical area that you can erase. Holding down Shift while you drag the eraser constrains the tool to erasing in a straight line.

But when you press Alt while clicking and dragging the Eraser tool, an amazing thing happens, as the following exercise demonstrates. Let's continue playing with MY_DESK.TIF, and you'll see how the Eraser tool can magically diminish your cash flow.

Easy Come, Easy Go

Pick the Eraser tool

Press and hold down Alt as you click the mouse and start to drag the Eraser tool over the duplicate coin	Temporarily halts Photoshop's actions while reading the last saved version of MY_DESK.TIF.
Continue pressing Alt while dragging the tool over the duplicate coin	Reveals the background of the last saved version of the area.

The Eraser tool changes into the Magic Eraser tool, and the cursor's appearance changes. Dragging the Magic Eraser over the image replaces the area with what *was* in that area the last time you saved. The coin appears to *disappear*, as shown in figure 5.9.

Release the Alt key, but continue dragging the tool	Removes the foreground image information to reveal the white background.

The Magic Eraser tool changes back to the Eraser tool.

Choose **E**dit, **U**ndo Eraser (or press Ctrl+Z)	Restores the background area.

Retouching: A Combination of Tools

Multiplying the coin in the last exercise is a good example of how you can use selection borders to modify part of an image. But the selection tools are only some of Photoshop's powerful retouching tools. To perform minor touch-ups or big-time overhauls to a digital image, you need to apply the right paint-type tools to your selection areas.

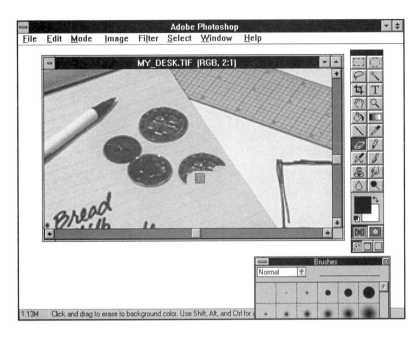

Figure 5.9
Holding down the Alt key while dragging the Eraser tool erases only the image information created since the last time you saved your work.

Chapter 4 explained how you can choose various colors, but there's a very easy way to set the exact color you need in an assignment *without* a trip to the Colors palette *or* the color selection boxes on the toolbox.

The Eyedropper tool is not a selection tool, but rather an editing tool. It doesn't create a selection border when you use it. However, the tool *does* select a color to paint with when using Photoshop's paint tools. The next exercise demonstrates how the paint tools apply Photoshop's electronic paint to an image area.

Pencil and Paint

Scroll down and to the left on MY_DESK.TIF	Moves your view to the cracker in the image.
Pick the Zoom tool, and then click once over the cracker area	Zooms into a tighter viewing resolution of the work area.

Good zoom ratios for this exercise are 3:1 or 4:1.

Pick the Eyedropper tool, and then click on the legal pad area where the cracker is	Samples the bluish gray color of the legal pad, and make this your foreground painting color.
Click on the Pencil tool, then from the Brushes palette choose Normal mode, a medium-sized tip, and **100**% opacity	Sets the characteristics of the Pencil tool.

continues

continued

If you aren't currently displaying the Brushes palette, press F5.

Click and drag the Pencil tool over a crumb, using one stroke	Applies a sharp-edged pencil stroke of your foreground color to the area over which you dragged, as shown in figure 5.10.
Choose **E**dit, **U**ndo Pencil (or press Ctrl+Z)	Removes the pencil stroke, if you previously made only one move.
Click on the Paintbrush tool	Changes your selection of painting tools.

The Brushes palette now offers a soft-edge characteristic to the available tips, unlike when the Pencil tool was selected.

Click and drag one stroke over the same crumb area	Paints over the crumb area with a foreground color that matches the bluish-gray legal pad, but leaves a soft edge to the stroke.
Choose **E**dit, **U**ndo Paintbrush (or press Ctrl+Z)	Cancels the last painting stroke you applied to the image.

Figure 5.10

The Eyedropper tool samples a color area in an image and then lets you paint with that color.

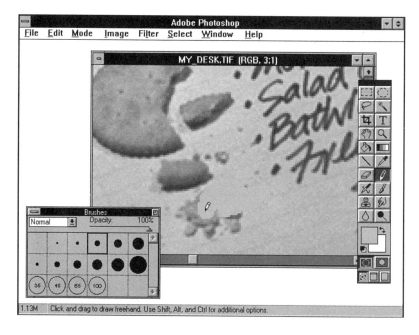

The Pencil tool is great for cleaning up an edge of an area at a pixel level; that is, you can zoom into an image area to a 16:1 resolution (the highest zoom field in Photoshop) and recolor a single pixel that's marring an image. The Pencil tool has no *spread* (the light application of semitransparent pixels to the edge of a stroke) like the Paintbrush tool does.

Photoshop has tool and menu commands that assist in blending image areas together. The Anti-Aliasing feature, the Feathering command, and the spread on brush tips all work to this purpose, while the Pencil tool creates clean edges.

Users sometimes associate the Brushes palette with characteristics that can only be applied to the Paintbrush tool. This is quite natural, but as the previous exercise demonstrated, the Brushes palette also sets the tip of the Pencil tool.

All the painting and editing tools in Photoshop depend on the characteristics you set on the Brushes palette to define how a tool or function works.

Characteristics—like the different Brushes modes listed in the drop-down menu (accessed by clicking on the down arrow next to the text box), and the intensity with which a stroke is applied—vary from tool to tool. For example, when you choose the Paintbrush tool, you can adjust the paint's opacity with the slider on the Brushes palette. When the Airbrush tool is selected, the slider on the Brushes palette changes and adjusts the *pressure* the Airbrush applies paint with, not the paint's Opacity setting.

When you select a different tool, be sure to check the Brushes palette to see which tool characteristics you can set.

Using the Rubber Stamp Tool

You can use the Pencil or Paintbrush tool effectively to paint in areas. But if your assignment is to paint over the cracker on the legal pad, the toolbox provides a tool that's better suited for this kind of work.

The Rubber Stamp tool paints over a foreground area with another section of image area. This is called *cloning*. The Rubber Stamp doesn't use Eyedropper color samples, but instead copies from *image areas* that you've sampled. You set a starting sample point by holding down Alt and clicking the Rubber Stamp tool cursor over the area you want to copy. When you move the Rubber Stamp to the area you are replacing, the sample point tags along (seen as a crosshair on the screen) and continuously supplies roving samples of the image to the Rubber Stamp tool.

The cracker in this image is on top of the legal pad. The legal pad consists of varying color values, texture, and a pattern of faint ruled lines running through it. To recreate the legal pad areas convincingly using only the Pencil and Paintbrush tools would take an impossibly complex set of moves. Fortunately, Photoshop's powerful Rubber Stamp tool is perfect for this job. In the next exercise, you experience the power of restoration that the Rubber Stamp brings to your everyday work.

Sayonara, Saltine

Press Alt while clicking the Zoom tool over the image	Zooms you out to a looser image resolution, 2:1, of the cracker area.
Pick the Rubber Stamp tool	Your cursor turns into a little rubber stamp.

When you choose a painting tool, the Brushes palette is automatically activated.

Click the paint tip third from the left on the second row of the Brushes palette	Selects a 13-pixel-diameter, soft-tip brush characteristic for the Rubber Stamp tool.
Place the Rubber Stamp tool to the left of the cracker	This is a good area to sample the legal pad image.
Press Alt while clicking on the legal pad area to the left of the faint red vertical line	Sets the sampling point for the Rubber Stamp tool.

The sampling point moves in tandem with the Rubber Stamp tool when it paints. The inverted triangle in the center of the cursor turns white to indicate that it is in sampling mode, and the status bar confirms this. Figure 5.11 shows the point at which you should set the start of the sampling. As you can see, you have plenty of clear legal pad that the traveling crosshair can sample, and then send these image samples to the Rubber Stamp to use when it clones.

Release Alt, place the cursor in the center of the cracker, and then drag from left to right	Replaces the area under the Rubber Stamp cursor with the area of the image that the sample point is currently over when you move the Rubber Stamp tool, as shown in figure 5.11.

The Rubber Stamp tool isn't very useful if your traveling crosshair moves into an undesired image area. By default, the cloning that the Rubber Stamp does takes the image under the sampling-point crosshair and copies it to the area indicated by the Rubber Stamp cursor. This is called *aligned cloning*. Aligned cloning is not the only method that the Rubber Stamp tool can use to receive samples, but it is the most common. Double-clicking the Rubber Stamp tool on the toolbox brings up a number of different methods you can use. You'll use From Pattern cloning method in Chapter 9 and From Snapshot cloning method in Chapter 14.

As you continue to wipe out the cracker in the next exercise, remember that if you sample (by pressing Alt while clicking the Rubber Stamp) directly over one of the legal pad's faint lines, a Rubber Stamp brush stroke in a direction that *follows* the line effectively recreates the pad and eradicates the cracker.

Avoid dragging back and forth in an area with the Rubber Stamp tool. Your strokes should be in one direction. Repetitious strokes with the Rubber Stamp results in an unpleasant and phony patterning effect.

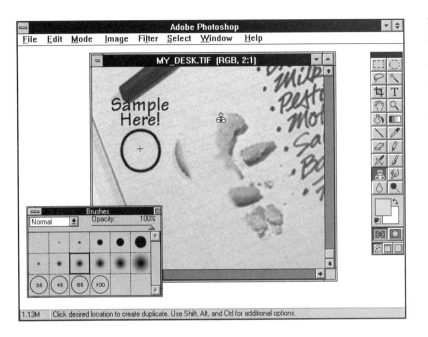

Figure 5.11
The Rubber Stamp tool moves its sampling point as you brush over an area with the tool.

Rubber Stamping a Selection Area

The highlight of the next exercise is a fairly sophisticated maneuver where you remove the cracker by cloning over it. If you continue to resample the Rubber Stamp tool's source point, proceeding down the legal pad page and staying on the pad's faint lines as you clone, you will convincingly remove the cracker. Keep checking the sample source cross hair to make sure this point doesn't run off the legal pad, or you'll clone undesired areas over the cracker.

In the next exercise, the faint red vertical line presents a problem. The cracker is sitting too close to the left side of the line, making it difficult to clone over the cracker precisely and still avoid the red line. Therefore, as a final step in cracker elimination, you'll use the Lasso tool to separate the cracker's left edge from the red line.

Protecting an Area from Cloning

Pick the Lasso tool

Click and drag the Lasso tool in a circle around the left side of the remaining cracker

Only this area is selected for editing.

The Rubber Stamp or any other Photoshop modifying tool can only edit the selected area within the circle.

continues

continued

Pick the Rubber Stamp tool	
Press Alt while clicking the Stamp in the margin of the legal pad	Sets the Rubber tool's sampling point.
Click and drag single strokes, laterally	Fills in the selection area with the legal pad's image.

Neatness doesn't count here. The red vertical line on the legal pad is unaffected. Only the area within the selection can be cloned over, as shown in figure 5.12.

Press Ctrl+D (or Choose <u>S</u>elect, <u>N</u>one)	Deselects everything in the active image, and your selection area becomes fused to the background image.

You can now edit the entire image.

Continue setting sampling points and brushing in one-directional strokes over the remaining cracker

You're finished when the cracker is gone.

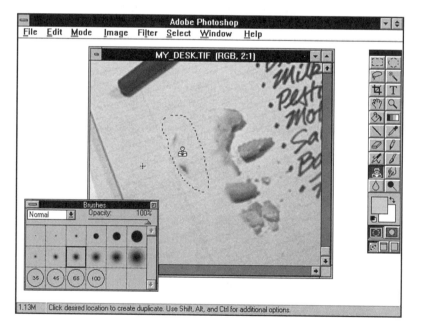

Figure 5.12
You can paint in an image only within a selection area, or if no area is selected at all.

Figure 5.13 shows the result of precision cloning. Maybe you can buy another cracker with all the coins you duplicated earlier.

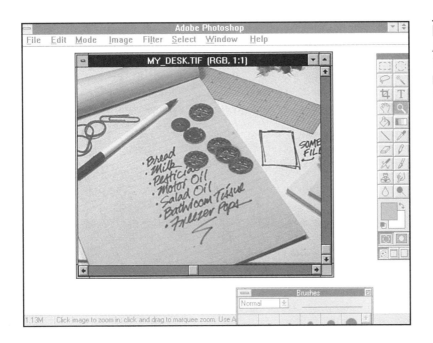

Figure 5.13
An example of two image areas professionally retouched with Photoshop.

Setting Different Painting Characteristics

As mentioned earlier, you can assign characteristics to each paint-application tool. The most common characteristic, that they all share, is the mode setting. You select which mode the tool will use from the small drop-down list that appears when you click the down arrow on the Brushes palette.

Modes control how the foreground application of color reacts to a selected image area. When you use a painting tool like the Paintbrush on an area, the modes affect how it works as follows:

Normal	Replaces the area with the foreground color, much like a physical paintbrush.
Darken	Darkens only the pixels in the image that are lighter than the foreground color. Equal or darker pixels are not affected.
Lighten	Affects only the pixels in the image that are darker than the foreground color you've selected.
Hue	Paints with the foreground shade of color only. The luminosity and saturation of the image area you paint over is unaffected. This mode is terrific when you want to tint areas.

Saturation	If your foreground color is black, this mode converts color areas to grayscale. If your foreground color is a color value, this mode, with each brush stroke, seeks and amplifies the underlying pixels' basic color value by reducing the gray component. The non-black foreground color you've selected doesn't affect what happens. You have to play with Saturation mode to understand its possibilities.
Color	Changes both the hue and saturation of a selected image. This mode can achieve a more thorough and convincing tinting effect on a selection area than the Hue mode.
Luminosity	Increases the lightness qualities in the image. This powerful mode doesn't change color values. You should use it sparingly when lightening, say, an over-saturated color area in an image. When using Luminosity mode with a brush, set the opacity on the palette down to about 30%.
Multiply	Darkens an image area to the selected foreground color. This differs from the Darken mode in that strokes over the same area intensify the effect. In effect, the mode multiplies the color values with each additional stroke.
Screen	Increasingly lightens or bleaches an area when you brush repeatedly over an area. It also tints the area to your chosen foreground color. The effect of the Screen mode is the inverse of that of the Multiply mode.
Dissolve	Creates a "splattering" effect by randomly coloring pixels in the area that you brush over. Darker pixels are more likely to be replaced than lighter ones. This mode is an excellent choice for creating weathering or sparking effects.

Your assignment in the next exercise is to change the fake plastic lemon image in MY_DESK.TIF to a fake plastic lime. Bear in mind that you can't simply paint over the image area without also painting over the lemon's visual detail—its texture and its face. To avoid this loss of image detail you need to use a special Brushes palette mode.

The Ever-Changing Faces of Fruits

Marquee-zoom into the plastic lemon area in the image

A 3:1 zoom viewing resolution is adequate for this exercise.

Click and drag the Lasso tool to trace an outline around the plastic lemon

Use the Alt and Ctrl keys to refine your first selection, adding to and subtracting from it until you have a fairly accurate border around the yellow area of the lemon.

Choose the Eyedropper tool and then click the lightest portion of the plastic lemon's green cap	Selects the foreground color for painting.
Choose the Paintbrush tool	Activates the options available on the Brushes palette.
Choose the 100 brush tip and Darken mode, and then set the opacity to **100**%	With these settings, you can darken a selected area to the chosen foreground color, using a large brush with spread.
Click and drag the Paintbrush cursor in the selection area	Darkens the light lemon colors within the area to the darker lime foreground color, as shown in figure 5.14.
Brush the area once or twice more until you cover it completely	

Repeated strokes won't darken an area once it's been completely covered with foreground color.

Press Ctrl+D (or choose **S**elect, **N**one)	Deselects the area.

Your image now should look like figure 5.15.

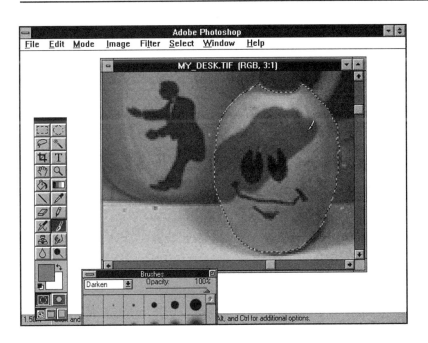

Figure 5.14
The Darken mode darkens only lighter pixels to the foreground color that you chose.

Figure 5.15
A completely recolored plastic lemon.

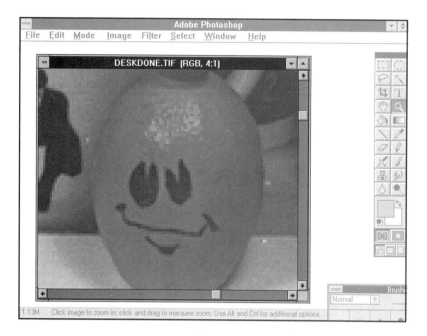

One advantage of using the Darken mode is that it doesn't affect the grayscale component of a selection area that you paint over. In the last exercise, using this mode to apply the paint retains the variations in tone and texture in the areas you work on. Using this mode, you can replace several color values within the selection area with darker ones.

If you double-clicked the Lasso tool before using it in the preceding exercise, and chose a two- or three-pixel radius in the Feather option, you probably have a plastic lime on your screen with a smooth border from its edge into the background of the image. You showed initiative, and put a feature to work for you. And this is good.

If you didn't, that's okay too. Sharp, telltale borders are a sign to a viewer that an image has been tampered with. In addition to Feathering and Anti-Aliasing commands, Photoshop provides several unique, manual tools that address telltale selection edges. These tools are so important to your Photoshop work that they are featured in several exercises throughout Parts II, III, and IV of this book.

Using the Gradient Tool

The Gradient tool is important in retouching work, and operates quite differently than any other paint application tool in Photoshop. Like the Paint Bucket tool, the Gradient tool floods a selection area, but it fills the area with a transitional blend between your foreground and background colors.

You can use the Eyedropper tool, Photoshop's Color Picker, or the Colors palette to set both the foreground and background colors, but the real fun begins when you select the *way* that the Gradient tool fills an area.

Before beginning the last exercise of your Photoshop test drive, double-click the Gradient tool. Figure 5.16 shows the Gradient Tool Options dialog box, which is where you go to specify how you want the Gradient tool to perform its blending wizardry.

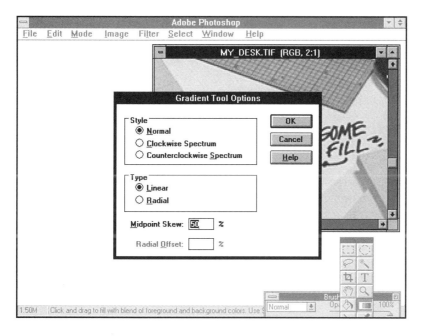

Figure 5.16

The Gradient Tool Options dialog box.

In the Style field of the Gradient Tool Options dialog box, you have the option to "cycle" the color spectrum between the foreground and background colors. You can do this clockwise or counterclockwise through the different hues that lie between your foreground and background color values. If you select an orange background and a red foreground, you won't notice a visible rainbow effect with the Counterclockwise **S**pectrum option selected, but you *will* with the **C**lockwise Spectrum option.

The most useful setting in the Style window for most of your Photoshop work is **N**ormal, which results in a straight transition between foreground and background colors. Leave this default selected for the next exercise.

From the Source to the Sample

In the Type field, you can choose the **R**adial option, which produces a color transition in seamless steps that move concentricity outward from where you first click the Gradient tool. The **L**inear option moves foreground colors toward background colors across a plane. Although this type of gradient is "flatter," you'll find more uses for it, so leave this setting selected as the default.

The default setting of the **M**idpoint Skew option is 50%. This means that when you click and drag a gradient fill, halfway between your beginning and ending points is a 50/50 blend of foreground and background colors. Setting this number lower increases the contrast within the gradient fill, because the halfway point between colors occurs less than halfway; conversely, a higher number decreases the contrast. Leave this default set at 50% because the next exercise shows you an easier way to manipulate the gradient than by adjusting the **M**idpoint Skew.

Fill 'er Up

Zoom out and drag the image with the Hand tool to reveal the SOME FILL? area in MY_DESK.TIF

This felt-tip pen scribble in the image was designed to easily hold a gradient fill.

Choose the Magic Wand tool, and then click within the area defined by the felt-tip boundary box	Selects the area inside the boundary box.

The inside area is selected because the felt-tip pen box prevents adjacent pixels of similar color value outside the box from being included in the selection.

Click on the Gradient tool

Click and drag with the cursor, starting above the selection area and finishing outside the bottom, but *don't* release the mouse button yet	Draws the path for gradient to follow.

The path starts with your foreground color on top and finishes with your background color on bottom.

Release the mouse button	Activates the gradient fill and floods the selection area.
Click and drag the cursor, starting inside the box at top and finishing inside the box at bottom, and then release the mouse button	Produces a more intense gradient.

The gradient is more intense this time because your starting and finishing points are located closer to each other, as shown in figure 15.17.

Click outside the left side of the box, drag across to the right side of the box, and then release the mouse button	Creates a gradient fill at an angle.

Any angle that you create by dragging is okay.

Figure 5.17
You can apply a gradient fill at any angle in a selection.

As long as a selection area is active, you can click and drag the Gradient tool in a totally unrelated part of an image and still fill the selection area. You can continue to modify your gradient without undoing the last step because the Gradient tool always paints over the entire selected area each time you click and drag it.

Using Fade-out Options

Although the Gradient and Paint Bucket tools are both paint application tools, the methods they use to apply paint are quite different than those used by the Airbrush, Pencil, and Paintbrush tools. Neither the Gradient tool nor the Paint Bucket tool have fade-out options because they are designed to flood an area with color. Adobe has segregated these two tools by placing them on different rows toward the bottom of the toolbox. This provides you with a visual clue that these two tools operate differently than the rest of the paint application tools.

If you double-click on the Paintbrush, Pencil, or Airbrush tools, you'll find an option to set the Fade-out **D**istance. The value entered here determines how soon a single tool stroke fades to the background image color or to transparency. The fade-out value ranges from 0 to 9999 pixels. You should set this value very high unless you're painting in Photoshop instead of retouching photos.

Why should you specify a long Fade-out **D**istance? To color a selection area evenly when retouching a photo, you need consistent brush strokes. If you set the fade-out on the Paintbrush tool to 45 pixels, the stroke that the tool creates fades to transparency (or to the background color) within 45 pixels. This is far too short a distance when your goal is to make long, even strokes. Short fades are usually best reserved for creating a painting instead of retouching a photo.

You may notice in dialog boxes that option names sometimes appear faded or grayed-out. This is because you're using a mouse as your input device rather than a digitizing tablet. Digitizing tablets offer users more natural expression when using painting tools, and more accuracy when selecting areas. Because Photoshop is "digitizing-tablet-aware," it offers those input devices options, like pressure and sensitivity, that a conventional mouse cannot support.

This does not mean you should run out and buy a digitizing tablet so that you can take advantage of the additional features Photoshop offers for this input device. Instead, honestly evaluate your need for a more precise input tool, try using a digitizing tablet at your local computer store, and *then* decide whether to take the plunge.

To maintain a totally consistent, evenly colored line, select the same background and foreground colors in Photoshop. Then select To Background as the Fade-Out Distance option from the paint tools' dialog box (double-click on the tool to get there). This forces Photoshop to "fade" a brush stroke into a background color that's the same as the foreground color you're using. In effect, the option extends your fade-out distance infinitely.

From the Image Test Drive to the Open Highway

This chapter explained how the selection tools and painting tools work, and gave you a taste of how they can function together. As you can see in figure 5.18, you've rearranged my desk a little and it looks that much better for it! You'll quickly arrive at different techniques for problem-solving if you continue to practice, which is the purpose of the next three parts in this book. In future chapters, you'll encounter various circumstances and assignments that are quite similar to those that occur in everyday, real-world situations.

Figure 5.18
Some basic changes you can apply to photos with a basic knowledge of Photoshop tools.

This chapter has not explored tools you use for tasks *other* than painting or selecting things. At the bottom of the toolbox are the Smudge, Sharpen/Blur, and Dodge/Burn tools. Each of these tools is used to modify parts of an image. These are Photoshop's editing tools. You use these tools extensively when you need to clean up problem areas in an image. You'll get a chance to work with them many times throughout the exercises in the following chapters.

Summary

We hope you'll continue to refer to this chapter and Chapter 4 as you move through the assignments in Parts 3, 4, and 5. These two chapters include useful reference information and some solid tips—perhaps too much to digest in one fell swoop. However, you've got half the secret if you remember that Photoshop's tools and effects are tightly integrated. When you do something in combination with something else, you usually arrive at a new effect or technique.

Here's a brief overview of some important points that you have learned so far in your adventure with Photoshop. You'll want to keep them in mind as you move upward and onward:

✔ Periodically check Photoshop's status bar at the bottom of your screen. It provides you with information about key combinations that you can use to access the other options that are available when you use a tool.

✔ If a selection or painting tool doesn't do exactly what you want, double-click the tool button. This displays its Options dialog box, which offers other settings for that particular tool.

✔ If you make a mistake, you can choose <u>U</u>ndo from the <u>E</u>dit menu or press Ctrl+Z to eliminate the last step that you performed. As you begin using Photoshop, limit your brush strokes to one at a time; you can Undo a modification you're unhappy with.

✔ Don't set unrealistic goals. At this point in your Photoshop career, you can't achieve the spectacular results that you may have seen Photoshop produce in magazines and movies. You have yet to explore filters, effects tools, and Photoshop's channels features. Mastery of the true power of Photoshop starts with an understanding of the basic tools and then how to use them in combination with the menu options, as upcoming exercises in the next chapters will show you.

The next two chapters in Part II, "Steak 'n' Potatoes Assignments in Photoshop," cover the process of restoring and retouching an heirloom photograph. In Part II, you step up from learning about Photoshop's theoretical underpinnings, to gaining the practical experience and acquiring the working skills that can be immediately put to good use in your everyday imaging work. The exercises in Part II of this book show ways to solve many of the most common, nagging problems that crop up when you work with images.

First you'll learn some incredible techniques that you can use time and again with damaged, aged photographs. These techniques use some of the tools that you've already used, some new ones, and some menu commands that effect global changes to an image to restore its quality.

Part II

Steak 'n Potatoes Assignments

Chapter Snapshot

In this chapter, you learn how to:

CHAPTER

Restoring an Heirloom Photograph

Photographic restoration is probably the most difficult task that you'll face when working with digital images. A photo that's faded and has surface nicks, creases, and abrasions leaves you very little information to work with when retouching. Whenever you add anything to the picture, you must be careful and keep a watchful eye for any *cosmetic* effect caused by the addition, to keep the picture from looking hand-tinted. To restore a photo, you must adopt skills similar to those of a detective *and* a plastic surgeon. Fortunately, Photoshop's features make this task much simpler.

Digital photo restoration has its advantages over the chemical photography darkroom. Traditionally, professional retouchers, using chemical photography, make a photographic copy of the original image and then apply filters and techniques in the darkroom to get a workable base image. They then apply transparent dyes to the photo. If they make a mistake, they have to copy the photo and start all over again.

But in Photoshop's digital world, there are Reset and Undo commands all along the way, so that you can undo each individual step without starting over from the beginning. If you save the image regularly to different file names, you also can return to an intermediate step and try a new strategy if a version isn't eye-pleasing. You use the wonderful, plastic qualities of the electronic pixel to apply adjustments, not dyes, to an image to *reveal* the truth behind the layers of time.

From an Old Shoe Box to the Monitor

The photo that you use in this chapter's assignment was dug out of my family's "virtual archive"—a shoe box in the basement. MY_MOM.TIF, shown in figure 6.1, is a scan of a photo of my mother when she was 11. My Uncle Alan took her picture while doing research work with some of AGFA's first color film. AGFA didn't know then that this photo would actually survive until 1994—sort of.

Figure 6.1
Almost no color is showing in this aged color photo.

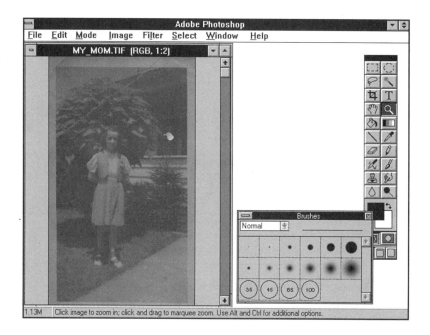

Open MY_MOM.TIF from the companion CD, and see the state of disrepair this photo's fallen into before you begin the exercises.

When restoring an heirloom photo, you have to break some rules. Normally, an image is scanned at the resolution that is the best match for your final, printed output. When restoring a faded, discolored, and damaged image like MY_MOM.TIF, you need to scan at *as high a resolution* as possible, *regardless* of final output considerations. You need all the information that you can possibly wring out of the image.

Working with huge files is time consuming and can bog your work down. For an assignment like the one you'll work on in this chapter, you have to work with large files to get the best results possible. The image of MY_MOM.TIF was originally scanned at 400 dpi and yielded an 8.3M file. For your own work, you may have to scan a faded photo to a file size this large, or perhaps a little less, to achieve a high enough resolution so you may edit with precision and

finesse. Your final goal, usually, is to print a copy of the image you restore, so you always need as much digital data from the source image as possible to do the retouching work.

Although working with a huge image file is necessary, you'll find that the process is slow and imposes a noticeable burden on a system. When you finish retouching such an image, you can use Photoshop's **I**mage Size command to decrease the resolution and file size.

But this chapter's assignment is a *practice* exercise, and you can learn the concepts, methods, and achieve good on-screen results without the burden of a huge file. Because you won't be giving a print of this image to your mom or anything, MY_MOM.TIF on the companion CD is a much more reasonably sized 1.3M file.

So in your own work, remember that when restoring a photo that's in poor condition, you need to acquire as much original image information as possible, so go ahead and break the rule and work with an image that has been scanned at a very high resolution.

Using the Levels Command *before* Variations

When working with properly exposed (brightness, contrast, and gamma-corrected) scanned photos, you should first color-correct the image. Starting with Photoshop's Variations command is *usually* a wise first step. However, MY_MOM.TIF is *not* a regular image. It looks like a sepia tone, but is actually a color photo where the color information is hidden beneath a layer of age. Although it may seem like common sense to adjust the color to remove the sepia color, the problem actually lies with the image's *brightness* values.

It's also a bad idea to color-correct first for a very basic reason: Photoshop's modifying filters (including variations as well as brightness levels) are all *relative*. Your first change is made to the *original* image, but each subsequent change is made to the image's current (changed) state. You can't go back to your starting point, the original image, without starting over again with a copy of the original.

For MY_MOM.TIF, you need to restore some perk to the overall brightness range *before* you adjust the color values. That is, you must get the brown out of view so that you can see the colors that you're correcting.

You can virtually eliminate the predominant sepia browns in MY_MOM.TIF by broadening the range of the brightness values of all the pixels. To do this, you must set a realistic white and black point for the image, as demonstrated in the next exercise. Setting these points will help you see what other global adjustments need to be done to this image in subsequent exercises.

Setting Realistic Black and White Points

Double-click on the Hand tool on the toolbox	Zooms the image to fit within the active window.
Click and drag the title bar MY_MOM.TIF to the top-left corner of the Photoshop workspace	Positions the image where you can see it and still have room for a palette and a dialog box in the workspace.
Choose **W**indow, Show **I**nfo (or press F8)	Displays the Info palette.
Click and drag the Info palette next to the MY_MOM.TIF image window	Helps organize your workspace so that there's enough room for another screen element to pop up.
Choose **I**mage, **A**djust, and then choose Levels (or press Ctrl+L)	Displays the Levels command.
Drag the Levels dialog box to a position where you can see both it and the image, as shown in figure 6.2	
Check the Preview option in the Levels dialog box	Displays changes in the image as you make them, but before you accept them as the new values.
Click on the far-right (white) Eyedropper button in the Levelsdialog box	Selects the tool used to define the image's white point.
Move the cursor over one of the white clapboards on the house, watching the right number in the B: column on the Info palette	

You are looking for a new white point for the image. By looking at the Info palette, find the highest brightness value in the overall image. (Hint: when the authors designed this exercise, they found 53% on the house's clapboards is the brightest value existing in this picture.)

Click your cursor over the area on the clapboard that reads closest to 53%	Sets the new white point, as shown in figure 6.3.

This ends the first part of the exercise. Take a break for a moment, and *don't* touch anything!

This is a break in the steps, but don't think of it as break in this exercise! You're not done yet, so don't click on OK, or leave the Levels command because you need to set a Black Point for MY_MOM.TIF next. Remember that all changes in the Levels command are relative, and that's why you need to change White *and* Black Points in the same Levels command session. You want to create more tonal balance in the image, and balance is achieved by editing the *entire* tonal range in one Levels session.

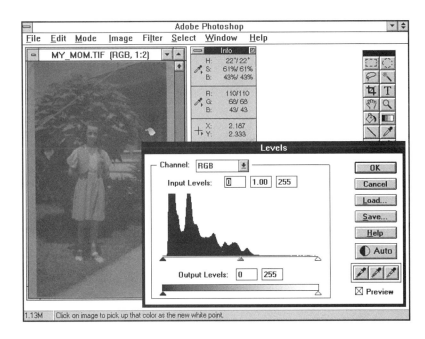

Figure 6.2
The Levels command displays a histogram of the brightness range in an image.

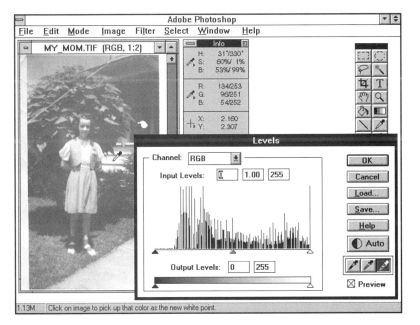

Figure 6.3
Setting the white point in an image redistributes all other color pixels to different brightness values.

II

Steak 'n Potatoes Assignments

As you can see in the Info palette shown in figure 6.3, the brightness value of the clapboard has changed from 53 percent to 99 percent. (Your white point value may vary, depending on

continues

continued

where you clicked.) Also in figure 6.3, notice that the white point in the Levels histogram changes to reflect the new range of brightness values in the image.

Now that you've set your new white point, you need to adjust the black point as well, so let's resume...

Click on the black point Eyedropper tool (the leftmost of the three Eyedropper tools) in the Levels dialog box	Selects the tool used to define the image's black point.

Move your cursor toward the shadows of the shutters in the MY_MOM.TIF image, and look for the darkest point in the image

You are looking for a new black point for the image. By looking at the right number in the B: column in the Info palette, find the lowest percentage of brightness.

Click the eyedropper when the cursor is over the lowest percentage of brightness	Sets the new black point, as shown in figure 6.4.

In figure 6.4, a brightness value of 16 percent is used as the new black point.

Type **1.03** in the middle box of the Input Levels options	Increases the gamma of the midranges by setting the midpoint slightly lower on the Levels histogram.

The arbitrary value 1.03 is a setting that results in a change that looks good when viewed in Preview. You can also click and drag the slider to make this adjustment.

Click on OK	Confirms your changes and returns to Photoshop's workspace.
Choose **F**ile, Sa**v**e As and save the file to a subdirectory of your hard drive Name the file MY_MOM.TIF	Saves your work to this point to your hard drive.

The Levels adjustment that you just performed resulted in a most dramatic change in this image—and it deserves a little explanation.

This image, as scanned, contained color pixels that were buried beneath the sepia tones. Setting a new black and white point redistributed the brightness values of all the pixels across the tonal range. Values that were whiter or blacker than the white or black point that you set were *clipped*—tonal information in these regions was ignored, discarded by Photoshop. The pixels that occupied these off-the-scale values were reassigned values between the new white and black points. This resulted in a broader midrange of values. As discussed in Chapter 3, the midrange is where you find most of a photo's valuable visual content. Slightly increasing the gamma—the midrange gray values—broadens the midrange even further, allowing still more detail to show in the darker registers in this range. The higher the gamma, the lower the contrast *only* in this *specific* range.

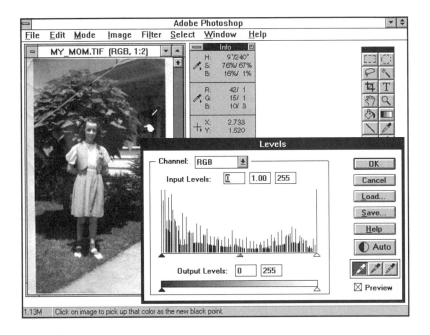

Figure 6.4
Setting a new black point in an image helps to sharpen its contrast.

The Info palette is an invaluable assistant in determining the value of changes that you create in the Levels dialog box before you click OK. You can also use this palette to determine the Hue, Saturation, and Brightness—or Red, Green, and Blue values of pixels when you're not in the Levels dialog box.

Photoshop's No Dummy

You should feel proud of the fine Black and White Point work that you just did, but you also have to give a little credit to Photoshop. Photoshop must do a lot of intelligent evaluation of all the pixels' tonal values between the black and white point to reassign them. The "comb" effect that results when the Levels histogram displays your changes, indicates that although Photoshop is redistributing many of the pixels, some remain the same. This is good, because if color pixels don't have the exact tonal (brightness) quality as their nearest neighbor, more *contrast* is created in the overall picture. When values are clipped off at either extreme of the brightness scale, vacancies are created for pixels in the midrange.

Before the chapter's end, you'll use the Curves command to fine-tune the tonal corrections to the Brightness range you just made using the Levels command. The next step in restoring this image, however, is a coarse color-correction.

Most faded photographic images need their brightness values remapped to create more contrast in certain areas of the image, which you can adjust in the Input Levels setting of the Levels dialog box. If, however, you need to create *less* contrast in an image area, you can adjust the Output Levels setting to *decrease* the contrast. When you move the Output Levels sliders, you're, in effect, telling Photoshop that the image has values that are darker than the current black point shown onscreen, and values far lighter than the current white point.

Be aware, though, that in both cases, lessening *or* heightening image contrast, you *redistribute* brightness values for color pixels, which results in some loss of quality to the image's visual content. By using the Levels dialog box to increase the image's contrast, you are actually *destroying* the brown sepia quality (an *unwanted* piece of visual content) found in MY_MOM.TIF.

You can also click the Auto button in the Levels dialog box to automatically bring more eye-pleasing tonal distribution to an image. When you do so, by default Photoshop arbitrarily lops off 0.5 percent of the upper white point and 0.05 percent of the lower black point. You can adjust how much Photoshop's Auto feature clips the image by double-clicking the Auto button.

If one evening you need to make 50 equally dull pictures presentable for the next morning, you'll want to use the Auto adjust feature. However, if you want more control over the mapping of brightness in an image, stick with the methods demonstrated in the preceding exercises.

Using the Variations Command

You aren't finished "shaping" the brightness map of MY_MOM.TIF yet. You used the Levels command first so you could see something in the image besides brown. Now, you can try to remove some of the awful bluish color cast that you have revealed in the image.

The Variations command is about the only straightforward command in Photoshop—if you want to see what the image would look like with a little more red or yellow, for example, this command displays thumbnail previews of the images with the proposed changes. Variations gives you hands-on control over an image's hue and saturation components in addition to minor contrast changes.

The Variations command operates using a color wheel as its *model.* Thumbnail images with contrasting color tints applied to them are arranged directly opposite each other, just as they would be on a color wheel, with the Current Pick thumbnail in the center of the wheel. For example, MY_MOM.TIF has a noticeable, unwanted blue color-cast. As you'll see in the following exercise, the opposite color, yellow, defeats the blue color-cast quite nicely when you select it.

Color-Casting Call

Choose **A**djust from the **I**mage menu, and then choose Variations	Displays the Variations dialog box, which shows different, miniature views of the image.
Click and drag the Fine/Coarse slider to the left two notches	Shifts the amount of color correction from average to subtle, causing the miniature selection photos, called *Picks*, to bear less difference in their variation.
Check the Show **C**lipping box	Displays a brilliant neon color in areas of the image where the pixels are either saturated or have reached the black or white point in the image.
Click the **M**idtones radio button	Constrains the effects of changes to only the midtones of the active image.
Click on the More Yellow selection photo	Changes the center photo, Current Pick, to show how adding yellow changes the image's appearance, as shown in figure 6.5.
Click Sh**a**dows radio button	Constrains color corrections to affect only the darker regions of the image.

Notice that some of the Pick selections display clipping (neon-colored areas).

Click and drag the Fine/Coarse slider all the way to Fine	Sets the finest degree of change that you can make to an image's saturation, shade, or color-cast.
Click on the More Red selection photo	Changes the tint of the shadows, mostly in the area of the leaves, and removes some of the cyan.
Click on OK	Confirms your selections and returns you to the workspace.
Choose **F**ile, **S**ave	Saves your work to your hard drive.

Variations is a most subjective command because everyone sees an image's color-casting differently. Some users prefer to be a bit stingy in using Variations color-correcting because there is a definite limit to what you can do with the command before a picture begins to look phony.

Also, there's a very good reason to limit your use of the Variations dialog box's Fine/Coarse adjustment. Although these thumbnail images can give you a good idea of the global scheme of an image's colors, their postage-stamp size makes them a tad inadequate for doing precision work. However, if you have a photo that just needs a little enhancing in one section, select it with the Lasso or Rectangle tool; then only the selected area appears as the Variations thumbnail, which makes the section a little easier to see.

Figure 6.5
The Variations dialog box enables you to control the color-cast in a selected area or all of an image.

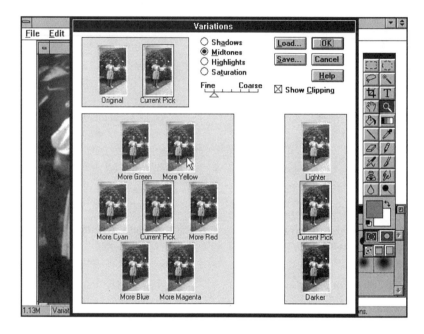

If you make a mistake with any of your Variations selections, you don't have to press Cancel, and then return to the Variations command. Instead, you can press the Alt key, which toggles the Cancel button to a Reset button, and then click Reset. Your image then changes back to the look it originally had before you entered the Variations command.

After you click OK and return to the full-sized image, if you don't like the change that you created in the Variations dialog box, press Ctrl+Z or select **U**ndo from the **E**dit menu to Undo Variations changes. This works only if you did no other editing between selecting OK and Ctrl+Z or **U**ndo.

To use the most processor- and time-intensive Undo command, which applies to Variations as well as every other series of steps performed in Photoshop, select **R**evert from the **F**ile menu. This command returns you to the last version of the image that you saved.

Clipping Is Obvious in a Photo

The Show **C**lipping check box activates a visual "flag" indicating when you reach a saturation point in areas of an image. In the last exercise, when you wanted to add more red to the overall image, the Fine/Coarse adjustment was too far to the right, resulting in brilliant green-cyan highlights peppering the Current Pick. If you selected the More Red image without adjusting the Fine/Coarse slider to the left, you would reach the maximum amount of color information possible for the highlighted pixels. Photoshop limits, or *clips*, any adjustment to a 100-percent saturation range. When you use the Variations dialog box, the trick is to add enough color to enhance the image without reaching a clipping point by adjusting the Fine/Coarse slider.

You usually don't want clipped areas in an image, and certainly not when restoring a delicate, faded photo. Clipping, which is caused both by pixels with 100-percent saturation and by those with a hypothetical value that *exceeds* 100 percent, results in flat areas of color with no variations within them. When you exceed 100-percent saturation at a black point, areas in the image fill in and seem to become a separate element from the rest of the image. A clipped white point creates "hot spots," undetailed highlights where the visual content is wiped out by "whiter than whites."

Whether you exceed 100-percent saturation at a black point, or clip a white point, you force pixels that formerly had varying brightness values into the same percentile. If you add too much color to any of the ranges, you also force an unrealistic contrast between specific areas and their neighboring pixels. Computer images are a digital display of samples from continuous-tone sources, such as chemical photographs. Inducing a harsh contrast within the *representation* of a continuous tone results in a posterized, phony-looking image.

Using Curves and Quartertones

You make the final adjustment to the color balance of MY_MOM.TIF after you make some additional changes to the color brightness map. With a typical image, you usually want to correct color in one fell swoop and then move on to tonal balance. The unique nature of this heirloom image, however, forces you to toggle back and forth between Photoshop features.

Photoshop's Curves command gives you total control over an image's brightness mapping. Unlike the Levels command, the Curves command fine-tunes not just the midrange but also the *quartertones* and any other specific tonal point in the image. Quartertones are regions at either end of the midtone range. Photoshop's capability to display these tonal regions in a visual, editable way is a welcome feature. The star of this image, my mom, has some harsh shadows casting on her. To correct this, you'll shape the Curve of the tones in the image.

You can lighten any area of an image in Photoshop without disturbing the rest of the image, by first selecting an area to work on and then using the Curves command to pinpoint a brightness range that needs adjusting.

Let's check out the Curves command and its usefulness in restoring this image.

Reshaping an Image's Brightness Curve

Double-click on the Zoom tool	Zooms your view of MY_MOM.TIF to a 1:1 viewing resolution.
Click on the Lasso tool, then click and drag a rough outline around mom from the top of her head to mid-torso	Defines the selection area that you will change using the Curves command.
Choose **I**mage, **A**djust, and then choose Curves (or press Ctrl+M)	Displays the Curves dialog box.

If necessary, reposition the box so that you can see the highlighted selection area in the image as well as the Curves dialog box.

Click the upper-right of the Curves graph line so that the Input is 180, and then pull straight down until the Output value is 140, making sure that the Input value remains 180 as you do so	Reduces the contrast in the upper region—the quartertone—of the selection area, as shown in figure 6.6.
Click the lower-left of the Curves graph line—the lower quartertone —so that the Input value is 68, and then pull straight up until the Output value is 77, making sure that the Input value remains 68 as you do so	Increases the contrast slightly at the bottom end of the midrange.

At this stage, you should have created an inverted "S" pattern out of the graph line.

Click the cursor over the highlighted area on mom's forehead in the image while holding down the mouse button	Turns the cursor into an eyedropper and marks the range of brightness in the forehead area with a little circle on the Curves graph, as shown in figure 6.7.

You may want to physically write down the Input and Output values at this highlight point because you will need to use this figure later. In figure 6.7, the value is 244, but yours may vary depending on the exact position over which you clicked.

Move your cursor over the Curves graph line and stop when the Input and Output values are 244	Positions your cursor to create a change in this specific brightness point.

Click and drag the 244 point on the graph down until the Output value is 235, and then click again

Lowers the brightness values of pixels in this range within the area that you selected with the Lasso tool and reduces the white point to a lower relative value.

The brightest value possible in the selection area is now the same for the blouse and the forehead highlights. This lessens the contrast and improves the detail in the fleshtones and blouse image areas, as shown in figure 6.8.

Click on OK

Confirms your changes in the Curves dialog box and returns to the Photoshop workspace.

Choose File, Save

Saves your work to your hard disk.

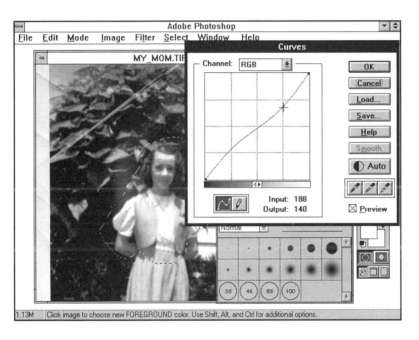

Figure 6.6

Lowering a quartertone's value diminishes contrast in the upper regions of an image's brightness.

Fine-tuning selected areas of an image is an important part of your photo-restoration work. You identify certain aspects of an image's flaws, and use Photoshop's precision adjustments to compensate for the flaws. The exercise also is an example of a good work methodology—to go from the general to the specific.

By selecting only the focal point of the image, the subject, and then adjusting it to display less harsh contrast, you leave the rest of the image unaffected.

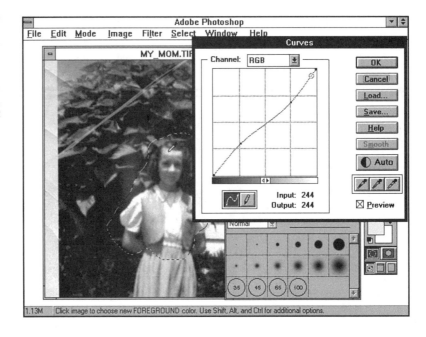

Figure 6.7
Increasing the tonal value in the bottom quartertone in a selected image area gets rid of muddy shadows.

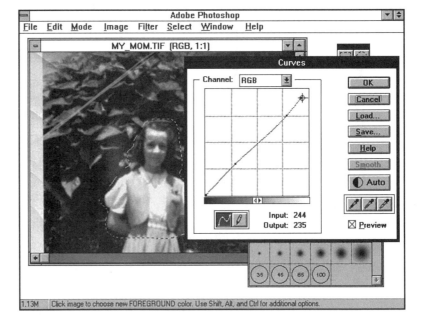

Figure 6.8
Lowering a white point to match a visual highlight in an image adds visual information to lighter areas in your selection.

The background in the MY_MOM.TIF image is of secondary importance when it comes to tweaking a photo's color balance and tonal scheme. You should always consider the subject of an image the primary target for corrections, filtering, and color balancing. You'll find the rest of an image generally falls into place after doing this.

Any good photographer will tell you to optimize the fleshtones in a photo first. If you correct them and make them look natural, the viewer will forgive less-than-perfect inanimate objects elsewhere in the image.

If you experience a problem with a specific area in the Curves dialog box, you can achieve more precise control over the image's tonal curve by using the Pencil icon than by clicking and dragging the graph line.

With the Pencil, you simply draw a new curve in the graph and then click the S**m**ooth button several times until you have the Curves mapping that you want.

A "contrary" image, such as the heirloom photo in these exercises, requires that you use a contrary procedure in Photoshop's Curves command. Imaging professionals often speak of an "S" curve in the midrange. An "S" curve is the exact *opposite* of the shape that you defined in the last exercise.

By shaping the Curves graph line like an "S," you add contrast to an image's midrange, and the overall picture gets a little snappier. You add some details in the image's upper shadow areas while losing some in the highlights. By using an *inverted* "S" pattern for the MY_MOM.TIF image in the Curves dialog box, you allocate more of a tonal range to the highlights and lose some detail in the upper shadow, quartertone range.

Understanding the Relativity of Changes

So far you have performed a lot of tonal and color adjusting to MY_MOM.TIF. If you've followed the steps, you can see that the image is coming back to life. But remember that your changes are all *relative*—that is, you can't click an Absolute button to return the image to the state it was three or four steps ago.

It also means that you currently may not have the ideal image on your screen, even if you believe you've followed each step in the exercises precisely. For example, if you clicked a different white point in the Levels command than the exercises specified, all the subsequent changes in the different commands can lead you further astray from the "ideal" images shown in this chapter's figures.

So how do you know whether you're on track or off at this stage? It's simple—use your eyes and your own evaluation. These tonal and color controls aren't self-governing, and these exercises are meant to give you the knowledge of why and how the controls work, and when you should use them.

Think about the information *behind* the various steps in these exercises. If the exercise tells you to enter a value of 120 when you think 128 looks better, go for it! As long as you understand the *principles* of Photoshop's tonal and color commands, there is no "right" or "wrong" evaluation. It's up to you. Eye-pleasing work is all relative.

Color-Balancing the Color-Corrected Image

While using the Variations command, you probably noticed that you were achieving a good *overall* change in the image's color cast, but that some areas were skewing heavily toward the wrong tint. This tendency is particularly evident in the darker areas of the background trees; the More Red option has left them looking parched. Photoshop's Color Balance command gives you an opportunity to separate the various colors in their respective ranges, refine your initial Variations changes, and shift *regions* of color values back in line with what looks most natural.

In the next exercise, you see some dramatic changes in the MY_MOM.TIF image, all because each primary additive and subtractive color in a color wheel model can turn toward its nearest neighboring color. And the next exercise shows you how to turn the colors *back*.

Balancing the Colors within a Range

Double-click the Hand tool on the toolbox	Restores the resolution of MY_MOM.TIF to a full-screen view.

You'll want to evaluate Color Balance changes performed on the *entire* image.

Choose **I**mage, **A**djust, and then choose Color Balance (or press Ctrl+Y)	Displays the Color Balance command, as shown in figure 6.9.
Choose the Preview check box and then choose the Midtones radio button	Displays changes as you apply them to the image and adjusts the color balance of the midtone range of color pixels.
Type **+15**, **–5**, and **–13**, or click and drag the sliders to get these values in the Color Levels boxes (or enter the values directly in the boxes)	Casts the midtone color pixels more toward red than cyan, more toward magenta than green, and more toward yellow than blue.
Click the Shadows radio button	Applies Color Balance changes to only the darker pixels in the image.
Type **–19**, **+4**, and **–5** in the Color Levels boxes	Casts the dark, shadow region pixels more toward cyan than red, more toward green than magenta, and more toward yellow than blue.

Click the Highlights radio button	Applies Color Balance changes to only the color pixels that lie in the image's brightest areas.
Type **+6**, **0**, and **–3** in the Color Levels boxes	Creates highlights in the image that are slightly more toward red than cyan, strike a neutral balance between magenta and green, and are a little more toward yellow than blue.
Click on OK	Confirms your changes and returns you to the Photoshop workspace.
Choose **File**, **Save**	Saves your work to your hard drive.

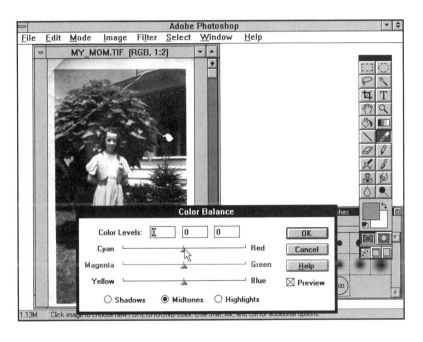

Figure 6.9
The Color Balance command's Color Levels boxes can achieve color balance in three individual tonal ranges of an image.

Additive primary colors (modeled as red, green, and blue on your monitor) and subtractive colors have an interrelationship that can be expressed as a color wheel, similar to the Variations command. When you use the Color Balance dialog box you can precisely control how the additive and subtractive colors in an image "lean" toward their neighbor. You can color-correct mom's face, which lies in mostly midtone values, and simultaneously "green up" the tree and shrubs a little, with each operation independent of the other. For this reason, you must learn how to evaluate an image, with your own eyes, in terms of the flow of the tones and colors in it. It's the only way can you take full advantage of Photoshop's commands.

Striking a Balance between Gray and Color

You've taken many steps toward restoring original color information to this heirloom photo. The picture now has better detail because of the tonal adjustments that you've made.

Details have been revealed because the brightness values of neighboring pixels show a contrast, yet are smoothly distributed throughout the web of image pixels to contribute to an eye-pleasing photo. This occurred because you have broadened, staggered, or otherwise reassigned the neutral-density grays in the color-pixel range.

You've also done some color adjustment to the image. You've corrected the color cast and refined the balance of the image's primary additive and subtractive colors. These are adjustments in Hue. If you had the Info palette on the workspace when you made the changes, you would notice a big shift in the Hue value at the top of the palette.

Saturation is your last stop in this photo-restoration. It's the only value in the HSB (Hue, Saturation, and Brightness) color model that you haven't directly addressed. Although a healthy tonal relationship exists among the relative brightness values in the image, the image contains too much gray information. When an image has too much gray, the color values are suppressed, and the overall picture is lackluster.

Let's change that with the Hue/Saturation command:

Balancing Values with Hues

Select **I**mage, **A**djust, and then choose Hue/Saturation (or press Ctrl+U)	Displays the Hue/Saturation dialog box.
Check mark the Preview check box	Displays the changes in the image as you make them.

Make sure MY_MOM.TIF is in a corner of the workspace so that you can see it when the Hue/ Saturation dialog box appears.

Click with the cursor over a medium-tone area in my mom's face	Displays in the Sample box the color of the selected area.

You can use the color displayed in the Sample box as a reference as you make changes to the image.

Click and drag the Saturation slider to a +16 value, or type **+16** in the box to the right of the slider	Increases the relative saturation in the whole image by a positive 16% out of a possible 100% relative saturation.
Click and drag the Lightness slider to a –2 setting, or type **–2** in the box to the right of the slider	Adds 2% black to all the additive and subtractive hue elements in the image, as shown in figure 6.10.

Click on OK	Confirms your settings and returns you to the Photoshop workspace.
Choose **F**ile, **S**ave	Saves your work to your hard drive.

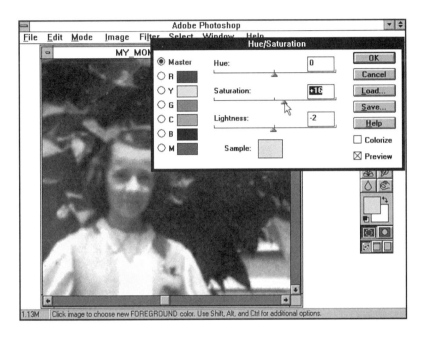

Figure 6.10

Saturating the Color Composite (RGB) channel of an image enhances the pure color component of the image and suppresses the gray component.

You didn't touch the Hue slider in the last exercise, because you have already balanced and corrected the hue of MY_MOM.TIF by using the Color Balance and Variations commands. Fully understand what you're getting into when you use command features that have overlapping functionality. Every tonal and color adjustment that you make to enhance this picture has an additive quality, because each is a *relative* command. One command *does not* neutralize the effect of another; with repetitious commands, you simply continue to change an image's property, spin your wheels a little, and ultimately degrade the quality of the image.

If your active image is positioned in the center of your workspace when you call an Adjust menu command item, like Levels or Hue/Saturation, the box can obscure your view of part of the image. This defeats the purpose of the Preview check box. Sometimes you must move the dialog box out of the way, but that may obscure some of its features. Even worse, you may have to select Cancel, move the image, and then select the command again—a frustratingly inefficient solution to the problem.

continues

If you want to move an image in its window, or zoom in or out of it without leaving a dialog box, the following are handy keyboard combinations to remember. With your cursor positioned outside of a dialog box, use the following keystrokes:

✔ Pressing Alt+spacebar turns your cursor into a Zoom In tool.

✔ Pressing Ctrl+spacebar turns your cursor into a Zoom Out tool.

✔ Pressing Shift+spacebar turns your cursor into the Hand tool. You can click and drag the active image around in its window frame with the Hand tool to get a better look at the image areas you want to work on.

From Restoring to Retouching

You have one last step for this chapter's assignment: Save the work that you've done so far as MY_MOM2.TIF. You need to save an additional copy of your work to a different file name now so that you can compare this image to the final retouched image you'll create in Chapter 7. This photo is by no means a complete work of art: The surface has abrasions, a lens flare, and a chemical stain that need expert attention with the aid of Photoshop. Restoring the color to an aged photo is only half the trick to bringing it back to life.

Figure 6.11 is a before and after, with the original image called back for an honest appraisal of the work done so far.

Figure 6.11
No chemical dyes or hand-tinting were used to help bring this aged photo back to life.

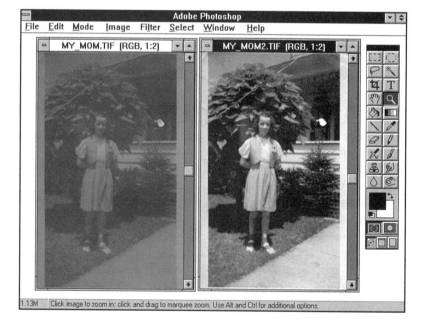

Ironically, it takes something as artificial as a computer to restore a damaged image accurately and aesthetically. In conventional photofinishing, a craftsperson must resort to hand-coloring a copy of a print to simulate the colors that *might* be buried underneath all this sepia. However, with Photoshop, you filter out the sepia and actually restore the original color values. Photoshop reassigns grayscale values based on your evaluations of the image's black and white points and does a lot of averaging to smooth out effects that are sometimes based on a pittance of original visual information.

But for just a moment, look *beyond* the technical details and simply admire the results of your photo-restoration work. It's awe-inspiring what you can do for an image after you have been introduced to Photoshop's restoration features and understand the principles behind them.

Summary

This book has repeatedly stressed the importance of the interrelationships among Photoshop's tools and functions, and in this particular chapter you have experienced evidence of this importance. Because color models are based on interdependence, so are Photoshop's features, which is why Photoshop offers so many different approaches to accomplish similar tasks. For instance, the Variations command features Darker and Lighter options. These options definitely belong in an overall evaluation of color-casting, but if you make shadows darker and highlights lighter within this command, you get an image that has more *contrast*. And isn't contrast a function of Brightness rather than Hue?

You have the opportunity at each step in Photoshop to adjust image qualities that you indirectly affect when you issue a specific command from the <u>A</u>djust menu. Photoshop's brightness controls may not affect an image's hue, but as you've just seen in this chapter, Brightness adjustments enable you to make the necessary changes to the Hue. What makes Photoshop such a special application is that it has adjustment controls in several different places within its workspace. Now that you know where to find many of the controls, take advantage of some of the features that overlap in the commands. Do this by experimenting with *combinations* of adjustments, and always let your own evaluation, your artist's eye, be the final arbitrator in image editing.

Chapter 7 focuses on Photoshop's tools more than its menu commands. Although the commands in the <u>A</u>djust submenu contribute heavily to restoring faded colors, they can't do much to correct the damage that a photo suffers from being passed from hand to hand. Nicks, dents, and a camera lens flare are all spoiling the picture of my mom at age 11. If you or a client has an image as valuable and as tarnished as MY_MOM.TIF, you'll definitely want to explore the tricks revealed in Chapter 7 for removing these defects.

Chapter Snapshot

In this chapter, you learn how to:

CHAPTER

Retouching an Heirloom Photograph

I n Chapter 6, you used commands from Photoshop's **A**djust menu to remove a layer of sepia dullness from an heirloom photograph. Using these commands restored enough visual content in the image to make it possible for you to evaluate the color information and then color-correct and balance it.

But enhancing an image that has weathered over a few years brings out both desired and *un*desired visual elements in the digital sample. By the end of your retouching work in Chapter 6, the MY_MOM.TIF image had color and balance, but also a few cracks and other flaws that make the picture less than presentable. The good news is that you can use Photoshop's selection and paint-application tools to recreate the damaged areas. These problems require a special use of Photoshop features, which is where the second phase of fixing an heirloom photo begins.

But your best tool in Photoshop is your own resourcefulness. With all Photoshop's features, the program still requires your input, and that means that you often must use your eye and judgment. In this chapter, as you retouch different areas of the MY_MOM image, each step requires that you identify a problem and then choose the best tool for the job.

Stain Removal Using a Copied Selection Area

Let's begin with an assessment of the stain to the right of my mom's head, as shown in figure 7.1. When this area was buried in sepia tones along with the rest of the image's visual content, the part that it played in the overall image was unclear. Now you clearly see that this stain has obliterated all visual information about an area that was part of the house's shutters.

Figure 7.1
Visual information about the shutters on the house has been completely destroyed by a stain in one area.

Let's take a look at the problem and decide on a course of action before beginning the first exercise. First, the image area of the shutters *directly beneath* the stained area has survived, and it can approximate, if not totally replace, the damaged area. Consider this area as source material you can use to replace the damaged section.

Second, consider the resolution of the obliterated area. Although you can clearly see a pattern in the shutters, the number of pixels that represents the shutters, when compared to the whole image, is relatively small. If you zoom into the area, you see that there's not much information to work with. In such instances, adopt the credo "less is more;" it's the key to disguising the blemish in this image. If you try to get fancy or overwork the area, it will show.

You will copy an area of the undamaged shutter image in the next exercise, then Paste the copied selection directly over the photo's stained area. This won't be a perfect fix, for several reasons to be discussed shortly. But it's only the beginning of several steps you'll perform to complete the image retouching, and through which you'll learn a little more about how Photoshop's integrated feature set makes the work easy!

Fixing a Window

Open MYMOM2.TIF from the directory on your hard drive that you saved it to in the last chapter if it is not already open in your workspace.

Click and drag an area around the window using the Zoom tool	Displays a closer view of the area.

A good resolution to start with is a 2:1 viewing.

Choose the Rectangle Marquee tool	This tool selects a rectangular area within the photo.
Click and drag an area of undamaged window shutter below the image's damaged area, with dimensions equal to those of the stain	Defines the area that you'll use to patch the damaged area, as shown in figure 7.2.
Choose **E**dit, **C**opy (or press Ctrl+C)	Sends a copy of the selected area in the image to the clipboard.
Choose **E**dit, **P**aste (or press Ctrl+V)	Places a *floating* copy of the selected area directly on top of the area you copied.
Press the up-arrow key until the pasted image covers the stain	Nudges the copied selection up into the damaged area of the image, as shown in figure 7.3.
Choose **S**elect, Hide **E**dges (or press Ctrl+H)	Hides the marquee lines around the selection so that you can see the placement of this copied selection more accurately.
Press the right- and up-arrow keys once or twice if necessary	Positions the copied selection so that the shutters line up in the image.

The alignment can't be perfect, so accept an eye-pleasing, if somewhat imperfect, match. At a 1:1 view, this dark background area won't be noticed.

Choose **N**one from the **S**elect menu, press Ctrl+D, or click outside the marquee area	Deselects the copied selection and blends it into the image.
Choose, **F**ile, **S**ave	Saves your work to your hard drive.

When you retouch a photo, maintaining its credibility is of prime concern. And you did the right thing, aesthetically, in copying the undamaged shutter area in to cover the chemical stain, for a number of reasons. First, the shuttered window is in the background, which is not where most people will focus when viewing a picture with a person in it. Also, the area is dark and low in contrast, which makes it easier to retouch without drawing suspicion.

II

Steak 'n Potatoes Assignments

Finally, because the resolution of the area is small, it's not made up of many pixels. This means that a relatively small effort to touch up the selection area is required, since there aren't that many pixels to paint in. Which is what you'll do next.

Figure 7.2
Copy an area that you feel will best cover the damaged area in an image.

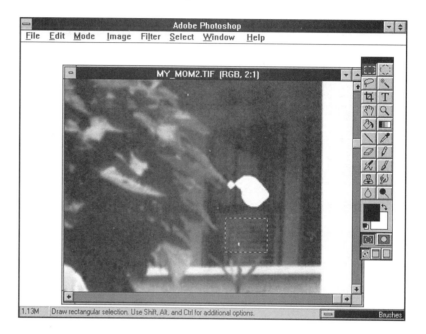

Figure 7.3
Use your arrow keys to nudge a selection one pixel per keystroke.

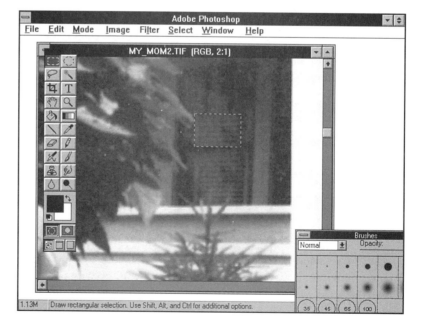

Fixing Edgework Using the Smudge and Paintbrush Tools

The top of the copied selection is where it fits into the background image the worst. This is because, although the copied selection has visual content that should be identical to the damaged area, its position relative to the camera at the time was slightly different. Perspective and the natural distortion of a camera lens has capture patterns that are slightly different from those perceived by the human eye.

As the following exercise demonstrates, you can change these captured patterns with a little assistance from the Eyedropper and Paintbrush tools:

Making the Shutters Fit the Window

Choose the Zoom tool and then marquee-zoom in on the copied selection area	Zooms you into a tighter view of the area.
A 4:1 viewing resolution is best here.	
Click on the Eyedropper tool	This tool selects an image's foreground or background color.
Click on a dark area of the shutters above the copied shutter area	Selects a foreground color to paint with that will match the shadow on the shutters.
Click on the Paintbrush tool	This tool applies color to an image area.
Choose a small tip with spread from the Brushes palette, then click and drag the Opacity slider to 100%, and select Darken mode	Sets the Paintbrush tip to apply the foreground color to only those areas that are lighter than the value that you selected with the Eyedropper tool.
Click and drag from the shadow area in the original image through the copied selection from left to right	Blends the shadow area of the original image into the copied selection, as shown in figure 7.4.
Choose the Smudge tool, then choose *Normal* mode on the Brushes palette, and Click and drag the *Pressure* slider to 58%	This tool treats areas under the cursor as if they were wet paint. The degree of intensity for the Smudge effect is about half.
Click and drag from just above the copied selection into the copied selection area	Destroys the hard-edge detail of the copied selection area, as shown in figure 7.5.
Continue to click and drag from outside the selection's edge to inside of it, using only two or three short strokes	Completely obscures the edges of the copied selection.
Choose **F**ile, **S**ave	Saves your work to your hard drive.

Figure 7.4
In Darken mode, the Paintbrush fills in only areas with color that is lighter than the selected foreground color.

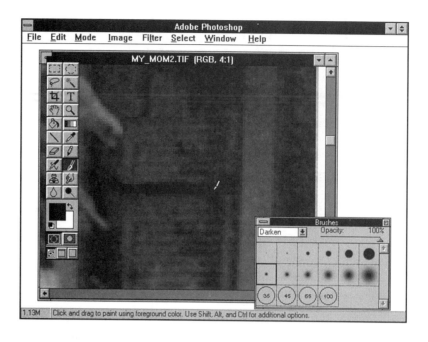

Figure 7.5
Use the Smudge tool to remove an image area's detail without losing the area's color values as well.

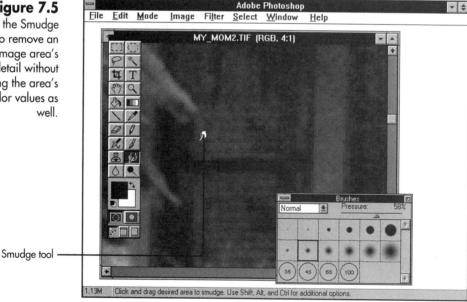

Smudge tool

Because the selected area is small and composed of only a few pixels, you don't have to use the Paintbrush and Smudge tools extensively to fix the edges and smoothly blend the copy of the shutters into the background image of MY_MOM. You'll want to use Darken mode a lot in your own retouching assignments because it's ideal for coloring in only the areas that are lighter than the foreground color you define. Chapter 12 has a good example of the use of the Darken and Lighten Brushes palette modes, to retouch the edges of image copies into background images.

The Smudge tool, as you've just seen, is the artistic equivalent of mumbling. When you have an area that can compositionally live without great visual detail, you simply "fake it" with the Smudge tool. Try using the Smudge tool in your own assignments in different Brushes modes. But always remember that the Smudge tool is used best when you have a *direction* for the wet paint in the image to flow. In other words, use the Smudge tool *from* an area *to* another area. But never drag the Smudge tool back and forth in one area, unless you want to create an abstract painting within a photo.

Fixing Chipped Emulsion with the Rubber Stamp

The next area that you need to fix with Photoshop is the upper-right corner of the image. Some of the emulsion on the original photographic print must have chipped off, and the flatbed scanner that was used to acquire this image compounded the flaw by bouncing a highlight off the image.

You shouldn't press a photo too tightly against the glass plate of a flatbed scanner in an attempt to avoid reflections as the light element passes over it. Many people place heavy books on the top of the scanner's image window to make sure the source image is flat. But this is a mistake because it distorts the surface of the photographic emulsion. Your acquired digital image can end up with blobs like those that you see when someone presses their face against a plate glass window.

Strive to get the best scan of an image without exerting unreasonable force to hold it in place beneath a flatbed scanner's platen. Then use Photoshop to correct whatever surface detail needs fixing.

You first need to find some unaffected areas next to the area of the damaged rain gutter and eaves, and then use the Rubber Stamp tool to sample this area so that you can clone it over the damaged area. You should mask off surrounding areas to avoid accidentally cloning into them. Don't worry about running into the white photo border because you'll replace the border later. You'll delete any stray cloning into the top edge when you define the new border.

Before using the Rubber Stamp tool, notice the diagonal lines that make up the eaves. You'll get the best results with your cloning work if you take your sample directly on an edge of the eaves in the image and then start cloning on the same edge in the damaged image area. The following exercise shows you how:

Fixing a Defective Edge with Cloning

Choose the Zoom tool, and then press Alt while clicking the center of the image	Zooms to a 2:1 resolution—a more complete, less pixellated view of the image.
Scroll or use the Hand tool to reposition the image in the window to show the image's upper-right corner	
Choose the Rectangle Marquee tool and then click and drag a selection border that encompasses the problem area of the house's eaves	Selects only the area that needs changing, while protecting the rest of the image from accidental cloning strokes.
Choose the Rubber Stamp tool, and then from the Brushes palette select a medium Brushes tip with spread, specify 100% opacity, and set the Brushes mode to Normal	Sets the characteristics of the Rubber Stamp tool's tip for the retouching work.
Press Alt and click on a point on the border of the eaves to the left of the damaged area	Sets the traveling sampling point for the Rubber Stamp tool.
Click on the edge of the eaves in the damaged area and drag diagonally (following the edge) to the right	Defines your initial cloning point with the Rubber Stamp tool.

You are recreating the border of the eaves by clicking and dragging in an area similar to that of the sample point, as shown in figure 7.6.

Click and drag a diagonal stroke above the first stroke, moving from left to right	Rubber Stamp samples and clones the eaves in the same diagonal direction as the eaves in the photo.
Continue clicking and dragging single strokes until you have retouched the damaged area	

You continue cloning in sample areas to the left of the damaged area in a diagonal direction that matches the angle of the house as it was photographed.

Choose **S**elect, **N**one (or press Ctrl+H)	Deselects the image area.
Choose **F**ile, **S**ave	Saves your work to your hard drive.

You'll find you'll want to create selection areas in images to be able to freely color in an area using Photoshop. The "virtual drop cloth" you used in the last exercise constrained the Rubber Stamp strokes to the damaged area. If you've ever seen a digitizing tablet in action with an application, you'll appreciate the relative imprecision of a mouse. When you use paint-application tools, selection borders help immensely to compensate for the mouse's lack of precision.

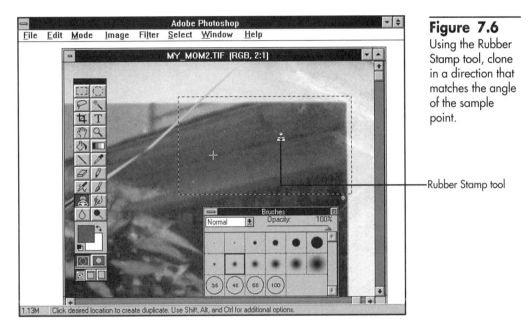

Figure 7.6
Using the Rubber Stamp tool, clone in a direction that matches the angle of the sample point.

Rubber Stamp tool

Setting a sample point that's on a diagonal line and then setting your initial cloning strokes on the same line helps you clone the entire area that was at an angle from the camera's point of view. See Chapter 5, in which you recreated lines on a legal pad by using the same technique.

Burning In Lens Flare

MY_MOM's image is also marred by a circular lens flare, which wasn't revealed until the sepia tones were removed from the image in the last chapter. Besides photographic film being in its infancy and my mother being in her childhood, the lens on Uncle Alan's camera wasn't the most mature player in this photo either.

You can correct this photographic problem by using a handy digital equivalent to the dodging and burning templates that the chemical photographer uses. In the chemical photography darkroom, you can burn in overexposed areas using a cardboard cut-out that you move under the condenser head as you shine light through the negative onto photographic paper. The result is an area with soft edges that's been treated to more light and becomes darker.

The following exercise shows how Photoshop's tools make "digital burning" much simpler.

Foiling a Lens Flare

Choose the Hand tool and then click and drag the image up and to the right	Moves the image in the window.

Stop when you can see the area to the left of my mom. The leaves on the tree require some burning in.

Choose the Lasso tool, which is the tool you use to define the selection area to be burned in	
Click and drag to encompass the area where you see the lens flare	Selects the area to be fixed and keeps the rest of the image from being affected by any changes.
Double-click on the Dodge/Burn tool on the toolbox	Displays the Dodge/Burn Options dialog box.
Choose Burn from the **T**ool drop-down list, and then click on OK	Sets the tool's default to Burn.

This sets the default of this tool to Burn, which is the only thing you need the tool for in the next exercise—no dodging is required. Setting the Dodge/Burn tool to burn as its default is more comfortable to work with than having to constantly toggle this tool to burn for minutes on end!

Set the Brushes mode to Midtones, click and drag the Exposure slider to 50%, and then select the 35-pixel tip	Assigns to the Burn tool characteristics that affect only the midtones in the image and apply burning at a mild, 50% intensity.
Click and drag over the lens flare once or twice until you remove it	Burns in the area to match the surrounding, unselected areas, as shown in figure 7.7.
Choose **S**elect, **N**one (or press Ctrl+H)	Deselects the area.
Choose **F**ile, **S**ave	Saves your work to your hard drive.

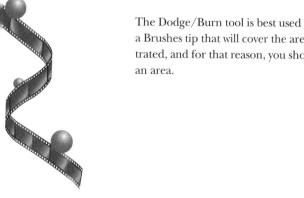

The Dodge/Burn tool is best used to correct an underexposed or overexposed area by setting a Brushes tip that will cover the area with a minimum of strokes. The effect is very concentrated, and for that reason, you shouldn't use repeated strokes. You can very easily overburn an area.

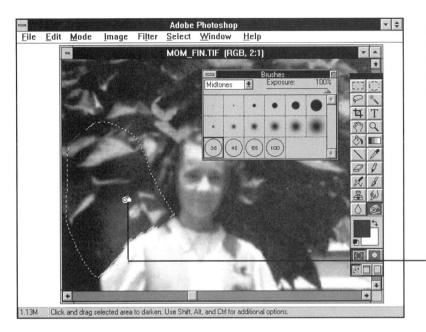

Figure 7.7
Use a large Brush
tip to burn in an
area evenly with
one or two strokes.

Dodge/Burn tool

II

Steak 'n Potatoes Assignments

Smoothing Out Saturated Pixels

If you've looked at other areas of this image while retouching, you may have noticed that mom's right forearm is a little funky. Certain areas have become oversaturated with color while neighboring pixels still contain a fair amount of gray component. The contrast within the area gives the appearance of video *noise*—the random distribution of color pixels in an image.

The best tool for correcting this kind of noise is the Blur/Sharpen tool. This tool decreases the contrast in an image area by increasing the similarity of the grayscale components in color pixels. The next exercise provides a quick example of how the Blur tool corrects oversaturation in an image without affecting color values:

Blurring an Oversaturated Detail

Choose the Hand tool and then click and drag the image up until you see my mom's right forearm

Positions the image for editing.

Choose the Zoom tool and then click once over the forearm area

Zooms you into a 4:1 resolution so that you can see what's going on.

continues

continued

Choose the Lasso tool, and then click and drag a selection around the area that looks oversaturated	Defines the image's active area where you can make changes.
Choose the Blur/Sharpen tool from the toolbox	

By default, this tool blurs areas. Do *not* change the settings as you did with the Dodge/Burn tool.

Choose the Normal mode on the Brushes palette, click and drag the Pressure slider to 83%, and select the third-smallest Brushes palette tip	Sets the characteristics for the Blur tool.
Click and drag across the image until you have completely gone over the selection area	Covers the area with the tool's blurring effect.

Try not to release the mouse button until you've gone over the entire area, as shown in figure 7.8.

Choose **F**ile, **S**ave	Saves your work to your hard drive.

The Blur setting of the Blur/Sharpen tool operates on a principle similar to that of Photoshop's Blur filters. As you saw in this exercise, the tool is quite useful in diminishing the contrast between pixel brightness in an area without disturbing color information. And if a 4:1 viewing resolution of an area looks okay, you may be certain that the image will print just fine at 1:1.

When doing detail work, zoom to a high-resolution view of the image. Make certain that your Brushes tip is set to about three pixels large at most. If you can see the pixellation in the image, you must apply color or effects with a *very small* tip. Using a small tip, as you did with the Blur tool, ensures that the amount of change you make with each stroke is in proportion to the area at that viewing resolution.

Before you start editing an image, you may want to double-click a Brushes tip to display the Brush Options box. This dialog box reports the diameter of a tip, measured in pixels, and you may want to change the diameter to a smaller or larger size. You especially should check the information in the Brush dialog box if you've customized any of the palette's tips because the picture icon of the tip on the palette is not all that informative.

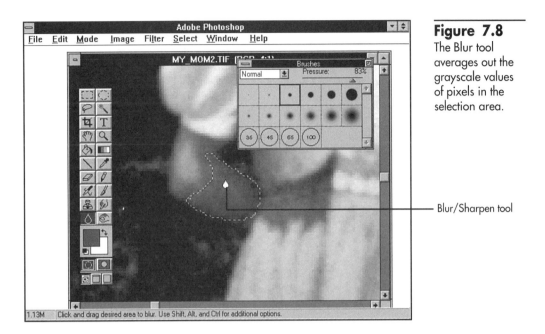

Figure 7.8
The Blur tool averages out the grayscale values of pixels in the selection area.

Blur/Sharpen tool

Putting Some Leaves Back on the Tree

The Rubber Stamp tool is great for cloning leaves, sand, and other organic material into an area. Masses of material with random patterns are perceived by the human eye as clumps of a type of material, which people then dismiss without examining closely. When you fix the crack that runs through MY_MOM.TIF, you can take advantage of the way people perceive background patterns. Even though the image's leaves have clearly defined edges, you can successfully clone over the crack with samples of other leaf areas, without spending much time trying to match precisely what's missing in adjacent leaves. The viewer's eye won't linger on anything in the background if the overall pattern looks correct at a glance.

A Little Visual Re-Leaf

Double-click on the Hand tool	Gives you a full-frame view of the MY_MOM2 image.
Choose the Zoom tool and then click in the center of the background tree	Zooms in to a 1:1 resolution of the image area.

continues

Steak 'n Potatoes Assignments

II

continued

Click on the Rubber Stamp tool, and then from the Brushes palette select a medium-size Brushes tip with spread, Normal mode, and click and drag the Opacity slider to 100%	Sets the characteristics of the Rubber Stamp tool.
Press Alt and click near the top of the tree, below the crack in the photo	Sets the sample point for the Rubber Stamp tool.

Be careful not to click too close to the crack, or you'll be using part of the photos damaged area for the cloning source.

Place your cursor directly on the crack, above and to the right of the sample point, and then click and drag down along the edge of the crack	Replaces the crack with samples of the trees leaves, as shown in figure 7.9.

Stop clicking and dragging when the sample cross-hair reaches the edge of the photo. You don't want to clone an area of the photo's border into the crack area.

Press Alt and click the middle of the tree	Resets the sample point for the Rubber Stamp tool.
Click and drag the remaining edges of the crack near the border of the tree	Eliminates the damaged part of the image over the tree.
Choose **F**ile, **S**ave	Saves your work to your hard drive.

The secret to convincingly cloning a crack away in an image with random, organic patterns is to resample the Rubber Stamp's source point constantly. You may also want to vary the size of the Rubber Stamp tool, to create a more random effect in the cloned-in areas. The sample point for the Rubber Stamp is always the same pixel diameter as the cloning point. When you have a small area of suitable sample material, don't set the brush diameter of the Rubber Stamp tool too large, or your sample will include unwanted fringe areas.

Fixing Emulsion Imperfections Using the Quick Mask

The last sore spot in this picture is the portion of sky in the upper left, which has specks of emulsion imperfections in it. Note that the sky is lit from the right of the image, so it's shaded unevenly. This makes it difficult to correct using Photoshop tools when they are configured to their default settings.

One of the Rubber Stamp tool's *non*default, special properties settings is the perfect choice to tackle the messed-up sky. Before you do so, you must mask the sky from the rest of the image. Working with a mask in place is quicker because you don't have to worry about spilling color onto the roof or the leaves that intrude on the sky area. The Quick Mask feature, the subject of the next exercise, makes the preparation for this cloning a breeze.

Figure 7.9
To avoid creating patterns in cloned-in areas of an image, reset the sampling point of the Rubber Stamp tool regularly.

II

Steak 'n Potatoes Assignments

Masking Off a Selection Area with Quick Mask

Double-click on the Quick Mask button on the toolbox

Displays the Quick Mask dialog box.

Click the Masked Areas radio button in the Color Indicates box, and then click on OK

Deselects the areas covered with masking (making them impervious to any changes) when you return to Standard mode.

When you return to Standard editing mode, the *un*masked areas will be areas that you can change.

Click on the Paintbrush tool

You can use the Paintbrush tool to apply and remove masking color when in Quick Mask mode.

continues

continued

Select from the Brushes palette a small, no spread tip from the top row, and then drag the Opacity slider to 100%, and select Normal mode	Sets the Paintbrush characteristics for applying solid masking color when in the Quick Mask mode.
Click and drag over the leaves in the image that are against the sky	Applies masking to the leaves, as shown in figure 7.10.

If you accidentally paint masking into the sky, click the inverse colors icon on the toolbox and then click and drag the Paintbrush tool over the unintentionally masked area. In Quick Mask mode, the black foreground color applies a mask and a white foreground color removes the mask.

Click the Default colors icon on the toolbox when you finish masking the leaves	Restores the foreground and background colors (which, when you're in Quick Mask mode, either adds or removes a mask) to their default position.
Double-click the Line tool on the toolbox	Displays the Line dialog box.

See this book's inside back cover for tool and icon locations.

Select 4 pixels for the Line option and then click on OK	Sets the Line tool to create a line four pixels wide.
Click and drag the Line tool from the right edge of the masked leaves to the house, across the top edge of the roof	Extends the masked area to the edge where the roof meets the sky.
Click and drag from the end of the last line to beyond the photo's border	Creates the second side of a masked border, around the sky area.
Click and drag from the end of the last line to a point to the left of the roof's edge	Creates the third side of the mask border.

At this point in the exercise your screen should look like figure 7.11.

Choose the Paintbrush tool and finish enclosing the sky area with mask color	Completes the masked border around the sky area.

You now have a masked border that will prevent you from changing the unmasked areas outside of the selection area.

Click on the Standard mode button	Changes your masked areas into an active marquee border, which includes the sky and areas of the house and excludes the areas you filled with paint.
Choose **S**elect, **S**ave	Saves your masking work to a new channel in the image.

Choose **S**elect, **N**one (or press Ctrl+D)	Deselects the active marquee in the image.
Choose File, Save	Saves your work to your hard drive.

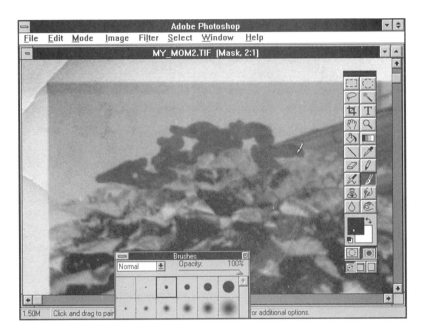

Figure 7.10
Use the Paintbrush tool in Quick Mask mode to apply or remove masking by setting the toolbox's color selection boxes.

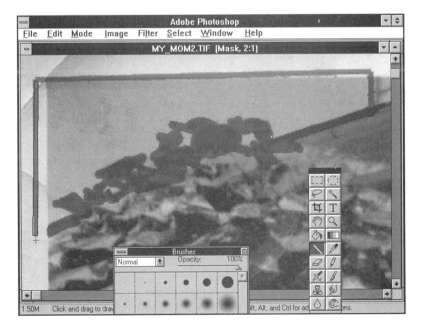

Figure 7.11
Use the Line tool to quickly Mask off large, angular areas.

When you click the Quick Mask button, your foreground and background colors are automatically set to their default black and white configuration. If you want to apply a *partial* mask, click on the color selection box foreground swatch and then pick gray from the Color Picker. The density of the gray you choose for the partial mask will be reflected in how opaque the mask becomes when you switch back to Standard mode.

If you should accidentally pick a color instead of a neutral tone, this will be represented as a shade of gray (a percentage of Opacity) while in Quick Mask Mode. How do you evaluate a color as masking material in terms of its opacity? You don't. You simply want to choose a neutral gray.

Choosing a neutral gray is easy. Instead of using the RGB or HSB numerical entry fields to the right of the color model window, use the CMYK fields. Type **0** in the C, M, and Y fields, then type in a value in the K (the black) field to give you the desired percentage for your partial mask.

Photoshop's Line tool can make quick work of the chore of selecting or masking a large, geometric area. But in the next exercise, bear in mind that your masked area is only four pixels wide, and that if you cross that part of the marquee while painting in Standard mode, you'll be painting over areas of the house. You can broaden the masked area at any time by loading the selection and then switching back to the Quick Mask mode. But if you use just a little care when cloning (and it doesn't require *that* much care), you won't have to spend time and effort increasing your "virtual drop cloth."

Pattern Fills for Retouching Sky Areas

You can use the Rubber Stamp and Paint Bucket tools to apply color and image source material as a pattern. Before you use these tools for this purpose, however, you must *sample* the pattern. The advantage of setting the Rubber Stamp tool to clone from a pattern is that a traveling crosshairs cursor isn't used to read the cloning sample areas. You do all your sampling from a constant image area that repeats a pattern that you can use to fill anything perfectly.

As the following exercise demonstrates, using a pattern is a great way to retouch a sky that has flaws like those in MY_MOM2.TIF.

Reach Up and Touch Up the Sky

Choose the Rectangular Marquee tool

The Rectangular Marquee is the only Photoshop tool you can use to define a pattern.

Click on and diagonally drag a portion of clear sky in the image

Marquee-selects the area as the pattern to use with the Rubber Stamp tool.

Make your selection as large a sample of the clear sky area as possible, as shown in figure 7.12.

Choose Edit, Define Pattern	Registers your selected area as the pattern to use with the Rubber Stamp tool.
Double-click on the Rubber Stamp tool	Displays the Rubber Stamp Options dialog box.
Choose Pattern (Non-Aligned) from the Option drop-down list, and then click on OK	Sets your Rubber Stamp tool to use the pattern that you defined as the cloning source wherever you apply the tool.

Non-Aligned means that every click and drag you make with the tool starts with an absolute, not relative, sampling point within the pattern. See the note that follows this exercise.

Choose a large tip, choose Lighten mode, and click and drag the Opacity slider to 50%	Sets the characteristics that the Rubber Stamp will now use.

The Rubber Stamp tool will now apply the pattern over any pixels in the image that are darker than those in the pattern. 50% Opacity ensures that the Rubber Stamp coverage is only partial and that the effect of patterning over the original sky area is a subtle one.

Choose Select, Load Selection	Loads the selection border that you created in Quick Mask mode in the last exercise.

The sky is a selection area, and the leaves and 4-pixel wide sides of the border created with the Line tool are masked areas (not selection areas).

Click and drag across the irregularities in the sky area	Gently replaces the flawed areas in the sky with the non-aligned pattern, as shown in figure 7.13.
Choose File, Save	Saves your work to your hard drive.

The practical difference between using an aligned and non-aligned pattern with the Rubber Stamp tool has to do with how repetitious a pattern you want to create. In retouching the sky in the last exercise, you didn't need any pattern, so you selected the Pattern (Non-Aligned) option from the Options drop-down list in the Rubber Stamp dialog box.

When you select the Aligned option, however, every time you click and drag the Rubber Stamp tool, the exact point of sampling within that pattern remains relative to the location at which you used the Rubber Stamp tool. Therefore, you have to complete the pattern "block" within a selection area in an image.

Non-aligned patterning starts its source from an absolute position within the pattern every time you click and drag. It creates a more random effect when

continues

you click and drag repeatedly over different selection areas in the image. In effect, you avoid a "pattern" effect when you choose Pattern (Non-Aligned) from the Rubber Stamp dialog box.

Figure 7.12
Use the Rectangular Marquee tool to select an area to use as a pattern.

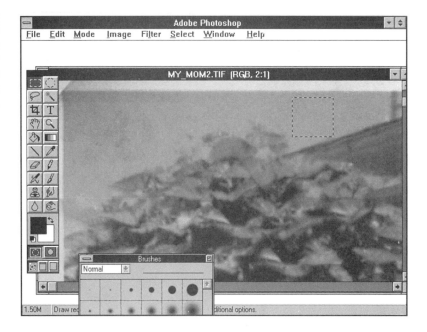

Figure 7.13
The Rubber Stamp tool clones from a pattern, eliminating the need for a traveling sample point.

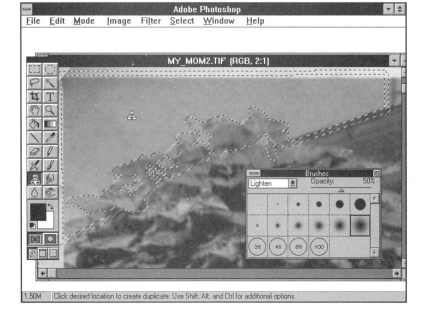

The Rubber Stamp tool is not the only tool you can use to define and use a pattern. The procedure for defining the pattern is the same, but you can also pattern in a selected area by using the **F**ill command from the **E**dit menu or the Paint Bucket tool. All these methods can use Post Script fills as source material in addition to the defined patterns you create.

The source of the pattern that you define in Photoshop doesn't have to be within your image. Photoshop installs a subdirectory called PATTERNS on your hard drive that contains patterns saved in the *.AI format (Adobe Illustrator, an encapsulated PostScript format).

If you open one of these files from the **F**ile menu, the EPS Rasterizer dialog box appears, as discussed in Chapter 18. You then can specify the size, resolution, and mode (grayscale, RGB, and so on) of the pattern. When the file opens, choose **A**ll from the **S**elect menu and then **D**efine Pattern from the **E**dit menu. You then can use the file's pattern with the Rubber Stamp tool, the Paint Bucket tool, or the **E**dit menu's **F**ill command.

By selecting the blandest, least distinctive area of the sky as a sample pattern for the Rubber Stamp tool and then setting the opacity to half-power, you can repair the damaged sky area without noticeable retouching. A large brush tip ensures adequate coverage with a minimum of strokes, which also helps to disguise your repair work. Brush strokes that are repeated more than twice or so in an area become evident, and when retouching an image, this effect obviously is not desired.

Adding a Border to Your Retouched Piece

If you followed the steps in Chapter 6 and in this chapter, you see that it's a long trail from a damaged, aging photo to a professionally restored one. Photoshop alleviates the tedium and frustration because it's a fresh medium for photo enhancing, and a powerful one as well. As shown in figure 7.14 , MY_MOM2.TIF has many fewer miles on it than before. The only thing left to retouch is the off-white, dented border of the photo.

Figure 7.14
The image looks
great, the
border... not so
great.

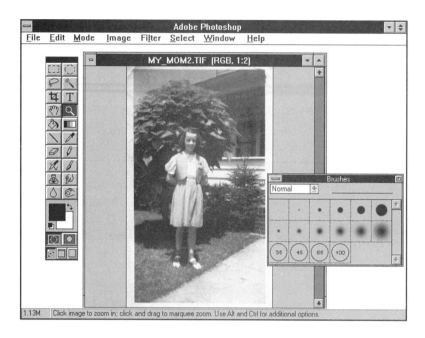

You can eliminate the rest of the dents around the border of the photo, and clean it up simultaneously, by simply deleting the border. As the following exercise demonstrates, the procedure is a quick one:

One Order of Fresh Border

Click on the Rectangular Marquee tool

This tool can create a rectangular selection area that you can use to replace the original image's border.

Click on the default colors icon

Sets the color of the foreground to black and the background to white.

Choose **File**, **S**ave

Saves the file.

You should save the file now because if you miss a step in the following process, you'll have to restore the previously saved version.

Click and drag diagonally (marquee-select) an area that contains the active area of the photo but not the "white" border around it, as shown in figure 7.15

Define this selection very precisely so that it contains absolutely no original border.

Choose **S**elect, **I**nverse (or press Ctrl + I)	Selects everything *except* the image area, so that the photo's border is selected and the retouched work is unselected.
Press the Delete key	Removes the selection of the photo's border, which is replaced by the white default background color.

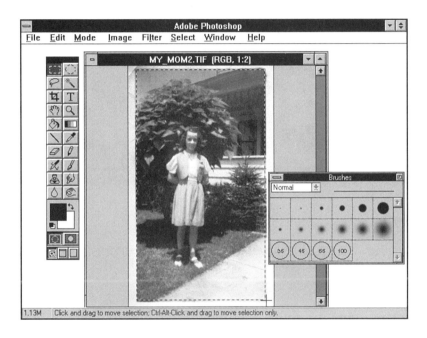

Figure 7.15
Select an area and then choose the **S**elect menu's **I**nvert command to select everything outside the original selection area.

Figure 7.16 displays the original, unretouched MY_MOM.TIF image from Chapter 6 alongside the final version of the image, which I've saved as MOM_FIN.TIF.

Saving Your Restoration and Retouching Work

At this point you should save your work as well. But first, you should remove the superfluous mask channel. Press F6 to display the Channels palette, and then click on the Channel #4 title on the palette. Then click the Channels palette's command button and choose Delete Channel from the drop-down list.

Then select Sa**v**e As from the **F**ile menu. Save your work as GIRL.TIF or something, though, because it's *my* mom, and probably not yours.

Figure 7.16
MY_MOM—three global adjustments, five tools, and a Quick Mask later.

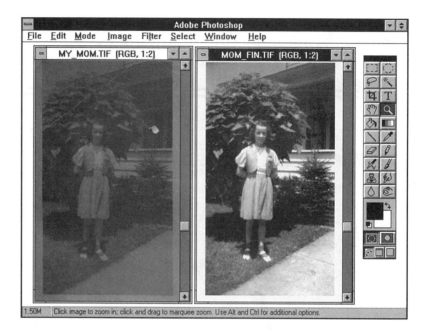

Summary

In the last two chapters, you have corrected image flaws specific to MY_MOM.TIF. You should apply the same techniques and rules, perhaps in different areas, to your own faded photographs or to your clients'. The following are some key points to keep in mind as you do so:

✔ Remember that you always need enough visual detail in an image to accurately assess its color-correction and balance. This means that you may have to make a couple of trips to the **A**djust menu for commands that affect brightness and color balance. But try to *limit* the number of changes you make to the image, with respect to both color and tonal qualities, because changes of this type *are relative to previous changes.*

✔ Try to scan an heirloom photo at the highest resolution your scanner offers, and limit the resulting file size to whatever system RAM you have divided by 3. Photoshop work requires about three times the megabytes in RAM as an image's file size. Gather as much original information about an aging photo as possible, but leave yourself enough system resources to let you actually *work* on the scan!

✔ Less is more, always. Don't push the saturation too high in an area. If you do, use the Blur tool to even out the contrast in the affected pixel region.

✔ Don't try to add detail in an image area that consists of only a few pixels. That's why the Smudge tool worked so well in blending the copy of the shutters back into the original—the shutters were an important detail when they were missing, but the detail in the image area itself contained little visual detail.

✔ Use patterns for your Rubber Stamp tool when you don't have a lot of source material to clone from.

✔ Remember to reset your tool options back to their defaults after you change them! This reminder applies to the color selection boxes on the toolbox, and especially the Dodge/Burn, and Rubber Stamp settings. If you forget to do so, you'll rudely surprise yourself when you unintentionally use the customized settings on your next assignment!

The next time you have to work with a cracked, aged photo, think twice about whipping out the transparent dyes and mending tape. Photoshop has the electronic tools that you need, and now you've got a guide.

II

Steak 'n Potatoes Assignments

Chapter Snapshot

In this chapter, you learn how to:

8

CHAPTER

Using Type in Photoshop

Part of Photoshop's ability to deliver clean, smooth text has to do with its Anti-Aliasing feature. The effect may appear subtle when you view an image at a 100% zoom, but when you select Anti-Aliasing from the Type dialog box, Photoshop places neighboring pixels of gray around type. Then, whatever you type into a picture takes on a photographic quality that blends into an image.

In this way, Photoshop treats type as a graphic. Consequently, editing text in Photoshop is a little trickier than in a word processing program (although this chapter will demonstrate a special technique for working around the trickiness). But the good news is, because Photoshop sees type as a graphic element, you can apply all Photoshop tools and filters to type the same way you can with any other part of an image. You can even mix Photoshop typography with scans of typing and graphics, and blend them into one seamless piece.

You'll find this chapter's adventures with Anti-Aliasing and the Type tool more rewarding if you first choose a 16.7-million-color driver for your monitor. So, if you aren't already running 24-bit color, now's a good time to boot it up. In this chapter, you work with color images from the companion CD, but you can also use the Type tool and Anti-Aliasing with grayscale images.

Creating a Really Hip Postcard

Everyone gets a kick out of a postcard that's been retouched to skew an original image toward the whimsical, like one a friend sent us from Mt. Rushmore, where Lincoln is wearing sunglasses and Washington is honking on a saxophone. But usually these postcards are done rather amateurishly, as though the perpetrators are still using their grade school art kit to retouch images.

For the first type-handling assignment in this chapter, you'll create a novelty postcard while you learn some new Photoshop techniques. The idea behind the postcard might be sophomoric, but the results will be nothing short of professional.

This assignment uses the file DEADEND.TIF from the companion CD. As shown in figure 8.1, the file's image is a pretty common sight: a dead end sign. You'll be changing the type on this sign to something a little more cheery. Except for a minor defect (which you'll retouch), the image is perfect for your first experiment with Photoshop's Type tool.

Figure 8.1
Road signs are perfect targets for retouching work using Photoshop's Type tool.

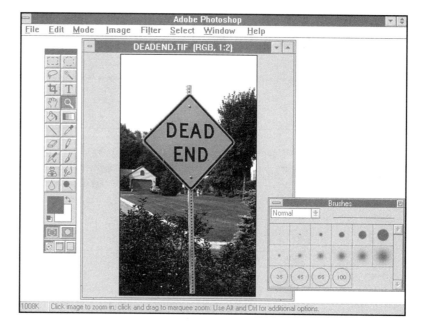

Notice that this photo didn't capture the dead end sign dead-on; that is, the sign was closer to the camera on the left edge than on the right. This makes your task a bigger challenge, but also presents an opportunity: if you can match the new lettering to the exact angle of the old lettering, you can enhance the illusion that the Department of Transportation actually posts signs with messages as stupid as the one that you'll create!

Using a Path to Define an Image Area

Before you remove the sign's type, you want to use the tools on the Paths palette to outline the border of the original text on the sign. You'll use this path as a reference later to shape the new type so that it follows the angle and slope of the original lettering.

The Path to a Dead End

Open DEADEND.TIF from the companion CD

Choose **W**indow, Show P**a**ths (or press F9)	Displays the Paths palette.
Choose the Pen tool from the Paths palette	The Pen tool creates outlines composed of anchor points and path segments.
Click once on the upper-left corner of the sign lettering	Creates the beginning anchor point for your path.
Click once on the upper-right corner of the sign lettering	Makes a corner of path segment from the first to second anchor point.
Click once on the lower-right and then the lower-left corners of the sign lettering	Makes the second and third sides of the path box around the lettering area.
Click on the upper-left corner, the first anchor point you created	A tiny circle appears next to the Pen tool cursor, indicating your click is closing the Path, with the fourth line segment connecting the anchor points.
Click on the Selection Pointer tool	The Selection Pointer tool (first button on the Paths palette) moves anchor points.
Click and drag the anchor points with the Selection Pointer tool as necessary to pre-cisely define the path box around the type	You can adjust a path segment between two anchor points by dragging one of the anchors with the Selection Pointer tool.

Notice that the path defined in figure 8.2 is not a parallelogram or a rectangle. Instead, the box cants ever so slightly in perspective—which contributes a quality of realism to this assignment.

Click on the command button on the Paths palette, and then choose Save Path from the drop-down list	Displays the Save Path dialog box with a default path name suggested in a text box.

The Save Path dialog box offers you a default name for the first path, Path 1, that you created.

Click on OK	Accepts the default path name, displays the saved path name on the Paths Palette and returns you to Photoshop's workspace.

continues

Steak 'n Potatoes Assignments

II

continued

Double-click on the Paths palette to hide it
and the path that you have drawn

Choose <u>F</u>ile, Sa<u>v</u>e As, name the   Saves your work to hard disk.
image, and save it to a directory
on your hard disk

Figure 8.2
Later you'll use the
path that you
draw as a
template for your
new type.

Removing Lettering with the Paintbrush Tool

The Rubber Stamp tool might seem like the painting tool to remove the black lettering.
However, if you used this tool, the results would be awful. In this image, you have very little
orange sign area to clone from, so if you constantly resample the limited source area for the
Rubber Stamp tool, an undesired texture effect is created and the overall image looks phony.

The sign has subtle variations in shade because the sunlight was striking it at an oblique angle
when the picture was taken. So, instead of using the Rubber Stamp tool, let's try a very simple,
painterly method for retouching the lettering.

Painting Over the Sign

Choose the Eyedropper tool	Changes the cursor to an eyedropper that you to choose a foreground color from the active image.
Click an orange portion of the sign	Selects the new foreground color.
Choose the Paintbrush tool	You'll use the Paintbrush tool to apply the foreground color.
Choose Normal Mode, a medium tip with spread, and an opacity of **100%** on the Brushes Palette	Specifies that the Paintbrush tool applies the selected color using a soft edge and total coverage.
Click and drag the Paintbrush cursor over the black lettering	Paints over the black lettering using a shade of orange identical to the part of the sign you selected with the Eyedropper.
Choose <u>F</u>ile, <u>S</u>ave (or press Ctrl + S)	Saves your work to hard disk.

Figure 8.3 shows what the image looks like as you paint over the light orange area. If you look carefully at the sign, you'll notice a slightly darker orange on the lower right. To finish painting over the lettering, you follow the same procedure as in the preceding exercise, except you resample the darker area with the Eyedropper tool before painting, so you can use this color to cover the lower area of the sign.

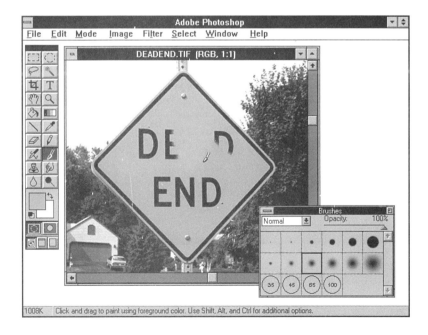

Figure 8.3
The End is near.

Use a brush with a "spread" characteristic to avoid having to blend the two slightly different shades of orange with an additional tool afterward. The two shades blend quite nicely if you join them by applying short strokes.

After all the lettering has been painted over, click on the Zoom tool and marquee-zoom in on the flawed area of the sign (see fig. 8.4). Time to do some quick touch-up work here.

Figure 8.4
A close-up view of a flawed detail.

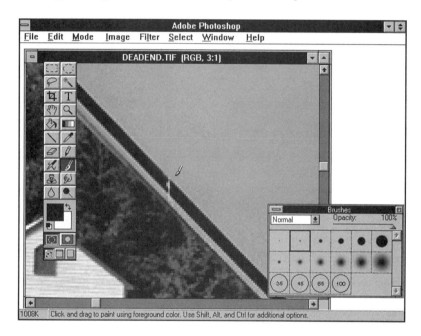

The next mini-exercise shows you how to handle some quick, minor retouching.

Reinforcing the Border

Choose the Eyedropper tool and sample a black area from the sign border

Gives you the right color for retouching the border.

Choose the Paintbrush tool and set the Brushes palette to Normal mode, 100% opacity, and the second smallest hard tip

Sets the characteristics of the Paintbrush tool for detailed retouching work.

Click and drag the Paintbrush over the sections of the black sign border that you need to fix

Choose **F**ile, **S**ave

Saves your work to hard disk.

While retouching a detail like the one shown in the last exercise, you should zoom out occasionally, not just to check the overall progress of your retouching work, but also to help relieve visual fatigue. You can saturate your eye's cones and rods while working in a close-up view, particularly if one area is a mass of one color, as is the case with this sign. Although the long-range effects aren't harmful to your eyesight, you can hinder your ability to evaluate a color accurately if you don't keep the picture moving a little. Take breaks, look out the window, change *After Dark* screen savers regularly.

You're now halfway through your assignment. Figure 8.5 shows what your DEADEND.TIF image should look like.

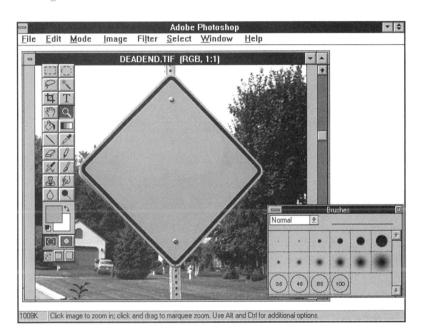

Figure 8.5
It seems like a lot of effort to say nothing. My ex-boss used to do this a lot.

You should save your work to your hard drive at this point (using a new file name) because you may want to reuse this blank sign later to apply your own slogans. After you save the image, it's time to proceed with your lettering adventure.

Measuring the Image Area for Type

It's important to measure correctly when fitting type into an image. Photoshop treats type differently than word processors do—it is entered as a graphical selection, not an editable one, as a floating selection above the background image. If you choose a wrong point size, you can't highlight and type over the typeface, change its style, or precisely adjust its size. The next exercise describes how you ensure that your type fits the image area:

Measuring with Photoshop's Rulers

Choose **F**ile, Pre**f**erences, and then Choose Units	Displays the Units Preferences dialog box, which enables you to specify how Photoshop measures things.
Click the **R**ulers Units drop-down box	Offers a selection of units that measure distance.
Choose Points from the **R**ulers Units drop-down box	Sets Photoshop's rulers to measure typeface heights, which are traditionally measured in points.
Click on OK	Applies the changes and closes the dialog box.
Choose **W**indow, Show **R**ulers (or press Ctrl+R)	Displays rulers on the edge of the image, with a Zero Origin box in the upper-left corner where the two rulers join.
Click and drag the Zero Origin box, as shown in figure 8.6, to a position where you want the new type to begin	Moves the rulers next to what you want to measure, which makes measuring accurately a lot easier.

With the point rulers in place, you can clearly see that 32-point type on two lines will fit inside the sign.

Now that you have measured the image area to fit your type, you need to select an appropriate foreground color for the new type. You always need to consider what color the type should be before clicking on the Type tool. When you click a type insertion point in an image, Photoshop sets the color attribute for the type to the current foreground color. Again, the Eyedropper tool is ideal for selecting a natural color found in the image to use as the type's color.

Selecting the Color for the Type

Click on the Eyedropper tool	Selects the tool used to pick a color from the image to use for the type.
Click with the Eyedropper on the black sign border	Sets the type color to black—not the same black as Photoshop's default black foreground swatch, but black nonetheless.
Click on the Type tool (the "T" icon on the toolbar)	Changes the cursor to an I-beam, which you can use to place text into an image.
Click the Type tool cursor in the top center of the sign	Sets the text insertion point (which specifies where the text will start) and displays the Type Tool dialog box.

Figure 8.7 shows the Type Tool dialog box. Now you see why you have to measure the available space where you want to place type beforehand—you don't enter type directly on the image.

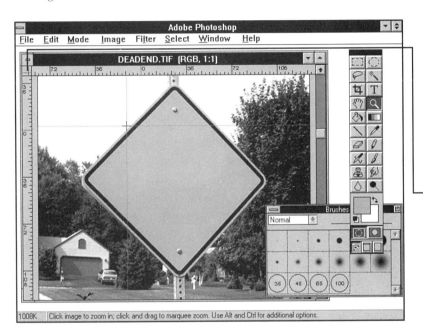

Figure 8.6
Use the vertical ruler to determine the height of the lettering; type is measured in point height.

Zero Origin box

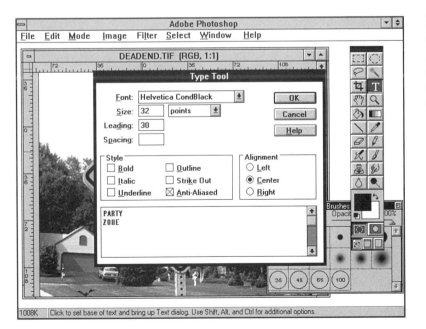

Figure 8.7
The Type Tool dialog box provides all the options for type specifications in Photoshop.

Speccing Type

The family of typeface, the weight, leading, and other typographic characteristics you'd normally assign to lettering are all chosen from the Type Tool dialog box. Here's how to specify type for the sign:

Selecting the Right Type

Click on the <u>F</u>ont drop-down box in the Type Tool dialog box | Displays a drop-down list of the typefaces installed on your PC.

You'll see in the next figures that the authors have used Helvetica Condensed Black (ITC by BitStream) for the type in this image. It's a pretty common face, but if you don't own it, use a different sans serif condensed, bold face to imitate the Department of Transportations lettering style. Arial Condensed, bold will work, for example, in this next part of the exercise:

Type **32** in the <u>S</u>ize box and click on OK | Makes each line of type 32 points tall, or a tad under a half inch.

Type **30** in the Lea**d**ing box and click on OK | Specifies the space between two lines of type, measured in points.

When using large typeface sizes, such as in this exercise, brief lines of type have maximum impact and good readability at a leading of 95 to 100 percent of their point size.

Click the **A**nti-Aliased check box | Ensures that your typeface looks clean rather than jagged.

Click on Center in the Alignment window | Centers the two lines of type relative to each other, just like the original type that you painted over earlier.

Place your cursor in the type entry field at the bottom of the dialog box | Turns the cursor into an I-beam, just like some word processing type tools.

Click, and then type **PARTY ZONE**, pressing Enter between the two words | Enters the text on two lines.

As you type, you can see your choice of typeface and style displayed in the type entry field. Make sure to use all capital letters. The Department of Transportation is authoritative, and has little regard for upper- and lowercase sign lettering.

Click on OK | Applies the settings and closes the dialog box.

Figure 8.8 shows the image after you click on OK in the Type Tool dialog box. The black type magically appears very close to our insertion point, with a marquee around every letter. The marquee indicates that Photoshop is treating the type entries as floating selections, so that you can reposition the entries until you click outside the selection area, or deselect the type.

Figure 8.8
Don't click outside the selection and blend it into the image yet, even after it's properly centered.

When you move your I-beam Type tool inside a selection area, it becomes a tiny arrow cursor. Use it to click and drag the type around as necessary until you've positioned it in the center of the sign. Do *not* click outside the selection border yet. For now, leave it as a floating selection.

Press F9 to display the Paths palette, as shown in figure 8.9. Note that the path of the original image's lettering falls inside of your new type. This discrepancy doesn't invalidate what you've done. You simply need to add an angle to the new type, specifically the angle described by the saved path you traced around the original image lettering.

Creating Perspective with Type

"PARTY" has one more letter than "DEAD" had, so you should condense the new type a bit. Although viewers tend to recognize a condensed typeface, they usually fail to notice the degree to which type is condensed. You can subtly condense your type by selecting **E**ffect from the **I**mage menu, and then choosing the Distort command, as shown in figure 8.10. A box then appears around the type that you can reshape to match the path outline, which also remains displayed. As you reshape the box, you also condense the type. The result is a wonderfully realistic, angled effect that closely matches that of the original sign lettering in the photograph.

Figure 8.9
Compare the
original text's
position to that of
the new text by
recalling the path
that you drew
around the
original text.

Figure 8.9
Compare the
original text's
position to that of
the new text by
recalling the path
that you drew
around the
original text.

Figure 8.10
The Distort
command
enables you to
adjust a selection
with the freedom
of a freehand
selection tool.

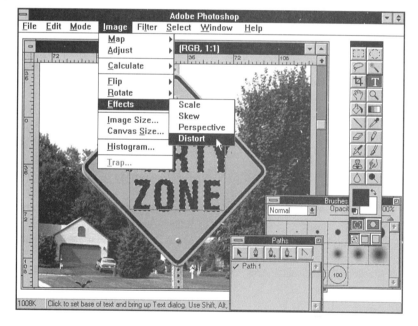

In the next exercise, you'll shape the type you entered to conform to the perspective of the
original lettering.

It's Party Time; Let's Twist

Press F9	Displays the Paths palette and also any saved paths on your image.
Choose **E**ffects from the **I**mage and then choose Distort	Displays a box in the image area that envelopes the selection area.
Click on a corner of the box around the type and then drag the corner toward the path outline	Moves the two lines surrounding the corner closer to the path lines, as shown in figure 8.11.
Repeat the preceding step with each corner until the Distort box aligns with all four sides of the Paths outline	Creates an envelope for the type that matches the angling of the original lettering.

Figure 8.11
Align the Distort box's border with the Paths outline that you previously drew.

The sign may say "PARTY ZONE," but it's not party time yet. Once you're satisfied with your changes, you need to make them permanent.

Locking Down the Party Zone

Click the center of the Distort box when it matches the Paths outline	Turns the cursor into a little gavel and "nails" the angles of distortion in place.

continues

continued

Click outside the marquee-selection borders around the lettering	Blends the floating type into place in the image.
Click on the command button on the Paths Palette	Reveals the drop-down list.
Choose Delete Path	Removes the path from the image file. You no longer need it.
Double-click on the command button of the Paths palette	Closes the Paths palette.
Choose <u>F</u>ile, <u>S</u>ave	Saves your work to hard disk.

Your image should now look like figure 8.12.

Figure 8.12
A really nice novelty postcard. Try the college market first.

From an ordinary scene, you've now created a wonderful "hyper-reality" that has commercial possibilities. The type on the sign looks completely authentic. The finished image will turn a lot of heads, especially if you use something more colorful than the phrase I've suggested here! Viewers will ask "How did you do that? Did you paint over a real traffic sign? How long were you sentenced for doing that?"

Adding Text and Graphics to a Photograph

You can use a scanner to bring a client's logo into an imaging program so that you can touch it up and use it later for a variety of purposes. For the next assignment, you have an imaginary customer, Fred Glough, who carts and hauls nuclear waste. Fred is considering having a painter reproduce his company letterhead on the side of one his trucks. But before he hires the sign painter, he wants you to show him what the truck would look like. This assignment provides an opportunity to use Photoshop's Text tool, as well as some scanned lettering and artwork, to create an image that's better seen on a monitor than driving down one of your neighborhood streets!

Refining a Scan

First, you need to clean up the scan of Fred's letterhead a little so that you can use parts of it in the image that you'll build. The letter spacing (kerning) in his letterhead is lousy. Besides, Photoshop can generate better type than the scan provides, so you'll want to replace some of the scan's type.

II

Steak 'n Potatoes Assignments

Cleaning Up Nuclear Waste

Open the image FREDLOGO.TIF from the companion CD	Displays the letterhead that you need to clean up.
Double-click on the Magic Wand tool	Displays the Magic Wand Options dialog box.
Set Tolerance to **127** pixels and then click on OK	Sets a "break point" for the Magic Wand's selection properties (see the following tip).
Click on the "E" in "FISSIONABLES"	Selects one of the letters that you'll kern.
Press Ctrl+Shift and then click the "S" in "FISSIONABLES"	Adds this letter to your selection.
Press the left arrow key repeatedly	Moves the selection one pixel to the left with each keystroke, as shown in figure 8.13.
Press Ctrl+D when the selection is in place	Deselects the selected areas—the E and the S—at their new positions.
Click on the default colors icon on the toolbox	Sets the foreground color to black and the background to white.
Click on the Eraser tool on the toolbox	Tool for removing foreground image areas, and exposing background color, which is now set to white.

continues

continued

Click and drag over the address
and telephone number areas

Erases the address and phone number
from the image.

You don't need this type in the scanned logo because you'll soon use Photoshop to replace it.

Choose **F**ile, Sa**v**e As, name the image, and
save it to a directory on your hard disk

Saves your work to hard disk.

Figure 8.13
By pressing an
arrow key, you
nudge a selection
by one pixel.

Adobe manufactures a handy utility, Adobe Streamline that can make quicker, simpler work of scanning business cards and logos to work with. Streamline is a bitmap-to-vector conversion utility that will auto-trace a TIF, PCX, or Macintosh PNT image file, and save a copy of it to an image format you can edit with a vector design program, like Illustrator, Micrografx Designer, or CorelDRAW!. Vector tracing eliminates the stairsteppy jaggedness in a bitmap image of type and graphic designs. Streamline saves the auto-trace of a bitmap to your choice of AI, DXF, or EPS file formats. Since these are vector, resolution-independent image formats, Photoshop can import them, and rasterize them to the dimensions you need.

The Magic Wand tool selects adjacent pixels in an image according to a range of 256 different tonal values (0 through 255), and by specifying different Tolerances, you can be choosy about which pixels are selected when you use the Magic Wand.

For this reason, the authors converted the FREDLOGO.TIF in the last exercise to Grayscale mode after scanning the original art at a Bitmap mode setting. Photoshop can't evaluate different pixel ranges in an image mode that only has black or white pixels.

The number 127 was arrived at for the Magic Wand Tolerance based on the reality that 128 is the midpoint (50% gray) in the tonal range the Wand can select from. Since the logo is still either black *or* white in different areas, even though it's an RGB image, a Tolerance of 127 will select everything except the black when clicked over a white area, as you did in the last exercise.

In actuality, a Tolerance value as high as 254 could have been used to select the white areas in the logo, since this setting would have selected all the tonal values in the image except one— the black. This is poor Photoshop practice, though, because whenever you resize a black and white image, or use Anti-Aliasing with a tool, Photoshop performs interpolation on the image, which places gray pixels around image edges to smooth the foreground/background transition from black to white. And a Magic Wand Tolerance of 254 would include (or exclude) these gray pixels, and you'd get fringing around a selection border.

Let 127 serve as your first choice of Tolerances when using the Magic Wand to select a black area out of a white one, and vice-versa. Then, readjust this Tolerance depending on how light or dark you've scanned an original image.

There's another way to select the white area in a black or white image that doesn't use the Magic Wand tool at all! If you create an Alpha channel for the FREDLOGO.TIF image (using the Channels palette, New Channel command), then copy the entire image to the extra channel, Photoshop will use this information to create a selection border you can call by using the **S**elect, **L**oad Selection command. The only thing you have to do before copying the image to the extra channel, is to specify Color Indicates Masked Area in the Channel Options dialog box when you create the new channel. This way, all the black areas are masked, and the white areas are selected when you Load the selection.

If this doesn't sound as quick as using the Magic Wand tool to select the white areas, it's because it's not! But it's important to remember that Photoshop usually offers more than one way to perform an imaging action.

Adding Attention-Getting Colors

FREDLOGO.TIF looks much better now and is ready for a little retouching. Before adding the logo to the image of the truck, you must ask yourself two questions:

✔ How large is the scan in relation to the available space on the truck image?

✔ How much easier would it be to color the logo before adding it to the truck?

Before adding one image to another, you should finish most of your retouching work on the image to be added *first*. This way, you have more control, and less opportunity to mess up the host image with the filters and tools that you use to apply changes to your selections.

Measuring the Logo To Fit the Truck

You need to size up the FREDLOGO.TIF scan and convert it to RGB mode so that you can add some color to it. Your first task, however, is to measure the relative sizes of both images.

Sizing Up the Images

Open FREDFISH.TIF from the companion CD	This image is the truck that will "host" the logo selection.
Choose **F**ile, Pre**f**erences, and then choose Units	Displays the Units Preferences dialog box.

You need to reset the unit of measurement because Inches, not Points (which you set in the last assignment) are the required Rulers increments for this assignment.

Click on the **R**ulers Units box, choose Inches from the Rulers drop-down list, and then click on OK	Sets Photoshop's rulers to measure in inches.
Press Ctrl+R	Displays the Photoshop rulers around the active selection.
Press Ctrl+Tab and then Ctrl+R	Toggles to FREDLOGO.TIF as the active selection and adds rulers to it.

Measure the borders of the design in FREDLOGO.TIF

Make a note on a piece of paper. You should get 3-3/8 inches.

Measure the "live space" on the truck's side in FREDFISH.TIF

Make a note of this, too. You should get a little less than 1-3/4 inches.

Choose Show **C**olors or press Ctrl+F7 from the **W**indow menu	Displays the Colors palette in your workspace, as shown in figure 8.14.
Click the minimize button on the window displaying the image of the truck	Minimizes FREDFISH.TIF.

Take a moment now to rearrange the image windows and open palettes on your screen so that your workspace is comfortable. Unless you manage this stuff prudently, your screen can get pretty cluttered.

Figure 8.14
Photoshop's rulers
provide an
accurate measure
for sizing images.

Adding Color to the Logo

Now that you've sized up the FREDFISH.TIF and FREDLOGO.TIF images, you need to change the mode for FREDLOGO.TIF so that you can add color to it.

Coloring the Logo Image in RGB Mode

Double-click the Zoom tool	Zooms your view of the active window, FREDLOGO.TIF, to a nice 1:1, 100% working size.
Choose **RGB** Color from the **M**ode menu	Changes the FREDLOGO image to a mode that enables you to add color and gradient fills.
Click on a dark orange-yellow color on the Colors palette, as shown in figure 8.15	Sets the foreground color.
Choose the Magic Wand tool, and then press Shift while clicking the white areas of the two symbols in FREDLOGO.TIF	Selects only the white areas where you need to apply a color.
Double-click on the Paint Bucket tool	Displays the Paint Bucket Options dialog box.

continues

continued

Set the Tolerance option to **127** pixels, select the **A**nti-Aliased check box, and click the Contents Foreground Color radio button	Specifies that flood-fill be constrained to the white area, none to the black, and that the fill have a smooth edge to it.
Click on OK	Returns you to the workspace.
Click the Paint Bucket cursor in the center of a selection area	Flood-fills a white selection area with the foreground color.
Continue clicking in the center of selection areas	Keeps flood-filling the white selection areas until they are all filled with the foreground color.
Press Ctrl+D	Deselects all the selected areas.
Choose **F**ile, **S**ave (or press Ctrl + S)	Saves your work to hard disk.

Figure 8.15
The Paint Bucket will completely color in a selected area when it's set to a Tolerance that includes *all* the values in the selected area.

It's not a mandate to select the areas you're going to flood fill with the Paint Bucket. But it's a really good idea to make a selection area first, and *then* fill with the Paint Bucket tool. If you're careful, you can get by without the selection borders and simply click in the center of a white area. However, if you're *not* careful, a simple misplaced mouse click can flood black areas or the background. Also, if you work with a scan where the black outlines around the areas to fill are broken, you will flood-fill an entire image. When you need to do precise work, selection borders act as Photoshop's "safety net."

Airbrushing a Van

The symbol portion of Fred's logo looks appropriate now, but the signature portion of it could use some attention. If you use the Gradient tool and select the right foreground and background colors, you can create an effect similar to those outrageous van murals you see on the interstate highways:

Gradient Filling the Logo

Move the sliders on the Colors palette so that the settings are: R158, G0, and B56	Sets the foreground color to the shade of red that you'll be using.
Click on the background color selection box on the Colors palette	Displays an outline around the swatch to indicate that it's active and can be changed.
Move the sliders so that the settings are: R20, G36, and B110	Sets the background color to a faded blue.
Choose the Magic Wand tool and then click on the black areas of the "Fred's FISSIONABLES" lettering	Selects the lettering and excludes (masks) all other areas from change.
Double-click on the Gradient tool	Displays the Gradient Options dialog box.
Set the Style option to **N**ormal, Type to **L**inear, and **M**idpoint Skew to **50%**	Sets the Gradient tool to an even, linear fill that progresses from the foreground to the background colors.
Click on OK	Confirms the settings and returns you to the workspace.
Click above the selection area and drag straight down to below it	Floods the selection area with a gradient fill from red to blue, as shown in figure 8.16.
Double-click the Colors palette's command button	Closes the Colors palette.
Choose **F**ile, **S**ave (or press Ctrl + S)	Saves your work to hard disk.

II

Steak 'n Potatoes Assignments

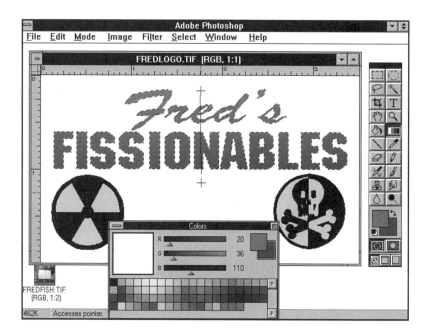

Figure 8.16
The Gradient tool
fills only the
selection area.

Resizing the Logo for the Truck

Now that you have Fred's logo in color, you need to resize it so that it fits in the clear space on the truck image. When you changed FREDLOGO.TIF to the RGB mode, you gained the ability to use Photoshop's color tools on the image. And you also gained a less obvious benefit—Anti-Aliasing.

An RGB image uses all 16.7 million colors in the PC system to perform Anti-Aliasing. At the heart of this "intelligent" gradating of neighboring pixels to achieve Anti-Aliasing is something called *interpolation*. Interpolation lets Photoshop make its best guess as to which neighboring color pixels should be shaded to form smooth transitions when you reduce or enlarge RGB image areas.

If you kept FREDLOGO as a bitmap file type, or changed it to an Indexed color image, the resizing that you do in the next exercise would produce jagged image outlines. This is because, to interpolate sizing changes, Photoshop must draw from the well of 16.7 million colors, which aren't available in Bitmap or Indexed Color image modes.

Remember those measurements that you jotted down in the exercise "Sizing Up the Images"? Have them handy because the following exercise requires some intricate math.

Fitting the Logo for the Truck

Choose **I**mage, **I**mage Size	Displays the Image Size dialog box, which enables you to alter an image's dimensions and resolution.
Type **1.625"** in the **W**idth box of the dialog box, then check the Constrain **P**roportion option but do *not* check the Constrain **F**ile Size option	Specifies the size of the image (1.625 inches), and that the image maintains height/width proportions.

You don't specify the 1-3/4 inches, you measured earlier because you need a little "breathing space" for the selection. Guesswork, trial and error, and experience can be your best guides in resizing things.

Click on OK	Confirms your settings and returns you to your workspace.
Click the FREDFISH.TIF icon at the bottom of the workspace and select **R**estore from the command drop-down list	Returns the truck image as the active image in your workspace.
Click FREDLOGO.TIF and drag its bar over the center of FREDFISH.TIF	Checks title to see that the new logo will fit nicely into the empty area on the side of the truck, as shown in figure 8.17.
Choose **F**ile, **S**ave (or press Ctrl + S)	Saves your work to hard disk.

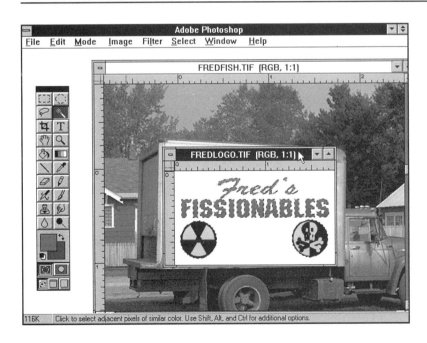

Figure 8.17
You can "eyeball" a resized image by placing the active window on top of the one you'll add the selection to.

Now that you've fitted the logo for the side of the truck, you still have some work to do before you paste the selection to the truck image:

Pasting the Logo to the Truck

Double-click on the Magic Wand tool	Displays the Magic Wand Options dialog box.
Set Tolerance option to 1 pixel and then click on OK	Specifies the narrowest value range for the Magic Wand's selection process.
Click a white area in FREDLOGO.TIF	The Magic Wand tool selects only absolute white in the image.
Choose **S**elect, Si**m**ilar	Selects all the *counters* in the type and other white areas that are non-adjacent and can't be picked up with the Magic Wand.

Counters are the typographic term for insides of "e"s, like in "Fred's."

Choose **S**elect, **I**nverse	Reverses the selection in FREDLOGO to select all type and symbols, but none of the white background.
Choose **E**dit, **C**opy (or press Ctrl+C)	Copies the selection to the clipboard.
Click the minimize button of the window displaying FREDLOGO.TIF	Changes the logo image to an icon on Photoshop's workspace and makes the image of the truck the active image.
Choose **E**dit, **P**aste (or press Ctrl+V)	Pastes your selection in the FREDFISH.TIF image.
Click and drag the selection to the center of the truck's side	Moves the selection to the area where you'll work with it.

Don't deselect the selection by accidentally clicking outside the marquee borders. Figure 8.18 shows a good example of the relative positioning that you need.

Choose **I**mage, **E**ffects, and then choose **D**istort	Creates a box around the selection.
Click on the corners of the Distort box (which look like little squares) and drag them until they're parallel to the edges of the truck's side	Skews the selection so that it appears to be at the same angle as the surface of the trucks side, as shown in figure 8.19.
Click inside the Distort box	Turns the cursor into a little gavel and "nails" the selection to the desired degree of distortion.

Don't deselect the selection yet. You continue the assignment momentarily with the floating selection.

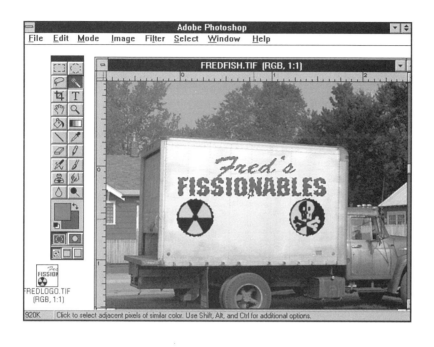

II

Steak 'n Potatoes Assignments

Figure 8.18
After you copy the selection, you can paste it to the truck image.

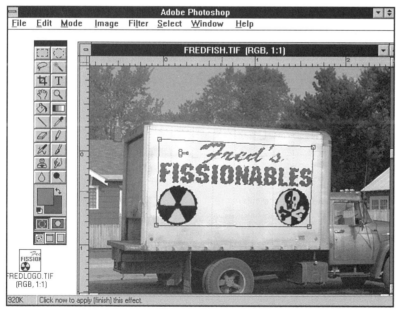

Figure 8.19
You make the image look more believable by angling the selection to conform to the angle of the truck side.

Weathering the Selection

If you've heeded the warnings in the past exercise, Fred's colorized logo is still in place as a floating selection in the FREDFISH.TIF image. Before compositing the logo into place as a final image element, you have to do something special with the floating selection.

A common problem occurs when you simply drop type or another graphic element into a scene. Instead of looking like an actual part of the scene, the element usually looks like you neatly pasted it over the image. For example, when you blend the pasted logo selection into FREDFISH.TIF, the logo will cover up the faint weathering on the side of the truck. To make this image convincing, you need to expose some of the mottling and weathering qualities of the metal side and still maintain the legibility of the logo. To accomplish this task, use Photoshop's Composite Controls feature as described in the following exercise:

Weathering the Logo

Choose **E**dit, Composite C**o**ntrols

Displays the Composite Controls dialog box.

The Composite Controls dialog box gives you enormous control over how a copied and pasted selection blends into an image, whether it's from the same image or a different one.

Set the opacity to **90%**, choose the Darken mode, check the Preview option, and then click on OK

Specifies the type of composite blend you want, then confirms selections and returns you to Photoshop's workspace.

These settings, as shown in figure 8.20, make the logo floating selection 10% transparent (or 90% opaque, so the truck's texture shows through a little). The Darken mode setting specifies that each pixel in the floating selection will only replace (paste over) a pixel in the host image if the selection pixel is darker than the corresponding host pixel it would replace.

Choose **S**elect, Fea**t**her

Displays the Feather dialog box.

The Feather dialog box enables you to blend edges of a floating selection into an image.

Type **3** for the Radius option, then click on OK

Subtly blends the selection's border into the image of the truck's side.

Press Ctrl+D

Deselects everything and locks the logo into place.

Choose **F**ile, Sa**v**e As and save this image to a directory on your hard drive by naming the file FREDFISH.TIF

Saves your work up to this point.

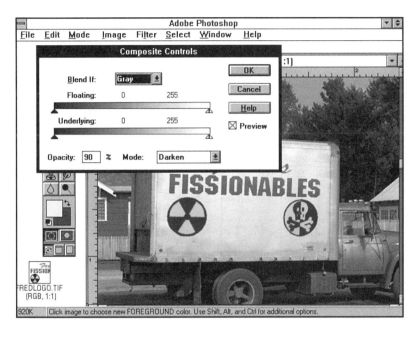

Figure 8.20
Composite Controls enable you to specify how a selection blends into an image.

As you can see, you're well on the way toward creating an image that will give Fred a good idea of what his logo will look like on the side of his truck.

Using the different modes the Composite Controls offer can produce unusual and useful effects. For example, you can use the Normal mode with varying degrees of opacity to "ghost" a selection, or to create shadows, as Chapter 15 describes in detail. Using the Darken mode in the previous exercise ensured that no value lighter than the truck's side appeared in the image after the logo was deselected and made part of the truck image.

The feathering effect provides a nice touch, but don't rely on it when you don't have a clean selection border because it will blend "impurities" into the background.

Feathering softens borders, so unless you want to paste a blurring selection into an image, make sure that you limit the number of pixels that you specify for the Feather dialog box's Radius option. Set the option for only a few pixels unless the dimensions of your image are extraordinarily large or you are trying to produce a noticeable soft-edge effect.

The Image Size dialog box shows that the FREDFISH image is about 4 by 3.5, or 613 by 512 pixels at a resolution of 150 pixels/inch. The result of using a three-pixel feathering radius was good, so calculate the ideal pixel-feathering amount accordingly for your own work.

Adding Photoshop Type to the Truck

Every good trucking company that hauls dangerous materials should advertise what its line is, so you now want to use the Text tool to embellish the side of Fred's mock-up truck. As you add this text to the image in the next couple of exercises, you'll discover several more of Photoshop's powers.

In the next exercises, you size up Fred's truck for the additional text and choose the color of the text. Keep in mind that you'll be entering the text directly, so you have to choose a good, "photogenic" color before you enter the text. Changing the color of text once it's been entered requires that you delete the present floating text selection, and start over again, so take the time to choose the right color.

Preparing Fred's Truck for Type

Choose **F**ile, Pre**f**erences, and then choose Units	Displays the Units Preferences dialog box.
Click on the **R**ulers Units drop-down list	Offers a selection of units that measure distance.
Choose Points in the **R**ulers Units drop-down list, and then click on OK	Sets Photoshop's rulers to use points to measure typeface heights, and returns to your workspace.
Evaluate how large four lines of type can be to fit under Fred's logo	

About 50 points of space are blank, so to include some leading, 10-point type seems ideal.

Click on the foreground color selection box on the toolbox	Displays the Color Picker.
Type the following color values and then click on OK: **R187**, **G37**, **B22**	Creates a "weathered" red color.

Not only is this approach to setting color values quicker than displaying the Colors palette for a one-time use, it also clutters up your screen less.

Now that you've sized up the space available on the side of Fred's truck and selected your color, it's time to enter the type:

Adding Type to the Side of the Truck

Click the Text tool and then click an insertion point on the truck image

Displays the Type Tool dialog box.

Choose HelveticInserat from the **F**ont scroll box, type **10** points for the **S**ize setting and **10** points for the Lea**d**ing, choose the **C**enter radio button in the Alignment field, and check the **A**nti-Aliased option in the Style field, as shown in figure 8.21

Specifies a size of type that will fit nicely on the truck's side. If you don't own this typeface, use a condensed sans serif one that's similar, like Arial Narrow.

Place your cursor in text field at the bottom of the dialog box and type the following, pressing Enter at the end of each line:

Specifies the text to enter into the FREDFISH image, as shown in figure 8.22.

`ISOTOPES`

`REACTORS`

`SHIELDING`

`CALL 1-800-MELTDOWN`

Click on OK

Returns you to the image, with the designated text in the foreground color as a floating selection.

Click on the floating text and drag it into position under the logo

Don't deselect the floating text yet.

Choose **E**ffects from the **I**mage menu, and then choose Distort

Creates a Distort box around the floating text.

Click the Distort box's corners and drag them to match box's angle to truck side

Skews the selection so that it appears to be at the same angle in the image as the side of the truck, as shown in figure 8.22.

Click inside the Distort box

Turns cursor into a gavel and "nails" the text into its distorted angle.

Don't deselect anything yet.

Figure 8.21
You can center multiple lines of text with the Type Tool dialog box.

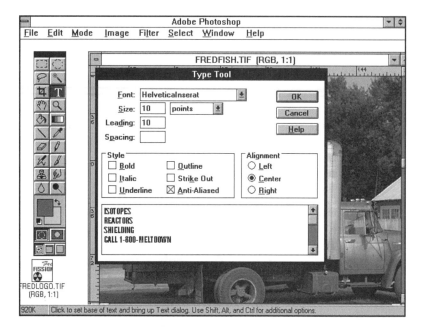

Figure 8.22
Use the edges of the top and sides of the truck's back as guidelines for the Distort command's boundary box.

Weathering the Paint

You already know half of the formula for making the text appear as though it's actually painted on the truck's side. The Composite Controls enable you to vary the degree of the floating text's opacity, so that some of the truck side's details can show through.

What a lot of folks overlook when using Photoshop's Type tool to place text on an image, is that the color of the text is usually too intense to look realistic. Fortunately, Photoshop keeps a selection active which enables you to refine the color, as long as you don't accidentally deselect the type selection along the way.

After you have chosen a basic color for the text, as you did in the exercise "Preparing Fred's Truck for Type," you can fine-tune the color so that it looks a bit more consistent with the rest of the paint on this early-model buggy. The following exercise shows you how:

Fading Text

Choose **E**dit, Composite C**o**ntrols	Displays the Composite Controls dialog box.
Set the opacity to **97%** and choose the Normal mode, and then click on OK	Defines the settings for the text selection.

The opacity setting leaves the text selection just a tad short of total opacity so that the truck's texture is evident. You use Normal mode because no portions of the lettering are lighter than the truck's color.

Choose **S**elect, Hide **E**dges (or press Ctrl+H)	Hides the edges of the text selection so that you can see what you're doing.
Choose **I**mage, **A**djust (or press Ctrl+U)	Displays the Hue/Saturation dialog box.
Move the Saturation slider to –5 and the Lightness slider to –6, as shown in figure 8.23	Makes the red color of the floating text selection less intense (desaturated) and bright.

Photoshop performs the desaturation by replacing some of the selection's color with an equivalent density of gray component.

Click the Preview option check box if it isn't checked now	Lets you see active changes in the image.
Click on OK when you're happy with the color in the active image	Accepts the changes and returns to your workspace.
Press Ctrl+D	Deselects the text selection and makes it a part of the truck image.
Choose **F**ile, **S**ave	Saves your work to this point to your hard drive.

Figure 8.23
The Hue/
Saturation dialog
box enables you
to vary the tone of
a selected area.

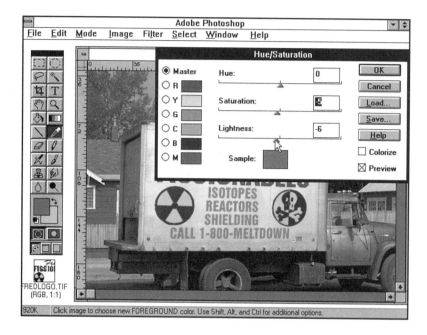

Viewing the Final Image

You're done! To look at the final image, click the window mode button (which displays a full-screen image view) at the bottom-right of the toolbox. Then press Tab to clear the toolbox and palettes from view. Your screen should now look like figure 8.24. You can get the toolbox back (which has the controls for the window modes!) by pressing Tab again. Think of the Tab key as another one of Photoshop's toggling functions.

You're now finished with Fred's truck. He likes what he sees, so he's now looking for a sign painter who can't read English.

You can use text generated with the Type tool in the same manner as any other graphical selection in Photoshop. It's because the text you type *is* a graphic, which you can't edit as you would with text typed using a word processor. But this also means that you can use the Distort command as well as filters, effects, channels, and any of the other tools with the type you create in an RGB mode image.

Figure 8.24
The finished piece
in the Full-Screen
Display Mode.

Summary

Besides getting familiar with the Text tool in this chapter, you've experienced how Photoshop's features integrate with each other, which makes creating complicated, photo realistic effects much simpler. The inter-relationship of Photoshop's features lets you achieve a *subtlety* in your work that's not available in other image-editing software.

For example, you didn't go overboard with the opacity setting in the Composite Controls, and you chose colors for the logo and text that might seem a little boring on the surface. This is because many times you want to create effects that blend into their surrounding subject matter, rather than leap out of it.

One of the keys to successful image editing is to match extra material to an image carefully so that the extra material doesn't draw extra attention. Let the idea speak, not the effect.

In Chapter 9, the spotlight is on Photoshop's Rubber Stamp tool. It's probably the funnest of all Photoshop tools to use because you paint a selection with *another* section of an image, rather than just a plain color. In Chapter 5, you took the Rubber Stamp for a test drive, but now it's time to apply this tool toward some very powerful image-editing purposes. In short, you'll correct some awkward, everyday photographic shortcomings by Rubber Stamping them out!

Chapter Snapshot

In this chapter, you learn how to:

9

CHAPTER

Stamping Out Photo Errors

Many of the exercises in this book use the Rubber Stamp tool to retouch little bits and pieces of an image that are flawed or damaged. But sometimes in your imaging work the Rubber Stamp tool moves out of the wings and into the footlights as the star!

As you've seen so far, the Rubber Stamp tool copies image information from one place and applies it to another. But the tool also has some special properties that make it much more versatile than you've seen so far. This chapter shows you two occasions where an understanding of the tool's properties and a technique that takes advantage of the special properties let you accomplish something that no other effect or filter can. On many occasions, the Rubber Stamp tool is the only one you'll use for *all* retouching work within an image.

Rubber Stamping a Portrait

Portrait photography is big business. Every department store and photo-portrait gallery offers special deals on packages for the family. They make a marginal profit by assembly-line photofinishing the film, which leaves little or no opportunity for retouching a blemish or other flaw in an image.

As you realize by now, no image is etched in stone when it's a digital sample. A larger-than-life mistake has been made in a portrait photo you'll be working with, to serve as an assignment on how to go about correcting a specific type of image. My brother Dave agreed to put a bandage on his forehead, as an example of something unwanted on the skin of the subject in a portrait. The bandage is a metaphor for blemishes, unwanted hair, or any number of a subject's imperfections in a picture.

Start with a Small Cloning Sample

In the next exercises, you concentrate on developing a technique to use with the Rubber Stamp tool. Open OUCH!.TIF from the companion CD, and you'll see the bandage-marred portrait shown in figure 9.1. Yes, the bandage is oversized, but because this assignment is larger than life, you'll master some techniques that will make your *own* assignments a breeze by comparison.

Figure 9.1
The bandage represents a skin flaw that you may find in a portrait image.

The big bandage on Dave's forehead doesn't leave much unblemished source material for you to use as a replacement for the bandaged area. Therefore, you'll start by selecting a small, unblemished area with the Rubber Stamp tool and use that area to build a larger area that you can continue to sample from. The trick is to work on this area with care and an observant artist's eye, to make sure that the retouched area of the photo looks natural and not ineptly retouched. To produce good results, don't tackle this problem area dead-on. Working with the Rubber Stamp tool from the outside edge of the bandage inward helps you preserve the continuity between the original forehead areas and the cloned areas that will cover the bandage.

Cloning To Build Up the Source Area

File, Open OUCH!.TIF from the companion CD if you haven't done so already.

Click on the Zoom tool, and then click and drag diagonally to define an area around Dave's forehead	Marquee-zooms to a higher resolution of the area.
Marquee-zoom a second time if at first you don't get a 2:1 resolution.	
Double-click on the Rubber Stamp tool icon on the toolbar	Displays the Rubber Stamp Options dialog box.
Set Option to Clone (aligned) and then click on OK	Sets the Rubber Stamp tool to its default properties, in case you didn't reset them after a previous exercise.
Choose a medium tip from the center row on the Brushes palette, Normal mode from the drop-down list, and 100% Opacity	Sets the characteristics of the Rubber Stamp tip for your first cloning maneuvers with this image.
Press Alt while clicking on an area in the center of Dave's forehead between the bandage and his eyebrows	Sets the point where the traveling crosshair cursor starts sampling source material.
Click and drag straight up with the Rubber Stamp tool, starting at the bottom edge of the bandage and stopping before the cloning-source crosshair cursor reaches the point where you first started cloning	Removes a small area of the bandage and replaces it with a clone of Dave's unbandaged forehead area, as shown in figure 9.2.
Press Alt while clicking to the left of your first cloning work, again halfway between the bandage's bottom edge and Dave's eyebrow	Sets a new sample source for the Rubber Stamp tool.
Click and drag from the bottom edge on the bandage straight up, stopping before the sampling crosshair cursor reaches the point where you started clicking and dragging	Removes still more bandage area and replaces it with the sampled skin area.
Choose File, Save As and save the file as OUCH!.TIF to a directory on your hard disk	Saves your work up to this point to your hard disk.

Figure 9.2

Don't let the cross-
hair cursor move
into the bandage
area, or you'll be
using it as source
material with the
Rubber Stamp
tool.

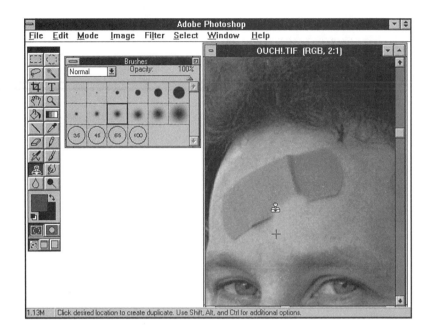

Figure 9.2

Don't let the cross-
hair cursor move
into the bandage
area, or you'll be
using it as source
material with the
Rubber Stamp
tool.

Chemical photo retouchers often make a fundamental mistake when handling an assignment like this one. They usually use an airbrush with a semitransparent dye to brush in an area like the one that you're retouching. Besides having to "guesstimate" the exact shade of the skin tone, this process usually airbrushes out *desired* visual information like freckles and pores.

When you use the Rubber Stamp tool, you paint not only the exact fleshtone but also the subtleties of the skin itself. Texture *and* visual content are cloned into this area, so that it looks as though the bandage is vanishing rather than being covered up.

Don't Make Cloning Obvious

The hardest part of this retouching assignment is to avoid creating *patterns* within cloned-in areas. When you lack a decent-sized, clear area to sample source material from, keep the following three tips in mind:

✔ Keep resampling from different areas that have the same tonal value when you use the Rubber Stamp. Frequent resampling helps you avoid creating obvious, repetitious patterns that tend to develop when you repeatedly use the same small sample.

✔ For most dimensional surfaces, the brightness and color varies. Use your eye to match the source and the cloning area for changing values.

✔ Reset your brush size as necessary. The Rubber Stamp sampling source point and the tip of the Rubber Stamp tool are both set to the same relative size. When working from a small sample area, using a small brush tip makes the traveling sample cursor take its samples from a smaller area. Use short strokes and change the tip sizes

frequently—this helps randomize a cloned-in area, which in turn keeps patterning out of the picture.

Cloning in the Right Direction

In the preceding exercise, you moved your Rubber Stamp strokes upward in a vertical direction for a very good reason: Dave's forehead is lit from the left, so the gradual shading of his forehead is vertical. If you made a horizontal stroke, you would clone a different shade of fleshtone into an area, and then the portrait would be better off with the bandage still in it!

Be patient when working with the Rubber Stamp tool. Many artists use it as though it's an instant cure-all for bad photography, but it's not. It's a tool, like any other one in Photoshop, and you need to build up your experience using it in order to master it.

The objective of the last exercise was to work up from the bandage's bottom edge with the Rubber Stamp tool. After you have a fair amount completed on the left of the bottom edge, it's time for you to start over from the *top* edge and work down, as you'll do in the following exercise:

Cloning Toward the Center of the Bandage

Press Alt while clicking as close as possible to the top of Dave's hairline above the far left of the the bandage	Sets a sample point for the Rubber Stamp tool.

Be careful not to sample too close to any hair, or you'll clone hair in where there definitely shouldn't be!

Click on just above the top edge of the bandage, and then drag down, stopping before the sampling crosshair cursor reaches your initial cloning point	Fills in the left part of the top of the bandage with samples of skin tone, as shown in figure 9.3.
Press Alt while clicking just below Dave's hairline to the right of your last sampling point	Samples a different shade of skin tone, to use to fill in another portion of the bandage area.
Click and drag down into the bandage portion, stopping when the sampling crosshair cursor reaches the first point in your stroke	Restores more forehead area.

If you feel like you're getting into an artist's role with this exercise, it's because you *are*! It takes *skill* to fit the right areas in the bandage area. But if you think the resampling isn't shaping up flawlessly at this point, don't worry; you haven't gotten to the finishing touches on the piece yet. Proceed with patience.

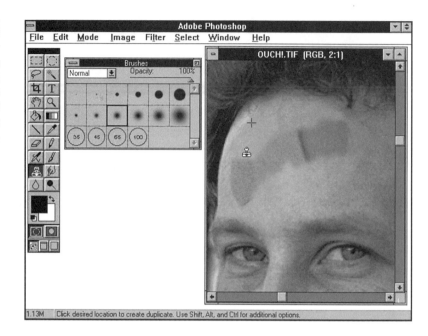

Figure 9.3
Resample your Rubber Stamp source area each time you move into a different shade of skin tone.

Bigger Brush, Looser Strokes

You've gained a lot more forehead area to sample from now, and you can put it to good use. You'll notice that after all these vertical cloning strokes, there's more skin tone in the overall area. It's a combination of original image blended with your cloning strokes. This means that you can now increase the size of the Brushes tip for the Rubber Stamp and polish off what remains of the bandage quicker.

If you've made the small, vertical strokes with the Rubber Stamp tool recommended in the preceding exercises, you'll notice that the shading on Dave's forehead is nice and even, with no cloned-in areas clashing with the original image areas. At this point, you can relax a little with these vertical strokes and combine a little lateral action with these last, large strokes. Use your eye to determine how best to clone in different shades of sampled skin tones. Dave's forehead isn't *perfectly* lit from left to right, so just follow the general flow of the lighting in the remainder of the bandage that needs covering up. In the next exercise, you'll remove the rest of the bandage from Dave's face.

Tearing Off the Last of the Bandage

Click on the second-to-last tip from the middle row of the default Brushes tip settings

Specifies a new size for sampling and cloning with the Rubber Stamp tool.

Press Alt while clicking on the Rubber Stamp tool in the area that you retouched in the first exercise	Samples an area that is a blend of the original and cloned image areas.

The size of this area has been expanded, so you can sample it with a larger Brushes tip.

Click and drag up and around into the remaining bandage area	Removes large portions of the bandage as shown in figure 9.4.
Press Alt while clicking above the bandage's remains on the upper left of Dave's forehead	Sets a new sample point for the Rubber Stamp tool.
Click and drag down and around the remains of the bandage to the left of Dave's forehead	Removes the left portion of the bandage.
Continue resampling in different tonal ranges, clicking and dragging into areas of the remaining bandage where the bordering skin tones match your sample point	Replaces the bandage remains with a combination of original and previously cloned-in areas.

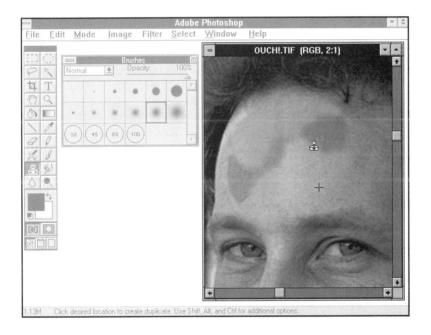

Figure 9.4
Now you can sample areas according to their tonal value instead of sampling only the original image area.

Pretty amazing, isn't it? You've used only *one* of Photoshop's tools to convincingly remove an oversize bandage from a portrait photo, and Dave didn't complain once.

Blur Surface Details

You'll want to add one final touch to the Rubber Stamp work that you've done. If you take a close look at your own skin, you'll notice that it's uneven; pores are distributed randomly, as are freckles. Because the formerly bandaged area of Dave's forehead is now covered over with cloned samples and even second-generation samples, the prominence of the pores and other skin characteristics are evenly distributed and are now visually wrong.

The Blur tool is great for softening the contrast that occurs when the grayscale component of two areas varies significantly. You can use the Blur tool to disguise the edges of an area that's been pasted over a background, but the tool also comes in handy (if used prudently) when you need to remove visual detail.

The texture of the skin on Dave's forehead in the photo looks a bit artificial because it has consistent detail, unlike natural skin. The following exercise uses the Blur tool to correct this problem.

The Rubber Stamp, Smudge, Blur/Sharpen, and Dodge/Burn tools belong to the editing, or modifying, family of Photoshop tools. Because they aren't paint-application tools, the foreground/background color selection box values don't apply when you use these editing tools.

When you choose the Darken, Lighten, or other mode from the Brushes palette to set a characteristic for these editing tools, these color characteristics are "built in" to your editing operation. In other words, to use the Darken mode effectively with the Blur tool, you have to click in an area where the values are darker, and then drag to a lighter area. The Blur tool then forces the grayscale value of the lighter color pixel toward that of the darker pixel you originally clicked over when you started your stroke.

So remember that while using the editing tools in any mode other than Normal, when you click an area, you select the color value that you're starting *from*; when you drag *into* another area, you change the color value of those pixels.

Final Touches

Click on the Blur/Sharpen tool on the toolbox	Chooses the Blur/Sharpen tool used in this exercise.

The Blur tool is the default button on your Photoshop toolbox. If you've changed the default prior to this exercise, double-click on the tool icon on the toolbar, and select Blur instead of Sharpen as the **T**ool option.

Choose the Brushes tip that is third from the left in the second row, choose Darken mode from the drop-down list, and set Opacity to **100**%	Sets the characteristics of the Blur tool.

The Darken mode sets the Blur cursor to affect pixels that are lighter than the pixels you first clicked on when you started a stroke with the Blur tool.

Click and drag in a circular motion over an area you have cloned in, but don't overdo it	Reduces the contrast in a cloned area to blur the skin details a little, as shown in figure 9.5.
Continue clicking and dragging other areas with the Blur tool as necessary	Reduces the detail in the forehead area.

Stop applying the tool after using it over three or four different areas. *Don't* ruin the entire focus of the forehead by blurring the entire area.

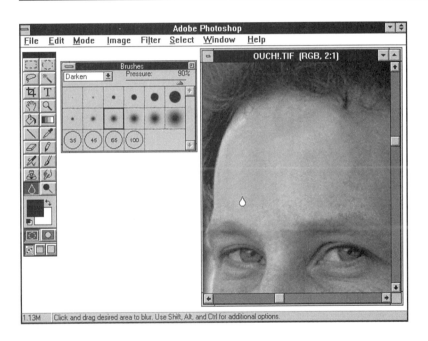

Figure 9.5
Use the Blur tool sparingly to fade image detail in the forehead area.

II

Steak 'n Potatoes Assignments

Figure 9.6 shows the image after completing the retouching work. You have now taken an obviously flawed area and corrected it! If you can successfully remove an object this large from a critical area in a portrait, imagine how easily you can erase a minor skin blemish in an otherwise perfect image!

Figure 9.6
You've removed
the bandage, and
left no scar!

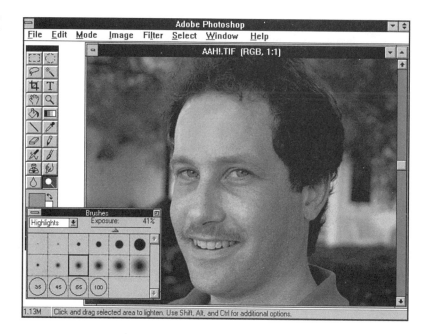

The Human Element in Retouching Work

Correcting a problem area in an image's composition is no different than fixing a problem that's the result of damaged photographic emulsion, or even a bad scan: you still must use patience and your own judgment. No Photoshop tool estimates and replaces what *would have been* in a damaged or missing area. However, with the Rubber Stamp tool, you can replace damaged areas by using samples from pixels that neighbor the area or from other complementary areas.

But there *is* a difference between filling an area arbitrarily and using Rubber Stamp strokes judiciously. It's called *technique.* Technique marks the difference between someone who simply works with a computer, and one who uses a PC as a part of his or her craft. If you're serious about imaging, you'll get out of it what you put into it. Photoshop makes it easy, but you alone make it an art.

Taking Photoshop Outdoors

If you thought removing a large bandage from a forehead was a big assignment, how do you feel about re-seeding a lawn now? The image TOYSET.TIF on the companion CD is of a wonderful children's playground. It's a scene with bright, primary-colored toys, a red slide, a lush forest background—and the lawn looks as though some four-year-olds use it for motocross practice or something.

If you need a picture of a house that's up for sale, and the season's spoiled the yard, this next assignment's for you. In fact, it's for *anyone* who wants to enhance an outdoor image that's been marred by nature *or* man.

Pick Your Tools Before Digging In

The TOYSET.TIF image on the companion CD looks a little rough around the edges; after all, kids play on grass, and this is a *play*ground. Because of the many scattered, exposed areas of earth, a cursory assessment of this photo would give a big thumbs down on its retouchability.

Fortunately, random, natural, organic textures, like grass, lend themselves to cloning with the Rubber Stamp tool quite well. As long as an area has a grassy texture, no one would ever spend the time picking out which one, or two, or a thousand blades of grass have been cloned in.

To do the retouching for this assignment, you'll depend quite heavily on the Rubber Stamp tool. But you'll also learn how using the pattern option with both the Rubber Stamp and the Paint bucket tools can make renovating this chewed up lawn a lot simpler. Just as with Dave's forehead, you first want to build up a decent-sized source area to do the initial cloning from, and then work on other cloning sources as the assignment progresses.

Throughout this assignment, pay careful attention to the shading in the areas that you clone over with the Rubber Stamp tool. Let's begin with a shaded area in the image. You need to create a small area that you can use as a cloning source for the first part of your assignment.

Finding a Little Shade

Open the TOYSET.TIF image from the companion CD	
Marquee-zoom to a 2:1 viewing resolution over the shadow of the children's slide	This is the first area to be worked on in the image.
Click on the Rubber Stamp tool	In its default setting of Clone (aligned), the tool can be used for straight cloning from image areas.
Click on the second tip from the left in the middle row on the Brushes palette, and select Normal mode from the drop-down list and set the Opacity to **100**%	Sets the characteristics for the Rubber Stamp tool to sample and clone small, soft-edged areas.
Press Alt while clicking on the Rubber Stamp tool on a shaded area of grass that is just above a section of barren ground	Sets the source point for your cloning work.

continues

continued

Click and drag over the barren ground area	Replaces the barren ground area with the shaded grass source.
Continue clicking and dragging until you have an even area of shaded grass that's about 1 by 1/2 inch, as shown in figure 9.7	Builds up a sample area to be used by the Rubber Stamp tool.
Click on the Rectangular marquee tool	In addition to its regular selection properties, you can use this tool to define a pattern.
Marquee-select the 1 by 1/2-inch perfectly shaded grass area that you cloned in the last step, as shown in figure 9.8	Specifies the area to be used as a pattern fill.
Choose **E**dit, **D**efine Pattern	Sets a repeating source area that can be used with the Paint Bucket or Rubber Stamp tool.
Choose **F**ile, Sa**v**e As; save the file to a directory on your hard drive; and name it **TOYSET.TIF**	Saves the work to your hard drive.

Figure 9.7
Use the Rubber Stamp tool to build up a sizable portion of perfect image area that you can sample.

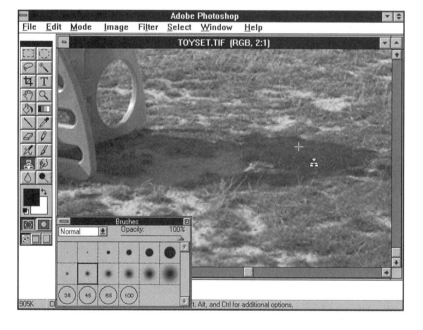

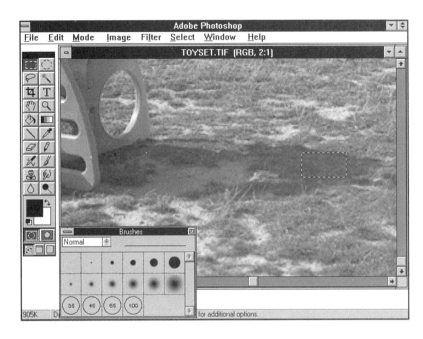

Figure 9.8
Use the Rectangular Marquee tool to select an area that you want to define as a pattern source.

When setting up a pattern, you should avoid sampling areas that display "character." For instance, if you marquee-select an area that includes a rock, you'll wind up with a pattern of the repeating, telltale rock everywhere you fill a selection area in.

Keep both pattern source areas *and* areas you use for the *other* Rubber Stamp options free from distinctive visual content. Instead, try to capture texture that you can weave into the image without drawing much attention.

Putting a Pattern in Its Place

Now that you have defined a pattern, you need to define the area that it will go into. It's ridiculous to try using the Lasso tool to neatly define all the shaded exposed earth in this image. Instead, you'll use the Quick Mask mode and the Paintbrush tool to mask the dirt areas. Photoshop will create selection areas from the masked areas when you click back to Standard mode. Then the fun begins!

Remember that a pattern consisting of *shaded* grass is loaded now. This means you want to define areas with Quick Mask that are *shaded* areas of exposed earth.

Masking a Selection Area

Click on the Paintbrush tool	The tool used for applying/removing Quick Mask in this exercise.
Set the Brushes palette for Normal mode and **100%** Opacity, and click on the brush tip that's third from the left on the top row	Sets the characteristics of the Paintbrush tip you'll use to apply the Quick Mask.
Double-click on the Quick Mask button	Displays the Mask Options dialog box.
Click the Selected Areas radio button in the Color Indicates field, and then click on OK	This doesn't change the way you apply Quick Mask to the image; it just makes the areas you paint over *selection areas* instead of masked (protected) areas when you switch back to Standard mode.
Click on the default colors icon	Sets your foreground color to black (applying Quick Mask) and the back ground to white (removing Quick Mask).
Click and drag in shaded, barren areas in the image	Applies Quick Mask to the areas that you paint over, as shown in figure 9.9.

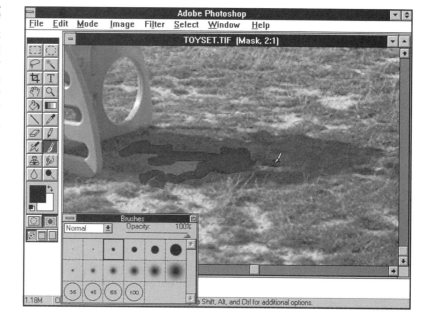

Figure 9.9
Use the Mask Options dialog box whenever you want to define either selection areas or masked areas.

Remember that, unlike the Pencil tool, the Paintbrush tool doesn't have a hard-edge characteristic. But even with a minimal to no-spread characteristic setting, the Paintbrush still has a fade-out distance, that creates a soft-edged stroke. This means that the selection area borders based on your Quick Mask work will have imperfect, soft edges around the shaded, exposed dirt areas you selected. This works to your advantage because you *don't want* a perfect selection area. You're painting grass onto grass, and unless you want this image to look like a putting green, it *should* include some flaws in its basic texture. In other words, relax a little with this assignment. Don't strive for perfectly masked areas, and your retouched image will actually look the better for it!

Pattern-Filling a Selection Area

Now that the area is "prepped," it's time to explore one of the real conveniences of electronic retouching: the pattern fill. For this exercise, you'll set the Rubber Stamp tool to the Pattern option. After this brief exercise, you'll be able to evaluate some of the benefits and disadvantages of pattern-filling an area.

Using the Rubber Stamp To Pattern-Fill an Area

Double-click on the Rubber Stamp tool	Displays the Rubber Stamp Options dialog box.
Choose Pattern (non-aligned) from the Option drop-down list, and then click on OK	Sets the Rubber stamp tool to sample from the pattern that you defined earlier, and to apply that pattern from the same relative point in the pattern each time that you click and drag.
Click on the Standard mode button	Changes the Quick Mask area into an active selection area that can be affected by changes you specify.
Click and drag in one of the selection areas with a stroke less than 1 inch long	Fills in the area with a pattern sample of the shaded grass that you defined earlier, as shown in figure 9.10.
Click another area with the Rubber Stamp and drag it for a stroke longer than 1 inch	Fills in the selection area again with the same pattern, yet this time a hard edge appears in your stroke.

The hard edge appears because you've reached the edge of the pattern sample. You should avoid making strokes longer than the size of your pattern sample in your own work.

Continue clicking and dragging until you cover all the selection areas	Fills in the barren ground spots with a pattern fill of shaded grass.
Choose Select, None (or press Ctrl+N)	Deselects the marquee areas.
Choose File, Save	Saves your work to hard disk.

Figure 9.10
Rubber Stamping from a pattern eliminates the need to watch where your trailing sample crosshair is wandering off to!

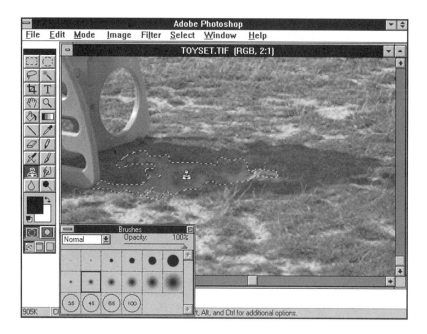

The Pattern Fill option for the Rubber Stamp tool makes quick work of filling in selection areas with the same patterned texture. You have to remember to periodically redefine the pattern you use, though. Otherwise, you won't be able to fill in areas of the image that have different *shades* of grass.

The problem that you encounter with the pattern fill—the hard edge of the Rubber Stamp strokes—is due to the fact that this is a pattern, and patterns come to an edge, and then they repeat.

One solution to avoiding pattern fill edges is provided in the Adobe Photoshop *Beyond the Basics* manual that shipped with version 2.5 for Windows. "Tiling Patterns" is a handy technique to learn after you've had some experience, and you have a need to create large, continuous pieces of texture.

In the next exercise, you'll fix any edges in the pattern fill you applied in the last exercise. The image should have only two or three tiling edges, depending on how long your strokes were when you filled in the selection areas.

Removing Pattern Edges

Double-click on the Rubber Stamp tool

Displays the Rubber Stamp Options dialog box.

Choose Clone (aligned) from the Option drop-down list and then click OK	Sets the Rubber Stamp tool to the default, regular operation of cloning from a source area.
Choose Lighten mode on the Brushes palette drop-down list	Sets the Rubber Stamp tool to only apply cloned material that's lighter than the background area where you click and drag.
Press Alt while clicking an area, at the extreme right of the shaded area where you did no pattern filling	Specifies the source sampling point for the Rubber Stamp tool.
Click on a pattern edge and drag with a small stroke	Blends the pattern edge into the rest of the grass, as shown in figure 9.11.
Repeat the last step until all the edges are gone	Completes the retouching of areas that were filled, yet marred by patterning.

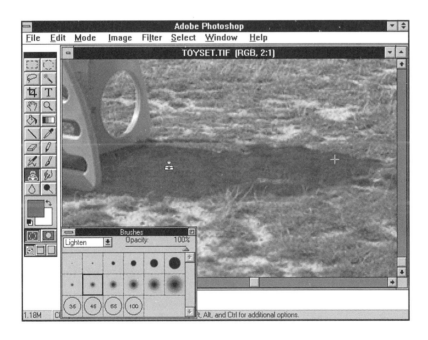

Figure 9.11
To blend in pattern edges, use the Rubber Stamp tool's default setting, Clone (aligned).

In the last exercise, there is a reason for setting the Brushes palette mode to Lighten. The setting brings out a little more texture to the shaded area of grass as you clone over the edge. If you had used Darken or Normal mode for your cloning, the area would take on a monotonous, detail-lacking appearance, and would tend to look phony. Using the Lighten mode for one or two brief strokes isn't a big detail in the overall scheme of the picture, but it's a good investment of one or two moments to help enhance the overall image.

Other Techniques for Different Image Areas

The pattern fill that you used in the last exercise is now worthless because there aren't any more areas in the shade in which to use it. So, it's time to resample a different part of the image—this time, the brightly lit parts.

You can sample an area for patterning from any part of an image to use in filling in other areas. So, let's scout for some green that will fit in with this image, and then put some Quick Mask over the dirt spots to select them for the pattern fill.

Always define a pattern in Standard mode *before* painting masks. When you're in Quick Mask mode, you can define only foreground black and background white as patterns, whether that's your intention or not.

Resampling a Pattern

Double-click on the Zoom tool	Zooms out to a 1:1 viewing resolution of the TOYSET.TIF image.
Click on the Hand tool, and then drag the cursor in the image all the way up and to the left	Scrolls your view in the active image window to reveal the bottom-right corner of the TOYSET.TIF image.
Click on the Rectangular Marquee tool, and then in the bottom corner of the image, marquee select as large a grass-covered area as you can, as shown in figure 9.12	Samples the pattern to be used next.
Choose **E**dit, **D**efine Pattern	Records the pattern.

This pattern can be used by the Paint Bucket, the **E**dit, **F**ill command, or the Rubber Stamp tool.

Click on the Quick Mask mode button	Allows the painting and selection tools to create and edit Quick Masks.
Marquee-zoom into the area beneath the first one that you pattern-filled	This brightly lit area of grass and dirt is where you'll retouch. A 2:1 viewing resolution is good.
Click on the Paintbrush tool, and then select Normal mode from the Brushes palette	Establishes tool and setting you use to create and edit a Quick Mask; the same way you did in the earlier exercise.
Click and drag in the exposed areas	Fills these earth areas with Quick Mask, as shown in figure 9.13.

Double-click on the Rubber Stamp tool	Displays the Rubber Stamp Options dialog box.
Choose Pattern (non-aligned) from the Op<u>t</u>ion drop-down list, and then click on OK	Sets the Rubber Stamp tool to apply the pattern that you defined at the beginning of this exercise.
Click on the Standard mode button	Creates selection-marquee areas out of the areas you previously masked.
Click and drag over the selection areas	Paints only the selected areas with the pattern that you defined earlier, as shown in figure 9.14.
Choose <u>S</u>elect, <u>N</u>one (or press Ctrl+D)	Deselects the selection borders in the image.
Choose <u>F</u>ile, <u>S</u>ave	Saves your work to hard disk.

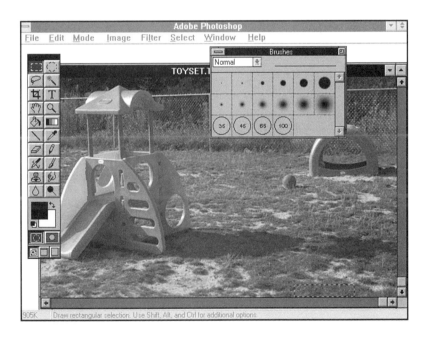

Figure 9.12
Sample a new area of grass to define it as a pattern to be used in brightly lit image areas.

The advantage of using this pattern-fill technique is that it's quick and that it lets you accomplish your assignment without requiring a high degree of accuracy. As soon as you have enough pattern-filled and original image areas woven into the retouched area, you can begin sampling areas of it with the Rubber Stamp tool with its Clone (aligned) option, and finish the retouching without depending on the pattern.

Figure 9.13
Cover all the barren parts of an area with the Paintbrush tool in Quick Mask mode.

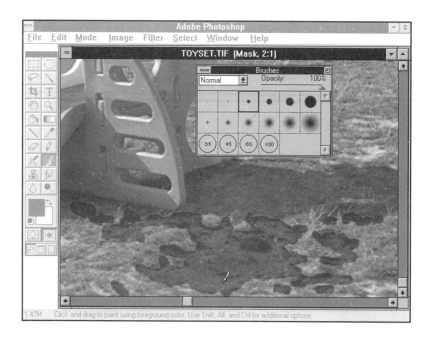

Figure 9.14
The Rubber Stamp fills in only the areas that you've selected.

Touch-up Work with the Paint Bucket

Now that you have restored some of the grass in a brightly lit area, you can use this restored area to create another pattern. However, you won't have to use the Rubber Stamp tool to apply the pattern. The area that you restored in the last exercise is large enough to create an excellent pattern that you can use with the Paint Bucket tool to fill other areas.

In the next exercise, you'll use this technique to restore the image's lower-right corner.

Paint Bucket-Filling with a Pattern Sample

Click on the Rectangular Marquee tool	Use this selection tool to define patterns in an image area.
Marquee-select a grass-covered area where you applied a pattern fill in the last exercise	Determines the content of the pattern fill.
Try to include both original image area *and* the area where you used the Rubber Stamp.	
Choose **E**dit, **D**efine Pattern	Defines the area as a source when you apply the pattern fill.
Click on the Paintbrush tool, and then click the Quick Mask mode button	Applies Quick Mask with the Paintbrush tool.
Click and drag over the exposed earth in the lower-right corner of the image	Defines areas as selection areas wherever you apply Quick Mask.
Click on the Standard mode button	Turns the masked areas that you've painted over into active selection areas.
Double-click on the Paint Bucket tool	Displays the Paint Bucket Options dialog box.
Set the **T**olerance option to **255**, check the **A**nti-Aliased option, click the Pattern radio button, and then click on OK	Allows the Paint Bucket tool to flood-fill an area with a defined pattern covering all the pixels in the selection areas.
Click a selection area with the Paint Bucket cursor	Flood-fills only the selection area you clicked over with the defined grass pattern as shown in figure 9.15.
Click on another selection area with the Paint Bucket cursor	Flood-fills that selection area with the grass pattern.
Continue clicking over selection areas until they are all flood-filled	Restores the grass in the lower-right of the image area.
Choose **S**elect, **N**one (or press Ctrl+D)	Deselects all the selection areas in the image.
Choose **F**ile, **S**ave	Saves your work to your hard disk.

II

Steak 'n Potatoes Assignments

Figure 9.15
The Paint Bucket
tool can flood-fill
a selection area
with a color or a
pattern that you
define.

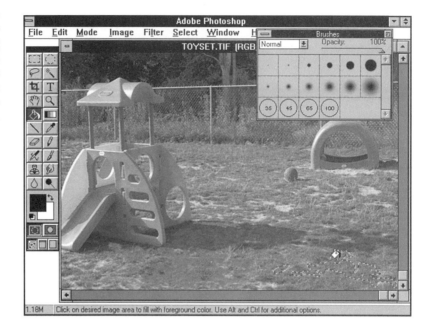

If you have many assignments that require pattern fills like you've seen in these exercises, you may want to leave the Rubber Stamp tool set to Clone (aligned) and set the Paint Bucket tool to apply flood-fill patterns. This way, you get the best of both worlds without having to toggle back and forth between Rubber Stamp options. If you don't want to constantly toggle between Rubber Stamp options, use the Paint Bucket for Pattern fills.

Because you defined such a large sample area for your pattern in the last exercise, you won't see a pattern edge in your flood fills.

You should always create a good, opaque mask in an area that you want to flood-fill with pattern or even a color. If your mask isn't 100-percent opaque in certain areas, the Paint Bucket tool can't apply a 100-percent dense pattern to the selection area, which results in a washed-out fill.

Masking Areas for Straight Cloning

The next area of TOYSET.TIF that requires some retouching is next to the ball in the upper-right corner. The grass near the base of the children's bridge is showing some wear, so the area needs the same sort of attention that you gave to the foreground grass in this image.

This task is an easy one because you have several nearby grassy areas to sample from with the Rubber Stamp tool. No pattern option is required, and the only prerequisite to fixing this area is to mask off the selections, the same way you've been doing all along.

Cloning In Some Background Grass

Marquee-zoom to a 2:1 resolution on the children's bridge area of the image	
Click on the Quick Mask mode button and then click on the Paintbrush tool	Sets up the Paintbrush tool to apply masking material to the image.
Click and drag over exposed earth areas in the image	Creates selection areas.
Click on the Standard mode button	Turns the masked areas into selection areas.
Double-click on the Rubber Stamp tool	Displays the Rubber Stamp Options dialog box.
Choose Clone (aligned) from the Option drop-down list, and then click on OK	Sets the Rubber Stamp tool to its default, which is to clone from a sample point within the image.
Press Alt while clicking to the left of the ball in the image	Sets a source point for the Rubber Stamp tool.
Click and drag over a selection area	Clones in image area from the source point, as shown in figure 9.16.
Continue clicking and dragging until you have cloned over all the selection areas	Restores an area of grass to the image.
Choose **S**elect, None (or press Ctrl+D)	Deselects the active selection marquees.
Click on the Quick Mask mode button	Returns you to masking mode with the selection and paint-application tools.
Click on the Paintbrush tool and drag over the exposed earth areas that are beneath the ones that you just cloned over	Masks the areas to produce selection areas when you return to Standard mode.
Click the Standard mode button	Displays the masked areas as active selection areas.
Click on the Rubber Stamp tool, and then press Alt while clicking the middle of the area that you cloned in beneath the children's bridge	Sets the source point for the Rubber Stamp tool.

continues

continued

Click and drag over the selection areas in the image	Clones in the grassy sample areas from your source point.
Choose **S**elect, **N**one (or press Ctrl+D)	Deselects all the selection areas in the image.
Choose **F**ile, **S**ave	Saves your work to hard disk.

Figure 9.16
After you retouch an area, you can use it as a source point with the Rubber Stamp tool to clone in other areas.

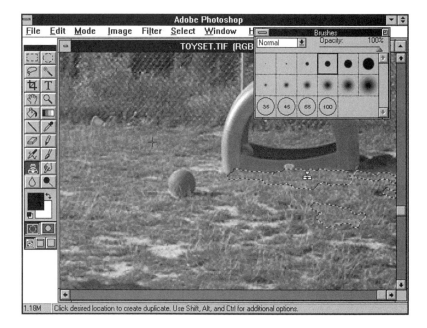

You should now have the right side of TOYSET.TIF completely manicured. If you start building perfect little areas with the Rubber Stamp tool, you can use increasingly broad strokes, and your sampling becomes less constrained by the available source area for the tool.

Mirroring a Sample to Pattern In

Because you didn't start the Rubber Stamp retouching of this photo with an abundance of grassy source material, some places may be showing unwanted patterning. You'll fix this noticeable repetition of the grass in the next exercise by sampling an area of contrasting visual content and then using one or two strokes of the Rubber Stamp tool to break up the unwanted pattern.

For example, if an area looks like it has a pattern of brownish grass, sample a greener area with the Rubber Stamp and clone one or two strokes of green into the area. If an area looks too flat and green, clone a weed or two into it. The point is to break up any obvious patterns

in this image's grass, and to create a random, textured surface that won't alert the viewer to your retouching work.

Through Photoshop, you can define a pattern that isn't even part of the active image. This feature is a life saver when you need to keep the grass texture looking well-defined, yet random.

Cloning or patterning with the Rubber Stamp tool can cause problems if your cloned-in area always looks the same as the rest of the image. You can't *mirror* a sample to use as a pattern source as long as it's in the image. Mirroring can help you create a more random, natural-looking lawn in TOYSET.TIF. To do so, copy a selection, paste it in a new image window, flip it, and then define it as a pattern source. The following exercise describes how to do this.

Using a Pattern from a Different Image Window

Double-click on the Zoom tool	Zooms you to a 1:1 viewing resolution of the TOYSET image.
Click on the Rectangular Marquee tool, and then marquee-select an area of grass in the center of TOYSET.TIF	Defines an area you'll use to make a pattern.

Make certain that your selection area doesn't include distinguishing characteristics that will be noticeable when the pattern is repeated.

Choose **E**dit, **C**opy (or press Ctrl+C)	Copies the selection area to the clipboard.
Choose **F**ile, **N**ew (or press Ctrl+N), accept the dialog box's defaults, and then click on OK	Reads the clipboard information and, by default, offers a New image window the same type and proportion as what's currently held on the clipboard.
Choose **E**dit, **P**aste (or press Ctrl+V)	Pastes a copy of your selection area into the new file, which is currently the active image, entitled UNTITLED-1.
Choose **F**lip from the **I**mage menu, and then choose Horizontal	Mirrors the copy from left to right.
Choose **E**dit, **D**efine Pattern	Makes the mirrored selection a pattern that you can use with the Rubber Stamp and Paint Bucket tools, as shown in figure 9.17.
Click on the title bar for TOYSET.TIF	Makes TOYSET.TIF the active image in Photoshop, and makes UNTITLED-1 the inactive image and sends it to the back of Photoshop's workspace.

continues

continued

Click on the Quick Mask mode button	Allows you to use selection or paint-application tools to create and modify a Quick Mask.
Click and drag over all the exposed earth areas in the lower-left of the TOYSET image	Masks the areas you paint over when you use black foreground color, and removes mask when you select white as the foreground color.
Double-click on the Rubber Stamp tool	Displays the Rubber Stamp Options dialog box.
Choose Pattern (non-aligned) from Option drop-down list, and then click on OK	Allows you to paint with the defined pattern when using the Rubber Stamp tool.
Choose a medium-size tip with spread from the Brushes palette	Increases the size of the tip that you're presently using with the Rubber Stamp tool.
Click on the Standard mode button	Converts the areas you covered with Quick Mask into active selection areas.
Click and drag the Rubber Stamp tool over the selection areas	Fills in the exposed earth areas with the mirrored sample pattern that you defined earlier, as shown in figure 9.18.
Choose **S**elect, **N**one (or press Ctrl+D)	Deselects all the selected areas in the TOYSET.TIF image.
Press Ctrl+Tab	Toggles UNTITLED-1 to the front and makes it the active image.
Double-click on the command button to UNTITLED-1, and then click on the No button in the dialog box	Closes UNTITLED-1 without saving it.

You're done with UNTITLED-1, and TOYSET.TIF becomes the only active image in Photoshop's workspace.

Choose **F**ile, **S**ave	Saves your work to your hard disk.

The more randomness that you achieve in your grass retouching work, the more credibility you instill in the image. Mirroring an area helps break up any discernible patterns in your work with the grass.

Figure 9.17
You can define a pattern from one image, and then use the pattern in another image.

Figure 9.18
The larger your sample or pattern area, the larger a Brushes tip you can use with the Rubber Stamp tool.

II

Steak 'n Potatoes Assignments

Switching Tools as an Option *and* as a Technique

You're now left with the upper-left corner of the image to retouch. You don't need another tutorial to finish the TOYSET image—simply choose one of the techniques that you've learned in this chapter that you believe would best fit the task.

By switching from Photoshop's default (aligned) cloning to patterning with the Rubber Stamp, you can address different problem areas of an image while also breaking up the monotony of the grass texture. Consider this a technique. Sometimes you don't *have to* use each of the various Rubber Stamp options, but you'll *want to* anyway, to create a visual randomness. Clouds, sand, leaves, and other natural shapes always should be portrayed as a *random* collection of things.

To finish this image, use the Quick Mask mode to mask the remaining exposed earth area in the upper left of TOYSET.TIF. Then decide on an existing area of the image that you think will fill in these areas best. Then experiment with the following:

- ✔ The Rubber Stamp's default, aligned cloning

- ✔ Defining and using a non-aligned pattern with the Rubber Stamp tool

- ✔ Defining a pattern and flood-filling the selections with the Paint Bucket tool

- ✔ Pattern-filling from a source that you've modified and sampled as a separate image, as you did in the last exercise

After you've finished retouching the remaining areas, you'll see how to perk up this newly seeded yard area with a little tweak from the **A**djust menu.

Color-Correcting the Retouched Image

If these exercises result in the same effects on your screen as you see in this chapter's figures, your work has come along wonderfully, and you've created some exciting enhancements to an image that *needed* enhancing!

But in addition to the turf of this playground being a little overrun, it was also a little underwatered this season. The grass isn't exactly a rich color that compositionally supports the brilliant colors of the children's toys. Some spot enhancement is in order here.

If you followed the exercises in the preceding chapters, you already know that you can use the Magic Wand tool to select areas based on a range of color similarity. The yard that you retouched in the preceding exercises consists of several shades of green, but they should all fall within a fairly *narrow* tolerance of color—green! Because of this narrow tolerance, the Magic Wand is the tool of choice to select the general area.

Don't concern yourself with precision-selecting in the next exercise. If you accidentally select part of the trees in the background, it's okay. Your objective in this exercise is to enhance the green *quality* in the picture, and the enhancement requires as random an application as that of the natural material in the image. Trees, weeds, and especially the grass, are all good candidates for a quick color boost. However, the brightly colored children's toys are *not*, which is why you'll need to begin the exercise by fine-tuning the Magic Wand's tolerance setting.

Adding Color to the Yard

Double-click on the Magic Wand tool	Displays the Magic Wand Options dialog box.
Set the **T**olerance option to 40 pixels, check the **A**nti-Aliased option, and then click on OK	Sets the Magic Wand to select pixels similar in color that are adjacent to the image area you click the Magic Wand cursor over.
Click on the center of TOYSET.TIF with the Magic Wand tool	Selects all the pixels in the image that share a moderate range of similar color.
Press Shift while clicking inside the areas of the children's slide	Selects these grassy areas as well.

The Magic Wand tool can't initially select these areas because the bright plastic slide borders separate them from the initial area you clicked over.

Choose **A**djust from the **I**mage menu, and then choose Variations	Displays the Variations dialog box, as shown in figure 9.19.
Click and drag the Fine/Coarse slider one tick toward the right	Makes the Picks offered by the Variations dialog box a bit more diverse.
Click on the More Green Pick, and then click on OK	Color-casts the selection areas to a more greenish tint than the Current Pick—the image presently in the center of the Variations Picks field.
Choose **S**elect, **N**one (or press Ctrl+D)	Deselects the Magic Wand selection in the image.
Choose **F**ile, Sa**v**e As, and save the file to the directory on your hard disk with a new name like TOYSET!.TIF	Saves your finished work to your hard disk.

Figure 9.20 shows the finished playground image, saved as TOYSET!.TIF, alongside the original image, so that you can compare them.

Figure 9.19
The Variations
dialog box lets
you tint all, or
only selected,
areas of an
image.

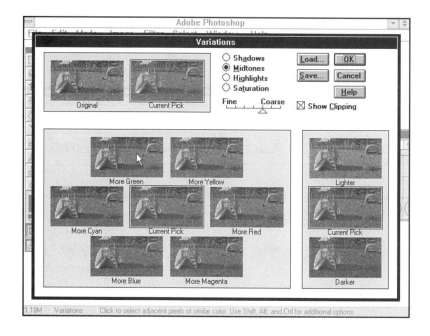

Figure 9.20
The reseeded
image and the
original.

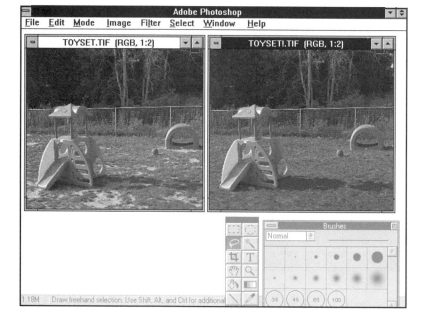

Summary

Although you used the Rubber Stamp tool in this chapter to do some miraculous retouching work, it still remains only one of many tools and filters that you can use to retouch an assignment. In fact, you often achieve the best results by constantly switching tools and by using them in various combinations. This chapter demonstrated several effective techniques that you can use with the Rubber Stamp tool, and just two of the many situations in which you can use it extensively.

These two exercises are actually "worst case" scenarios, meant to give you experience and a feel for working with flaws in images. You are developing a wonderful faculty, through these exercises, for using judgment, skill, and technique with Photoshop's tools.

But if you're actually confronted with images as completely and embarrassingly *wrong* in a paying assignment, you may want to consider the possibility of a photographic re-shoot to remedy the flaws. This is a serious imaging professional's option, and it's one you don't select from any menu bar.

Get to know what your tools can do and master a technique or two to use with them. Experiment and pay attention to what works and what doesn't in different situations. This will develop your ability to quickly evaluate a project and select the right tools and techniques for each assignment.

Chapter Snapshot

In this chapter, you learn how to:

CHAPTER

10

Using Effects and Tools Together

At some point in your career as an imaging professional, someone will hand you a photo and ask, "Can you fix this?" The photo might be a beautiful product shot for a print advertisement that includes a glaringly obvious mistake in it—like the label on the product is crooked.

This is not as unlikely an occurrence as you might imagine. In the confusion and with the tight deadlines that surround a typical photographic shoot, strange things do happen. Without Photoshop, the only recourse for correcting a mistake like this would be to try to schedule a reshoot of the product, or hire the services of a traditional, chemical retoucher. Both of these options are expensive, and time consuming. Having Photoshop in your graphics arsenal gives you another option—one that will save you money and a world of aggravation when faced with many of these situations.

This chapter uses an exaggerated example, a "sore thumb" of an image, and takes you through the process used to restore it to commercial usability. You'll see how to save post-production costs, and you'll pick up a few tricks that you can apply to an image that looks as though it should be rephotographed.

When photographing an image, it's always best to lay out all the elements correctly. But sometimes you can't be present at a photographic shoot and must trust the stagehands, which often yields the same result as trusting your pussycat to mind your goldfish. It's enough to give a soul coffee nerves.

Your assignment in this chapter is to fix a fictitious coffee ad for the Tropicafé company. While you were out, perhaps getting a cup of coffee, your Property Manager, Henry "Hap" Hazard, stuck the label crooked on the coffee can, marring an otherwise glorious image.

Using the Pen Tool

To fix a label on a package that is planar (flat and essentially one-dimensional) is a fairly simple feat: you would use Photoshop's rotate effect to spin the selected area back to normal. But an area that lies on a dimensional, *cylindrical* object represents three dimensions with angles that are determined by the angle of the camera. At the beginning of the next exercise, you'll see that the coffee label is dimensionally distorted.

In the exercise you'll adjust the label so that it fits properly on the can by using two of the Image menu commands—Rotate and Distort. These two commands will fix the problem with the orientation of the label, but this alone won't fix the problem. Shifting the shape and orientation of the label creates empty space in the image in the areas where the original label was that the new label doesn't cover. You'll use Photoshop's painting and editing tools to complete this assignment.

The first task at hand is to select the coffee can label so that you can modify it. In this instance, the Lasso tool is a poor choice for your selection tool. Because the geometry of the label's borders is well defined, but curved, the Lasso's freehand drawing capability isn't necessarily desirable for the task. Instead, let's see how the Paths palette can provide the features for accurately defining the label.

Making a Path for the Coffee

Open the TROPCAF.TIF image (shown in fig. 10.1) on the companion CD	This is the image you'll be working with in this chapter.
Click on the Zoom tool, then click and diagonally drag around the area of the coffee can label	Results in a 2:1 viewing resolution of the label, giving you a better view the work area.
Choose **W**indow, Show P**a**ths (or press F9)	This calls up the Paths palette to the workspace.
Click on the Pen tool	Specifies the tool you use to create path segments between Anchor points.

Click on the upper-left corner of the label	Sets your first Anchor point.
Click on the upper-right corner of the label	Sets a second Anchor point and draws a straight path segment between the two Anchor points.
Click on the lower-left corner of the label	Adds a second path segment between Anchor points, as shown in figure 10.2.
Click on the first Anchor point	Closes and completes the path.

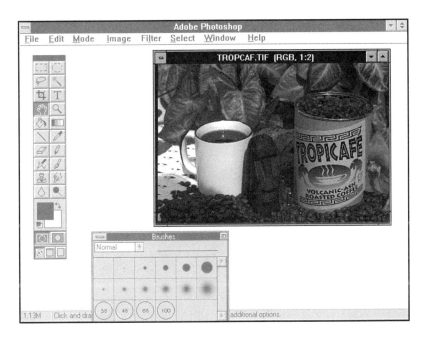

Figure 10.1

Find the mistake in this picture.

Figure 10.2
The Pen tool on the Paths palette creates anchor points and path segments between them.

Defining a Path

The Paths palette is an anomaly in Photoshop's host of tools. Although you always work with bitmap-type images in Photoshop, paths belong to the *vector* family of computer graphics. A path is a representation of a math equation, not a map of where each pixel should be. As a representation, it can be freely designed in smooth curves that are resolution-independent and have no jagged edges.

A path can be used to define a precise outline, but as long as the path is a vector, it can't interact with your image. To make the outline interact with the image in Photoshop, you need to convert the path to a selection border. Selection borders, as you've seen in this book, *can* and *do* affect bitmap-type graphics. Think of paths as blueprints for an action to be performed later. The advantage Photoshop offers with paths is the precision that you achieve when defining a selection border.

So far, you've used the Paths palette to complete a coarse outline around the coffee can label. The outline doesn't contain any of the corresponding curves that make up the label's top and bottom because you created the path with the simpler of the two Photoshop techniques for creating paths—the "click" method. You can also click and drag with the Pen tool to produce curved path segments automatically, but it's sometimes easier modifying straight path segments than using the click and drag path-making technique. In the next exercise, you use another Paths palette tool, the Corner tool, to modify these straight path segments in your path.

Bending a Path

Click on the Corner tool of the Paths palette	This is the angle-shaped tool on the far right of the palette.

The Corner tool creates direction lines from Anchor points and curved path segments from straight ones.

Click on the upper-left Anchor point and drag it to the right	Bends the two path segments that that meet at the Anchor point.

A straight line that goes through the Anchor point appears. This is the *direction line*. At the end of each half of the direction line is a *direction point*. You're dragging the direction line by its handle, or direction point. This changes the shape of the adjacent path segments symmetrically.

Release the direction point, then click on the right direction point and drag it further to the right and down	Breaks the symmetrical relation to the opposing direction line.

The direction points now operate independently of each other. You're fitting the curved top path segment to the shape of the coffee label's upper edge.

Click on the image window's left border and drag it further to the left	Broadens your view in the active image window so that you can see the left direction line and point.
Press Ctrl while clicking and dragging the left direction point so that it lies on the left path segment	Straightens the left path segment by dragging the direction point toward the coffee can, as shown in figure 10.3.

By pressing the Ctrl key while you click and drag, you toggle from the Corner tool to the Arrow Pointer tool.

Release the Ctrl key and then click the bottom-right Anchor point and drag it to the left with the Corner tool	Gives the two path segments that meet at the Anchor point a curved property direction, and pulls the direction point to the left.

Repeat all the preceding steps with the two remaining path segments

You should end up with two straight path segments and a curved top and bottom to the path that fits the label pretty accurately.

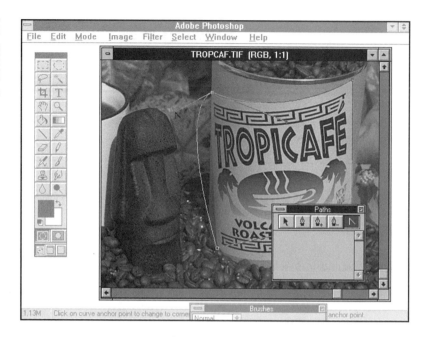

Figure 10.3
The Paths palette's
Corner tool
creates curved
path segments
from straight ones.

Understanding Paths and Path Tools

Before continuing the assignment, let's review some of the phenomena you've just seen. If you've previously used a computer drawing package, like Adobe Illustrator, you're probably an old hand at this Anchor point and direction point stuff. If not, you need to review the properties of a path and the tools that you use to change them.

Paths

A path has a direction to it. It starts where you click the first Anchor point with the Pen tool. When you complete a path, a tiny circle appears to the right of the Pen cursor, which indicates that you're about to close the path. If you don't close the path, you won't be able to convert it to the selection border that you'll soon need. You can choose not to close a path, by either Saving a path before you've completed it, or be deselecting the Pen tool before you've drawn a complete path. Photoshop calls the unclosed path a *"path segment"* and there is not a lot you can do with an open path segment in Photoshop.

Path Directions

A closed path travels either clockwise or counterclockwise. The path's direction depends on which direction you went originally in creating the Anchor points. When working with direction points, it's important to your sanity that you remember which way the path was

constructed. You should click and drag direction points in the direction of the path. If you drag a direction line in the opposite direction of a path, you're looking for trouble—the path will twist and cross itself and generally frustrate you and your work.

You can also create curved path segments between the Anchor points if you click and drag the Pen tool while making Anchor points instead of just clicking the individual points. If you're familiar with the creation of Bézier curves, you may want to use this method to create paths. If you're not, you'll find it much simpler and less confusing to create the Anchors first and then modify them with the Corner tool. The method you use to create a path is a matter of work preference.

To preview the next path segment that you draw, double-click the Pen tool icon on the Paths palette. Then check the Rubber Band check box on the Pen Tool Options dialog box. Turning this option on can be quite useful if you use the click and drag method for designing a path with curved path segments.

Putting a Wave in a Path

When you create a path by clicking the Anchor points (not the click-and-drag method), direction points aren't automatically created. If you want to edit the curve between the Anchor points, you have to use the Corner tool. The Corner tool creates symmetrical direction lines and points when you click and drag an Anchor point. Symmetrical direction lines and points move in unison in opposite directions to identically modify the path segments on each side of the Anchor point. You may be a bit surprised if you click and drag an anchor and suddenly find that you're dragging a direction point. But *don't* go back to the Anchor point if your intention is to shape a path segment, because that *is* what you're doing as you drag the direction point.

If you release the direction point and click the Anchor point again, the direction lines and the point vanish and you toggle the function of the Corner tool to change the path segments back to straight lines. This can be very frustrating. The primary function of the Corner tool is to create direction points, but its secondary function is to change the symmetrical nature of the two opposing direction lines. You do so by clicking and dragging a direction point, not the Anchor point. When you click and drag a direction point with the Corner tool, the function of the tool toggles between symmetrical and asymmetrical direction points. Which leads us to our last point!

The Arrow Pointer tool can be accessed by pressing the Ctrl key while using the Corner tool. (The Arrow Pointer tool is also available as the leftmost tool on the Paths palette, but why switch tools when it's so easy to toggle between them?) The Arrow Pointer tool can move Anchor points and direction points, but can't create direction points. This is to your advantage, though, because you can use it to modify path segment angles and curves without disturbing the symmetrical/asymmetrical properties of direction points that you've already established using the Corner tool.

The Pen Plus and Pen Minus tools that make up the rest of the Paths palette are very straightforward: click with one to create another Anchor point on a path, and use the other to remove an unwanted Anchor point. These are the only tasks that the two tools can accomplish. You can easily toggle to them when you have the Arrow pointer tool selected by holding down the Ctrl+Alt keys and clicking on a point to delete it, or by clicking on the path segment to create a new anchor.

Paths come in very handy when you want to precisely mark an area in your work without the slightest possibility of accidentally changing it. But for all the power that you can apply to your work with the Paths palette, paths can't help you much unless you convert them to something that can act as a foundation for applying changes to an image—which is what you'll do in the next exercise.

Creating a Path from a Selection

Adobe Systems took great care to keep users from accidentally deleting the paths that they create. Creating a path sometimes requires a substantial investment of time and effort, and often you can modify and reuse paths ad infinitum. However, the path that you created in the last exercise ultimately has only one use: to create a selection that is based on it.

Paths and selections aren't the same, although you can make one from the other and vice versa. A path will remain in your image even after you create a selection from it. This is because you don't convert a path into a selection; rather, you create a selection from the geometric information that the path contains.

In the next exercise, pay close attention to the steps you take to create a selection around the coffee can label from the path you have defined. You will eventually delete the path when it has outlived its usefulness.

Saving a Selection and Removing a Path

Click on the command button in the Paths palette	Displays a drop-down list of Paths options.
Choose the option Make Selection	Displays the Make Selection dialog box.
Set the Feather Radius to **0** and check the Anti-Aliased option (you can find both options in the Rendering field), and then click on OK	Creates a selection marquee that accurately describes the path you created, with edges that are smooth.
Press the Backspace key twice	Removes the path from the image.
Choose <u>S</u>elect, <u>S</u>ave	Saves the selection border to an Alpha channel in the TROPCAF.TIF image.

Choose **F**ile, Sa**v**e As. Save the image to a directory on your hard drive. Save the file as TROPCAF.TIF and be sure to check the **S**ave Alpha Channels box is checked when Photoshop's Save TIFF dialog box comes up.

Saving and Deleting Paths

In the last exercise, you deleted the path as soon as you made a selection from it. Because paths are vector-based, they are easy to edit once you get the hang of how they work. And there are times when you may want to save the path, so that you can either reuse it as is, or edit its shape and then use the new shape in your work.

While both saved and unsaved paths are a valuable feature in Photoshop, they can sometimes produce some very unexpected and unwanted results in your work. The following sections discuss how to save paths, how to know when they are active, how to delete them, and when you should be on the lookout for path-related problems.

Saving a Path

You can use the Save Path command from the Path's Palette drop-down list to save a path. Choosing this command brings the Save Path dialog box to the screen. You are then given the option to name the path or accept a default number as the path's name.

Discerning when a Path Is Active

Paths are only visible and active when the Paths palette is open in your workspace. Unsaved paths are displayed on your screen when the palette is open. A Saved path is active and visible in the image when it has a check mark next to its name in the Paths palette, or inactive and invisible when unchecked.

Deleting Unsaved Paths

Although an unsaved path can be quite helpful when you need to create a selection border that is based on it, unsaved paths will also linger around longer than you want unless you delete them when you're done with them.

There are several ways to delete paths. When an unsaved path is visible and active, you can press the Backspace key twice or you can marquee-select the entire path with the Pen tool and press the Delete key. It's important you don't have an active selection in the image when you press the Delete key, though, because this will also remove foreground image areas! Pressing the Backspace key three times in succession will delete all unsaved paths that are visible and active in the workspace *and* any saved paths that are currently active and visible. Use this command with caution.

Also when you have an unsaved path in an image and use the **F**ile, **C**lose command, Photoshop displays the attention warning box that reads:

```
This window contains an unsaved path. Close anyway?
```

If you choose **Y**es, the file is closed and the unsaved path is discarded. If you choose cancel, you are returned to the workspace with the file still displayed in its window. Photoshop never warns you when you save or close a file that contains *saved* paths—only if you have unsaved paths.

Deleting a Saved Path

When you've saved a path, there are two ways to delete it. Both ways require you to select the path first by clicking on its Paths palette title to make it visible and active. (There's a check mark next to it.) Then you have your choice of either pressing the backspace key once or choosing the Delete Path option from the Paths palette's drop-down list.

Problems Paths Can Create

Saved paths in files that are used by programs other than Photoshop will often fail to open or they may cause the application to crash. If you intend to use this file in another program, be sure to delete any paths in the file, then use the Save As command to make a copy of the file without the saved paths. Then use this pathless file with the other program.

Another problem that most new users of Photoshop face with paths occurs when they create a selection border that is based on a path. If you copy the selection, but haven't deleted the path or if the path *has* a check next to it on the Paths palette box, you're in for a rude surprise. The selection that is based on the path is not copied to the clipboard—the path itself is copied instead.

To avoid confusion when working with selection areas that are based on paths, delete or save the path, and then remove the check mark next to its name on the Paths palette's dialog box.

Rotating a Selection Area

In the next exercise, you use one of the Rotate features to straighten the coffee can label. As mentioned before, the label was photographed dimensionally; in addition to exhibiting height and width, the label exhibits the same degree of depth as the can to which it's applied. This means that rotating the label is only half the solution. You'll use another Photoshop effect, Distort, to finish straightening out the image.

When you rotate the label, you'll expose areas of the background that it no longer covers. So before rotating the selection, you'll want to set a color for the background that's a little more *brown* than Photoshop's default of white!

Rotating the Coffee Can's Label

Click on the Eyedropper tool	Activates the tool used to select a color within the image.
Press Alt while clicking on the top front center of the coffee can as shown in figure 10.4	Selects the background color for the image.

Skip the following step if you never deselected the selection border that you saved earlier.

Choose **S**elect, **L**oad Selection	Displays the selection border that you saved earlier.
Choose **I**mage, **R**otate and then choose Free	Sets a Free Rotation box around the selection.
Click on the upper-right corner of the Free Rotation box and drag the corner downward	Rotates the selection clockwise.

Continue dragging until the right side of the label is parallel to the right side of the coffee can, as shown in figure 11.5.

Click inside the rotation box	Locks the floating selection into the degree of rotation that you've set.

Don't click outside the selection yet.

II
Steak 'n Potatoes Assignments

Figure 10.4
By pressing the Alt key, you toggle the Eyedropper tool to pick up background color.

Figure 10.5

Free rotation lets you specify exactly how much a selection is rotated by hand.

In addition to the Free option, you may also want to check out the Arbitrary option from the **R**otate menu. Although you sacrifice the manual, hands-on qualities and advantages of the Free option, the Arbitrary option lets you make minor corrections to a selection that's just a little off kilter. This rotation option can make corrections of as little as one degree and can apply the correction either clockwise or counterclockwise. This is much more accurate than your hand/mouse moves can accomplish.

Distorting a Selection Area

If you followed the exercises in Chapter 8, you're already familiar with the Distort command. This free-form effect tool can change the selection based on the shape of a boundary box (like the Rotate's boundary box), whose sides can be arranged at any angle. The Distort command reshapes a selection area to fit inside the boundary box. You can pull the boundary box's sides to make a trapezoid out of a square, or any other shape that has four sides.

In the following exercise, you'll use the Distort command to adjust the sides of the label manually. Be aware, however, that the correspondence between the coffee can label's edges and the Distort boundary box isn't exact, it's *relational.* To straighten the coffee can label's sides, you don't align the Distort box's sides. Instead, you must check your screen at every stage as you adjust the Distort boundary box, until you align the label's edges with the side of the can. Because the image of the can comes slightly toward the viewer, the can's sides are at a slight perspective. So forget about evaluating your work according to parallel lines, and instead use your eye. (You may want to prop up your book as you do the following exercise, so you can keep an eye on both the steps and your screen.)

Stretching a Label

Choose Image, Effects, and then choose Distort	Displays a boundary box around the selection.
Click on the lower-right corner of the Distort box and drag it down and to the right of the selection	Distorts the selection area of the label to cover most of the missing background in the corner, as shown in figure 10.6.

Your PC may need a moment to process this transformation. Be patient, and *don't* click outside of the Distort box.

Click on the upper-right corner of the Distort box and drag up to the left of the selction	Reshapes the label to cover the can from the other side, as shown in figure 10.7.
Repeat this step for each corner of the box	Distorts the label's borders to make them even with the sides of the can.
Click inside the border when you're satisfied with your work	"Nails" the selection to the degree of distortion that you want, and removes Distort boundary box.
Click outside the selection border	Blends the selection into place in the background image.
Choose File, Save	Saves your work up to this point to your hard disk.

II

Steak 'n Potatoes Assignments

Figure 10.6
You can shape the
Distort boundary
box, which
reshapes the
selection
according to
where you've
clicked and
dragged the
boundary box
corners.

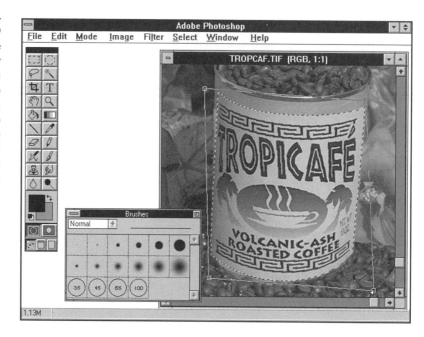

Figure 10.7
Use your eye to
determine which
corner of the
Distort box you
should move to
produce the
desired effect.

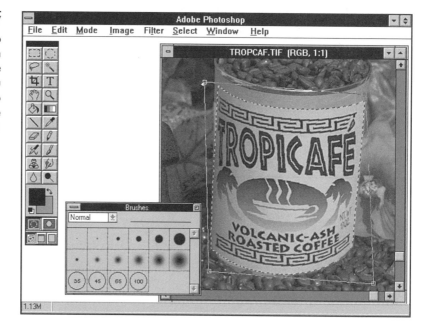

Reducing Your File Size

You're done with the selection you previously saved of the crooked label's outline. When you saved the selection, it was saved to an Alpha channel, which allowed you to recall it when you needed to use it again. Being able to save selections in Alpha channels is one of the most useful and important features in Photoshop. But it does have a price—each Alpha channel you have in an image substantially increases the size of the file. This ties up more of your precious system RAM and uses more hard disk space when you save the file.

When you are sure that you won't need to use a selection again, you should delete the selection by deleting the Alpha channel it's stored in. A little bit of housekeeping as you go along in your work keeps your file sizes manageable. You can work faster, and the chances of overtaxing your resources and crashing out of Windows and Photoshop is reduced. In the short exercise that follows, you'll delete the now unnecessary channel in TROPCAF.TIF.

Deleting an Unnecessary Alpha Channel

Press F6 to display the Channels palette if it is not already onscreen.

Click on the #4 channel	Activates the channel that your selection was stored in.

Photoshop automatically takes you to a view of this channel. Look at the contents of Channel #4 to be sure that it is the channel that contains the selection you want to delete, and that you haven't accidentally gone to one of the color channels or some other channel you may have created. Photoshop does *not* ask for a confirmation when you choose Delete Channel.

Click on the Channels palette's command button	Calls up drop-down list of commands.
Choose Delete Channel	Deletes the unwanted channel from your image, and returns you to the RGB Composite channel.
Choose File, Save	Saves a smaller version of the file to your hard disk, and economizes hard disk space.

Cloning Over Defects

The newly rotated and distorted label has introduced a few problems to the image. First, the bottom of the can is a photographic mess because distorting the label to the proper perspective covered up some of coffee beans on the right.

As often happens when working with images, you have to make an artistic decision here. In the next exercise, you use the Rubber Stamp tool to clone in a few coffee beans along the bottom edge of the can, where the distortion of the label is the most obvious. At a 1:1 viewing resolution (the final printing resolution), viewers don't see the coffee beans as separate items but rather they see all the beans as a single texture within the image. Because the beans in this image are viewed as texture, you won't have to be as painstakingly accurate with your cloning work as you usually need to be when cloning in image elements.

Now, it's time to begin cloning in the coffee beans and repairing some of the mess.

Amounting to a Hill of Beans

Choose the Rubber Stamp tool

Double click on the Rubber Stamp button on the toolbox to bring up the Rubber Stamp Options dialog box. Make sure that the default of Clone (aligned) is set in the Option drop-down list. Then click on OK.

Choose from the Brushes palette a medium tip with spread from the second row of tips, set to Normal mode, and **100**% Opacity	Sets the properties of the Rubber Stamp tool to a size and mode that works best for this task.
Press Alt while clicking in the the lower-right corner of the image	Specifies the sample site for the Rubber Stamp tool.

The sample *crosshair* moves along as you "paint" with the Rubber Stamp tool in its Clone (aligned) setting.

Click and drag a stroke from right to left along the telltale edge of the coffee can label	Clones over the offending area with a bean image sample, as shown in figure 10.8.
Continue to click and drag in single strokes until you cover the edge	Disguises the label's imperfect edge with samples of the coffee bean image.
Choose **F**ile, **S**ave	Saves your work to this point to your hard disk.

When you repair leaves, sand, and other natural, random patterns, you usually can use the Rubber Stamp tool without having to maintain a high degree of accuracy. Your goal in these cases is to create a random effect in an area that the viewer will "read" as texture rather than an important visual element to focus on.

But when the area you are fixing has a repeat pattern, like grillwork, you must pay careful attention to how you use the Rubber Stamp tool. You must be certain that the sample point you choose to start cloning from is lined up perfectly with the point in the image where you begin cloning. Chapter 5 provides a good example of using the Rubber Stamp tool for precision cloning, and Chapter 11's exercises demonstrate how to break up natural, nonrepeating patterns.

Figure 10.8
Coffee bean samples are cloned into the label's edge with the Rubber Stamp tool.

Protecting Areas from Change

After you have the bottom edge of the label obscured with coffee bean texture, it's time to address the top of the label. Before you rotated and distorted the label, you used the Eyedropper tool to change the color of the newly exposed areas. Matching this new background color to the label's color helped to disguise most of the effect your work had on the label. But some telltale edges remain that you will need to fix.

Fixing these edges is another problem that is easily dealt with when you use the Rubber Stamp tool. Your two biggest challenges when using the Rubber Stamp tool are to keep the cross-hair sampling cursor from moving into undesired sampling areas and to avoid accidentally cloning material into areas you don't want to cover. In the next exercise you need to allow yourself enough freedom of motion to clone over the miscolored areas with a broad stroke or two without crossing into the label itself with the Rubber Stamp.

Creating a "digital drop cloth" before you start cloning will solve both these problems. It will give you the freedom of movement to make broad strokes and preserve the nice, clean edge of the label. Creating the "digital drop cloth" with a selection border is the focus of the next exercise.

Creating a Digital Drop Cloth

Choose the Zoom tool

Marquee-zoom into the area near the top right of the can

You should be comfortable working at a 2:1 field of view over the problem area.

Choose the Lasso Tool

Click on the Lasso tool and drag it around the area of the can where the background color protudes from the original image's colored texture, as shown in figure 10.9	Selects an area of the image, leaving the rest of it unselected.
Double click on the Quick Mask mode button on the toolbox	Calls up the Mask Options dialog box.
From the Color Indicated field, choose Selected Colors	Areas covered with the mask color will be included in the selection area you create with the mask.
Click on OK	Places you in Quick Mask mode so that you can create a mask.

You can refine a Quick Mask with selection or paint-application tools.

Click on the Paintbrush tool

Choose from the Brushes palette a very small tip, Normal mode, and **100%** Opacity	Defines the Paintbrush characteristics for removing or adding mask, not color.
Click on the default colors icon	Sets the foreground color to black.

With this setting, you apply mask when you paint in Quick Mask mode.

Click and drag across an area next to the coffee label that you have not masked but needs to be added to the area you selected with the Lasso tool	Extends the mask to cover background area that doesn't have original label texture in it.
Click on the default colors icon (double-headed arrow) on the toolbox	Sets the foreground color to white.

When applying mask, white always represents the removal of mask, not the color white.

Click and drag across a masked area of the coffee label and the label's edge	Removes the mask from the edge of the label and from the label.

You don't want to mask any part of the edge or the label. Painting over such areas with white removes unwanted mask material from the label, as shown in figure 10.10.

Click on the Standard Mode button	Returns you to editing Mode.

Figure 10.9
You can loosely define a selection border with the Lasso tool and then refine it later.

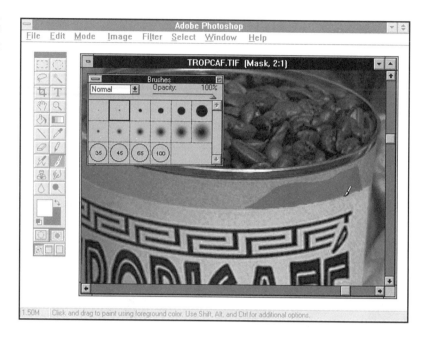

Figure 10.10
The Quick Mask mode lets you refine a selection border with paint-application tools.

Cloning into the Can

Now you can freely clone over the areas that you revealed when you rotated the label and exposed background areas. The trick with the Eyedropper tool disguised the revealed background color pretty well. However, the coffee can is lit from the right, so the shading on the can is uneven.

The last step to correcting the sloppily labeled coffee can is to apply neighboring sample areas over the telltale areas:

Adding Texture and Visual Content to the Selection Area

Click on the Rubber Stamp tool	This tool will clone an area of the can.
Choose from the Brushes palette a medium tip with spread, Normal mode, and **100%** Opacity	Sets up the Rubber Stamp tool to do its cloning work.
Press Alt while clicking on an area of the can to the left of the selection area	Sets the source area for cloning.

Click on the Rubber Stamp tool and drag it over the blemishes in the selection area, as shown in figure 10.11

Replaces the drag areas that you revealed when you rotated the coffee label with properly textured and lit material.

Continue doing the last step until the area looks right to you.

Choose **S**elect, **N**one (or press Ctrl+D)

Deselects the selection area when you finish using the Rubber Stamp tool.

Choose **F**ile, **S**ave

Saves your work to your hard disk.

Figure 10.11

Use the Rubber Stamp tool to finish retouching the coffee can.

The property that sets the Rubber Stamp tool apart from the rest of Photoshop's paint-application tools is its use of source material within an image as its "paint." This adds texture and other visual content across the area over which you move this tool. The result, as you can see, is picture-perfect image retouching.

The Steps to Undetectable Image Retouching

Correcting a label as you've now done provides a valuable lesson that you can apply to different situations. Suppose, for example, that you have an image of a building whose sides are crooked. No problem—simply rotate a selection around the side of the building and then retouch the edges. Or perhaps you want to create a special effect with an image of an airplane. With some planning and careful retouching, you can change the angle of its ascent by selecting it and then sending it into a nose dive. The lesson here is to use Photoshop's tools to do a coarse readjusting of a scene and then refine the rough edges. If you use Photoshop's effects features and *then* the paint tools, your imaging prowess will increase greatly through practice.

Adding a Steaming Effect to the Image

The product shot looks great now , but you can also enhance the image a bit by adding some steam coming from the coffee cup to create the impression that it's filled with piping hot coffee. Creating this effect in Photoshop requires just two easy steps. In contrast, if you've had experience with table-top photography you know how hard it is to choreograph *actual* steam in a photographic session.

It's much easier using the Paint Brush, a custom-tailored Brushes tip, and a special mode setting from the Brushes palette. Here's how:

Getting Steamed

Click on the Paintbrush tool	Activates the Brushes palette.
Set the Brushes palette to Screen mode and **39**% Opacity	Sets the characteristics for how you'll apply color to the image.
Double-click on a vacant tip slot on the bottom row of the Brushes palette	Brings up the New Brush dialog box, as shown in figure 10.12.
Set Hardness to **0**%, Angle to **45**%, and Roundness to **50**%	Specifies the settings for creating a special, angled, soft Brushes tip for retouching in this exercise.

Leave the rest of the New Brush dialog box's defaults as shown in figure 10.12.

Click on OK	Adds a new Brushes tip with the characteristics that you specified in the New Brush dialog box to the Brushes palette, in the slot you double-clicked on.

Click on the default colors icon and then click the inverse colors icon

Selects white as the foreground color and black as the background color.

Click and drag a wavy line, starting from the coffee in the cup and extending into the leaves

Screens (or bleaches) the active image area and creates a subtle steam effect, as shown in figure 10.13.

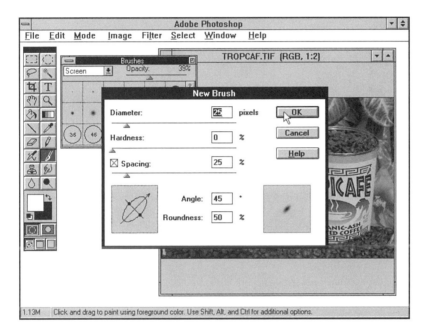

Figure 10.12

Design as many custom Brushes tips as you like by double-clicking on a vacant Brushes slot.

Although Chapter 4 demonstrated how to access the CUSTOM.ABS file to add all sorts of wacky tips to your palette, the preceding exercise demonstrates the best probable usage of the customizable Brushes palette. You can create large and angled tips for special assignments, and create exotic tips to wow clients when they drop in to snoop on an assignment.

In the last exercise, you added some flair to the imitation steam by angling your Brushes tip. The Screen mode came into play because it bleaches an area toward the foreground color that you've selected. If you increase the opacity, you can achieve a less subtle effect than the one in this exercise. But painting something into a photo always demands subtlety. Let observers paint their own picture when they recognize a glimpse or trace of a highlight. Besides, if you make the coffee steam too strong, people might conclude that the coffee is too hot to drink!

Figure 10.13
Bleach out an image area by using the Screen mode setting.

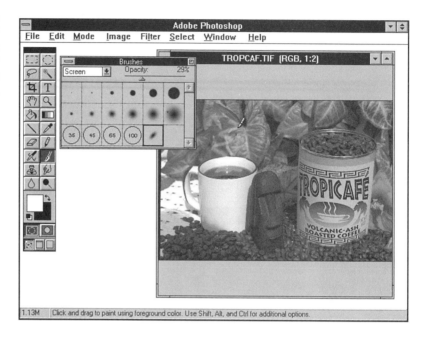

In addition to defining a new brush for the Brushes palette, you can also modify an existing one by double-clicking it. It's almost always better to create a new brush rather than editing a default brush tip. If you change a default Brushes tip, you'll never get it back unless you write down that particular tip's attributes or reinstall Photoshop.

Photoshop remembers your tip additions and changes from session to session. If you want to add custom Brushes tips, or redefine them and still leave your default set of tips intact, select the Save Brushes or Append Brushes commands from the drop-down list that appears when you click the command button of the Brushes palette. Then choose a unique file name and choose Load Brushes from the drop-down list the next time that you want to work with the brushes you've created.

Summary

This chapter introduced you to the mysteries, the frustrations and the rewards of Photoshop's vector-based paths. They work differently than Photoshop's paint and editing tools, but they are worth mastering. When you need to make precise, smooth selections, nothing else does it as well. Paths can also be used to create some stunning special effects—something you'll see how to do in Chapter 15.

Using vectors in a bitmap program is just another example of how interrelated Photoshop tools and features are. In the exercises you used vector paths, the Rotate and Distort commands, masks, a variety of paint tools and custom brushes and settings to produce your finished piece. One tool, command or setting rarely does the whole job, but several tools used together can do most anything you would ever require when working with an image. This book shows you a number of useful tool combinations, but there are many more out there just waiting for you to discover how they can be applied to solve each special problem your work brings you.

This chapter concludes the Steak 'n Potatoes assignments in Photoshop. And it's only upwards from here. Part III covers tougher assignments with richer rewards. Now that you have a good working knowledge of Photoshop's interface, and a grasp of techniques you can use for simple problem-solving, you can concentrate on enhancing images. In Part III's assignments, none of the images that you'll correct have glaringly obvious mistakes—in fact, the images are quite serviceable. The objective of this book is to familiarize you with Photoshop's tools, and show you how you can use them in combination with other tools and effects, so that you can create your own Photoshop techniques for getting the results you expect *and* the ones you've always hoped to achieve.

When the exercises start coming effortlessly, you then understand the techniques. Then you can tackle truly advanced assignments using Photoshop.

Part III

Gourmet Assignments

Chapter Snapshot

In this chapter, you learn how to:

11

CHAPTER

Enhancing a Poorly Staged Photo

J ust as every image you capture is unique, the *flaws* you perceive in an image have their own unique characteristics. The secret to correcting and enhancing a near-perfect photo is to first isolate these flaws and then decide which Photoshop tools, filters, and effects can best address the problem areas.

By now, you should be fairly familiar with the functions of Photoshop's tools. When used in combination with some of the menu items, you virtually arrive at *new* tools you can use to retouch specific spots in an image. Learning to work a combination of tools with filters is a *technique*. But being able to recognize a photo's problem areas and then call on the appropriate combination of tools is a *skill*, an invaluable one in your career as an imaging-type person.

Find the Mistakes in the Picture

At a cursory glance, your assignment in this chapter is nothing short of impossible. A friend wants a nice picture of the family homestead for a genealogy album. You have a beautiful image of a storybook house, marred by such real-world intrusions as a basketball hoop and a set of unsightly utility lines. Although the picture is good and sharp, it sports a bland gray sky. Reshooting it will not fix much because neither the utility company nor an 11-year old Michael Jordan fan is going to appreciate their removal.

You can steer around the real-world flaws to this photo and create a different, ideal reality from this image by isolating each of the problems and selecting the right Photoshop feature to correct it.

Correcting the Contrast

The image of the Tudor house shown in figure 11.1 came on a Kodak PhotoCD, which not only saved time but also cost less than having a color-corrected dye transfer print made that could be scanned. Kodak also digitized more detail than most commercial scanners are capable of (roughly 1,200 dpi) and—because no color print was involved—saved a generation of image quality.

Figure 11.1
Nice house, but the photo needs Photoshop's help.

As mentioned in Chapter 3, PhotoCDs are optimized for display on television sets and look great there. But straight-out-of-the-box PhotoCD images are *not* so great for PC imaging because television and computer monitor displays are different.

A PhotoCD's unadjusted color balance emphasizes midrange values but has a very weak *black point*. Although the image fairly oozes with color, the overall dynamics of the picture are a little wimpy. Fortunately, using Photoshop, you can put life back into the photo in only a minute or so. The following exercise shows you how.

Finding a New Level

From the companion CD, open HOME.TIF	PhotoCDs tend to look like this when you open them on a PC; brilliant, with no "bottom" to add punch to image.
Choose **I**mage, **A**djust, and then Levels (or press Ctrl+L)	Displays Levels dialog box. (Notice that the histogram shows almost no black at black point—common with PhotoCD images.)
Type **16** in the first Input Levels box	Raises black point of image to point at which actual values exist in this range. You can also use cursor to move black-point slider to the right.
Type **.85** in the middle Input Levels box	Removes a hint of gray component from photo.

By reducing the gray component (known as image *gamma*) you gain some image "snap" without sacrificing the luminosity in midranges.

Type **235** in the last Input Levels box	Sets new, lower white point for the image. Few images have a "whiter-than-white" 255 level. As you can see from the Levels histogram in figure 11.2, values near 235 are fine for white point here.
Click on OK	Applies corrections and closes Levels dialog box.

Before you click on OK in the Levels dialog box, you can use the **S**ave command button to save the settings. This is great when you work with a PhotoCD image because you can correct brightness and contrast for the image *without* saving the image to your hard drive. By saving the Levels setting, you can quickly and consistently apply the same Levels adjustment the next time you use the image.

continues

III

Gourmet Assignments

Always save Levels files for images with which you need to do "trial-and-error" experimenting. When you install Photoshop, the program makes a *calibrat* subdirectory—a good place to store these settings. Photoshop automatically stores Levels settings that you've created with the ALV file extension.

Figure 11.2
The Levels command enables you to reassign values for gray-scale densities across the spectrum of a photo.

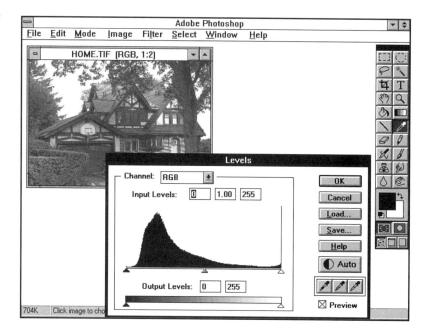

Making Gray Skies Blue

The sky in this image is typical Syracuse Overcast. It contributes less than nothing as a backdrop for the Tudor home. With enough time and skill using Photoshop, you can add a totally different sky. Or you can work with the one you have.

The droopy branches in the foreground make a total sky-ectomy unfeasible. Although accurately selecting the foreground branches and leaves is possible, to do so would take a long time. Without a precise "mask" of the flora, fringing will be evident when you paste in a new sky. And because of their complex organic outlines, trees are usually difficult to mix into new background elements, even with the assistance of the Defringe and Feather commands.

But you can add a little to the sky in the image *without* an accurate selection border around the trees. The next exercise is a prime example of how to "tint" an area of a photo. The beauty of this technique is that the light sky is enriched but the leaves and branches that outline the sky seem unaffected because they are darker than the sky.

The Sky's the Limit

Press Ctrl+plus	Zooms in so that you can see what you are doing.
Choose **W**indow, Show C**h**annels (or press F6)	Displays Channels palette.
Click on the command button in the upper-left corner of the Channels palette, then click on New Channel	Displays Channel options box.
In the Name box, type **Sky** and then click on OK	Replaces default name (#4) with something you can remember. Note that creating a new Channel view always switches you to that view.
Click on the Blue channel (Ctrl+3) in the Channel palette	Provides clearest view of both house and sky.
Choose **S**elect, **A**ll (or press Ctrl+A): then choose **E**dit, **C**opy (or press Ctrl+C)	Selects entire image and copies it to clipboard. Use this copy as a visual reference of the RGB channel as you work.
Click on the Sky channel (or press Ctrl+4)	Selection will be deposited here.
Choose **E**dit, **P**aste (or press Ctrl+V); then choose **S**elect, **N**one (or press Ctrl+D)	Pastes copy into Sky channel and then deselects it.
Click on the Lasso tool in the toolbox	Use this freehand selection tool to create irregular borders.
Press Alt and click at the left edge of the photo, just where the bushes meet the trees	Starting point of freehand selection. Alt key constrains selection border to straight lines.
Click around the border of the house, moving from left to right	Bottom of selection border. You need to move up, then left, in a counterclockwise direction to include the sky (from image border to border) in the selection.

continues

continued

Click up and off the image border to the right	Second side of selection border. Don't worry about clicking outside image. This is the way to continue a border that is flush with the active image window—if your image fills the window frame.
Click to the upper left, outside the image window border	Third side of selection border. Includes everything up to the image border (because you clicked outside the active window).
Release the Alt key and the left mouse button	Photoshop completes selection border. Done correctly, selection border looks like the one in figure 11.3. Leave it selected.

Figure 11.3

In full frame view clicking outside an image window with the Lasso tool includes everything in the selection, up to the outside border of the image.

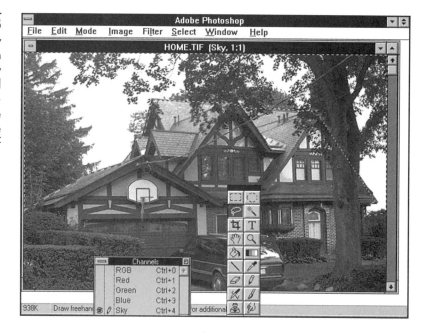

Touching (Up) the Sky

Right now, the sky is a uniform shade of blah. And you can't do much with Photoshop's Hue/Saturation command because the sky selection contains too much gray color information. Pumping up the Saturation only adds more gray; colorizing the selection area makes it look phony.

You can add color in a different way, though, by using the Gradient tool in combination with the Composite Controls. By fitting a gradient into the picture, you can add a gradual, naturalistic color shift in the sky, with motion and interest in an area that currently is pretty static.

The Sky channel now comes into play as the target for a Gradient fill. This channel serves as both the position of a selected area and a safe space where you can add visual information. A Gradient fill in any of the four native HOME.TIF channels is a big-time mistake—having control over the effect, and *how* the effect is added to the overall picture is important. This is yet another example of the important part channels play in your Photoshop work.

In the last exercise you selected the sky and treetop area in a channel. In the next exercise you fill only the selection in the Sky channel with a gradient fill, leaving the house and ground alone.

Creating Shades of Blue with a Gradient Fill

Press Ctrl+minus and then click on the middle Window mode box at the bottom of the toolbox

Zooms out middle to 1:2 view and eliminates scroll bars from active image window, making room for next few steps.

Click on the default colors icon on the toolbox

Sets colors to default setting of black foreground and white background.

Double-click on the Gradient tool on the toolbox

Displays Gradient tool options dialog box.

Choose Style Normal and Type Linear; set Mid-point Skew to 50%, then click on OK

Applies settings and closes dialog box.

With the Gradient tool, click on a point about one inch above the center of the photo, drag down to the roof of the car, and then release the mouse button

Applies Gradient fill (see fig. 11.4).

Choose Edit, Copy (or press Ctrl+C)

Copies Gradient-filled selection area to clipboard.

Click on the RGB channel (or press Ctrl+0) in the Channels palette

Displays full-color view of active image.

continues

continued

Choose **E**dit, **P**aste (or press Ctrl+V)	Pastes copy of selection into RGB channel.
Press Ctrl+plus	Zooms in for closer view of active image to give you better view of changes you are about to apply. Also, you should move palettes out of the way.
Choose **A**djust, **I**mage, then Hue/Saturation (or press Ctrl+U)	Displays Hue and Saturation dialog box.
Check the Colorize box and type the following numbers in the appropriate boxes: Hue **-137**, Saturation **69**, Lightness **0**, and then click on OK	Grayscale Gradient is now a brilliant blue (see fig. 11.5). *Don't* deselect anything yet!
Choose **E**dit, Composite C**o**ntrols, set Opacity to **40**%, set Mode to **Multiply**, and then click on OK	Areas of pasted Gradient fill that held white color information are now transparent, Blue values are now more predominant than HOME.TIF file's original sky values.
Choose **S**elect, **N**one (or press Ctrl+D), then, from the **F**ile menu, choose Sa**v**e As and name the file **HOME.TIF**	Saves the file to your hard disk.
Choose **S**elect, **N**one (or press Ctrl+D). Then, from the **F**ile menu, choose Sa**v**e As and name the file **HOME.TIF**. Save it to your hard disk	You can choose LZH compression to conserve hard drive space when you save the file.

Choose **F**ile, **C**lose, to close the file now if you need a break, or skip this step and leave it open and continue the assignment.

Cool, huh? You created a great, natural-looking sky, you didn't mess up the foliage, and you did it faster than weather forecasters change their mind! This trick works best with dark foliage values that can absorb some of the bluish tint without a noticeable shift in color. Don't try this exercise with an image that includes a rosebush (or other brilliant blossoms or foliage) unless you want to wind up with some interesting hybrid horticulture.

Replacing Parts of an Image without Leaving Holes

Home-court demolition is on the agenda in the next set of exercises. Because the basketball backboard and net are easy to select, you could easily just delete them. But that would leave a hole in the image because (unlike the real world) nothing but a background color is behind the photographic backboard. You "replace" the backboard, net, and hoop by borrowing from other nearby areas in the image.

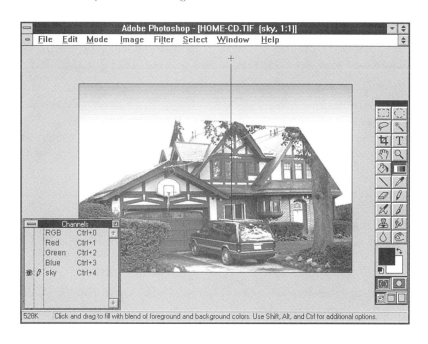

Figure 11.4
Start above the photo, then drag down to the car to create the gradient fill.

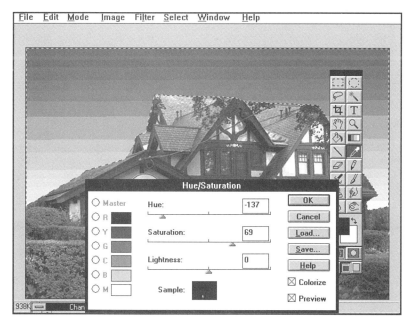

Figure 11.5
A gradient fill fills only the area you have selected.

Here are some observations worth keeping in mind when you begin the next exercises.

Careless cloning and pasting often leaves telltale marks. Be sure to watch color matching and avoid pattern repetition while you reconstruct a fairly detailed background. Because you don't have much clear image area to "borrow" from, you need to use your artist's eye and evaluate each step you take. Take your time. If your work doesn't look right, immediately select **E**dit, **U**ndo and try again.

When a section looks good, if you have extra disk space, save the file to a new name before you continue. You'll end up with a large collection of files, but you'll be able to retrace your steps without redoing all the work. If you're short on disk space, a regular save will do—you can use **R**evert to go back to the last saved version if you need to.

Also, Zoom in and out frequently to check your work from different perspectives. An area that looks a little rough and less than perfect at a 6:1 view can look perfect at 2:1 or 1:1. Don't drive yourself nuts trying to perfect something that *already* looks perfect at a 1:1 resolution.

The basketball backboard and net have obscured two boards in the image. Whenever you can, you may want to check out the physical location where an image was taken so that you can get a realistic idea of what is actually behind something you plan to remove or alter. Then you can accurately reconstruct the image in Photoshop. A little survey around the house when the photograph was taken showed that the board behind the basketball net is actually *wider* than the vertical board above it (behind the backboard).

You'll use similar techniques in the next two exercises to change the home court into just the home.

Removing a Net To Restore the Facade

If HOME.TIF is not already open in Photoshop's workspace, open the file from your hard drive.

Zoom in on the net hanging from the basketball hoop	An 8:1 viewing ratio is comfortable.
Click on the Rectangular Marquee tool in the toolbox	You can "borrow" from the image area to the left of the netting.
Click and drag a selection area (see fig. 11.6)	Avoid the dark row of pixels adjacent to the net, but *include* the dark area where the garage door recedes.

Choose **E**dit, **C**opy (or press Ctrl+C), then choose **E**dit, **P**aste (or press Ctrl+V)	Pastes a copy into the original area.
Choose **I**mage, **F**lip Horizontal	Minimizes repetitious patterns between edges and patterns of copies pasted next to original areas.
Press the right-arrow key a few times	The right-arrow key nudges the selection laterally, one pixel per nudge. Seven times will do the trick.
With the Rectangular Marquee tool, click and drag a new selection area to the left of the remaining net	A selection area of 7 x 13 pixels is good (see fig. 11.7). Be sure to get the dark edge of the board and the first row of pixels that make up the image's shadow.
Repeat the procedure (**C**opy, **P**aste, **F**lip Horizontal, drag seven pixels)	No more net!

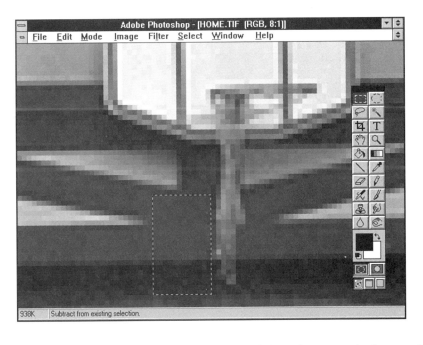

Figure 11.6

Selecting an area to copy to replace the bottom of the net.

The next target is the double horizontal board above the area you've been working on.

Figure 11.7
Flip this piece to
replace the net
and create the
new board's edge
and shadow.

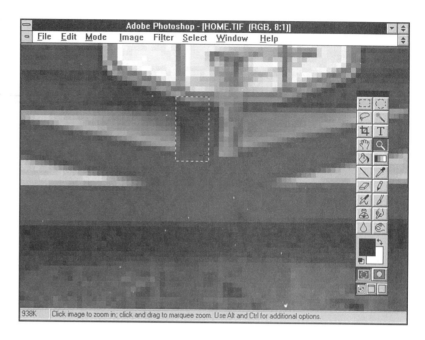

Making Room for Boards

Using the Rectangular Marquee tool, click and drag a new selection area to the left of the backstop (see fig. 11.8)	*Avoid* three-pixel-wide shadow (to left of backboard) and edge of vertical boards (to left and below). *Do* get upper edge and shadow.
Repeat the **C**opy, **P**aste, **F**lip Horizontal procedure used in the previous exercise	Modifies pasted piece, creating same effect as in preceding exercise.
Drag (or use the arrow key to nudge) the selction to the right	Left edge of selection should cover the three-pixel-wide shadow.
Choose **S**elect, **N**one (or press Ctrl+D)	Deselects image area and locks it in place.
Choose **E**dit, **P**aste (or press Ctrl+V) again	Places an identical selection area from clipboard onto image.
Choose **F**lip Horizontal and drag the selection into place next to the previously placed section	Now both pastes cover most of backboard.
Choose **S**elect, **N**one (or press Ctrl+D)	Deselects image area and locks it in place.

With the Rectangular Marquee tool, click and drag an 11-pixel-wide selection area to the right of the backboard	You'll copy this new area shortly. *Avoid* including one-pixel-wide shadow (to right of back stop) and edge of vertical boards (to right and below). *Do* include upper edge and shadow in selection, as before.
Choose **C**opy, **P**aste, and then **F**lip Horizontal	Creates replacement piece for more of backboard area.
Click and drag (or use the arrow key to nudge) the selection so that its right edge is adjacent to the area from which you selected	"Removes" more backboard.
Choose **S**elect, **N**one (or press Ctrl+D)	Deselects image area and locks it in place.

Paste in another copy of the selection, repeat the **F**lip Horizontal procedure, then drag the floating (pasted) selection into the remaining space to replace the remainder of the backboard.

Choose **S**elect, **N**one (or press Ctrl+D)	Deselects image area and locks it in place, completing a *coarse* retouching phase you now must refine. Screen should look like figure 11.9.
From the **F**ile menu, choose **S**ave	Saves your work.

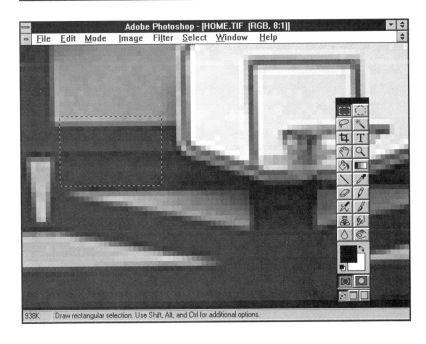

Figure 11.8
This selection is used twice to reconstruct the home's board area.

III

Gourmet Assignments

Figure 11.9
The pieces are in place but need some blending work.

Turning Wood "Paneling" into a Wooden Beam

Here's a quick recap of what you've done so far. You restored what *would* have been behind the basketball net had it not been in the photo. The values and colors of the replacement pastes are identical because the sources you copied them from were lit and colored identically to the home itself. Now you're going to *blend* the copies to suggest a continuous piece of wood.

In the next exercise you use the Rubber Stamp tool to blend the copies. But before you begin, you need a plan. Natural textures, like sand, water, and wood, can be cloned very successfully with the Rubber Stamp because the patterns in the textures are random. But multiple pastes, no matter how skillfully arranged, contain a telltale repetitious pattern that points to Photoshop trickery.

You need to blend the edges of the pastes and go a little farther into them with the Rubber Stamp tool. And you constantly need to resample the Rubber Stamp tool's source area, every three or four brush strokes. A cloned-over area needs to integrate visually with the rest of the picture, look absolutely boring, and not call attention to itself. Rubber stamping that has an abrupt beginning and end in a confined area looks just as obvious as the seams between pasted selections!

Start outside the pasted selections and work your way in. It is always best to "sample outside, clone inside" an area you want to blend in. Beware of repetitious brush strokes and begin the next exercise.

Blending in Wood Grain

Open the HOME.TIF file you saved in the last exercise, if it is not already open.

Zoom in on the reconstructed section under what remains of the hoop	Use a 4:1 ratio, full screen.
Choose Rubber Stamp tool from toolbox	Only tool used in this exercise.
Choose **W**indow, Show **B**rushes (or press F5)	Displays Brushes palette.
Choose second smallest hard-tip brush (3 pixels diameter) from top row of default tips	Double-click on this one if you need to confirm size in Brushes options box.
Set Mode: to **Normal** and Opacity to **100**%	For this task, you need a very small brush tip with a minimum of spread.
Press Alt and click the Rubber Stamp tool in the center of brown beam, to left of original paste	Sets sample point where the Rubber Stamp tool begins copying (see fig. 11.10).
Press Shift while you click and drag the Rubber Stamp cursor to the right	A short stroke copies Rubber Stamp sample across pasted selection's hard outline and breaks up wood grain in image.

If you like the way your work looks, go on to the next step. If you don't like the way it looks, press Ctrl+Z to undo it, then try again.

Hold Alt key down and click on the image, to the left of the pastes but lower than before	Sets new sampling point for Rubber Stamp tool.
Press Shift while you click and drag the Rubber Stamp tool, starting to the left of the paste edge and following through with a longer stroke than before	Constrains Rubber Stamp tool to a straight line; by lengthening the stroke, you continue to blend grain of wooden beam.
Continue varying stroke length and sample areas until left edges of pastes are hidden	Work your way across left edges of pastes, disguising them with random patterns of sampled areas.
Hold Alt down and click to right of pasted areas	Sample an original image area for cloning out right edge of pastes.
Click and drag from the right of the pasted edges to center of pasted area	Keep the random effect by using varying strokes and several sample areas.

continues

continued

Repeat the last steps from right side

Blend left clone strokes as well as pasted selections to finish the job.

Choose <u>F</u>ile, <u>S</u>ave

Saving your work at this point is wise!

Figure 11.10
Setting the place where the Rubber stamp tool samples is critical when clone-retouching.

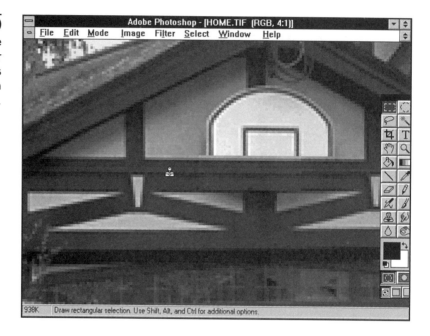

The top and bottom edges of the pasted selections also require a little work. A few simple, short strokes with the Rubber Stamp tool remove all the unnatural evidence of the restoration work.

The preceding wood-grafting adventure is a good example of how to change an image by using your artistic talents. Skill and a good eye are needed to literally *paint* some random wood-grain texture back into the section of board that was never photographed! The good eye depends mainly on your artistic disciplines but the *skill* part of the formula comes from repeating exercises—and some experimenting.

I first tried using the Smudge tool to quickly obscure the detail of the beam's wood grain. This method was unsuccessful because it *defocused* the pattern instead of blending it. The human eye sees funny things. Even the blandest design elements, like the wood beam, fairly shout at you when the calming natural order of its design has been tampered with.

Sometimes, when you have an area that contains an unwanted repeat pattern, putting the Rubber Stamp over the area and clicking once without dragging can be useful to break up the pattern. Doing this "blasts" an area with material from the location of the sampling crosshair, so make sure that the crosshair is set in a place that will provide good pattern and proper color value.

Stucco Repair

The next series of exercises wipes out the rest of the backboard. You eliminate the left half of the backboard by using the Rubber Stamp to add "new" stucco. A different approach to the right side of the backboard is necessary, however, because that side doesn't have enough material to take cloning samples from. Work on the right side goes much faster because the left side can be reused after it has been retouched. A little fancy pasting into the right side completes the work in just a few steps.

You begin by retouching the left triangular section of stucco from the bottom up, using a combination of horizontal strokes and strokes that parallel the roof line to work the material into place. You'll have to rely in part on inspiration and artistic flair to complete this section. And you'll have to zoom in and out often because the task—painting in a convincing panel— must be evaluated at various stages from a complete image perspective.

Stay away from the soft shadow under the eaves as much as possible. The stucco, because it is naturally swirly and uneven, can be "faked." But shadows are hard to restore after they have been altered.

Cloning Stucco

Open the file HOME.TIF that you saved in the last exercise, if it is not already open.

Zoom in on the garage peak	The rest of the backboard needs to be replaced here. An 8:1 viewing ratio is good.
Choose Rubber Stamp tool	Use this tool for first part of retouching task.
Choose **W**indow, Show **B**rushes (or press F5)	Displays Brushes palette, if it is not already displayed.
Select third brush from left in top row. Set Mode to **Normal** and Opacity to **100**%	You need a medium-hard brush with no spread to work in this area.

continues

continued

Press Alt and click the Rubber Stamp tool along the bottom left edge, about 1/4 inch from the corner	Sets sampling point for Rubber Stamp tool.
Move cursor up into position just before start of shadow on backboard, then click and drag Rubber Stamp into the backboard image	Rubber Stamp tool now clones over this area (where the backboard obscures brown vertical board).
Place cursor above and slightly to the left of the place where you started in the last step; repeat last step	Continue cloning stucco from a sampling area that moves as the cursor moves.
Repeat a third time	Three passes with the Rubber Stamp is about all you can do before you start copying in roof-line shadow, which you don't want.
Click on next-smaller-tip brush on Brushes palette	You need a smaller tip for precise work.
Press Alt and click the Rubber Stamp in the middle of panel, but not in a shadow	Sets *new* sampling point relative to the Rubber Stamp's position when it clones.
Make a few more short horizontal strokes into the backboard	Refines previous cloned strokes to eliminate any "patterning" effect in cloned area. Your screen should resemble figure 11.11.
Press Alt and click Rubber Stamp in lower left part of area	Sets new sampling point for tool. Do *not* sample over a shadow area!
Click and drag strokes at an angle parallel to the roof line, over the top section of backboard	Again, not only covers up backboard but also varies the angles to prevent an unwanted patterning.
Repeat last two steps, resetting sampling point and varying size of brush, make short strokes	If pattern develops, resample from area that does not have that pattern, move cursor over pattern and click once to "burst" away the offending pattern.
Choose medium-sized soft brush with spread (middle row on Brushes palette)	Sets new size and spread attribute to Rubber Stamp tool.
If you have cloned into a shadow area and left a hard edge, press Alt and click Rubber Stamp in shadow area	Sets sampling point for cloning in shadow value and texture.

Click and drag over hard line between shadowed stucco and illuminated stucco	Evens out hard line between the two areas.
Choose <u>F</u>ile, <u>S</u>ave	Save your work when you are happy with it. It should look like figure 11.12.

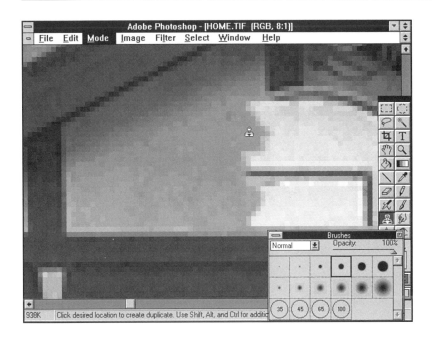

Figure 11.11
Stucco reconstruction in progress.

Pasting with Stucco

In the last exercise, you spent some time and effort generating a good-looking stucco panel. Now, by copying that panel, you'll restore the right stucco panel. Although the two panels are not identical in real life, they are similar in color, lighting, and size.

You do not want *exactly* the same shadow pattern under the eaves on both sides because nature's lighting does not work that way! In the next exercise, you use the Paste Into command to "tuck" some of the excess shadow area under the eaves.

Now get your trowel so that you can do some fast stucco restoration.

Figure 11.12
A nice, naturalistic
piece of stucco.

A Perfect Patch

Open the HOME.TIF file you saved in the last exercise, if it is not already open.

Zoom in on garage peak area, to an 8:1 viewing ratio	As you work on this area, a close zoom ratio ensures precision.
Choose the Lasso tool from the toolbox	For a freehand selection.
Press Alt and click and hold the Lasso on lower-left corner of left panel of stucco	Constrains the tool to a straight line with anchor points and begins selection. Include shadow edges but *not* the brown boards themselves.
Keep holding Alt and click points around the stucco panel's border	Creates a selection border (see fig. 11.13), which should consist of straight, non-parallel lines.
Choose **E**dit, **C**opy (or press Ctrl+C)	Copies the selected area to the clipboard.
Hold Alt key down and click to create selection border around right stucco panel that includes shadow edge next to the boards	Creates active selection area, target for the paste (see fig. 11.14).
Choose **E**dit, Paste **I**nto	Pastes clipboard selection *into* right-panel selection.

Choose **I**mage, **F**lip, and then Horizontal	Mirrors pasted copy but is too "perfect," viewed next to the original.
Press up-arrow key two or three times	Nudges selection up behind selection area by 2 to 3 pixels.
Press Ctrl+minus (or select Zoom tool, then press Alt and left click)	Zooms out of tight-resolution ratio so that you can better evaluate work.
Press Ctrl+plus (or select the Zoom tool)	Should return you to original viewing resolution.
Click on toolbox's Rectangular Marquee tool	You need to fix gap at bottom, formed by double row of shadow lines.
Click and drag a long rectangular selection area just above the double shadow area that needs correcting	Creates a sample area you use to correct the problem area.
Choose **E**dit, **C**opy (or press Ctrl+C), then **E**dit, **P**aste (or press Ctrl+V)	Copies selection back into image at the same relative position as the copy point.
Press down-arrow key several times	Nudges copy into location to be covered.
Stop nudging when it is covered (see fig. 11.15)	
Choose **S**elect, **N**one (or press Ctrl+D)	Locks the copied selection into place in HOME.TIF.
Choose **F**ile, **S**ave	You want to save your work at this point!

Dragging a Board through Stucco

The last element in the stucco and board reconstruction is the center board. The plan is to clone what little remains in the top area by dragging the Rubber Stamp tool straight down.

Because the sample area is in shadow in the image, the cloned area you create is also shadowed. This is not a problem because Photoshop's Brightness and Contrast controls can adjust the selection after it has been cloned.

Let's do it.

Figure 11.13
Select a section of
stucco to paste into
the opposite
panel.

Figure 11.14
Select the area to
be pasted into.

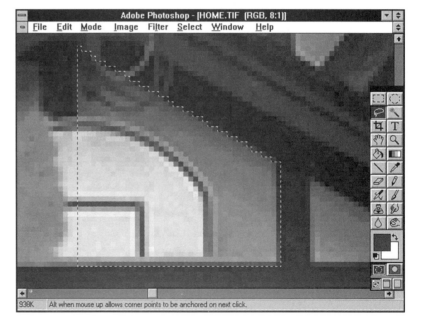

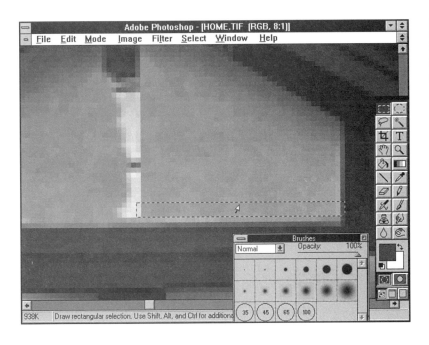

Figure 11.15
Stop nudging the copy when it covers the area.

Restoring House Areas by Rubber Stamping

Open the file HOME.TIF that you saved in the last exercise, if it is not already open.

Zoom in on the garage peak where you will restore the center board	An 8:1 ratio, full screen view is comfortable.
Choose Rubber Stamp tool from toolbox	Use this tool to complete retouching.
Click on second brush from left in top row of the Brushes palette	You need a small, hard brush with no spread.
Set Mode to **Normal** and Opacity to **100**%	Same brush characteristics as in the preceding exercise.
Press Alt and click on a point near the top center of the board	Sets the sampling point of Rubber Stamp.
Click and drag long straight lines	Creates missing portion of board. Stop brushing when you reach the horizontal board.
Choose small, soft-tipped brush from the Brushes palette (second row of default tips, second from right)	For precise, soft-edge work.

continues

continued

Resample from top of board, slightly off center; click on a "problem" area	On visible patterns in this cloning work, one click with Rubber Stamp tool "bursts" a clone beneath the Rubber Stamp cursor, "randomizing" the area's texture.
Press Ctrl+minus (or select Zoom tool, then press Alt and left click), then press Ctrl+plus key (or click, using the Marquee Zoom tool placed over the area)	Check your progress from different perspectives (resolutions).

Click on **E**dit, **U**ndo if you are unhappy with last Rubber Stamp cloning move. Complete the cloning process. When you are happy with restoration, move on to next step.

Choose Lasso tool from toolbox	Freehand tool for selecting cloned area.
Click and drag selection border around the cloned board	You must make this area lighter, to match the other boards (see fig. 11.16).
Choose **I**mage, **A**djust, Brightness/Contrast (or press Ctrl+B)	Displays Brightness/Contrast dialog box.
Type **-17** in Contrast: text box, then click on OK	Evens out board's appearance to more closely match unretouched, similar boards in image. (17 is an arbitrary number that worked.)
Choose **S**elect, **N**one (or press Ctrl+D)	Deselects decontrasted selection area.
Choose **F**ile, **S**ave	Saving your work at various stages is important.

The sky is blue, the stucco is all set, and basketball is no longer played in front of the image of this house. At this point, you may want to click on the right Display Mode button at the bottom of Photoshop's toolbox. You deserve an uncluttered view of all your work!

All that's left now in this fairly sophisticated home-remodeling job is to remove the utility lines. Removing power lines that mar a clear blue sky is an easy trick with the Rubber Stamp tool, but when the wires run through the tree and part of the house, you definitely need the techniques you have just learned.

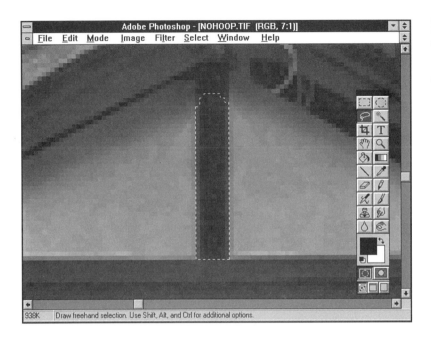

Figure 11.16
This selection area needs to be decontrasted to match the other boards on the peak.

Power Outage—Removing Lines that Cross the Roof

The Rubber Stamp tool is very effective for removing all sections of the utility lines, *except* where they cross the roof. You don't need a step-by-step exercise for most of this phase of reconstruction because you learned the necessary techniques in your basketball work. To avoid a shock, keep the following pointers in mind while you work on the utility lines.

✔ To clone over wood areas, move the Rubber Stamp cursor in the direction indicated by visible grain or bark. If the bark grew straight up and down in an area of trunk, clone that way. If a piece of board is at an angle, brush at that angle with the Rubber Stamp.

✔ Resize the Brush tips according to your work. Because using a brush that is sometimes too large is easy to do, be ready to Undo (press Ctrl+Z) after each stroke.

✔ *Where* you sample with the Rubber Stamp tool is critical. Resample often to avoid "painting" patterns or adding areas that are the wrong color.

✔ Some sections of the wire can be seen only when you zoom out to a 4:1 or greater resolution. Choose the degrees of magnification to suit the task.

✔ The "burst" versus the click and drag method of cloning with the Rubber Stamp tool is *especially useful* for removing wires. You need to replace only a very small amount of utility line at a time. Clicking without dragging the Rubber Stamp also works best in

III

Gourmet Assignments

tight areas on the house, where you have an extremely limited area to sample from. Don't be afraid to clone in a few leaves in areas where you remove power lines—and then clone in a few more to balance the new ones.

By removing the utility wires over the tree and the front of the house, you reinforce your experience with the tools and menu options that are part of this retouching technique. The skill becomes one you own.

Rubber stamp out all the wires *except* the ones that cross the roof tiles. When you have finished, save the image. The next section has some special copy and paste methods that make short work of patching the roof tile.

Fixing a Roof

The regular pattern of the roof tile is distorted by perspective when it is on the different roof planes. You can't use the Rubber Stamp tool for the mend because the Rubber Stamp only re-creates from samples across a 2D plane. You can't access a feature to compensate for the perspective, and the Rubber Stamp will make confetti of the irregularly spaced roof tiles. You don't want to ask precision work from a tool whose forté is blending.

Pasting works well here because you can "adopt" the fixed angle and perspective of the roof tiles if you carefully and accurately select the source for copying. In the next exercise you learn how to make a perfect selection.

Patching the Roof on a Sunny Day

If the HOME.TIF file you saved in the last exercise is not already open, open it.

Marquee-zoom in on large section of roof on right, where the utility lines cross just below the standpipes	An 8 :1 ratio, with active window at full screen, is the best view of area.
Choose Lasso tool from toolbox	Use this freehand selection tool to create irregular selection borders.
Using the Lasso tool, press Alt and click around the wire only	Make selection area very tight-fitting. The Alt key constrains to straight lines the anchor points you click. Selection area should be only two to three pixels wide (see fig.11.17).
Choose **S**elect, **S**ave Selection, New	Selection area is now Channel 5.

Figure 17.17
With the Lasso tool, make a tight selection around the wire on the roof only.

Upon close examination, the wire looks as though it should be replaced by a light-colored copy. A promising piece of roof is four or five pixels down from the current selection. To preserve the angle of the material to be copied, use the *same* selection border you created in the last exercise.

To do this, move the selection *border*—*not* the contents of the selected area— down. After the empty marquee is moved into place, the section of roof can be copied and pasted into the Channel #5 selection area with the Paste **I**nto command. This is the technique you used with the stucco panel, but with a new twist!

Picking Up a Section of Roof

Place Lasso tool over selection you created in the last exercise	Lasso cursor becomes an arrow.
Press Ctrl+Alt and drag the selection border down the roof line four or five pixels	Ctrl+Alt key combination moves selection border only, not the contents. One white pixel should be in middle of first column of pixels inside selection border (see fig. 11.18).
Choose **E**dit, **C**opy (or press Ctrl+C)	Copies selected area to clipboard.

continues

continued

Choose **S**elect, **L**oad Selection, and then choose #5	Displays wire area saved earlier as a selection.
Select **E**dit, Paste **I**nto	Pastes copied roof-tile image into selection border.
Choose **S**elect, Hide **E**dges (or press Ctrl+H), then Zoom out	Hides selection marquee. Pasted-into selection is still a floating selection, but hidden marquee lines afford better view of work.
Press left-arrow key twice, down-arrow key once	Nudges pasted-into selection; aligns pattern of roof tiles.
Choose **S**elect, **N**one (or press Ctrl+D)	Locks floating selection into main image.
Click on the Rubber Stamp tool on the toolbox	You repair remaining tiny area of utility wire by cloning.
Choose **W**indow, Show **B**rushes (or press F5)	Displays Brushes palette (if closed earlier).
Choose Normal, 100%, small, hard brush	For precise cloning with no brush "spread."
Press Alt and click on some nearby foliage	Sets sampling area for Rubber Stamp tool.
Click once or twice over remaining wire, then click once or twice on tree	Removes rest of wire and mottles area where tree area met wire.
Choose **F**ile, **S**ave	Saves finished work to disk.

Zoom out to a 1:1 resolution and look at the whole picture. The only retouching left to do is on the small gable roof over the garage and a little on the main gable roof next to it. With the same roof-repair technique, using the small Brushes tip for the Rubber Stamp to sample with, moving the selection border only, and then cleaning up with the Rubber Stamp tool, you can finish retouching *sans* an additional exercise.

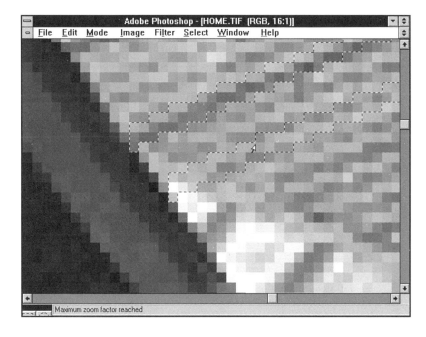

Figure 11.18
Drag only the selection border by pressing Ctrl+Alt while you hold down the left mouse button.

Who Says Housework Is Easy?

The example provided here is solid, and you now have a good example of how to approach restoration of a house. You can use the techniques learned in this chapter on images of houses, buildings, and other structures. Chapters 6 and 7 in this book detailed the best way to retouch an image of a person. But cosmetic renovation of a physical *location* requires different techniques and disciplines, and in some respects, is more difficult.

After you apply the final touches to the cleaned-up version of this Tudor home, you face one more piece of "house-cleaning"—but it requires no precision and no Rubber Stamp tool.

Cleaning Up Your File after Cleaning Up the House

Before you save your file for the last time and astound your client, you need to do a little file management. In the course of this assignment, you created several extra Alpha channels that hold valuable but *temporary* image information. Each of these channels increases an image file size significantly. Most programs—other than Photoshop—get confused or crash when they attempt to read an image that contains channels. Should this happen, you might be forced to restart your machine, and you could lose data. The solution to this problem is in the Channels palette. Delete the channels you no longer need. The experience is gratifying, akin to trashing that clearinghouse sweepstakes notice you received in the mail last week! The next exercise shows you how.

Removing Channels

If the Channels palette is not displayed, press F6 to display it.

Click on the Sky channel	Displays active view of channel used earlier to mask sky.
Click on the command button in Channels	Displays drop-down palette list of options.
Choose Delete Channel	Deletes sky channel and displays RGB channel.
Repeat process for Channel #5	Deletes roof-tile selection channel.

Do not delete the Red, Green, Blue, or RGB channels! When only these four original color-information channels remain, file management is complete.

Choose **F**ile, **S**ave	Saves HOME.TIF image with all retouching work but no extra, temporary information channels.

Take a good long look at what you have accomplished. If you have followed along, your file will look like figure 11.19. Look back at figure 11.1—it has come a long way, hasn't it?

Figure 11.19
Picture-postcard-perfect landscaping, courtesy of Photoshop.

Light on the Razzle, Heavy-Duty Dazzle

People, landscapes, and architectural structures require that the Photoshop retouching work done to them must be invisible. It's because they are "real" image objects, and you should strive for a *verisimilitude*, a faithful rendering of what things *should* look like in an image, even when in reality, they *aren't!* This is an important distinction to make early in your photoshop experiences, because we'll be getting into *fantastic* image retouching in future chapters, when the objective is to *show* the viewer that something's been tricked-up using computer art.

This assignment was designed to familiarize you with a process you can use to retouch a realistic scene. Experience, practice, and perspective is the "hard stuff." After you have mastered a technique such as copying, pasting, and positioning, you can move on to many similar assignments in your own work. The Rubber Stamp tool has a place not only in simple situations (like those in Chapter 9) but also in those that require utmost care and precision. If you are beginning to feel that Photoshop's tools belong to something larger, you are right—it is called *technique.* And when these techniques become effortless, it is called skill.

Summary

You have learned how to retouch people and landscapes without once copying and pasting between the two image types. Such copying and pasting is done every day in professional imaging—this exciting technique is a logical outgrowth of the exercises you have done so far.

The next chapter shows you how to use Photoshop to transplant a landlubber to a surfside spot without even booking a flight! Set aside a little time, put on a Beach Boys cassette, and get ready to say, "Like, oh, wow!"

Chapter Snapshot

In this chapter, you learn how to:

CHAPTER

Combining Photos

Although cutting and pasting photos into *other* photos has been the practice of grade school students and amateur publishers for fun and humorous effects for a long time, electronic imaging has increased the accuracy, power, and capability of cutting, copying, and pasting. It's no longer kid's stuff. You can transport images to entirely different locales, and do it convincingly with Photoshop. And still have fun!

This chapter is a double-header on the subject of combining photos. First, you learn how to disguise glaringly obvious image edges into the background so that they are undetectable! Then, you get a chance to flex those artistic muscles and paint a convincingly realistic shadow. Shadows add depth and realism to a retouched scene, and if done properly, separate amateur work from professional imaging.

The tools you use are in Photoshop, and the materials are on the companion CD. Set your sights for some serious fun as you learn how to paste into images, Photoshop-style.

Plan Your Photos before Using Photoshop

To create believable composite images in Photoshop, you need to do a little pre-photography planning and carefully select the images. The following are a few ground rules for successfully combining photographic images:

✔ Make sure that the lighting in the two photo sources is the same. If the lighting source appears to come from the upper-left in one image, the second image must also be lit this way. Similar lighting is the biggest hurdle to portraying a composite scene realistically.

✔ Use your camera's viewfinder to compare relative sizes of the two images to be composited before you photograph or digitize them. For example, it's usually best to capture an image of a person at the same camera lens field size as the person would fit into a background of a different scene. If the scene's captured from a distance, the person should be photographed that way, too. It's easier to photograph, then digitize your source images in *proper relation to each other,* than to fuss with different image resolutions and sizes later using Photoshop.

✔ The *angle of photography* must match in the two images. If you take a picture from the ground floor of a skyscraper, the picture of the person you want to paste in front of it must *also* be photographed from the ground floor.

Pictures Perfect for Use with the Magic Wand Tool

The two images you are going to use in the following exercises were taken at different times in different places. The background image, DAYTONA.TIF, was captured at about three o'clock in the afternoon in sunny Florida. The time here is important because the shadows cast in the image go to the right, almost parallel to the horizon. SRFNDAVE.TIF, the image you are going to paste into DAYTONA.TIF, was taken several months later in New England. I was able to plan how large the subject would be in the picture, and how to get the overall lighting to match the DAYTONA image. Matching the shadows was almost impossible, however, because Florida is closer than New England to the earth's horizon. But that's okay because shortly you are going to see how to *create* a realistic shadow, using both images as references.

One of the last considerations before I took the SRFNDAVE.TIF image was how to set up the background. I wanted a material that would make separating the model from the background easy to do in Photoshop. As you will see, a simple white sheet behind the subject is much easier to select than the New England grass he posed on!

The reason for explaining this, is that you'll be using Photoshop's Magic Wand tool to separate the model from the sheet he's posed on and place him in a second image. The Magic Wand tool, unlike the other selection tools in Photoshops tool box, selects image area based

on color, not on geometric areas. This is the ideal tool to use when faced with picking an image area out of a background that has very little tonal variation.

By double-clicking on the Magic Wand button on the toolbox, you can specify the <u>T</u>olerance (the range of different colored adjacent pixels) the Magic Wand will select relative to the specific point you click over in the image with the cursor. A Tolerance setting of 1 or 2 pixels will only select pixels adjacent to your clicked-over area that are fairly identical in their color value. A Tolerance setting of 255, the maximum, will select the entire image area because every tonal value has been chosen! You'll want to tinker with different settings to get the best results when selecting areas in images.

Start Photoshop, and then open the SRFNDAVE.TIF image from the companion CD and begin preparing for vacation!

Removing an Unwanted Background

Double-click on the Zoom tool	Zooms in to a 1:1 viewing resolution of SRFNDAVE.TIF, a good viewing angle for establishing a rough selection border around the model.
Double-click on the Magic Wand tool	Displays Magic Wand options box.
Set Tolerance to **35** pixels; make sure that Anti-Aliased option is on	Sets tool to select a medium range of pixels that neighbor the pixel you click on and creates a smooth selection border.
Click on the white sheet in the middle of the image, toward the top	Selects a good portion of the top sheet area, as shown in figure 12.1. For best results, try to click in the area indicated in this figure.
Press Shift and click in an unselected white sheet area	Adds to the first Magic Wand selection. You cannot select *all* the white sheet area in one Magic Wand swoop because the variation in tone, hence color, is too great.
Press Shift and click on the bluish shadow area on the sheet, behind the model's left shoulder	Adds the area to your original selection.
Continue pressing Shift and clicking until most of the white and shadow area is selected	Object is to select as much of the unwanted background sheet as possible with one tool.
Choose the Zoom tool, then click+ diagonal drag to the right of the model's head	This marquee zooms your view to an unselected, unwanted sheet area. A 4:1 resolution is good. Marquee zoom a second time if necessary.

As with most tasks you set out to accomplish using Photoshop, you'll want to use a combination of tools. In this exercise, "pulling the sheet" from under the model requires two selection tools; the Magic Wand and the Lasso tool. The previous exercise used the Magic Wand tool to do the bulk of the selecting work. In the next exercise, you'll use the Lasso to refine the selection outline you've created with the Magic Wand tool. The Lasso tool is best for selecting precise, little areas, whereas the Magic Wand's forte is usually reserved for selecting large areas that have similar color values.

Refining the Selection Outline

Click on the Lasso tool	Use this tool to add and subtract from selection areas.
Press Shift while you click and drag the Lasso around the unselected shadow area	Adds to the sheet selection area. Don't worry about including some grass—soon you will select the grass area also. (Fig. 12.2 shows the area to select.)
Press Shift while you click and drag around other unselected areas in the sheet image	Adds to sheet selection. You can stop after selecting a fairly good, but not flawless, sheet area that excludes the model.
Choose **S**elect, **S**ave Selection	Saves selecting work into an Alpha Channel.
Choose **S**elect, **N**one (or press Ctrl+D)	Deselects everything in RGB image.

Figure 12.1
The proper Magic Wand Tolerance helps you select an image area based on color values.

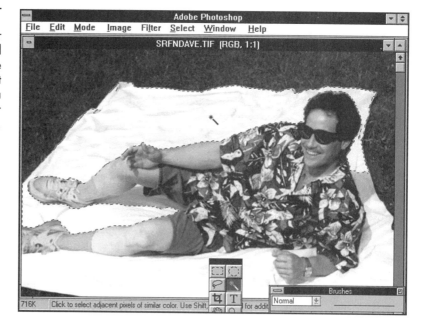

Figure 12.2
The Lasso tool can be used to modify a Magic Wand selection.

You can use a combination of selection tools to make quick work of defining an area. In the preceding exercise, the Lasso tool was useful for "carving out" an area the Magic Wand couldn't. Yet using the Lasso tool to define the entire border would not be wise because the border is too complex. A color selection, combined with a geometric selection, has brought you to a point at which you can use a *third* way of selecting things to polish off this selection.

If you are a professional photographer, you're probably keeling over with laughter about using a sheet as a backdrop for the model on the grass in the image. Nonprofessional photographers may find the following tip useful for backdropping a subject. It's a tip that can eliminate some of the selecting processes in assignments similar to this one.

Go out and buy a paper seamless to put under or behind your model. This kind of paper, available at commercial art supply stores, comes in rolls and does not exhibit the same variations in tone as the sheet did when photographed.

The selection process in Photoshop goes a little faster when a selection has less variation in background tone. Then you can set the Magic Wand Tolerance to a smaller value.

Quick Mask to the Rescue

Presently, the Saved selection area includes some areas that run into the model's border and other areas that are not selected but that you *want* selected. The goal is to create a selection border that includes everything *except* the model. Later, you simply select the inverse of the defined area to exclude the entire background, and include the model. When defining a border is your goal, the task involves much less fuss when you select a simple background and then invert the selection.

You have made a good start, using only two of Photoshop's selection features. Now it's time to clean up the border areas with a drawing tool and Photoshop's Quick Mask feature.

The Quick Mask button, next to the Standard view button, on the toolbox, shows a "film," or mask over a selection area. Besides being a more helpful visual reminder than the marquee lines you get every time you select something, you can edit a Quick Mask with painting tools, then turn it back into a marquee selection again! You can't do any image editing while in Quick Mask mode, but you can do *selection* editing, with all the precision and refinement you'll find in using Photoshop's painting tools.

When you "paint" with a dark foreground color, you are actually adding to a selection. And when you paint with a light foreground color, masked areas are removed from the original mask that becomes a selection area again when you click the Standard mode button. A mask is simple and clear in its visual representation of a selection area, and editing this mask is what you'll do next.

The Border Watch

Click on the default color icon on the toolbox	Sets foreground color to black, background to white.
Click on the inverse colors icon at the top right of the selection boxes	This little two-headed bent-arrow shape reverses foreground color to white and background to black.
Select the Zoom tool, then click+ diagonal drag over the model's left hand	This marquee-zooms you to the area you work on first.
Double-click on the Quick Mask button on the toolbox (second row from the bottom, on the right)	Displays Quick Mask options menu.
Choose the Selected Areas radio button, then click on OK	Sets Quick Mask to display colored Quick Mask over areas included in selection border.
Choose the Standard Mode button to the left of the Quick Mask button	Returns you to regular editing mode.
Choose **S**elect, **L**oad Selection	Retrieves selection border from alpha channel and displays its marquee in RGB channel. (You are viewing the image in this channel.)
Click once on the Quick Mask button	Displays all selected areas in deep-tinted color.

Select the Pencil tool from the toolbox, then choose a small tip from the Brushes palette	Sets cursor for a tool that applies or removes Mask areas in Quick Mask mode, with a well-defined, no-spread, small tip.
Click and drag over the wristwatch area on the image	Pencil tool removes some of the mask (see fig. 12.3).
Click on the invert colors icon on the toolbox	Switches foreground color back to black.
Click and drag over the border area of the model's forearm	Applies foreground Mask color in Mask mode. You will "paint" Quick Mask areas the Magic Wand tool missed in your original selection.
Scroll (or use the Hand tool) to move your view to other model-meets-background areas	Look for other areas where Quick Mask overlaps or does not meet model image.
Continue to click on the invert colors icon and to remove and/or apply Quick Mask color with the Pencil tool	You are refining the selection border. Stop after checking the entire periphery of model and finishing all edge work.
Choose File, Save As (Pick a name like SRFNDAVE.TIF for the file and save it in a directory on your hard drive)	You are saving your work at this phase of completion.

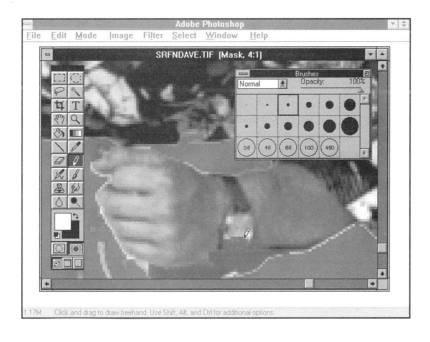

Figure 12.3

You can apply and remove mask in Quick Mask mode with selection or paint application tools.

Making a Splash before Hitting the Beach

The Quick Mask should now include all of the sheet backdrop, maybe a little of the grass area, and absolutely none of the model. It's not the selection border of our dreams because most of the grass area and the model would be excluded if you clicked from Quick Mask to Standard mode at this stage. The trick here is to exclude everything *except* the model so that you can invert the selection area later.

The quickest, easiest way to fill the remaining grass area is to use the Paint Bucket tool—but only if the Quick Mask completely borders the model. Like the Magic Wand tool, the Paint Bucket has a user-definable Tolerance, which is set by double-clicking on the Paint Bucket button. Using the Paint Bucket tool, you can quickly fill an *enclosed* area with a uniform color (or mask, when you're in Quick Mask mode).

If the Quick Mask does not surround the model completely, the Paint Bucket leaks through a separation in the border and flood fills the model, too!

Take one last look at the Quick Mask border around the model in SRFNDAVE.TIF to check for "leaks" before you dive into the next exercise!

Flood Filling with the Paint Bucket

Double-click on the Paint Bucket tool on the toolbox	Displays Paint Bucket Options dialog box.
Set **T**olerance to **219** pixels, check Anti-Aliasing, then click on OK	Establishes a tolerance for the area to be flooded to less than the "break point" of the Quick Mask color. A higher Tolerance would include the Mask color itself. See following *tip*. The contents of the Paint Bucket is always set to foreground color when in Quick Mask mode and no pattern is available.
Click on the default colors icon on the toolbox	Icon below and to left of color selection boxes resets foreground to black, background to white.
Click in an area above the Quick Mask in SRFNDAVE.TIF	Fills unmasked grass area with mask's foreground "color" (see fig. 12.4 for exact position).
Click on Standard mode on the toolbox	Displays marquee selection area, with marquee lines around border of image window and around model. Selection area is between the two marquees.

Choose **S**elect, **I**nvert	Inverts selection area to include only the model; excludes all grass and the white sheet (see fig. 12.5).
Choose **S**elect, **S**ave Selection, then click on #4	Refined border work overwrites previous selection. You no longer need previous selection. Overwriting Alpha channel selections keeps files small.

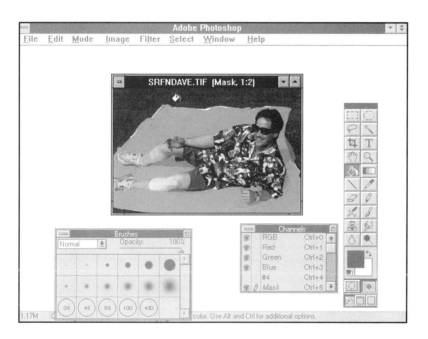

Figure 12.4
Use the Paint bucket tool to flood-fill the unmasked area of an image with Mask.

III

Gourmet Assignments

The Paint Bucket tool can be used as a normal paint application tool in Standard mode. In Quick Mask mode, this tool also applies (or removes) Quick Mask areas with the same Tolerance sensitivities.

Thus, if Tolerance is set too high on the tool in Quick Mask mode, you flood fill the *entire* image window when its Tolerance includes a range of neighboring pixels that include the Quick Mask color itself.

How do you know the correct Tolerance when you use the Paint Bucket in Quick Mask mode? Try setting the tolerance very low, apply the tool, then set Tolerance higher if the flood fill produced only a trickle of foreground Quick Masking. Click again with the Paint Bucket. Stop clicking when you have flooded the desired area.

continues

The goal is *coverage* with the Paint Bucket. If you set the Tolerance too high, you must use the Edit, Undo commands to restore your previous Masking efforts.

Figure 12.5
A selection
can be inverted
only when it's
viewed in
Standard
mode.

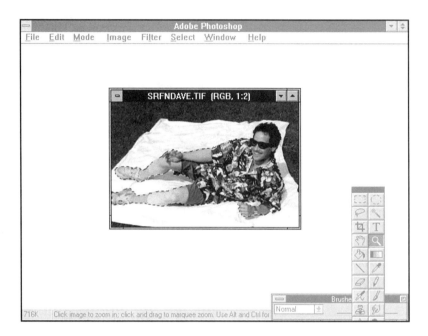

Further Refining a Saved Selection

After you save the selection of the model, you can display it again as a Quick Mask and edit it. Click on Channel #4 on the Channels palette now to evaluate how well the selection border you created fits the model. Some areas that you want covered, such as seams between the Paint Bucket fill and your Pencil work, may not be covered at all. In a view of Channel #4, you can correct them with the Pencil or Paintbrush tool. Just zoom into an area and apply a black foreground color to the area outside the selection, white background where the selection border is a little too tight.

Combining Photos

It's time to haul this guy over to the beach scene captured in DAYTONA.TIF. After you position the copied selection, you blend the selection border into the background to complete the overall effect. Selection borders with Anti-Aliased edges eliminate jagged edges around selection areas but also leave unwanted gray edge pixels between the selection area and background image.

This is when the Select, Defringe command comes into your Photoshop work. Think of Defringe as the opposite of Anti-Aliasing. When you click on this command, an options box pops up in which you can specify how many pixels you want removed from a selection's border. In most cases, you'll find your work only calls for one or two pixels to be Defringed around a selection. Defringing actually replaces edge pixels around a selection border with pure colors found in the selection area, but not the background image. This sometimes gets rid of an Anti-Aliasing "halo effect" perfectly, but there are times you'll want to work manually on an area that's been Defringed to get a border perfect.

In the next exercise, you'll copy and paste the image, and then learn how to get rid of the superfluous pixels.

Finding a Spot on The Beach

Click on the RGB composite channel title of the Channels Palette	Gives you the full-color view of the SRFNDAVE.TIF image.
Choose **S**elect, **L**oad Selection, then choose #4	Loads previously defined selection marquee created by combining Magic Wand selection and Quick Mask editing.
Choose **E**dit, **C**opy (or press Ctrl+C)	Copies selection of model to Clipboard.
Minimize or close the SRFNDAVE.TIF file	Reduces screen clutter while you move to next background image. If you close file now, save Alpha channel.
Open the DAYTONA.TIF file from the companion CD	"Host" image for selection area in SRFNDAVE.TIF.
Choose **E**dit, **P**aste (or press Ctrl+V)	Pastes the selection area into DAYTONA.TIF.
Click and drag the selection area down onto the beach area in DAYTONA.TIF	Pasted selection arbitrarily pops into a new image file (see fig. 12.6). Drag selection into place, using tiny arrow cursor(what the selection tool turns into when positioned inside a selection border).
Click and drag the selection so that the extreme left border butts against the left image frame of DAYTONA.TIF	Making bottom of model's foot (accidentally clipped off in original photo) flush with DAYTONA.TIF image border creates appearance that sneaker is also out of frame in *new* background image.

continues

III

Gourmet Assignments

continued

Choose **S**elect, Hide **E**dges (or press Ctrl+H)

Selection is still active but marquee border is invisible. You can position more precisely when selection's edge is visible.

When selection is positioned, Marquee Zoom to the model's head

Use a 2:1 resolution as you retouch this area (see fig. 12.7).

Choose **S**elect, **D**efringe, then select **2** pixels and click on OK

Removes edge pixels added by Anti-Aliasing when selection border around model was created.

Choose **S**elect, **S**ave Selection, then click on New

Saves defringed selection to new channel 4, which you can display later.

Choose **F**ile, Sa**v**e As, name the image, and save it to a directory on your hard disk

Saves your work to hard disk.

Figure 12.6

To reposition a Floating selection copied from another image before you save it, use any of the selection-tool cursors.

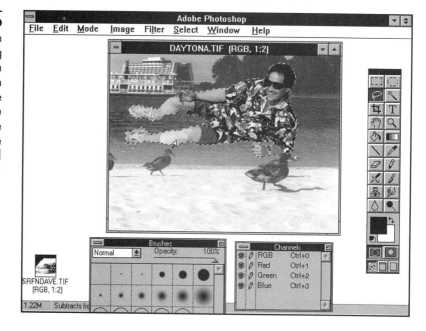

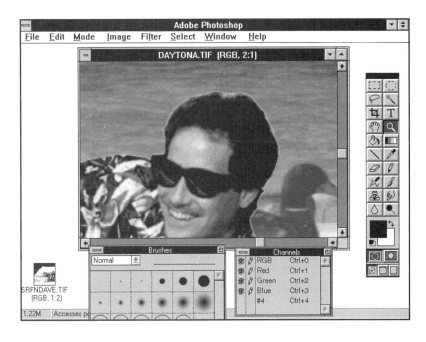

Figure 12.7
The Defringe command removes pixels from the edges of a selection area.

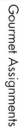

Correcting a Defringed Border

When you define a selection area, Photoshop's Anti-Aliasing features offer many advantages. In addition to smoothing edges created by selection tools, or paint strokes in Quick Mask mode, Anti-Aliasing fits special pixels into sharp edge areas. The pixels Photoshop applies through interpolation contain evened-out grayscale components, that cause a gradual color fall-off at the extreme edges of the border.

This is great when you paste a selection from a light background into a new background that's similarly colored. But the effect of Anti-Aliasing in figure 12.7, in which the model selection was pasted into a darker, seascape background, made using the Defringe command necessary. This command removed the telltale edges in which Anti-Aliasing extended the absolute border of the selection area and deposited light-colored pixels.

The disadvantage of the Defringe command is that, because it has no Anti-Aliasing feature, it gives the selection border a hard edge. You correct this in the next exercise, using a smoothing tool and a paint tool.

A Little Off the Top

Press Ctrl+minus key

This brings you out to a 3:1 resolution of the active image, where you have a better overall view with which to work on the image.

continues

continued

Select the Eyedropper tool on the toolbox	With this tool, you pick up a value of foreground color to be used by Photoshop's paint application tools.
Click over the model's hair	Sets foreground color to color of model's hair.
Click on the Paintbrush tool	Use this tool to eliminate hard top edge of pasted selection.
Select a small, hard brush tip, set Brushes palette mode to Darken, **58**% Opacity	Creates small-tipped Paintbrush tool that applies semitransparent color only to regions *lighter* in value than foreground color of model's hair.
Click and drag over the selection border area	Applies a percentage of darker foreground color to edge of border selection (see fig. 12.8).
Continue to drag and click *only* around the model's hair area of selection edge	You use a different Brushes mode to smooth the rest of the selection edge.
Choose **F**ile, **S**ave (or press Ctrl+S)	Saves your work up to this point.

Figure 12.8

A percentage of opaque color gently covers a harsh selection edge.

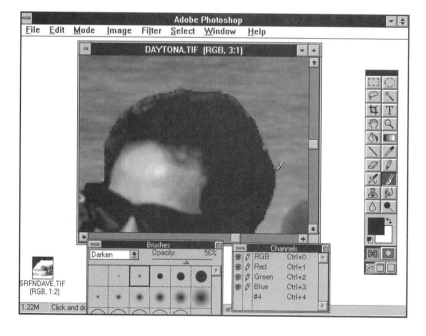

The model's hair is a really tricky area to blend convincingly into a background image. Because it has a cotton candy sort of texture, the best way to handle it is to paint into the edges with a semitransparent foreground color so as not to disturb the *visual* content while you modify the *color* content in an area.

A Different Blend Color for Different Areas

The Darken Mode on the Brushes palette can be used in combination with the Blur/Sharpen tool. The Blur/Sharpen tool is a Photoshop *editing* tool, but you can still access the Brushes palette modes controls when using editing tools. This Brushes palette feature is great because the next step for this image is to soften *and* ever so slightly change the color tone in the selection area edges, and the Brushes palette control makes this easy.

The Blur/Sharpen editing tool in Photoshop's toolbox obeys the same modes on the Brushes palette as any paint-application tool. In Darken mode, it softens an edge by gently blurring an area to a shade you first define when you initially click over an image area to click and drag over with the tool. The Darken mode only goes into effect when you've clicked over an area that's darker than most of the pixels in an image area in which you're using the Blur/Sharpen tool. In the Darken Brushes palette mode, the Blur tool can reduce the hard edge detail created by the Defringe command.

If you use a pressure-sensitive digitizing tablet instead of a mouse with Photoshop, you have more options for the Airbrush, Dodge/Burn, and Blur/ Sharpen tools on Photoshop's Brushes palette. You can increase the size of your brush stroke by applying pressure to the tablet, or you can intensify the effect of a brush stroke by selecting Pressure.

For mouse-users, Pressure on the Brushes palette slider refers to a *combination* of intensity and size of the brush stroke. The higher the percentage, the greater the effect applied to an area and the more noticeable the effect. If you don't use a tablet, think of the Pressure slider as *Subtlety*.

Everything's Soft on the Beach

Scroll over (or use the Hand tool) to the model's right shoulder

First target area for retouching.

Marquee zoom to a 4:1 resolution of the shoulder area

View of target area, almost at pixel level, is good for gauging amount of retouching evident or invisible, compared to *original* pixels in background image.

continues

continued

Select Darken mode, Pressure **78**%, and use the same brush tip size as before (a small, hard tip) on the Brushes palette	This "trial & error" setting for intensity of Blur tool works for this step.
Click and drag over the selection edge of the shirt area	Blurs area beneath cursor, muddying image detail toward darkest pixel value that you started your click and drag over.
Continue to click and drag, starting the click over a darker shirt area, moving into a light shirt area	Softens selection edge outside original selection border, and darkens lighter areas to the value you started your click and drag over (see fig. 12.9).
Choose **F**ile, **S**ave (or press Ctrl+S)	Saves your work up to this point.

Figure 12.9
Blurring the selection edge by using a Darken mode smoothes the edges toward the foreground color.

The first time I tried this, I was shocked! No upstanding photographer or scientist would ever entertain the idea of blurring something to a darker tonal value based on neighboring pixels. Things don't blur to another value in the real world—they simply fuzz out! But this is not the real world. This is Photoshop, where every pixel is plastic and can be pushed around according to parameters the user defines. In plain English, this trick works beautifully.

The Converse of Making Areas Darker

The last exercise provided you with a way to soften the edges of a dark selection toward another dark area. But when you move into an area such as the model's forearm and legs, you'll want to blur the edges toward a *lighter* value that more closely resembles the skin tone values. Why? Because the Anti-Aliasing selection border added pixels *darker* than skin tones around the edge areas where a shadow was cast on the sheet. The next exercise shows you how to solve this problem.

Lightening Areas with the Blur/Sharpen Tool

Double-click on the Zoom tool	Zooms to a 1:1 resolution of DAYTONA.TIF.
Select Lighten Mode from the Brushes palette; leave everything else alone	Sets Blur tool to lighten pixels to the value you first click over.
Click and drag, starting on the selection edge of the model's left leg, moving to darker areas	Blurs and lightens selection edge to foreground flesh tone (see fig. 12.10).
Continue alternating between Lighten and Darken on the Brushes palette and click and drag around the selection edge	Completes perfect blending of selection into new background image.
Choose File, Save (or press Ctrl+S)	Saves your work up to this point.

After you completely blur the periphery of the model selection, the telltale signs of photo-foolery—the sharp edges—disappear. Always remember that an editing tool can be more powerful if you set a mode from the Brushes palette to use with it. If you want to lighten dark pixels in an area, click on a light area, then drag over the dark area. If darkening is needed, click in a dark area, then drag into the lighter image area. This only works if you click and drag in one stroke (you *don't* click, release, *then* drag!).

Sometimes plain old, normal mode Blurring isn't enough for a special assignment, and the Darken and Lighten modes are important features in your arsenal of imagery tools. You can use this technique on virtually any pasted-in selection. Practice this technique and add it to your skills.

Something is still missing from this composite of images. Doesn't the model seem a little lighter than air?

III

Gourmet Assignments

Figure 12.10
Use Lighten and Darken on the Brushes palette to "push" a Blur stroke to the value you first click over.

Everything Casts a Shadow

Whenever an opaque object sits on a surface, and the scene is illuminated, a shadow is cast. Even in outer space, where you'd think there's no background, shadows are cast—they cause phases of the moon and eclipses. Here on earth, the model—surrounded by mighty fine edge retouching—looks fairly unrealistic because, unlike the ducks in the scene, he's not casting a shadow. Yet.

You and Your Shadow

Now you are going to learn why selecting a shadow with an image area you transplant into a new background makes little sense. Shadows are notoriously uncooperative. They don't take root convincingly in new locales. Shadows are almost always tinted with color from the original image. And because they contain little visual content, softening around their selection edges is a pain.

In the next exercise, you use SRFNDAVE.TIF as a guide, referring to it as you create brand-new shadows. If you packed the file away earlier instead of minimizing it, get it handy on screen now. Remember—the shadows in the original model file are *for reference only*.

The shadows in SRFNDAVE.TIF were cast at a steeper angle than the ones cast by the ducks in DAYTONA.TIF. Note the general direction and feel of the shadow from the SRFNDAVE.TIF image so that you can imitate it, compensating for the angle as it *should be* rendered by looking at the duck shadows in the DAYTONA.TIF image. The task is a "painterly" one, but it's part of

"Inside Adobe Photoshop"

Ingredients: Photoshop, MacroMedia MacroModel,
Pixar RenderMan, Fractal Design Painter, scanned images.

"Daylight Savings Time"

Ingredients:
Photoshop, Fractal Design Painter, scanned images.
(Chapter 18: DST.TIF)

"Fred's Fissionables"

Ingredients:
Photoshop, CorelDRAW!, scanned images.
(Chapter 8: FREDDONE.TIF)

"Sinkin' the Eight"

Ingredients: Photoshop, Visual Software Renderize for Windows, CorelDRAW!, Fractal Design Painter.

"Games"
Ingredients:
Photoshop,
CorelDRAW!,
scanned
images.
(Chapter 14:
GAMEDONE.TIF)

"Surfin' Dave"
(Before)

Ingredients:
Camera, queen size
percale bed sheet,
suburban climate,
Dave.
(Chapter 12:
SURFNDAVE.TIF)

"Surfin' Dave"
(After)

Ingredients: Photoshop, scanned background image.
(Chapter 12: SURFSUP!.TIF)

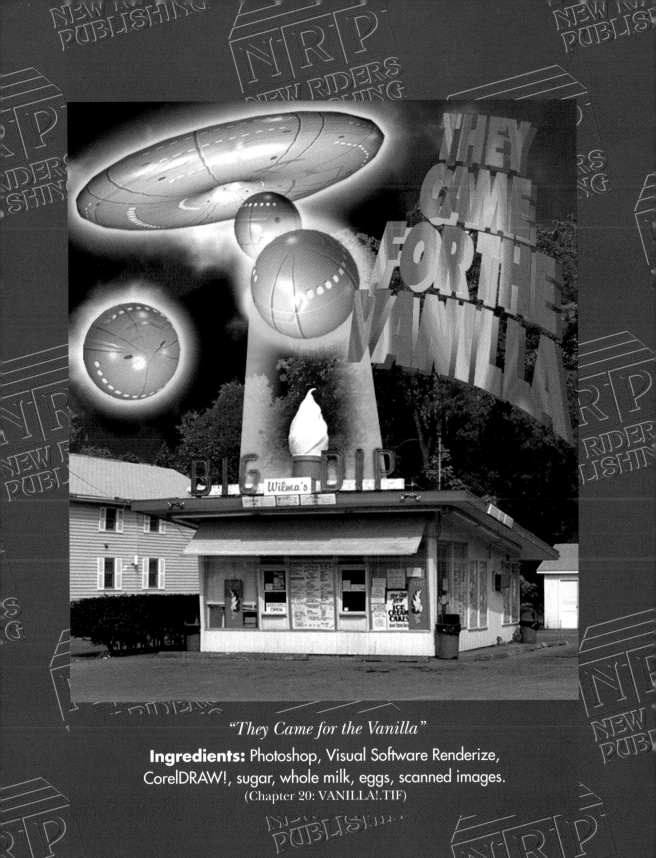

"They Came for the Vanilla"

Ingredients: Photoshop, Visual Software Renderize,
CorelDRAW!, sugar, whole milk, eggs, scanned images.
(Chapter 20: VANILLA!.TIF)

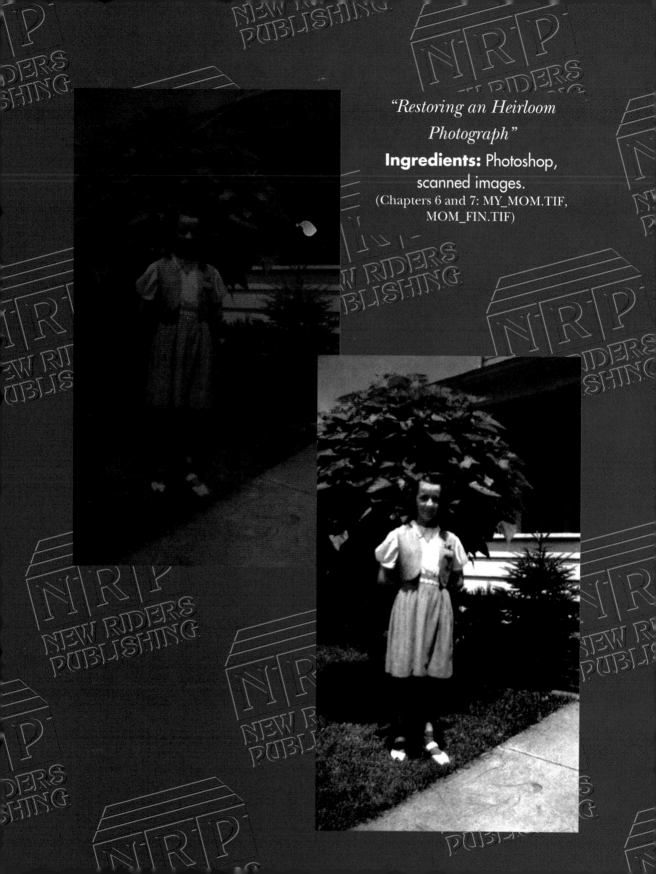

"Restoring an Heirloom Photograph"

Ingredients: Photoshop, scanned images.
(Chapters 6 and 7: MY_MOM.TIF, MOM_FIN.TIF)

"PlusZeroMinus"

Ingredients: Photoshop, MacroMedia MacroModel,
Pixar RenderMan, HSC Software Kai's Power Tools,
Visual Software Renderize for Windows,
CorelDRAW!, Fractal Design Painter,
Aldus Gallery Effects II, scanned image.

"Aurene Splendour"

Ingredients: Photoshop, MacroMedia MacroModel, Pixar RenderMan, HSC Software Kai's Power Tools, Visual Software Renderize for Windows, CorelDRAW!, Fractal Design Painter, Aldus Gallery Effects II, scanned image (possibly. It's hard to tell at this point).

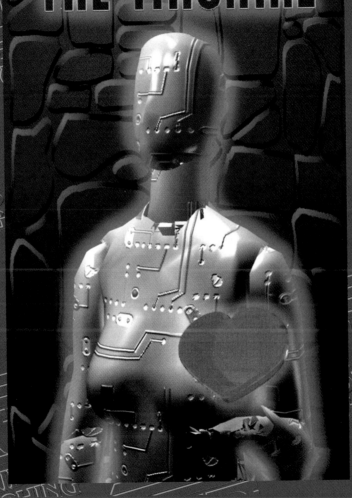

"The Heart of the Machine"

Ingredients: Photoshop, BioMechanics Corp. of America Mannequin, Visual Software Renderize, CorelDRAW!.
(Chapter 19: HARTMACH.TIF)

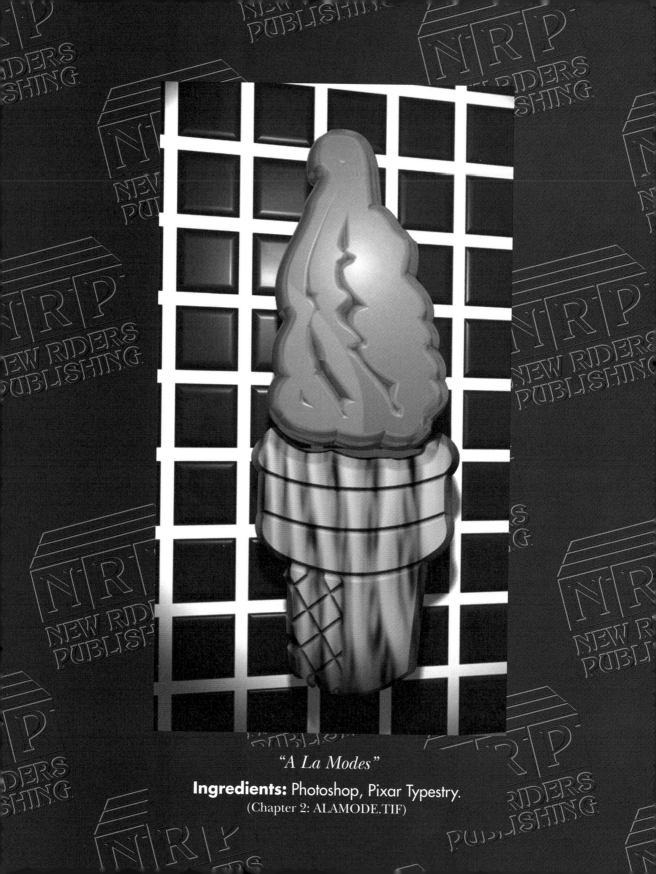

"A La Modes"

Ingredients: Photoshop, Pixar Typestry.
(Chapter 2: ALAMODE.TIF)

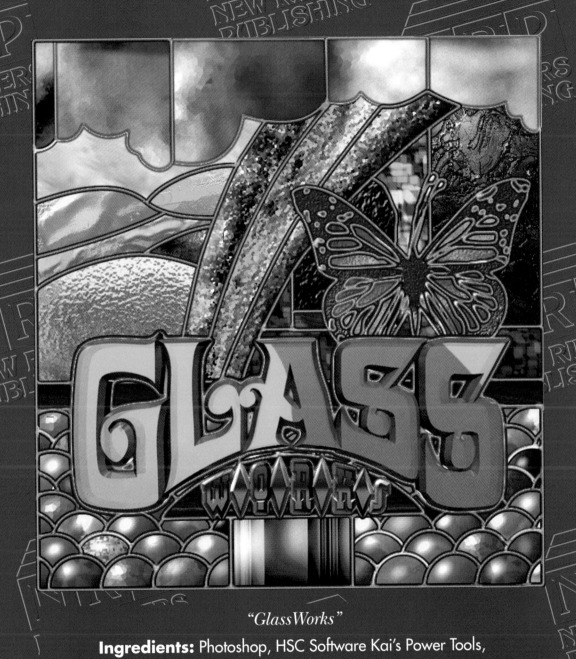

"*GlassWorks*"

Ingredients: Photoshop, HSC Software Kai's Power Tools, Fractal Design Painter, CorelDRAW!, Pixar Typestry.

"The Enchanted Gazebo"

Ingredients: Photoshop, scanned images.
(Chapter 13: PARKBLAH.TIF, PARKWOW!.TIF)

Teamwork begins with one person.

"Teamwork"

Ingredients: Photoshop, Pixar 128, scanned images.
(Chapter 15: TEAMWORK.TIF)

"Weather Report"

Ingredients: Photoshop, Pixar Typestry, scanned images.
(Chapter 17: W_REPORT.TIF)

"Better Hoops & Gardens"

Ingredients: Photoshop, scanned images.
(Chapter 11: HOME.TIF, HOME_FIN.TIF)

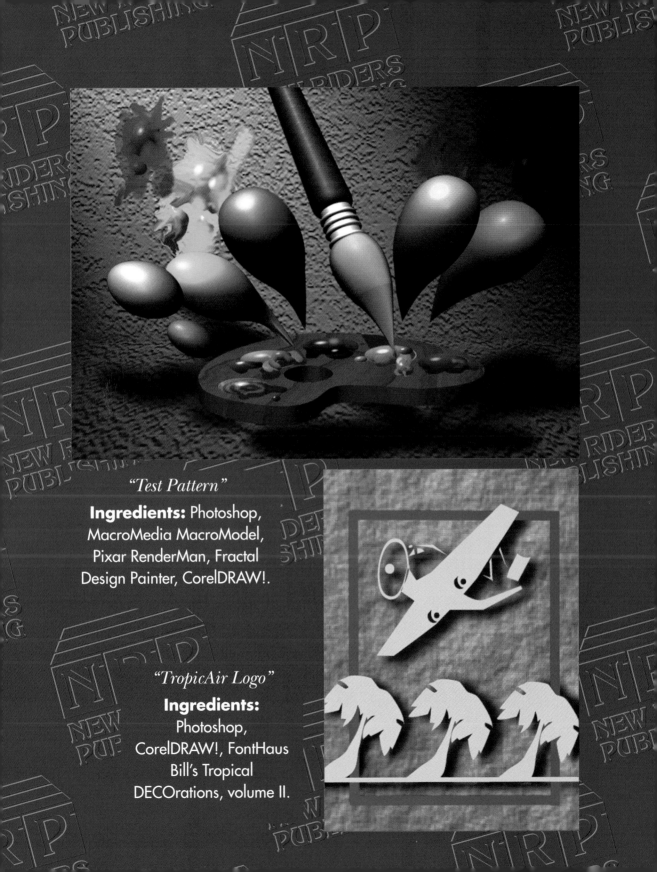

"Test Pattern"

Ingredients: Photoshop, MacroMedia MacroModel, Pixar RenderMan, Fractal Design Painter, CorelDRAW!.

"TropicAir Logo"

Ingredients: Photoshop, CorelDRAW!, FontHaus Bill's Tropical DECOrations, volume II.

"Toons"

Ingredients: Photoshop, Visual Software Renderize for Windows, BioMechanics Corporation of America's Mannequin, scanned images.

any sophisticated imaging work. And because Photoshop's features have eliminated much of the other guesswork in this exercise, you have little to worry about except painting.

Before beginning the exercise, lets do what classical painters and other artists do when they need a small "thumbnail" reference before creating a masterpiece on a large canvas. Restore SRFNDAVE.TIF to a 1:2 resolution and position it in the upper-right corner of the Photoshop workspace. This is equivalent to pinning a small snapshot of your source guide up on a wall, for quick reference to how the shadows look in the original. Click on the DAYTONA.TIF Title Bar, and then double-click on the Zoom tool. This places DAYTONA in front of SRFNDAVE and makes DAYTONA the active image window for editing. Double-clicking on the Zoom tool restores the active image to 1:1 resolution, so that DAYTONA fills screen.

Now we're all set!

Finding a Little Shade on the Beach

Click and drag the image window until an upper torso view of the model in SRFNDAVE is visible behind DAYTONA	Positions image windows so that you can see the shadow of model's head *and* same relative area in active DAYTONA image.
Select the Eyedropper tool and sample an area of duck shadow	Picks up the color an opaque object casts on beach area; use this color to paint new shadows.
Choose **S**elect, **L**oad Selection, then choose **S**elect, Inverse, and then **S**elect, Hide **E**dges (or press Ctrl+H)	Loads selection area around model, changes it to everything in image *except* model, then hides marquee edges to provide better view of image area.
Select the Paintbrush tool from the toolbox	Tool used for creating shadows.
Select a medium-tip brush with spread from the Brushes palette, set Opacity to **35**%, Mode to Darken	Paints foreground color at 35% opacity over *only* those pixels in selected area that are *lighter* than foreground color. Paint does not touch pixels darker than foreground color.
Click and drag a stroke (moving away from the model's head) parallel to the duck shadow above the model's head	Casts shadow of model's head, mimicking angle of shadows cast by ducks in DAYTONA scene (see fig. 12.11).
Continue single strokes closer to the edge of the selection border	Saturates area closest to base of model, where shadows naturally are darkest and most intense.

continues

continued

Click and drag short, single strokes behind the model's shoulder and under the arm areas	Use SRFNDAVE image as reference for placement of shadows, but make angle of strokes conform to angle of shadows cast in DAYTONA image.
Choose File, Save (or press Ctrl+S)	Saves your work up to this point.

Figure 12.11
In Darken Mode, successive strokes with a medium-opacity Brush tip continue to darken the selection area until it's a flat foreground color.

Think back for a moment to where we found this guy. He was stretched out on a white sheet in the suburbs. Now, with a few shadows added to the right half of the picture, he actually looks as if he's frolicking with the water fowl in sunny Florida!

The exercises throughout this book show you many ways to create shading and shadows in images, but I have a personal fondness for the near-miraculous transformations accomplished with Photoshop's Darken and opacity settings. You see, even though a grain of sand has almost no distinct form, a sand dune definitely has texture. Using an opaque color, no matter how light, to paint a shadow destroys visual content. By darkening the sand area with multiple semitransparent brush strokes, you have control over the amount of sand texture that shows through the shadow. And the spread on the brush carries the stroke into oblivion, as with a natural shadow whose outline has no distinct edge.

Switching Halves

When designing this piece, evaluating where to put the shadows on the left of the image was more difficult than deciding where to put them on the right. The next exercise also includes the set-up steps for continuing to use SRFNDAVE for a thumbnail reference because it proves to be a real help in completing the new image.

Doing the Legwork

Choose Title Bar; move it down, almost off screen	Provides unobstructed view of SRFNDAVE.TIF.
Move SRFNDAVE.TIF to the upper left of the Photoshop workspace	Provides clear view of left side of image when DAYTONA.TIF is brought back into view.
Click and drag DAYTONA.TIF by the Title Bar; move it back to center screen	Make sure left side of SRFNDAVE.TIF is still visible when you reposition DAYTONA.
Scroll (or use the Hand tool) to the left side of DAYTONA.TIF	Area where you complete painting shadows.
Choose **S**elect, **L**oad Selection, then choose **#4**. Next, choose **S**elect, **I**nverse (or press Ctrl+I); then choose **S**elect, Hide **E**dges (or press Ctrl+H)	Ensures that background area is selected and marquee edges are hidden before you apply foreground color. Make sure that model *is not selected* before you start painting.
Increase the Brushes palette's opacity to about **70**%	Creates more opaque shadow. Model's legs are closer to ground (and therefore cast denser shadow) than his head, which is elevated.
Click and drag the Paintbrush cursor to create a stroke similar in shape to the shadow in the same area in SRFNDAVE.TIF	Paintbrush leaves shadowy area in background area only (because model is not selected).
Click and drag some strokes where the model's left side meets the sand	Multiple passes with Paintbrush tool in Darken mode create dense shadow area, mimicking shadows cast when background is close to object (see fig. 12.12).
Choose **F**ile, Sa**v**e As **SURFSIDE.TIF**	Saves your image as a new file on your hard drive.

After you finish, admire your handiwork from a good vantage point. Why not click to Menuless Display Mode (the middle button) in Photoshop's toolbox, then use the Tab key to toggle off the toolbox and palettes to see the completed image *sans* tools. Figure 12.13 shows a full-screen view of the completed work, saved as SURFSIDE.TIF (mostly because KAWABUNGA is more than eight characters).

Figure 12.12
Denser shadows are created by multiple passes with the Paintbrush in Darken Mode.

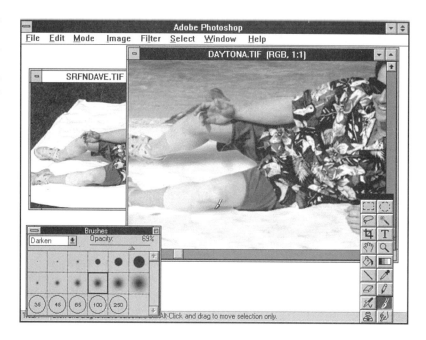

Figure 12.13
A well-depicted, if not well-deserved, vacation.

Summary

This assignment may have been humorous—but then again, maybe not. If one of your clients is a travel agent who needs a model posed on a sunny beach in the dead of winter, consider the techniques you learned in this chapter. You can transport someone from the studio lights to some of nature's own, courtesy of Photoshop and some stock photography.

This assignment was about as difficult as assignments for copying a selection area into another image can be. With no other object—such as a palm tree or beach ball—to disguise selection edges, you had to smooth out the edges very carefully. Should you ever want to add a late-comer to a group photograph, you could get away with much less edge and shadow work. In that instance, you could paste a copy **B**ehind or into a selection area. To be able to convinc-ingly paste something **I**nto a new background, with the edge work *in full sight* of the viewer, you need patience, practice, and a good eye developed through experience. That's what these exercises are all about. That, and a little fun.

Chapter 13 is a great guide to doing the exact opposite of what you accomplished in this chapter. Instead of moving a subject to a better background, you learn how to bring a new *background* to a subject that is hurting compositionally. You'll use some of the techniques you used in this chapter, and learn some different ones using Photoshop, as we dress up a charming gazebo that was photographed on a lousy day.

Chapter Snapshot

In this chapter, you learn how to:

Enhancing a
Boring Photo

Many things in life cannot be controlled—the weather, deadlines, or when opportunity strikes. In the field of photography, you're often forced to take an image under less-than-ideal circumstances.

For example, we wanted a photograph of a lakeside gazebo to use as a stock image, but had only one opportunity to take the picture—on a day it had rained. Although the sun was out, the sky and light were gray and hazy. This dreary, overcast element ruined the composition in what could have been an enchanting picture. The bright side of this story (and this image) is that it's an ideal example for some exercises in this book! If this "nice landscape/crummy weather" scenario sounds familiar, you're reading the right chapter; it holds the remedy for this situation.

You may not be able to change the deadline or the weather, but with Photoshop, you can enhance a lackluster picture to compensate for prevailing conditions at the time of the photo session. With a little ingenuity and Photoshop's features, you can add life and drama to *any* boring photo—and still meet a deadline.

Visiting Beautiful Park Blah

The photo that needs a bit of lift is PARKBLAH.TIF. As you can see from figure 13.1 (or by opening the image from the companion CD), the sky is a uniform gray and the entire image looks hazy. Although the water has some interesting movement and tree reflection, its overall color is too monotonous to be inviting. The image has a lot of charming elements, but the lighting makes you want to put on a sweater.

Figure 13.1
PARKBLAH.TIF is an example of good composition, but poor color and lighting in an image.

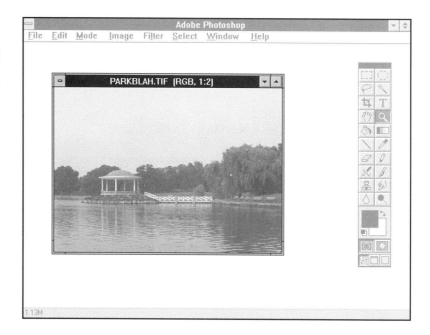

To be fair, some of the lack of vibrancy is because this TIF was taken directly from a PhotoCD. As you learned in Chapter 3, all PhotoCD images need to have Levels adjustments made to their White and Black points, and to the image gamma. You'll make these corrections in an upcoming exercise, but these corrections are only a small part in the process of adding visual interest to the image.

The Action Plan

To change the scene from blah to wow, you need to enhance each area of the image—the sky, the land, and the water. You will work on each of these elements separately. The plan for this image is to add drama to the sky, warmth to the scene, and reflections to the water. First, you replace the original sky with a more dramatic one from a different photo. To do this convincingly, you must cut and paste precisely.

The image also needs a healthy dose of color to add warmth to the scene. You raise the temperature of this scene by using Photoshop's Color Balance commands to change the color scheme of the sky and land from cold colors to warmer ones.

The water gets a treatment all its own. Water should reflect both the surrounding land and the sky. Warming up the water and providing reflections that make the image plausible is easy when you use the Composite Controls commands.

For the plan to work smoothly, you must create accurate selection borders that define the three areas: sky, land, and water. You begin by making a good selection border for the sky.

Don't Adjust Before You Select!

The intricate tree line that borders the sky in PARKBLAH.TIF poses a problem. The pixels that form the transition between the sky and the trees are a blend of the two areas, and therefore contain elements of both.

A Levels command adjustment is usually the recommended first step with a PhotoCD image. But in this case, such an adjustment would increase contrast in the image pixels, forcing the tonal value of some of them toward the sky and others toward the trees' values—sharpening up overall image quality. Although this *sounds* good, it creates a sharp border between sky and tree tops. Because of the increased contrast in the transition area, the task of making a good selection border around the sky without leaving a harsh fringe around the trees is more difficult. The solution is simple. Break the "rule." Select the sky first, and adjust the Levels to compensate for the PhotoCD image's tonal qualities later.

Lowering the gamma of an image with the Levels command increases contrast. The color pixels that form the transition between two objects in an image become more striking in their contrast when the Levels command is applied. This increase in contrast defeats Photoshop's Anti-Aliasing capability to smooth the selection edge by adding neutral grayscale information to the edge pixels. The greater the contrast in an image, the greater the difference in the grayscale components of color pixels. In this case, when Photoshop's Anti-Alias feature adds edge pixels with similar grayscale content, the result is obvious, harsh, and looks phony.

Finding a Better Sky

A number of approaches can be taken for enhancing the sky area in this image. One is to accept the image area "as is," and enhance its color (as you learned in Chapter 11). Or you can generate a new sky entirely at the computer (as you will learn in Chapter 14). The third approach, the one taken in this chapter, is to *replace* the blah sky with a dynamic, natural sky from a different photo.

III

Gourmet Assignments

Having a collection of photos available, whether they are stock photos you have purchased or photos you have taken, is invaluable in Photoshop imaging work. Often, you need to replace an element in your current composition—a sky, a tree, a pair of hands—and a stock image is the best place to find these replacement parts. With a varied collection of source material, and Photoshop's capability to *edit* this material, your tool kit for any imaging assignment is pretty complete.

Figure 13.2. is a "private stock" sunset photo with lots of drama—one you can substitute for the sky area in PARKBLAH.TIF. But this photo also needs work. It needs the gamma correction typical for a PhotoCD, and it is also a *cold* sunset. The predominant colors in it are dark blues and cold yellows. Because this sunset photo was taken late in the day, its tonal and color values are too dark to match those in the park picture. Later in this assignment, you use Photoshop's Adjust commands to bring warmth and light to the sky image.

Figure 13.2
Tonal and color correction will make this image better fit into PARKBLAH.TIF.

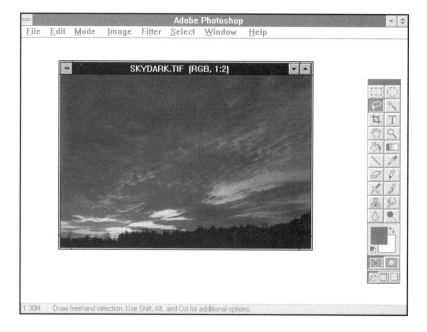

This picture will work beautifully with the park photo because its *visual content* is good. When you sift through source material, you have to use your eye and your judgment to evaluate the composition and the details in a photo. Don't be put off by a photo because it's too dark or light, or because it has the "wrong" colors. All of this can be changed in Photoshop.

The Magic Wand: First Step toward a Magical Sky

The color range in the PARKBLAH.TIF sky is minimal, which makes the Magic Wand the ideal tool for selecting most of the sky in one fell swoop. You can select into the nooks and crannies where sky meets tree much faster with the Magic Wand tool than with the Lasso tool. With its **T**olerance set to 32, the Magic Wand will pick up all of the sky and some of the transition pixels between the sky and the trees. This Tolerance setting is the result of trial and error; a value greater than 32 picks up more of the troublesome transition pixels, but also tends to blunt the shape of the trees.

After you use the Magic Wand to select most of the sky, you use other Photoshop selection techniques to *refine* the selection border. By using a combination of selection tools, you can work quickly and accurately. First, let's wave that Magic Wand.

Waving the Magic Wand

Choose **F**ile, **O**pen, then open PARKBLAH.TIF from the companion CD	Opens image of park.
Double-click on the Magic Wand tool on the toolbox	Opens the Magic Wand Options dialog box.
Set the **T**olerance to **32**, make sure that **A**nti-Aliasing is on, then click on OK	Sets characteristics of the Magic Wand tool and redisplays Photoshop's workspace.
Click on the Magic Wand tool in the sky, about an inch above the gazebo roof	Places selection marquee border around sky (see fig. 13.3).
Pick the Zoom tool from the toolbox; marquee-zoom into the gazebo roof; check whether the selection border forms a smooth curve for the roof, as shown in figure 13.4	Depending on exactly where you clicked, the sky selection may have "leaked" into the roof. You don't want this.
If Magic Wand does *not* form a smooth boundary, choose the Lasso tool, then press Shift while you click and drag around pixels	Adds to Magic Wand selection area.

(Conversely, pressing Ctrl while you click and drag removes areas from the selection.)

Double-click on the Hand tool on the toolbox	Zooms to full view of image with no scroll bars.
Choose **S**elect, Save Selection	Saves the selection border that holds the sky to selection #4.

continues

III

Gourmet Assignments

continued

Figure 13.3
Use the Magic
Wand tool to
select the
PARKBLAH.TIF
sky area.

Figure 13.4
Check for a
smooth selection
between the sky
and the roof.

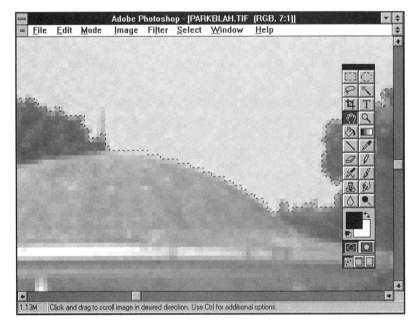

File, Save As PARKBLAH.TIF
on your hard drive. Make sure
the **S**ave Alpha Channels box is
checked in the TIFF Options dialog box

This saves the image and your
selection border at this point
to your hard drive.

Refining a Complex Selection Border

The Magic Wand's selection of the sky is pretty impressive for just one click of the mouse, but it's not perfect. You could use the Lasso tool to adjust this border all along the tree line, as you may have done in the area where the sky and the gazebo roof meet, but that's a tedious method. An easier, more naturalistic way to refine the sky selection is to use the Quick Mask and the Paintbrush tool.

Using the Quick Mask To Refine Selection Borders

The goal is to add as many light-colored pixels to the sky selection as possible, without blunting the shape of the natural irregularities found in the outline of trees. The Quick Mask mode in Photoshop is great: adding mask material (using the default black foreground color) extends the sky *selection border,* and removing mask material (with a white foreground color) *subtracts* from the sky selection. To help keep the edge of the tree line irregular, natural looking, and, well, *tree-like,* you use a small Paintbrush (with spread) to increase the area the mask covers. In the next exercise, you set up the Quick Mask and the Paintbrush tip.

Preparing To Mask the Sky

Double-click on the Quick Mask
button on the toolbox

Displays Quick Mask Options dialog box.

Choose Selected Areas in the box's Color
Indicates field, leave Opacity and Color
set to their defaults of 50% and Red (see
fig. 13.5), then click on OK

Displays image and covers the *selected* sky
area with a red tint.

Choose the Zoom tool from the toolbox; click
four times just below the tree line at the
extreme right of the image

Zooms to 8:1 view of tree line at the right
edge of image.

continues

continued

Click on the up arrow in the image's title bar	Maximizes image to occupy all of Photoshop's workspace.

Use the scroll bars, if necessary, to bring tree line into view.

Pick the Paintbrush tool on the toolbox, then choose **W**indow, Show **B**rushes (or press F5)	Displays Brushes palette so that you can set characteristics of Paintbrush before you use it.
Set the Brushes Palette mode to Normal; move Opacity slider to **100%**	Sets Paintbrush characteristics to paint full-strength with foreground color.
Double-click on the smallest brush with spread in the Brushes palette (far left, middle row)	Displays Brush Options dialog box.
In the Diameter text box, type **3** to replace the default (5) pixels, then click on OK	Makes brush smaller; you accept the rest of the defaults for this tip (see fig. 13.6).

You are ready to paint in or remove mask from the image.

Figure 13.5
Set Photoshop's Mask options to mask the selected area.

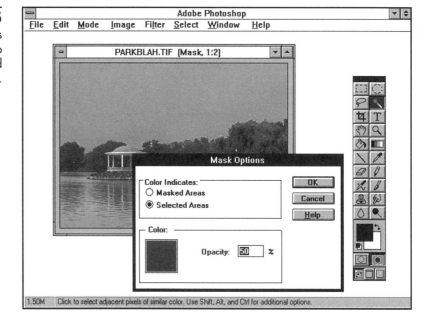

Refining the Mask

The mask and Paintbrush are set up to refine the sky-selection border. The key to retouching the PARKBLAH.TIF image is to accurately select the border so that you can paste a copy of the stock photo into the sky area to replace it. If the selection area is not defined with care, the finished image will scream "Tricked-up Photo!" That is why you should take a *reasonable* amount of care in creating the selection border.

"Reasonable" doesn't mean that you need to sweat over this refined selection border for hours on end, though. You are going to use several other techniques after this to make the overall image look as though it were photographed on a glorious day. In your Mask-refining labors, don't mask in the white "cut-out" areas where the sky shows through the trees. Concentrate on the edge—you will take care of the light areas that peek through the leaves after you add the new sky.

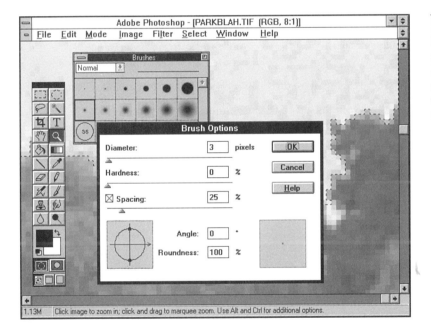

Figure 13.6
Brush options provide control of the tip characteristics with which you apply color.

When black is the foreground color in Quick Mask mode, you apply a mask that displays a red tint—or whichever color you have defined from the Quick Mask Options dialog box—with Photoshop's tools. And when the foreground color is white, you *remove* the mask with a tool. You can use almost any tool to do masking in Quick Mask mode: the Paintbrush, Pencil, Paint Bucket, Gradient, Rubber Stamp, Airbrush, Lasso, and Elliptical and Rectangular Marquee tools are all valid. You can even apply and remove Quick Mask with the Text tool, but that would call for a really special purpose!

continues

The point is that you can remove or apply mask material by clicking on the inverse color icon beneath the color-selection boxes to switch mask activity with the tool you're using. Just remember to switch the color-selection boxes back when you are done.

Painting the Mask

Click and drag the Paintbrush (carefully) above the Quick Mask, where the light-colored edge pixels between the sky and the trees meet (see fig. 13.7)	Applies mask to these pixels, making them part of sky selection area.

Try to color only light-colored pixels that don't look tree-like; maintain as much irregular tree-line shape as possible.

Paint in the edge until you reach the gazebo dome	Applies mask to areas you want included in sky selection area.

Use scroll bars or the Hand tool to move the view across the image in the window frame.

Paint in the edge pixels between the Quick Mask and the gazebo's dome	Continues adding to sky selection border. Pay special attention to shape and smoothness of this curve.
Press Ctrl+plus key, then press Ctrl+minus key	Zooms out to a 2:1, then a 1:1 viewing resolution.

Check the shape created with the mask around the gazebo dome; zoom back in and paint in or remove mask, if necessary.

When you are satisfied with the roof, continue masking edge pixels above the tree line to the left of the image	Completes accurate mask of sky area.
Click the Standard mode button on the toolbox when you reach the left side of PARKBLAH.TIF	Displays *editing* window of image; the active selection border reflects changes "painted in" in Quick Mask mode.
Choose **S**elect, **S**ave Selection, choose #4	Saves the refined selection border that then holds the sky to selection #4.
Choose **S**elect, **N**one (or press Ctrl+D)	Deselects the active selection in image.
Choose **F**ile, **S**ave	Saves your work at this stage of retouching.

Adjusting the Levels

Now that the sky selection is made and saved, you can safely make Levels adjustments to the image. Any shift in contrast in PARKBLAH.TIF that would have affected the Magic Wand selection of the sky area is a moot point now. You defined and saved the selection area after evaluating the *visual detail* in the image. Heightening or reducing gamma and Black or White points in the image won't affect your ability to accurately select the sky for editing, since it now has an accurate selection border that has been saved for future use.

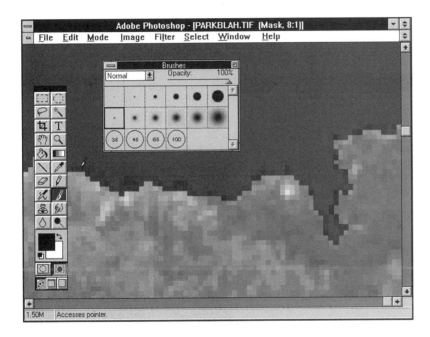

Figure 13.7
Masks are modified by adding or removing Masking material with almost any Photoshop tool.

Correcting Brightness Values Using Levels

With PARKBLAH.TIF still open in the Photoshop workspace, press Ctrl+L or choose **I**mage, **A**djust, then choose Levels

Displays Levels dialog box.

Make sure Preview is checked in the Levels box

Preview shows changes made in image as you make them.

Move the box by dragging its title bar

Position box so that you can see the entire box and get a good view of the land and water in the image.

continues

continued

In the Input Levels text boxes, enter the following values from left to right: **49**, **.88**, **228** (see fig. 13.8), or move the three sliders under the histogram to get these values

Values were determined by what looked best in the image.

Click on OK

Displays changed image.

Choose **F**ile, **S**ave

Saves the changed image to your hard disk.

Choose **F**ile, **C**lose

Closes the file. You're done with it for the moment.

Figure 13.8
The Levels adjustments to the image compensate for its high gamma, which PhotoCD images tend to have.

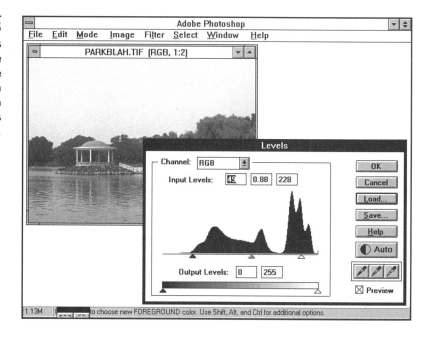

The changes you made with the Levels command changed the look of the image dramatically. Moving the Black and White points toward the midtones snapped the image up by increasing the contrast—narrowing the range of available tones the pixels in the image could occupy. And lowering the gray midpoint narrowed the midtones' brightness values to a more visually appealing contrast, without making a noticeable shift in the image's shadows or the highlights. PCs read lower gammas than PhotoCDs, televisions, and Macintosh systems; their higher gamma calibration makes digital images seem washed out on IBM-compatible computers.

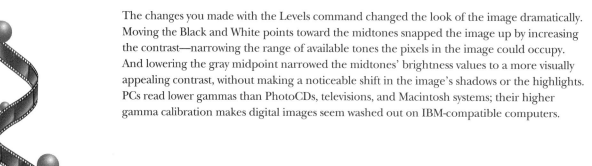

Prepping the Sky

The next step in park restoration is to get a new sky ready for transplant. The image you use is SKYDARK.TIF from the companion CD. Straight out of the box, SKYDARK is a striking, dramatic image, but in the context of the PARKBLAH scene, it needs to be warmer and lighter. Using Photoshop's suite of commands from the **I**mage, **A**djust menu, you are going to learn a new technique that will become routine, with a little practice. The right set of commands can produce a radically different image, one that's better suited to this assignment and retains the realism needed for a convincing, unretouched, realistic landscape scene.

Check Your Aesthetics Before You Begin

Keep two things in mind before you begin. All settings suggested in the exercise are arbitrary, in that they were determined by the authors' artistic eye and judgment. When you do this kind of work in your own assignments, trust your *own* eye. The second point to keep in mind is that the trees and the very bright spots above the tree line in SKYDARK.TIF will not be visible in the final composite. These areas won't be cropped out of the SKYDARK.TIF image, but rather, they will fall behind the selection area in PARKBLAH.TIF, vanishing after the two images are composited together. Focus on what happens to the image *above* these areas.

Doing a Balancing Act with Photoshop

Your first stop on the **I**mage, **A**djust menu is the Color Balance options. You want to shift SKYDARK's cold colors to warmer colors to see what you have to work with! When you use the Color Balance command, the changes are made to the individual Red, Green, and Blue channels. You have quite a lot of control with this command because three brightness ranges of the image are addressed individually: the shadows, the midtones, and the highlights. In the next exercise, you make changes in all three areas.

Warming Up the Sky

Choose **F**ile, **O**pen SKYDARK.TIF from the companion CD	Opens image in Photoshop workspace.
Choose **I**mage, **A**djust, then choose Color Balance (or just press Ctrl+Y)	Displays Color Balance dialog box.
Check the Preview box, if it is not already checked	Displays changes as you make them.
With the Midtones radio button selected, enter the following values in the Color Levels input boxes,	Slightly increases amount of cyan, dramatically increases amount of blue in midtones of image;

continues

continued

from left to right: **-2, 0, +49** (see fig. 13.9) (or use the sliders to perform the same actions)	magenta and green values remain the same. Produces much bluer, more day-like color scheme.
Click on the Shadows radio button to adjust the color values in the shadows	Sliders and input boxes move to zero.
Enter the following values in the Color Levels input boxes, from left to right: **-13, 0, -28** (or move the sliders)	Settings increase cyan and add a great deal of yellow to shadows. Image is less blue overall than it was with just midtone adjustment; yellow warms shadows.
Click on the Highlights radio button to adjust the color values in the highlights	Sliders and input boxes move to zero.
Enter the following values in the Color Levels input boxes, from left to right: **60, 20, 90** (or you can move the sliders)	Dramatically increases red and blue in highlights; green cuts magenta to keep highlights more blue than purple. Previously yellow-highlighted clouds now have warm pink glow.
Click on OK	Displays image with color changes set.
Choose **F**ile, **S**ave	Saves the changed image to hard disk.

Figure 13.9
Color Balance values are adjusted to alter the midtones in the sky.

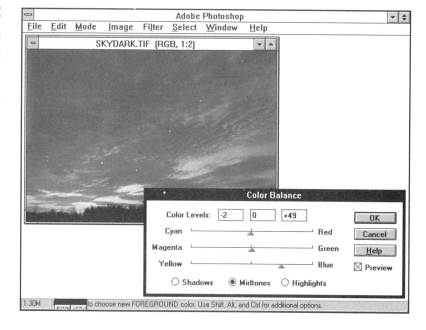

You've shifted the color values to produce a much lighter, warmer color balance. The wispy cloud highlights—the predominant element of this sky—have changed from a cold yellow to a warm pink-yellow.

Although you have made positive alterations to the color scheme, the scene still needs some tweaking in terms of the range and allocation of *tones*. In the next exercise, you'll use the Levels command with assistance from the Info palette to plot the brightness mapping of the image.

Tweaking the Sky

Choose **W**indow, Show In**f**o (or press F9), click and hold on the top eyedropper, then drag down to choose HSB Color mode	Displays Info Palette and sets it to display HSB color values in top section of palette.
Choose **I**mage, **A**djust, choose Levels (or press Ctrl+L), then check the Preview box (if it is not already checked)	Displays Levels dialog box and sets it to display changes as you make them (see fig. 13.10).
Click on the Black-point Eyedropper (the one on the left) and position it over the black tree area in SKYDARK.TIF	You are looking for a better Black point for the image by scouting for the darkest point in this image.
Move the Eyedropper around in the trees, look for an HSB value close to 120/100%/5% on the Info Palette, then click on the Eyedropper	Selects new Black point.
Click on the White-point Eyedropper (the one on the right) and put it over the long white cloud, just over the tree line	The "set-up" for picking a new White Point in the image.
Move the Eyedropper around, look for an HSB value close to 24/13%/100% on the Info Palette, then click on the Eyedropper	Selects new White point.
In the Input Levels boxes, enter the following values: **6**, **.94**, **228** (or move the sliders under the histogram), as shown in figure 13.11	Increases contrast, narrows range of brightness in midtones, slightly diminishes highlight-brightness areas in midtones.
Click on OK	Displays image, which now has much more snap and glow.
Choose **F**ile, Sa**v**e As SKYDARK.TIF to your hard disk	Saves all changes made to companion CD image to your hard drive.

Figure 13.10
The Levels command box first displays a histogram of the image before any changes are made to brightness mapping.

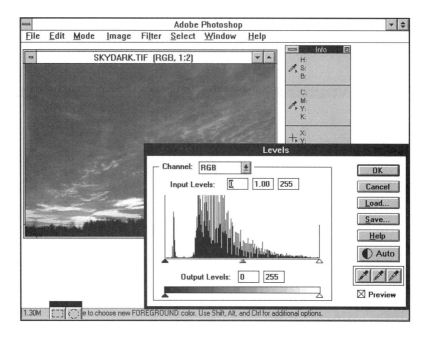

Figure 13.11
The histogram shows the effect of your changes—some pixels have been redistributed, others retain their original brightness values.

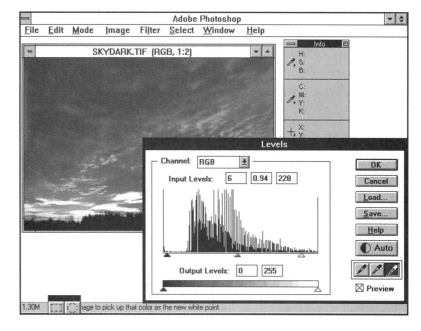

A trip to the **I**mage, **I**mage Size command would show that SKYDARK.TIF's height and width dimensions are a little larger than PARKBLAH.TIF's. The difference in dimensions gives you room to move the sky after it's placed in the PARKBLAH image. The larger size gets the most eye-pleasing areas of the sky selection in view as it's pasted into the picture. The SKYDARK image also was made slightly larger to compensate for some fogging on the left edge of the photo.

Having the image you are pasting from a different height and width than the image you are pasting into is often desirable, but they should *never* have different resolutions. SKYDARK.TIF and PARKBLAH.TIF both have a resolution of 150 dpi. Photoshop automatically changes the resolution of the floating selection image to match the resolution of the background image, *interpolating* the floating selection to make the resolutions match. This often degrades the quality of the floating selection image. It also throws your precise image dimension-measuring down the drain because image resolution has an inverse relationship to image dimensions. You may think that a 72 dpi selection fits wonderfully into a 3 1/2-inch space, only to find the selection much smaller because the image you measured from and pasted to is at 150 dpi.

Whenever you assemble a piece from different sources, always make sure that all the sources have the same resolution.

Warming the Landscape

This wonderfully warm sky is ready for transplant into the park scene. But the recipient, PARKBLAH.TIF, still has a color scheme akin to frostbite. The color balance that warmed up SKYDARK.TIF can warm the land, too. As you saw in the last exercises, a quick trip to Color Balance can make a cold world warm. Destination Balance command in the next few steps.

Warming Up a Cold Day

Choose **F**ile, **O**pen PARKBLAH.TIF from your hard disk	Image modified earlier (and selection of sky saved in it to an Alpha channel); when opened, becomes the active image window.
Choose **I**mage, **A**djust, choose Color Balance, then make sure that the Preview box is checked	Displays Color Balance dialog box.

Move the Color Balance dialog box, if necessary, so that you can see all the land in the image.

continues

III

Gourmet Assignments

continued

Click on the radio button next to Highlights	When you move the sliders or enter values, this causes changes in color values for pixels in the highlight tonal range of the image.
Enter the following values in the Color Levels input boxes, from left to right: **52, -11, -11** (see fig. 13.12)	Skews highlight pixels toward red, magenta, and yellow; adds warmth to scene.
Click on the radio button next to Shadows	Moving sliders or entering values causes changes in color value to focus on pixels that make up shadows in image.
Enter the following values in the Color Levels input boxes, from left to right: **-9, 0, 0**	Pushes shadows toward magenta to warm and deepen shadows ("punches up" and warms image).
Click on OK	Displays image with new color values.
Choose File, Save	Saves altered image.

Figure 13.12
Image warmth is easy to achieve with the Color Balance command.

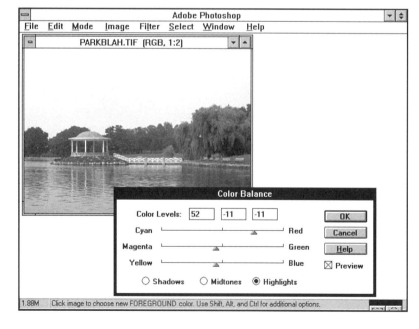

Tip

Again, the values used to warm up the scene were arrived at by personal aesthetics—the author's eye, not secret formulas. Whenever you adjust for color or tonal balance, your own eye must guide you. Staring intently at the monitor for a while can make seeing subtle changes difficult. In such cases, take a short break before you click on the OK button. Walk around the room, look out the window for a minute or two, or close your eyes for a while. When you return to the assignment, you can better evaluate the scene with an impartiality you can't aspire to with retinal fatigue!

A Bright New Sky for the Park

With the new sky prepped for transplant, the park color corrected, and the same resolution for both images, it's time—literally and figuratively—to create some atmosphere in this image.

You don't have to crop the trees out of the new sky or worry about making it the exact size of the old sky, because you are going to use the Paste Into command. With Paste Into, you can reposition the new sky to get it where you like it. Photoshop ignores parts of a floating selection (like the new sky) that extend beyond the selection borders of the background image. No fuss, no muss, and the information contained in the excess pixels vanishes! It's time to make the big switch!

Creating a Brand-New Day

Choose **S**elect, **L**oad Selection	Marquee selection border surrounds sky; you'll paste into this background image selection.
Click on SKYDARK.TIF's title bar to make it the active image window	Image must be active so that you can copy from it.
Choose **S**elect, **A**ll (or press Ctrl+A), then choose **E**dit, **C**opy (or press Ctrl+C)	Copies entire image to Clipboard.
Choose **F**ile, **C**lose	Image is no longer needed; copy of image is on clipboard and PARKBLAH.TIF is the active image.
Choose **E**dit, Paste **I**nto	Displays new sky in park image. Sky is floating selection whose border is defined by the marquee that runs all around the image. *Do not deselect the image!*
Click on the Lasso tool on the toolbox, then position the small arrow cursor over the image	Lasso tool, which becomes small arrow when over selection, is used to move floating selection.

continues

continued

Click, hold, and drag the floating sky selection up and to the left; release when it looks like figure 13.13	Bright white clouds above black tree line should not be visible in image; the bottom marquee line should be about one inch from bottom of PARKBLAH.TIF.
Press the up-, down-, left-, or right-arrow key	Precisely positions floating selection by nudging it one pixel at a time in the direction of the arrow key pushed.
When the sky is where you want it, click once with the mouse over the image (or press Ctrl+D, or use **S**elect, **N**one)	The SKYDARK pasted selection is now composited into the PARKBLAH image; all non-exposed pixels in selection area are now gone.
Choose **F**ile, **S**ave	Saves altered image to your hard disk.

Figure 13.13
Coarsely adjust a
pasted selection
with the mouse,
then use the
keyboard arrow
keys to nudge the
selection precisely
where you want it.

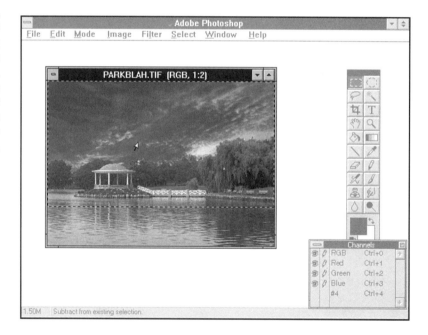

Touching Up the Skyline

The new sky makes a dramatic difference in this image, but the *edge* where it was pasted into the PARKBLAH image leaves something to be desired. Some fringing exists along the border, and gaps are visible in the trees (where the old sky was not selected and replaced by the new sky). Removing the original sky areas takes two different exercises and a variety of techniques. None of the techniques is particularly difficult or time consuming, but each has its own place and function in this assignment, as well as in your own work.

Making a Beeline for the Tree Line

In the next exercise, you concentrate on the tree line. To fix the original sky areas poking through the leaves, you'll use several different tools. To remove the telltale edge between the trees and the new sky, you use Photoshop's Defringe command and Blur tool. These powerful features always need to be used in moderation if you don't want the viewer to notice the effect. The Defringe command replaces the color of the edge pixels in a floating selection with pure colors (no gray components) obtained from neighboring pixels—tree pixels, in this assignment—that do not contain any background color (the new sky). Ironically, if Defringe is set too high, it creates a fringe of a different color!

The Blur tool reduces the contrast between adjacent pixels by averaging the gray component contained in the color pixels. The Blur tool, used sparingly, creates a smooth visual transition. But when applied full-strength (large Brushes tip, 100% Opacity), it noticeably fuzzes image *details* as the pixels take on more and more gray component. Whenever you use the Blur tool, be sure to zoom out frequently to a 1:1 image view to see what the effect is accomplishing. Be prepared to use the **U**ndo command if your eye tells you that you have overdone it.

The next exercise is an example of using both tools sparingly to achieve a natural, gradual transition between sky and tree line. The prudent use of Defringe and Blur together is a technique you might apply to a variety of situations in your own work. This set of steps for producing subtle transitions is essential, not just for sky-ectomies, but whenever you bring different elements together.

It's time to go where the trees meet the sky, to restore a sense of harmony to nature.

III

Gourmet Assignments

Taking the Edge Off a Nature Scene

Choose **S**elect, **L**oad Selection, then choose **S**elect, **F**loat/De**f**loat (or press Ctrl+J)	Loads sky selection and changes it into a floating selection that can be defringed.
Choose **S**elect, **D**efringe	Displays Defringe dialog box.
Set the **W**idth to **1** pixel (see fig. 13.14), click on OK	Defringe command executes; less fringe shows in image.
Choose **S**elect, **N**one (or press Ctrl+D)	Deselects the sky.

continues

continued

Click on the Blur/Sharpen tool on the toolbox, press F5 to display the Brushes palette, then (from the Brushes palette) set mode to **D**arken and pressure to **100%**; choose the second tip from the left on the top row	Sets Blur tool to darken gray component of color pixels you drag over (to shade closer to area first clicked on).
Choose the Zoom tool from the toolbox, click twice just below the tree line at the extreme right of the image, then click on the up arrow on the image's title bar	Zooms in to 2:1 view of tree line at right edge of image.

Use the Hand tool, if necessary, to bring the tree line into view.

With the Blur tool, click on the sky side of the tree/skyline and (without letting go of the mouse button) drag a single stroke to the left, following the tree/skyline edge (see fig. 13.15)	Darkens light edge pixels.

Zoom out to a 1:1 view after each stroke with the Blur tool to make sure that you haven't over-fuzzed the border. If it's too fuzzy, choose **E**dit, **U**ndo. Go over the edge once more, if necessary, checking whether you have over-blurred.

With the Hand tool, reposition the image as necessary to keep moving along the edge with the Blur tool. Keep zooming out to check across each section, until you reach the left border.

Double-click on the Hand tool on the toolbox to change to a 1:2 view of the full image	Completed image should look like figure 13.16.
Choose **F**ile, **S**ave	Saves completed image to your hard drive.

Was the last exercise a test of your mousing prowess? Perhaps. When you make short, precise mouse movements, you can work faster and get immediate feedback on the effect. Blurring was done to the image while working at a 2:1 viewing resolution of PARKBLAH.TIF. We choose this view to work in because if you zoom into a view that's too close, what you see may not accurately reflect the impact of your editing work on the image. A pixel that may look dark enough is not dark enough, and vice versa. A view from different resolutions of an image enables you to assess your work at various stages of completion.

And this is why large monitors are vital to the imaging profession. You avoid eyestrain and mousing errors when your field of vision isn't constrained by small, physical boundaries.

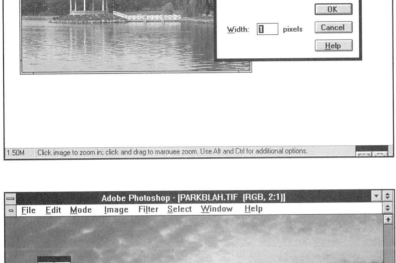

Figure 13.14
Most Defringing requires only a 1- to 2-pixel setting.

Figure 13.15
Use the Blur tool to softly blend the sky and tree line.

Figure 13.16
The Blur tool
reduces contrast in
neighboring
pixels.

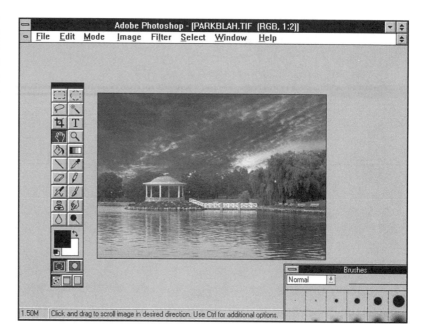

Filling In the Trees

Although the overall image is a glorious attraction now, the *distraction*—the original hazy sky areas between the leaves—is still painfully obvious. In this type of situation, you have an artistic call to make. Do you keep faith with reality and fill the holes with new sky? Or do you use artistic license to improve upon nature?

You try *both* techniques in the following exercises. The object is to demonstrate the problem-solution approach to using Photoshop in assignments. The type of image enhancement a client would pay good money for requires a working knowledge of a *variety* of image editing tools and techniques. The creative solution to the problem in this example is to restore some areas of the sky to the trees and, in other areas, replace original sky portions with tree samples.

Fixing Background Areas within Trees

Here's the scoop on each approach to the areas in the trees in question, and on the applicability of Photoshop's tools from an aesthetic point of view. The small flecks of sky in the maple trees to the right of the gazebo add reality to the image—some bits of sky usually show through the treetops. Using the Paintbrush tool, you give these pixels a sky color. The large holes in the tree line are ideal candidates for the Rubber Stamp tool, which applies not only the colors of the sky or tree but also the visual detail (not easily accomplished with the Paintbrush tool). Because the holes in the maples to the right of the gazebo, when filled with sky, distract the eye from the gazebo—the focal point in the image—you will fill them with tree. The holes between the maples to the left of the gazebo look better filled with sky, to show the natural break in the trees.

A Soft Touch for Invisible Retouching

These approaches require some care to avoid creating hard edges. To make your retouching invisible, use Anti-Alias, soft brush tips, and resample for color and pattern at points along the way. Don't be afraid to practice initiative in areas *you* feel need work beyond the basic steps we guide you through. Every artist sees things differently; developing your individual artistic sensibilities is as vital to an imaging career as a working knowledge of Photoshop.

In this next exercise, you may come across small bits and pieces that could use special attention. Fix them last, after you have tried different approaches to the larger areas.

Oh—and before you retouch an area, zoom out and make sure that you're looking at a hole, not one of the three lampposts in the image!

Picking a Few Pixels and Darkening Them

At this point, a single, oddball pixel or two from the original PARKBLAH sky is probably sticking through the dark maple trees to the right of the gazebo. Funny, isn't it, how zooming into an incongruous image area shows the cause of the damage to be much less severe than you estimate at a 1:1 view? This sort of situation calls for light artillery, not for something as heavy-handed as the Rubber Stamp tool. The appropriate strategy is to use the Eyedropper tool to pick up a color from the sky, then paint the light areas with the Paintbrush tool set to Darken mode.

When you use Darken mode with the Paintbrush, only pixels lighter than the color you chose with the Eyedropper (the foreground color) are painted in. You need to select several colors and use as few brush strokes as possible to cover the offending pixels. The best view for this retouching work is at 1:1, actual size because if you have obliterated the pixels at a viewer's resolution, laboring in the area one nanosecond longer than necessary is pointless. Learn to identify and analyze a sore spot in a picture at a high resolution, but (wherever possible) do the actual retouching work with as large a sense of the whole image as possible. In many instances, precision retouching in Photoshop requires a magnified view of the problem area, while other times, like in the last exercise, it doesn't. If you can see what you're doing at 1:1, and can do the required image editing comfortably at this view, stick to it.

Lightly Painting

With the Zoom tool, click once on the maple trees to the right of the gazebo, then click on the up arrow in the title bar	Displays 1:1, full-screen view of PARKBLAH.TIF image.

continues

continued

Click on the Eyedropper tool, then click over the sky above the trees until you find a dark purple	Sets foreground color you'll paint with.
Click on the Paintbrush tool on the toolbox	Activates available options for tool on Brushes palette.
On the Brushes palette, select Darken mode, set the Opacity slider to **71**%, then choose the second brush from the left in the top row	Sets characteristics for Paintbrush to apply color with partial transparency that colors only pixels lighter than specified foreground color.
Click and drag with short strokes over the light-colored, dappled areas (see fig. 13.17)	Colors original sky pixels with darker foreground-color selection.

Go for effect, not precision with the Paintbrush tool; leave large areas of original sky alone. They are covered (no pun) in next exercise.

Continue using small, short strokes to fill in areas of original sky	Retouches only "pinholes" between leaves in image. (Stop when all pinholes are filled.)
Choose **F**ile, **S**ave	Saves image at this point.

A wise decision that takes only a moment between exercises: To safeguard your investment of time and labor, progressively **S**ave an image that takes time to complete.

By applying the color at 71% Opacity in the last exercise, you preserved some of the tonal values in the pixels you stroked. Gray, tonal information constitutes much of the visual detail in images. You do yourself (and the image) a service when you change only the *color* aspect of an image area.

Let your eye be your guide when you set opacity and select which pixels to color. Your intent should be to create the impression (for viewers) that the sky is filtering through the leaves of the tree.

Doing Mother Nature One Better

If you followed the exercises in sequence, two fairly large holes should be in the center maple-tree section. An imaging person's natural instinct would be to fill these holes with new sky color also. But the holes are caused by one of Nature's quirks. The real reason for the holes is that the trees have grown twisted and slightly crooked. There is no artistic reason not to *correct* one of nature's flaws instead of accentuating the homeliness by adding a piece of new sky. You second-guess nature in the next exercise by filling the gaps with tree samples instead of sky. Painting samples into an image area is always a call for the Rubber Stamp tool.

Figure 13.17
Painting in sky color, using the Brushes palette's Darken mode, affects the image's lighter pixels only.

Tree Repair

Marquee-zoom into the area that contains the two large holes in the trees

Double-click on the Rubber Stamp tool, make sure that the Rubber Stamp options are set to Clone (aligned), then click on OK

Choose Darken mode from the Brushes palettes command button drop-down list, and slide the Opacity to **100%** on the Brushes palette, then choose the third soft tip from the left, second row

Press Alt while you click the Rubber Stamp tool on the lighter green area under the lowest large hole

Area you work on in this exercise.

Now Rubber Stamp tool continuously samples from trailing crosshairs.

Sets characteristics of Rubber Stamp tool to affect only the pixels (under the cursor) that are lighter than the pixels under the sampling crosshairs.

Sets initial point from which Rubber Stamp will clone.

continues

III

Gourmet Assignments

continued

Move the Rubber Stamp tool over the hole, click (see fig. 13.18), then move it slightly to get the rest of the hole, click again. Do *not* drag the Rubber Stamp tool	"Bursts" some pattern in the area, replacing hole with sample of tree image.
Press Alt while you click the Rubber Stamp tool on the darker green area to the right of the highest large hole	Sets new sample point, with color values more in keeping with section of tree addressed next.
Move the Rubber Stamp over the right side of the highest large hole, click, then move the tool over slightly and click again	Fills in the hole.
Press Alt while you click over the darker green area to the left of the hole, move the cursor over the remaining portion of the hole, then click	Both large holes are filled.
Choose a smaller brush tip; repeat this procedure of sampling and then clicking over the smaller holes in this area. Try not to go into the sky	Fills in old sky areas in this section only.
Double-click on the Hand tool on the toolbox	Displays full-frame view of PARKBLAH.TIF, to give you some perspective on your accomplishment!
Choose **F**ile, **S**ave	Saves changed image to your hard disk.

Identical Situations Call for Similar Techniques

You use this same technique to correct other isolated areas, such as the willow trees on the right, that have fairly large holes. When a hole is very near the sky, you might prefer to clone sky material into the area. Use your artistic judgment as to whether sky or tree would look best.

We heartily recommend that you spend some time experimenting on your own with this unsupervised retouching work. You have some new techniques and approaches to solving the problems at hand; if an area in PARKBLAH displays some obvious visual dissonance, you can travel not one, but several avenues to fix an image area. Take a good look at the composition of this image; using your eye and a little ingenuity, decide what needs to be rectified to make the image appear more natural.

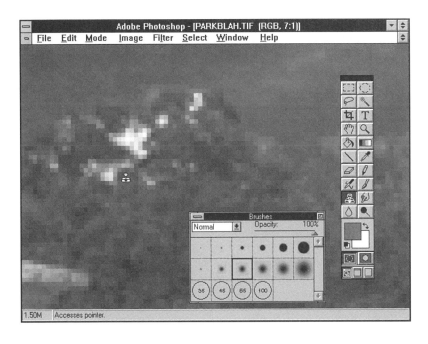

Figure 13.18
Use the Rubber Stamp tool to hide areas, rather than re-create them.

For instance, in a break in the middle of the trees, the sky shows through in three or four places to the left of the gazebo. When you work on this area, set the Brushes palette to the smallest brush you have with spread. Position the Rubber Stamp over a bright area of the sky above these trees, and then press Alt and click to set the Rubber Stamp's sampling point. Brightness is expected here because the sun would actually set here. Use your eye and the **E**dit, **U**ndo commands to achieve a pleasing effect. Be sure to save your file after you finish retouching the trees.

Adding Reflections of New Sky in the Lake

One more area in this image—the water—needs a touch of Photoshop magic. Water, by its nature, is reflective. The current image has nice reflections of the land, but no reflection of the sky. The original sky had nothing to reflect *into* the water except a shade of humdrum! The new sky would look great in the water, though, and if you think about it, it's only natural!

In the next exercise, you'll use Photoshop's Channels, Gradient tool, and Composite Controls to precisely and realistically add the shimmer, the colors, and the pattern of the sky to the water's surface. And you do this without destroying the equally necessary and interesting reflections in the lake of the image's land areas.

When you create or modify scenes in Photoshop, you often will want to consider how image areas interact (or should interact) with other, pasted-in selections. The two features most often overlooked in image retouching and composition are the shadows and reflections. Everything in our world has a shadow, a reflection, or both. If you add or change an element in an image without restoring or creating the shadows and reflections, your work will look unreal. Readers may respond directly or just have a subconscious feeling that something about the piece is hoked-up.

Selecting a Place for the Reflection

Before you can put the sky into the water, you need to create a selection border around the water. Because anything contained within this border gets the sky treatment, this border needs to be fairly accurate. The Lasso tool is the tool of choice for making this selection. And pay careful attention to the stone walls, which reflect rather heavily into the water. Zoom out to determine where the water line is, so that you can accurately select only the water, not the wall.

A good approach to this water-definition is to first use the Lasso tool to create a coarse outline of the area you want. Next, refine the selection area a little by using the Shift key with the Lasso tool to add to the first selection, including image areas of the lake you originally missed. Then press and hold the Ctrl key while you lasso areas you want to subtract from the selection. Put on your imaginary wet suit for the next exercise!

Gathering the Water

Double-click on the Hand tool, then click on the up arrow in the corner of the image's title bar	Displays image window in middle of screen at 1:2 viewing resolution to make clicking around the image easy.
Click on the Lasso tool on the toolbox	Selection tool used for this exercise.
Press Alt and click at the waterline in the center of the gazebo, then (still pressing the Alt key) click completely around the water, back to your starting point; when you reach the edge of the image, click outside the image to select right up to the edge	Alt key constrains Lasso tool to create straight lines between successive click points. Clicking outside image window enables you to create a selection border edge flush with edge of the image window.
Marquee-zoom into the left edge of the gazebo's island	Area of imprecise selecting (with Lasso tool) that needs attention now.

Press Shift while you click and drag an image area not included in your present selection marquee	Pressing Shift key while clicking and dragging adds to selection border (see fig. 13.19).
Press Ctrl while you click and drag an image area you don't want included in the selection marquee	Ctrl key lets you subtract an area from the present selection when you click and drag with the Lasso tool.
Reposition the image with the Hand tool or the scroll bars	Moves your view of PARKBLAH.TIF to different areas in the image that must still be included in or excluded from active selection.
Continue pressing Ctrl (or Shift) while you click and drag near the selection border, as necessary	Creates refined selection border around water area in PARKBLAH.TIF (for editing you'll do shortly).
When all the water is selected, double-click on the Hand tool	Zooms to 1:2 viewing resolution.
Check the entire selection border for any missing or "wrong" areas in the selection	If border looks fine, continue with next step; otherwise, correct it by using Ctrl and Shift keys with Lasso tool.
When your selection looks like figure 13.20, choose **S**elect, **S**ave Selection, then choose New	If the image looks fine, saves the selection to a new channel (5).
Choose **S**elect, **S**ave Selection, and again choose New	Creates duplicate copy of selection in new channel (6).
Choose **F**ile, **S**ave	Save your work to your hard drive.

Selective Selecting with a Gradient Fill

Before you "float" a copy of the sky on the water to form the reflection, you need to create a *partial mask* for the water selection. Certain areas of the sky paste should be more predominant as reflected images than others. The cloud forms on the right of the SKYDARK image are very strong, with some delicate wisps on the left side. Although compositing the image at a certain opacity doesn't solve the problem of being able to control which elements predominate in the image when you paste, creating a partial mask *does*.

The Gradient tool and Photoshop's method for determining selection borders are the key to creating a believable, photogenic reflection in the water. In the next exercise, you create a mask that doesn't affect the wispy clouds on the left, but quite literally "tones-down" the heavy clouds on the right.

Figure 13.19
Adding to the
selection border
with the Lasso tool.

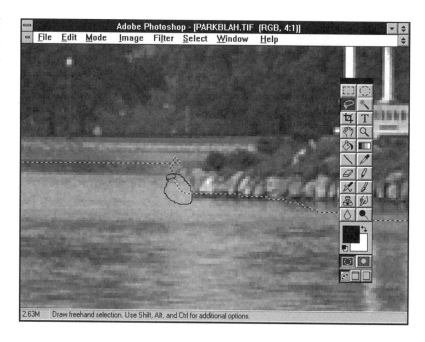

Figure 13.20
Selecting just the
water so that you
can paste the sky
into it.

A Completed Assignment with a Partial Mask

When you create a selection with any of the selection tools except the Magic Wand, you *appear* to be defining an area based on the geometry of the lines that you drew. Actually, you are creating and saving a *mask*, which is saved in an Alpha channel. When you apply a filter or an effect, or perform any kind of action to an image which has a mask in place, Photoshop decides how to carry out the action based on information in the *tonal value* of the mask that's covering each underlying pixel. When the mask over a pixel is 100% opaque, the underlying pixel is ignored. When the mask is transparent, the underlying pixel gets the full treatment of the effect, the blend, whatever. When the mask is a percentage of black, however, (shades of gray are percentages of black), the action performed on the underlying pixel is inhibited to an extent determined by how deep a shade of gray covers the pixels in question.

Creating Partial Masks with the Gradient Tool

When you worked with the Quick Mask earlier in this chapter, you learned how to edit a mask by painting with the Paintbrush tool. In this next exercise, you paint the mask with the Gradient fill tool. When you use a Gradient fill in a channel, you create a mask with a smooth transition from white, through various shades of gray, to black. The properties of white and black vary, according to the settings in the Channel Options dialog box's Color Indicates field, but gray always means that the pixels covered by the gray are *partially* masked.

Setting the Color Properties of Masks

When Channel Options is set to Color Indicates **M**asked Areas, painting with white adds to the selected area in the image (permitting changes to the area), whereas painting with black excludes areas (protecting them from change). If you have chosen Color Indicates **S**elected Areas, you've reversed the areas that the mask color covers.

Channel Options are set by default to whatever the Mask Options are set to when the channel is created. Mask Options are set by double-clicking on the Quick Mask button on the toolbox and clicking one of the radio buttons. When a specific channel is your active view of an image, you can set the Color Indicates options for that channel by clicking on the Channels palette command button and pressing one of the radio buttons. This setting goes into effect immediately if your image contains a defined selection.

If the marquee border displayed when you load a selection *doesn't* have the same shape as the original selection you saved to a channel, don't panic. It's most likely because you have created a partial mask in that selection area. That's what you'll do in the next exercise when you fill the original selection area with a gradient fill.

When a mask is based on *grayscale* information in a channel, the shape of the resulting marquee selection border may be deceiving. Photoshop evaluates the

continues

tonal density in the channel to determine how to draw the visible marquee selection border, but it actually uses all the grayscale information when creating partially masked areas. It "draws the line" rather arbitrarily based on a break point of 56% gray. Pixels with values above this percentage but below 100% are indeed included in the active selection area. Adobe just doesn't include them in the area defined by the visible marquee selection border.

Filling the Channel

Choose **W**indow, Show C**h**annels (or press F6)	Displays Channels palette.
On the Channels palette, click on the #6 title (or press Ctrl+6)	Displays editable view of Channel 6.
Click on the Channels palette command button, choose Channel Options, then click on the Masked Areas radio button in the Color Indicates field, click on OK	Specifies that the channel's black areas are masked and not affected by change.
Click on the default colors icon in the toolbox	Sets foreground color to black, background color to white.
Double-click on the Gradient tool in the toolbox	Displays Gradient Tool Options dialog box.
Set Style to **N**ormal, set Type to **L**inear and **M**idpoint Skew to **70**%, then click on OK	Sets the Gradient tool characteristics.

The gradient fill produced by these settings will shade from the foreground color to the background color linearly, with the midpoint between the colors occurring at the 70% point-of-direction line you created with the Gradient tool.

From the right edge of the selected area in Channel #6, click and drag the Gradient tool straight across to the center of the selected area, then release the mouse button	Graduated fill should resemble figure 13.21.
If it doesn't, try again	New gradient replaces previously created one.
If you accidentally deselect the water area in Channel #6, reload the selection by choosing **S**elect, **L**oad Selection #5	Selection in Channel 5 is a backup selection of water.
Choose **F**ile, **S**ave	Saves changed image to hard disk.

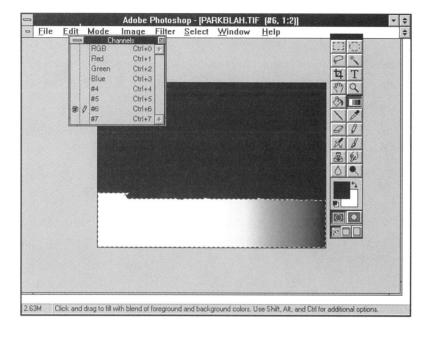

Figure 13.21
A gradient fill created in a channel can be used as a mask.

Creating Water Reflections Using the Partial Mask

All your selection work is done now. You made and saved all the necessary selections and created a mask that will help you add beauty and realism to the image's reflections. In the next exercise, you use the Paste Into command with two slight twists. Because reflections are images mirrored across the horizontal axis, you take a quick trip to the Flip, Vertical command. And you don't want to paste this image in at full opacity. Although the mask you created provides the transition you need to cut back the intensity of the clouds on the image's right side, it doesn't provide the control you need over the opacity of the entire image. Photoshop's Composite Controls feature gives you precise control as you fit the two images together.

In this exercise, you put the finishing touches on the PARKBLAH image (which no longer really merits this name!).

Bringing the Sky to the Water

Click on the RGB title in the Control palette (or press Ctrl+0)	Displays RGB image; marquee selection border is still active.
Choose **S**elect, **L**oad Selection #4	Deselects water and makes sky the current selection.

continues

III

Gourmet Assignments

continued

Choose **E**dit, **C**opy	Copies selection to clipboard.
Choose **S**elect, **L**oad Selection #6	Selection border surrounds part of water. This is OK—result of using selection that contains a partial mask.
Choose **E**dit, Paste **I**nto	Pastes sky into water.
Choose **I**mage, **F**lip, then choose Vertical	Flips sky into its proper orientation as a reflection.
Choose **E**dit, Composite C**o**ntrols	Displays Composite Controls dialog box. Move box by dragging its title bar so that you can see water in image.
Set the Opacity to **65**% and the Mode to Normal (see fig. 13.22); click on OK	Sky melts (composites) nicely into water.
Choose **S**elect, Hide **E**dges, (or press Ctrl+H)	Hides marquee selection so that you can see where image lies.
Zoom in and check the borders along the wall; if you need to adjust the sky, use the keyboard's arrow keys to nudge it into place	Each press of an arrow key moves floating selection one pixel in that direction.
Double-click on the Hand tool on the toolbox for one last look at the whole image; if it looks all right, press Ctrl+D to deselect the floating selection and make it part of the image	Sky is now a real part of water's reflection in image.

Before you save your retouching endeavors, you want to delete the Alpha channels you created. They dramatically increase the size of the file, and you no longer need them, unless you plan to experiment with this piece on your own. You might want to store the file in JPG compressed-file format. Although JPGs can't save Alpha channels, they do help reserve hard drive space for your *own* imaging work!

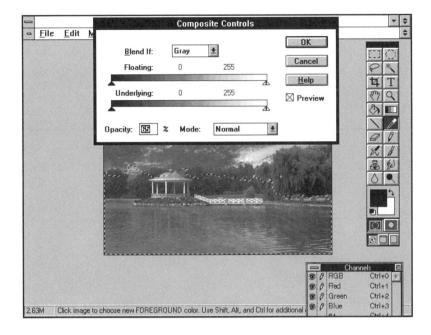

Figure 13.22
With the
Composite
Controls, you
reduce the floating
selection's opacity
to create the
reflection in the
water.

III

Gourmet Assignments

Cleaning Up

Click on the #6 title in the Control palette, click on the command button in the palette, then choose Delete Channel	Deletes channel and reduces file size.
Repeat the preceding step with Channels #5 and #4 remain	Only the RGB Red, Green, and Blue and the RGB Color Composite channels.
Select File, Save As PARKWOW.TIF	Saves finished image to a different name. (You might want to pick something snazzier than PARKWOW.)

You're done. Take a nice long look at your handiwork. As you can see from figure 13.23, you've come a long way with this image. It's a place you'd like to visit, a place to dream about. Creating idyllic situations, making the pedestrian seem special, and painting a dream with realistic strokes is what imaging with Photoshop can be all about.

Summary

This chapter has shown you that a beautiful image of a photograph doesn't always just happen. Sometimes, creating a beautiful image takes a little pushing and prodding, a good selection of stock images you can choose from to augment the budding image, and a midwife as capable as Photoshop to assist in the creation.

Figure 13.23
The Enchanted Gazebo.

But all the fancy moves and techniques you'll continue to pick up about computer imaging won't automatically generate a breathtaking landscape unless you tip your *own* vision into the recipe. You have to start with a dream, discover the possibilities in images you take (or have taken for you), and polish the rough edges to create the appearance of a calm, quiet beauty in the picture. To be able to convey this while you're frantically rushing to beat the deadline, the weather, or the time of day is the *real* magic Photoshop can help you with.

For the average viewer, the art of digital imaging is "magic." A well-executed magic trick always hides what the magician doesn't want the audience to see. But when you reach the point in your imaging career at which you have total control over what the viewing audience sees and takes away from one of your pieces, it's no longer magic—it's called Art.

Chapter Snapshot

In this chapter, you learn how to:

CHAPTER 14

Special Effects with Ordinary Photos

What happens when you paste an out-of-scale, totally unrelated image into a different background? Unless you have read this chapter, you probably will get garbage! But if you read on, you will discover some of the abstract truths about images and imaging work that can make a collection of common pictures positively remarkable.

In Chapters 12 and 13, you learned how to paste a good image into the appropriate scene to express an idyllic, realistic situation. But when, by all rights, the images don't belong together, yet the lighting and other aspects are right, you have used your imagination and Photoshop to create art.

This chapter goes into the details of creating imagery to make an impression. A special effect can come from inspired use of image composition—it can be surreal, striking, fantastic, evocative, even humorous. In this chapter, you are going to plant some one-inch-tall plastic chess pieces on a golf course and make them look like twenty-foot-tall bronze statues. Convincing lighting, some good stock photos, and an understanding of Photoshop techniques are the tickets to creating outrageous, Magritte-influenced, yet believable images.

Creating a Surreal Image Using Real Photos

The image you design in this chapter is both preposterous and credible. With the advent of digital imaging and programs like Photoshop, a photograph no longer ensures reality. Digital imaging can trick the viewer into believing that a politician is shaking hands with a mortal enemy or that the prize in a cereal box is as big as a yacht.

This chapter forsakes commercial and political motivations, however, to pursue art for art's sake. You learn, right here, how to create a fantasy photograph from a real golf green and real (plastic) chess pieces. Photographic illustration is in constant demand by magazines and motion pictures. The greater the sense of realism you convey in the fantasy, the greater the wonder you instill in the viewer. The closer the viewer looks, the more photo-fakery he or she expects to see. But if you follow the steps in this chapter and develop a technique of your own through these exercises, viewers will never see the magician's strings or trap door. No matter how long they look—they will sense only wonder.

Part of your success as a digital-imaging person is to make the viewer look as long as possible at a piece, isn't it?

Using a Fantastic Sky for a Background Element

The image GREENS.TIF is the host for this chapter's imaging work. The reason this image contains virtually no sky is that the weather was uncooperative on the only day (during an entire week) that offered a clear chance of capturing the beautifully manicured golf course. You too, will have to deal often with uncooperative weather during your imaging career. If this were a golfing advertisement, you would want to drop in a more dramatic sky from a different photo, using the techniques you learned in Chapter 13.

But this is a *fantasy* composition, and the rules you play by are your own (within reason). As a creative point of contrast to the well-sculpted, lush greenery in this image, you'll use a fractal sky generated in CorelDRAW! As you'll see, the fractal sky needs a little Photoshop bending and shaping to keep it from clashing with the realism of the trees. But the GREENS.TIF image will take shape immediately after you enhance it in this way.

Be sure to notice something about complementary colors as you go through this first exercise. With its natural sky as a background, the image looks pale. But when you add the rich bluish fractal image to the picture as the sky, the green of the trees truly comes to life.

When I first photographed GREENS.TIF, I almost didn't realize what a useful image it is! The lesson before the exercise: Always evaluate a good *area* of an image, separate from the other elements. Put your hand over the top of your monitor, or use Photoshop to crop away an area. Image *areas* can be more useful than a first glance sometimes suggests.

Selecting the Sky Area for Replacement

Open the GREENS.TIF image from the companion CD	First image you work with.
Double-click on the Magic Wand tool	Displays Magic Wand dialog box.
Set the **T**olerance to **40** pixels, make sure that **A**nti-Aliased is on, then click on OK	Sets range of adjacent pixels of similar color value that Magic Wand will select.
Click on the sky area to the right of the GREENS.TIF image	Selects most of sky area (see fig. 14.1).
Choose **S**elect, Si**m**ilar	Picks up pixels of similar value but not adjacent to area clicked over. (Similar command picks pixels within same Tolerance range as Magic Wand tool, but don't expect *miracles.*)
Click on Lasso tool	Selection tool for editing Magic Wand selection.
Press Shift while you click and drag over the remaining sky area (to the left of the GREENS.TIF image)	Shift combination adds to existing selection area.
Choose **S**elect, Save **S**election	Saves sky selection to new channel.
Choose **F**ile, Sa**v**e As GREENS.TIF to an appropriate location on your hard disk; be sure **S**ave Alpha Channels is checked!	Saves image to hard disk.
Choose **F**ile, **C**lose	Closes image. (In next step, you work with a distortion filter on another image; two open images can strain computer system.)

Determining what Tolerance value to set the Magic Wand to when approaching a specific task is a trial-and-error process. The value you chose in the last exercise (40 pixels) works in this instance; it is the result of earlier trial-and-error work by the authors. In your own assignments, try an arbitrary value, and then adjust the Tolerance up or down to find the value that works.

Alternatively, you can press F8 to display the Info palette, then run the cursor around an image area to see the different color-model values in an area bound for selection. In this example, a lack of differences in an area's RGB or HSB values suggests that you can use a fairly high Tolerance to select only the sky image area. With a high Magic Wand Tolerance, the marquee border around the tree line is a tight one; later, removing any telltale Anti-Alias pixels where the edges of the trees meet the new selection area will be a fairly easy task.

III

Gourmet Assignments

Figure 14.1
The Magic Wand
tool can select
most of an even
sky area.

No matter what you do with the Magic Wand Tolerance setting, you can never select an area bordered by trees "perfectly." Trees are extremely complex, irregular, natural shapes; although their boundaries might appear well-defined in the real world, they aren't (as you can see by looking carefully at the resulting image file).

If you still experience Anti-Alias fringing after you make a selection in your own work, try one, or all of the following techniques on your virtual forest:

✔   Set the Magic Wand Tolerance a little higher than you think you should. Although your selection of the sky will include some leaves and branches, you can always add a few here and there later, using the Paintbrush and Pencil tools.

✔   After you've made a selection of the sky, use the **S**elect, **I**nverse commands on the selection area. Then copy the selection area and paste it into a new channel in the image. In the new channel, issue the **S**elect, **D**efringe command. Then select and save the selection to the same channel in which you defringed. Defringing removes the Anti-Alias pixels around the tree. Saving the selection to the same channel destroys the copied paste, but you're trying to create a *selection border* here, not preserve a copy of the image. This technique gives you a better selection border for the RGB channel.

✔ Click on Quick Mask mode to turn the Magic Wand selection into one that can be edited by the paint-type tools. Trees always have nooks that the Magic Wand tool and the **S**elect, **S**imilar commands ignore. The best way to address these areas is to use the Quick Mask mode and the Paintbrush or Pencil tool after the Magic Wand selection. Then you can click back into Standard view and use the **S**elect, **S**ave Selection commands to save the edited selection.

Making a Fractal Sky More Natural

Next, you'll use Photoshop's Distort Fi̲lters commands (*not* the same as the **I**mage, Effects, Distort command) to lend a more natural sweep and flow to the FRCTLSKY.TIF image from the companion CD. Although fractal designs are wonderful to work with in Photoshop, their synthetic qualities are sometimes obvious when the fractal designs are positioned next to a natural area, such as the trees in GREEN.TIF. Figure 14.2 shows you how glorious, fluffy, and static the FRCTLSKY.TIF image is.

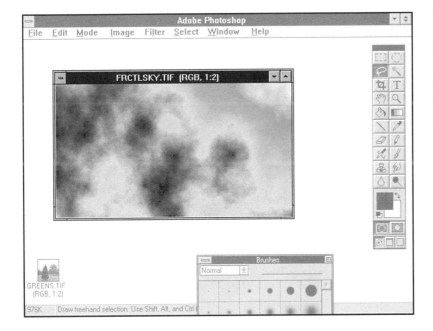

Figure 14.2

Fractals are mathematical formulas that express random patterns similar to those found in nature.

Each element in the piece you are creating will have its own level of believability. Together, the plausible and the implausible balance each other, influencing your perception of the whole image in much the same way that a painter does by playing with color. In the next exercise, you'll shape and modify the artificial FRCTLSKY.TIF image so that it adds some hyperrealistic tension to the finished image but remains the backdrop for the stars of the design—the giant chess pieces.

Adding Clouds, Movement, and Drama to the Sky

Open the FRCTLSKY.TIF image from the companion CD	Fractal sky image used to replace original GREEN.TIF sky.
Choose Fi*l*ter, Distort, then choose Twirl	Displays Twirl dialog box.
Enter a value of **-50** in the **A**ngle box, then click on OK	Applies mild counterclockwise spin to entire image.
Choose Fi*l*ter, Distort, then choose Pinch	Displays Pinch dialog box.
Enter **50**% in the **A**mount box, then click on OK	Creates mild vortex in center of image (see fig. 14.3).
Choose **S**elect, **A**ll (or press Ctrl+A), then choose **E**dit, **C**opy (or press Ctrl+C)	Copies entire FRCTLSKY.TIF image to Clipboard.
Click on the down button on the FRCTLSKY.TIF image window	Minimizes FRCTLSKY image (now an icon).
Choose **F**ile, **O**pen, then click on GREENS.TIF under the files list of images saved to your *hard disk*	Image of golf course you created (and in which you saved a selection).
Choose **S**elect, **L**oad Selection	Activates selection area you defined earlier in GREENS.TIF image.
Choose **E**dit, Paste **I**nto	Pastes copy of fractal sky into selection area of GREENS.TIF (see fig. 16.4).
Choose the Lasso tool from the toolbox, then click and drag the fractal sky copy to a compositionally pleasing area in the pasted-into selection area	Fractal sky is marginally larger than section area you defined; you have some "play" for positioning the copy.
Choose **S**elect, **N**one (or press Ctrl+D)	Deselects pasted-into fractal sky, making it part of image.
Choose **F**ile, **S**ave (or press Ctrl+S)	Saves your work up to this stage.

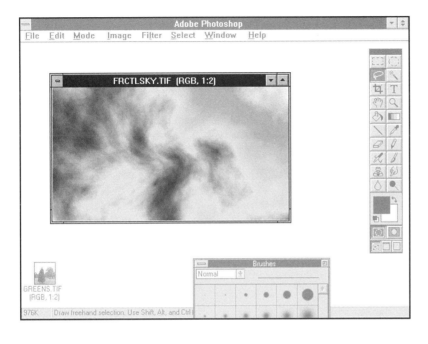

Figure 14.3
To add a sense of motion to a static image, use the Pinch and Twirl Distort commands.

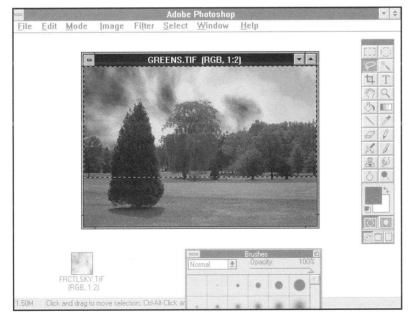

Figure 14.4
The Paste Into command enables you to replace a selected area with Clipboard selections.

III

Gourmet Assignments

The nice thing about the Paste Into command is that it saves you from the hassle of deleting an area you want to replace. In the last exercise, the fractal sky copy covered the original sky; when you deselected the fractal sky, it became part of the image.

Blurring the Line between Trees and Sky

At a 1:2 viewing resolution, you probably have noticed that the Anti-Aliasing around the trees is visible. The gray pixels Photoshop adds around the edges of an Anti-Aliased selection (in an attempt to create a smooth selection border) are brighter than the fractal sky you pasted in behind them.

In a similar situation in Chapter 13, you learned that you can use the Blur tool to fix this problem quickly and effectively. In a photographic image, trees don't starkly pierce the sky—they fuzz off into it. Throughout this book, a technique is used for fixing pasted edge areas; a quick refresher follows:

1. Select the Blur tool, then set the Brushes palette for Darken mode, at about 2/3 Opacity.

2. Zoom into an area in which edges are most visible at a low viewing resolution (1:1 or 1:2).

3. Click on the Blur tool in a dark area near the pasted edge (see fig. 14.5), then drag across the edge into a lighter area.

Figure 14.5
Click in a dark area, then drag to a lighter one, using the Blur tool set to Darken mode on the Brushes palette.

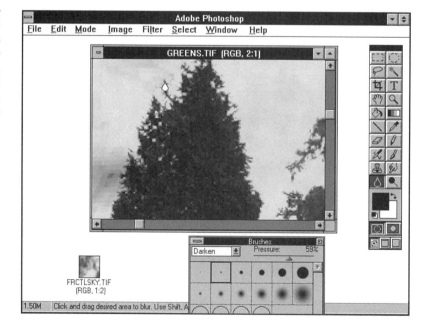

Editing tools like the Blur/Sharpen, Dodge/Burn, and Smudge tools are great for lessening detail in image areas. These tools don't add color to the image; they simply start where you click and apply their special editing characteristic in the direction you drag.

Try the technique now on parts of the trees in the image. Notice that if Darken mode is selected on the Brushes palette, you can easily Blur a dark tree area into a lighter, fractal sky area. Blurring an area with a selective preference of tonal values is a weird concept, but it works. You are blurring one area *toward* another when you click and drag. With the Brushes palette, the mode setting for editing tools determines how the editing is applied, just as the setting for paint-application tools determines how paint is applied.

Consider Resolutions Before You Get to Photoshop

Now it is time to introduce one of the lead characters in this fantasy image—the pawn. Part of the secret to building convincing images with photographic pieces that don't scale well naturally is to photograph them with different camera lenses. For this assignment, the pawn occupied the same field size in the lens as the golf course; a 55mm lens was used for the golf course, a macro zoom lens for the plastic chess pieces.

Don't think for a second that you can use the same lenses for a background and a miniature, then hope to combine them in Photoshop with any degree of success. You can increase a miniature's size to make it comparable to the background, but at the expense of *resolution*.

Bit-mapped images contain a finite number of original pixels. Photoshop interpolates additional pixels into an image you want to enlarge. But the results look grainy and phony because Photoshop has to "best guess" what the pixels *would* have been had more detail originally been captured. For better results, do some "editing" with your photographic gear *before* you use Photoshop.

When photographing or choosing stock images for this kind of scale-warping composition, you need to shoot for identical lighting and camera angle in the images. The pawn in the next exercise was lit and photographed from the same direction as the golf course so that the highlights in the plastic chess pieces are where the sun in the GREENS.TIF image would have put them. Using natural highlights in an improbable composition adds a reality difficult to achieve with Photoshop retouching only.

Creating a Selection Border for the Pawn

As you can see from figure 14.6, the PAWN.TIF image scales nicely into the GREENS image. Because PAWN.TIF has the same lighting, a similar camera focus, and (most important) the same resolution as GREENS.TIF, you can copy a pixel in the PAWN image to the GREENS image without any interpolation work by Photoshop.

Figure 14.6
A one-inch-tall chess piece can hold its own in a golf course image, provided that field sizes are the same in both images.

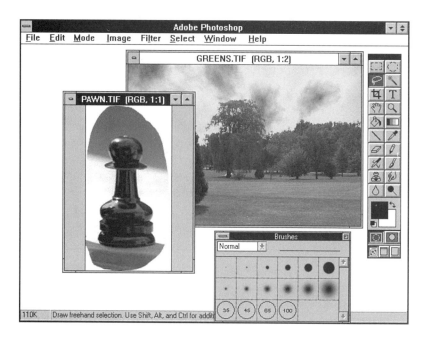

You need to create a selection border around the pawn, so that it can be selected and copied into the GREENS.TIF background. Usually, you use the Lasso tool, or Quick Mask mode with a painting tool, to create a precise selection border. But the pawn's predominant geometric lines and curves make the Paths palette's Pen tool a much better choice for defining this outline. If you are not familiar with the Pen tool, the next exercise gives you directions for using it. (Chapters 4 and 8 contain detailed instructions for using Paths and the tools.)

PAWN.TIF has all the necessary detail to transplant successfully to the 18th hole, except that it lacks a shadow like the one cast by the trees in GREENS.TIF. The outline you create for the pawn with the Paths Pen tool has an additional purpose beyond basing a selection border on it to use when copying the pawn into GREENS.TIF. Instead of hand-rendering a shadow for the pawn, you'll learn how to reuse the selection border, tailoring it to be the pawn's shadow.

First, you need to define the pawn's outline:

Creating a Pawn Path

Click on the FRCTLSKY.TIF icon to display the command menu, choose **C**lose, then click on No in the Save Changes? dialog box	Fractal sky no longer needed (and you cannot save changes to a CD-ROM).
Click on the down button in the upper right of the GREENS.TIF image's window	Minimizes image to icon; conserves workspace; temporarily relieves video driver of unnecessary redraws.
Choose **F**ile, **O**pen	Open PAWN.TIF from companion CD.
Choose **W**indow, Show P**a**ths (or press F9)	Displays Paths palette.
Choose the Zoom tool from the toolbox, then Marquee-zoom into top of pawn image	Starting point of Path. (Tight viewing resolution promotes accuracy; 3:1 zoom field is good.)
Click on the Pen tool in the Paths palette	Tool used to create Anchor points and path segments in an image.
Click on the top edge of the pawn	Places first Anchor point.
Click on the extreme right of the top "bulb" on the pawn	Sets second anchor point and creates path segment between the two. Path direction is now clockwise; you must continue in this direction.
Click on the base of the bulb on the pawn	Creates another Anchor point and a path segment between the two anchors.
Click on the Hand tool, push the image up in the window	Pushes down view of PAWN.TIF, providing better view so that you can continue Path.
Continue clicking anchor points clockwise around the pawn outline at edge points where the outline's geometry takes a different direction	Adds anchors, with direction lines in between (that will be molded to pawn outline).
Click on the first anchor with the Pen tool	Tiny circle at bottom right of cursor indicates that Path is now closed (can be used to create an enclosed selection).
Click on the Corner tool in the Paths palette	Tool used to create direction lines and bend path segments.
Click and drag clockwise from an Anchor point	Produces direction point now held by cursor; curves the two neighboring line segments (see fig. 14.7).

continues

continued

Click and drag on a direction point	Controls only path segment to right of Anchor point; you can fit line segment to curve of pawn's outline.
Press and hold the Ctrl key while you click and drag on the point directly opposite the one you're working with, to fit the path segment to the left of the Anchor point to the pawn's outline	Corner cursor toggles to Pointer cursor so that you can manipulate direction point independently of opposing direction point.
Continue to click while dragging anchor points to create direction points, then pressing Ctrl while you click and drag the direction points, fitting them to the pawn's outline	Shapes Path to fit pawn's outline.
When you finish shaping the path, click on the Paths palette command button, choose Save Path, then accept the default Name: Path 1 and click on OK	Saves path.
Choose File, Save (or press Ctrl+S)	Saves your work to hard disk.

Figure 14.7
Click and drag on an Anchor point to produce direction points that bend and shape path segments to an image outline.

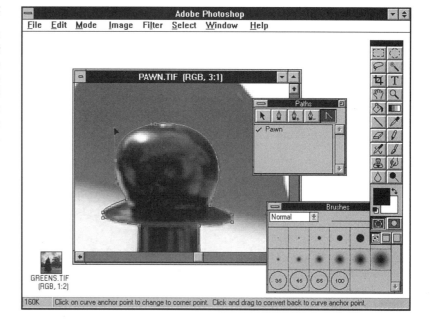

The Paths Pen and Corner tools can make quick work of precisely describing the pawn's outline because the pawn has a hard outline composed only of straight lines and curves. This past exercise is only one way to render a path segment. Another technique, which produces curved line segments from the get-go, entails clicking while dragging at each Anchor point. This second technique eliminates the need for the Corner tool but is more difficult for someone new to the concept of paths (vector art) to work with.

Practicing making paths—using this exercise and the others in the book—is a good idea. Paths are ideal for situations like this one, but the properties of the tools don't operate very intuitively. The only way to develop an understanding of how they behave and to learn how to work quickly with them is to practice, but it's well worth the effort.

If you have invested a substantial amount of time building a path, and you are called away often in your work, consider saving a path between steps. Specifying a name for the path is easy. Simply click on the Paths command button, select Save Path, then use the dialog box to name the path. After you save the path, Photoshop automatically saves subsequent path segments to the image file you can later recall from the Paths palette.

But getting rid of a path when you no longer need it in an image is *not* easy! When you create a selection from a path, as you will in the next exercise, an unsaved path still exists. When you copy the selection, *the unsaved Path* (*not* the selection) is copied to the clipboard. To avoid this unexpected substitution, you must do one of the following three things:

✔ If you have saved a path, you must deactivate it by removing the check from the space next to its name in the Paths palette.

✔ Or you can check the space next to the path's name, then select Delete Path from the Paths palette's command button drop-down list.

✔ Finally, and *only* when you have a selection made from the path, you can press the keyboard's Backspace key twice to eliminate an unsaved path you have created.

Integrating the Pawn and the Golf Course

Now that you have fitted a path to the Pawn's outline, it is time to create a selection based on the path. In the next exercise, you also save the *selection area* so that you can use it as the pawn's shadow on the golf course. After you paste the pawn onto the GREENS.TIF background image, you'll learn how to transform it from plastic to gleaming bronze. This "material" transformation, from plastic to bronze, contributes to a more visually exciting photo illustration.

Transforming the Pawn in the Image

On the Paths palette, click on the space to the left of the Path name (Path 1) you saved in the last exercise	Makes path visible and active.
Click on the command button in the Paths palette, select Make selection	Displays Make Selection dialog box.
From the Rendering option field, set Feather Radius to **0** pixels, make sure that **A**nti-Aliased is checked, then click on OK	Creates active selection based on path you designed earlier. Path you saved is no longer checked in Paths palette (see fig. 14.8).
Choose **S**elect, Save **S**election	Saves selection created from Path outline as separate Channel 4 in PAWN.TIF image.
Choose **E**dit, **C**opy (or press Ctrl+C)	Copies pawn selection to Clipboard.
Minimize PAWN.TIF, then restore GREENS.TIF by double-clicking on the thumbnail of it in Photoshop's workspace	Makes GREENS.TIF image window active.
Select the Zoom tool, then Marquee-zoom to a 2:1 viewing resolution on the light-green patch of land in the foreground, to the right of the pine tree	Provides good working view of area to paste pawn.
Choose **E**dit, **P**aste (or press Ctrl+V)	Pastes pawn copy into GREENS.TIF image.
Click and drag the pawn image into place on the green	Position pawn image so that it seems to sit on light-green area of image.
Choose **S**elect, **D**efringe, then select **W**idth: **1** pixel, click on OK	Removes Anti-Aliasing edge pixels from pawn's selection border.
Choose **I**mage, **A**djust, then choose Hue/Saturation (or just press Ctrl+U)	Displays Hue/Saturation dialog box.
Check the Colorize box, type **+40** in the Hue box or drag the Hue slider to the right to a value of +40, then click on OK	Colorizes pawn, giving it a bronze color (see fig. 14.9).
Choose **S**elect, **S**ave Selection, then click on #4	Overwrites sky selection area (no longer needed) and creates selection border of pawn in GREENS.TIF image's Channel 4.

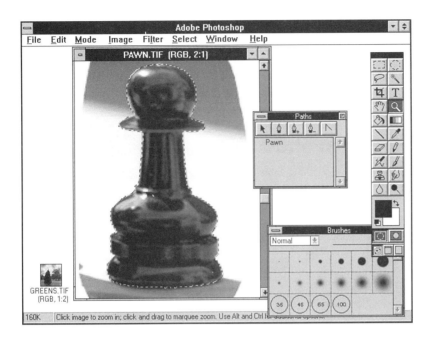

Figure 14.8
To create a precise selection border from a path, use the Paths palette's Make Selection command.

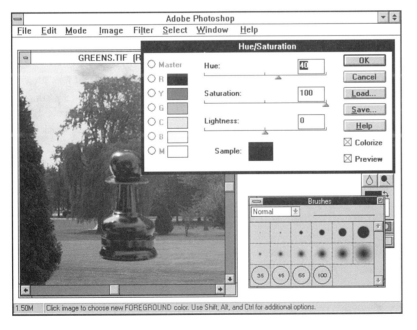

Figure 14.9
Colorizing a naturally monochrome image gives it a different "look."

The colorizing trick works beautifully because the pawn was originally black, with a few highlights. Colorizing a selection doesn't normally yield such realistic results after the colorized image is positioned against an RGB background. It worked in this case because the hue used to colorize affected only the lighter areas of the pawn. Bronze and gold are traditionally portrayed as having highlights, a few colored areas, and a great deal of black shadow area—the effect the Colorize command produced.

The Pawn Gets a Shadow

If you look at the pine tree (by scrolling down or zooming out), which is now close to the pawn in the GREENS.TIF image, you can see that the tree casts a fairly short shadow. The shadow points at about 4 o'clock from the base of the tree onto the golfing green. Your task in the next exercise is to duplicate the angle of the tree's shadow, using the pawn outline as the shape. You then paste this shape behind the bronze pawn and composite it to blend into the scene.

This next exercise involves copying the selection from the PAWN.TIF's Alpha channel for use as a design for the pawn's shadow. When you create a new document for the copy of the Alpha channel, Photoshop will give you a lot of choices about the creation of the New File. Alpha Channels are grayscale information channels, and when you copy one to the clipboard, Photoshop "senses" what image type is on it, and intuitively offers you all the image options, like Height, Width, and Mode to accommodate the image you have on the clipboard.

So, by default, Photoshop will offer you a grayscale Mode for the **F**ile, **N**ew you're about to create. And this is okay because when you eventually bring the modified copy of the alpha channel into the RGB GREENS.TIF image, Photoshop automatically converts the "client" image into the "host's" color format.

But don't freak if you only see a Black Channel from the Channel's palette, instead of Red, Green, and Blue for the copied shadow image file. All is well, and if you can intuitively guess how they get 47 clowns in a Volkswagen at the circus, you're a long way ahead in your understanding of Photoshop.

First things first, though. You are going to create a copy of the saved selection in PAWN.TIF, then modify it by using the **I**mage, **E**ffects commands.

Creating an Angled Shadow

Double-click on the PAWN.TIF
thumbnail in Photoshop's workspace

Restores image and becomes active
image window.

Click on the Channel #4 title in the Channels palette	Displays channel that holds selection you saved earlier.
Choose **S**elect, **L**oad Selection	Activates marquee border in channel (see fig. 14.10).
Choose **E**dit, **C**opy (or press Ctrl+C)	Copies selection to Clipboard.
Click on the down arrow in the upper right of the PAWN.TIF image window	Minimizes PAWN.TIF to an icon. You don't need it for a while.
Choose **F**ile, **N**ew (or press Ctrl+N)	Displays New dialog box.
Choose **W**idth:**200** pixels, H**e**ight:**300** pixels, then click on OK	Specifies new file larger than image on Clipboard.
Choose **E**dit, **P**aste (or press Ctrl+V)	Pastes copy of pawn selection area into Untitled-1 image window. New file, by default, becomes active image window.
Choose **I**mage, **F**lip, and then choose Vertical	Creates mirror image of pawn "silhouette."
Choose the Lasso tool, then click and drag the selection to the left of the Untitled-1 window	Prepares for next step.
Choose **I**mage, **E**ffects, then choose Skew	Puts Effects boundary box around selection area.
Click and drag the lower-right corner of the boundary box to the right	Angles silhouette selection to match angle at which tree shadows are cast in GREEN.TIF (see fig. 14.11).
Click inside the Skew boundary box	Cursor becomes gavel; clicking with it "nails" selection area to degree of Skew created.
Choose **I**mage, **E**ffects, and then choose Scale	Puts Scale boundary box around image.
Click and drag the lower-right corner of the boundary box straight up	Scales only the vertical aspect of selection. Stop when selection is stubby and angled (similar to pine-tree shadow in GREEN.TIF image).
Click inside the Scale boundary box border	"Nails" scaled selection to degree you want (see fig. 14.12).
Choose **S**elect, **S**ave Selection	Saves skewed, scaled selection area to new channel in Untitled-1.

Figure 14.10
You can copy the contents of a selection marquee in a channel by loading the selection first.

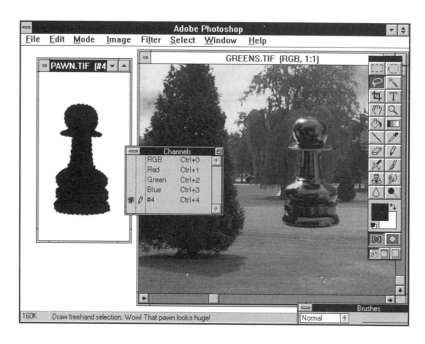

Figure 14.11
A selection skews horizontally or vertically, depending on the direction in which you first drag the corner.

Figure 14.12

You can scale a selection area proportionately or disproportionately with the Scale command.

Don't try to perform horizontal *and* vertical skewing moves in a single session with the Skew boundary box. The box skews only horizontally *or* vertically, depending on which direction you click and drag first. You can, however, continue to click and drag on any of the boundary corners. This enables you to move a boundary corner independently of the adjacent corner, but then the effect is no longer a true skewing effect.

To scale a selection area proportionately, hold down Shift while you click and drag.

You have learned the secret to creating a complex shadow from a selection border of the object that *needs* the shadow!

Using a Selection Area as an Image

In the real world, shadows fade at the point farthest from the base of the shape that's casting the shadow. In the next exercise, you add a gradient fill to the shadow, to imitate the way a natural shadow behaves.

But Photoshop evaluates selections based on the *brightness* of the pixels found in an Alpha channel. If you shade a selection area in a channel with a gradient fill, the lighter parts of the fill form *partial masks*—they are opaque in darker areas, transparent in others. And although this was useful in Chapter 13, when you pasted the reflection of the sky into the lake, you don't want the effect for this shadow image. You need to be able to select the *entire* shape, which happens to contain a fill with shades of gray in it. The following exercise shows you how to select the entire grayscale image:

Creating Some Realism with the Pawn Shadow

Choose **S**elect, **L**oad Selection	Displays marquee border around shadow in Untitled-1.
Click on the background color selection box on the toolbox	Displays Color Picker model.
Enter the following values, C **0**, M **0**, Y **0**, and K **50**%, in the CMYK field on the Color Picker dialog box, then click on OK	Specifies neutral, 50% gray for background color in Photoshop.
Double-click on the Gradient tool, then (from the Gradient Options box) select **Style** **N**ormal, **Type** **L**inear, click on OK	Sets Gradient tool to characteristics needed to create realistic shadow.
In the Black channel, click and drag in the active selection area, starting at the bottom third of the shadow and ending just outside the selection area	Creates gradient fill from black to gray (see fig. 14.13).

Giving the Pawn Some Substance

The pawn in the GREENS.TIF image still has no shadow, which makes it an unnatural and unrealistic element in the image. But when you add the realistic, accurate shadow you have designed, it's a whole 'nother ball game.

In the next exercise, you take a snapshot of the GREENS.TIF image before you paste the shadow into it. You can use snapshots to "reclaim" original areas that have been edited. To place the shadow in the image, you use the blending function of the Brushes palette's mode rather than the Edit menu's Composite Controls. In this assignment, you access a mode from the Brushes palette simply because it's convenient and you don't need the more sophisticated extra options of Composite Controls. Using the information saved with the Snapshot command, you enhance the reality of the shadow by restoring some of the underlying texture that is obscured by the shadow. It's time to place and tweak the shadow.

Figure 14.13
A gradient fill can
be applied only to
a selection in an
image.

Adding Realism to the Pawn

III
Gourmet Assignments

With PAWN.TIF as the open, active window, choose **S**elect, **L**oad Selection	Loads selection #2, the selection area you saved earlier.
Choose **E**dit, **C**opy, then click on the down-arrow button on PAWN.TIF's title bar	Copies gradient shadow selection to clipboard and minimizes image to thumbnail in Photoshop's workspace. GREENS.TIF should now be the active image window.
Choose **E**dit, T**a**ke Snapshot	Loads copy of GREENS.TIF image into system RAM for Photoshop to reference later.
Choose **S**elect, **L**oad Selection	Displays marquee selection border around bronze pawn image.
Choose **E**dit, Paste **B**ehind	Pastes gradient shadow selection on top of GREENS.TIF, but behind selection of bronze pawn.
Press Ctrl+H	Hides marquee edges so that you can see what you're doing.

continues

continued

Click and drag the gradient-shadow floating selection to a point at which its base touches the base of the bronze pawn	Positions floating selection so that it seems to be bronze pawn's shadow.
On the Brushes palette, set the mode to Multiply, set the Opacity: to **84**%	Creates semitransparent, dense shadow from gradient floating selection (see fig. 14.14).
Choose **S**elect, **D**efringe, select **W**idth: **1** pixel, then click on OK	Defringe removes some gray edge pixels Anti-Aliasing added to selection's border.
Choose **S**elect, **N**one (or press Ctrl+D)	Composites gradient shadow area into GREENS.TIF background image.
Choose **F**ile, **S**ave (or press Ctrl+S)	Saves your work up to this point.

Figure 14.14
The Brushes palette can be used to composite a floating selection into a background image.

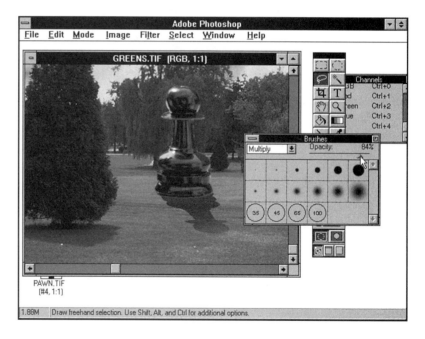

Now that the shadow is in the GREENS.TIF image, you can evaluate its verisimilitude against the real shadow beneath the pine tree. The pawn's shadow is in the right place and it's the right shape, but two things mark it as an unrealistic shadow. First, the shadow is far too crisp around its edges to be believable. Second, there is too much black and too little original grass image showing through in the shadow area. Unfortunately, that's what a gradient-filled shadow *looks like* against a natural texture! But you can easily enhance the look. You can gently reapply the original grass area with the Rubber Stamp tool—but not by cloning from another area of the image. Now that you have a Snapshot of the GREENS image, the Rubber Stamp can read it as a source for samples so that each Rubber Stamp stroke you apply corresponds to the identical image area in the Snapshot! Now you perfect the pawn's shadow.

Adding Photorealism to a Shadow

Choose the Blur tool, choose a small tip from the Brushes palette's top row, then set it to Lighten mode, **70**% pressure	Sets Blur tool to lighten tonal values of pixels darker than area you first click over.
Click and drag from a point outside the shadow area into the shadow area	Decreases contrast between lighter grass pixels and darker shadow pixels (see fig. 14.15).
Continue to click and drag from outside the shadow to inside	Blur/sharpen shadow border when it falls on grass; stop when edge is completely blurred.
Double-click on the Rubber Stamp tool	Displays Rubber Stamp Options dialog box.
Choose From Snapshot as the Option, then click on OK	Sets Rubber Stamp tool to "paint" from samples of GREENS.TIF image before shadow was added.
Choose the 45-pixel-diameter tip from the Brushes palette, set a **12**% Opacity level	Sets Rubber Stamp tool to reapply a faint degree of original image over shadow area.
Click and drag one or two strokes in the pawn shadow area	Restores slight amount of original, Snapshot image to shadow area (see fig. 14.16).
Choose **F**ile, **S**ave (or press Ctrl+S)	Saves your work up to this point.

Reusing the Pawn Image To Create a Virtual Second Pawn

If you're "game" for embellishing this fantasy illustration a little more, read on. You are going to learn how to reuse the pawn to create a second one in GREENS.TIF. Adding perspective in a digital image is easy if you think about what things look like at a distance—they seem smaller. If you reduce the size of PAWN.TIF by, say, a quarter, you can place the second pawn a little to the right of the first one—it will seem to be a different pawn, farther from the camera.

Figure 14.15
The Blur tool in Lighten mode changes only the pixels that are darker than the area you are blurring from.

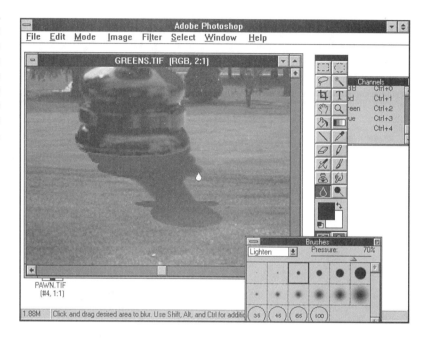

Figure 14.16
The Rubber Stamp tool "paints" by using image information from a Snapshot rather than from areas presently in the image.

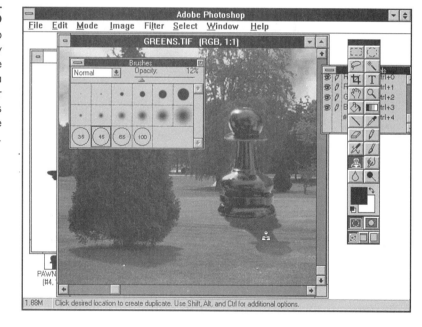

In the following exercise, you learn a trick for easily scaling the Untitled-1 shadow so that it precisely matches the size of the smaller pawn. The technique for colorizing the pawn and dropping it into the GREENS.TIF image is the same one you used before, but with a few twists and turns you might want to use in work of your own. Let the pawn shrinking commence!

Creating a Second Pawn from the Same Image

Minimize the GREENS.TIF image for the time being	Frees some workspace.
Double-click on Untitled-1, then on PAWN.TIF	Restores image windows and makes PAWN.TIF the active one.
Press Alt and click on the file-size box in Photoshop's status bar	Displays Width and Height of PAWN.TIF (152 pixels by 269 pixels).
Choose **W**indow, Show In**f**o (or press F8)	Displays Info palette.
Click on the Untitled-1 title bar	Makes Untitled-1 the active image window.
Choose the Crop tool from the toolbox	Tool used to crop images.
Click and drag with the Crop tool to marquee-select the pawn shadow in Untitled-1; stop when the Info palette's W: and H: areas read 152 and 269	Makes Untitled-1 image dimensions exactly those of PAWN.TIF (see fig. 14.17).
Click inside the Crop marquee border	Cursor becomes scissors and image is cropped.
Choose **I**mage, **I**mage Size	Displays Image Size dialog box.
In the New Size field, click on the **W**idth drop-down list, choose Percent, then type **75** in the **W**idth text box; make sure that Constrain: Proportion is checked	Sets width; Constrain: **P**roportion adjusts Height accordingly (see fig. 14.18).
Click on OK	Confirms changes and redisplays Photoshop's workspace.
Click on PAWN.TIF's title bar	PAWN.TIF becomes active image window.
Repeat the **I**mage, **I**mage Size steps used for the Untitled-1 image	Shrinks pawn image to exactly same size as Untitled-1; now both have same image dimensions.

By using Percentage as a unit of measurement (instead of a linear unit), you ensure that two or more identically sized image windows scale up or down exactly. You don't use the Canvas Size command to make the images identical in size, because the Canvas Size command gives you very little control over *cropping* the image. Photoshop even flashes a warning before you try to execute such a command. Use the Crop tool when you want a say in the way an image is cropped.

III

Gourmet Assignments

Figure 14.17
Use the Info palette to get precision results when you crop an image.

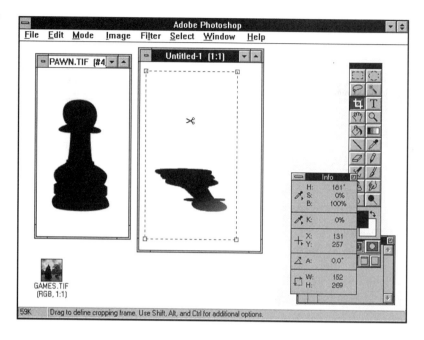

Figure 14.18
Use Percentage instead of pixels or inches to scale an image with the Image Size command.

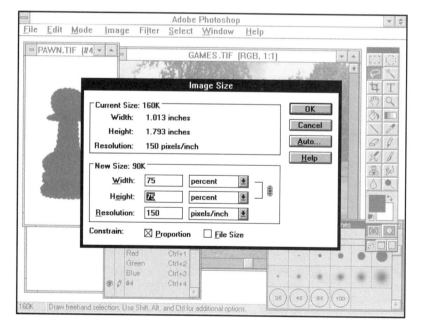

Adding the Second Pawn's Shadow

With the first pawn's selection border active, you can use a simple Paste Behind command to place the second pawn. But the second shadow has to be pasted behind *both* pawn 2 and *part* of pawn 1. Pawn-der this point as you move into the next exercise. As soon as you've placed the "smaller" pawn in the background image, you're going to learn how to create a selection border that encompasses both pawns.

Let the game continue!

Adding the Second Pawn

Click on the PAWN.TIF title bar	PAWN.TIF becomes active image.
Click on the RGB title in the Channels palette	Displays view of RGB pawn image.
Choose **S**elect, **L**oad Selection	Activates marquee border around pawn.
Choose **E**dit, **C**opy (or press Ctrl+C)	Copies RGB selection to Clipboard.
Click on GREENS.TIF's title bar, choose **F**ile, then Sa**v**e As GAMES.TIF. Be sure that the **S**ave Alpha Channels box is checked!	Saves file under different file name to protect your work.
Choose **S**elect, **L**oad Selection	Loads active marquee selection border around bronze pawn.
Choose **E**dit, Paste **B**ehind	Pastes second pawn behind first.
Choose **I**mage, **A**djust, then choose Hue/Saturation (or press Ctrl+U)	Displays Hue/Saturation dialog box.
Check Colorize, enter **40** in the Hue text box, then click on OK	Colorizes second, smaller pawn to same color as first pawn.
Click and drag the second pawn into position so that it peeks out from behind and to the right of the first pawn	Positions second pawn (see fig. 16.19 for exact positioning).
Choose **S**elect, **D**efringe, choose **W**idth: **1** pixel, then click on OK	Defringe removes Anti-Aliasing fringe around second pawn's border.
Choose **S**elect, **S**ave Selection, then choose New	Creates new Channel 5 in GAMES.TIF, for second pawn's selection outline.
Choose **F**ile, **S**ave (or press Ctrl+S)	Saves your work up to this point.

III

Gourmet Assignments

Figure 14.19
A smaller pawn,
slightly eclipsed by
the first, suggests
depth to the whole
image.

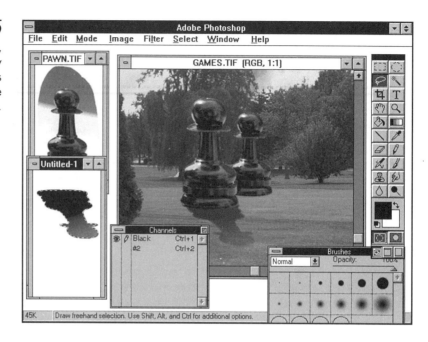

Now that you have Alpha Channels #4 and # 5, each of which contains the outline of a single pawn, it's time to create a third, compound outline by adding one selection to the other. This third outline is the selection border you'll Paste **B**ehind when you place the smaller pawn's shadow.

Creating a New Selection Border from Existing Ones

Choose **I**mage, **C**alculate, and then choose Add	Displays Add dialog box.
Choose (Source **1**) Document GAMES.TIF, Channel **4**, (Source **2**)Document GAMES.TIF, Channel **5**, (Destination) Document GAMES.TIF, Channel New, Scale **2**, Offset **0**	Adds contents of Channel 4 to Channel 5, places addition in New Channel 6.
Click on Untitled-1's title bar	Untitled-1 becomes active image.
Choose **S**elect, **L**oad Selection, then choose **E**dit, **C**opy (or press Ctrl+C)	Copies shadow to Clipboard.
Click on GAMES.TIF's title bar window	GAMES.TIF becomes active image.

Choose **E**dit, T**a**ke Snapshot	Saves copy of image, GAMES.TIF, in system RAM.
Choose **S**elect, **L**oad Selection, then choose #6	Loads selection border created with Add command.
Choose **E**dit, Paste **B**ehind	Pastes small shadow on top of GAMES.TIF image but behind selection border of two pawns.
Click and drag the floating shadow selection so that its base is hidden behind the second pawn's base	Positions second pawn's shadow.
On the Brushes palette, set the mode to Multiply, set Opacity: to **84**%	Reduces opacity of floating shadow selection (see fig. 14.20).
Choose **S**elect, **D**efringe, choose **W**idth **1** pixel, then click on OK	Trims Anti-Aliasing edge pixels from shadow selection.
Choose **S**elect, **N**one (or press Ctrl+D)	Deselects floating shadow selection and makes it part of GAMES.TIF image.
Choose **F**ile, **S**ave	Saves image.

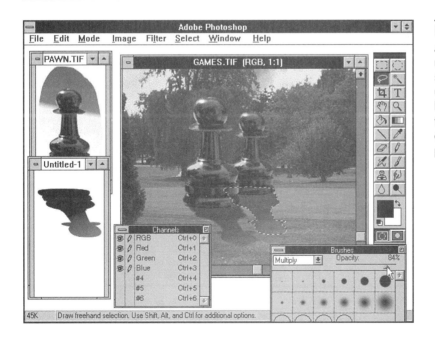

Figure 14.20
After loading the new, Added selection border, use the Paste Behind command to put the pasted area behind both pawns.

The Calculate, Add command does not operate properly when Alpha channels contain "inverted" information. If you have Color Indicates Selected Areas checked in either the Channel Options or Quick Mask **O**ptions dialog box, a selection area's color will be black and the masked, unselected areas will be white in the Alpha channels. If the Add command is not working as it should, click on the Channel's title bar in the Channels palette and look at the Channel's contents. Are both selection areas the same shade? If not, press Ctrl+I to invert the channel you are viewing.

Never choose `Selection` for the destination of your addition work. Choose an existing channel or a new one. The Photoshop Add command cannot calculate the average of two channels' contents as a selection. Channel+channel = channel. Otherwise, you are asking for apples plus apples and telling Photoshop to give you the answer in oranges.

Making the Second Shadow More Convincing

To make the second shadow more realistic, you go through the same routine you used for the first one. Use the Blur tool in a Lighten mode on the Brushes palette to blend the edge of the grass into the shadow area. Then use the Rubber Stamp tool, still in the From Snapshot Op**t**ion, to wash over the shadow area, revealing some of GAMES.TIF's grass (see fig. 14.21).

Figure 14.21
The Rubber Stamp tool can work from a Snapshot, but you have to remember to take a snapshot before you make changes in the image.

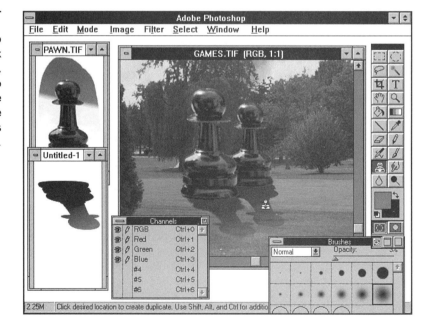

Don't forget to reset the Rubber Stamp tool to its default of Cloning (Aligned) before you go on to the next chapter! In this chapter, you used a special-purpose setting for the Rubber Stamp. Unless you restore its default setting, you might start messing up your work the next time you use it!

Photo-Reality-Check Time

You have been building the composition in this chapter to the grand finalé—adding the QUEEN.TIF image from the companion CD as the crowning glory, to the far right of the GAMES.TIF image. The visual focus of the completed image is the collection of gigantic chess pieces marching across the fairway. If they are skillfully integrated into the image, folks will probably never notice the fractal sky in the background!

When you reach the phase of your career at which you can control what the viewer sees in a piece without you even having to be present, you have accomplished a great deal. You have art that speaks for you and for itself. You have mastered retouching as well as image composition. And by taking charge of an application's features, you have discovered a wealth of dynamic self-expression.

The Arrival of the Queen

You have done a lot in this chapter, learning by *doing* it. The QUEEN.TIF image in the next exercise already has a selection path created and stored in a channel. The selection was created by using the same Pen Paths technique used with the pawn. In the next exercise, you get to skip the selection-building step so that you can focus on building and refining the selection and shadow. Shadows play a key role in your retouching work. They spell the difference between a pasted image selection that *belongs* in a background image and one that hovers about a scene in an obvious retouch.

Enter the Queen

Double-click on the GAMES.TIF image	Zooms view of image out to full-frame view.
Click on the Channel #6 title in the Channels palette	Switches to view of #6 selection channel.
Press the command button, and then choose Delete Channel	Removes channel and redisplays view of GAMES.TIF's RGB channel.

continues

III

Gourmet Assignments

continued

Repeat the last two steps with Channels #5 and #4 in the GAMES.TIF image	Deletes unnecessary channels and reduces GAMES.TIF's file size, as you can see on Photoshop's status bar.
Open the QUEEN.TIF image from the companion CD	Final image you work with in this chapter.
Choose **S**elect, **L**oad Selection	Selection marquee appears around queen. (Border was created by using Paths Pen technique described in an earlier exercise, as shown in figure 14.22.)
Choose **E**dit, **C**opy (or press Ctrl+C), then press Ctrl+Tab	Copies selection in QUEEN.TIF's RGB channel to Clipboard. Ctrl+Tab toggles active image window to GAMES.TIF.
Choose **E**dit, **P**aste (or press Ctrl+V)	Pastes queen selection area into GAMES.TIF image.
Select the Lasso tool from the toolbox, then click and drag the queen selection to the lower right of the GAMES.TIF image	Positions queen in background image (see fig. 14.23).
Choose **I**mage, **A**djust, then choose Hue/Saturation (or press Ctrl+U)	Displays Hue/Saturation dialog box.
Check Colorize, set Hue to **40**, and then click on OK	Colorizes queen to resemble bronze pawns.
Choose **S**elect, **D**efringe, choose **W**idth **1** pixel, then click on OK	Removes any Anti-Aliasing around queen's border.
Choose **S**elect, **S**ave Selection	Creates Channel 4 in GAMES.TIF; contains queen's outline.

You're in the home stretch—it's time to kick into high gear and polish off this chess piece with the realistic shadow techniques. The gradient fill is unnecessary this time, because the top of the queen's shadow will run out of the image frame. Also, you can skew and scale the queen's shadow without creating a new, larger image window. Because the queen's shape is narrow and tall, you can simply copy the entire selection channel without changing Photoshop's defaults for a New File.

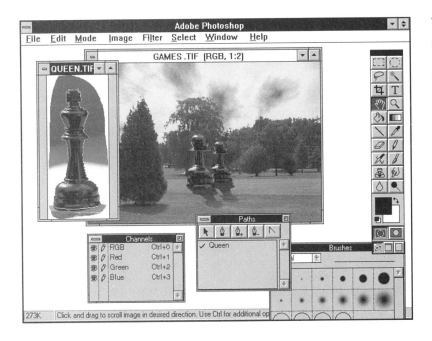

Figure 14.22
QUEEN.TIF's selection border was created from a Path.

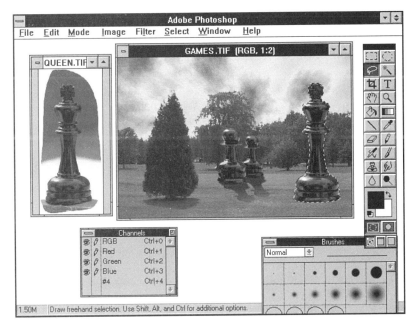

Figure 14.23
Place the queen selection area so that it creates an asymmetrical image composition.

III

Gourmet Assignments

Subjects and Shadows Follow the Queen

Click on QUEEN.TIF's title bar to make it active, then click on the Channel #4 title in the Channels palette	Displays Alpha Channel authors created in active image window, QUEEN.TIF.
Choose **S**elect, **A**ll (or press Ctrl+A)	Selects entire Channel 4.
Choose **E**dit, **C**opy (or press Ctrl+C), choose **F**ile, **N**ew (or press Ctrl+N), then click on OK	Copies entire Channel to Clipboard and creates new file based on selection's dimensions.
Choose **E**dit, **P**aste (or press Ctrl+V)	Pastes selection into Untitled-2's image window.
Choose **S**elect, **S**ave Selection	Saves silhouette part of entire image window as selection border (border is based on brightness in entire image).
Choose **S**elect, **L**oad Selection	Activates selection border around silhouette part of Untitled-2 image.
Choose **I**mage, **F**lip, then choose Vertical	Turns queen's silhouette upside-down.
Click and drag the silhouette to the far left of Untitled-2's image window	Positions silhouette.
Choose **I**mage, **E**ffects, and then choose Skew	Displays Skew boundary box around selection.
Click and drag the bottom right corner of the boundary box to the right	Skews selection to approximate shadows cast in GAMES.TIF image.
Click inside the boundary box	Locks image into desired degree of skew.
Choose **I**mage, **E**ffects, and then choose Scale	Displays Scale boundary box around selection.
Click and drag the bottom corner of the Scale boundary box straight up	Stop when image resembles figure 14.24.
Click inside the Scale boundary box	Fixes selection to desired degree of scaling.

Think of *channels* as views of an image that Photoshop uses to make intelligent decisions about selections. What you see and what Photoshop sees is different. When you look at an Alpha channel you see a black silhouette or a grayscale photographic image. Photoshop sees *information sources* on which to base the creation of selection areas and masked areas. The darker the color, the higher the degree of opacity assigned to the selection. Photoshop creates the marquee selection by encompassing the highly opaque pixels. In this case—a solid black queen—you were able to select just the queen's silhouette, even though you pasted the entire selection channel into a new document's Alpha channel. Photoshop looked at the colored areas in this information channel and created the selection marquee based on the colored areas only, not on the entire paste.

Now you can finish the image.

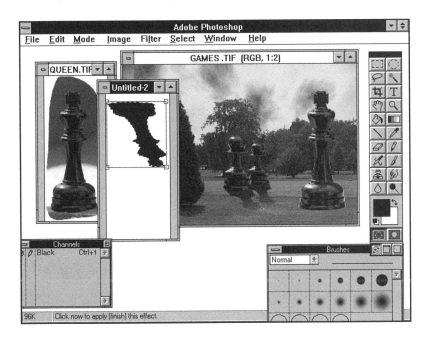

Figure 14.24
Even unsaved new files can have Alpha channels.

III
Gourmet Assignments

Pulling the (Chess) Pieces Together

Choose **E**dit, **C**opy (or press Ctrl+C), then press Ctrl+Tab	Copies selection to clipboard and toggles display to active view of GAMES.TIF.
Choose **S**elect, **L**oad Selection	Activates the selection border you saved earlier around the queen's figure.
Choose **E**dit, Paste **B**ehind	Pastes queen's shadow behind active selection border but on top of GAMES.TIF image.
Click and drag the shadow so that its base fits under the queen's base	Positions shadow (part of it is supposed to go outside image border).

continues

continued

From the Brushes palette, set the
mode to Multiply, click and drag the
Opacity: slider to about **80**%

Creates semi-transparent shadow
beneath queen.

Choose **S**elect, **D**efringe, select
Width 1 pixel, then click on OK

Removes Anti-Aliasing from selection.

Choose **S**elect, **N**one (or press Ctrl+D)

Composites floating shadow selection into
GAMES.TIF background image.

Select the Blur tool from the toolbox,
then (on the Brushes palette) select
Darken mode and set Pressure **71**%

Sets characteristics of Blur tool.

Click and drag, starting inside the
shadow's edge and moving outside it

Blurs edge of composited shadow
selection, decreasing contrast between
edge pixels by moving them to darker
shade (see fig. 14.25).

Continue to click and drag until the
edge has been completely covered

Completes cosmetic blend of shadow
into GAMES.TIF image.

Choose **F**ile, **S**ave (or press Ctrl+S)

Saves your work for good!

Figure 14.25
Use the Blur tool
last, to blend the
edges of the
pasted selection
into the
background
image.

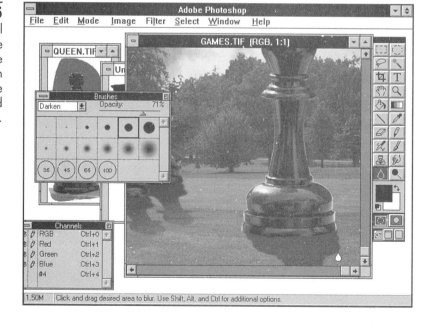

The amazon chess pieces are pasted in, the highlights are in corresponding places to original areas in the background, and all the shadows, natural and synthetic, look the same. Figure 14.26 shows the image after we clicked on the middle View mode button in the toolbox to banish the scroll bars, and pressed the Tab key to toggle off all the palettes and the toolbox. Why don't you do the same now, to fully appreciate your photo-realistic illustration?

Figure 14.26
A very different definition of "miniature golf"!

Can you use the techniques in this chapter with other images? Absolutely. Hopefully, you have developed a speedy way to create realistic shadows from selections, as well as an artist's eye that can scout a background image first to see the intensity and angles of natural shadows on which to base your own creations.

You can use these techniques also to create the opposite artistic effect. If you want a tiny person standing on someone else's palm, set up your lighting and angles to match before you photograph. Then define the selection borders carefully and create the shadows by using a flipped, skewed, scaled silhouette of the original selection area.

Summary

You have half the problem licked in your conventional Photoshop assignments if you understand what channels do by the time you finish this book. Masks and their inverse (selections) may seem to be based on the simple geometry of a selection border. But as you see time and again in *Inside Adobe Photoshop for Windows* exercises, a selection is defined by *tonal* variations, like those found in a grayscale photographic image. And the amount of grayscale density (percentages of black) in a channel determines how completely a selection marquee envelops an area in the RGB channel.

We'll be playing more with creating shadows, surrealistic effects, and the wonder of Channels in our next chapter, but to less fanciful ends. Can you image a group of individuals at work that all look identical? Is it photo-fakery? Is this a supermarket magazine headline? Do they all get equal health benefits?

People will stop and stare at your design skills, as you stretch your imagination and photographic believability a little in our next adventure with Photoshop!

Chapter Snapshot

In this chapter, you learn how to:

CHAPTER

The Photo Collage

As you've seen in other chapters, it's remarkably easy to copy and paste your way to stunning collages, Photoshop-style. *Collage*, loosely translated from the French, means "pasting stuff from different media onto a page." The photo collage, as redefined by Photoshop's remarkable features, can be used to create powerful, eye-catching artwork, from a combination of digital images, synthetic software-based designs, and a Photoshop brush stroke or two. Collage is an art form that lends itself equally well to both the fine and commercial arts. And Photoshop's capability to bring together diverse materials and seamlessly integrate them makes Photoshop the software tool of choice for doing great collage work.

The corporate motivation poster is a good example of how collage artwork can be used in business. Those dramatic, impactful, color signs of the times can be seen in every worker's cubicle at firms both large and small. They usually feature an awe-inspiring image accompanied by a sage slogan about Success or Ambition. Following this line of thought, this chapter's goal is to create an original corporate motivation poster. The topic of Teamwork is the idea for the poster's catchy slogan, and to illustrate it, you'll work with a number of images found on the companion CD to create the collage.

The images used in this assignment are of the same person photographed in several different poses. Skillfully combining pictures of the same person in one poster creates an unusual, powerful effect. You may have seen ads that attempt to use multiple images to convey a single person, but they usually leave telltale edges or other signs that the image has been tricked up. With Photoshop's tools, you can hide your "fingerprints" and handle this effect with style and professionalism.

Masking Your Intentions

You explored the virtues of the Photoshop Quick Mask feature in Chapter 5. In that chapter, you took a simple fake lemon and colored it fake lime. You will be using Photoshop's Quick Mask feature extensively in this chapter, along with masks you'll create in Alpha channels. You'll discover that after a mask has been made, it can be reused, and then deleted when you're through using it. You'll also be working with image areas that block *other* image areas. The big boys in Hollywood sometimes call this type of mask a *matte*. A matte can be applied to a series of 70mm images, to hide the wires of a flying superhero or place a computer-generated dinosaur on a hillside among human actors. But before you can actually use a mask or a matte, you first must have a *background* to mask *against*.

You begin the following exercise by opening TILEBACK.TIF from the companion CD. The background was created after the model had been photographed. The photos were scanned into Photoshop, where the model's image height and the width were measured. These measurements were used to determine how large the background, TILEBACK.TIF, needed to be. TILEBACK.TIF was created inside the computer using the PIXAR *One-Twenty-Eight* collection, a Photoshop third-party plug-in filter capable of producing seamless, tiled patterns in an active image window, to any dimension or resolution.

Creating a Neon Graph

Companies love graphs and charts, especially when the figures are on the rise. In the next exercise, you'll take this plain tile pattern and turn it into a graph. With Photoshop, you never have to settle for boring—an impressionistic, dimensional neon line is just the sizzle this background needs. Let's begin by creating the path that the synthetic neon should follow in the TILEBACK image. For the creation of the path, you'll need the tools found on the Paths palette.

Creating a Path for Neon

With TILEBACK.TIF open in the Photoshop workspace:

Click the default colors icon on the toolbox	Sets up a black foreground and a white background.
Choose **W**indow, Show P**a**th (or press F9)	Opens the Paths palette.

Click the center Window mode button on the last row of the toolbox	Removes the scroll bars from the image display.
Choose the Pen tool from the Paths pallette	Creates paths and subpaths.
On the extreme left edge of TILEBACK.TIF, move two tiles down from the top and click on the left edge of the tile	Serves as the starting point for the path. Be sure to click anchor points only within a three-tile range at the top of the background; you need room at the bottom of the background for your subject.
Click to the right of the first path anchor point about two tiles up	Creates a second anchor point, with a path segment in between.
Continue clicking to the right, alternately up and down	Creates a graph effect against the tile (see fig. 15.1).
Click a final point on the extreme right edge of the background	End of the path's segments needed to create the neon design you'll create.
Press Ctrl, then click on the Paths pallette's pointer tool	Frees you from creating additional anchor points on TILEBACK.TIF.
Click on the command button on the Paths palette, then choose Save Path	Calls up the Paths dialog box to the workspace.
Click on OK	Accepts the default name for the saved path, and you are returned to the workspace.
Choose File, Save As TILEBACK.TIF to a directory on your hard drive	Saves changed image to your hard drive.

Now that you have the connected path segments drawn and saved as Path 1, it's time to apply color to the path to create the neon graph effect. You'll be using a special Brushes mode, Screen, normally used as a painting and compositing mode, to create this effect. Screen is used as the mode and is set on the Brushes palette even though you won't be using a paint-application tool in the process.

Subpaths (connected path segments are considered to be "open" in that they don't end where they begin and form an enclosed area) and Paths (segments that form an enclosed area) can be "stroked" in Photoshop. Choosing the Stroke command from the Paths palette command button drop-down list automatically applies color on top of the path. Since paths are like EPS files, and contain vector information but no bit-map qualities, the Stroke Path (or Subpath) command needs information about what tool you'd like it to access to perform the operation. This means that if you don't have a tool currently selected, a Stroke Path dialog box will pop up asking you for more information. The settings on the Brushes Palette and the color tool that is selected from the toolbox determine how the paint is applied along the path segments.

Figure 15.1
Use the Pen tool on the Paths palette to create connected path segments.

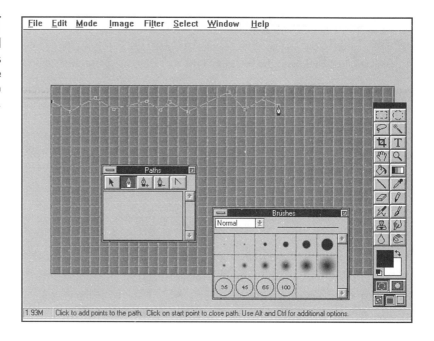

Stick with the Paintbrush tool most of the time for your stroking paths adventures. The Stroke Path command allows you to use several other editing and selection tools, like the Smudge tool, to perform the path stroking, but the results typically range from childish to hideous.

Applying Color across a Path Segment

Choose the Show **B**rushes option from the **W**indow menu, or press F5, if the Brushes palette is not visible at the moment	Brings the Brushes palette to Photoshop's workspace.
Click the Paintbrush tool	Activates the Brushes palette and chooses the Paintbrush as the tool that the Stroke command will emulate.
Click on the 65-pixel-diameter brush tip on the Brushes palette	Sets the width of the tip used for paint application in Photoshop.
Choose Screen from the Brushes palette mode drop-down list	Bleaches present color areas, tinting them toward the foreground color.
Move the Opacity slider to **45%** on the Brushes palette	Creates a mild bleaching effect by using a faint stroke to draw the path.

Click on the foreground color selection box on the toolbox	Accesses the Color Picker.
Enter H:**10**, S:**82**, B:**73** in the numerical entry fields, then click on OK	Specifies a reddish-orange color for the neon foreground. Feel free to select a different hue, but make sure the color is a pastel rather than a deep shade.
Click on the command button on the Paths palette	Reveals a drop-down list of Paths options.
Choose Stroke Subpath	Applies a 45% opaque; reddish-orange bleach (Screen); with a 65-pixel-diameter along the path. No physical painting is required.
Click on a 17-pixel-diameter soft brush (shown in fig. 15.2) from the Brushes palette	Chooses a smaller, soft-tip brush tip.
Set the opacity to 70% by moving the slider on the Brushes palette	Specifies a more intense shade for the second stroke.
Click Stroke Subpath again from the command button drop-down list on the Paths palette	The path is stroked again and the neon effect is enhanced.
Click on the inverse colors icon (the upper right of the foreground/background color selection boxes) on the toolbox	Makes the foreground color white.
Increase the Brushes Opacity to 100% using the slider	Sets color to be applied with total opacity.
Choose a new tip, from the top row, second tip from the left, on the Brushes palette	This small, hard-edge tip will create an intense, white core for the neon when used with the Stroke Subpath command.
Click on Stroke Subpath from the control button drop-down list on the Paths palette	The white core that finishes the neon effect is applied.
Double-click on the command button on the Paths palette	Closes the Paths palette and removes the path.

You have now completed the first phase in creating your corporate motivation poster. This neon effect also can be used to highlight photos of UFOs, simulate lightning in a picture, and generally dress up a boring picture in a surrealistic way. Tuck this secret away for now, because it's time to move on to phase two.

III

Gourmet Assignments

Figure 15.2
Using the screen
mode to Stroke a
path bleaches the
area under the
path to the
foreground color.

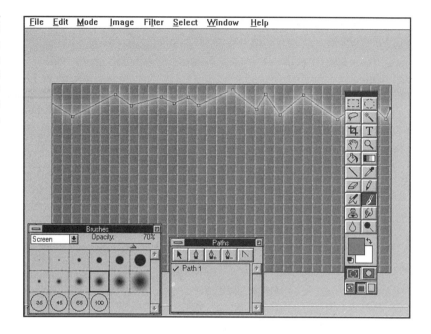

Many Images, One-Color Correction Setting

Next, you'll pay a call to the "bottomless" companion disk for CRAN2.TIF, the first of seven images of the actor that you'll mask and place in the background image to create the poster. The actor was photographed against a blank backdrop. He wore different clothes and assumed different poses for each picture taken. Part of the secret of creating a whole "scene" using only one actor, is to get him to pretend that he's interacting with "other" actors while you photograph him. The first image, CRAN2.TIF, shows a guy with his arm around empty space. Don't worry; it won't be empty when you finish creating the poster.

The following exercise addresses one of the photographic problems you may run into even before you use Photoshop. I took 36 photos to come up with the seven best ones to use in this assignment—and wouldn't you know that each one had a slight, hazy, bluish tint to it! Do you need to fine-tune each picture individually? No, the culprit producing the same blue haze in all these pictures is actually a high midtone value, which is common in many images that are digitized to a Kodak PhotoCD.

If you take a look at Chapter 3, you'll see that the Levels command can restore tonal balance to an image by redefining the image's black-and-white points. You can *automate* tonal corrections for similar images that share a common tonal imbalance by correcting the Levels for one

image and then saving those settings. Whenever you open another, similar image that needs the same kind of Levels correction, you can reload the settings you saved and apply them to that image. This way you can quickly and efficiently correct the Levels in a whole batch of images. "Batch" color correcting images is as easy as using a word processing macro you've written! Here's how you do it.

Making and Saving Color Corrections

Open CRAN2.TIF from the companion CD

Choose **I**mage, **A**djust, then choose Levels (or press Ctrl+L)	Displays the Levels dialog box.
Shift the left Input Levels slider so that it reads 50 on top	Brings the black point in the photo to a level at which more *actual* blacks are in the photo, as in figure 15.3.
Click on the **S**ave button	Opens the Save As dialog box.
Use the Dri**v**es and **D**irectories fields to locate your PHOTOSHOP directory and double-click on Photoshop's CALIBRAT subdirectory to go to it	Of Photoshop's many subdirectories, CALIBRAT is ideal for storing Levels settings, calibrations, monitor gammas and the like.
In the File **N**ame text box, type in the file name CORPMOV.ALV	
Click on OK in the Save **A**s dialog box, then click on OK in the Levels dialog box	Returns you to Photoshop's workspace with the image corrections made and the settings saved to the CORPMOV.ALV file.

That was pretty simple, wasn't it? Actually, not much was wrong with the image to begin with. Most new users are eager to "overtweak" an image with various filters and the like. That's why this book discusses Photoshop features one at a time. The image did need some Levels-tuning, but that wasn't the entire reason you went through the last exercise.

The Levels setting you saved can now be used with every other picture of the actor that you open from the CD. You won't have to hand tweak or remember settings to correct these images. Tonally balancing these images is as easy as opening the image file, pressing Ctrl+L to display the Levels dialog box, and choosing **L**oad. Then choose the CORPMOV.ALV file and click OK and Photoshop does the work for you. Using the saved setting speeds up your work and ensures a consistency amongst the similar images.

You'll find this feature very useful when you get a CD or roll of film back, and there's the same lighting flaw in each image. Let Photoshop do the correcting, precisely and perfectly, from your original instructions.

Figure 15.3
You can save
Levels settings and
apply them to
other images.

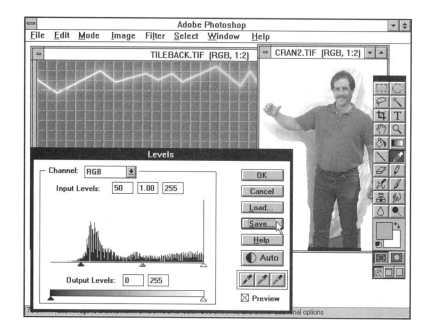

Levels, Curves, Hue/Saturation, and Variations all have Save options. If you do a lot of image editing, you may want to save these custom settings and then reuse them with similar images. They help you produce precise, consistent work.

Working with Channels

Now that the TILEBACK.TIF background image is completed and one of the images of the actor has been color-corrected, it's time to start adding the many images of the actor to TILEBACK.TIF. And this means using Photoshop's Channels to their fullest. All the actor images files were scanned and saved in RGB Color mode. The RGB Color mode organizes the information that comprises the image into three discrete color channels—the Red channel, Green channel, and Blue channel. Together these channels produce the RGB channel view that is the normal, full-color editing view of the image you see on your screen.

As you've seen in other chapters, the Photoshop user can also assign up to 16 extra-user definable channels to an image. These are called Alpha channels, and like each individual color channel in an RGB image, Alpha channels can hold up to 8-bits of grayscale information. It's important that you understand the inter-relationship between selections, masks, and channels at this point in the exercise. Much of Photoshop's power as an image editing program is directly related to the ability to create, work in, and save Alpha channels. In this

next exercise, you'll be doing some sophisticated manipulation of information contained in Alpha channels.

Creating Masks

Masks and selection areas are created the same way in Photoshop, but they serve different functions. Every time you create a selection border around an area using a selection tool (like the Lasso tool), and then use the Select, Save Selection command, you are saving the geometry of the border as a solid shape area to an Alpha channel. This area can be recalled (Select, Load Selection) at anytime. When it is recalled, the area within the border becomes the active area in the image window—everything outside that border is masked from any effects, paint, or other editing you perform.

Because saved selections are stored in Alpha channels as grayscale information, you can view and edit the selections without affecting any other channel or the image as a whole. You edit these selections by clicking on the appropriate channel title on the Channels palette. The *density of grayscale information* in an Alpha channel determines how completely a selection area is defined.

As you saw in Chapter 13, when you define an area with a selection tool *and* the Channel Options are set to Color Indicates $\underline{S}$elected Areas, the pixels within the selection border are stored and displayed in the Alpha channel as being 100% opaque (black) density value. When you are in the Alpha channel view for that selection, you can instantly turn the selection area into a mask (something that protects an image area from editing changes) by pressing Ctrl+I ($\underline{I}$mage, $\underline{M}$ap, Invert). The Invert command reverses the grayscale scheme and produces a negative of the selection area. In this case, the black areas turn white, and the area you originally defined with a selection tool is a full, 100% opaque mask that can be used from the RGB composite view of an image. A mask can be modified, by adding or subtracting areas using painting tools or editing tools like the Eraser tool. You can lighten the density of the selection area using painting tools and $\underline{I}$mage command controls. Altering the density (changing opaque and transparent pixels to semi-transparent ones) creates a Partial Mask. Pixels that are partially masked are only partly affected by changes you apply with filters, effects, editing, and paint tools when you use the $\underline{L}$oad Selection command from Photoshop's $\underline{S}$elect menu.

Modifying the Grayscale Information in a Channel

A selection area, or a mask, can be modified with selection tools or painting tools, from the Alpha channel's editing view. But defining a selection border while in the composite, or any other color channel view, isn't the only way to create masks and selections. You can create a new Channel by clicking on the Channels palette command button, and either paint in the new channel, or copy grayscale information into the channel. In the next exercise, you'll create a selection area around the actor in CRAN2.TIF that will be used to separate the actor's image from the background in the image. This selection border will also be used to create a realistic shadow to go behind the actor when he is placed on the TILEBACK image.

To create an accurate selection border as intricate as the outline of the actor would take time, and would be tedious work if done with the Lasso tool. The work wouldn't go much quicker using the Quick Mask mode because you'd still need to "paint" a complete outline and fill in the mask on top of the actor's image area. Instead, let's start with a copy of the CRAN2.TIF image placed in an Alpha channel.

It's much easier to use a combination of Photoshop tools to darken and define the actor's image area when you work in a channel. When a copy of an image is pasted into an Alpha channel, it immediately becomes information that Photoshop can use to create a selection (*or* masked) area. Refining the actor's image area by adding contrast, removing areas, and adding color will result in an image area that basically becomes a shadow of the actor. Photoshop can use this contrasting shadow of the actor in this channel to accurately determine the actor's outline and create a selection border that you can use in the composite view, the RGB channel of the image file.

If you currently have the Color Channels in the Color check box marked in Preferences, General (press Ctrl+K to get there), now's a good time to uncheck this option before beginning the next exercise. This is because you need to know which one of the Red, Green, or Blue channels—when viewed as a grayscale image—shows the clearest contrast between the CRAN2.TIF actor and his background. You'll copy the color channel that has the best contrast to an Alpha channel (where it becomes a selection area) and with a minimum of work, refine the outline of the border. This refined border will serve as an accurate mask for the actor.

Creating an Alpha Channel from a Color Channel

Choose Show Channels from the **W**indow menu, (or press F6)	Displays the Channels palette.
Click on Blue (or press Ctrl+3)	Displays a view of the Blue channel (as seen in fig. 15.4), which shows more contrast between actor and background than the RGB composite channel, or the Red or Green channels. Try clicking on the other channel titles to see for yourself.
Click on the Lasso tool on the toolbox	Tool used to create a freehand selection within an image.
Trace a rough outline around the actor in the Blue channel	Creates a selection marquee that specifies the area inside the border as active and the outside area as masked.
Choose the **C**opy option from the **E**dit menu (or press Ctrl+C)	Copies only the selected area of the image.

Caution: Do not deselect the area by clicking outside the selection area.

Click the command button on the Channels palette, and then select New Channel	Calls up Channel Options box to the screen.
Leave Channel #4 as the default Name for the channel, choose Color Indicates: Selected Areas, then click on the Color: swatch	You are setting the characteristics for how the new channel displays Quick Mask color, and calling the Color Picker to set a Quick Mask color.
Enter **282** for H, **95** for S, and **84** for B, then click on OK	You've selected a color that Photoshop displays over selected image areas while in Quick Mask mode. The color contrasts with the image so you can see the mask better.
Click on OK in the Channel Options box	Confirms your selections and returns you to Photoshop's workspace.
Choose **E**dit, **P**aste (or Ctrl+V)	Places a copy of the selection in the same *relative* position as it had in the Blue channel (see fig. 15.5).

Now you can click outside the border. This deselects the copy, making it a permanent part of the Alpha channel #4's background, and the basis of the selection area you'll refine in future steps.

III

Gourmet Assignments

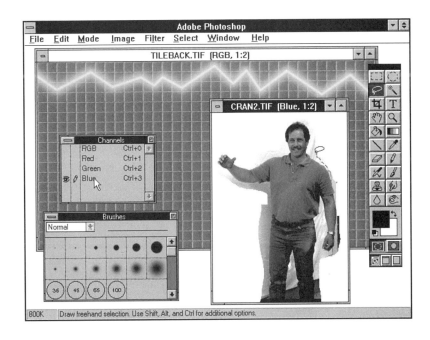

Figure 15.4
A view of the Blue channel in CRAN2.TIF.

Figure 15.5

The grayscale image placed in the Alpha channel is evaluated by Photoshop as a basis for a selection area.

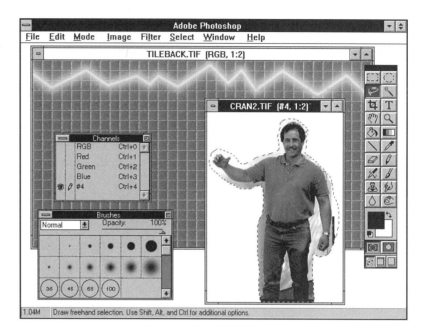

In the last exercise, you created a channel in CRAN2.TIF that clearly shows the outline of the subject. By clicking the name of any channel in the palette, you can view and edit that channel. If you clicked on the individual color channels of CRAN2.TIF before the last exercise, you saw that, for this particular image, the Blue channel shows the most outline detail of the actor, more than even the RGB composite channel does. This enhanced detail is the reason that we copied the image from the Blue channel.

Before you modify this grayscale (partial mask) image area in the #4 channel, there's something you need to bear in mind. In order to completely select the actor from the background area, there must be a clear definition between the colored (selected) areas, and the noncolored (masked) areas. For this reason, it's usuallly easiest to work on both areas, lightening a little here and darkening a little there, until Photoshop can clearly distinguish between the two areas when it creates a marquee selection border from the brightness information present in the Alpha channel. This will be your approach as you refine the selection created by copying a grayscale version of the actor image to this channel.

Selection Refinement

Part of the magic of channels is that they're all different, and yet they're spatially identical views of one image. When you copy a selection to a new channel, and you *don't* deselect the image before you use the Paste command, the copied image falls in exactly the same position as it had in the channel you copied it from. Selection borders also appear with the same x and y coordinates from channel to channel, regardless of what channel view you're in when you Load or create a selection border.

The task at hand is to remove the extraneous background areas around the actor in Channel #4, and at the same time darken the grayscale area inside the actor's figure, so you can use this channel information to create an accurate selection border and shadow for the actor. As you do this, you must choose your tools, filters, and methods carefully so that you don't create any telltale hard edges.

Contrast and the Lasso Tool

Different areas of the grayscale image in Channel #4 require different techniques to silhouette the actor from the background. The area you'll work on first in the next exercise is the actor's head and shoulders. Understand that this grayscale image of the actor in Channel #4 isn't going to look very aesthetic as you work on it, but that's not the intent.

By increasing the contrast and brightness in an area selected with the Lasso tool, you will push the grayscale densities in the actor's face toward black to make it a selection area. At the same time, the brightness/contrast controls will force the areas of light-gray background to white.

The object is to accentuate contrast in the channel in selected areas to separate the actor from the background. You'll soon see that this technique cannot be used on the entire grayscale selection because some of the background areas are too dark and match the actor's jeans too closely. So we'll use a different technique there when we've worked our way to that area. First, let's concentrate on the actor's head area.

Using Contrast To Separate Image Areas

Pick the Lasso tool, then click and drag an area around the actor's head down to his collar-line; be sure to include original image background areas

You are selecting this area of the grayscale information to be separated by adding contrast to it.

Choose Image, Adjust, Brightness/Contrast from the menu (or press Ctrl+B)

This Brightness/Contrast dialog box appears on your screen.

continues

continued

Click and drag the Brightness slider to **+28**, click and drag the Contrast slider to **+31**, then click on OK	Forces light grayscale areas in the background area to turn to white, and the already dark areas in the actor's face to turn black (see fig. 15.6).
Click OK, then press Ctrl+D	You confirm the Brightness changes you've made, return to the Photoshop workspace, and deselect the marquee border.
Use the scroll bars or Hand tool to scroll left in the image window	Reveals the actor's right arm and shoulder, the next selection area that needs refining.
Click and drag the Lasso tool around the shoulder area; inlcude the original background area	Selects the area to be worked on next.
Choose Image, Adjust, Brightness/Contrast (or press Ctrl+B)	Calls up the Brightness/Contrast dialog box again.
Click and drag the Brightness slider to a **+29** value, and the Contrast slider to a **+37** value, then click OK	Increases the contrast in the selection area to hclp scparate the actor's outline from the background (see fig. 15.7).
Choose File, Save As, type **CRAN2.TIF** as the image file name on your hard drive, and then click on OK	Saves your work to a directory on your hard drive.

Using Quick Mask Mode To Edit a Selection Area

As you continue down the actor's figure in the Alpha Channel #4, it will no longer be practical to use the Contrast/Brightness command to separate actor from background. Because the Alpha channel that the grayscale image information is in can hold only 256 shades (densities) of gray, some of the background shadows share a similar density as the actor's arms and shirt. But Photoshop's resources include different tools and views that can be used for this part of the selection refining.

A Quick Mask is a temporary application of a visible "film" over an image area that, although you can't edit the underlying image while in this mode, you can use both editing *and* painting tools to reshape the masked area.

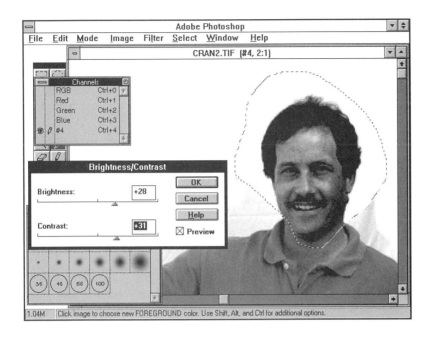

Figure 15.6
Applying Contrast to a selected area forces the lighter shades to white, and the darker ones to black.

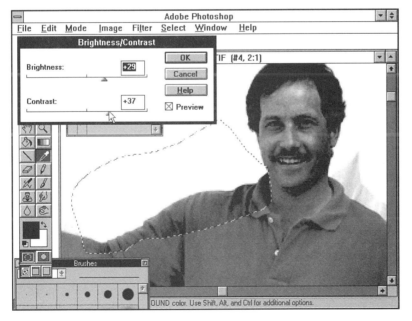

Figure 15.7
Different selection areas require different Brightness/Contrast adjustments to separate the actor from the background.

III

Gourmet Assignments

Photoshop's capability of displaying different channel views of the same image areas means that you can switch channels while editing. You'll use this display feature to create a selection area while in Quick Mask mode in the composite view of CRAN2.TIF, where it's easier to see the border of the actor's shirt and arm. But you'll then switch to Alpha channel #4 before changing from Quick Mask to Standard mode. Because you need to edit the grayscale information to create the selection border around the actor, and not around the composite, RGB image itself, you'll need to do some last-minute channel switching.

Quick Mask-ing a Selection Area

Click on the RGB title on the Channels palette	Switches your view to a color composite of the CRAN2.TIF image.
Pick the Zoom tool, and click once over the actor's right, outstretched arm area	Zooms you to a 4:1 viewing resolution of the area you'll be working on.
Click on the Quick Mask mode button on the bottom right of the toolbox	Masked image areas will now remain the same, while any application of foreground mask color will turn an area light purple, which represents a selected area.
Click on the Paintbrush tool on the toolbox	This is the tool for applying foreground color in this exercise.
Choose the second tip from the left, on the top row of the Brushes palette	This is a good size tip for doing initial, precise masking work.
Click and drag the Paintbrush tool on the outside edge of the actor's right arm	You are applying mask color, which means this area will be included in the selected area when you switch to standard viewing mode.

Caution: Don't paint on any area of the actor's arm!

Complete applying mask to the outside edge of the arm, then select a tip from the second row, second from the right on the Brushes palette	Selects a good size tip to cover other areas of the image now that a precise border has been created.
Click and drag the Paintbrush tool across any original background image areas you see (see fig. 15.8)	You will add these areas to the selection area when you return to standard mode.
If you accidentally wander into the actor's arm area with the Paintbrush, click on the inverse colors icon on the toolbox, and stroke over the area where you went into the arm	Reverses the foreground color to white, which allows the Paintbrush to remove Quick Mask color from areas.
When the area is covered, and the actor's arm border is precisely defined, click on the Standard mode button (left, bottom toolbox button next to the Quick Mask button)	Returns you to an editing mode for the image, with a marquee selection running around the area you Quick Masked.

Click on the Channel #4 title on the Channels palette (or press Ctrl+4)	Shows you an editable view of the channel's grayscale information.
Click on the default colors icon on the toolbox	Restores the foreground color to black, the background to white.
Press the Delete key	Removes the selection area, and replaces it with white background information, as seen in figure 15.9.

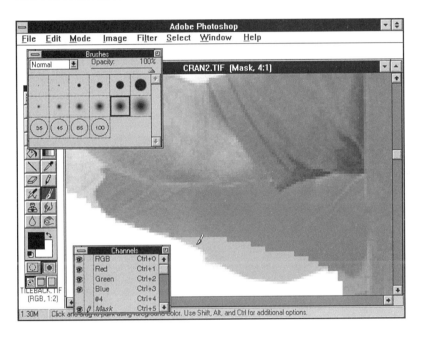

Figure 15.8
Use different Brushes palette tips to apply foreground color in Quick Mask mode to select an area.

Tip

You'll soon be using the little icons of eyes and pencils on the Channels palette to select how your view of the CRAN2.TIF image displays on Photoshop's workspace. Up until now, you've been asked to click on the name, or Channel title, when switching between channel views. This action has made each channel you view both visible and editable. But there will be times you will want a view in one channel, but be able to edit a *different* channel at the same time.

This is what the little eye and pencil icons are for on list of channels at the far left of the Channels palette. A pencil icon next to the channel name means that you can edit the view of the channel it is next to. An eye means that the channel view is presently visible. By default, you are sent to a visible, editable channel when you create a new one, and when you are in Quick Mask mode.

continues

In the next exercise, the Mask title is italicized in the channels title list. Photoshop italicizes the title because Quick Mask mode isn't permanent and because it really isn't a discrete image information channel. But as with any other channel listing, when you click on a pencil, you turn off the editability of the channel, and when you click on the eye icon, you lose your view of the channel. Both eye and pencil icons are *toggling functions*—click once in their space to turn them on, and a second time to turn them off.

Figure 15.9
When a selection area is deleted, it's replaced with background color.

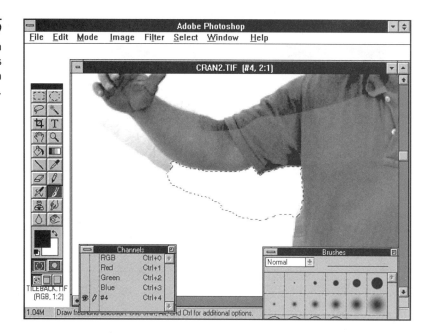

Using the Magic Wand Tool for Selection Refinement

You've used the Brightness/Contrast command and the Quick Mask mode so far to refine the selection edge in the Alpha channel. You can use these two techniques in your own work, and we have two more in store for you. You may have put the Magic Wand tool in the closet for a while, but dust it off for the following short exercise. Notice that there's a uniformly dark background area to the left of the actor's right pants leg that needs to be separated from the actor's outline. And since it is a uniformly colored area, it's a perfect candidate to be selected and deleted using the Magic Wand tool.

When you learn to use a combination of tools and commands to accomplish a single task, the task goes quicker, and your mastery of image editing becomes more of a reality!

Deleting an Area Based on Tonal Value

Double-click on the Zoom tool	Zooms you out to a 1:1 viewing resolution of the CRAN2.TIF image.
Scroll down to the lower torso of the actor	This is the image area.worked on next.
Double-click on the Magic Wand tool	Activates the Magic Wand Options dialog box.
Type **32** in the **T**olerance box, and make sure the **A**nti-Aliased box is checked, then click on OK	You've specified that the Magic Wand tool should select a moderate range of adjacent, similarly colored pixels, and the edge of the selection border should be smooth.
Click on the background area to the left of the actor's pants leg	Selects the background area (see fig. 15.10).
Press the Delete key	Removes the selected area, and replaces it with white background color.
Choose **F**ile, **S**ave (or press Ctrl+S)	Saves your work to hard disk.

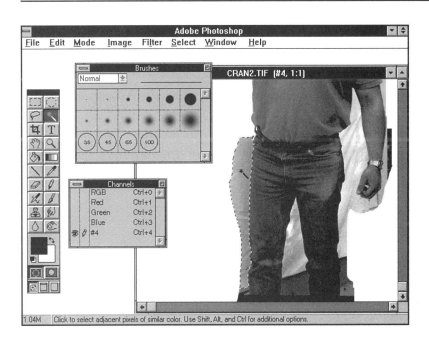

Figure 15.10
The Magic Wand tool can select as wide a range of similarly colored pixels as you specify in its Tolerance setting.

III

Gourmet Assignments

Using the Delete key to remove unwanted selection areas is a very quick way to edit in Photoshop. However, you should also understand the perils that accompany its use. You can wipe out an image area, and be three or four steps along in your work before realizing you've made a mistake. Using keystrokes to edit is quick and easy, whereas more conventional paths to menu commands require some time to think about the action and catch your mistakes.

Choosing **E**dit, C**l**ear from the menu takes more time to accomplish the same result as using the Delete key, and if your personal experience with PC programs has been that haste does make waste, you may want to adopt this slightly longer, yet safer, way to remove image areas in Photoshop.

Using the Magic Wand to select the unwanted background area in the last exercise may not have given perfect results. Cleaning up by deleting surrounding original background areas in the CRAN2.TIF image is necessary so that the ultimate selection border you're creating and refining will precisely match the figure of the actor in the color composite channel. Between exercises, you may want to use the Eraser tool to remove some of the remaining grayscale debris. You can also use the Lasso tool to define and delete an area.

An Undocumented Secret about Mask Colors

Up to now, your experience with Photoshop Quick Masks has been with RGB color composite Channel views. But there's absolutely no reason why you can't put a Quick Mask over *other* color channels, or even a user-defined Alpha channel! And this is what you'll do next to eliminate some complex background areas in the remainder of the #4 Alpha channel.

Channel #4 contains grayscale information that Photoshop bases a selection area on. So when you click on the Quick Mask mode button while in a view of this channel, the actor, who is mostly dark at this point, will turn a fairly solid purple, since the density of grayscale in this channel represents a *selection area*, whereas the white areas represent a mask, an *un*selected area that displays no purple tint.

It's an undocumented secret, though, that you can specify a *different* color to represent *temporary* Quick Mask selection areas. You can do this if you double-click on the Quick Mask mode button and set the Mask Options *before* you begin applying the mask. Even though the grayscale information in Channel #4 represents a selection area in the CRAN2.TIF image when Loaded, the little pencil icon will toggle off next to this channel, and your view is one of the temporary Mask channel (indicated by the italicized title on the Channels palette). With the pencil tool toggled off, no image area, not even the grayscale that defines a selection area in Alpha channel #4, is *editable* while applying or removing Quick Mask from this temporary view.

You will set the Quick Mask's Color Indicates: Selected Area color to a brilliant green in the next exercise, which will sharply contrast with the purple tint the selection area becomes in Channel #4 while in Quick Mask mode. Your goal here is to cover all the original background areas *outside* the actor's figure with green Quick Mask, without leaving a gap between the green and the purple selection tint areas of the Alpha Channel #4. You'll be editing in the temporary Mask channel created by the Quick Mask mode, but your view of what is happening is as if you were applying the green mask in the Alpha channel that has the purple selection mask. You'll see that the Alpha channel will have an eye icon (which stands for visible), but the pencil icon, which stands for editability, will automatically toggle off when the Quick Mask mode is activated. The green you'll apply stands for active selected areas you'll later remove from the Alpha channel selection when you switch back to Standard mode.

Stop *Don't overlap* the green "paint" with the purple areas because this *will* remove some of the grayscale information area if you delete these areas while in Standard mode!

The whole point of creating a temporary mask, and viewing the permanent selection area in different colors, is to make it easier to create a precise selection around the actor. Before beginning, remember that there shouldn't be gaps between the green and purple, and it's also a mistake to overlap the two colors around the actor's border.

Using Two Colors To Show Selections

Click on the Zoom tool, then click once over the actor's knees area	Zooms you to a 2:1 viewing resolution of the area where you'll create a selection mask.
Double-click on the Quick Mask tool on the toolbox	Accesses the Quick Mask Option dialog box.
Click on the Selected Areas radio button in the Color Indicates field, then click on the Color swatch	Specifies that when you apply color, you're defining a selection area, and you've called the Color Picker to specify this color.
Enter **127** in the H field, **97** in the S field, and **68** for B	Specifies a green tint for areas to be selected in an image area.
Click on OK	Returns you to the Photoshop workspace and CRAN2.TIF, working in Quick Mask mode. The actor should appear in a purple tint.
Click on the Paintbrush tool on the toolbox	This is the tool for applying Quick Mask in this exercise. Clicking on a tool activates the Brushes palette.

continues

continued

Select a tip from the top row, third tip from the left on the Brushes palette	This is a small, hard-edge tip, ideal for precise brushing or stroking of a selection area in Quick Mask mode.
Click and drag over the outside edge of the actor's pants leg	This area is included in the selected area when you switch back to Standard mode.
Continue clicking and dragging strokes to define the outside edge of the actor's pants legs	Defines a selection edge with Quick Mask color.
Select a larger brush tip, and fill in the area your Quick Mask edgework has defined	You are completing an area for selection in Standard mode.
If you make a mistake, click on the inverse colors icon on the toolbox, and paint over the areas	After inverting foreground and background colors, you can remove Quick Mask areas that you stroke over, like overlapping green and purple areas, as seen in figure 15.11.
Scroll up to the actor's wristwatch image area	This area needs edgework correction and selecting also.
Click on the default colors icon on the toolbox	Resets your foreground color to black, which applies Quick Mask when using the Paintbrush tool.
Click and drag across original background image areas, right up to the edge of the actor	Adds the areas to the selection when you return to Quick Mask mode (see fig. 15.12).
Double-click on the Hand tool	Returns you to a full-frame view of CRAN2.TIF.
Click on the Standard mode button on toolbox	Turns the Quick Mask area in Channel 4 into active selection marquees.
Click on the default colors icon on the toolbox	Ensures that your background color is white at this time.
Press the Delete key	Removes the selection areas, and replaces them with white.
Choose File, Save (or press Ctrl+S)	Saves all your work to your hard disk.

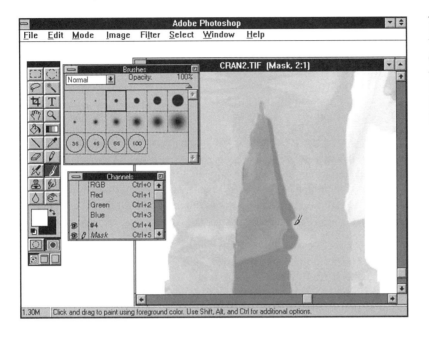

Figure 15.11
You can erase
Quick Mask as
well as apply it
by clicking the
inverse colors
icon.

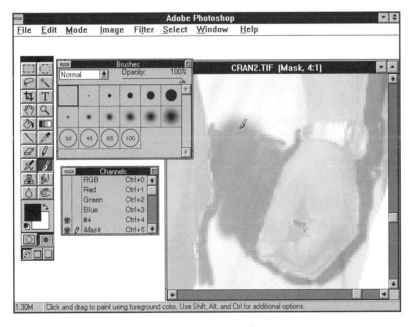

Figure 15.12
Paint the Quick
Mask over all of
the background
image areas, but
don't paint into
the purple
selection areas!

III

Gourmet Assignments

A Recap on Selection Techniques

One or two background areas may be left that should not be included in your finished selection area. But you have four techniques under your belt right now, for addressing the problems that pop up when you modify grayscale information that has been placed in an Alpha channel. Let's review the situations that call for each technique. Afterward you should finish the selection border refinement so that it is accurate when used to select the actor, and when creating a shadow to go behind him.

- ✔ When the selection area is mostly denser than 56-percent gray, and the background is light, define the border between background and foreground areas in the Alpha channel view, by using the Lasso, Rectangular marquee, or Elliptical marquee tools. Then increase the Brightness and Contrast of this defined area until the edge between the foreground and background areas is clear.

- ✔ When an Alpha channel's grayscale view of the image doesn't show enough tonal contrast to define an accurate selection border, change your view to one of the image's color channels (R, G, B or color composite). Here, you can use the Quick Mask mode and a painting tool to select the area, return to the *Alpha channel*, and switch back to Standard mode view of the Alpha channel. The Mask becomes an active selection marquee whose contents can then be deleted.

- ✔ When you have a large area that's mostly the same tonal value, but different from the tones you want included in a *selection area*, use the Magic Wand tool to select it, and then delete it.

- ✔ If you have a geometrically complex area that you want to delete, but it's bordering an area you want to save, use a different color for the Quick Mask areas than the one in which the Alpha Channel selection areas appear while viewed in Quick Mask mode. Then, switch back to the Standard viewing mode of the Alpha channel image, and delete the marquee selected areas in that Alpha channel.

Additionally, you can use the Eraser tool to clean up the background areas.

Finishing a Selection Mask

You've seen the interchangeable roles that selections and masks play in Photoshop design work. When you are finished with the selection area, there's one last thing you need to do with it, so it can play both shadow and selection border for the actor.

Your selection area should be totally opaque, in other words, it should consist of a black silhouette of the actor, and the background should be white. You will still have some areas within the outline of the actor; the wristwatch face, the actor's forehead, and highlights on his shirt buttons are still less than 56-percent dense, and that means that a selection border won't include them.

Rather than trying to color in all the little highlight areas at this point (which, FYI, is ridiculous to determine and frustrating to attempt), in the next exercise you'll Load the selection, and then save it to another channel. This will force the pixels that are lighter than Photoshop's selection tolerance to become visible in the new selection and make areas darker gray turn to a 100-percent opaque black. After this has occurred, you can easily spot and color in the remaining, unselected white areas you want to include in the selection of the actor.

Creating a Selection Area from Grayscale Information

Choose **S**elect, **L**oad Selection	Loads the Alpha Channel 4 selection areas, based on tonal densities in this channel.
Choose **S**elect, **S**ave Selection, then choose New	Creates a new selection in a new Alpha Channel 5, based on the #4 channel's selection area, as shown in figure 15.13.
Click on the Channel #5 title on the Channels palette	Moves you to a view of the new channel.
Select the Zoom tool, click and diagonally drag on the wristwatch area in the image	You marquee-zoom into a selection area that still has white, unselected areas in it.
Choose the Pencil tool, then click the white wristwatch area	You are including this white and drag on area in the selection in this channel by coloring it black.
Scroll to other areas inside the silhouette of the actor that are white; fill them with black, too	You are completing the selection area.
Click on the Channel #4 title on the Channels palette when you are finished with Channel #5	Gives you a view of the original Alpha channel that you used to make Channel 5.
Click on the Channels palette's command button, and select Delete Channel from the drop-down list	Deletes Channel 4. You no longer need it. It increases CRAN2.TIF's file size needlessly. Channel 5 immediately gets renumbered/renamed Channel 4.
Choose **F**ile, **S**ave	Saves your work on the CRAN2.TIF image.

III

Gourmet Assignments

Depending on the visual content of a grayscale-saved selection in an Alpha channel, you may want to try loading the selection, inverting the color selections so that black is Photoshop's background color, and then pressing the backspace key a few times. Grayscale information constitutes a partial mask, so that when a selection of this type is loaded, it's only partially covering an area. Pressing the backspace key is equivalent to deleting a selected area to reveal the background color. You can only partially delete a grayscale selection in an Alpha channel by backspacing, but each backspace keystroke serves to succesively delete the area to the background color of black. This trick doesn't work all the time, and especially not with a faint gray selection area against a white (non-selected, masked) background.

Figure 15.13
A selection based on a previous selection area has more contrast than the original.

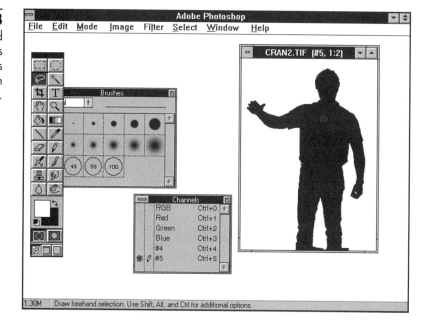

Compositing Different Image Areas into a New Image

The work you've done up to this point will almost immediately show its rewards now that you're almost ready to copy the actor's image into the TILEBACK.TIF image. But before you copy him to his new background, you have to copy his shadow to TILEBACK.TIF.

Giving Actors Depth by Using Shadows

This corporate motivation poster would look flat, and perhaps even a little phony, if you were to simply paste image after image behind and in front of one another. You need to take into account that if all these images of an actor really were photographed in front of this tile wall, they would cast shadows on it. It's a small point, but one that adds realism to retouched images when you create collages.

The next exercise shows you how to copy and paste the actor's black silhouette in CRAN2's Alpha channel on top of the TILEBACK image. The Brushes palette tips and the Magic Wand and Lasso tool selections you've used in the previous exercises all had Anti-Aliasing properties, which will produce some telltale fringing on the edge pixels of your selection. The Defringe command will take care of these pixels.

You'll also use Photoshop's Composite Controls to paste the shadow into the background image. Shadows should never be 100-percent opaque. Instead, they should allow some background detail through them. Setting the Composite Controls to less than 100-percent Opacity when pasting the shadow into the TILEBACK image will allow some of the background to show when the images are pasted together. The Composite Controls command is a less resource-intensive method of compositing the images than using the Brushes palette to achieve the same semi-transparent effect. You've used composite blending using the Brushes palette's Opacity controls in several other chapters, but never with a 2M file, plus another 1.3M file actively stored in system RAM! Using the Composite Controls after performing a lot of processor-intensive stunts, as we've done in the last few exercises, is quite simply a safer avenue to travel.

You're ready now to select the shadow and drop it into the TILEBACK.TIF image.

III

Gourmet Assignments

Me and My Shadow

To start this exercise, CRAN2.TIF is the active window in your workspace, and you should be in the Channel #4 view of this file. This is where you left off in the last exercise.

Choose **S**elect, **L**oad Selection	Loads the selection area saved in the new Channel 4 in the CRAN2.TIF image.
Select **E**dit, **C**opy (or press Ctrl+C)	Copies the contents of the selection—the black silhouette of the actor to the clipboard.
Click on the down arrow on the CRAN2.TIF image window	Minimizes the image to a thumbnail view on Photoshop's workspace, conserving system resources.
Choose **F**ile, **O**pen, TILEBACK.TIF from your hard disk	This is the version you saved earlier with the neon effect in it.

continues

continued

Choose **E**dit, **P**aste (or press Ctrl+V)	Pastes the shadow on top of TILEBACK.TIF as a floating selection. *Be careful not to deselect it accidentally.*
Place the cursor inside the selection border and drag the image to the right of TILEBACK.TIF	Turns the cursor into a small arrow so that you can move the floating selection freely.
Choose **S**elect, Hide **E**dges (or press Ctrl+H)	Makes the irritating marquee invisible, but keeps the selection floating (and selected).
Choose **D**efringe from the **S**elect menu, then enter **2** pixels in the Defringe dialog box	Removes **A**nti-Aliasing edge pixels created when you used selection tools and soft-tipped brushes to define the selection border in CRAN2.TIF earlier. (See the tip following this exercise.)
Choose **E**dit, **C**omposite Controls	Displays options that you can use to specify how an image is blended into another.
Set Opacity to **65**%, Mode to Normal, Blend If to Gray, as shown in figure 15.14, then click on OK	Displays the shadow faintly against the TILEBACK.TIF tiles.
Click outside the shadow's border	Deselects the shadow.

Because you turned off the selection marquee earlier, you can't see it. Nevertheless, clicking away from the selection locks the marquee into place in the background.

Choose **F**ile, **S**ave (or press Ctrl+S)	Saves your work to hard disk.

This exercise reveals one of the secrets to creating believable shadows. But the Normal mode is only one of the ways you can composite two images together. Experiment with the other modes available from the Composite Controls and the Brushes palette to create different effects when pasting in selections. The Multiply and Screen modes produce dramatic effects when a pasted image is copied to a background, and there are other examples of using composite modes throughout this book.

If the Defringe command negates the Anti-Aliasing property you use when selecting the shadow in the channel, why go through the bother of Anti-Aliasing in the first place?

Using the Anti-Aliasing property before the Defringe command helps you avoid the hard edge associated with clumsy cutting and copying. When dealing with images of natural subjects, it's important to give a little slack to their borders because images in a bitmap don't simply have a beginning or an ending—they blend into the next series of pixels.

When you reach the pasting phase, however, the problem with Anti-Aliasing is that these semitransparent edge pixels can clash with the tonal values of the background image you're pasting on top of. The Defringe command removes edge pixels inward from the selection border, drawing replacement color values from adjacent pixels in the selection (no background colors are involved). Usually, this process results in a non-jagged transition. A Defringe command setting of 2 to 3 pixels, tops, helps greatly to disguise a pasted selection.

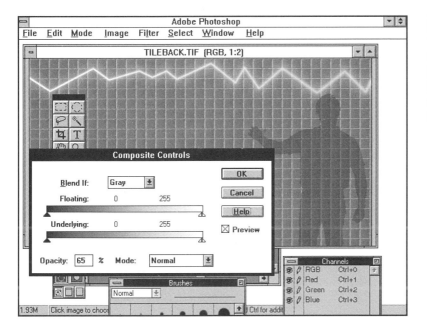

Figure 15.14
The Composite Controls dialog box enables you to create a faint shadow against the background.

The Multipurpose Mask

Now that you have created the actor's shadow and pasted it into the TILEBACK.TIF image, it's time to concentrate on the image of the actor himself. You can now reuse the same selection border to go around the RGB image, which shares an identical shape and orientation in the CRAN2.TIF image window. The following exercise demonstrates this part of channel selecting.

Selecting the RGB Image for Compositing

Click on the thumbnail image of CRAN2.TIF, then choose **R**estore from the **W**indow menu

Makes CRAN2.TIF the active image window in Photoshop.

The selection marquee should still be active on channel 4. If it isn't, use **L**oad Selection from the **S**elect menu to make it active.

Click on the RGB title on CRAN2.TIF's Channels palette (or press Ctrl+0)

Switches channels from the Alpha to the color composite channel, as shown in figure 15.15.

Choose **E**dit, **C**opy (or press Ctrl+C)

Copies the RGB channel selection to the clipboard.

Press Ctrl+Tab

Toggles you to an active view of TILEBACK.TIF.

Choose **E**dit, **P**aste (or press Ctrl+V)

Pastes the selection on top of TILEBACK.TIF.

Choose Hide **E**dges from the **S**elect menu

Makes the marquee border invisible.

Move the selection to a position slightly above and to the left of the shadow

Creates the appearance that the actor is casting a shadow on the tile wall as shown in figure 15.16.

Choose **S**elect, **D**efringe, enter **2** pixels in the Defringe dialog box

Removes the Anti-Aliased edges from the active selection.

Choose **S**elect, **S**ave Selection

Saves the area inside the border, but not the image contents within the selection border, to a new TILEBACK.TIF channel that you will use later.

Click outside the selection border (or press Ctrl+D)

Deselects the subject and blends the selection into TILEBACK.TIF.

Ctrl+Tab

Toggles your active image window back to CRAN2.TIF.

Double-click on the CRAN2.TIF window command button

Calls up the Photoshop dialog box for saving changes to an image that is about to be closed.

Double-clicking on a command button is a shortcut that instructs Windows' applications like Photoshop to close a document, image, window or dialog box.

Click on **Y**es

Photoshop closed the CRAN2 image, with changes saved to your hard disk, and TILEBACK.TIF is now the active image window.

Choose **F**ile, **S**ave

Saves the most recent version of the TILEBACK.TIF image.

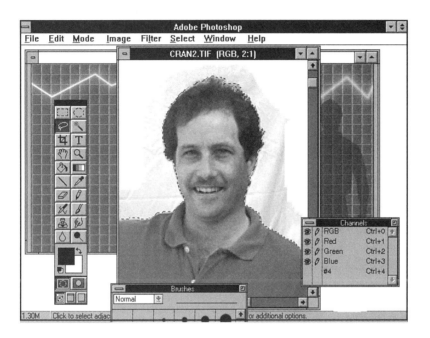

Figure 15.15
The selection is reused to select the actor's image in the RGB composite channel.

Retouching Pure Color Pixels from the Image

The Defringe command, although useful, can leave a tell-tale deposit of pure color (color without gray component) just inside the pasted image's edge when it's composited into a background image. However, because you saved the selection border of the actor in the last exercise, you can easily correct such problem areas caused by the Defringe command. You may notice pure colors on the edge of the actor's fleshtones, where bright red (a pure color) has replaced part of the Anti-Aliased edge. This bright red is the pure color Photoshop found in the skintones to replace the Anti-Aliased edge pixels. This bright red is obviously unappealing because there are very few, if any, pure colors found in photographs of natural subjects.

Fixing this is easy. First, display the selection border by selecting **L**oad from the **S**elect menu, and then choose Selection #4, your only saved selection in TILEBACK.TIF. This selection border protects the background image, so you can safely paint over flaws like the red pixel created by the Defringe command. Use the Eyedropper tool to sample a medium fleshtone from the hand. Using a soft-tip brush in Normal mode, simply brush a few strokes over any

III

Gourmet Assignments

flaws you find. The selection border stops you from running over into the background, and the soft tip adds a little spread outside the border to disguise a hard-edge retouch. Use the Eyedropper sampling technique in other areas where the Defringe command left obvious, pure color pixels around the actor's edge.

Figure 15.16
The actor is in a position to cast a shadow!

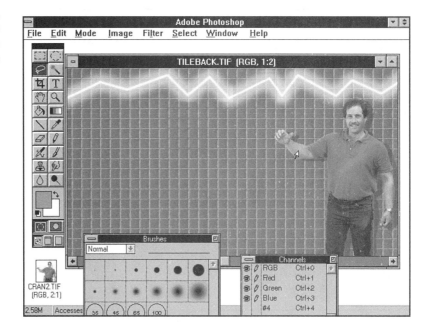

Pre-Made Masks on the Companion Disk

The point to any exercise in this book is to get you familiar with a new technique or Photoshop feature. If you successfully created the selection border in CRAN2.TIF, you now should have the ability, if not the experience, to create six others for the rest of the CD images of the actor. But this chapter is assignment-oriented, too, and if you're anxious to complete the corporate motivation poster, we've provided a "shortcut" to levels adjustments and selection borders you may be interested in!

The authors completed the steps you went through earlier on the rest of the poses of our actor. Five of the other subjects on the companion CD were color-corrected using the same CORPMOV.ALV file you created earlier. All six of the remaining images have Alpha channels with masks created that are all ready for you to use. Completing the poster is simply a matter of copying the correct channels to the TILEBACK.TIF image.

But before completing the assignment, let's spend a moment on the "art" of the design, and two other ways Photoshop helps flesh out our idea here. You will be placing a second image, SPRING2.TIF from the companion disk, to the left of the CRAN2 image in TILEBACK.TIF, to create the impression that one figure is leaning on another. But as you continue adding the actor, in his many poses to the background, compare SPRING2 to SPRING1. He's wearing a white T-shirt in both poses, but the T-shirt isn't white in the SPRING2.TIF image! This was done to give the completed poster more color variation. A Photoshop feature you may want to know about was used to do this retouching before it was mastered to the companion CD!

Dying a Shirt, Photoshop-Style

When you open the SPRING2.TIF image for the next exercise, look closely at it for telltale signs of retouching. Even though it was painstakingly executed, we've given you the clue now, and even the best retouching is detectable when the viewer's been tipped off! We used the same techniques you learned earlier about using combinations of painting and selection tools to define the shirt area. This was a difficult undertaking because parts of the actor's shirt areas "bled" into the white background. Don't *ever* photograph a model wearing white against a white background if you want a fair chance at selecting the model off the background later!

After the selection border was created, we went to **A**djust from the **I**mage menu, chose Hue/Saturation and then selected **C**olorize. This all worked pretty well, and helped to create yet another "wardrobe change" after the actor was photographed. You may want to try out this trick sometime when you have too many people in a crowd wearing similar colors.

In the next section, you select the SPRING2 actor image and place it into TILEBACK.TIF. You want to position the SPRING2 selection in such a way as to create a believable interaction between the two images. The next exercise shows you how to paste SPRING2's shadow behind the CRAN2 figure in the TILEBACK image because, as always, the shadow needs to come before the RGB selection.

III

Gourmet Assignments

Compositing a Second Shadow

Open SPRING2.TIF from the companion CD.

Choose **I**mage, **A**djust, and then choose **L**evels (or press Ctrl+L)	Displays the Levels command.
Click **L**oad, and then find and choose CORPMOV.ALV	Tells Photoshop to apply the same tonal adjustments as were defined for CRAN2.TIF.
Click on OK	Confirms the application of the new Levels settings and returns you to the Photoshop workspace.
Click on the Channel #4 title on the palette	Displays the mask the Channels authors created for the SPRING2.TIF image, using the same techniques you used for CRAN2.TIF.

continues

continued

Choose **S**elect, **L**oad Selection	Loads the saved selection border to encompass the black selection shape in Channel 4.
Choose **E**dit, **C**opy (or press Ctrl+C)	Copies the selection to the clipboard.
Press Ctrl+Tab	Toggles TILEBACK.TIF to the active image.
Choose **S**elect, **L**oad Selection	Activates the selection border that you created around CRAN2.TIF in the last exercise.
Leave the selection marquee visible.	
Choose **E**dit, Paste **B**ehind	Places the shadow next to the loaded selection.

The shadow now appears behind the active selection, which is still a floating selection while the channel 4 selection is loaded (see fig. 15.17).

Choose **E**dit, Composite C**o**ntrols	Displays the Composite Controls dialog box.
Set Opacity to **65**%, the Mode to Normal, then click on OK	Creates a transparent shadow, just as you did in the previous exercise.
Choose **D**efringe from the **S**elect menu, and enter **2** pixels as the Defringe value in the dialog box	Removes the anti-aliased edges from the shadow.
Deselect the shadow selection by pressing Ctrl+D, or by clicking outside of the selection marquee	Blends the shadow into place in TILEBACK.TIF.
Choose **F**ile, **S**ave (or press Ctrl+S)	Saves your work to hard disk.

The Paste Behind command is incredibly useful for doing photo-collage work. It's the next best thing to having "layers" in a bitmap editing program! You can use the Paste Behind, the Paste Into, and the plain Paste commands with copied selection areas in your own work to eliminate some of the planning ahead normally required in compiling a *physical* collage!

As you move along with the corporate motivation poster, you'll accumulate extra channels in the TILEBACK.TIF image, which will dramatically increase the file size. Therefore, you should delete any extra channels by selecting the Delete Channel command from the drop-down menu from the Channels palette's command button when you're certain a selection area has outlived its usefulness.

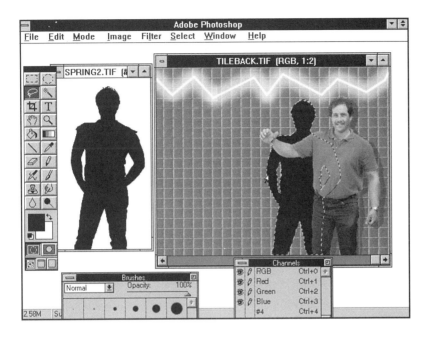

Figure 15.17
The Paste Behind command enables you to position a selected image behind an active selection area.

Next you need to select the SPRING2.TIF's RGB channel to get the actor's color image and paste it into the background image. You don't want to just plop SPRING2 into TILEBACK because you want the outstretched hand of the CRAN2 image to appear as though it's actually on the shoulder of the SPRING2 pose. To create this interaction, you'll use the saved selection in the TILEBACK image, but you must do a little mask-editing before you use it. The right hand of the CRAN2 actor is the only image area that needs selecting—your task is to subtract from the selection after its loaded. Using the Lasso tool for this editing procedure will work a lot quicker than if you use Quick Mask editing, so let's make the Lasso the first tool you'll use in the following steps.

Give the Man a Hand

Marquee-zoom over the right hand of the CRAN2 actor in the TILEBACK.TIF image

Choose **S**elect, **L**oad Selection

Recalls the selection border you saved in TILEBACK.TIF.

Select the Lasso tool, then Ctrl+drag trace around the bottom of the fingers

Begins defining a selection area used to remove the fingers from the overall selection, as shown in figure 15.18.

Arc away from the trace, releasing the mouse button and Ctrl

Closes the selection area, leaving the fingers and a gap in the active selection.

continues

III

Gourmet Assignments

continued

Double-click on the Hand tool on the toolbox	Displays a full-frame view of TILEBACK.TIF.

The view shows two marquee-selected areas: the fingers and the remainder of CRAN2.TIF's image.

Ctrl+click and drag to trace the around the selection area that is *not* the fingers selection	Subtracts the torso shape from the fingers selection.
Release the Ctrl and mouse button	The torso selection area disappears, leaving only the fingers selection.
Choose **S**elect, **S**ave Selection, and then choose #4	Overwrites the previous selection area to create fingers selection area in TILEBACK.TIF.
Choose **E**dit, Paste **B**ehind	Pastes the SPRING2 copy on the clipboard behind the finger selection.
Click and drag SPRING2 into position behind the active finger selection	Places the selection in a natural looking pose relative to the CRAN2 actor.

Before you proceed, your screen should look like figure 15.19.

Choose **D**efringe from the **S**elect menu, then type **2** pixels in the **W**idth text box on the Defringe dialog box	Removes the anti-aliasing from the SPRING2 image area.
Deselect the loaded selection by pressing Ctrl+D, or clicking outside the selection border	Blends the SPRING2 image into the background image.
Choose **F**ile, **S**ave (or press Ctrl+S)	Saves your work to hard disk.

This exercise is about as tough as an assignment gets. For the five other images on the companion CD, you can create shadows from the extra channels you have learned to create, and place them in front of or behind each other, as long as you save a selection border before you use the Pasting Behind command with the next image.

Soon you will see the completed corporate motivation poster, which was finished using the techniques you've learned in this chapter. But first, let's take a look at one more effect you can create using the Channels palette.

CRAN2's hand, which is apparently placed on SPRING2's shoulder, is missing a shadow. You saved the fingers selection, so in the following exercise you'll reuse the saved fingers selection area to create the missing shadow. No copying or pasting is involved this time out. You can use the Levels command to darken the pixel's tonal values within the selection area to create a believable shadow.

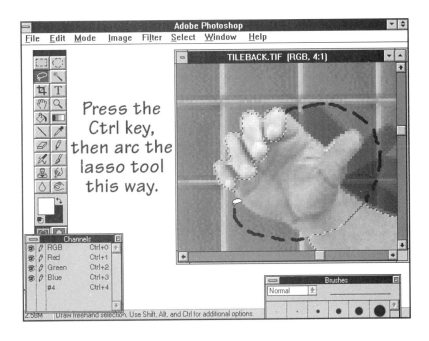

Figure 15.18
You can subtract from the original selection border by using the Lasso tool while pressing the Ctrl key.

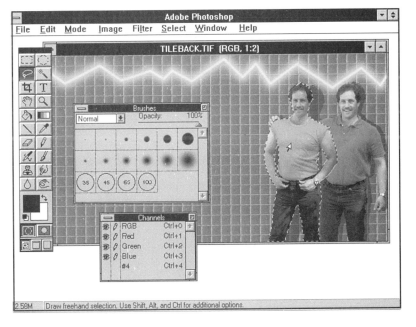

Figure 15.19
Figures seem to interact when you place image elements behind, and in front of each other.

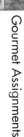

III

Gourmet Assignments

Creating a Shadow Using the Levels Command

Marquee-zoom into the finger area on SPRING2's shoulder	This is the area you'll be working on in this exercise.

To get into this area, you need about a 4:1 viewing resolution, as shown in figure 15.20.

Choose **S**elect, then **L**oad Selection	Loads the fingers selection area.
Press Ctrl and Alt while you Click and drag the selection down and to the right	Moves only the selection border, not the image area inside (see fig. 15.20).
Click on the Quick Mask button	Turns the selection area to a tinted color you can edit with a painting tool.
Click on the inverse colors icon on the toolbox	Makes your foreground color white, which in Quick Mask mode, removes mask color.
Select the Paintbrush tool, then select the second smallest tip from the top row of the Brushes palette	You need a fine tip to remove areas of the Quick mask.
Click and drag over the Quick Mask area presently covering the fingers, but not in the area covering SPRING2's shirt	You are removing Quick Mask from the fingers area (see fig. 15.21).
Click on the Standard mode button on the toolbox	The remaining, Quick Masked areas become active selection areas.
Choose **I**mage, **A**djust, Levels (or press Ctrl+L)	Accesses the Levels command.
Set the middle Input Levels value to 0.44, by typing it in the middle text box or moving the slider, and then click on OK	Darkens the selected area (See fig. 15.22).
Choose **S**elect, **N**one (or press Ctrl+D)	Deselects the active selection area.
Choose **F**ile, **S**ave	Saves changed image to your hard disk.

Unlike using the Composite Control features to make a semi-opaque shadow from a black silhouette, increasing the midrange values of a selection using the Levels command redistributes the tonal values of color pixels and assigns them darker tones than they originally had. In other words, you're darkening a color, not adding a film of grayscale to an image.

You'll note from this chapter's exercises that selection areas can act on identical parts of different channels because the *channels are actually part of the same image.* You must, however, be in the desired channel when you cut, paste, or move a selection area. And if you've deselected the pencil icon next to a channel name, you can't edit in that channel.

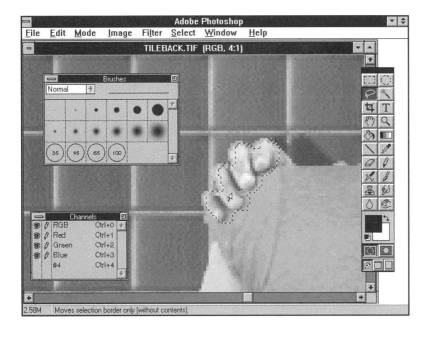

Figure 15.20
Move the selection border, but not the image within the border, by using the Ctrl+Alt combination when you drag a border.

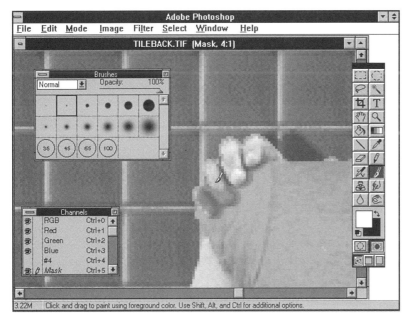

Figure 15.21
Use the Paintbrush to remove mask from the fingers.

Figure 15.22
Another way to
create shadows is
by using the Levels
command.

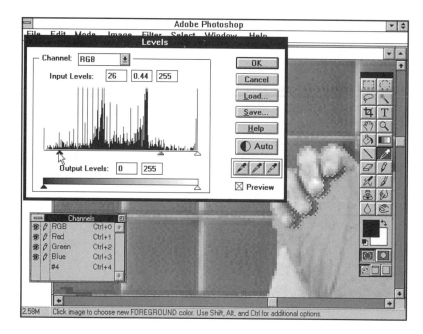

Flash Forward to the Finale

There are a few intermediate steps between the results you see in figure 15.22 and figure 15.23. These steps include much copying, loading of selection borders, repositioning pasted selections, and extensive use of the Paste Behind and Defringe commands—but the work should go quickly because the selection areas have already been created for you in the rest of the image files on the companion CD. And we believe the time invested in creating a professional photo-collage is well-spent. Through creating this visually striking corporate motivation poster, you've discovered a visual "hook" that can be used with other types of collages.

Your ability to do this kind of professional retouching work depends on remembering that different image areas require different tools and Photoshop commands to make the time spent finishing a piece the most productive.

Many contemporary films and magazines feature surreal, provocative, fantastic, and humorous images as a centerpiece, not just an illustration that accompanies a story. Don't underestimate Photoshop's capability to produce commercial work. Nothing is as eye-catching as a photographically impossible image.

Adding Type to the Corporate Motivation Poster

Before your masterpiece is complete, however, it needs a caption. It, too, should be as dynamic as the image you've created. You'll be using the Gaussian blur filter in this final exercise to create a realistic drop shadow for the text string you create with the Type tool.

The Type tool's capability to "remember" what you've typed in the Type tool dialog box from Photoshop session to session saves you from having to create an additional Saved Selection in the TILEBACK.TIF image. Usually, you'd want to type a Text string once, then save the resulting floating selection to a new channel, where you can blur it, and bring it back into the RGB composite view. But the TILEBACK.TIF image's file size is quite large, and an additional channel would increase demands on your system RAM by more than a third if you did this. It's needless— you can blur a text selection right in the RGB channel, then enter the text again as the main text with only a couple of clicks. Here's how.

Corporate Titles

Click on the background color selection box on the toolbox	Displays the Color Picker.
Type **31** in the R field, **31** in the G field, and **38** in the B field; then click on OK	Makes the new background color a neutral, corporate, cold gray.
Choose **I**mage, Canvas **S**ize	Displays the Canvas Size dialog box, with which you can make the canvas larger than the active image, and thus reveal the background.
Select H**e**ight 4.75", and then click Placement's upper-middle box	Adds three-fourths of an inch of background canvas to the image and places the image on top of the background.
Click on OK	Returns you to the image.
Choose the Type tool (the one with the "T" on it) from the toolbox	Turns the cursor into an insertion tool when you place it over the active image.
Click on the bottom of the active image	Indicates where the text should begin on the image, and activates the Type Options dialog box in which you compose the phrase.
Select a typeface from the **F**ont drop-down list, check the **B**old Style box, and type **48** in the **S**ize field, with points selected from the drop-down list	There are 54 points in three-fourths of an inch (1 inch equals 72 points). Therefore, a 48-point height fits comfortably inside the 54-point canvas you added to the image area before.
Type **Teamwork begins with one person.**	This is your corporate motivation phrase. Catchy, huh? (See following Tip.)
Click on OK	Places black type (the foreground color) as a floating selection on the image.

continues

continued

Drag and center the type in the extra canvas space	The type remains a floating selection as long as you don't click outside the border.
Click outside the border	Deselects the text, and it becomes part of the background image.
Select the Rectanglular marquee tool and click and diagonally drag an area around the text, but within the new canvas addition	Marquee selects the text and a portion of the the neutral gray canvas area.
Choose Blur from the Filter menu, choose Gaussian Blur, and then set **R**adius to **4** pixels, then click on OK	Gently blurs the type into the neutral gray background, as shown in figure 15.23.
Choose **F**ile, **S**ave (or press Ctrl+S)	Saves your work to hard disk.

Figure 15.23
You can build
a convincing
shadow for type
by blurring dark
type into the
background.

Finishing the caption for the assignment is simple. In the Color Picker, specify R:**91**, G:**105**, and B:**165** to create the foreground color for the type a second time, and then click the Type tool in the neutral gray canvas area. You then drag the floating text to a position above and to the left of the Gaussian blurred text, deselect it by clicking outside the marquee border, and you're home free!

The color values we've recommended throughout these exercises are arbitrary ones, based on personal taste. Feel free to choose colors, typefaces, and degrees of effects, filters, and color corrections to suit your personal aesthetics. Values we've suggested were intended as a reference for the exercises, and nothing more. There is no "right or wrong" when it comes to creating art—with the *possible* exception of mixing argyle patterns with khaki.

To create the caption as shown in figure 15.23, the ITC Windsor Condensed font was used. Although you may not own Windsor Condensed, a creative substitution can do the trick as well. The key word here is "condensed"—just about any 48-point typeface works to create this caption, but you may run out of space if you don't use a condensed version of Windsor, Arial, Bodoni, or a similar typeface. If you don't have a condensed typeface available, simply shorten the phrase you typed in the Type dialog box, or reduce the type size to complete the exercise.

Figure 15.24 shows the completed work. It takes only a few hours to create this poster in Photoshop, and the secret is in knowing how to work with *combinations* of tools.

Should you decide to create a photo-collage like the one shown in this chapter as an original assignment of your own, plan your photography carefully, and create accurate selection areas you can re-use as selections and masks. You can even copy and paste selections from the RGB, Green, Blue, or Red channels into new channels you've created if you mess up your masking work along the way.

Figure 15.24
The completed corporate motivational poster.

Summary

The reason why professionals get better, quicker image editing done using Photoshop, is because of the incredible power of selections and masks in Channels. You always have more than one view of a selection area you've created in an image—as a representation based on tonal densities in the channel view of the selection, and as a selection marquee border when it's active in an image.

When grayscale information is created in a channel, the Photoshop user can create partial masks, or further edit the visual information to create complete, 100-percent opaque masks and selections. You can invert a selection by pressing Ctrl+I to make the area a mask, and you can specify not one, but two different colors to represent a selection while in Quick Mask mode viewing an Alpha channel.

It's the plastic quality of the digital image and the versatility of Photoshop's tools that you can use to create reality out of fiction—to bring dreams into the real world.

Chapter 16 is not paced at the breakneck speed of our last few exercises. In fact, it should seem as familiar and comfortable to you as an old friend.

Your friend in the next chapter is the monochrome image—the black-and-white still. Black-and-white photography represents the infancy of the captured image, but in the next chapter you learn a few new twists using image-editing software from the here and now on this timeless image type.

There's still a great demand for professionally enhanced black-and-white images—for newspapers, company newsletters, and personal use. So let's take a look next at how to bring some uncommon qualities out of the common snapshot.

Chapter Snapshot

In this chapter, you learn how to:

The Wonderful World of Black and White

Color imaging is emphasized in this book because color is the way people see the world. For the PC platform, the ability to do professional color imaging has only recently become a reality. But as exciting as color photography and imaging is, black and white photography still has a place in the world of media—it's an art form in its own right. And Photoshop has much to add to the traditional craft of black and white imaging.

In your career as an imaging-type person, you probably face having to produce black and white work for a newsletter, flyer, or other promotion. The good news is that working with a grayscale digital image puts less of a strain on your system resources. Files are a third the size of a full-color image, and you can actually get a proof copy from a laser printer with a grayscale image.

But if you think of black and white images as bargain-basement, second-best images, Photoshop will severely challenge that belief as you move through this chapter. Grayscales *can* be creative, sparkling images. Working with these images can be a fascinating and dynamic experience *if* you know how to use Photoshop's power.

This chapter is a potpourri of helpful techniques and special effects you'll want to adopt in your own work with monochrome, grayscale, black-and-white photographic images. In this wonderful digital world, an image created or photographed in color can be manipulated as a grayscale, and vice versa. You have complete flexibility. In this chapter, you start with a color image and learn how to create the ultimate black-and-white masterpiece out of it. And after a sidestep to Photoshop's Filter effects (and a couple of homemade ones), you find out how to put color back into a grayscale photo! Photoshop handles image data adeptly, regardless of color mode. You will soon see how to get the most out of any type of image you have to work with.

From 24-bit Color to 8-bit Grayscale

Chapter 2, which dealt with capturing a photographic image with a scanner, advised against acquiring a color image with a grayscale scanner. The rationale is that the 8-bit sampling of a grayscale scanner *does not* take into account the *color densities* in a color image. Luminosity, the way brightness is evaluated in an image, should actually be *weighted* when an RGB image is converted to Grayscale, to the tune of about 30 percent red, 60 percent green, and 10 percent blue. When you scan a color image in a grayscale mode, most color scanners *won't* weigh the color components this way. The result is often a grayscale image with darker areas where red is found in the original image, or blue areas that fail to register, or other areas that are lighter or darker than they should be in the grayscale image.

You can avoid many headaches by scanning a color image in an RGB mode, then letting Photoshop do the conversion to Grayscale. The process is ridiculously simple, but read on to learn how a grayscale image can be *balanced* after the conversion so that it reproduces at its best when printed on a laser printer or commercial press.

Your introduction to the wonderful world of black and white starts, paradoxically, with the color image, LAURIE.TIF, on the companion CD. You will work with this sample image as you explore the techniques and special effects in this chapter.

First, you will sample and preserve some of the original colors from the image before it is converted to grayscale. The Colors palette is the ideal storage place for these sample colors. When this chapter comes full circle, from RGB to Grayscale to RGB, you will have custom-specified colors that you can use to hand-tint a black and white image.

The Colors Palette

Think of the Colors palette as an alternative to Photoshop's foreground/background color selection boxes. The Colors palette is a great place to mix custom colors, save entire custom palettes, and work from PANTONE or other color-matching specifications, if that's your assignment. And it's only an F7 key away.

In addition to a Color Picker of its own, the Colors palette sports a scratch pad area that acts exactly like an image background. You can paint on it, mix colors on it, and even put image samples on it. The default Colors palette comes with color samples, or *swatches*, based on a color model, but you can add to them, or eliminate some (or all!) of the default samples.

Tip

If you decide to drastically alter the Colors palette in an assignment of your own, choose Save, or Append from the Colors palette's command button drop-down list. If you have Restore Windows selected as a General Preference for your workspace environment (press Ctrl+K to access this preference quickly), Photoshop remembers the changes you have made to the Colors palette from session to session. But...if you make changes to any of the Colors palettes that Photoshop ships with, including the default palette you're working with in this chapter, and then change to a different one without saving or appending your arrangement, you lose those changes forever.

Because you are going to remove the color qualities in the LAURIE.TIF image shortly, the first exercise shows you how to save sample colors from an image, in case you want to use them later. Or you may want to do some quick color-matching between two different images someday. The following exercise shows how color sampling and saving is done.

Color Sampling an Image

Open the LAURIE.TIF image from the companion CD	One of the image files you work with in this exercise.
Press Ctrl+plus key	Zooms to a 2:1 viewing resolution of the image so you can see it better.
Choose **W**indow, Show **C**olors (or press F7)	Displays the Colors palette in Photoshop's workspace.
From the command button on the Colors palette, select HSB colors	The color model you use in this assignment to adjust sampled colors.
Click on the Pencil tool, then set the Brushes palette to the fourth, top-row tip, click and drag the Opacity slider to 100%, and choose Normal mode	Sets characteristics of Pencil to apply solid color with small tip.
Press Alt and click on a facial area in the LAURIE.TIF image	Pencil tool temporarily toggles to the Eyedropper as you sample color beneath cursor on Laurie's face. Color appears on color selection boxes on the toolbox and Colors palette (see fig. 16.1).
Release the Alt key, then click on the scratch pad area on the Colors palette	Applies dot of the color sampled with Eyedropper tool to the square, white area on the left of the Colors palette.

See this book's inside back cover for tool and icon locations.

III

Gourmet Assignments

continues

continued

Press Alt and click on a background area in the LAURIE.TIF image	Samples another color from image.
Release the Alt key, then click on the scratch pad area on the Colors palette	Applies dot of the color sampled with Eyedropper tool.
Continue the Alt+click process, sampling on the image, then clicking on the scratch pad area	Collect predominant colors of LAURIE.TIF image to scratch pad area (see fig. 16.2). Stop after sampling about 12 predominant image colors.

Figure 16.1
Use the Alt key to toggle between the Pencil tool and Eyedropper mode.

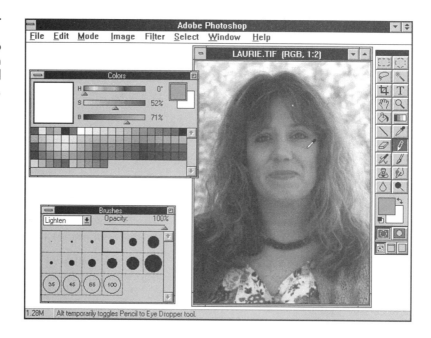

When you want to create several variations in tonal qualities from a single sampled color, use the number keys (or the numerical pad) on your keyboard before you apply the Pencil tool to the scratch pad area. The numerical keyboard pad changes the opacity on the Brushes palette in increments of 10. If you sample a color area and want only 40 percent of it as a color to use later, for example, type **4**. Photoshop's Brushes palette will automatically lower the percentage of opacity.

No matter which Colors palette model you choose, if you specify a "tint" of a color by key stroking a numerical percentage, the RGB, HSB, or LAB values on the Colors palette and the Color Picker do not change. The reason is that you

are specifying the same color, but at a different opacity than the one with which it is being actively applied. If you want to add this percentage of color to a more permanent collection, you have to resample the percentage of color from the scratch pad area, using the Eyedropper tool.

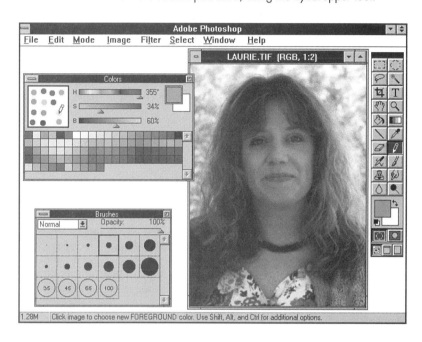

Figure 16.2

Create a collection of color samples on the scratch pad area of the Colors palette.

III

Gourmet Assignments

Although you cannot copy the scratch pad area on the Colors palette with a selection tool, you sample it for use as a pattern fill, which in turn can be saved as an image file! Here's how:

Marquee-select the scratch pad area with the Rectangular Marquee tool, then click on **E**dit, **D**efine Pattern. Then, create a new document (**F**ile, **N**ew, or press Ctrl+N). There are four ways to put the defined pattern into your new image document. First, you can use the **E**dit, **F**ill command. Or second, you can double-click on the Rubber Stamp tool, set the cloning Op**t**ion to Pattern (aligned or unaligned), and then clone away on the new document! Third, you can flood-fill a selection area in the new document with the Paint Bucket tool, by double-clicking on the tool, selecting Pattern as the fill Op**t**ion, and pouring the paint Bucket into the new image. A fourth way is to clone a color sample area into an open document by pressing Alt and clicking in the scratch pad area with the Rubber Stamp tool. This sets the sample point, then you can clone into the active image window, just as though the sampling crosshair was in the same document!

continues

Whatever method you choose, you can save the "art" you created on the scratch pad area in a file!

As was mentioned earlier in this chapter, the color samples you are taking from the LAURIE.TIF image are for an exercise at the chapter's end. In the real world, you seldom have the opportunity to sample original colors when your job is to hand-tint a grayscale, black and white image. This lesson is important, however, because real world colors are extremely difficult to create using only your imagination. You might even want to save the values from a color image and later apply them to a *different* grayscale image. In any event—in this assignment, investing a moment's work sampling actual RGB image colors is easier than guesstimating them later.

Enhancing Samples To Add to the Palette Swatches

In the next exercise, you add the colors you sampled to the Colors palette, next to the default swatches. You can have as many color swatches as you like on this or any other Colors palette. The scroll bar on the right side of the palette becomes active when you have added swatches that, along with the default swatches, exceeds seven rows' worth of swatches.

You get exceptionally eye-pleasing color matching if you build a sample color collection from LAURIE.TIF. But there's a trick to making these samples work properly with a grayscale image. You have to *change* the gray component of the color dots *before* you save them as swatches for grayscale tinting.

Colors you sample directly from an image have a gray component because they are exact color samples from a photo in which all pixels contain both gray and color components. The reason you switch from RGB to HSB mode on the Colors palette before you begin this process is that you can't discern or manipulate the amount of gray component in a color sample when you use the Red, Green, Blue color model.

By increasing the saturation of each sample dot before adding it to the swatches, you decrease the gray component of the color without changing its color value. Think about it this way— traditional photo retouchers use pure dyes when they hand-tint a photo, and pure colors are the analogy for specifying a tint in Photoshop. The less gray in a color, the purer it is. Don't worry if the colors you add to the swatches in the next exercise bear little resemblance to the original sample points in LAURIE.TIF. What you're doing is correct in the context of the hand-tinting exercise at the end of the chapter. These are special-purpose colors. You'll see how increasing the saturation makes them ideal choices later.

Temporary Changes to the Colors Palette

If this were a long-term project, which it isn't, you probably would want to clear a palette (the default one, for example) and add only the colors you specify. You can delete a color swatch

by pressing Ctrl and clicking over it. Then, after deleting all the default swatches and adding all your custom colors, you can save the palette with a new name. You can reload this newly named custom palette whenever you need to use the colors. But with a simple trick found in the next exercise, you can forego building the custom palette. By placing a "marker" in the rows of color swatches, you can get away with loading a dozen or so colors to the default palette and still remember which colors are the ones you defined.

Adding to the Default Colors Palette

Click on the Eyedropper tool on the toolbox	The tool you use in this exercise.
Click on the default colors icon on the toolbox	Sets foreground color to black, background to white.
Position the cursor over the blank area immediately to the right of the last default color	Turns Eyedropper into a paint bucket-shaped cursor.
Click once	Fills blank area with foreground black color.
Click to the right of the blank you filled in	Creates black swatch in this area, too.
Click to the right of last blank you filled in	Creates a quick visual reference separating the default colors from any new colors.
Click over a dark, skin-colored sample on the scratch pad area	Samples a color you placed on scratch pad area in last exercise.
Click and drag the S slider to 100%	Specifies 100% Saturation for this color.
If the exclamation button (a "flag" that the color you specified can't be reproduced by commercial print presses) appears, click on it	Photoshop automatically moves the color to closest value in the printable range.
Click over the empty space to the right of your black swatches on the Colors palette	Adds this color to swatches.
Click over a slightly darker skin-tone sample on the scratch pad area	Samples another color in same color family as first sample.
Click and drag the S slider to 100%	Specifies 100% Saturation for second color.
Click on the exclamation button if it appears	Moves color to closest value in printable range.
Click to the right of the first skin-tone color you added on the swatches	Adds this color to custom color-swatch collection.

continues

continued

Continue sampling from the scratch pad area, moving the S slider to the right and clicking in empty areas in the swatches area

You are building custom colors according to groups (see fig. 16.3).

Stop after sampling all colors in scratch pad area.

Figure 16.3
Create groups of modified colors in the Colors palette swatches by adding them from samples in the scratch pad area.

You can add sampled colors directly to a palette by simply hold the cursor over a blank portion of the swatches area on the Colors palette, then clicking. And you can replace a color by pressing Alt and clicking over it when you have a foreground color defined. But the point of this exercise is to *organize* colors sampled from the image so that you can find them when you need them later.

By entering samples of the image as little dots in the scratch pad area, you can fine-tune the values, then select the order in which they appear as swatches on the palette. You're forced to enter color samples *sequentially* when you do it directly from an image. I can't imagine that an individual would know exactly which group of colors should be organized on-the-fly this way!

If you checked Restore Windows in Photoshop's General Preferences, the new colors are now a part of the Colors palette swatches collection—until you load another palette. In any event, your palette now sports a very special collection of saturated color swatches from the original LAURIE.TIF image as well as the exact original colors in the scratch pad area. Now, with all the important color information archived, it is time to convert this RGB image to grayscale and to introduce the commands you need to familiarize yourself with to perfect this process.

Converting and Balancing the Black-and-White Image

In the last exercise, you removed the gray component from the sample pixels in the scratch pad area to arrive at only the color components of the LAURIE.TIF color samples. It stands to reason, then, that removing all the *color information* from the *photo* will cause the grayscale information to step in and represent the visual content of the image.

This is exactly what Photoshop does when you switch an RGB image to Grayscale mode. When you make this Mode change, Photoshop pops up a dialog box that asks whether you want to remove all color information from the image. After you answer Yes, Photoshop displays an image that consists only of the *tonal* relationships—the grayscale components—in the image.

Unfortunately, the human eye can't switch modes as Photoshop does; our evaluation of an image's *visual content* is always influenced by color. The LAURIE.TIF image, although pretty and informational in color, is somewhat less evocative when displayed in 256 shades of gray. When color information is mixed with the tonal values, the viewer has a great deal of visual detail to assimilate. But without color information to help separate visual areas, the gray components tend to look too similar, and the image is dull. Lesson number one after you convert an image is to *reevaluate* the visual content and then use Photoshop's filters to correct the tonal balance in the new grayscale image.

When you switch the image's Mode, pay attention to what the happens to Laurie's skintones. In the next exercise, after you convert the image to Grayscale, you define and save an area that needs tonal correction. Then you learn how easily a grayscale image can be selectively balanced for tone.

Switching Modes/Creating Selections To Correct

Choose **M**ode, **G**rayscale	Displays Photoshop exclamation dialog box, which asks whether you want to discard color information.
Choose Yes	LAURIE.TIF image becomes Grayscale image.
Pick the Lasso tool from the toolbox	Tool used to create freehand selection borders in an image.
Click and drag a border around Laurie's face and collar line in the image	Creates selection area that defines image area which needs tonal balance.

continues

continued

Choose **W**indow, Show C**h**annels (or press F6)	Displays Channels palette; click and drag it to place where it doesn't interfere with your view or your work.
Choose **S**elect, Save **S**election	Saves Lasso selection area to new Channel 2.
Click on the #2 title in the Channels palette, click on the command button, then select Channel Options from the drop-down list	Displays Channel Options dialog box for Channel 2.
In the Name: box, type **Face** (or anything you choose), then click on OK	Labels selection channel, so that you can locate it easily later.
Click on the Black Channel title on the Channels palette	Displays grayscale view of LAURIE.TIF, shown in figure 16.4.
Choose **F**ile, **S**ave As, then choose a directory on your hard disk, and name the file **LAURIE.TIF**	Saves changed image to hard disk.

Figure 16.4
Even in a Grayscale image, an area can be saved to an Alpha channel.

This Face channel comes in handy when you start adding special effects to the image. Because LAURIE.TIF is a portrait image, the area of greatest visual interest—the subject's face—needs special handling. You can control the subject using this saved selection, or the inverse of it (Laurie's hair and the background), without affecting the unselected areas.

Balancing and Smoothing an Adjustment

Because a grayscale image contains no colors, the commands for color, hue, and saturation are not available. But the Curves command, which adjusts the relative relationship of pixel brightness, *is* functional in Grayscale mode.

Selecting areas to balance is much easier in a grayscale image than when you work with an RGB image. You don't have to think about color casting or over-saturation. And the Feather command makes an easy job of the transition between edited areas and the background. The next exercise shows how beautifully you can correct the tones in this converted image.

Tonal Balance in a Grayscale Selection

Choose **S**elect, **L**oad Selection, Face	Loads the selection you saved earlier.
Choose **S**elect, Fe**a**ther, type **12** in the **R**adius entry field, then click on OK	Sets feathering to active selection. Feathered border is *not* saved to the Face channel.
Choose **I**mage, **A**djust, then choose **C**urves (or press Ctrl+M)	Displays Curves command.
Check the **P**review box	Enables you to see changes in an image as you map changes to Curves graph.
Place the cursor over the graph on the Curves dialog box, moving it up the graph line until Input and Output are at 178	Upper range of image's quartertone, area that contains highlight information in the image.
Click on the graph line, and drag it straight up until Output reads 194	Heightens tonal value in this range and slightly increases overall range of midtones.
Place the cursor over one of the darker areas on Laurie's face, then click	Defines tonal value on Curves graph (see fig. 16.5). The value in this figure is 44; your value may be different, depending on where you clicked.
Place the cursor on the graph line so that the Input and Output boxes read 44	The tonal area in the photograph you clicked on earlier with the Eyedropper.
Click and drag the line on the graph straight up, until Output reads 56	Decreases contrast in light shadow areas in image, further broadening midtone range, but only in selection area you defined earlier with the Lasso tool.

continues

continued

Click on OK	Confirms selections and redisplays the workspace.
Choose <u>S</u>elect, <u>N</u>one (or press Ctrl+D)	Deselects marquee border in the image.
Choose <u>F</u>ile, <u>S</u>ave	Saves your changes to hard disk.

Figure 16.5
Broadening the midtones in the selection area brightens it and reduces harsh contrast.

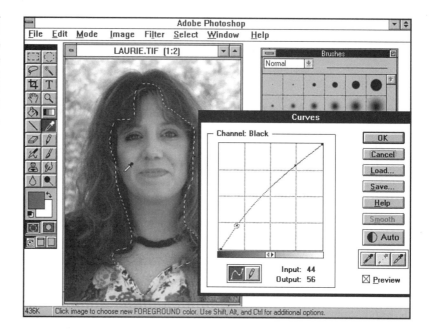

The curve you just designed in the Curves dialog box is not a "conventional" one. It isn't an "S" curve that adds snap to an image, or an inverted "S" that restores detail to a faded or murky image. It is a purely artistic call *that works.* In portraits of men, you can get away with displaying harsh contrasts in the tonal ranges that represent skin tones because a male image typically is thought of as rugged, stark, and full of contrast. But portraits of women should not display such harsh contrasts. By increasing the frequency in the upper quartertone of LAURIE.TIF, you diminished the contrast in the highlight areas of her face; the lower quartertone adjustment also allowed for less contrast.

Feathering Smoothed the Transition

By selecting a fairly broad Feathering radius in the last exercise, you were able to keep the background area of LAURIE.TIF constant and a little harsh. The background now plays nicely off Laurie's soft facial tonal values. Feathering's contribution to this adjustment was to take 12

pixels outside the selection edge and 12 pixels inside the border, and make a gradual tonal transition between them. You don't see the selection border's hard edge in the image, and you have restored a pleasant tonal balance to the most important part of the photo. Feathering a border before tuning tones in a grayscale image is the conventional equivalent to using a really soft-edge cardboard cutout to dodge or burn in an area of photographic paper when you're printing from a negative.

Alpha Channels and the Grayscale Image

Channels in a grayscale image are the same as those in an RGB image, except that, by default, you have one channel (Black) instead of separate Red, Green, and Blue channels. But *extra* channels, such as the one you used to save the Face selection, can hold as many as eight bits of information, just like an Alpha channel in an RGB image. And the magic eight-bits number just happens to be the maximum amount of tonal information in the grayscale image's Black channel!

So you can store an exact copy of a grayscale image in a user-defined Alpha channel. This is great because you can create tonal and effects variations on an image in a channel without ever having to save another copy of the image until you arrive at a particular variation that pleases you.

And you can composite and combine variations of the same image, all in the same image file—which is what you do next, as we explore Photoshop's special-effects filters.

Stylizing Part of a Grayscale Image

The Filters menu in Photoshop comes packed with many dramatic, processor-intensive effects you can apply to selections or to entire images. Although these effects are useful for distorting and randomizing simple still life images, they are absolutely inappropriate to apply full-force to a portrait image.

Nevertheless, if you use your artist's eye to evaluate a portrait image, you can see how applying a *few* of these filters to *parts* of the portrait can produce some interesting artistic effects. The Crystallize filter creates a pebbled, almost painterly effect in an image, and it is only one of many Photoshop filters you may want to experiment with in your imaging work. Although the Crystallize filter destroys much original composition detail in the process, the effect can be "worked into" a portrait image in such a way that the Crystallize filter enhances, rather than disrupts, a pretty picture.

Creating a Painting from an Image

Choose **S**elect, **A**ll (or press Ctrl+A)	Selects entire LAURIE.TIF grayscale image.
Choose **E**dit, **C**opy (or press Ctrl+C)	Sends a copy of entire image to clipboard.
Click on the command button in the Channels palette, then choose New Channel	Displays New Channel Options dialog box.
Click on OK	Accepts default values of New Channel Options; LAURIE.TIF now displays channel view, marked as 3 on Channels palette.
Choose **E**dit, **P**aste (or press Ctrl+V)	Pastes copy of image into new channel. Consider Channel 3 "spare image" to use later.
Click on the command button on the Channels palette again, choose New Channel, then click on OK	New channel, labeled Channel 4, is active view in image.
Choose **E**dit, **P**aste (or press Ctrl+V)	Pastes another copy of entire image in Channel 4 (channel to which you apply Crystallize filter).
Choose **F**ile, Sa**v**e As LAURIE.TIF to your hard disk; make sure the **S**ave Alpha Channels box is checked	Saves your imaging work in preparation for Crystallize filter.
Choose Fil**t**er, Stylize, then choose Crystallize, type **10** in the **C**ell, size field, and click on OK	Sets size of "crystals" you will create out of the image, as shown in figure 16.6.

Wait a little while. Crystallize, like most Stylize commands, is extremely processor-intensive; it takes half a minute or more to execute, even on a fast PC. Why not read ahead while you wait?

Choose **S**elect, **A**ll (or press Ctrl+A), then choose **E**dit, **C**opy (or press Ctrl+C)	Copies entire crystallized selection (see fig. 16.7) to clipboard.
Click on the Black channel (or press Ctrl+1) on the Channels palette	Redisplays main channel view of LAURIE.TIF.
Choose **E**dit, **P**aste (or press Ctrl+V)	Pastes crystallized copy onto original in Black channel.

Set the Brushes palette to Normal mode, then click and drag the Opacity slider to 71%

Blends crystallized copy of Channel 4 into Black channel (see fig. 16.8).

Choose **S**elect, **N**one (or press Ctrl+D)

Composites selection into Black channel; deselects everything in image.

Do not save the image at this point

You need the uncrystallized version as your last saved version for the next exercise.

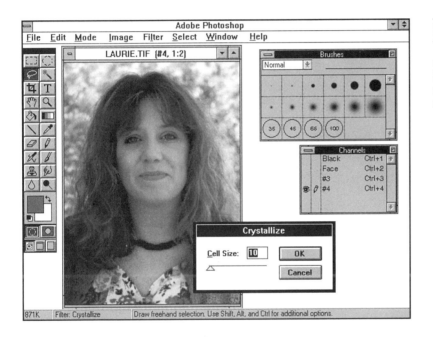

Figure 16.6
To specify the size of the crystals your image is composed of, use the Crystallize filter.

III

Gourmet Assignments

You aren't finished yet! Although it's an interesting, abstract image now, you want to *augment* LAURIE.TIF with the Crystallize effect, not let the effect become the main visual attraction. By combining the Crystallized copy with the original, you have gained a less intense effect. In fact, you may notice that some areas of the combined image now show no strong crystallized effect. You can take advantage of this visual diversity in the image by selectively restoring original image areas to the image from the last saved version of the file—the one you saved just *before* using the Crystallize filter. With the original image still available, you can make this painted version of LAURIE.TIF a photo-realistic painting!

Remember the special property of the Eraser tool? You use it next.

Figure 16.7
The Crystallize
filter creates an
impressionistic
variation of a
digital image.

Figure 16.8
The Brushes
palette's Opacity
setting controls
the degree
of blending
between a
floating
selection and
an original
background
image.

Erasing Back to Last-Saved Versions

Pick the Eraser tool from the toolbox	Tool used to erase foreground image areas.
Press Alt while you click and drag the Eraser tool over Laurie's face in the image	Toggles Eraser tool's function to expose last-saved version of image, rather than background color (see fig. 16.9).
Stop when you have "erased" enough crystallized image area to expose the facial details in the original Black channel	Creates effect of portrait gently fading to rough, impressionistic paint strokes in unimportant detail areas.
Choose **F**ile, **S**ave	Saves your work to hard disk.

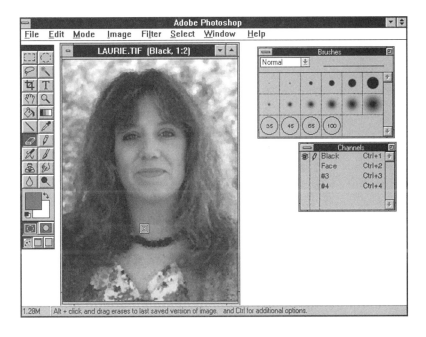

Figure 16.9
The Eraser tool restores original image areas, but only back to the last-saved version of an image.

The Eraser tool's work would be obvious if you hadn't *blended* a crystallized version into the original first, to lessen the effect in the image. The Eraser tool, unlike the Paintbrush tool, has no soft-edge option, and you cannot set a size to it.

Another way to perform this last exercise is to take a Snapshot of the Black channel before pasting the crystallized copy into it. To do so, choose **E**dit, T**a**ke Snapshot. These commands load a copy you can work from into system RAM that the Rubber Stamp tool can work with.

continues

Take the Snapshot, then double-click on the Rubber Stamp tool, and select *From Snapshot* as the Rubber Stamp Option. Then you can set Brushes tips and Opacity for cloning the original image back into the blend of the Black and crystallized image.

This technique is processor-intensive because Photoshop has to hold an additional image (to work from) in system RAM.

The Pen-and-Ink Grayscale Photo

Textures can be combined with grayscale images to produce other effects that simulate natural renderings, rather than photography. A texture can be created in Photoshop, created in another program (like Fractal Design's Painter), or you can acquire an image by scanning one, or purchasing a texture image file from a host of vendors.

The next exercise shows you how to apply a humanistic, line-drawing type of effect, using a texture of grain as another source to be applied to the LAURIE.TIF image. But instead of compositing it into the original, you'll load it as a selection, much like you did with the actor's finger shadows in Chapter 15.

By using the texture as grayscale information in an Alpha channel, you create a *partial mask*, and you then adjust the tonal balance of the Black channel with this selection Loaded to create an effect. The next exercise shows you how.

If you want to save the image now, save it under a different file name and close the image. Reopen LAURIE.TIF from your hard disk (the version you saved before the Crystallize process). Keep the number of extra channels in a grayscale image to the bare minimum in your imaging work. This means only keeping channels for the purpose of seeing the variations you've created. Three or four Alpha channels are reasonable for a grayscale image, but additional ones slow down your work because your system has to hold the grayscale and the Alpha channel information in system RAM while you work.

If you want to dive right into the next exercise without saving, however, press Alt and click with the Eraser tool over the entire Black channel now, removing the Crystallize effect completely.

Creating a Hand-Drawn Image

Open the TEXTURE3.TIF image from the companion CD	File you will add to LAURIE.TIF image.
Choose **S**elect, **A**ll (or press Crtl+A), then **E**dit, **C**opy (or press Ctrl+C)	Copies entire texture image to Clipboard.
Click on the title bar to the LAURIE.TIF image	Makes image the active window in Photoshop.

Click on the Channel #4 title on the Channels palette	Texture will replace image information (crystallized image) in this channel.
Choose **E**dit, **P**aste (or press Ctrl+V)	Pastes copy of texture into Channel 4 (see fig. 16.10).
Click on the Black channel on the Channels palette	Restores view to grayscale channel of LAURIE.TIF. A copy of the portrait that's been tonally corrected, but not Crystallized should be in this channel before you proceed.
Choose **S**elect, **L**oad Selection, then choose #4	Loads texture Channel 4 as selection (see fig. 16.11).
Choose **I**mage, **A**djust, then Brightness/Contrast (or press Ctrl+B)	Displays Brightness/Contrast dialog box.
Enter **+48** for Brightness, **+71** for Contrast (or use the sliders), then click on OK	Increases Brightness and Contrast of only selection areas in LAURIE.TIF image.
Choose **S**elect, **N**one (or press Ctrl+D)	Deselects everything in image.
Choose **I**mage, **A**djust, then Brightness/Contrast (or press Ctrl+B) again	Displays Brightness/Contrast dialog box.
Enter **+2** for Brightness, **+36** for Contrast (or use the sliders), then click on OK	Adds to contrast of original selection area and creates more contrast in overall image (see fig. 16.12).
Choose **F**ile, **S**ave	Saves your work to your hard disk.

As you saw in this exercise, when you save a tonal image to a channel, the variations in its tonal values can be used to affect only certain areas when it's Loaded as a Selection. In this example the Brightness/Contrast editing, based on the same tonal densities as the selection marquees, brought out the texture of the selection. Then forcing the contrast with the Brightness/Contrast controls, when the entire Black image channel was selected, produced the pen-and-ink effect.

The companion CD has other texture samples in the TEXTURES subdirectory you can experiment with in your own assignments.

III

Gourmet Assignments

Figure 16.10
You can use an entire image as a selection in a channel.

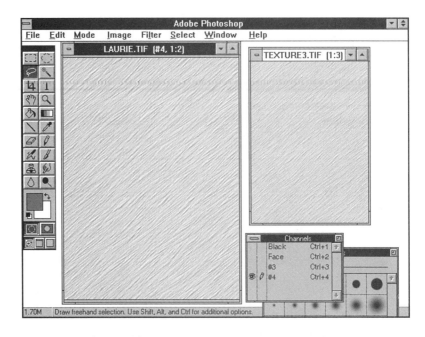

Figure 16.11
The levels of brightness in the texture image serve as selection borders in the Black channel image.

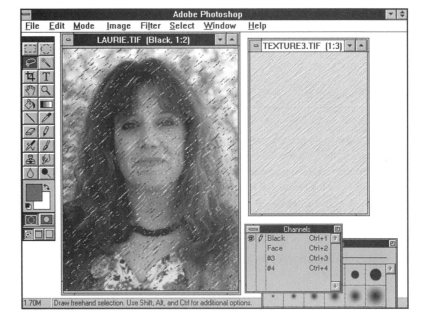

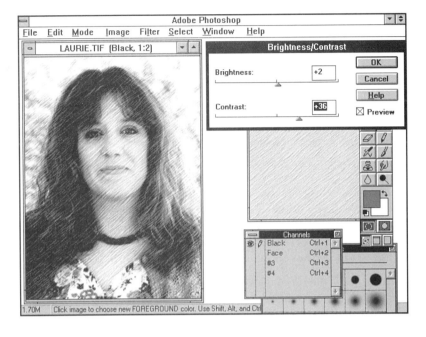

Figure 16.12
Each Brightness/
Contrast
adjustment you
make is relative
to a preceding
adjustment.

Why Grayscale Is Sometimes Better for Effects

The human eye is subliminally attracted to a color image over a grayscale one, often for the
wrong reasons. The eye is attracted to flashy hues and saturated color areas and often
overlooks poor composition in a color image. When you look at a grayscale image, which
contains no distracting color information, you are forced to analyze the image solely on its
visual detail. The special effects you are working with in this chapter are particularly effective
when applied to an image that only contains visual detail, and spares the viewer the distraction
of the element of color. Photoshop's Filters work as artistic enhancements within grayscale
images for the following reasons:

✔ Shifting the focal point in a color photo by adding a special effect is almost impossible.
The eye is drawn primarily to an interesting color area and registers an effect as a
secondary consideration.

✔ Blending a special effect into a grayscale image is much easier than blending it into a
color image. You don't have to worry about matching saturation and hue values
between special and not-so-special areas of the image because there are no hues!

Think about the uses you have for black and white photography in everyday assignments.
When the budget is tight for a flyer or newsletter, process color printing is out of the question.
And that puts the brunt of the printed material's attraction on the composition of art and
photographic images. So why not make them as eye-catching as possible with a few Photoshop
effects?

Tidying Up Your Channels

You need to do a little housecleaning again before you create the next effect. If you followed these exercises in sequence, you should now have the following:

✔ A pen-and-ink effect in the Black channel of LAURIE.TIF

✔ A Face channel that contains a selection border you created earlier

✔ A copy of the original image on Channel #3

✔ A texture image in Channel #4

If you want to save the pen-and-ink effect now, copy the Black channel to the Clipboard, open a new file, paste the effect in there, and save it as a TIFF image with a different name than LAURIE.TIF. You may have noticed that, by default, Photoshop automatically creates new files to the dimensions and image mode of what is stored in the Clipboard—which makes saving a copy on occasions such as this a no-fuss operation.

After you've decided the fate of the pen-and-ink-effect image, choose **S**elect, **A**ll in Channel #3, then copy it to the Black channel. Then delete Channel #4 (the texture selection) and rename Channel #3, calling it **Copy**. When you do this, you do away with extraneous channels, reduce the size of the LAURIE.TIF file, and have everything clearly labeled in the channels.

The Zoom Blur Effect

You've seen how to use the Gaussian Blur effectively to create convincing shadows in images. But Photoshop has *other* Blur Filters in that also come in handy. Each one can be applied in different ways to achieve a special look.

The Radial Blur comes in two flavors—Spin and Zoom. The Zoom is particularly nice because it does a faithful reproduction of the "rack/zoom" effect photographers use to focus the center of attention on an area in an image. This effect is difficult to achieve in real time in conventional photography because your subject doesn't always remain motionless while the camera squeezes off a relatively long exposure time.

With Photoshop's Radial Blur, you can pick the focal center of the blur. But the Radial Blur Options box lets you define only a small central area of the image that remains in focus. This is not a problem, because you made and stored a selection of Laurie's face in a channel. Inverting the Face selection (which protects her face from change) enables you to apply as much blurring as you like to the rest of the image. The next exercise shows you how this is done.

The "Forced" Focal Point of an Image

Click on the Black channel title in the Channels palette	Displays view of grayscale image in LAURIE.TIF.
Choose **S**elect, **L**oad Selection, then choose Face	Loads selection marquee-designed earlier in this chapter.
Choose **S**elect, **I**nverse	Inverts marquee border so that current selection excludes Laurie's face and includes rest of image and background (see fig. 16.13).
Choose **S**elect, Fea**t**her, make sure that value is set to **12**, then click on OK	Confirms that Feather Radius value is set to 12 pixels, last value you set it.
Choose Fi**l**ter, **B**lur, then choose Radial Blur	Displays Radial Blur dialog box (see fig. 16.14).
Set Blur Method to **Z**oom, Quality to **B**est, type **10** in **A**mount field, then click on OK	Sets parameters for blur.

Be patient. The effect is processor-intensive, as most Filters are.

Choose **S**elect, **N**one (or press Ctrl+D)	Deselects marqueed area; image should resemble the one in figure 16.15.
Choose **F**ile, **S**ave	Saves your work to your hard disk.

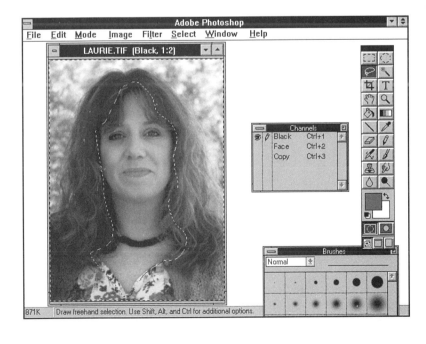

Figure 16.13

Use the Inverse command to allow only the background in the image to be selected.

III

Gourmet Assignments

Figure 16.14
The quality of the Radial Blur is a function of processing time. The longer the processing, the better the results.

Figure 16.15
The Zoom Radial Blur forces the focus of the image on the subject.

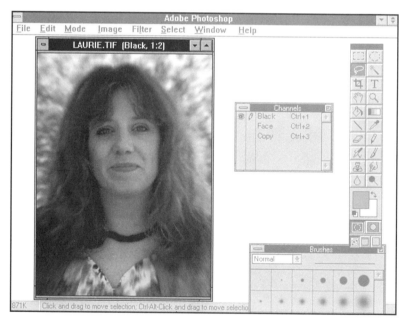

To avoid a telltale selection border when you applied the powerful Radial Blur effect to the image's background, the Feather command came to the rescue again.

The Radial Blur, like the Gaussian and Stylize Filters, needs to use as much of your system's resources as possible to execute an effect. Some heavy-duty interpolation is going on behind the digital scenes. Which is sort of reason number two and a half why grayscale images and special effects go hand in hand—executing this sort of Filter on an RGB image would require a lot more processing power, and possibly swapping out to hard disk if you don't have a lot of system RAM. Anytime you swap to hard disk, the time it takes to accomplish the effect increases substantially.

Black and White in Your Profession

With any luck, this chapter's excursion into converting, balancing, and applying special effects to the Grayscale image has given you some insights and you can put the tips to practical use. Because very few run-of-the-mill photofinishing places do custom work on black and white images these days, people are likely to hand you a *color* image for a newsletter or other in-house organ.

A typical example of this situation was a black and white corporate annual report we worked on. The photos submitted for the report were an odd assortment of black and white *and* color images. Scanning everything with a grayscale scanner would have been a quick, one-step solution to converting the color photos for placement in a desktop publishing document destined for one-color printing. But the results of grayscale scanning would have made the report look amateurish. The board members' RGB portraits would have been converted in an *unweighted* fashion to 256 grayscale shades which would have emphasized skin blemishes, muddied the highlights in their eyes, and made the printed product resemble a photocopy. Instead, we scanned the color photos in color, then used the same Photoshop techniques you have learned in this chapter to quickly reveal and balance gray components. Happy client, handsome report, professionally finished digital photographs.

Black and white printing is still a popular medium, for technological and monetary reasons. If you know how to make the most of the Grayscale image, your talents will always be in demand in the business community.

Picking Colors for a Grayscale Image

For video slide shows, avant garde presentations, and the simple pleasures of restoring a monochrome family photo, Photoshop offers you the capability of hand-tinting a grayscale image. At the beginning of the chapter, you sampled the predominant colors in the RGB version of LAURIE.TIF and learned how to modify and save the colors to your Colors palette. These digital tints are good for hand-coloring the grayscale version of LAURIE.TIF because they are based on the original image.

If you intend to hand-tint an image when you *have* no original RGB values to sample, take samples from a different RGB image that contains the range of colors you want in your hand-tinted image. Follow the steps outlined at the beginning of the chapter for creating and saving these colors as "pure dyes."

If you rely solely on your eyes to get the right shade of skin tones for hand-tinting, the chore is laden with "ifs." Time and experience will show you that sampling a natural color is easier than trying to create a color. As color-enabled humans, we are drawn to the point of distraction by colors that are too brilliant and vibrant to be natural. If you doubt me, think about all the detergent boxes and flashy sports cars sold in America!

Grayscale Goes to RGB

In the next exercise, you need to convert the Grayscale LAURIE.TIF image back to RGB mode (and you know that a mode change is permanent). Switching from Grayscale to RGB mode does not restore original colors. Photoshop *converts* images between modes.

The mode switch you'll make from Grayscale to RGB in the next exercise allows Photoshop to expand the color capacity of the image and express up to 16.7 million possible shades of color, including the 256 grayscale tones already in the image. You'll also set the Brushes palette to use Color mode instead of Normal mode when you apply any of the colors from the swatches you defined earlier. Painting in this Brushes mode changes the hue and saturation of the pixels you paint over, but does not affect the *luminosity* (the measure of brilliance) in the pixels. In other words, the gray levels in the LAURIE.TIF image are preserved when you tint them.

You should restart Windows with a 16.7 million color-capable video driver loaded before you start the next exercise if you aren't using a 16.7 million (TrueColor) driver already.

Color-Enabling a Grayscale Image

Switch to the Copy Channel in the Channels palette

Displays view of copy of original LAURIE.TIF image.

Choose **S**elect, **A**ll (or press Ctrl+A)

Copies Copy channel to Clipboard.

The next step is optional:

Save LAURIE.TIF to a new file name if you want to save the version with the Radial Blur. Then open the previously saved version of LAURIE.TIF from your hard disk. You don't have to save the blurred version, but if you want to, this is your last chance. The next step destroys it by pasting original copy over it.

Click on the Black channel title in the Channels palette

Displays view of Radial Blur image created earlier.

Select **E**dit, **P**aste (or press Ctrl+V)	Copies Copy image into Black channel.
Click on the Copy channel title in the Channels palette, click on the command button, then select Delete Channel	Removes Copy channel from LAURIE.TIF image file and displays Black channel.
Click on the Face channel title in the Channels palette, click on the command button, then select Delete Channel	Removes Face channel from LAURIE.TIF image file and displays Black channel.
Choose **M**ode, RGB	Converts Grayscale LAURIE.TIF image to an RGB image. Colors palette again displays color; Channels palette has three color channels (in addition to the color composite channel).
Select the Paintbrush tool, select **Color** mode from the Brushes palette drop-down list, click and drag the Opacity slider to **23**%, choose the last Brushes tip on the second row as your brush tip	Sets characteristics of Paintbrush tool to apply color broadly, with a very mild concentration.
Click on a skin tone color you defined earlier on the Colors palette	Chooses a saturated color to paint with Color mode with the Paintbrush tool.
Click and drag over the facial areas in the LAURIE.TIF image until you have covered all the facial area	Applies flesh tint to image. Do not release mouse button until entire area you intend to cover is covered.
Click on a darker skin tone you defined earlier on the Color palette	Color you will apply to shaded facial areas in image.
Click and drag the Opacity slider on the Brushes palette to **16**%	Reduces coverage of Paintbrush tool, prevents mottling between new Paintbrush stroke and previous one.
Click and drag over areas you already tinted, which are shaded darker with grayscale component	Applies deeper color tint over previously tinted image area.
Click on a color swatch (on the Colors palette) that represents the original leafy background area	Selects foreground color with which Paintbrush will fill some background image areas.
Set the Opacity on the Brushes palette to **23**%, then click and drag in the background area of the LAURIE.TIF image	Applies stronger shade of tint to background of image (see fig. 16.16).

continues

III

Gourmet Assignments

continued

Continue applying tints to the image, reducing the Brushes Opacity when you click and drag over an already tinted area	You are well on the way to creating a digital hand-tinted image.
Choose **F**ile, **S**ave	Saves your work to your hard disk.

Figure 16.16
Reduce the Opacity of the Brush tip when you tint over an image area you have already tinted.

The biggest secret to creating an authentic-looking hand tint from a black-and-white image is to keep the Opacity on the Brushes palette set to less than 30 percent, dropping way back into the teens when you apply tint over an area that *already* contains some tint. In Color mode, Photoshop's "virtual" tints behave like real world tints. Progressively stroking in the same areas produces a mottling effect around the edges of an area in which the two tints saturate each other. Reduce the opacity and play with different-sized Brushes tips in your tinting. The spread amount, which you can reset by double-clicking on a Brush tip, contributes greatly to an extremely naturalistic effect.

Summary

Working with grayscale images doesn't have to be an uninspired task, as this chapter has shown you. And if you have a laser printer capable of at least 600 dpi, the printed results of your labors can be immediately gratifying. When your client has a modest imaging need, you now have the tools and some understanding of techniques to far surpass this client's expectations. If you are a dyed-in-the-wool photographer just adopting some of the new computer-imaging powers, Photoshop might be your very last stop for digital equivalents of familiar real world imaging tools. And the cross-over between color and grayscale is effortless with Photoshop. Most of the tools and effects featured throughout this book can be applied identically to both grayscale and RGB images.

Grayscale images are a pleasure to work with. You can perform the same magic with them as you do with color images. And if you're a really *good* magician, your work will call attention to the *results*, not to the effect or the tools used. And that's called mastering a *technique*.

Part IV

Fantastic Assignments

Chapter Snapshot

In this chapter, you learn how to:

Integrating Applications with Photoshop

O nly recently has the PC world enjoyed the tight integration of different software
applications that Macintosh users have had. Microsoft Windows was the first step
toward establishing common conventions that applications could adopt, so that users
could cut and paste between applications. Then an incredible thing happened. Application
developers actually started talking to each other! This led to the TWAIN standard, which many
manufacturers currently follow. You can scan directly into any Windows application that
features this standard.

Just as importantly, the files created in many Windows applications can be imported to
Photoshop. Two programs highlighted in this chapter, PIXAR Typestry and CorelDRAW!, can
be used to your advantage in your Photoshop work. Typestry can generate three-dimensional,
realistically lit text. You can control the "stage lighting" and the "skin" you place on text.
Typestry produces eye-catching, almost startlingly realistic TIFF or BMP files from TrueType
or Type 1 typefaces.

CorelDRAW! has long been called the "Swiss Army Knife" of design programs, and for good reason. This vector-based application also "speaks" the TIFF format. Because it additionally speaks Adobe PostScript Type 1 and Windows TrueType formats, you can design an illustration in Corel, export it as a typeface to Typestry, work on it there, and produce a design element for your Photoshop work! Do you see where this is leading?

Creating Newsworthy Images

For some time, television stations have used proprietary computer software running on special computers to produce station identification and news bulletin "billboards." These graphics were produced with extremely expensive applications designed for RISC-based computers (Reduced Instruction Set Commands).

PIXAR markets its own class of workstation, which runs proprietary software that the motion picture industry uses to wow audiences. The entry-level PC system requirements for PIXAR's Typestry program, however, are about the same as those for Photoshop. And although Typestry is not as feature-laden as a high-end imaging application, it excels at producing wonderful results with type.

Typestry's only requirement for creating textured, dimensional, dramatically lit text is that you use a Type 1 or TrueType typeface. The assignment in this chapter is to create a weather bulletin for a fictitious television station, using two Typestry-rendered TIFF images. A unique typeface would be nice, though. Something a tad more special than Times New Roman!

This is where a third application comes into play, and where this chapter's work begins. CorelDRAW! is an exceedingly versatile design program and a handy companion to your Photoshop work. CorelDRAW! is a vector program that can export vector file information, raster information (bit maps, TIFF images), and even supports font information! You can create a typeface in CorelDRAW!, export it to be used by Typestry, then enhance the fruits of your labors in Photoshop.

The first part of this chapter is a behind-the-scene view of the how-tos with CorelDRAW! and Typestry. You don't have to have the programs—the ride's on us in this first part (the file we ultimately produced is on the companion CD). If you do have these applications as well as Photoshop, however, feel free to follow along! In the second part of this chapter, you fit the Typestry files (found on the companion CD) to another image using Photoshop. The assignment is to take PIXAR's rendered TIFF image files of the CorelDRAW! typeface, and bring them into Photoshop, where you'll composite them into a background TIFF image of a stormy sky. Then you'll add a few special effects to this fake weather bulletin to make it look as professional as those billboards you see on TV!

The adventure begins in CorelDRAW!'s workspace.

CorelDRAW!-ing a Font

First, the custom typeface needs to be created for a hypothetical television station—WXYZ, Channel 3, in sunny Mount Morris, New York. The best way to create a unique typeface is to base it on one that already exists. We're not condoning font "piracy." Rather, what you can do here is *modify* a typeface. (Font foundries and the law take a dim view of appropriating someone else's design!)

Bold, italic lettering is ideal for station call letters. Eras Black (manufactured by Bitstream for ITC) is a novel choice, but it doesn't seem to have an italic version. No problem. You can type the call letters in CorelDRAW!, and then click on them to perform a skew—the same effect as the one featured in Photoshop. Figure 17.1 shows the lettering setup for skewing.

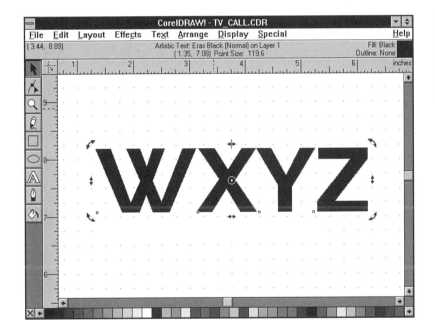

Figure 17.1
Like Photoshop and Typestry, CorelDRAW! can "read" Type 1 and TrueType fonts.

After the WXYZ characters have been skewed, they are converted to graphics (which means that the phrase can no longer be edited). The conversion to graphics is necessary because a Contour effect can be applied only to a graphical object in CorelDRAW!. *Contouring* is an automatic process that draws an outline around an object in steps and widths you can define. Because the station call letters would be more striking if they were a little bolder, the next step is to apply a .07-inch Contour to each individual graphical object, starting with the "W" (see fig. 17.2).

IV

Fantastic Assignments

Figure 17.2
Contouring an
object repeats
its outline,
"thickening"
the piece.

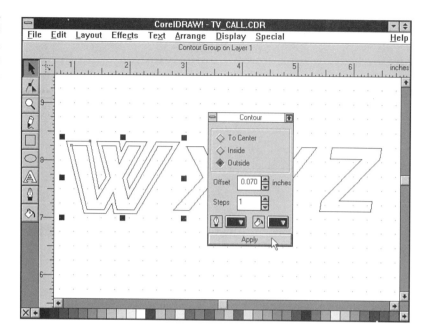

Creating the Station Bullet

Networks usually like their station number inside a bullet that they can use on the side of microphones, trucks, and particularly next to their call letters. A numeral 3 was set in Peignot Bold, centered in a circle, and then the two objects were combined to produce a good, clean graphic. That left the bullet and the call letters—for a total of five objects to export as a typeface (see fig. 17.3).

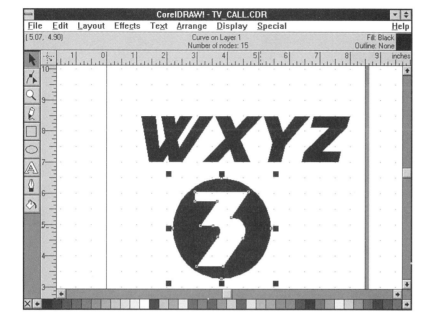

Figure 17.3
Graphical objects
can be exported
as typeface
characters, using
CorelDRAW!

Exporting Graphics as Type

By selecting one object, and then selecting File+Export, CorelDRAW! offers a number of
different file formats for exporting. For this example, I have chosen the TrueType format (see
related Note), a new typeface name (StationType), and the character (3), which is my first
typeface character export. As you can see from figure 17.4, the procedure is fairly automatic.

I have chosen TrueType as the typographic format because I intend to delete
StationType after Typestry has created its contribution to this assignment.
StationType's only purpose is to give Typestry specific font metrics information
so that the program can render an image.

Although CorelDRAW! can also export characters to create a typeface in the
Adobe Type 1 PostScript descriptor language, removing TrueType from a hard
drive is easier than going through Adobe Type Manager, uninstalling a font,
and then deleting the typeface from File Manager.

IV

Fantastic Assignments

Figure 17.4
StationType is the
TrueType font
face; the character
is set as the
keystroke "3."

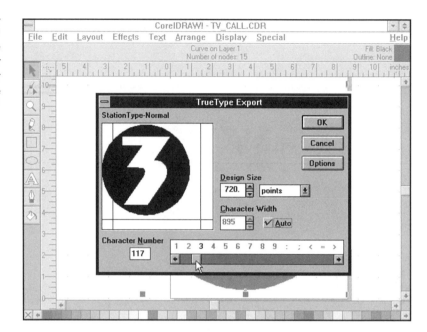

Figure 17.4
StationType is the TrueType font face; the character is set as the keystroke "3."

Sizing Up the Background

After the five characters are exported as the StationType font, a quick trip to the Windows Control Panel to install the font is in order. If you're following along with your own copy of Typestry in this assignment, here's the trick to creating the graphic to fit in the stormy sky TIFF image:

Before opening Typestry to design the station logo, you need to measure the dimensions of the STORMSKY.TIF background image in Photoshop. Typestry creates a bit-mapped image from font metric information. Although Typestry can render a TIFF file out of a font to any dimension, the final TIFF file is resolution-dependent. The best move is to tell Typestry to render the type at its final size for work in Photoshop. If you don't measure the dimensions to make sure that they fit within the background image, you are forced to resize the Typestry files. In that case, Photoshop rearranges (interpolates) the pixels, which invariably degrades image quality.

Next (in Photoshop), open STORMSKY.TIF and press Ctrl+R to display rulers around the active image area (see fig. 17.5). You want to tuck the WXYZ logotype into the lower right corner of this image. As you can see from the vertical ruler, 2.5 inches is a good size for the station call-letter type. The horizontal ruler shows that the overall width of the background image is 5 inches and a squeak, which is important to know when you render the *main* title, the second piece of graphical text for this weather forecast bulletin.

Additionally, to eliminate any need for resizing, the resolution of the Typestry image should match that of STORMSKY.TIF. To find the resolution of the image in STORMSKY.TIF, press Alt and left-click over the image size on the Status Bar. As you can see in figure 17.5, the resolution is 150 pixels/inch.

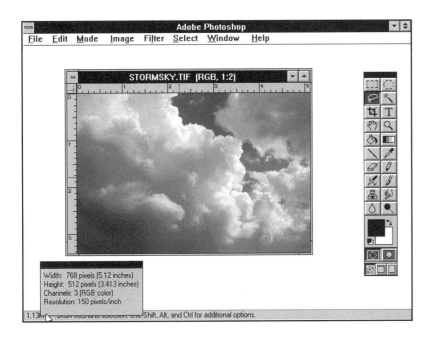

Figure 17.5
Press Alt and click the left mouse button to reveal image size and resolution on the Status Bar's image-size window.

In Photoshop, a simple left click of the mouse (with no key held down) over the file size box displays the proportions of the image that would print on an 8 1/2 by 11-inch page. A gray border shows where the "bleed" for most printers will cut off the image.

If you press Ctrl while you left-click over the active image's file size on the Status Bar, Photoshop displays information about the image's tile size. This information pertains to the way an image is redrawn on the screen whenever you call up a file. Don't worry about tile information unless you're grouting a new kitchen wall or something!

Weaving a Tapestry out of Type

Now that you know how wide the text can be, the next stop is Typestry. Although you can design some rich graphics in Typestry, it is a fairly "hands-off" program. You set some parameters, then Typestry renders the image (giving you about a 10-minute coffee break). In figure 17.6, the Image Format is set to 5" by 3" with a resolution of 150 pixels/inch, then tapping on the workspace with Typestry's Text Tool cursor activates the text field entry box for the program. The Text Object menu is where you type the station call letters, specify the CorelDRAW! StationType face that was created, and set the width and type of bevel on the face of each character object.

Figure 17.6
In both Photoshop and Typestry, text is entered in a dialog box and not directly on the image.

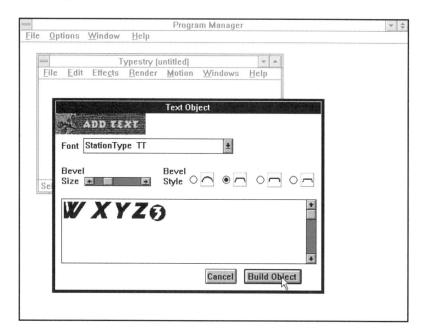

PIXAR's tool palettes are slightly different from Photoshop's; they float over Program Manager or any other Windows program shell you may have installed. By pressing the appropriate key combinations, you can display Looks and Lights palettes and select a texture, light position, and light color for the final render of the scene. Typestry also features a 3D cursor that can rotate the text object to various pitch, yaw, and roll positions relative to the "camera" position.

In this example, Brushed Chrome was chosen for the WXYZ type, with a deep blue Plastic for the number 3 bullet; the type is extruded to make it look powerful and attention-getting. Lighting the type with various key lights that have colored gels on them adds some flair to the brushed-chrome Look. Figure 17.7 shows the wireframe view of the type; creating it involved all of about five minutes of tinkering.

If you are uncertain about a look or the lighting, you can save rendering time by previewing a piece in Typestry. *Rendering*, which is covered in more detail in Chapter 18, is fundamentally the rasterizing of mathematical information. CAD designs, EPS images, and CorelDRAW! vector designs are all examples of images that must be rendered (or rasterized) before they can be viewed.

You can tell Typestry to show you a preview of the WXYZ logo before creating the final TIFF image for use in Photoshop. Figure 17.8 shows a test image rendered to screen on top of the

wireframe view. It looks fine and is ready for a final rendering of the scene to the TIFF format that can be used in Photoshop.

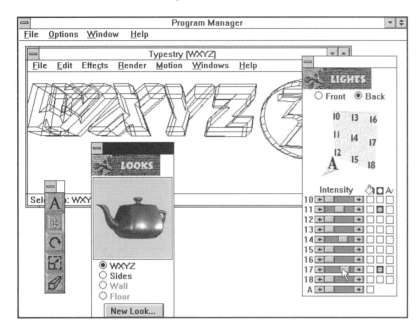

Figure 17.7
Looks and lighting are applied to a wireframe of text in Typestry.

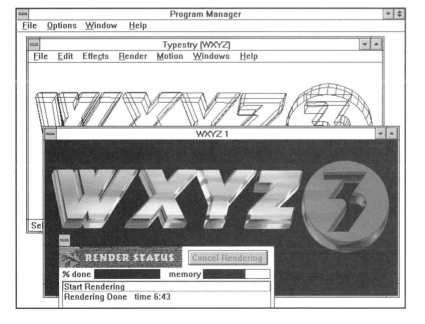

Figure 17.8
Typestry can render a high-resolution test image to the screen before rendering the final scene to a file.

IV

Fantastic Assignments

Channels, Channels Everywhere

The particularly easy thing about creating a Typestry image to work with in Photoshop is that both programs understand channels. As you know, channels play a prominent role in Photoshop work. Because Typestry can save an object's outline and shadow to an Alpha channel, you don't need to use Photoshop's tools on the image to separate the foreground text image from its background.

In Photoshop, the terms *Alpha channel*, a *user-defined channel*, and *Saved Selection* are synonymous. To software developers, an *Alpha channel* is an extra one, added to an image's RGB color information channels. Alpha channels are capable of holding 256 levels of shade densities (usually considered grayscale information), which only Photoshop, Typestry, and a few other image-editing programs support.

Cleaning these channels out of a TIFF image is important when you are going to send copies of the image to someone who will view them in a normal image-viewing program. Norton Desktop Viewer, for instance, is a wonderful image and text-file utility that is unaware of Alpha channels. If you try to view a TIFF image that contains extra channels and paths in Norton Desktop Viewer, the utility gags, churns, then blows up.

The Changing Faces of the Weather

Part 2 of the Typestry adventure created the title for the fictitious TV station's bulletin. There was no need to create a custom typeface, though, because Serpentine Bold-Italic looks extremely contemporary and powerful, and complements the WXYZ logotype. To create the title shown in figure 17.9, you would specify Gray Granite as the look for the phrase, light the text object a little differently, and put a spin on it so that the bottom of the extruded type comes forward slightly. The color scheme of the WXYZ image is simple and needs to contrast with the stormy sky it will be blended into in this chapter's assignment.

Figure 17.9
Rendering a type-
face in Typestry is
automatic. No
user input is
required after the
Render to File
command is
issued.

Bringing the Pieces Together

Now, with the assignment's components rendered and saved, it's time for a Photoshop exercise in selecting and copying. Selecting the station logo is effortless because of the extra information channel—the Alpha channel Typestry created from the outlines of the text objects to mask the type.

Since Typestry uses the RGB image's Alpha channel to save *masking* information, you'll need to reverse this in Photoshop to make the Alpha channel represent *selection* information. But this is a simple operation, very much like the steps you took if you did the exercise in chapter 15.

In Photoshop, open the STORMSKY.TIF and WXYZ.TIF files from the companion CD. You are going to build a bulletin graphic worthy of a television network!

Getting a Handle on Alphabet Soup

Click on the title bar of WXYZ.TIF

Makes WXYZ.TIF the active image window.

Choose **W**indow+Show c**h**annels (or press F6)

Displays channels palette in workspace.

continues

continued

Click on the channel #4 title in the Channels (press Ctrl+4)	Displays active view of the Alpha (extra palette information) channel Typestry created.
Click on the command button on the Channels palette, then select Channel Options from the drop-down list	Displays the Channel Options dialog box.
Click on the Selected Areas radio button in the Color Indicates field of the options box	Makes the colored areas (the black ones) in the Alpha channel (#4) the selection areas instead of masked areas (see figure 7.10).
Click on OK	Confirms your selection, Channel 4 inverts color areas, and you are returned to Photoshop's workspace.
Click on RGB Channel (or press Ctrl+0) on the Channels palette	Redisplays full-color view of WXYZ.TIF file.
Choose **S**elect, Load **S**election	Loads the selection area you just inverted, and the WXYZ lettering is selected.
Choose **E**dit, **C**opy (or press Ctrl+C)	Copies selection area from RGB channel to Clipboard.
Minimize WXYZ.TIF (click on the down arrow at the upper right of the image window)	Makes WXYZ.TIF file an icon at bottom left of Photoshop workspace; STORMSKY.TIF becomes active image window.
Press Ctrl and the plus key	Zooms STORMSKY.TIF image to a 2:1 viewing resolution.
Scroll to the lower right corner of STORMSKY.TIF image	Area where you will paste.
Choose **E**dit, **P**aste (or press Ctrl+V)	Pastes WXYZ.TIF selection into STORMSKY.TIF.
Click and drag the selection to the bottom right of STORMSKY.TIF	Position it to resemble figure 17.11.
Choose **S**elect, **N**one (or press Ctrl+D)	Deselects pasted selection.
Choose **F**ile, Sa**v**e As, then pick a spot on your hard disk and name the file **STORMSKY.TIF**	Saves your work to hard disk.

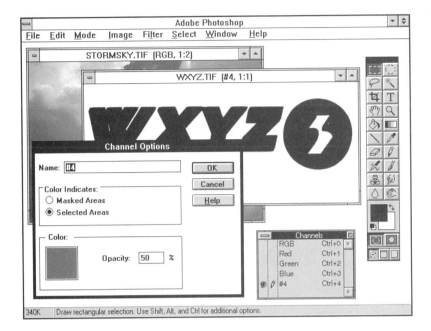

Figure 17.10
Choose Color Indicates: Selected Areas, to make the Alpha channel information create a selection out of a mask.

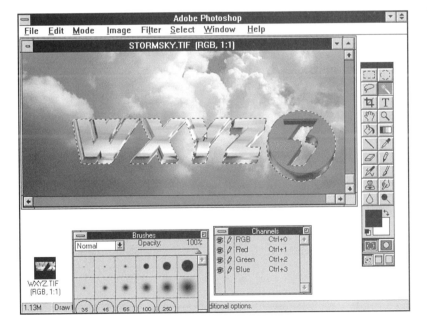

Figure 17.11
Don't deselect or click outside a selection's border until the selection is positioned where you want it to be!

IV

Fantastic Assignments

Always remember that Photoshop defines a mask as the inverse of a selection area. We wanted you to see how Photoshop redefines the black color area when you made the selection from the Channel Options dialog box in the last exercise. It really isn't necessary in your own work to view the Alpha channel in order to make this switch.

The next exercise shows you an even easier way to select PIXAR Typestry's text object out of the background. Load UPDATE.TIF, the second Typestry image from the companion CD, and take a look.

Foreground Forecasting

Open the UPDATE.TIF image
from the companion CD

Choose **S**elect-**L**oad Selection	Loads the background area from the Alpha channel Typestry built into this image (see fig. 17.12).
Choose **S**elect, **I**nverse	Reverses selection area; now PIXAR's text object is selected.
Choose **E**dit, **C**opy (or press Ctrl+C)	Copies selection to Clipboard.
Minimize UPDATE.TIF (Click on the down arrow in the upper-right corner of the window)	Makes UPDATE.TIF an icon at the bottom of the workspace; STORMSKY.TIF becomes the active image.
Choose **E**dit, **P**aste (or press Ctrl+V)	Pastes selection into STORMSKY.TIF.
Click and drag the selection to the upper center of STORMSKY.TIF	Titles belong in this area (see fig. 17.13).
Choose **S**elect, **S**ave Selection	Creates a new Channel #4 that contains the "Weather Update" selection border in the same position as the full-color selection in the RGB channel.
Choose **S**elect, **S**ave Selection, and then click on New	Creates duplicate of last selection, also in exactly the same position relative to the pasted color selection.
Choose **S**elect, **N**one (Ctrl+D)	Deselects pasted selection. Life is good.
Choose **F**ile, **S**ave (or press Ctrl+S)	Saves your work to hard disk.

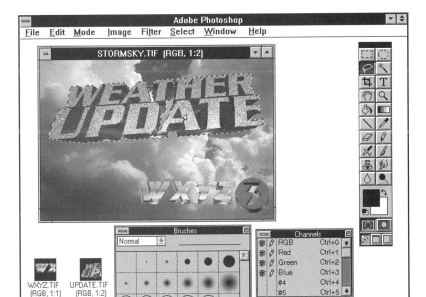

Figure 17.12
The inverse of the desired area is selected when you choose **S**elect, **L**oad Selection.

Figure 17.13
When you position the pasted selection, give it enough "air" around the edges (no pun intended).

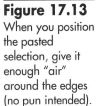

The roles of selection areas and masks are reversible in your imaging work. Although Typestry always defines its Alpha channel in the finished rendered TIFF file as a mask, you can invert the selection area in the channel, as you did in the first chapter exercise. You can also leave Typestry's Alpha work alone, and simply choose the **S**elect, **I**nverse command when viewing the image from the RGB composite Channel view, as you did in the last exercise.

There may be times when you *want* a mask instead of a selection in your work. If, for instance, you wanted to copy the STORMSKY.TIF image to place behind the lettering in the WXYZ.TIF image, you'd Load the WXYZ Alpha channel, then use Photoshop's Paste Behind command to achieve the same order of image areas stacked upon each other. Fortunately, it's easy in Photoshop for the user to specify whether an Alpha channel is supposed to mask, or select an area.

Tip

If you want to make a permanent change to an Alpha channel, and make a mask into a selection area, using the Channel Options dialog box is just one way to do this. You can also use Photoshop's **I**mage, **M**ap, Invert command (Ctrl+I) while you are in the Alpha channel view to make masks into selections, and vice-versa.

You *must* be in the Alpha channel view of an image when issuing this command. Otherwise, you'll wind up with a negative image in a color channel.

Also, you mustn't Load the selection when you are in the Alpha channel, or any other view of the image. This will cause only the selection area to invert, and you'll wind up with meaningless information in the channel.

Unless you're fairly comfortable with Photoshop's commands at this point, the safest way to invert a selection area is to use the **S**elect, **I**nverse command. No permanent changes to the image file information are made by doing this because you are choosing the inverse of an active selection area, not reassigning the tonal information in the Alpha channel from which the selection is made.

Creating a Neon Lettering Effect

You probably are wondering why you created two identical selections out of the selection border you pasted into STORMSKY.TIF in the last exercise.

They are both used to create a rather unusual effect in the assignment. Have you ever noticed that titles not only roll and swoop in TV promos, but also glow a lot? The next exercise creates this effect in the still image. The "Neon Glow" effect can be used (and frequently is *overused*) to emphasize a graphical element in a very stylized manner. And if you follow the steps in order, creating the effect is almost as easy as pasting in an object.

To learn more about the Neon Glow effect and different ways to create it, see Chapter 19, *"Virtual Reality: The Ingredients of Dreamwork."*

There's a Glow in the Sky!

Click on Channel #5 (or press Ctrl+5) on the Channels palette	Displays view of last Saved Selection in active STORMSKY.TIF image area.
Choose Filter, Blur; then select Gaussian Blur, **R**adius: 12 pixels	Sets naturalistic blurring effect to a moderate degree.
Click on OK	Closes Gaussian Blur dialog box and applies effect to Channel 5 only. Because no selection border is active in this channel, effect is applied to all of Channel 5.
Choose **S**elect-**A**ll (or press Ctrl+A)	Selects all of Channel 5.
Choose **E**dit, **C**opy (or press Ctrl+C)	Copies Channel 5 to Clipboard.
Click on RGB on the Channels palette (or press Ctrl+0)	Restores active image window to full-color view.
Choose **S**elect, **L**oad Selection, and then select #4	Loads unblurred selection; the marquee border precisely defines the Typestry letting area.
Choose **E**dit, Paste **B**ehind	Pastes the selection behind the loaded selection #4 and on top of everything else that was not selected.
Choose **I**mage, **A**djust, then select Hue/Saturation (or press Ctrl+U)	Displays Hue and Saturation dialog box.
Check the Colorize checkbox if it isn't already checked	This allows you to color image pixels to a monochrome hue in the active selection.

continues

Fantastic Assignments

continued

Click and drag the sliders to set Hue:**-112**, Saturation: **100**, Brightness: **0** (or enter the values directly into the boxes)	Colorizes lighter portions of blurred, pasted-in copy to a deep blue. Look at the Preview of the effect in the main image window to see what's happening, as shown in figure 17.14.
Click on OK	Confirms your choices and returns you to the workspace.
Choose **E**dit, Composite C**o**ntrols	Displays Composite Controls Menu (see fig. 17.15).
Choose Screen Mode from the drop-down list, then click on OK	Causes lighter portions of pasted selection to show through RGB channel over which it was pasted; darker portions become invisible.
Choose **S**elect, **N**one (or press Ctrl+D)	Deselects selection and blends paste into main RGB channel.
Choose **F**ile, **S**ave	Saves your work to hard disk.

Figure 17.14
The Colorize feature causes noticeable results only to the lighter areas of the pasted selection.

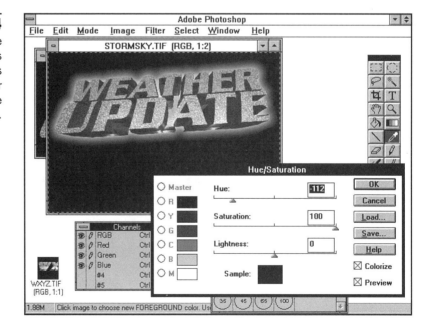

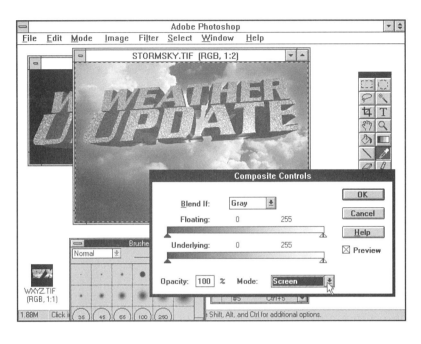

Figure 17.15
Screen Mode
washes out darker
portions of the
pasted selection,
leaving lighter
areas alone.

This exercise shows you how to use a selection area in a channel as a piece of art. You can use this neat trick for putting a glow behind an object, provided that you remember to save *two* copies of the selection area. If you don't keep an original unblurred selection, you'll have nothing to paste the blurred selection behind.

In addition to the Gaussian Blur, you may want to try the motion blur effect on the UPDATE black and white copy before Colorizing and blending the paste into the STORMSKY image. Motion blur is also in the Filter, Blur dialog box. The effect you can achieve is that of a glowing trail behind the lettering that suggests motion along with the brilliance.

Adding Photoshop Type

The image looks pretty striking now, but still needs one element traditionally seen on TV bulletins—the name of the town. You can fit some Photoshop type into the space in the WXYZ logotype, giving the lettering the same sort of flair as the rest of the image.

Adding a Shadow Before Adding Type

In Chapter 15, you saw how to use a drop-shadow effect, directly applying it to a background. The technique is a little different when you want to apply text to an image area with color and tonal variation. You need to position and edit text in an image channel before applying the drop shadow effect to the RGB image of STORMSKY. The steps in the next exercise make positioning new selections between channels a breeze.

Creating Shadow Text

Marquee-zoom in on the corner where WXYZ 3 is located	A 1:1 viewing ratio zoom provides a good view of the area.
Click on Channel #5 in the Channels palette	Provides a view of the blurry channel created earlier.
Click on the default colors icon (the mini-swatches) on the toolbox	Sets foreground to black, background to white.
Double-click on the Eraser tool in the toolbox, then click on Yes	Wipes out Channel 5 with white background color. Clicking on Yes in confirmation dialog box completes the action.

The Blurry selection is no longer useful; wiping out the selection to clear space for new text entry is easier than creating a new channel.

Click on Type tool, then click an insertion point in the lower left of the active image window	Displays Type tool dialog box.
In the drop-down box, select a sans serif, bold, italic typeface from your personal type collection	If you don't own Futura Black (the font used in this example), Arial Bold Italic, which ships with Windows 3.1, is a good substitute.
Type **MOUNT MORRIS, NEW YORK** in the Type entry field	Text to be added to image.
Choose <u>S</u>ize **10** points, <u>B</u>old, <u>I</u>talic, and Alignment: <u>L</u>eft	Specs type for Type entry. (Backstage calculations indicate ideal size for this image is 10 points; see Tip following the exercise.)
Click on OK	Confirms selections and returns to Channel 5. Now text is floating selection you can reposition (see fig. 17.16).
Click on the left column, next to the RGB channel on the palette	Eye icon appears in column; displays Channel 5 text selection with marquee border and Quick Mask shading (see figure 17.17).

Press Ctrl+Alt and drag the text selection under the WXYZ logo	Moves selection without editing RGB channel (see fig. 17.18).
Choose **S**elect, **S**ave Selection, then click on #5	Repositions text in Channel #5 but does not change RGB channel.
Click on the eye icon next to the RGB Channel title in the Channels palette	Toggles "view" off in RGB channel and returns to Channel 5.
Choose **S**elect, **N**one (or press Ctrl+D)	Deselects floating text selection in Channel 5.
Choose Fi**l**ter, Blur, then Gaussian Blur; type **2** pixels in the **R**adius: field	Displays Gaussian Blur options box; resetting radius of blur to minimal value applies blur of fairly small resolution to text.
Click on OK	Displays workspace, which features fuzzy Type.
Choose **F**ile, **S**ave	Saves your work to hard disk.

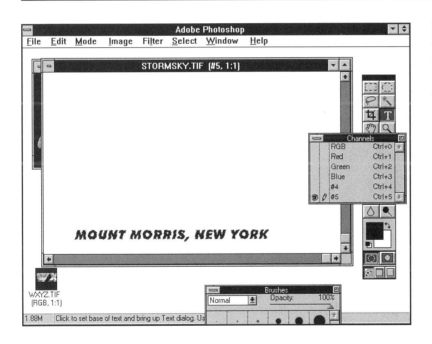

Figure 17.16

Type can be a floating selection in a channel, or it can be a mask.

IV

Fantastic Assignments

Figure 17.17
The absence of a pencil mark in the column next to a Channel tells you that channel is not in editing mode.

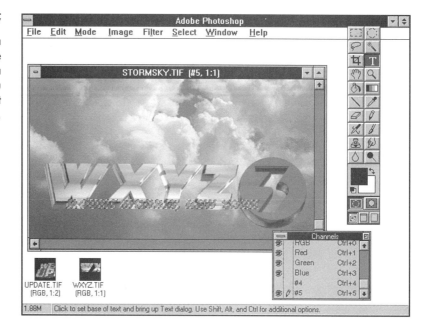

Figure 17.18
Be sure to use Ctrl+Alt when you click, to reposition only a selection area, but not what it contains.

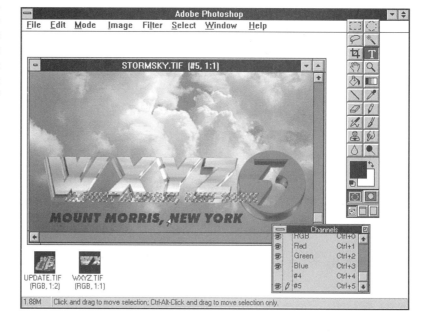

Sizing text in Photoshop can be a frustrating experience if you come from the Desktop Publishing School way of doing things. Photoshop does not provide for point-and-a-half sizes (such as 10.5 point) and offers no real method for evaluating what the width a line of text should be. You can evaluate Type height only.

On assignments like these, try using a *wild guess* and then, if your first try is wrong, use the backspace key to delete the text. Photoshop remembers your last Type entry in a Photoshop session. You can fairly quickly enter a line of type at a given point size, delete it, click an insertion point again, then estimate the type size a second or third time til it's perfect.

A Recap on the Channels Editing and Viewing Modes

Now to review a very important feature in Photoshop—one that has to do with positioning stuff *between* channels. The Quick Mask feature is an excellent visual clue to a selection's position. Moreover, the reddish tint (or whatever color you may have changed it to) indicates which area of an image is selected, and the areas that are not.

Photoshop automatically invokes the Quick Mask feature when you click on the left column of an Alpha channel while the RGB composite view of an image is your active one. This View-only Mode is different from the Editing and Viewing Mode displayed when you click on a channel title (or press Ctrl+number). You can use Ctrl+Alt and drag a floating selection to reposition it (safely!) only when the eye icon (View-only Mode) is displayed in a channel other than the one your selection is in. When it is in "view only mode" (eye icon present, pencil icon absent) you can "edit between channels" in Photoshop.

To create a duplicate selection, use the Ctrl+Alt+Drag method while the pencil icon (Editing Mode) is displayed in a channel. The image inside the selection area is duplicated, creating a floating selection out of the image inside the selection border at the time. The selection border can be moved as many times as you like to create multiple images. The effect is artistic, giving an image of simple textures with subject matter that is not complex.

You've been using a powerful aspect of Photoshop's channels feature to do some complex image editing so far. But don't forget that a selection area can also be *created* when you're in an Alpha channel view. Photoshop always evaluates the density (how dark/how light) of the pixels in an Alpha channel when saving or loading a selection area from it.

You can copy visual information, up to 8 bits (256 shades of gray) into a channel. Defining a border with selection tools isn't the only way to define a mask or selection.

Adding the Shadow Text to the RGB Channel

The Gaussian-blurred Channel 5 is about to get a new home in the RGB channel, as a shadow for the Type to perch on. The shadow exists in the channel as black type on a white background, the inverse of the "mask" channel Typestry created for the UPDATE type.

You don't need to invert Channel 5 before you copy it, because Photoshop's Modes for compositing and painting are sort of paired-off in opposing functions. In this exercise, to create the shadow in the RGB channel, you use the Multiply Mode, the inverse function of the Screen Mode.

Adding Shadows to the Sky

Click on the Title area of Channel #5 (or press Ctrl+5)	Displays active, editable view of repositioned text.
Choose **S**elect, **A**ll (or press Ctrl+A)	Selects entire Channel 5.
Choose **E**dit, **C**opy (or press Ctrl+C)	Copies entire channel to Clipboard.
Click on the RGB title in the Channels palette (or press Ctrl+0)	Displays full-color, fully editable view of image.
Choose **E**dit, **P**aste (or press Ctrl+V) channel	Pastes copy of Channel 5 onto RGB.
Choose **E**dit, Composite C**o**ntrols	Displays dialog box where you specify how to blend pasted copy into RGB channel.
Choose Multiply from the Mode drop-down list, leave the Opacity: at **100**% then click on OK	Multiply treats darker areas of the paste as *additive* elements to RGB image area, lighter areas as transparent when Preview is checked (see fig. 17.19).
Choose **F**ile, **S**ave	Saves your work to your hard disk.

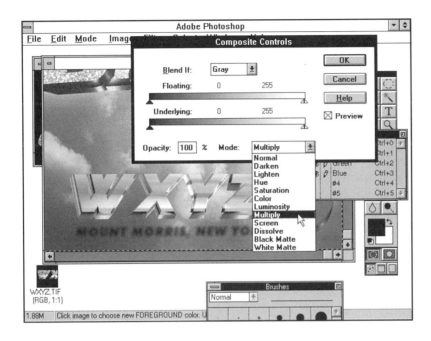

Figure 17.19
Multiply and
Screen, opposite
functions, are
paired next to
each other on
the Composite
Control's Modes
drop-down list.

Non-Shadow Text Is Next

Another nice feature about Adobe Photoshop is that a type entry keeps its size, font, and other attributes during a Photoshop session. You don't have to retype MOUNT MORRIS, NEW YORK, a second time to complete the lettering over the shadow. All you really need to do in this final exercise is pick a nice color for the text!

Where Is Mount Morris?

Click on the Eyedropper tool on the toolbox	Used for "picking up" a foreground color value to paint with.
Click on part of the neon glow around the UPDATE image	Sets foreground color to light blue on the toolbox for paint tools and text entry.
Click on the Type tool, then click an insertion point on STORMSKY.TIF	Sets point where text entry starts and displays Type options dialog box (see fig. 17.20).
Click on OK	Dialog box's Type field already contains text entry from last exercise, with identical Size and Font values.

continues

IV

Fantastic Assignments

continued

Click and drag the floating Type selection to position above and to the shadowed type	Standard artistic convention for left of the shadow displaying type drop-Shadow seems to be cast below and to right of text (see fig. 17.21).
Choose **S**elect, **N**one (or press Ctrl+D)	Deselects text and makes it part of STORMSKY.TIF image.

It's time to Save your work now, but you have two channels that have outlived their purposefulness at this point. They contribute to a wastefully large TIFF image file size.

Click on the Channel #5 title on the Channels palette	Shows you an active view of Alpha Channel 5.
Click on the Channels palette's command button, and select Delete Channel	Deletes Channel 5 from the STORMSKY image, and returns you to an RGB color composite view of STORMSKY.TIF.
Click on the Channel #4 title on the Channels palette	Shows you an active view of Alpha Channel 5.
Click on the Channels palette's command button, and select Delete Channel	Deletes Channel 4 from the STORMSKY image, and returns you to an RGB color composite view of STORMSKY.TIF.
Choose **F**ile, Sa**v**e As	Name file something other than STORMSKY.TIF so that you have unadorned sky image to experiment with later. Name can be **W_Report.TIF** or something more inventive.
Choose **F**ile, **S**ave	Saves your work to your hard disk.

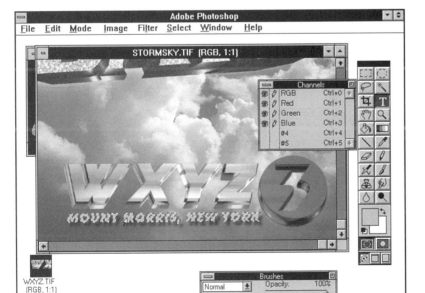

Figure 17.20
Photoshop remembers your last type entry— very useful for creating exact duplicates of a text block!

Figure 17.21
Dragging the text selection above the shadow creates the drop-shadow effect.

IV

Fantastic Assignments

Beyond the Weather...

Figure 17.22 is a full-frame view of the finished piece.

Io create a nice, large screen capture here, I click on **I**mage, **I**mage Size, and then change the proportions of W_REPORT.TIF to 480 pixels wide. Shortly thereafter, I click on **E**dit-**U**ndo. A neat, potentially reckless thing to do with a carefully edited image—but it *does* maximize a full-frame view of a design. You just have to remember to *undo* this command to avoid files that are sized wrong!

Figure 17.22
A full-frame view of the finished assignment.

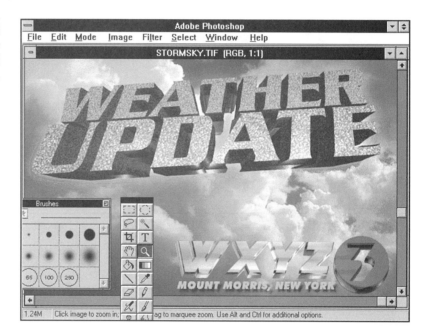

Summary

So you say you never get television-bulletin assignments at work. The WXYZ.TIF design is pretty, but how practical is it? Being able to integrate Windows applications gives the serious designer a great deal more latitude with tools and different ways to create images. You've seen how quickly and obligingly the three applications in this chapter worked together to express an idea. Imagine the possibilities for your next slide presentation! With a program like Typestry, and Photoshop's image-editing capabilities, your next sales chart can have the kind of snap and appeal long available only in the Big Leagues in Hollywood!

Even if you don't pop for other applications today or tomorrow, the Neon Glow effect and photorealistic drop-shadows are now at your command, and type set against a photo is much more eye-catching than the primary-colored Clip Art most folks settle for today. The reward for using Photoshop to create your own presentation graphics is that people acknowledge an original creation—which puts the serious designer way ahead of the pack.

Photoshop's Channels are a powerful tool we use frequently in both everyday and extraordinary assignments. If you learn how to use them, your work will always feature the icing on the cake.

Chapter Snapshot

In this chapter, you learn how to:

CHAPTER

Fractal and Photoshop

T he term *fractal* is used in computer graphics to describe mathematics that simulate natural, organic shapes and textures. Depending on the way a fractal math *model* is written, incredibly detailed, resolution-independent landscapes and textures can be produced. With fractal images, the larger the size you specify for rendering the model, the more detail you can see!

Photoshop does not generate fractal textures by itself, but you *can* use them in Photoshop to produce outstanding effects. You are going to work with several fractal elements in this chapter. They were created in Fractal Design Painter, a "natural media" paint program developed by the Fractal Design Corporation. The program provides a wide array of realistic artist's materials—such as chalk, oils, and watercolors—that the computer imagist can apply to virtual canvas surfaces. It's a great source for fractal textures and an extremely useful addition to your imaging tools.

Photoshop's tools and effects are not suitable for creating photo realistic textures, and Painter lacks the powerful editing features found in Photoshop. But by putting the two programs together on an assignment like the one in this chapter, you can create whole, real, even *surreal* scenes upon which you can build by adding a real world photograph.

The highlight of this chapter is how Fractal meets Photoshop. You are going to learn one of the many ways the two can help you convey a visual idea with drama, detail, and uncanny realism.

The assignment in this chapter is to create a stock illustration that can be used to accompany an article or advertisement whose theme is the world and time. If this sounds a tad vague, think about the many uses and reuses served by a well-executed stock illustration. A globe and a clock in an abstract setting can appear in a magazine's feature story about daylight savings time. Or it might be the cover of an in-flight brochure about the different time zones traveled through by an airline. When you create a stock clip-art or photographic piece, the object is to be interesting but *general* so that the customer can decide its many uses.

The Painter Workspace

Before you begin this chapter's exercises, we'll take a backstage look at how to create the textures Painter provides as raw materials for a scene. You do not have to own Fractal Design Painter to do the exercises in this chapter; the book's companion CD includes the assignments' textures already designed for you, saved as TIFF images. But if you already have Painter, you might want to follow along.

Creating a Canvas

This chapter relies on Painter's capability to generate a colored, textured, realistically lit canvas. You reshape it and add other things to the results in Photoshop. Painting isn't even an exercise here!

Painter's first assignment was to generate an image that looks like rough plaster, to be used as the face of a clock in this chapter's assignment. A new file was opened and the dimensions, resolution, and color of the image "canvas" (you may call it a background) was defined. Then, from the Paper palette, Watercolor2 was chosen as the canvas Surface Texture, and it was applied, as shown in figure 18.1. When you create a Surface Texture with Painter, you can specify the direction the light falls on the texture, and whether the surface is reflective. All the objects built in this assignment were lit from a specific angle.

In figure 18.2, you can see the many Apply Lighting options available in Painter. We chose Plane Light, although there are many exotic, intricate arrangements to select from. It's best not to "over-render" an image that has several additional changes waiting for it later in Photoshop.

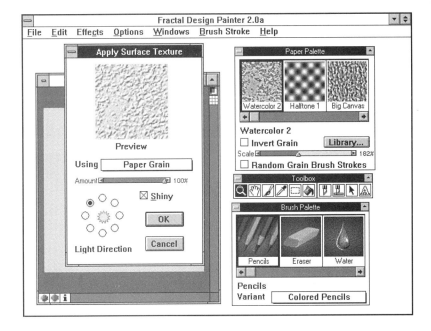

Figure 18.1
Fractal Design Painter lets the user specify many details about a canvas background's appearance.

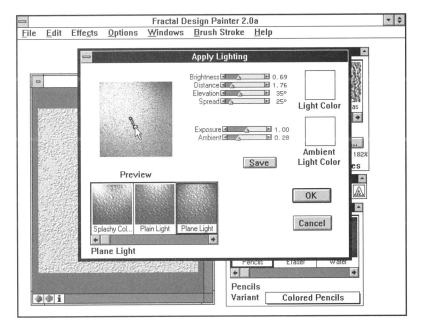

Figure 18.2
Painter's "virtual lights" can be adjusted to create a dramatic effect on the canvas.

IV

Fantastic Assignments

From Plain Pixel to Virtual Texture

After texture and lighting are applied to the surface, the image is saved as a TIFF file in Painter. CLOCKTOP.TIF, shown in figure 18.3, is a 24-bit, RGB image you can use in Photoshop just like any other digital image. The amazingly realistic detail Painter has rendered to this file helps you portray a 3D object convincingly.

Figure 18.3
CLOCKTOP.TIF, as rendered in Painter's workspace.

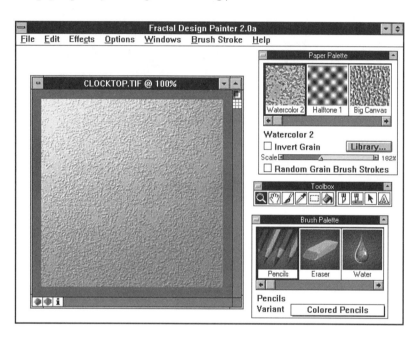

To create this chapter's assignment, you are going to use a combination of Painter's *.TIF renderings of texture, a TIFF photograph, two Encapsulated PostScript line-art drawings, and Photoshop's effects and tools. Painter's contribution to the assignment includes CLOCKTOP.TIF and two other files (EARTH.TIF and DST_FLOR.TIF) created by using the same canvas-coloring, texturizing, and lighting procedures. Figure 18.4 shows the three completed TIFF files in Painter's workspace.

Describing Fractal Design Painter's amazing brushes and effect filters in detail would require a book by itself! They work in much the same way Photoshop's paint application tools work, except that they *interact* with the texture of the canvas, just the way real paint and drawing tools do. If you decide that Painter belongs in your imaging arsenal, you will have a powerful *companion* for Photoshop.

Additionally, Photoshop's Plug-ins (and other third-party effects filters) can be used directly in the Painter workspace. You can apply the Photoshop Extrude filter, for example, to an image—in Photoshop *or* in Painter.

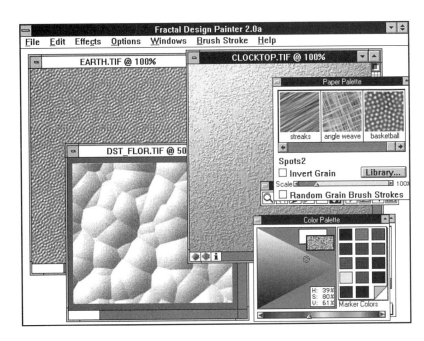

Figure 18.4

Painter can generate a diverse range of image textures.

The Fine Art of Clock Building

Now, using the textures Painter generated for this illustration, it's time to start building the first object in the illustration. The stylized clock face in this assignment is an EPS file placed on top of CLOCKTOP.TIF. *EPS files* are vector-oriented images designed in programs like CorelDRAW! and Adobe Illustrator. When you open an EPS image, Photoshop converts the EPS image to any size bitmap-type image you want.

The first exercise shows you how CLOCKTOP.TIF and CLOKFACE.EPS are combined and then modified to enhance the dimensional quality of the clock as it fits into the entire illustration.

IV

Fantastic Assignments

Putting Your Hands over Your Face

Open the CLOKFACE.EPS image from the book's companion CD	Displays EPS Rasterizer dialog box where you select the way PostScript data is converted to bitmap information.
Click on OK	Accepts defaults. Because CLOKFACE.EPS was created to fit perfectly into the design, no guesswork or calculating is necessary here.

continues

continued

Choose **S**elect, **A**ll (or press Ctrl+A), then **E**dit, **C**opy (or press Ctrl+C)	Copies entire CLOKFACE.EPS image area to Clipboard.
Open CLOCKTOP.TIF from the Companion CD	This Painter image file was measured, designed, and saved as texture for clock.
Click on the default colors icon on the toolbox	Sets foreground color to black, background to white.
Choose **I**mage, Canvas **S**ize, then set the **W**idth to 5 inches, the H**eig**ht to 5 inches in the New Size fields, and then click on OK	Increases image's background to add white border around it.
Choose **W**indow, Show C**h**annels (or press F6)	Displays Channels palette in Photoshop workspace.
Click on the Channels palette command button and select New Channel	Creates Alpha Channel 4 in CLOCKTOP.TIF image.
Click on the Channel #4 title, then choose **E**dit, **P**aste (or press Ctrl+V)	Makes Channel 4 viewable and editable; pastes CLOKFACE.EPS into Channel 4.
Click on the eye icon in the RGB channel in the Channels palette	Shows RGB view of image window, with Alpha channel displayed as a mask.

You can move the pasted copy in Channel #4 without changing what's in RGB Channel (see fig. 18.5). You can view the RGB Channel, but you cannot edit it right now.

Use the keyboard arrow keys to move CLOKFACE.TIF so that it is centered in the RGB view of CLOCKTOP.TIF	Arrow keys nudge CLOKFACE paste by one pixel in the direction determined by the key pressed.
Click on the eye icon next to the RGB title in the Channels palette	Toggles back to Channel 4; mode is the same (editable and viewable) as it was before you toggled to RGB channel's view-only mode.
Choose **F**ile, **S**ave As, specify the TIF extension by clicking on the Save File as Format **T**ype drop-down list, then find a suitable directory on your hard disk	Saves CLOCKTOP.TIF to your hard disk.
Accept the default name CLOCKTOP	

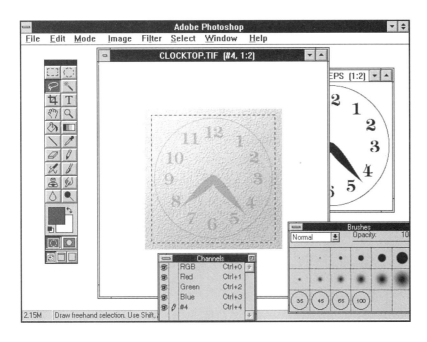

Figure 18.5
With the eye icon displayed and the pencil icon hidden, a channel can be viewed but not changed in any way.

Adding Dimension to 2D Art

Shortly, you'll do something very special with respect to how the numbers and the clock take shape in this assignment. First, you create a dimensional feel by adding the CLOKFACE image to the RGB channel twice; once as a shadow, then as the usual numbers and hands on a clock's face.

Then you learn how to add perspective to the piece *and* make changes to an Alpha channel without even viewing the Alpha channel!

Shadows are on deck—time to start the exercise.

Creating a Five O'Clock Shadow

Choose **S**elect, **A**ll (or press Ctrl+A), then **E**dit, **C**opy (or press Ctrl+C)

Copies entire Channel 4, with CLOKFACE image in its new position, to Clipboard. *Do not deselect anything!*

Click on the command button on the Channels palette, then select New Channel

Creates Alpha Channel 5 in CLOCKTOP.TIF image; by default, creating a new channel switches your view to a display of it.

continues

continued

Choose **E**dit, **P**aste (or press Ctrl+V)	Pastes a copy of CLOKFACE image into the selection border still active from copying the the first time; this copy now shares same relative position in both Channels 4 and 5.
Click on the Title Bar to Channel #4 (or press Ctrl+4)	Displays viewable, editable CLOKFACE image.
Choose **S**elect, **A**ll (or press Ctrl+A), then select Fi**l**ter, Blur, then Gaussian Blur	Calls the Gaussian Blur dialog box.
Type **8** pixels in the **R**adius field, then click on OK	Creates soft shadow out of CLOKFACE image; you add this shadow to RGB channel (see fig. 18.6).
Choose **E**dit, **C**opy (or press Ctrl+C)	Copies blurry channel 4 to the Clipboard.
Click on the Title of the RGB channel on the Channels palette (or press Ctrl+0)	Shifts to editable, viewable display of full-color Channel in CLOCKTOP.TIF.
Click on the Lasso tool on the toolbox	Choosing a selection tool prior to pasting enables you to use the Brushes palette to perform composite blends using the mode feature on the palette.
Choose **E**dit, **P**aste (or press Ctrl+V)	Pastes blurry copy of channel on top of RGB channel.
Choose Multiply from the Brushes pallette, move slider to **85**% Opacity	Composites pasted image into RGB channel, using Multiply Mode.

(Multiply Mode affects only the darker areas, ignoring the white in pasted selection.)

Choose **F**ile, **S**ave	Saves your work to your hard disk.

You can use the Brushes palette to composite blend a pasted selection into a background image instead of using the Edit, Composite Controls feature. Executing a composite from the Brushes palette takes a little more PC processor umph, and you must have a selection tool (Lasso, Rectangular, Elliptical) selected in order to paste a selection into an image. And if you use the Brushes palette instead of the Composite Controls, you can't set the range of brightnesses you want to include in the blending of the two images.

Whether you use the Composite Controls or the Brushes palette, compositing works only on a selection pasted from the Clipboard, *not* on a selection *area* in a channel. Use the **S**elect, **F**loat command if you ever have an area in an image that you want to composite blend into a different area in the same channel. This produces a floating copy of the selection area, with the original still present as part of the background image.

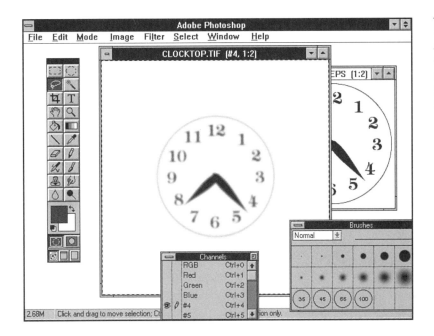

Figure 18.6
A Gaussian Blur creates realistic shadows from simple line-art renderings.

Adding Perspective to the Clock

Now that the shadowy details are on the texture of the clock's face, it's time to carve a round clock-face shape out of the CLOCKTOP texture image, adding perspective to the whole thing to angle it away from the viewer.

You haven't finished adding the *real* hands and numbers to the clock, though, right? Aha! A technique you learn soon enables you to change an Alpha Channel, even though it isn't *visible* while you *change* it. The secret is that (by default) when you select a Channel, all others become invisible and uneditable. But if you select the pencil icon (which represents an editable view) on a channel *other* than the one you are viewing and editing, the changes made to the viewable channel also occur to the channel tagged with the Pencil icon. You can distort the Channel 5 clock face in exactly the same way as the textured image with the shadow, then position it later!

This technique has advantages in your own work. But first you have to see it to believe it!

IV

Fantastic Assignments

Adding Perspective to an Image

Choose **S**elect, **N**one (or press Ctrl+D)	Deselects active image border in RGB view of CLOCKTOP.TIF.
Click on the Pencil icon on Channel #5 in the Channels palette	Enables you to edit Channel 5 as well as RGB channel.
Select the Elliptical tool from the toolbox	Selection tool for trimming out shape of clock face.
Place the cursor where the blurry hand shadows meet in the CLOCKTOP image	Center of image, where selection image will begin.
Press Shift+Alt while you click and drag away from the selection point	Creates a constrained ellipse (a circle) from center starting point outward.
Release the mouse button and the Shift and Alt keys when you reach the shadowy circle that borders the blurred clock hands and numbers	Selection area of clock face has been defined (see fig. 18.7).
Choose **I**mage, **E**ffects, then choose Perspective	Creates boundary box around selection area; manipulating box creates perspective in a selection.
Click and drag the handle on the box's lower-right corner toward the right edge of the image window	Creates a perspective on the selection that makes bottom of the image appear closer to viewer. ***Do not click outside boundary box!***
Click and drag the handle on the upper-right corner down and toward the clock-face image	Increases illusion that clock's bottom is coming toward viewer; figure 18.8 shows where perspective boundary box edges should be now.
Click inside the perspective boundary box	Gavel cursor "nails" image to desired degree of perspective.
Choose **S**elect, **I**nverse (or press Ctrl+I)	Inverts the active selection border from clock selection to everything except the clock.
Press the Delete key	Wipes out everything except clock, replacing it with default white background.
Choose **S**elect, **I**nverse (or press Ctrl+I)	Changes selection again to include clock image, exclude white background.
Choose **S**elect, **S**ave selection, then choose #4 selection	Saves oval border around the clock, over-writing blurry clock face (no longer needed in Channel 4).

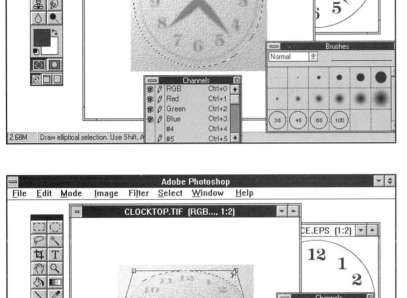

Figure 18.7
The selection border affects every channel that displays the pencil icon.

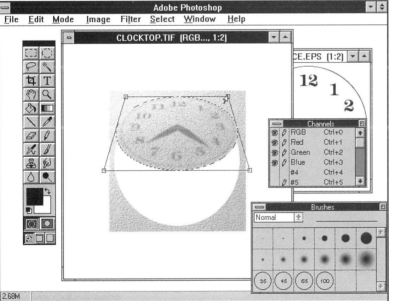

Figure 18.8
Perspective is added in the direction from where you make the first drag.

IV

Fantastic Assignments

Extra Channels create larger files when you work on an image. A good practice is to overwrite channel information whenever you need a new channel and no longer need the information in another. This way, only one or two Alpha Channels exist while you work. (This is the reason you overwrote the blurry clock face channel with the new clock outline in the last exercise.)

To preserve your work and your sanity, though, be sure to keep track of what is in each channel! If you are unsure about this, click on the channel in question before overwriting it.

At any time, you can click on a channel title, then click on the command button to access the Channel Options dialog box so that you can assign the numbered channel a name more evocative than 4, 5, and so on.

Adding a Face to the Clock

Now that you've given the clock perspective and cleaned it up, it's time to add Channel 5. To make a clock face "float" above the dial, as we'll do next, you needed to keep the image separate until after the dial is put in perspective. You now have complete control over how much you want the hands to float. You wouldn't have been able to achieve this if you had copied the Channel 5 image area to the RGB channel earlier.

Moving Time

Click on the Title of Channel #5 in the Channels palette	Reveals the clock-face image pasted in earlier (but it has undergone perspective change identical to RGB channel).
Choose the Rectangular Marquee tool from the toolbox	Used to select area to be modified.
Click and drag around the clock-face image	Marquee-selects clock-face image area; make sure it is entirely selected (see fig. 18.9).
Press the up-arrow key three times	Nudges selection area up three pixels.
Choose Select, None (or press Ctrl+D), or click outside the selection area	Deselects all areas; the image is now repositioned relative to the original blurred copy on RGB channel.
Click on the command button on the Channels palette, and select Channel Options from the drop-down list	This calls the Channel Options dialog box.

Make sure Color Indicates Selected Areas radio button is checked	This makes the colored areas (the black) in Channel 4 the selection areas, and the white areas masked.
Click on the RGB title in the Channels palette	Displays full-color view in editable mode.
Choose **S**elect, **L**oad selection, then choose #5	Makes selection border around clock face in Channel 5 editable in RGB-channel view.
Click on the inverse colors icon on the toolbox	Switches color selection boxes on toolbar to white foreground, black background.
Press the Backspace key	Removes contents of selection area, replacing them with background black.
Press the Backspace key again	Further darkens background color in selection area (see fig. 18.10).
Choose **S**elect, **N**one (or press Ctrl+D)	Removes Marquee selection border from around clock face.
Choose **F**ile, **S**ave	Saves your work to your hard disk.

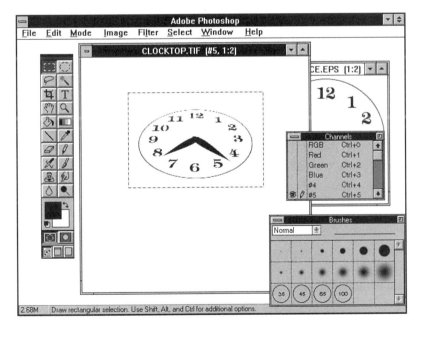

Figure 18.9

You can move a selection area in a channel to set it apart from common elements in other channels.

Figure 18.10
The finished face
of the clock.

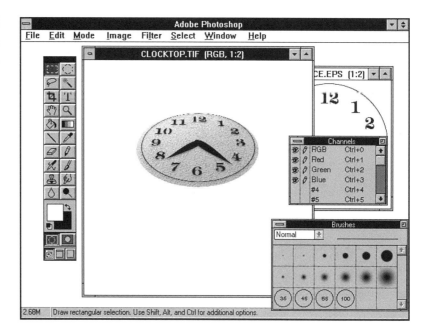

Finishing Off the Timepiece

Because the clock is at an angle now, it looks phony because it has no depth, no second point of view. There is a side that should be visible from this perspective. No problem. With Photoshop's Calculate command, you can create most of the clock's side selection area, then reuse the CLOCKTOP.TIF texture file created in Painter to paste into the new side area. The only problem is that you are using CLOCKTOP.TIF at the moment! You solve the problem in the next exercise.

Creating a Side Selection Area

Save CLOCKTOP.TIF as CLOCK.TIF, check Save Alpha Channels box

Frees CLOCKTOP.TIF to become original source of design texture again.

Zoom to 1:1 viewing resolution of CLOCK.TIF (if you're not already at this view, Press Ctrl+plus)

Zooms to 1:1 resolution of CLOCK image, a better view for upcoming work.

Choose **S**elect, **L**oad Selection, then choose #4

Loads ellipse shape you saved earlier.

Press Ctrl+Alt while you press the down-arrow key about 10 times

Moves ellipse selection (not the contents) down in RGB channel. Stop when bottom is a good "depth" for side of clock (see fig. 18.11).

Choose **S**elect, Save **S**election, then choose New	Ellipse selection area becomes Channel 6.
Choose **I**mage, **C**alculate, then choose Subtract	Displays Subtract dialog box (see fig. 18.12).
Enter Source **1**: Document: **CLOCK.TIF**, Channel #6; Source **2**: Document: **CLOCK.TIF**, Channel #4; **D**estination Document **CLOCK.TIF**, Channel Selection, **S**cale:**1**, **O**ffset:**0**	Creates new selection border, calculated from Brightness value of Channel 6 minus Brightness value of Channel 4.
Click on OK	Displays Photoshop's workspace, with nice bottom lip selection area beneath clock image (see fig. 18.13).
Choose **S**elect, **S**ave Selection, then choose #5	Overwrites clock's numbers and hands selection (no longer needed); saves selection.
Click on Channel #6, then from the command button drop-down list, select Delete Channel	Deletes second ellipse nudged down to make part of clock-side selection (no longer necessary) and makes CLOCK.TIF file smaller.
Choose **F**ile, **S**ave	Saves your work to your hard disk.

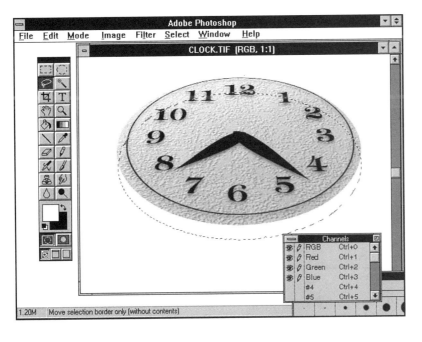

Figure 18.11

Press Ctrl+Alt+ arrow keys to nudge the selection border only, not its contents.

Figure 18.12
You can subtract
one selection from
another selection
by using the
Image, Calculate,
Subtract
command.

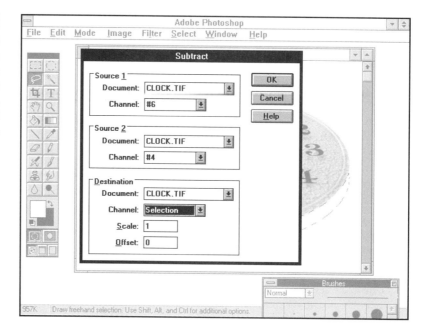

Figure 18.13
A new selection
area, created from
two other saved
ones.

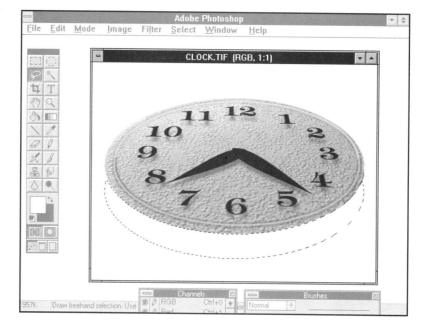

Tip

Calculate's Subtract and Add dialog box is confusing if you associate it with the way mathematical equations are laid out. You are calculating the brightness value contained in the two source Channels, not subtractive or additive geometry. The Add dialog box is explained later in this chapter in another exercise, but here is what you always need to do when you want to subtract one channel from another to get your selection:

In the Subtract dialog box's first entry field, Source 1, you stipulate which area of the **selection** acts as a "knife," carving out to a second **selection**. You select the document and the channel from the drop-down list that does the carving.

The area to be carved out is the second entry field, Source 2. You select the same document, but specify the area to be carved out by choosing its channel here.

When you subtract one Brightness value from another, you make the value you subtract a **selection** in the Destination field. The reason you need to make the subtracted creation a **selection** rather than a new channel is that saving the selection as a new channel causes the selection to be inverted when you load it from the Select menu. By saving it as a selection in the Destination field, you can select and save the selection to a new channel later.

Use a Scale setting of 1 when you subtract one channel from another. Scale is an averaging feature, but when you subtract, you don't want an average of the brightnesses found in the two channels involved in the Subtract command. You want the same brightness values, so the Scale of the subtraction should be divided by itself, or a value of 1.

You don't use Offset at all when subtracting, unless you want the pixels that make up the subtracted result to be lighter in value than the original density of the pixels involved in the Calculation. This is something you almost never want because gray is the result of a positive Offset value, and this constitutes a partial mask when displayed in an Alpha channel.

The Calculate, Add command works a little differently. Another Tip explains it when you come to it.

Refining the Edge Work

The area you just created for the clock's side is good, but because you subtracted one oval shape from another oval shape, it doesn't have straight lines for sides. You can easily correct this before you paste in the texture.

IV

Fantastic Assignments

On the Edge of Time

Choose **S**elect, **L**oad Selection, then choose #5	Loads selection border created in last exercise.
Click on the Quick Mask button on the toolbox	Displays selection area in Quick Mask color. Selection and painting tools can now be used to modify the mask colored areas.
Marquee-zoom to the left edge of the clock	First area of Mask to be straightened; 3:1 zoom viewing resolution is good.
Click on the default colors icon on the toolbox	Restores color selection defaults to black foreground, white background.
Select the Pencil tool from the toolbox, then select the smallest Brushes tip from the Brushes pallette; set Mode to Normal, **100**% Opacity	Good tool for touch-up work around Quick Mask area (see fig. 18.14).
Click and drag around the "dimple" in the Quick Mask's left edge	Fills in an area not defined by the Subtract calculation in the last exercise.
Choose the Hand tool, click and drag to the left until you see the edge of the Quick Mask	Displays right edge of Quick Mask, right area also needs touching up.
Click and drag the Pencil tool to fill in the gap on the Quick Mask's right edge	Refines Quick Mask, creating a selection border that looks more like a cylindrical section than two overlapped ellipses.
Press Ctrl+minus three times	Displays 1:2 complete view of the clock image.
Click on the Standard Mode on the toolbox	Quick Mask becomes active selection border again; marquee shows the modifications you made while in Quick Mask mode.
Choose **S**elect, **S**ave Selection, then choose #5	Overwrites unretouched border in Channel 5, replacing it with refined border selection just created.
Click on the RGB title in the Channels palette	Displays full-color view of CLOCK.TIF, with Channel 6 selection border still active.
Choose **F**ile, **O**pen CLOCKTOP.TIF	Reopens texture image in its original condition.

Choose the Rectangular Marquee tool on the toolbox, then drag and click a selection border across the bottom third of CLOCKTOP.TIF	Selects a texture selection for filling in the active selection area in CLOCK.TIF.
Choose **E**dit, **C**opy (or press Ctrl+C)	Copies texture selection to clipboard.
Double-click on CLOCKTOP.TIF's command button	Closes file. After copying section of texture, you no longer need it. CLOCK.TIF is the active image window again.
Choose **E**dit, Paste **I**nto	Pastes texture into selection area (see fig. 18.15).
Choose **F**ile, **S**ave	Saves your work to your hard disk.

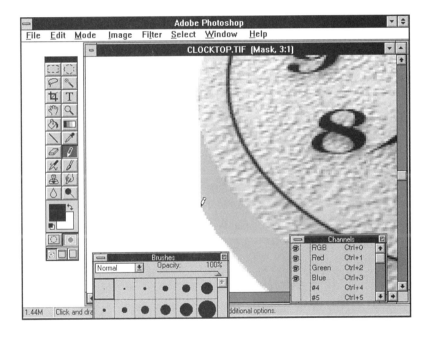

Figure 18.14

Use the Quick Mask feature and a tool to refine a previously saved selection area.

IV

Fantastic Assignments

Figure 18.15
Use the Paste Into command to place a large selection into a smaller area.

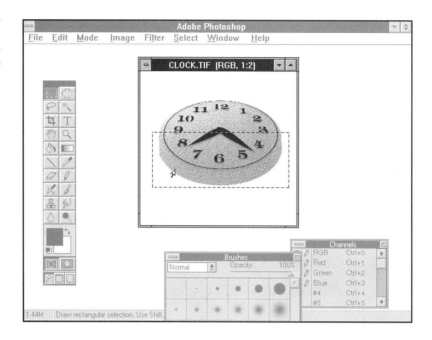

The Clock's Final Details

Now the clock image is good-looking and fully dimensional. The only thing missing from the image is some shading to suggest that the clock edge is pointed away from the light source in the scene it will ultimately become part of. Think about this for a second. If the face of the clock is lit from a light source above it, the edge facing you would miss that light source, right?

In the next exercise, you color in a selection that adds drama to the scene. The selection you color is in a selection area you've already defined.

It's Twilight Time

Double-click on the Zoom tool on the toolbox	Displays a 1:1 view of CLOCK.TIF.
Click on Channel #5, then choose **S**elect, **A**ll (or press Ctrl+A). Now choose **E**dit, **C**opy (or press Ctrl+C)	Copies entire Channel 5 to clipboard.
Click on the command button in the Channels palette, choose New Channel	Creates Channel 6, where you will fill in the selection border.
Choose **E**dit, **P**aste, then **S**elect, **N**one	Pastes copy of Channel 5 into Channel 6.
Choose **S**elect, **L**oad Selection, then choose #5	Displays marquee border from view of Channel 6.

Choose the Lasso tool from the toolbox; press Ctrl while you click and drag through the center of the active selection marquee, then complete the lasso around the right half of the active marquee border	Causes right half of marquee border to disappear; left side of marquee selection is still active.
Double-click on the Gradient tool on the toolbox; from the Options box choose Style **N**ormal, Type **L**inear, then click on OK	You use Gradient tool to apply fills to selection area in Channel 6.
Click and drag from left to right in the marquee selection	Flood-fills marquee area from white to black, as shown in figure 18.16.
Choose **S**elect, **L**oad Selection, then choose #5	Again, displays marquee border from view of Channel 6.
With the Lasso, press Ctrl while you click and drag through the center of the active selection marquee, then complete the lasso around the *left* half of the marquee border	Left half of marquee disappears; right side is still selected.
Select the Gradient tool, then click and drag from right to left over the selection	Fill completes the Gradient shading of the new selection (see fig. 18.17).
Click on the RGB channel title in the Channels palette	Displays full-color view of image.
Choose **S**elect, **L**oad Selection, then choose #6	Loads Gradient-fill selection.
Choose **I**mage, **A**djust, then choose Brightness/Contrast (or press Ctrl+B)	Displays Brightness/Contrast dialog box.
Drag the Brightness slider down to **-100%**; make sure that the Preview box is checked, then click on OK	Decreases brightness in RGB channel, (see figure 18.18) based on densities of Gradient applied to Channel 6 selection.
Choose **F**ile, **S**ave	Saves your work to your hard disk.

When the selection you save in an Alpha channel is based on pure geometry, you have saved a mask of an area that can be reused at any time. But when a gradient fill is in a channel, the selection *masks* the area in the RGB channel from filters, to various extents. This is called a *partial mask*. The darker areas in the gradient fill allow the Brightness/Contrast to darken the areas in the RGB selection, whereas the white areas in the gradient mask the corresponding areas in the RGB channel completely.

IV

Fantastic Assignments

Figure 18.16
Subtract from the loaded selection with the Lasso tool, then apply a gradient fill to half the remaining selection.

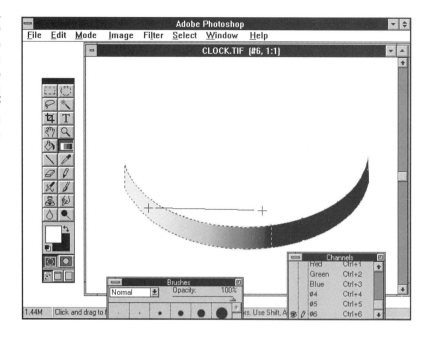

Figure 18.17
Complete the lighting effect by clicking and dragging in the opposite direction with the Gradient tool, on the opposite half of the selection.

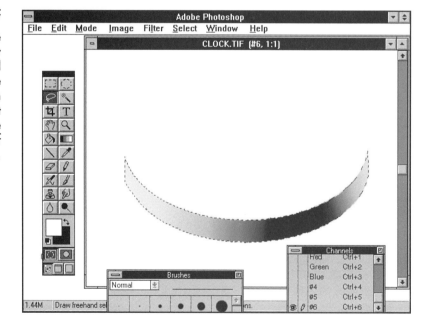

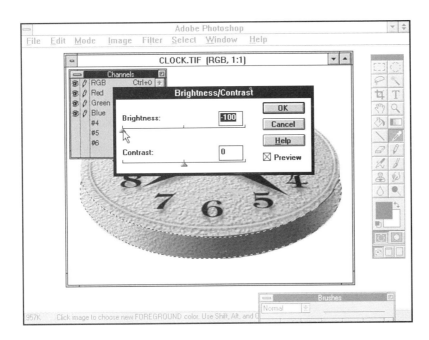

Figure 18.18
In the RGB channel, shift the Brightness slider to **-100**% to darken the selection area.

This gives you another way (besides compositing a black image paste using multiply mode) to shade an RGB image without destroying visual content, such as texture. The advantage in using the Brightness/Contrast command with a partial mask selection is that you are not introducing another color to the RGB channel—but you can never get absolute black in an area as you can by using Composite Controls with a pasted selection.

Creating the Earth

Put the clock away for the moment. Now you need to spend some quality time building the other main piece for this assignment. For the next Photoshop exercise, I scanned a map, tinkered around with continent placement, and then exported it as an EPS file from a drawing program.

When you open EARTHMAP.EPS, you'll notice that East meets West to the point of silliness (and for good reason). You are going to use Photoshop's Spherize filter to distort the EPS file so that it looks more dimensional. When Spherize does its thing, it gives preference to the center of a selected area, squeezing the surrounding areas outward toward the selection edge. Because Africa is much too close to South America in the EPS file, the two continents will distort away from each other and the effect will look more natural, albeit somewhat inaccurate.

But we're all artists at heart, not cartographers. Now it's time to learn more about Photoshop and *our* craft!

IV

Fantastic Assignments

What Goes Round, Comes Round

Choose File, Open, then choose EARTHMAP.EPS from the companion CD	Displays EPS Rasterizer dialog box, which offers options for the Size, Resolution, and the Mode of the image when brought into Photoshop.
Click on OK	Accepts the defaults. EARTHMAP.EPS was scaled correctly when created for use in this exercise.
Choose Mode, RGB	Converts grayscale image to RGB color so that it can be colored in Photoshop.
Choose the Elliptical marquee tool, then press Shift and Marquee-select to include include the world, from Alaska to Africa	Constrains selection area to perfect circle around interesting parts of continents (see fig. 18.19).
Choose FiLter, Distort, then choose Spherize	Displays Spherize dialog box.
Set Amount **100**, Mode: **N**ormal, then click on OK	Produces maximum amount of spherical distortion to selection area, both horizontally and vertically (see fig. 18.20).
Choose Select, Save Selection	Saves circle outline around spherized earth to Alpha Channel 4 in EARTHMAP.EPS.
Click on the default colors icon on the toolbox	Sets background color to white; foreground color to black.
Choose Select, Inverse	Selects background and excludes spherized earth area.
Press Delete, then Select, None (or press Ctrl+D)	Removes rest of map, replacing it with white background.
Choose the Cropping tool from the toolbox, then marquee select an area that includes only the spherized earth	Displays boundary box—border of crop.
Click inside the boundary box	Image crops down in size and image file gets smaller.
Choose File, Open to open EARTH.TIF from the companion CD	File contains earth's texture (created in Fractal Design Painter).
Choose Select, All (or press Ctrl+A), then choose Edit, Copy (or press Ctrl+C)	Selects entire earth texture and copies it to Clipboard.

Double-click on the command button in the EARTH.TIF image window	Closes image file (no longer needed).
Choose the Magic Wand tool from the toolbox, then click on a black area on EARTHMAP.TIF	Selects the black pixels adjacent to the area you clicked over.
Choose **S**elect, Si**m**ilar	Selects all black pixels in image.
Choose **S**elect, **S**ave selection, then choose #5	Saves a silhouette of continents to Channel 5.
Choose **E**dit, Paste **I**nto	Pastes copy of EARTH.TIF into black selected areas (see fig. 18.21).

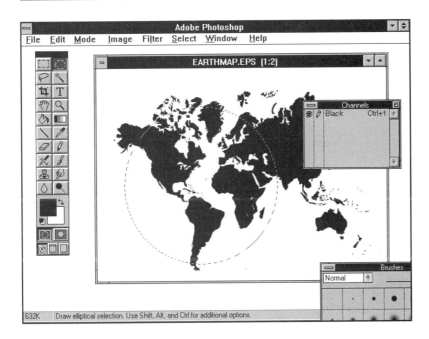

Figure 18.19
Photoshop rasterizes EARTH.EPS to a bitmap-type image you can work with in Photoshop.

Figure 18.20
The Spherize Filter gives flat objects a feeling of roundness.

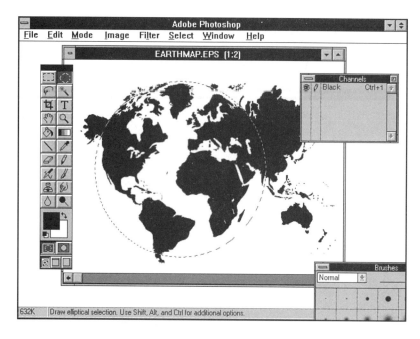

Figure 18.21
The Paste Into command keeps pasted images inside the selection borders.

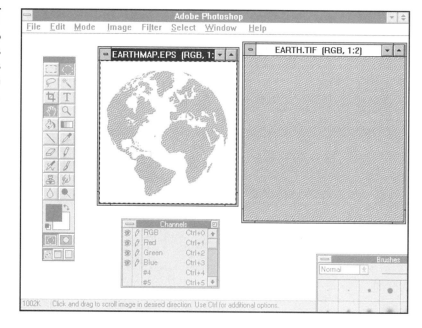

Lighting a Selection Area

You are well on the way to creating a digital masterpiece, but the continents, now composed of a Painter texture, lack global lighting—pardon the pun. Because you have selection borders saved for the sphere and the continents, you can use Photoshop's Gradient tool to color in the ocean and put better shading on the land masses.

Color My World

Click on the inverse colors icon at the upper right of the Foreground/Background color selection boxes on the toolbar	Switches foreground color to white, background to black.
Click on the background color	Displays the Color selection box Picker used to select a new background color.
Enter H **51** degrees, S **74**%, B **45**%, then click on OK	Sets background color to rich earth brown.
Double-click on the Gradient tool, set Type to **R**adial, then click on OK	Sets Gradient to apply foreground-to-background color with concentric transition.
On the Brushes palette, select Multiply mode and set opacity to **82%**	Causes heaviest application of color in darker areas of Gradient fill, almost no color in lighter areas.
Choose **S**elect, **L**oad Selection, then choose #5	Loads selection of continents you saved earlier.
Click and drag from Nova Scotia to South Africa with the Gradient tool	Fills continents with semitransparent shade of brown, creating appearance of light cast from 11 o'clock angle (see fig. 18.22).
Click on the foreground color selection box, choose H **175**, S **47**, and B **73**, then click on OK	Sets foreground color for ocean Gradient fill.
Click on the background color selection box, choose H **241**, S **56**, and B **53**, then click on OK	Sets background color for ocean's depths.
Choose **I**mage, **C**alculate, then choose Subtract	Displays Subtract dialog box.

continues

continued

Enter Source **1**: Document: **EARTHMAP.EPS**, Channel: **#6**, Source **2**: Document: **EARTHMAP.EPS**, Channel: **#4**, and **D**estination Document: EARTHMAP.EPS, Channel: **Selection**, **S**cale: **1**, **O**ffset: **0**. Then click on OK

Removes continents from sphere selection and creates a selection area containing only the oceans.

With the Gradient tool, click and drag from Nova Scotia to South Africa again

Floods only the ocean areas with foreground radiating to background color, so that ocean areas seem to be lit from same point as land masses (see fig. 18.23).

Click on the Channel #5 title in the Channels palette, then click on the command button and choose Delete Channel select **F**ile, Sa**v**e As WORLD.TIF to a directory on your hard disk, and make sure that the Save Alpha Channel option is checked

Deletes continents masking selection, saves sphere outline selection, and saves file as TIFF image that is easier to work with.

Figure 18.22
A selected area is partially covered by using the Brushes palette's Multiply mode and a partial opacity.

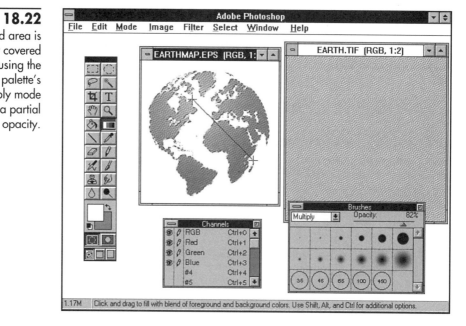

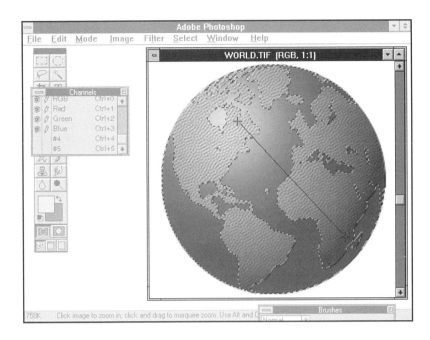

Figure 18.23
Applied to round shapes, the Radial type Gradient fill simulates a point of light.

Creating a Background with Dimension

This book gives you not only the time and the world, but also a place to store them!

The background for CLOCK and WORLD.TIF combines a real world image and a little supporting digital texture. Be careful not to build a scene with too many artificial elements, or it will look, well, artificial! In the next exercise, you use the Perspective command again and make quick work of a nicely stylized background.

Getting Behind a World Effort

Click on the default colors icon on the toolbox

Sets foreground color to black, background to white.

Choose **F**ile, **N**ew (or press Ctrl+N); set Width: **5** inches, Height: **5** inches, Resolution: **150** pixels/inch; select RGB Mode, then click on OK

"Canvas" in Photoshop for illustration background is the same resolution as the pieces you've built and accepts RGB color model.

Choose **F**ile, **O**pen DST_FLOR.TIF from the companion CD

One of two background images for this design.

Choose **S**elect, **A**ll (or press Ctrl+A), then choose **E**dit, **C**opy (or press Ctrl+C)

Copies entire DST_FLOR image to clipboard.

IV

Fantastic Assignments

continues

continued

Double-click on the command button in DST_FLOR.TIF's window	Closes image (no longer needed).
Choose <u>E</u>dit, <u>P</u>aste (or press Ctrl+V)	Pastes DST_FLOR.TIF copy into new image window.
Choose <u>I</u>mage, <u>E</u>ffects, then choose Perspective	Creates a boundary box around entire pasted selection.
Click and drag the boundary box's lower-right handle clear outside of the window	Creates illusion that top of selected image is pointed away from viewer.
Click and drag the upper-right corner of the boundary box straight down, about 3/4 inch	Enhances perspective effect (see fig. 18.24).
Click inside the Perspective boundary box	Cursor becomes a gavel and "nails" image to desired degree of perspective.
Click and drag the selection so that the bottom of the image is flush with the bottom of the image window	Final position for selection.
Choose <u>S</u>elect, <u>S</u>ave Selection	Saves selection to Alpha Channel 4.
Open FARMDUSK.TIF from the companion CD	File that completes background to new file.
Choose <u>S</u>elect, <u>A</u>ll (or press Ctrl+A), then choose <u>E</u>dit, <u>C</u>opy (or press Ctrl+C) and close FARMDUSK.TIF	Copies entire FARMDUSK.TIF image to Clipboard (you no longer need it).
Choose <u>E</u>dit, Paste <u>B</u>ehind	Pastes copy of FARMDUSK image behind abstract image in new file (see fig. 18.25).
Select the Cropping tool from the toolbox, start cropping point at the upper-left corner of the FARMDUSK copied paste, then Marquee-select across to the other edge and then down to the bottom of the window frame	Includes full-frame height of window in Cropping tool's boundary box, but eliminates white space and excess perspective image area.
Click inside the Cropping tool boundary box. From the <u>F</u>ile menu, choose Sa<u>v</u>e As DST.TIF on your hard disk; do *not* save Alpha Channels	Crops image, names it, and saves it as an RGB image. You no longer need saved Alpha Channel.

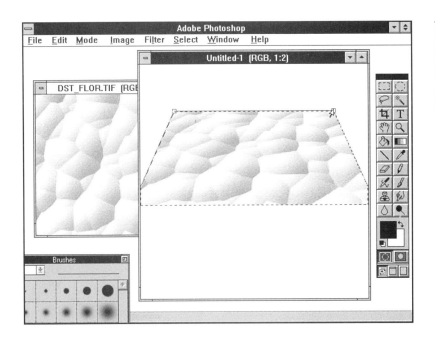

Figure 18.24
Use the
Perspective
command to
create great
fake floors!

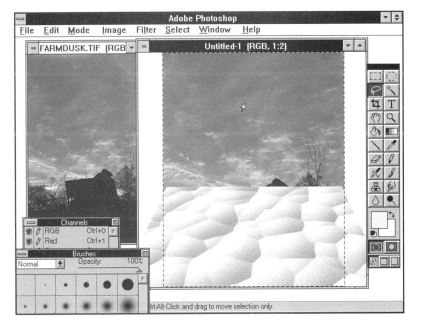

Figure 18.25
Set the new file to
dimensions that
allow positioning
and perspective
that go outside the
final crop.

IV

Fantastic Assignments

Composing a Bizarre Foreground on a Weird Background

If you positioned the two background elements so that you achieved an image like the one in figure 18.25, you now have a nice blend of the surreal and a bare tree, and the tip of a run-down barn that rather resembles a pyramid. The sky, which had a spectacular sunset reflected in it the day the image was taken, both enhances and contrasts with the abstract "floor." Learn to choose image elements according to their intrinsic visual content—you can adjust color, shading, and shaping later in Photoshop.

In the next three exercises, you add the clock and world to the background image and learn a few lighting tricks to bring the elements together.

Time Is on Your Side

Choose File, Open CLOCK.TIF (the image you created earlier)	The lower of the two elements you add to background next.
Choose Image, Calculate, then choose Add	Displays Add dialog box.
Enter Source 1 Document: **CLOCK.TIF**, Channel #4; Source 2 Document: **CLOCK.TIF,** Channel #5; Destination Document: **CLOCK.TIF**, Channel Selection, Scale:2, and Offset:0	Creates inverted selection marquee of Channels 4 *and* 5 in RGB channel.
Choose Select, Inverse (or press Ctrl+I)	Inverts selection in RGB channel to include entire clock image and exclude white background area.
Choose Edit, Copy (or press Ctrl+C)	Copies entire clock image to clipboard.
Press Ctrl+Tab, then choose Edit, Paste (or press Ctrl+C)	Toggles active window to DST.TIF image; pastes clock image into scene (see fig. 18.26).
Click and drag the selection with a selection tool so that the clock selection is centered and slightly above the horizon	Positions clock selection so that you can paste world over it.
Choose Select, Save Selection	Saves clock selection border to new channel in DST.TIF.
Choose File, Save (or press Ctrl+S)	Saves your work to hard disk.

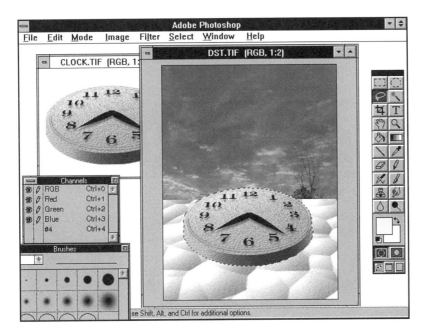

Figure 18.26
Save the selection of the pasted clock image so that you can call it back later in the new document.

The Add command combines the Brightness values of two channels to create a New Channel selection. The rules you follow are different than those for the Subtract command, because you are using a different math function. To add one channel selection to a second one, always choose Source 1 and 2 from the same document, choose the different channels, then specify the Destination in the same document as New Channel (*not* as Selection, as you did with the Subtract command).

The reason you use New Channel is that the new selection in the channel is inverted (the background instead of the combination of selection areas) because you are adding Brightness values instead of subtracting them to create a selection shape.

Calculate is not a straightforward command because it can be used also to combine channels that contain grayscale visual information in addition to the geometry of a selected area. The last step in adding two channels together is always to set **S**cale to **2**. This averages the Brightness values of the two channels, making the result a combination of selection shapes. Leave **O**ffset at **0** (unless you want to lighten the overall selection shape and ruin your new precisely defined selection borders).

Finishing the Earthy Illustration

Before you paste the WORLD.TIF image above the clock in the illustration, you need to create the *shadow* it would cast so that the image fits realistically into the illustration. Usually, shadows are rendered after a selection is in place in an image; the selection area is masked off and then detailed shadow work is painted in around it.

In this one instance, however, you can render the shadow *before* you paste the selection because you know the shape of the shadow (it is round) and its location (on top of the clock). One of the advantages of pasting images into a background image is that, by planning ahead, you can decide the order that elements are added. You save time and conserve file size when you don't have to save a selection to a channel after every other step!

I Feel the Earth Move

Choose **S**elect, **N**one (or press Ctrl+D)	Deselects everything in DST.TIF image.
Double-click on the Paint Bucket tool	Displays Paint Bucket Options dialog box.
Set a high value for Tolerance (even **255** is good); then click on OK	Ensures total coverage when you apply paint with Paint Bucket tool.
Click on the default colors icon on the toolbox	Sets foreground color to black, background to white.
Double-click on the Elliptical Marquee tool on the toolbox	Displays Elliptical Marquee Options dialog box.
Choose **S**elect Fea**t**her **12** pixels, then click on OK	Sets selection tool to create medium-sized Feathering border wherever you create an Elliptical selection.
Click and drag an ellipse selection over the clock image that covers the top half of the clock	Defines selection area where you create shadow of WORLD.TIF image.
In the Brushes palette, select the Paint Bucket tool, then select **Normal** Mode, **75**% Opacity	Setting causes Paint Bucket to pour semi-transparent "paint" into selection area.
Click inside the Elliptical Marquee selection with the Paint Bucket	Floods selection area with foreground color and creates WORLD.TIF shadow (see fig. 18.27).
Choose **F**ile, **O**pen and select WORLD.TIF, the image you saved earlier	Displays final element to be pasted into illustration.
Choose **S**elect, **L**oad Selection, then choose #4	Displays border selection to world (saved earlier).

Choose **E**dit, **C**opy (or press Ctrl+C), then press Ctrl+Tab	Copies world selection to clipboard, then toggles to DST.TIF as active image window.
Choose **E**dit, **P**aste (or press Ctrl+V)	Pastes world image onto DST.TIF background.
Click and drag the world image into position, centered and above the shadow you designed	Places world selection in its compositionally correct position in DST.TIF image (see fig. 18.28).
When the world image is in a good location, choose **S**elect, **N**one	Composites world image into DST.TIF image.
Choose **F**ile, **S**ave	Saves your work to your hard disk.

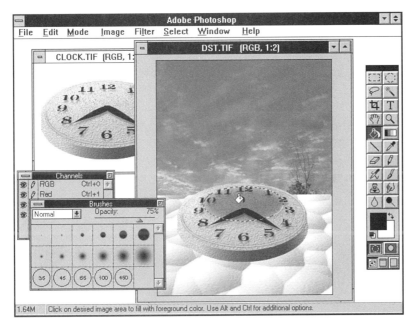

Figure 18.27

The Feather command causes a gradual color transition around the selection edge when paint is applied inside it.

You have done a good deal of shading, creating highlights, and adding shadows in this assignment. When you start using Photoshop to create your own illustrations, try not to obliterate visual content, such as textures, in the images when you apply digital paint. Feathering destroys visual content; because the Opacity was turned down on the Brushes palette in the last exercise when you created the world shadow, detail in the clock face was mostly retained. Use the Opacity setting on the Brushes palette to "hedge your bet" when you apply paint to intricate areas. In this way, if the coverage in the selection area is not ideal, you can always make a second paint pass.

IV

Fantastic Assignments

Figure 18.28
Place the world
image where it
belongs—over its
own shadow!

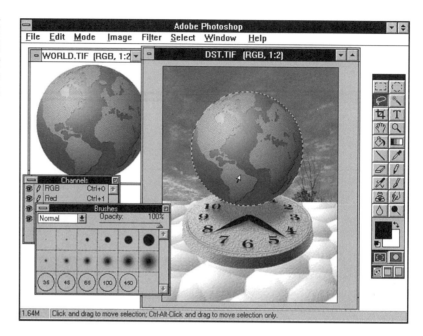

Oh—and be sure to reset the Elliptical Marquee tool's options for Feather, now that you've finished using it! If you don't, you might get a nasty surprise the next time you try to select with it!

As We Fade into DST

Creating a shadow to go under the clock image when you completed the DST.TIF background did not make sense. Because the clock image was the first to be placed in the background image, and because you can never be certain where a shadow will be placed without a reference point, creating the clock's shadow is reserved for the last step. Placing the world's shadow was an easy call—you knew it would be centered toward the top of the clock image area.

Incidentally, the rather cryptic DST prefix used in this assignment stands for *daylight saving time.* If you can think of a better title, I'm open.

In the next exercise, you polish off this illustration, then reflect on some of the finer points of the entire assignment.

The Floating Timepiece

Choose **S**elect, **L**oad selection illustration	Displays only selection channel in DST.TIF
Choose **S**elect, **I**nverse (or press Ctrl+I)	Selects everything except clock image; selection can now be colored into.
Click on the foreground color selection box on the toolbox	Calls Photoshop's Color Picker so that you can choose a foreground color.
Enter H **51** degrees, S **74**%, B **45**%, then click on OK	Selects same brown used earlier to create shading with Gradient tool and continents.
From the Brushes palette, select the Paintbrush tool; then select Multiply Mode, the **65** pixel tip, and **78**% Opacity	Settings for a fairly large brush and semi-transparent color to apply to selected areas.
Click and drag a short stroke under the selection border around the bottom of the clock image	Applies color to background image only; clock image is masked from changes.
Click and drag another short stroke above the first one	Multiply Mode for Paintbrush tip saturates previously colored area a little deeper and gently applies color to other area for first time (see fig. 18.29).
Deselect the selection border, get rid of the extra Channel #4 in DST.TIF, then **F**ile, **S**ave the image	Completes the illustration, and saves changes to hard disk.

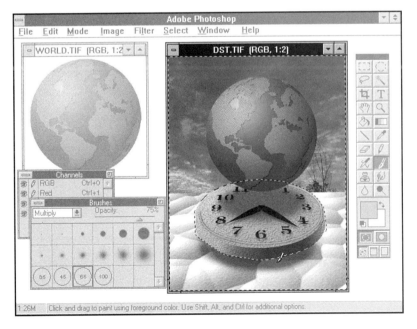

Figure 18.29
The finishing touch is the shadow beneath the clock image in DST.TIF.

The illustration looks terrific—and you have no paint on your hands!

Summary

You did not really need the FARMDUSK.TIF image in this assignment. It added a small touch of photorealism to the scene, but the objects you created were the *real* heroes, with a realism of their own that could have carried off the idea easily.

DST.TIF is a study in two techniques you should continue to practice on your own. The first is the use of textures, artificially created in Painter or elsewhere. You can use the images from the companion CD under the TEXTURES subdirectory as practice items, but you can also create your own textures in many different ways.

Fractal Design Painter is extremely useful for creating textures on-the-fly without ever having to leave your PC. You can also scan textures directly, using a flatbed or handheld scanner, and then trim, shade, and distort these images to suggest the shape you need to build cylinders, cubes, or globes. You can even reuse and recombine the images created in this assignment to create different scenes!

None of this would be possible without the power of Photoshop's channels. You learned several ways to modify a selection area and then save it. Try using different methods in your own work to achieve the most precise, creative way to approach a problem. Masking, coloring, and Photoshop filters are all affected by the combination of settings you use to carry out a command. There is no right or wrong way to do something in Photoshop. By using the features with an understanding of their properties, you will be able to solve any problem.

You are working your way up to total independence from using digital photography in your Photoshop work. In fantastic assignments in Photoshop, which rely more on synthetic images and your own imagination, you can create virtual lighting, virtual objects, and virtual settings. The resulting images transport the viewer from the humdrum to "How did they do that?" The next chapter walks you through a fantastic illustration that uses a 3D modeling program to create virtual reality images you can manipulate, using Photoshop.

Chapter Snapshot

In this chapter, you learn how to:

Virtual Reality: The Ingredients of Dreamwork

The time has come, having devoted a great deal of space in this book to redefining the art of retouching real-world photographs, to work on *non*-real-world images. Photorealistic, virtual-reality images can be created inside the computer. New software has given the entertainment industry tools to create all sorts of science fiction creatures and spacecraft. Scaled-down versions of the software have trickled down from RISC-based graphics workstations to our own PCs.

One such program is Renderize for Windows. It is a *rendering* program, which can light and apply textures to CAD *modeled* designs and present you with lifelike creations directly from your imagination.

But these images still need "cleaning up" to achieve seamless integration with other image sources to complete a scene—which is where Photoshop *always* enters the picture. For the exercises in this chapter, you use rendered designs, a texture we built, and other premade pieces, all of which are on the companion CD. Using these components, you'll build a "Virtual Reality" scene in Photoshop. And you're going to learn a little about how other high-end computer graphics programs work. The Reference Guide at the end of this book includes a list of names and addresses of the program developers, in case you want to use programs like these in your Photoshop work.

The Fantastic Concept Comes First

Suppose that your assignment is an illustration for a magazine article about industrial robots, entitled "The Heart of the Machine." For the composition, you need to generate the elements of a robot, a heart, some sort of background, and the title. First you tackle creating a robot. Two ingredients go into the rendering of a photorealistic image: the wireframe (a CAD design) of the robot, and the "skin" that is mapped to the wireframe.

Mapping, a term frequently used in computer imaging, means to plot information to a set of coordinates—the set of coordinates usually being on a 2D or 3D plane. The most common usage of mapping is in Windows—you map something to the monitor and then map it to a printer. The term *WYSIWYG* (What You See Is What You Get) means that the two mappings are identical (most of the time).

Computer information can be arranged to create visual information out of numbers that are associated with other numbers, which is how you get data graphs—visual representations of statistics. To design the robot image, an image of a circuit board is mapped to the wireframe of the robot. *Image-mapping* is used to cover the body of the robot with a repeating design that follows the robot's dimensional curves. Image-mapping is the plotting of a graphical image (like a TIFF or Targa file) to a 3D topology, as opposed to the flat, 2D way one usually views a graphical image. The *bump*-mapping of the same circuit image creates a 3D topology from a 2D circuit image. *Bump-mapping* makes lighter areas of an image recede and darker areas come forward (the effect is similar to conventional embossing). The first stop is a vector-image program, where CorelDRAW! is used to design the circuit board.

Designing "Skin" for a Dimensional Wireframe

Although the circuit board *could* be designed in Photoshop, using the right tool for the right task is always a good rule to remember. CorelDRAW! isn't a bitmap-design program like Photoshop, but the program's precise design tools make quick work of building a circuit board and this work can be exported as a TIFF image. Figure 19.1 shows the finishing touches being put on the circuit board. This is how the CIRCUIT.TIF image on the companion CD was created. You'll be using the image shortly to perform a little image enhancing for practice with images you may come by professionally that were created this way. (F.Y.I.—I have no idea what this circuit board does; I looked inside my Sony Walkman, found some good-looking parts, and drew them!)

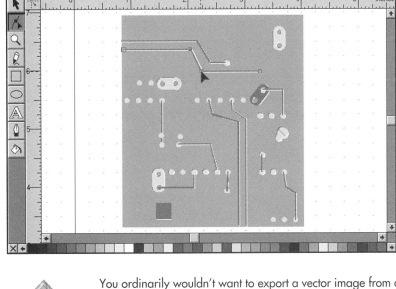

Figure 19.1
Vector-design
programs make
quick work of
technical (and
pseudotechnical!)
illustrations.

You ordinarily wouldn't want to export a vector image from a design program like CorelDRAW! or Adobe Illustrator as a TIFF image format. We made an exception in this instance because the design is in color. EPS is a preferred format for exporting drawing-type designs into Photoshop because Encapsulated PostScript is an information-style format that is resolution-independent, and can be scaled before it's imported by Photoshop to any dimension the user chooses, with no jagged, stairsteppy edges in the design. Photoshop offers its Anti-Aliasing feature for EPS files, so the edges are smooth.

The only problem is that color EPS format technology is in its infancy at this writing, and very few programs can export in this format. Presently, EPS designs in Grayscale mode are the highest degree of tonal image information a user can import for use in Photoshop from another application with any degree of certainty. So the CIRCUIT design was exported as a TIFF, which requires Photoshop's help to lend a measure of finesse and polish to the image before it looks realistic in the context of this chapter's assignment.

Humanizing a Design in Photoshop

In the following exercise, you are faced with the task of "softening" the Corel vector design. Unlike bitmap programs, vector programs tend to export images to a bitmap format with sharp, hard, precise pieces that can look unphotogenic and fake to the human eye. This is because vector design programs treat design elements as discrete objects with no regard to a viewer's focus on the design—it's always perfectly sharp and precise. To make CIRCUIT.TIF a suitable image to map on the surface of the robot's wireframe, it needs to be toned down a little. Now, *you are* not going to do any of the mapping in this exercise because you may not *have* the Renderize program! But you can use the techniques described here to enhance *any* vector design, not just one used for texture mapping. And you may find the results good "art" in their own right.

Softening a Vector Graphic

Open CIRCUIT.TIF from the companion CD	The image to be modified in Photoshop.
Choose **W**indow, Show C**h**annels (or press F6)	Displays Channel selections for active image.
Click on the Green title on the Channels palette (or press Ctrl+2)	Displays Green Channel for the active image window of CIRCUIT.TIF; clicking on the Green title makes this channel both visible and editable (indicated by the tiny eye and pencil icons to the left of the channel title).
Choose Fi**l**ter, Blur, then choose Gaussian Blur	Displays Gaussian Blur dialog box for this effect.
Type **1** pixel in the **R**adius box, then click on OK	Applies the slightest degree of Gaussian blur to the Green Channel only.
Choose **W**indow, Show **C**olors (or press F7)	Displays Colors palette, which is used soon.
Click on RGB in the Channels palette (or press Ctrl+0)	Displays blurred Green Channel's contribution to softening overall image.
Click+diagonal drag with the Zoom tool once, or twice in the center of the image	Marquee-zooms into the center of CIRCUIT.TIF, to a 3:1 viewing resolution.
Change your color selection to R **80**, G **180**, B **234** (or use Color Picker to enter these foreground color values manually)	Sets foreground color values.

Click on the unbordered bottom color selection box on the Color palette	Calls up the Color Picker for selecting a background color.
Pull sliders on the Colors palette to R **37**, G **38**, B **113** (or use Color Picker to enter values manually)	Sets background color value.
Double-click on the Gradient tool	Displays Gradient dialog box.
Click the Style **N**ormal and **R**adial radio buttons, then type a value of **50**% in the **M**idpoint skew field	Creates radial fill from foreground and background color.
Click on the Elliptical marquee tool	Tool used to create a light on CIRCUIT.TIF.
Press Shift while you click and drag diagonally with the Elliptical marquee tool (see fig. 19.2)	Constrains selection to perfect circle. (Stop when circle is about three times size of another round doodad on CIRCUIT.TIF.)

Choose the Gradient tool, then click and drag from an 11 o'clock position inside the selection area to a 4 o'clock position slightly outside the selection area. Creates radial fill, also shown in figure 19.2.

Press Ctrl+D	Deselects everything in active image.
Choose **I**mage, **A**djust, then choose Brightness/Contrast (or press Ctrl+B)	Displays Brightness and Contrast dialog box.
Type **-20** in Brightness, **+4** in Contrast, then click on OK	Darkens image and creates a little more contrast in the selection area.
Double-click on the Hand tool	Displays Zoom field of entire active image.
Save the image to your hard disk, or Close (Alt+4) the file and click on No when in the Photoshop's exclamation dialog box	This image won't be used in the remainder of this chapter's assignment. You're done with it, so you may elect to close it without saving it.

In the last exercise, you applied photographic, bitmap-type qualities to an imported vector art file that was a little too "clean" to be passed off as a real-world image. By blurring the Green channel, you "defocused" the image without ruining its overall visual information. You may want to experiment, using different channels in an image to sharpen or blur it to simulate different camera focuses at which a real-world photo might be captured.

IV

Fantastic Assignments

Figure 19.2
The Radial
Gradient-fill tool
can simulate
spherical objects.

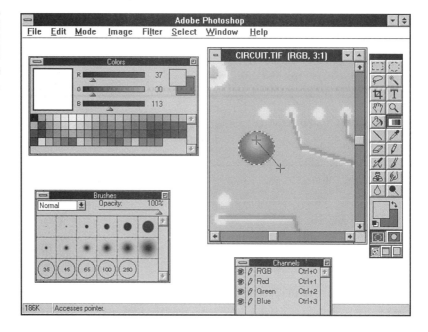

Creating a light on the circuit board was simple. Soon you will see how it fits into the scheme of the wireframe mapping. Figure 19.3 shows the finished hybrid of vector design and bitmap enhancement.

Figure 19.3
A TIFF image that
began as a vector
type.

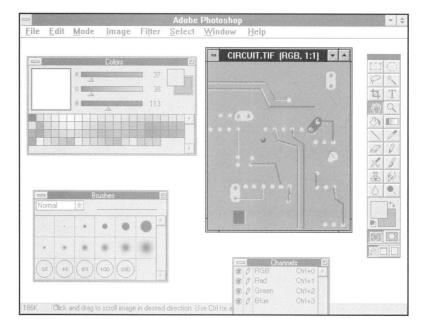

In the last exercise, you blurred a color channel, then sharpened the overall RGB image by applying contrast. A casual observation might be that you did an effect, then *undid* it. Nothing could be farther from the truth!

Color pixels *shift* in an image when you issue commands such as Blur, Sharpen, Contrast, and apply other effects. And they'll never, never be the same, even after you apply an "inverse" command. The pixels *continue* to shift in color and position, regardless of which effects you choose. It's the same concept as demonstrated with successive Levels adjustments in Photoshop—all changes are *relative*, based on a previous change. For this reason, saving an original of a file is important if you are experimenting with it.

Think of an image as a deck of cards, and Photoshop's effects as shuffling the cards. If you shuffle cards once, you cannot restore their original order by shuffling them a second time!

Instant Robots

The second part of creating a virtual subject for the illustration is to make a model to which the rendering program can map the CIRCUIT.TIF image. Biomechanics Corp. of America makes a splendid DOS program, called Mannequin, that automatically creates a DXF (*Data Exchange Format*, a CAD file format standard) model according to gender, weight, height, and even nationality! Mannequin's ability to almost instantly create human, 3D shapes takes days, if not weeks, off the process of designing of the human figure used for the robot. No CAD experience is necessary. In minutes, with a pull and tug here and there, the model is posed and ready to be rendered. Figure 19.4 shows the Mannequin interface, along with the robot-to-be.

For in-depth information about dimensional modeling and rendering, you may want to pick up a copy of *Learn CAD with AutoSketch*, (New Riders Publishing). This is a fascinating way for designers to use industrial-design packages in a fine-art manner.

IV

Fantastic Assignments

Figure 19.4
A DXF file can contain 3D information about an object, or several objects grouped together.

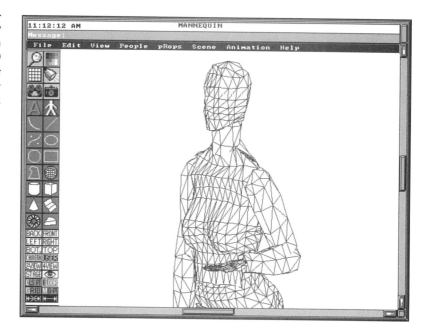

Putting the Pieces Together

Renderize for Windows maps bitmap images to vector information (like DXF files) to produce a rendered piece. After loading the CIRCUIT.TIF image, along with HARTPOSE.DXF (the Mannequin creation), into the Renderize program, we set lighting, a background color, and specified the method in which CIRCUIT.TIF is mapped to the wireframe model.

It's simpler than it sounds. Renderize lets the user drag on virtual spotlights as well as on the wireframe in a 3D workspace, and to set a bump-mapping to the wireframe's surface to create "texture" from the little doodads and light that are part of the CIRCUIT.TIF image design.

The most important concern at this phase is to specify a flat, colored background for the rendered robot—a background that doesn't contain any of the colors used in the CIRCUIT.TIF image. Why? Because you want to create your own, science-fictionesque background for the design. You need to use Photoshop's Magic Wand tool to separate the robot from its background when Renderize finishes building the image. The job can be easy or difficult, depending on the background color selection.

As this book goes to press, Visual Software has released an upgrade to their rendering program, called Renderize Live. In addition to extra features and other enhancements, Renderize Live is now Alpha channel "aware." This means the user can specify an additional information channel about a mask in

the finished, rendered image that Photoshop can read and separate rendered models from, without the fuss of specifying a solid background of unique color.

This doesn't mean you should forget how to use the Magic Wand tool, though! There are plenty more programs that can generate images for use in Photoshop that still haven't adopted the Alpha channel convention.

We chose purple for the background. After a few dialog box settings, Renderize assembled the robot from a TIFF image and Mannequin's 3D wireframe file (see fig. 19.5). You can specify how large an image is rendered in Renderize; we chose 3 by 5 inches as the total area.

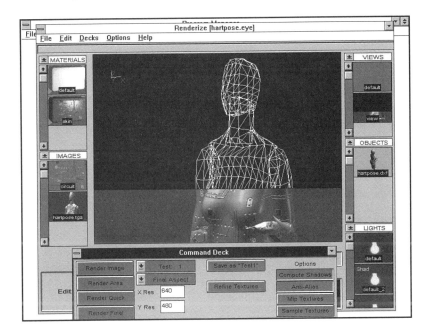

Figure 19.5
Many photo-realistic computer images are created by rendering a model.

Creating a Surreal Background

Soon, you will use the rendered robot (saved as HARTPOSE.TIF) and a heart TIFF image we created, by using a CAD program and Renderize to produce a *second* photorealistic image. They remain on the companion CD for the moment, because you now need to concentrate on a background for the design first.

I wanted a setting with a spacey sort of background that still conveyed an organic, natural quality. Again, CorelDRAW! made designing many irregularly shaped "stones" a snap. You can see their wireframe construction in figure 19.6.

Figure 19.6

Vector designs use Bézier curves, which are just like Photoshop's Paths.

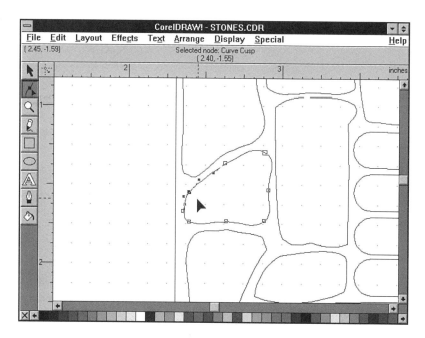

Photoshop Goes 3D!

The STONES image was designed larger than the HARTPOSE.TIF image (about 3.5-inches by 6.1-inches) so that it could accommodate type and frame the robot image. The image was exported from CorelDRAW! as a TIFF image. Now you are going to open the image in Photoshop and turn a good graphic into a superb photo(surreal)istic image! Photoshop does *embossing*, which is similar in theory to Renderize's bump-mapping, but produces a different effect.

Embossed Stones

Open STONES.TIF from the companion CD	The image to which you will apply an effect.
Choose Filter, Stylize, then choose Emboss	Displays Emboss dialog box (see fig. 19.7).
Click and drag the line in the circle to about 118 degrees (or type **113** in the Angle box)	Creates embossed effect with light source matching that of Renderize TIFF image.
Type **8** for pixel Height, **100**% for Amount	Embosses design to depth of 8 pixels (maximum of 10), with about one-fifth of the original color information retained in the emboss. (For more explanation, see following Tip.)

Click on OK	Confirms selections and displays active image.
Double-click on the Magic Wand tool on the toolbox, type **1** pixel for Tolerance, and make sure that **A**nti-Aliasing is checked OFF	You want to pick up only one density in the image. Anti-Aliasing seeks to select similarly colored pixels to include in the selection area, and 50% gray would be included in the white selection otherwise.
Click on a white area of STONES.TIF	Selects highlight in embossed image.
Choose **S**elect, Si**m**ilar	Selects all remaining highlights (see figure 19.8).
Choose **S**elect, **S**ave Selection	Saves all highlights in embossed image to new channel, by default entitled Channel 4.
Press Ctrl+D	Deselects everything in the image.
Click on the Channel #4 title on the Channels palette	Displays view of the saved selection areas.
Click on the command button on Channels palette, then choose Channel Options from from the drop-down list, click on the Color Indicates Masked Areas radio button, and then click on OK	Displays masked areas as black and selected areas as white from the Alpha channel view of the image, which you'll be working in shortly.
Click on the RGB channel title on the Channels palette	Displays composite (normal) view of image.
Choose **F**ile, Sa**v**e As, then find a working directory and name it STONE.TIF; make sure the Save Alpha Channels box is checked in the Save As dialog box	Saves your work to hard disk.

The emboss effect that comes with Photoshop can be applied to color images as well as to the monochrome STONES image. In either case, most of the color information is discarded during the embossing process. This didn't matter with the black and white STONES image, but you might want to keep some original color if you were working on an emboss of a 24-bit RGB image. To do so, you can set the Amount from the lowest value (1) to the value of highest color retention (500). This creates an interesting effect, but "interesting" is about as far as you can take this option. I have never found a commercial illustration purpose for a high emboss Amount (which takes a great deal of PC processing time to achieve).

IV

Fantastic Assignments

Figure 19.7
Embossing can be
set to any angle.

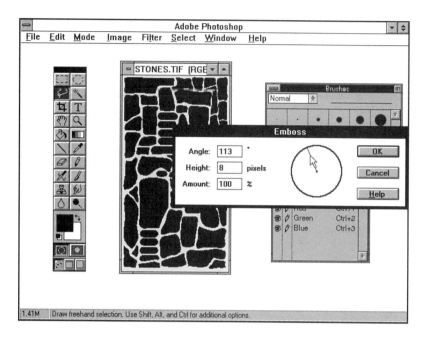

Figure 19.8
The highlights of
the embossed
image can be
saved as a
separate selection.

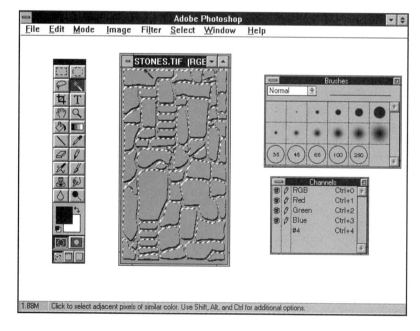

Adding Light and Color to an Image

Now that the white values have been assigned to a different channel, you can select them again—regardless of the changes you make to the overall piece. STONES.TIF now has some interesting dimensional value, but it lacks lighting and color information to make it as "real" as the robot you are going to add.

To give this image more drama, and a slightly moody look , you need to colorize the gray areas to make them seem less sterile. You also need to add some interesting color lighting to the highlights you saved earlier. You begin with the entire image, then concentrate on the specifics.

An important "art" lesson I learned early in the imaging game is to work from the general to the specific. This rule applies to both physical artwork, and the digital art you create on the PC. Start with a canvas, rough out the design, and save the finishing touches for last.

Giving the Wall Some Depth

Choose **M**enu, **R**GB Color	Converts the STONES.TIF image to color. The image was originally rendered as a Grayscale file to conserve file space until it needed to be larger.
Click on a gray area of STONES.TIF with the Magic Wand tool	Selects gray areas only.
Choose **S**elect, Si**m**ilar	Picks up other gray areas that might be bounded (hence separated from area you clicked on) by neighboring white and black values.
Select **I**mage, **A**djust, then choose Hue/Saturation (or press Ctrl+U)	Displays Hue/Saturation dialog box.
Check the Colorize box	You can assign a color for the gray value (see fig. 19.9).
Enter the following numbers: Hue **-178**, Saturation **23**, Brightness **-71** (or use the sliders to change the values), then check Preview	You can see changes you are making in gray selection areas; you are colorizing gray to a darker slate color.
Click on OK	Confirms selections and displays the image.

continues

continued

Click on the Channels Command button, select New Channel	Adds Channel 5, a blank channel, to STONES image.
Choose **S**elect, **N**one (or press Ctrl+D)	Deselects the gray areas you just colorized. Nothing should be selected in the image now.
Double-click on the Gradient tool on the toolbox	Displays Gradient tool Option box.
Make one change only: change Midpoint Skew to 40%	Adjusts "meeting point" of foreground and background values in a Radial Gradient fill closer to foreground color. This will produce a fill with less contrast the way you'll use the tool next.
Click on the default color icon on the toolbox	Sets foreground color to black, background to white.
Click on the inverse colors icon on the toolbox	Reverses foreground/background default setting.
Click and drag the Gradient cursor from 1/3 of the way down from the top center of the Channel 5 view of the image to 4 o'clock near the bottom of the image (see fig. 19.10)	Creates a spotlight effect in the channel.
Choose **S**elect, **A**ll (or press Ctrl+A)	Selects Channel 5, from border to border.
Choose **E**dit, **C**opy (or press Ctrl+C)	Copies Channel 5 to Clipboard.
Select the RGB channel from the Channels palette (or press Ctrl+0)	Displays main view of image.
Choose **E**dit, **P**aste (or press Ctrl+V)	Pastes Channel 5 copy on top of RGB channel, in the exact position it had in Channel 5.
Choose **E**dit, Composite C**o**ntrol	Displays Composite Controls dialog box.
Choose Multiply from the Mode drop-down list, type **100**% Opacity	Makes copied selection invisible at lighter values and pushes darker areas of pasted selection toward black in smooth pattern created with Gradient tool (see fig. 19.11).
Click on OK	Confirms selections and displays the image.
Choose **F**ile, **S**ave	Saves your work to hard disk.

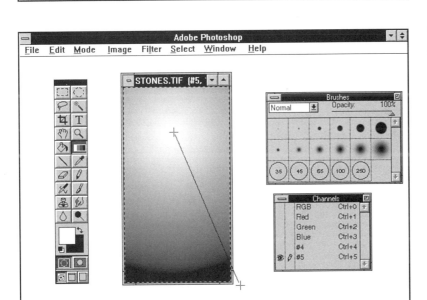

Figure 19.9
Check the Colorize box of the Hue/ Saturation dialog box to assign a color for the gray value.

Figure 19.10
The Gradient tool can suggest a lighting source in a "flat" image.

Figure 19.11
The Multiply Mode
darkens areas to
the foreground
color.

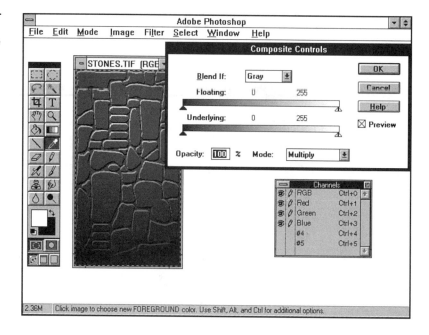

The modes and painting/editing slider on the Brushes palette can also be used to blend a pasted image into a background image, but only if you have a selection tool active at the time of the pasting.

If Multiply mode seems a strange way to achieve the single-source lighting effect of last exercise, you might want to know why the effect happened this way. Multiply mode will darken an image's pixels in a Composite blend toward the foreground value, which you specified as white. But because no "whiter than white" pixels were in the STONES colorized selection areas, they remained the same color. But when the Gradient Fill selection you copied over the RGB channel faded to black, the effect of Multiply mode is visible. It darkened the bottom "stones" and created an overall lighting effect that gives the illusion of a soft spotlight cast on the scene!

You can use different angles when you design the Gradient Radial fill to highlight different areas in your work. You can even use a Linear Gradient, or several of them in different areas of an image, to simulate light reflecting off different flat selection areas. Experiment with the technique you learned in the last exercise, creating different lighting situations in different images.

To automate the process of creating elegant gradient and other type fills, check out Kai's Power Tools for Windows, from HSC software. It's a collection of plug-in filter effects designed for use in Photoshop that's extremely useful for creating compound gradient fills, in just about every conceivable variety.

Spotlight on Highlights

Now, to address the stone highlights you saved earlier. The Radial Gradient can be used also to suggest intense highlight areas on smooth, round objects such as these fake stones. You learn the technique in the next exercise.

Polishing Stones

Click on the Channel 4 title on the Channels palette	The stone highlights are saved here.
Marquee-zoom to a 1:2 view anywhere on Channel #4	You need to see highlights clearly to select them.
Double-click on the Magic Wand tool on the toolbox	Displays Magic Wand options dialog box.
Set Tolerance to **127** pixels, click on OK	Establishes "break point" for selecting adjacent, similarly colored pixels, just short of 50% black.
Click on a white area in Channel #4	Selects stone highlight (see fig. 19.12).
Click on the RGB channel in the Channels palette	Highlighted area is selected in color view of STONES.
Click on the foreground color selection box on the toolbox	Calls Photoshop's Color Picker for selecting a foreground color.
Type R **110**, G **76**, B **255**, in the appropriate field boxes then click on OK	Sets foreground color to a warm purple.
Double-click on the Gradient tool, reset Midpoint skew to **50**%	Returns Radial-fill option to default.
Click and drag the Gradient tool, starting in selection area, down to 4 o'clock, outside selection area	Floods selection area with radial fill, starting with purple and gradating to black (see fig. 19.13).
Choose <u>F</u>ile, <u>S</u>ave	Saves your work to hard disk.

If you are thinking, "One down, five million to go" after the highlight-coloring exercise, relax. Now that you understand how to color the highlights, you don't have to repeat the exercise and fill in *all* the highlights! The completed background is already done—it's the STONE2.TIF image on the companion CD.

Figure 19.12
Selected white area in Channel 4 corresponds to highlight area in the RGB channel.

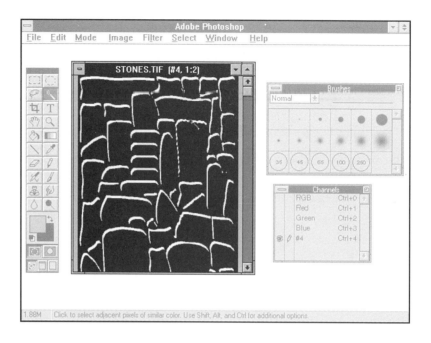

Figure 19.13
The Gradient tool "softens" the highlighted selection area, in addition to coloring it.

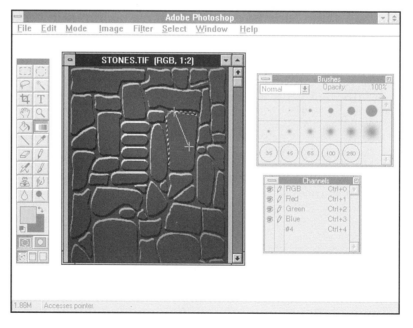

Just repeat the last steps a few times now to get the hang of it. You can use the Radial Gradient to imply a "rounded" texture to a selection area. And by saving the highlights to a separate channel before you start compositing Channel 5 into the RGB image, you can create some drama in highlight areas that have been obscured and are difficult to select now. You've just tasted some of the power of Photoshop's selection tools and Channels.

By the way, to minimize any potential confusion about channel numbers in the following exercises, we've deleted the extra channels in STONE2 after finishing the STONES exercise image for you.

Adding the Robot as a Foreground Image

The time has come to add the HARTPOSE.TIF image to the STONES2.TIF background. Whether you completed the last exercise or not, the robot image has been kept out of Photoshop until you're ready for it—for good reason. With the two extra information channels in the STONES image, this TIFF file now tips in at almost 2.5M! With a 1M robot image added to your system's RAM, we're talking about serious strains on any PC with less than 12M of RAM! These exercises were designed on a 486 DX2/66 with 20M of RAM, but it sometimes ran sluggishly because Photoshop needs about three times the active image size in RAM and swap-disk space to function. A word to the wise: For smooth Photoshop performance, keep only the image windows which you are actively working on open.

Be aware of a few telltale signs that you should save your work and exit Photoshop because your memory pool is getting filled and Windows is running out of resources. If images don't completely redraw, save and get out fast! If images redraw slowly after you apply an effect, Windows resources are low.

Resource Monitor (RESMON.EXE) is an invaluable Windows utility included on the companion CD, in the BOOLEANS subdirectory. It gives you current information on how your Windows memory resources are doing. See the documentation on how to install this utility that accompanies the executable file in the same subdirectory. It's a good idea to put RESMON in your Windows Startup Group so it loads when you begin a Windows session. If you're getting sluggish performance from Photoshop while working on an image, press Ctrl+Esc to call Windows Task List to your workspace, and check out what Resource Monitor is telling you that you presently have for GDI (Graphics Device Interface) resources in Windows. If the number is below 60%, seriously consider saving your work at this point and restarting Windows.

This is preferred practice over allowing Windows resources to become depleted, and letting Windows close you out of your work (read *crash!*) rather unceremoniously!

You'll be adding the robot image to the STONE2 background image in the next exercise. You'll also be adding a special effect around the outline of the robot eventually, so it's important you use the right selection tool now, and save the selection area within the STONES2 image file, to create a special effect with it later.

Borderline Robotics

Open STONE2.TIF and HARTPOSE.TIF from the companion CD	The two images you will composite together.
Double-click on the Magic Wand tool, set Tolerance to **50** pixels, make sure that Anti-Aliasing is checked, then click on OK	Sets Tolerance to perfect balance for creating sharp border around robot image (see following Note).
Click on the purple background in HARTPOSE.TIF with the Magic Wand tool	Selects neighboring pixels in this color-value family.
Choose <u>S</u>elect, Si<u>m</u>ilar	Picks up little areas tucked inside robot's arm and other areas of purple background.
Choose <u>S</u>elect, <u>I</u>nverse	Selects only the robot, with no background in selection (see fig. 19.14).
Choose <u>E</u>dit, <u>C</u>opy (or press Ctrl+C)	Copies robot selection to Clipboard.
Double-click on the Control button in the HARTPOSE.TIF window	Closes image, reducing stress of having two active images held in your system's RAM.
Press Ctrl+plus, then scroll down to the bottom of STONES2.TIF	Displays image in 1:2 zoom field; bottom of image area is visible.
Choose <u>E</u>dit, <u>P</u>aste (or press Ctrl+V)	Pastes robot onto STONE2 image.
Press Ctrl+H	Hides selection border's edges, for accurate positioning.
Click and drag inside the robot selection border	Position selection with its bottom touching bottom of STONE2 image, aligned to center of STONE2 (see fig. 19.15).
Choose <u>S</u>elect, <u>S</u>ave Selection	Saves robot outline to Channel 4 in STONE2.TIF.
<u>S</u>elect, <u>N</u>one (or press Ctrl+D)	Deselects the robot image and it becomes part of the STONE2 background image.
Choose <u>F</u>ile, Sa<u>v</u>e As, pick a subdirectory on your hard drive, and call the image **STONES.TIF**	Saves the image to your hard disk.

Whether you've been using the STONES image, or have skipped ahead and actually used the STONE2 image, name the file STONES.TIF at this point, so you can reference it in the next exercise. You'll change the name shortly.

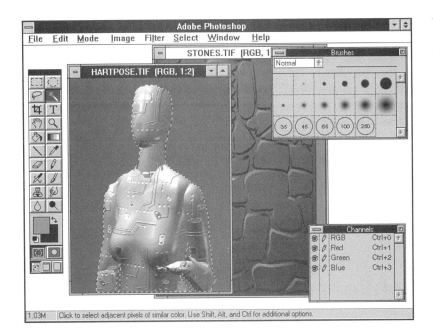

Figure 19.14
Use the Magic Wand tool with the Inverse command to select something with a solid background.

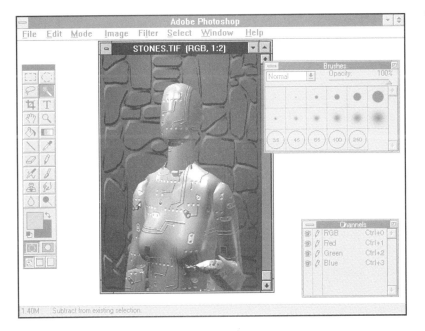

Figure 19.15
Be sure to save the selection area before deselecting the robot!

IV

Fantastic Assignments

In the last exercise, you reset the Magic Wand tool to 50 pixels for a special reason. The image Renderize created in HARTPOSE.TIF has a clean, solid background, which usually could be selected with a Magic Wand Tolerance of 1 pixel. But because Renderize simulates camera views and focal depth, in addition to its other "virtual" qualities, the robot was ever-so-slightly out of focus around its edges when "photographed." This is an Anti-Aliasing function common to most rendering applications.

Therefore, when selecting the background, we wanted to include *more* than just one value of purple so that we could include some pixels near the edge of the robot itself. Some trial and error work—one pixel, 12, and so on—led to the ideal 50 pixels, which worked. You might want to fine-tune your Magic Wand selection tolerances according to how fuzzy a background is in relation to what you want to select. The right tolerance varies from image to image.

Neon Highlights

The selection border you saved to a new channel in the last exercise can help you do some special stuff around the robot's border. Glowing borders around objects can be wonderful—unless they're around Fred's truck, seen in Chapter 8!

To create the effect around the robot, you need to modify the border selection in Channel 4 with—what else?—the Border effect! In the next exercise, you modify the selection, then use some familiar tools to create a neon outline around the robot.

Bending Some Neon

Double-click on the Quick Mask mode button on the toolbox	Calls the Mask Options dialog box.
Click on the Color Indicates Masked Areas radio button, then click OK	Sets masked areas to display as black and selection areas to display as white when viewed from an Alpha channel.
Click on the Standard mode button on the toolbox	Returns you to the regular editing mode for images.
Click on Channel #4 (or press Ctrl+4) in the Channels palette	Displays channel selection created earlier.
Choose **S**elect, **B**order, type **12** pixels, then click on OK	Creates selection border 6 pixels inside and 6 pixels outside Channel 4 selection outline.
Select the Lasso tool from the toolbox	Tool used for subtracting from bordered selection in next step.

Press Ctrl and drag around the very bottom edge of the marquee selection	Subtracts very bottom of selection area (see fig. 19.16).
Choose **S**elect, **S**ave Selection	Creates Channel 5, with border 12 pixels wide but no "bottom."
Choose **S**elect, **A**ll (or press Ctrl+A)	Selects everything in Channel 5, not just the selection border.
Choose **F**ilter, Blur, then Gaussian Blur, set to **12** pixels, then click on OK	Applies soft blur to border selection (see fig. 19.17).
Choose **F**ile, **S**ave	Saves your work to hard disk.

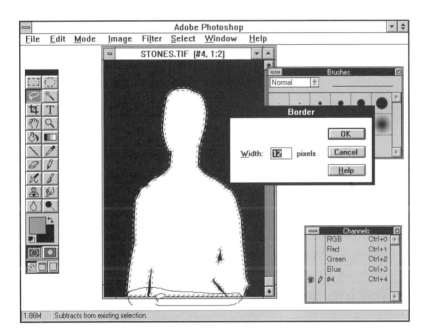

Figure 19.16
Pressing Ctrl and dragging with the Lasso tool subtracts from the selection border.

Tip

If you didn't remove the bottom edge of the border selection in the last exercise, your Gaussian blur will not be ideal to apply to the next effect. Try this instead: use the Border command again on Channel 4 and save Channel 4 to overwrite your present Channel 5. Then use the Eraser tool to wipe out the bottom of the border before you apply the Gaussian blur. This will work if your background color is still set to black. A good thing to remember is not to delete extra channels until you are certain you no longer need them!

Figure 19.17
A Gaussian blur affects a grayscale channel, producing a soft glow.

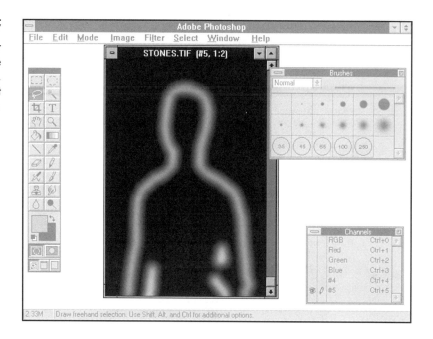

Creating a Neon Effect

The results of using the Gaussian blur to fuzz a selection and using it to fuzz a border are different. Fuzzing a border does not affect the inside of the selection. In the next exercise, you are going to create a neon "glow" around the robot. If you had simply blurred the entire selection in Channel 4, the neon effect would be inside the selection as well as around the border of the robot, ruining all the fancy detail work that went into creating the robot!

Taking a Shine to the Robot

Click on Channel #5 (or press Ctrl+5), then choose **S**elect, **A**ll (or press Ctrl+A)	Selects entire bordered, blurred image.
Choose **E**dit, **C**opy (or press Ctrl+C)	Copies selection to clipboard.
Click on RGB in the Channels palette (or press Ctrl+0)	Restores view of STONE2 to normal.
Choose **E**dit, **P**aste (or press Ctrl+V)	Copies Channel 5 selection to RGB channel. Do not deselect or move anything! You haven't finished yet!

Choose **I**mage, **A**djust, then choose Hue/Saturation (or press Ctrl+U)

Displays Hue/Saturation dialog box.

Check Colorize, then type Hue **-101**, Saturation **49**, Lightness **0**

Colorizes only blurred area of selection, leaving background black (see fig. 19.18).

Click on OK

Confirms selections and displays image.

Choose **E**dit, Composite C**o**ntrols, set Opacity at **95**%, select Screen mode from the drop-down list, then click on OK

"Bleaches" out lighter areas into RGB area; darker areas have no effect on RGB image (see fig. 19.19).

Choose **F**ile, Sa**v**e As STONE2.TIF HARTMACH.TIF, click OK, then check **S**ave Alpha Channels box when TIFF Options dialog box appears, and then click on OK

Saves your work.

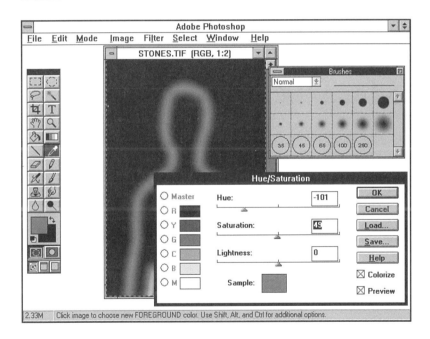

Figure 19.18

You can colorize a grayscale (Channel) selection only after it has been copied to the RGB channel.

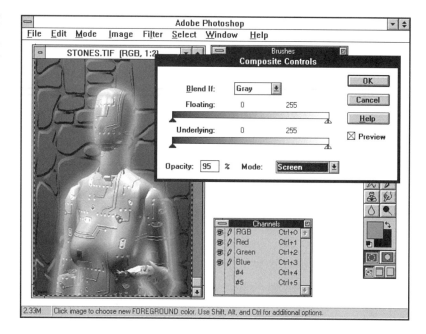

Figure 19.19
Screen mode is the
inverse of Multiply
mode.

Adding a Little Heart

Having completed the last exercise, you can get rid of the extra channels in the STONE2.TIF image. To do so, click on Channel 5, click on the Channels palette Command button, and select Delete Channel. You will see the file size of this image shrink substantially.

You use some of the same techniques you've learned before to add a glowing HEART.TIF image to the scene, with a minor variation. A neon glow effect will be added to the heart image, but you'll be creating the blurred outline to create the effect a little differently.

Before you begin, remember that the image file you're presently using, whether it's been constructed from the STONE or the STONES2.TIF image, should have no extra Alpha channels in it. You are finished with the border used to create the neon effect around the robot. This means the Channels palette should only be displaying four channels—the RGB composite, the Red, the Green, and the Blue. If you have channels numbered beyond this, click to the superfluous channels, and select Delete channel from the Channels palette's command button drop-down list. You'll be adding channels to the present image of robot and stone background, and don't want the image file to be larger than it has to be while performing the next steps.

The Droid Gets a Transplant

Open HEART.TIF from the companion CD	Image to be added to scene.
Select, Load Selection	Loads the selection border the authors created for your use with this image.
Choose Edit, Copy (or press Ctrl+C)	Copies selection to Clipboard.
Double-click on HEART.TIF's command button	Closes file (no longer needed).
Choose Edit, Paste (or press Ctrl+V)	Pastes heart selection into active image window, STONE2.TIF.
Click and drag the heart selection to position above the robot's hand	Positions heart in image (see fig. 19.20).
Select Save, Save Selection	Saves heart floating selection to new Channel 4.
Select Save, Save Selection	Saves selection, again, to new Channel 5. You need two copies because you are going to mess one up and you need another, untouched one to work with later.
Press Ctrl+D	Deselects floating heart selection.
Click on Channel #4, then select Filter, Gaussian Blur (or press Ctrl+F)	Photoshop remembers last effect applied, with its previous effect settings (suitable, in this instance).
Choose Select, All (or press Ctrl+A), then Edit, Copy (or press Ctrl+C)	Copies all of Channel 4 to Clipboard.
Select the RGB Channel (or press Ctrl+0) on the Channels palette	Target for copied Channel 4.
Choose Select, Load Selection, then select #5	Activates selection border around heart image.
Choose Edit, Paste Behind	Copies Channel 4 to RGB channel, on top of the robot and background, but behind the selection of the heart image.
Select Image, Adjust, then choose Hue/Saturation (or press Ctrl+U), check Colorize, and click on OK	Same technique as the one used for neon outline. Default Colorize settings are appropriate this time.
Choose Edit, Composite Controls, then type 100% Opacity, select Screen mode, and click on OK	Technique and result (see fig. 19.21) are almost the same as those for robot's border selection.
Choose File, Save As and name the hard disk	Saves your work to image HARTMACH.TIF.

Figure 19.20
The Paste Behind command allows the heart image to sit on top of the Pasted copy from Channel 4.

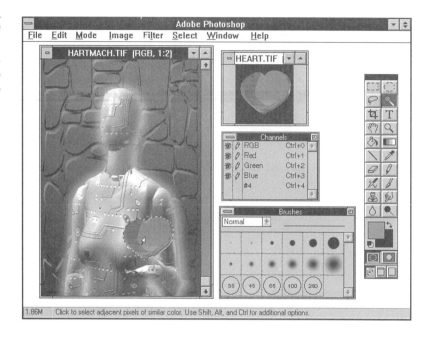

Figure 19.21
A 100% Screen mode in Composite Controls makes the heart image appear to be glowing!

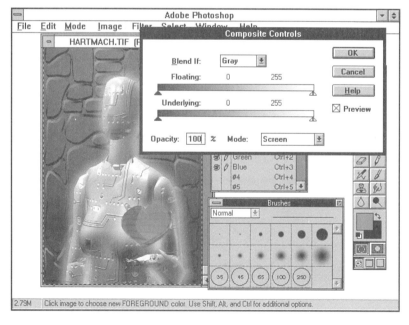

In the last exercise, you did a variation on the neon effect that viewers will not notice (and rightly so). The heart image now glows, but the glow comes from *behind* the heart (because you pasted behind selection #5). An aura is *around* the robot because you pasted over it, using the Composite Controls. The two different techniques are creating a spectacular image!

The robot's outstretched palm looks a little pale. You can correct that now. This step does not merit a exercise. Use the Eyedropper tool to sample the color in the heart image area. Then get the Airbrush tool from the toolbox. Set the Brushes palette to **100**% Opacity, Multiply mode, and the 100-pixel diameter tip. Marquee-zoom in on the hand (see fig. 19.22) and "hit" the palm of the robot's hand only once. You can create a much more diffuse and subtle effect with the Airbrush tool than you can with the Paintbrush tool. It's an easy way to create a soft reflection of the heart's glow on the robot's palm.

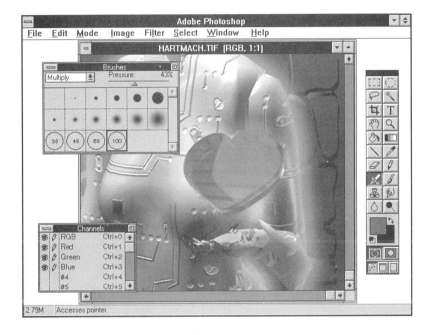

Figure 19.22

Use the Airbrush tool to create subtle tonal and color variations.

Text Appeal

You have accomplished some serious work and (from a technical standpoint) you have added new techniques to your retouching arsenal. Now for another example of how you can use other programs with Photoshop. The last piece of this assignment—the type—was generated in another design program. Because the typeface, Bitstream Industria, needed some kerning (interletter spacing) and a little stretching to look "ideal," HARTLOGO.EPS was produced using CorelDRAW! Setting the logo and exporting it was quicker and simpler than using Photoshop's native Type Tool.

As mentioned earlier, Encapsulated PostScript files are the preferred format for importing vector-type graphics into Photoshop's bitmap image type domain. You'll see in this next exercise how clean and smooth EPS images become when Photoshop rasterizes them.

To ensure that you're working with the same channel numbers referenced in the next exercise, and to keep HARTMACH.TIF's file size as low as possible, take a moment to delete channels 4 and 5 from the image. Click on the channel title, then choose Delete Channel from the command button drop-down list on the Channels palette. Be careful not to delete the RGB composite channel, since every time you delete an Alpha channel, Photoshop returns you to the RGB view of an image!

To conclude the session with "The Heart of the Machine," you add the text, using your "glowing" experience gained in this chapter!

Adding Backlit Text

Open HARTLOGO.EPS from the companion CD	Calls Photoshop's EPS Rasterizer dialog box.
Make sure **W**idth in the Image Size says 3.5 inches, the **R**esolution is 150 pixels/inch, and the Mode is RGB color, then click on OK	These are the field specifications for rasterizing the HARTLOGO.EPS file to bitmap format that will scale properly for use in the HARMACH.TIF image.
Press Ctrl+minus key	Reduces the HARTLOGO.EPS image to 1:2 viewing resolution, so it doesn't hog the workspace.
Choose **S**elect, **A**ll (or press Ctrl+A), then choose **E**dit, **C**opy (or press Ctrl+C)	Copies the entire composite view of the HARTLOGO.EPS image to the Clipboard.
Select New Channel from the Channels palette, and click the Color Indicates Selected Areas, accept default channel name of #4, and then click on OK	This specifies that colored areas in the Alpha channel will be selection, not masked areas.
Choose **E**dit, Paste (or press Ctrl+V)	Pastes copy of HARTLOGO.EPS image into channel 4, where the black lettering now serves as Photoshop's selection information about the image.
Click on the RGB channel title	Returns you to the color composite view of HARTLOGO.EPS.
Choose **S**elect, **N**one (or press Ctrl+D)	Deselects the active marquee border.
Choose **I**mage, **A**djust, then select Hue/Saturation (or press Ctrl+U), check Colorize	You are going to shade the black type.

Type Hue **-180**, Saturation **48**, Lightness **+14**, then click on OK	Sets values to closely match stone color in HARTMACH.TIF. Different Colorize settings are required to colorize black (instead of dark gray, as you did before).
Select, **L**oad Selection	Activates the selection border around the lettering you defined earlier by copying the HART-LOGO.EPS image to a new Alpha channel.
Choose **E**dit, **C**opy (or press Ctrl+C)	Copies type to Clipboard.
Click on the Title Bar to HARTMACH.TIF, then press Ctrl+V	Selects HARTMACH.TIF as active image window, then pastes text on top of image.
Drag the text to location above robot, then center text	Positions text (see fig. 19.23).
Choose **S**ave, **S**ave Selection, New, then choose **S**ave **S**election, New again	Creates two copies of text: one for a "mask," one to work with.
Choose **S**elect, **N**one (or press Ctrl+D)	Deselects active selection border around text.
Click on the title to Channel #5 on the Channels palette	Displays an editable view of your last saved selection in the HARTMACH.TIF image.
Press Ctrl+I	Inverts colors in Alpha channel. Text should be white against black now.
Choose **F**ilter, Gaussian Blur (or press Ctrl+F)	Photoshop applies 12-pixel Gaussian blur to Channel 5.
Choose **S**elect, **A**ll (or press Ctrl+A), then **E**dit, **C**opy (or press Ctrl+C)	Copies blurry Channel 5 to Clipboard.
Select RGB Channel (or press Ctrl+0) on the Channels palette	Displays complete view of HARTMACH.TIF image.
Choose **S**elect, **L**oad Selection, then choose #4	Displays marquee selection border around text.
Select **I**mage, **A**djust, then Hue/Saturation (or press Ctrl+U)	This is getting familiar, isn't it?
Check Colorize, set Hue **-130**, Saturation **64**, Lightness **+3**, then click on OK	Creates beginning of blue neon effect behind type (see fig. 19.24).
Choose **E**dit, Composite C**o**ntrols, then choose Screen mode, at **100**% Opacity, and click on OK	Bleaches out area around text, thereby highlighting it (see fig. 19.25).
Press Ctrl+D	Deselects everything.
Choose **F**ile, **S**ave	Saves your work to hard disk.

Figure 19.23

The Colorize option has its most visible effect on the lighter areas of the image.

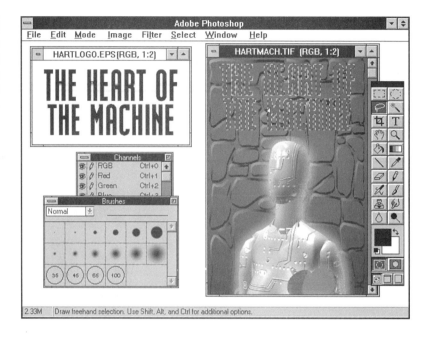

Figure 19.24

Don't increase the lightness too much, or it will "tint" the image into which you are compositing the pasted image!

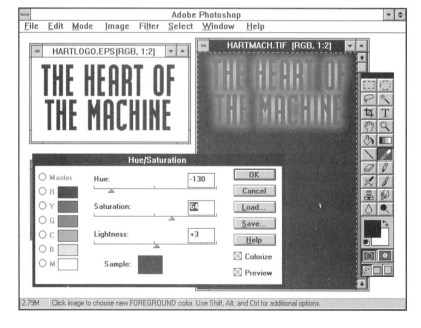

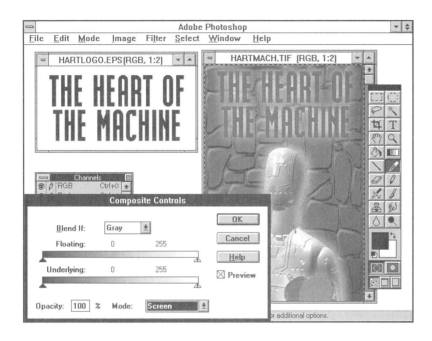

Figure 19.25
The complementary Colorized Paste helps separate the text selection from the background of the image.

Summary

The view shown in figure 19.26 was created by clicking on the rightmost Display Mode at the bottom of Photoshop's toolbox, then pressing the Tab key to clear the toolbox and palettes from the screen so that we could take a gander at the finished product. You can do this, too. Just remember that you need to press Tab a second time to make the toolbox reappear, so that you can select Normal display mode and eventually close Photoshop!

This chapter has showed you how to apply "photogenic" features to images created in the computer and has given you a taste of the power of rendering programs. You always need a program like Photoshop, however, to integrate different images and to blend them in an eye-pleasing way.

In this chapter, you have devoted a great deal of time to the "neon" effect—only one of the many ways you can use Photoshop's commands to create an effect. You know how to create a neon halo (as applied to the robot) as well as "backlit" neon (used with the heart image and the text). Backlighting text that is similar in color value to the background is a particularly rich effect, one you can use (sparingly, please!) in slide presentations to highlight an important piece of text.

Speaking of presentations, you have reached the part of this book that makes all the Photoshop experiences in earlier chapters a little more real. Great imaging has a significant life outside your computer, on real world hard copy and 35mm slides. In the next part of your Photoshop adventure, you explore the world of printing, and take a virtual trip to the Service Bureau—a strange and wonderful place that will turn your Photoshop files into tangible copies.

IV

Fantastic Assignments

Figure 19.26
The finished piece.
What a shame this
illustration won't
actually
accompany any
writing!

Part V

Inking Up and Doing Yourself a Service

Chapter Snapshot

In this chapter, you learn how to:

The Basic Guide to Printing Options

P rinting, like photography, is an art. Unfortunately, this craft has more fine
points than can be thoroughly documented in a single chapter of a book. But you *do*
need to familiarize yourself with some important considerations and concepts to have
some control over the way your Photoshop work prints.

As you begin your career as a Photoshop-savvy, imaging-type person, you'll have the most
hands-on control with the outcome of your artwork as black-and-white, halftoned images. This
chapter focuses on this aspect of printing, providing an understanding of how the pixels you
see on the screen can best be represented as dots on the printed page. Use this chapter as
your guide for the tips, tricks, and modifications you need for grayscale images as they are
transformed into hard copy.

Commercial offset process *color* printing also is touched upon in this chapter, but as you travel
up the rungs of quality printing through your imaging experiences, you'll find this to be
mostly a "hands-off" sport. You have less control, partially because you don't *own* a high-speed
four-color printing press. They not only run between five and six figures, but two or three of
them take up the floor space typically found in a *warehouse*, not your office. Commercial
printers and prepress service bureaus are usually staffed by capable, diligent folks who've
spent many years mastering and perfecting their craft—which is more time than you can
spend, while still developing your *own* craft.

But you *do* need to know how to deliver a digital copy of your color *and* grayscale work to commercial printing houses. TIFs and other format images must be specially prepared to make it easy for the press folks to make proper press plates from them. This chapter shows you how.

Whether you use the familiar laser printer or a four-color process offset print press, the digital image undergoes *transformations.* The data is converted from pixels to dots.

What's the correlation between the monitor and the hard copy? How can you ensure the most faithful translation of data from one medium to the other? What's the best way to get your work out the door and to a commercial print press? These are the questions you'll ask yourself, even before you've completely mastered Photoshop. And here are the answers.

Ground Zero: the Laser Printer

Laser printers are the most common way PC people get a hard copy of their work. They're affordable, most businesses buy handfuls of them for their work force, and they all have one thing in common with print presses—they produce work composed of tiny dots.

How your application, the printer driver, and the laser printer decide where to put these dots of toner depends on several factors. Your finished piece can benefit or suffer, depending on the options you choose during the laser-printing process.

Although resolution—the frequency of toner dots on a page—has a direct bearing on the quality of the finished print, let's focus on the actual dots first.

From Sample to Screen to Printed Page

Chapter 2 discussed the way a scanner collects and interprets information from a traditional, continuous-tone photograph to create a digital version of the image that is measured in *pixels per inch* (often called *dots per inch* by both scanner manufacturers and application software designers). This misnomer isn't relevant during imaging work, but when a digital file meets the printed page, the distinction between pixels and dots is a critical one for you to understand and be able to communicate to others—*especially* the folks who run a commercial print press, discussed a little later in this chapter.

A laser printer is not capable of expressing shades of gray the way you see them onscreen. A grayscale image might contain as many as 256 densities, whereas a laser printer is limited to toner color (usually black) and paper (usually white) to convey all this grayscale information. This is where halftoning enters the picture. A *halftone* is a simulation of the grayscale value(s) in a digital image. The aesthetic value of the finished, printed copy depends on both the dots per inch (the printer's *resolution*) and *how* the halftone dots are arranged on the printed page.

The PostScript Halftone Dot

Most laser printers use either Hewlett-Packard's Printer Command Language (PCL) or Adobe Systems' PostScript Language. Both languages render an image with dots of dry, fused toner, but they handle the information about the graphical image entirely differently. The PCL language was designed to print text quickly, whereas the PostScript language was designed to expertly handle high-quality graphics and text.

Although one of today's PCL printers can handle text and certain types of graphics quite well, the printer language is limited in its rendering smooth, even gray shades on the printed page. It's a good language for a report, an interoffice memo or two, or a simple chart, but it's not quite up to the task of tackling a grayscale digital original because *halftones* are not in its vocabulary.

A PostScript printer, however, can render halftones to represent a grayscale image. A halftone image is composed of dots whose size varies according to the corresponding density found in the original image. The different-sized halftone dots, when printed at a high frequency (measured in *lines per inch*), convince the human eye that it's seeing shades of gray. But when you look closely at the printed image, or use a magnifying loop, you see only dots of toner surrounded by areas of no toner.

Imagine a grid that covers the area on the printed page where you want an image. This grid, or *line screen*, is composed of *cells*, each capable of holding a dot of toner. The size of a single PostScript halftone dot has a direct relation to the shade, or degree of density, in the original image. Figure 20.1 is a representation of this halftone screen with halftone dots placed inside. The percentages of black at the top of the figure correspond to the size of the halftone dot in the cell. When arranged in a line and viewed from a distance, these halftone dots convey the feeling of the continuous tones in a grayscale image.

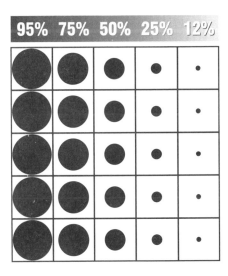

95% 75% 50% 25% 12%

Figure 20.1
Different densities in a grayscale image are expressed by different-sized halftone dots.

Although figure 20.1 shows how the size of halftone dots is related to their grayscale counterparts, it fails to show how halftones look in action! TONAL!, the grayscale image in figure 20.2, was printed at 2,540 halftone dots per inch, as are all the grayscale images in this book. When you can't easily see the dots that make up the image, you've achieved the truest representation of a grayscale image possible on a printed page.

Figure 20.2
A high-resolution halftoned image, expressed at 2,540 dots per inch.

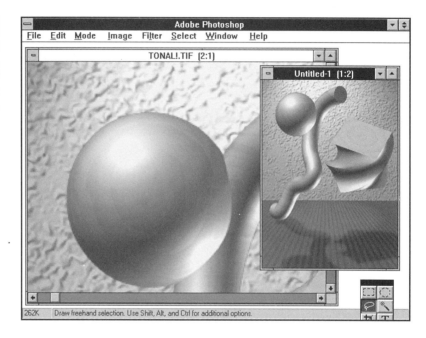

Figure 20.2 was produced by an *imagesetter*, a distant relative of the laser printer. Laser printers can't generate halftones at as high a resolution as that shown in the figure. The maximum number of dots a laser printer can fuse to a piece of paper is 1,200 dpi, less than half the number a high-end imagesetter can place. Higher-resolution output is discussed later in this chapter. But for now, you are going to see how the most common and affordable PostScript printer, the 300 dpi business workhorse, arranges halftone dots.

Figure 20.3 is a magnified view of the TONAL! image, printed at 300 dots per inch.

A PostScript printer with a high dots-per-inch resolution can produce a finer halftone than the image in figure 20.3 because it can produce smaller dots, and therefore more lines per inch of toner. The *line frequency* used to create the halftone pattern also directly affects the number of shades of gray you can simulate. This is a separate issue, covered shortly.

The 300 dpi Printer Command Language laser printer is even more common than the PostScript printer in today's business office. In the next section, you'll see how *it* renders dots.

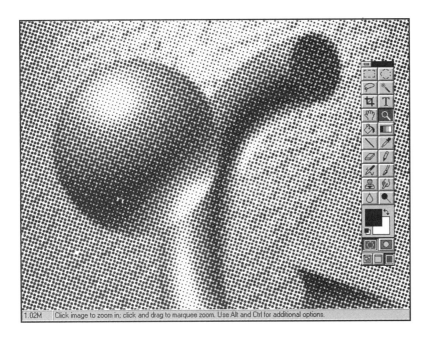

Figure 20.3
Different-sized
halftone dots are
used to express the
original shades of
gray in an image.

PCL Printers: Dots Made To Order

PCL printers are quick, but they are inaccurate when describing a grayscale graphical file because they aren't able to generate halftone dots. *Resolution enhancement,* a scheme developed by the Hewlett-Packard company for use in their PCL laser printers, helps smooth out square, *non*halftone laser dots in an image. Other PCL-based printer manufacturers have also developed schemes similar to HP's, but they all work on the same principle—small dots are placed between larger dots to create smoother tonal transitions in a rendered image. Most of these printers can also apply a default line screen to the image. This default screen should not be confused with a *halftone line screen* because the dots used in each line of a PCL screen are not halftone dots.

Although resolution-enhancement schemes sometimes provide adequate, even pleasant printed results, they still do not render the file based on a descriptor language of what's *in* a grayscale image. And the results, compared to PostScript's intelligent interpretation, are invariably a looser, less precise interpretation of graphical information.

Figure 20.4 is a magnified view of TONAL! printed by using a Windows printer driver for an HP III, Printer Command Language, 300 dpi laser printer. As you can see, the printed image is harsher and displays much more contrast than the same file rendered PostScript-style. PCL printers lack the information and the capability to intelligently render different-sized halftone dots that translate different grayscale densities to corresponding halftone-dot densities.

Figure 20.4
PCL laser printers depend on a print driver to send a rasterized byte stream of data about an image for rendering.

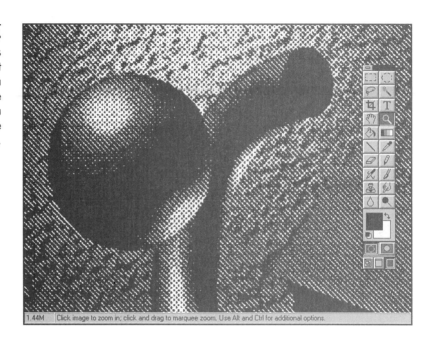

The good news on the PC imaging front is that the prices of *higher-resolution* PostScript- and PCL-based printers are becoming more reasonable. Faced with competing technologies to the PostScript descriptor language (such as Microsoft's TrueImage), Adobe has lowered the price of the PostScript interpreter that OEM manufacturers license so that their printer can speak PostScript. And more and more PC software (in addition to Photoshop) supports the PostScript language.

Consumer demand for graphics has driven the stakes up, and the prices down. If you're buying your first laser printer, keep this thought in mind: You can get high-resolution copies of a digital file by using either PostScript or non-PostScript standards for your printer's language. Both will look great, but if you want to take your laser copy to a commercial printing place as camera-ready art, the dots that represent your image *should* be of the halftone variety—and that means PostScript. Commercial printers rely on halftones to simulate continuous tones with ink on paper, and that's not about to change soon.

Managing Halftone Dots

PostScript dot management, the art of *lines per inch*, is another factor that affects the quality of the printed piece. If you think about it, a 600 dpi PostScript-rendered image is *not* twice as refined as a 300 dpi copy. It actually produces *four* times the number of dots in an area. Each square inch of an image has 600 × 600 = 360,000 dots instead of the 90,000 dots that 300 × 300 produces. And this is where the line screen *angle*, the line *frequency*, and the *shape* of these halftone PostScript dots come into play.

The Halftone's "Line"age: The Line Screen

Before the PostScript laser printer, imagesetter, or Personal Computer, there was the *line screen*. Commercial printers lay a piece of film with a line pattern on top of a photosensitive material and then project a negative, continuous-tone image onto the screen and photosensitive material "sandwich." The resulting screened image is then used to create the printing plate. When the image is projected onto the sandwich, it partially exposes areas on the photosensitive material, which in turn produces a composite of line pattern and image positive on the printing plate. This was the *only* way, pre-PC, the press operator had to convert a continuous-tone image to a black-and-white halftone that would represent shades of gray on the printed page.

Times have changed, but the convention of a line screen lingers in our quest for hard copy from grayscale images. And this is good because a laser copy that contains a halftone line screen can be used to produce a copy printed from a commercial press. But if you aren't going to send this grayscale image to press, you still need to know about halftones, line angles, and frequencies to print a good-looking photo on a laser printer. Image quality depends on the *lines per inch*, which is calculated from the dots-per-inch capability of your laser printer. An uneducated guess at frequency and angle yields a very poor laser copy, which would be criminal because these parameters are really easy to figure out!

Line Angles

In nature, continuous-tone images contain many right angles, such as the sides of buildings and the stripes in someone's shirt. For this reason, setting a halftone line angle at zero or 90 degrees is not a good idea. Most applications, including Photoshop, offer a default line angle of 45 degrees for halftone dots. In Photoshop, you have the option of adjusting this angle, but you'd only really need to do this if you'd photographed an image containing strong diagonal stripes.

You should specify a halftone line-screen angle that's *oblique* to the elements in a digital image—45 degrees works in most cases. Line-screen patterns that closely resemble the patterns in images visually resonate, creating unwanted, unappealing *moiré* patterns. Figure 20.5 illustrates the way different-sized halftone dots are arranged in a 45-degree-angle screen.

To define specific halftone screens for printing, you use Photoshop's Page Setup, Screens command, although you can specify the halftone screen parameters from the Setup option in the Print dialog box as well.

The options in Photoshop's Halftone Screens dialog box include Frequency and dot Shape, in addition to halftone Angle (see fig. 20.6).

Figure 20.5
Lines of halftone dots are arranged at an angle to create a line screen.

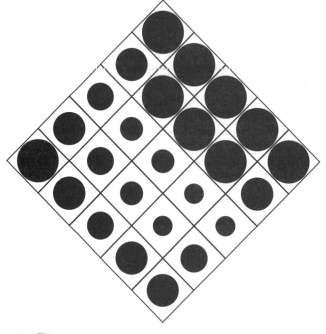

45-degree line screen

The Accurate Screens option in the Halftone Screens dialog box refers to a technology designed for PostScript Level 2 and Emerald controllers. PostScript Level 2 interpreters are installed in some of the newer PostScript printers, and they produce better halftone prints faster than the older PostScript standard. Check the documentation for your printer to see whether your printer supports PostScript Level 2; if it does, be sure to check this box so that you can get the maximum benefit from your hardware.

Halftone screen frequency is another option to specify when you print from Photoshop. The frequency of the lines per inch used when printing halftone dots has a direct correlation to *the number of shades of gray* you can simulate in a print. And there's a very simple way, using your eyes and a little math, to achieve the best line frequency for a grayscale image.

Line Frequency

Usually, the lines that make up an image printed from a 300 dpi printer are visible to the naked eye. (Shortly, you learn how to compensate a little for this by stylizing the halftone dot shapes.) When you specify the *lines per inch*, the line frequency of halftone dots, you need to strike a compromise. The default setting for a 300 dpi laser printer is usually about 45 to 60 lines per inch, and this number varies from one manufacturer to another. But the basic truth about medium- to low-resolution laser-printer output is that to increase lines per inch, you decrease the number of grayscale values you're simulating on the printed page. There is a direct correlation here.

Two factors govern the maximum number of tonal values that laser printing can simulate: the resolution of the *digital* image, expressed in pixels per inch, and the number of densities that can portray the gray shades in the printed image.

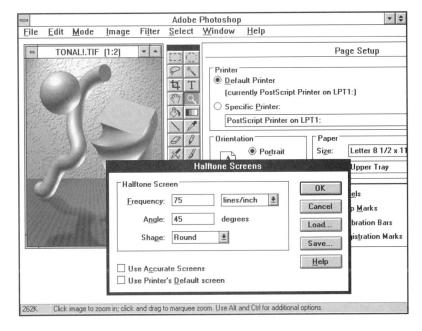

Figure 20.6
You can set a custom angle for halftone dots from the Photoshop Halftone Screens dialog box.

The Times-Two Rule

An accurate halftone print of a grayscale image should have a lines-per-inch value no less than half the pixels-per-inch value of the original file. This chapter's TONAL! image, for example, has a resolution of 150 pixels per inch, which means that to portray this image with any sense of aesthetic value, the halftone screen should be no less (or more) than 75 lpi.

Keep this rule in mind when you specify image dimensions and resolution for a *copy* of an image you want printed. When you create a piece, "shooting for the stars" is good practice; if you're particularly proud of some work you've done in Photoshop at 300 pixels/inch, save it this way. (You might get to print it at a high resolution some day.) But then make a *copy* of it, keeping in mind the resolution of your *present* target printer. You can use Photoshop's **I**mage, Image **S**ize command to specify a lower resolution for an image.

The Math for Determining Lines per Inch

To calculate the optimal resolution for a digital image to print, use this mathematical formula:

Printer Line Frequency (in lpi) x 2 = Image Resolution (in pixels/inch)

Photoshop pops up a warning when you try to print an image with a resolution of more than 2.5 times the line frequency specified for laser printing. You can continue with the operation, but it's futile to try to squeeze more visual detail out of an image than the printer is capable of producing.

The Times-Two Rule, however, is only half the equation for printing a grayscale image from a laser printer. As mentioned earlier, you have some flexibility in determining the lines-per-inch value when you use a PostScript printer. You can adjust the coarseness of the lines (the space between them) by specifying a lower line frequency, but depending on your printer's resolution in dpi, you may not get a very good-looking print. The print may look blocked in or muddy, and lack refinement. This is why you need to understand how to determine *how many of the grays* in a grayscale image can be represented by halftone lines.

Digital Copies Are Disposable

Tip

After you finish printing, you can free up hard disk space by deleting the copy of the image (it's served its purpose). By specifying a lower resolution for the copy, you *degrade* the image quality by substituting larger, fewer pixels/inch to portray the scene that a laser printer with limited resolution can translate to toner dots more easily. After you degrade an image in this way, you can never retrieve the pixel information that's now been simplified for printing purposes. That's why you should always specify digital image dimensions and resolutions for printing from a *copy* of the work you've labored over.

The Number of Grays in a Grayscale Image

An 8-bit grayscale image can contain up to 256 unique tones. Your laser printer has a definite threshold of capability for expressing all the grayscale information; this may become particularly obvious when you print to a low-resolution, 300 dpi printer.

You need to strike a fine balance between line frequency and the number of gray shades the halftone dots can represent. The balance is expressed as this mathematical equation:

$$\frac{\text{Printer Resolution (in dpi)}}{\text{Printer Line Frequency (in lpi)}} = \text{n (squared)} = \text{shades of gray}$$

You'll "plug and play" with this equation next to see how faithfully a 300 dpi printer can represent the tonal values in a grayscale image.

Using Calculations To Determine Image Quality

Suppose that you have an image with a resolution of 150 pixels/inch like the one used earlier as an example. You know, from the first equation, that the setting for the halftone screen's lines-per-inch frequency should be half the image's pixel-per-inch resolution, or 75 lines per inch. The following calculation is for a 300 dpi printer:

$$300\text{(dpi)}/75\text{(lpi)} = 4 \text{ (squared)} = 16 \text{ shades of gray}$$

Pretty pathetic, right? When a 256-shades-of-gray image is reproduced at 75 lpi with a 300 dpi printer, all the tonal information is arbitrarily lost and squashed into 16 shades! This is unacceptable for the serious imaging-type person.

To be fair, a 75 lpi halftone screen is way too high a value for a 300 dpi printer. Most manufacturers recommend a value between 45 and 60. Which line-screen frequency to use with a printer capable of this resolution, then, is really a question of aesthetics. The fewer lines per inch used to express the halftone patterns, the more shades of gray they simulate—but the more visible the lines are in the image. A line-screen frequency of *less* than 45 per inch becomes *painfully* obvious on the printed page, to the extent that the line pattern overwhelms *the composition* of the printed image!

Higher-Resolution Printers

To get a reasonable facsimile of your digital image, a printer capable of 600 to 1,200 dpi is more in keeping with hard-copy proofing needs. Laser printers that produce 600 dpi are becoming as affordable as 300 dpi printers were a few years ago. And several add-on cards are available that can step up a 600 dpi printer's resolution to 1,200 dpi. The following equation shows the gamut of grayscale a 600 dpi PostScript printer can simulate with a halftone line screen of 45 lpi:

$$600\text{(dpi)}/45\text{(lpi)} = 13.3 \text{ (squared)} = 176.89$$

Not bad! 177 of the 256 possible gray shades in a grayscale image can be represented at 600 dpi with a line-screen frequency of 45 lpi.

The Laser Printer Approaches the Imagesetter

The message you should take away from this section is that laser printers capable of greater dpi resolution can more faithfully reproduce your grayscale art. And at higher resolutions, you can use the laser copy not only as a hard-copy proof of an image, but also for another purpose. Medium-quality newsletters, flyers, and advertisements can actually be sent to a commercial printer as camera-ready art to make the photographic plates for offset printing! You'll explore the hows and whys of commercial presses and your digital images shortly. But first, you make one last stop in Photoshop to learn about *stylizing* the PostScript information to enhance the printed image.

You can define the *dots* in "dots per inch" by using Photoshop's Halftone Screen dialog box's Shape option. Although round dots are the convention when you create a halftone image, *other*-shaped dots can add detail also, as a refinement to the image rendered from a laser printer.

Shaping the Dots in a Laser Copy

In a newspaper, have you ever come across a photographic print that seems to have been printed through a special-effects screen? The image might look diffuse, or stylized, and may have been unusually printed for a number of reasons. Newspaper is highly absorbent. When a dot of ink is applied to it, the dot spreads out and, if not controlled, bleeds into its nearest neighbor. Many presses use line screens with specially shaped halftone dots that help control this problem.

Newsletters printed on "copy paper" use the same frequency of line screen (85 lpi) that newspapers do, but because "copy paper" is less porous than newsprint, folks usually don't have to resort to using custom-patterned halftone dots. And newsletters and other medium-quality business materials are printed on different kinds of presses than newspapers, which also affects the way the ink reacts with the paper.

Whether for practicality's sake or purely for an effect, a special line screen composed of irregularly shaped halftone dots can be specified for printing. You can do this straight out of Photoshop to your laser printer or a high-end imagesetter.

How a Squashed Dot Fits in a Screen

In figure 20.7, you can see the Halftone Screen Shape option's drop-down list of shapes in which Photoshop can render the halftone dots. If you intend to take a laser copy to a commercial printer, ask whether they prefer a specific dot shape, angle, and frequency of halftones for reproducing work. Print presses have many variables, such as the speed of the press and ink formulation, and the dot shape of halftones has a bearing on how effectively a grayscale image is expressed as a halftone.

But if you want a stylized halftone print for the sake of Art, and a laser copy of your masterpiece is considered *finished*, you can create several special effects by using different-shaped dots. The relationship between a digital halftone cell and a single line of a line screen is a fixed one; a dot representing 50% black (a medium gray) occupies half a cell's dimensions, regardless of line frequency. But the *shape* of this dot influences the overall design of the print. Figure 20.8 is a representation of Photoshop's Ellipse dot shape, as the halftone dots sit in a line screen set to a 45-degree angle.

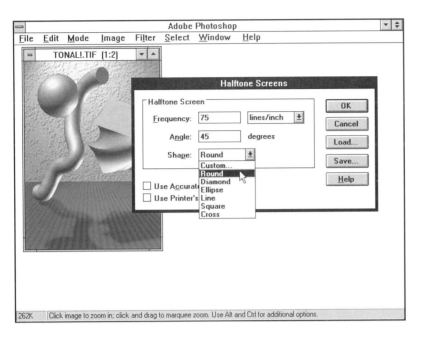

Figure 20.7
Drop down list of possible halftone dot shapes.

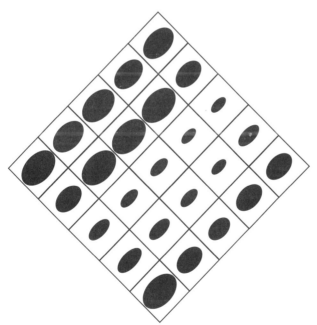

Figure 20.8
Changing the halftone-dot shape stylizes the printed grayscale image.

Elliptical dot shape

A particularly striking effect, as you can see in figure 20.9, can be accomplished by using Line as the halftone-dot shape. You may have seen this effect in publications. Owners of lower-resolution printers can achieve very pleasant results with this halftone-dot shape. Keep in mind, though, that altering halftone dots to more exotic shapes detracts from the composition of the original image. Sometimes an irregular dot shape even becomes *part* of the image's composition. You should experiment and evaluate, on an image-to-image basis, which "effects screen," if any, produces the most eye-pleasing results. Figure 20.9 is a magnified view of a 600 dpi image with a Line dot shape and a line-screen angle of 45 degrees.

Figure 20.9
A Line dot shape can add another dimension to the printed grayscale image.

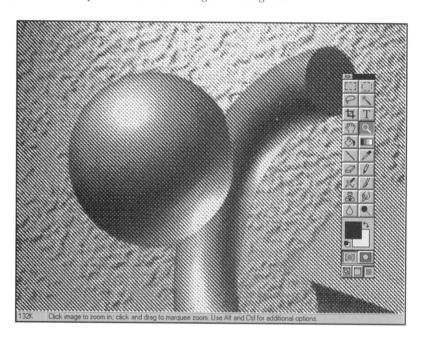

Different-shaped dots in a halftone line screen can add excitement and drama to the printed image. But you may need to do a little special preparation work on a copy of the original image before you print it. The higher the *contrast* in an original image's composition, the better that image lends itself to special dot shapes. When tonal densities in the original display only mild variation, the effect of the irregularly shaped dots in the screen pattern is not visually pronounced. An image with higher-than-average contrast will produce halftone dots that vary widely from one neighboring dot to another—and you can see the *effect* of the distorted dots more clearly.

Printing for the Masses

By its nature, the laser printer is not intended to mass-produce documents, particularly not a halftone copy of a digital image. Laser printers are slower than most other reproduction methods and limited as to the size and kind of paper they can print on. And a PC has to be dedicated (*tied up!*) while a massive quantity of copies is printing. Only in the most lavish office environments are laser documents distributed to more than, say, 50 people at a time. The prudent, pragmatic approaches to mass distribution of computer documents are by electronic mail (e-mail), photocopies of a laser copy, or the printing press.

The first two options are not suitable for getting the world to appreciate your digital master-piece. You have to use the third option—commercial printing presses. The next section describes a few dos, don'ts, and tricks you'll want to be aware of before your work is commer-cially printed.

Two Ways To Get Your Image to Press

Hopefully, this book reinforces the idea that you should always talk to the person who will be *doing* a commercial print of your digital image *before* you prepare a copy of the piece to take to the printer. A digital image can travel in two basic ways to a commercial house that does black-and-white or color printing. The next section covers four-color process printing, but you need to treat the black-and-white (grayscale) image with equal foresight *before* taking the image to a press house.

To get the digital image to press, you can print a laser copy of your work and have the printer make the press plates from the laser copy. This is commonly referred to as *camera-ready art*. Or you can give the commercial printer a copy of the digital image file, in which case, you obviously have to use a printing firm that's computer-enabled. The following section examines the route that gives you personal control over an image's outcome—the delivery of a camera-ready image to the print house.

The Quality of Home-Brew, Camera-Ready Imaging

Camera-ready halftoned images from a laser printer can produce images suitable for a medium-quality publication. We're not talking fashion-magazine or coffee-table-book quality; *medium-quality* publishing is the thrust behind hard-copy communications in America today. Today's laser printers are capable of generating up to 1,200 dpi resolution prints. To print smaller dots with toner requires finer toner particles. Toner is already extremely small—making it any smaller would be terrifically expensive and impossible at present. That's why *film*-based *imagesetters* will reign supreme for quite a while to come, and why magazine-quality publications don't use camera-ready laser copies.

But something irresistible in the budding imaging person's soul craves the instant gratification of producing a high-resolution laser copy of his or her work. With the help of some special tricks that can be performed using Photoshop, and a shareware utility that's included on the companion CD, creating a camera-ready image can be a gratifying experience.

To make the experience *rewarding* as well as gratifying, the next section is devoted to the steps you need to take to optimize a copy of your grayscale image file before you click on <u>F</u>ile, Print.

How Many Shades of Gray Should You Render?

A fairly common screen used for printing a medium-quality publication at 1,200 dpi is 85 lines per inch at a 45-degree angle. Many commercial printers use this same screen to *physically* process the continuous-tone, physical photos they get. Plugging these numbers into the mathematical formula we took you through earlier (1200/85=14.12; $14.12 \times 14.12 = 199.34$) tells you that the printer (your laser printer or the print press) will be able to represent a maximum of 199.34 shades of gray.

What happens when you use these settings for a grayscale image that contains *more* than 200 shades of gray? You lose control over the finer visual details in the image. You leave the extra shades to chance and run the risk of a final, ink-on-paper print that has harsh, contrasty areas where you least expect them because you gave a machine more visual information than it could handle.

Instead of permitting the print presses to arbitrarily mess up your image, consider an alternative. Although you can't change the screen, you *can reduce* the number of grays in a *copy* of the image with such subtlety and finesse, and viewers won't ever notice that anything's missing. To reduce the grays, you first calculate the number of grays in an image, then reduce that number with Photoshop so that the number of grays corresponds to your printer's upper limit.

Paint Shop Pro: a Utility with an Angle

Despite Photoshop's imaging prowess, it can't (to date) tell you how many unique colors are in a digital image. But JASC's *Paint Shop Pro* can. It's the program used in the next exercise to determine how many shades of gray the image has, so that you can make intelligent decisions about how to reduce the number of grayscale shades, instead of "guesstimating."

JASC distributes a shareware version of *Paint Shop Pro* through computer user-group meetings, bulletin boards, nationwide online services, and the companion CD.

Shareware is distributed with the expectation that folks who evaluate the program and find it useful will register (buy) it by paying a small fee to the software author. Shareware is *not freeware*. It's uniquely marketed software—you can evaluate its worth (to you) before you buy it.

For the next exercise, which is optional, you need to install the *Paint Shop Pro* program found in the SHAREWAR subdirectory of the companion CD. If you didn't install it when it was first mentioned in Chapter 1, now's the time. But even if you want to sit out this exercise as a spectator, you'll see how *Paint Shop Pro* can help you in the early stages of preparing a digital image.

Counting the Shades in a Grayscale Image

Double-click on the Paint Shop Pro icon in Windows Program Manager	Launches Paint Shop Pro application.
Choose **F**ile, **O**pen (or press Ctrl+O)	Opens a drive directory structure.
Find TONAL!.TIF on the companion CD in your CD-ROM drive, then select it and click on OK	Displays TONAL! image in Paint Shop Pro's workspace.
Choose **C**olors, **C**ount Colors Used	Paint Shop Pro counts unique color values in TONAL! image (see fig. 20.10).
Click on OK, then select **F**ile, E**x**it (or press Alt+F)	Exits program and redisplays Windows Program Manager.

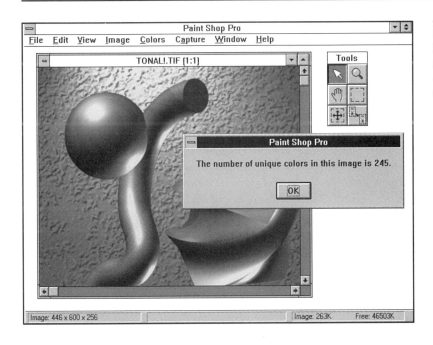

Figure 20.10
Paint Shop Pro counts the unique color values in a digital image.

V

Inking Up and Doing Yourself a Service

If you followed the last exercise, you saw that the TONAL! image contains 245 unique shades of gray. To print this image successfully with a halftone line screen at a frequency of 85 lpi from a 1,200 dpi printer, 45 of these unique shades in the image must go!

But which ones? The range of grays in an image that you ask Photoshop to produce, versus how many your laser printer can reproduce, is best decided after a talk with your commercial printer. They know the capability and limitations of printing from a plate made from your camera-ready image on their presses.

Ink Is Different Than Toner

A print press and a laser printer are two different *physical* ways of rendering a halftone image. Halftone dots of ink on paper soak in, whereas laser toner dots sit on top of the paper. Good commercial printers will tell you to avoid absolute whites and blacks in the halftone you give them; the reason for this is that although a halftone screen printed from a laser is capable of fusing a 100% dense, black area *onto* a page, print press inks soak *into* a page and spread. Depending on the paper, the ink, the presses, and the line screen used, an area that screens at, say, a 90% or 95% density won't "hold." When a screen doesn't "hold" on the press, the dark grays become black and bleed together into a muddy area.

The converse is true with white areas. A no-coverage area on a laser copy sent to a commercial press sometimes results in an image area that contains a "hot spot," a glaring reflection caused by an absence of halftone ink dots in the image. Densities of 0% and 1% in an image expressed as ink halftone dots create an unwanted border within the image. Think about this one for a moment. The 1% dots have to *start* someplace, don't they? The idea is to cover even totally white areas in the original image with at least a 1% density of halftone dots.

Decrease Contrast in the Laser Copy

To handle these extremes, go back to your original digital image and make a *copy* of it for modification. Then, in the copy, reduce the contrast of the image so that there are no "black" blacks or "white" whites. Although the modified image will look flat and dull on the monitor, the image *will* snap up when printed from a plate made from your laser hard copy. When you know that an image file contains an excess of grayscale information, and where that information lies, the areas of extreme contrast are the ones that usually need to be modified.

For instance, if the press operator tells you that the press doesn't handle halftone percentages of less than 12% density, the solution is to change the distribution of values in your image so that the first 12% (the very light grays) are reassigned to darker values. This shifts the tonal range of the image into a printable range of tonality. Don't think of it as degrading your work, but rather as optimizing the image for display in a different medium. And now for an example of how you optimize the image.

The Math behind Optimizing an Image for Press

The first thing you need to do is figure out which levels of gray occupy the upper 12% of the image's tonal range. A brightness gamut that ranges from 0 to 255 doesn't correspond directly to a density percentage that ranges from 0% to 100%. You use the following equation:

$$256 - [\text{Halftone Density (in \%) x 2.56}] = \text{Brightness Value}$$

Now to plug the 12% minimum density value for the print press into the equation:

$12 \times 2.56 = 30.72$, then

$256 - 30.72 = 225.28$

The solution, then, is to bring the output level for an image's upper range down to 225.

Similarly, if your printing person tells you that 90% black is *the densest* halftone dot the press can render, you should apply this same rule, as follows:

$90(\%) \times 2.56 = 230.40$, then

$256 - 230.40 = 25.60$

In this case, you'd enter a 26 in the left Output Level box in the Levels command.

You actually experiment with the TONAL! image in this exercise, gaining some hands-on experience with the grayscale-reduction process that's usually necessary to create accurate camera-ready art.

Decreasing Image Contrast for the Print Presses

Open the TONAL! file from the companion CD | The image that needs adjusting to produce good laser-printed, camera-ready copy for a commercial printer.

Choose **I**mage, **A**djust, Levels (or press Ctrl+L) | Displays Levels command.

Enter **238** in the right Output Levels box (or use the white Output Levels slider) | Reassigns pixels above 225 brightness point in tonal range to darker ranges.

Enter **26** in the left Output Levels box (or use the black Output Levels slider) | Reassigns pixels below 26 brightness point in tonal range to lighter ranges(see fig. 20.11).

Click on OK, then choose **F**ile, Sa**v**e As, pick a name *other* than TONAL!.TIF, and choose a location on your hard disk | Confirms modification, saves *copy* of original image as one that can be printed from a 1,200 dpi laser printer, and optimally used by a commercial press with requirements outlined earlier.

Figure 20.11
Reduce the output
level in an image
whose range
exceeds the print
press's capability to
render it with
halftone dots.

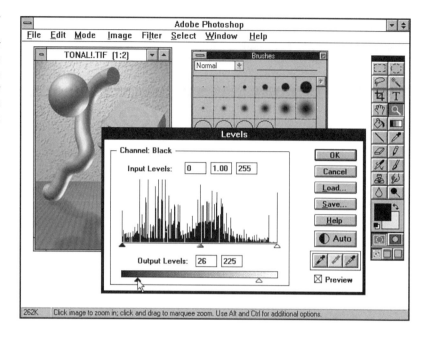

If your commercial printer specifies *only* a top *or* a bottom density threshold, don't use Levels to readjust both the bottom *and* top ranges. Photoshop recalculates and redistributes all the pixels in an image when you make a change in a particular area of brightness. Photoshop's ability to reproportion the scheme of tonal values so that they look smooth can wreck your chances of an optimal print if you specify an Output Level that the commercial printer has not!

Generally, when you follow the specifications a commercial printer gives you for maximum and minimum halftone densities, the number of unique colors in the image file falls below the maximum capability of a 1,200 dpi laser printer to render halftones at a medium-quality, 85 lpi screen frequency. If, after doing the *last* exercise, you were to repeat the Paint Shop Pro exercise outlined earlier, you'd find that the unique number of colors in your saved copy of the TONAL! image is now 196. A 1,200 dpi laser printer can faithfully render a halftone dot to represent each of the grayscales found in the new image.

Increasing Print Quality, Decreasing Artist Involvement

We've shown you what you can do by yourself with a high-resolution laser printer and Photoshop methods for optimizing your grayscale image to reproduce the best. But as you gain experience with imaging, you'll find that you are spending equal amounts of time at your PC and at the commercial printer. You'll become familiar with the special requirements of a specific print press and learn to trust the people who render your work as ink on the printed page.

And this is the time when you might consider abandoning the "home brew" halftone from your laser printer and letting the commercial printer render your computer file directly to an *imagesetting* device. Imagesetters don't depend on toner dots to render halftones. They can produce film positives and negatives from which a pressman can make press plates. Increasingly, commercial printers offer magazine-quality printing created from high-resolution line screens made possible only by imagesetting the computer file.

And you'll need to be aware of some things that have to do with Photoshop: how to prepare the file for the commercial printer and what to expect when you take the plunge into printing at resolutions the pros use.

Schemes for Getting an Image Out the Door

Most of the image files on the companion CD are "lightweights" in terms of file size. A grayscale image with a 300 dpi resolution will print beautifully from a 2,540 dpi printer, using a line-screen value of 133 to 150 lines per inch. This is magazine-quality. But an 8 1/2-inch-by-11-inch grayscale image, which is not an uncommon size for magazines, takes up more than 8M of file space!

As you gain experience with Photoshop, you *will* become more ambitious—which means higher-resolution images, RGB images, and files that can't possibly fit on a floppy disk!

So how do you get them out the door and down the street to the commercial printer? There are several ways, as you'll discover in the next few sections.

JPEG Compression

In Chapter 2 you learned about JPEG, a *lossey* compression scheme, and how it affects color work. A quick refresher: Photoshop gives you the option to save an RGB image in the JPEG format, which can compress the file size of an image anywhere from 5:1 to 100:1, depending on the composition in the image and how much compression you specify in Photoshop. JPEG technology compresses the file by averaging almost imperceptible neighboring pixel color differences in a color image.

Although the purist in most artists shuns the idea of removing information from a piece of work, JPEG is becoming a preferred file format for many service bureaus and commercial printers. JPEG files are easier for printers and service bureaus to handle: their small file size fits comfortably on a floppy disk, they transfer quickly from your media (floppy, tape, removable drive) to a network's hard disk, and they don't take up much space on the commercial printer's hard disk.

Most graphic software today directly supports JPEG files. Because JPEG images decompress when loaded into system RAM, you or your commercial printer doesn't have to own or run a separate decompression utility. Saving files and transporting them as JPEG images can not only relieve an overcrowded hard disk, but also gives you a chance to get large, high-resolution images onto a floppy disk!

The next exercise shows you how to use JPEG on an oversized file, but don't think that you're missing out on a Photoshop feature if you don't participate. In its present state, HUGEFILE, a 3.25M RGB image on the companion CD, obviously won't fit on a 3 1/2-inch high-density disk. And if this were an image *you* created, you would need at least 10M of free system RAM and a healthy amount of *virtual* memory space on your hard disk to work quickly and comfortably with it. The reason is that Photoshop needs multiple copies of the same image loaded into memory to calculate effects you may apply to it.

For this reason, some of you may decide to sit out this next exercise. But if you're up to the challenge, here's one way to make a large image file portable.

JPEG Squeezing Your Image

Open the HUGEFILE image from the companion CD	The 3.25M image you'll work with.
Choose **F**ile, Sa**v**e As	Displays Photoshop's Save As dialog box.
Choose JPEG (*.JPG) as Save File As Format **T**ype from the drop-down list, select a **D**irectory that has a little room on your hard disk, name the file HUGEFILE, and then click on OK	Displays JPEG Options dialog box.
Drag the Quality slider to Excellent	Saves HUGEFILE image as a JPEG with least amount of image loss, hence least amount of compression (see fig. 20.12).
Click on Save	Saves HUGEFILE.JPG to directory you specified.

If you followed the preceding exercise, you should close Photoshop for the moment and check the file size of HUGEFILE.JPG from Windows Program Manager. You'll see that it takes up about 500K, depending on how far to the right you pushed the Quality slider. Unfortunately, Photoshop can't be more specific about the compression ratio because it varies according to the visual complexity of any single image.

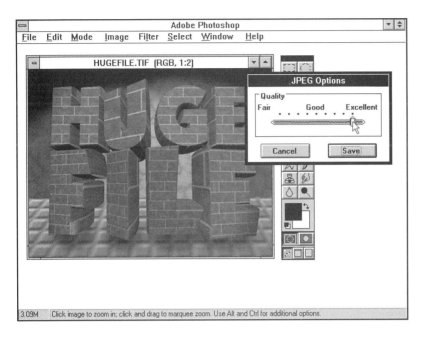

Figure 20.12

JPEG quality ranges from Fair (best compression) to Excellent (least amount of compression).

Because you picked the Excellent quality setting for your JPEG compression in the last exercise, you can transfer this high-quality image to a floppy disk. It can now be used by a commercial printer who owns Photoshop, or any number of other software applications that understand the JPEG compression scheme.

RGB color images, such as HUGEFILE, can take advantage of JPEG compression; but grayscale images, in their native grayscale mode, cannot because JPEG is a color-image compression scheme.

If you have a grayscale image with a file size larger than will fit on a floppy, you can convert the grayscale image to RGB Mode in Photoshop, then use JPEG on it. The converted image scales down in file size exactly like a native RGB image. In RGB format, the image will take longer to print because the printer will have to read, then discard irrelevant information about the non-existent color qualities about the image before it renders the black-and-white image. For this reason, you may decide to convert the image back to grayscale once again, when your image file on floppy has reached its destination.

Grayscale images saved to a 24-bit RGB format, and grayscale written to 8-bit (grayscale) will print identically to a black-and-white imagesetter. The only difference is in the time they take to print. But the image can't be printed at all if you don't use JPEG or some other compression scheme to make the file portable!

If lossey compression simply isn't your style, though, you can always use loss*less* compression to make a large file portable. PKZIP, a shareware program, is a very popular utility that performs lossless compression. The following section explains how a somewhat more complicated compression scheme can ensure that every pixel in your image is in place when you arrive at the commercial printer.

Using PKZIP To Span Disks

PKZIP, developed by Phil Katz, is marketed as a shareware, "try it before you buy it" compression utility used by practically everyone who needs more hard disk space on a PC—which means everyone who has a pulse. You'll find a copy of it in the SHAREWAR subdirectory on the companion CD.

If you've used on-line services or BBSes where file compression is necessary to reduce modem-transmission time, you may already be familiar with PKZIP. Unlike the JPEG image format, PKZIP is not compression-on-the-fly. The format of a ZIP file cannot be read until it's decompressed. The type of compression PKZIP offers is not as dramatic as that of JPEG, but then again you don't lose any image information with it, either. Your file has complete integrity when you "ZIP" it.

Perhaps the nicest thing about the latest version of PKZIP is its capability to *span* disks. A single file that is larger than the capacity of a 1.44M floppy can be safely broken into pieces onto separate floppies and transported. When you get your disks to the commercial printer, the PKUNZIP utility restores them to the single image file on their hard disk.

Yet another shareware utility in the companion CD's SHAREWAR subdirectory makes the process of spanning a large file to several floppy disks as hassle-free as one could imagine. WinZip, by Niko-Mak, is a ZIP "shell" that makes program calls to PKZIP directly from the Windows environment. PKZIP is a DOS-based utility, and WinZip addresses the Windows-oriented user's need to work completely within the Windows environment.

You learn how to ZIP an image file in the next exercise. Although HUGEFILE is used here as an example, feel free to experiment with an oversized image of your own. PKZIP is risk-free. It uses a *copy* of your original for the compressed version of your image. Before you begin, the PKZIP and WinZip programs must be installed on your hard disk. To do this, look at the documentation that accompanies each program in its own subdirectory.

Spanning and Zipping a Large Image File

Have two formatted 1.44M disks handy	Target disks for HUGEFILE.TIF image you ZIP in this exercise. Have more handy if you decide to experiment with files larger than HUGEFILE.
From Windows Program Manager, double-click on the WinZip icon	Launches WinZip. (WinZip creates an icon in a program group of your choice when you install it.)
Place a 1.44M disk in your floppy drive	This exercise assumes B drive is your 3 1/2-inch drive; if not, substitute A for B throughout exercise.
Click on the New button	Displays New Archive dialog box.
Choose your B drive from the **D**irectories list	Specifies 3 1/2-inch floppy drive as target for Zipped, spanned file you create.
Type **HUGEFILE.ZIP** in the Archive **N**ame: box; check the **A**dd Dialog box	Name for file PKZIP copies from original (see fig. 20.13). **A**dd Dialog box is your next stop.
Click on OK	Displays **A**dd Dialog box.
Choose **C**ompression Fast, **M**ultiple Disk Spanning No format, then select the HUGEFILE image from the Se**l**ect Files box (see fig. 20.14)	Sets compression with speed more important than compression rate; No format because floppies are already formatted.
Click on OK	PKZIP compresses HUGEFILE image to floppy disk.
When a DOS window pops up over WinZip, remove the first disk, place the second one in your hard drive, then press Enter	You instruct PKZIP (from a DOS window) that second disk is ready to be written to.
Choose **F**ile, E**x**it (or press Alt+F4) when a screen similar to that in figure 20.15 is displayed	After WinZip finishes using PKZIP, file is compressed and spanned to floppy disks; WinZip displays specifics on how compression went.

Figure 20.13
A file with a ZIP extension is a compressed copy of the original. (It can have the same eight-character name as the original.)

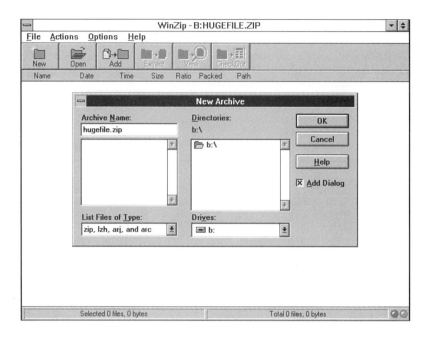

Figure 20.14
ZIP-type compression can be done to a single file over multiple floppy disks.

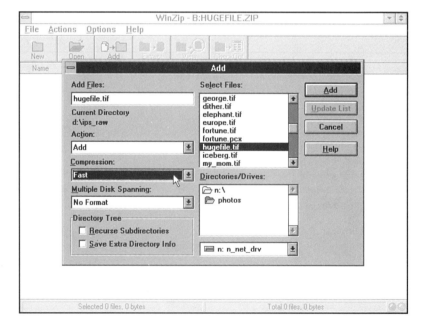

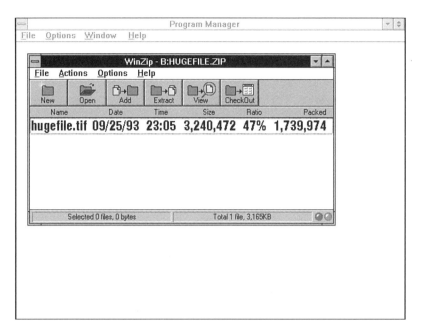

Figure 20.15
WinZip, a shell for the PKZIP utility, gives a report of each compressing session.

After your file is "spanned" to the necessary number of floppy disks, copy PKUNZIP.EXE to *another* disk to take along to the commercial printer. (PKUNZIP.EXE is in the directory from which you originally extracted the PKZ204G.EXE file.) Your printer may not have PKZIP, or may not have the version included on the companion CD, and PKUNZIP is the only key to restoring your file on another PC.

The capability of PKZIP to span floppy disks means that compression is not of tantamount concern. You can get away with a minimum of compression which, in fact, makes the process of restoring the image, or images, much faster at the commercial printer.

Some file types, like Kodak's PCD PhotoCD images, are already compressed in their native format. Don't use compression when you ZIP these files; they simply won't squish more than the way they're written to PhotoCD. In fact, because PKZIP creates a header for its ZIP copy of your image, a file that's already compressed (a PCD file, for example) actually becomes *larger* than the original because this header information is added to it.

In such a case, you'd want to set the Spanning option for your file(s) and specify None as the compression type when using WinZip, or PKZIP alone.

Large-Format Removable Media

You can use more exotic forms of transporting your digital images to a commercial printer. Large-format, removable media come in a wide range of formats from a variety of manufacturers. SyQuest, Bernoulli, and MO cartridges, optical disks, DAT and QIC 40 or 80 tapes can hold anywhere from 21M to well over a gigabyte of image data, depending on which one you use. They are ideal for moving large amounts of data.

The catch with these drives is that each kind of removable media drive usually reads only media produced on a similar, or identical, drive. If you have a large-format, removable media drive, check with your printer or service bureau before making your copies to see whether they have a compatible model. If you are *thinking* of buying one of these devices, find out what kind of removable media your favorite printer or service bureau uses, and get one like theirs. It makes life much simpler.

What can you do when you or your printer doesn't have a high-capacity removable media drive, or theirs doesn't match yours, and floppies just aren't practical?

Send your hard drive to the printer. It's a pretty drastic move, and not one to be done on a whim. But if it's the only way to move tens of megabytes of image files, and your commercial printer is capable (and willing to share some of the responsibility/liability), you can do it.

Questions (and Answers) for the Commercial Printer

It's a foregone conclusion that if you want your commercial printer to image Photoshop files, the printer must have a computer. But do they have an IBM-compatible like yours, or a Macintosh? Computer graphics began on the Mac long before the IBM-compatibles, and many commercial printers who have computers chose the Mac.

Do They Have the Right Drive?

The IBM/Mac issue is not a problem if you are transporting your image on a floppy disk (or disks). But if you are using some of the other removable-media mass-storage devices, such as tapes or SyQuest or Bernoulli cartridges, you may run into a stone wall because these media types can't always be read in IBM-standard *format* by the Macintosh.

All except the most ancient Macs have SuperDrives that can read an IBM-formatted floppy disk. Because Macs don't have 5 1/4-inch drives, make sure you send 3 1/2-inch disks to a Macintosh-based printing place. And if you're working "cross platform," ask your printer what *kind* of 3 1/2-inch disk they can read. Older Macs read only 720K disks, but newer ones can read the high-density, IBM-formatted 1.44M disks as well as Macintosh-formatted disks.

If your commercial printer has a computer *network*, you may have no problem dealing with a "Mac-based" print shop when you take your work in on something *other* than floppies. At least one IBM-compatible PC is usually involved in a multicomputer environment, whether it's specifically to accommodate a user like yourself or for a receptionist doing DOS word processing. If that computer's drive matches yours, it can read your tape or cartridge and put the information on a network drive that the Macs can read.

Does Your Printer Own Photoshop?

Even though TIFF images are platform-independent, as you've seen throughout this book, Photoshop can do some pretty special things with them. Alpha channels and paths in a TIFF image are *not* understood by some other imaging software applications. And no hard-and-fast rule exists as to which applications don't understand Alpha channels and paths because more and more software manufacturers are adopting the Alpha-channel convention every day.

If your commercial printer owns Adobe Photoshop, either the Macintosh or the IBM-PC version, you'll have no problem getting them to print an image file, regardless of what you've stuck in an Alpha channel. The reason is that Adobe has written Photoshop to both platforms with identical features and file compatibility in mind.

But you may have some problems if you take a TIFF file you've enhanced using Photoshop to a printer who uses an imaging software application *other* than Photoshop to drive his or her imagesetter. The printer's application may not be able to read Alpha channels—and your file won't make it to press. That's if you're *fortunate*. This other-than-Photoshop application *may crash* trying to read an Alpha channel, and your printer or service bureau is not likely to thank you for the experience.

A Word on Corruption

If you happen to leave an Alpha channel or path in your TIFF image and don't remember doing it, and the printer's imaging application succeeds in *partially* reading your file, the file can appear corrupted. TIFF images corrupt more easily than other types of files, such as databases and spreadsheets. File corruption can happen when Windows crashes and you have an image open—or even when you've done nothing at all with the image, and it resides on a hard disk partition that is subject to a crash.

The point here is to determine whether a Photoshop Alpha channel is to blame for a file's lack of readability at the commercial printer, or whether your image file has indeed become corrupted.

Figure 20.16 is a copy of the TONAL! image after it went through the wringer on the authors' hard disk during one of Windows "unexpected enhancements." You can see horizontal areas of "noise" that streak the image. This file is corrupted. The image can't be restored by any of the software "recovery" schemes you may have purchased as utilities. It's a goner and should be deleted. Hopefully, the author has a spare copy of the image.

On the other hand, a file that can't be understood by an imaging application because it contains a Photoshop doo-dad, such as an Alpha channel, looks quite different than a corrupt file.

Different programs respond in different ways to this weird stimulus. Figure 20.17 shows what an image with an Alpha channel looks like when Logitech's PhotoTouch software tries to load it.

Figure 20.16
Video "noise" running across an image file is the most common sign of file corruption.

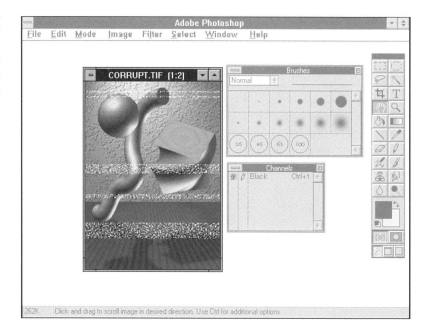

Figure 20.17
An imaging program that doesn't have the same features as Photoshop won't be able to understand channels or paths.

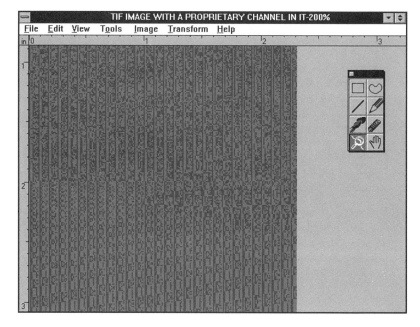

The point here is not to confuse a corrupt file with one that contains additional information you set up using Photoshop. Always bring *copies* of your images to the commercial printer. Make sure they are stripped of channels and paths if your commercial printer doesn't use Photoshop. Even if the printer does own Photoshop, he or she doesn't need the channels and paths unless your work is going to be edited. And remember, channels increase the size of your files and make file transfers take longer. To see how easily superfluous channels and paths can be deleted, read Chapter 10 in this book about working with these features.

Whether they are image files you send to a printer or files you create for use in other applications, clean Alpha channels and paths out of image file copies before you proceed. Desktop-publishing applications, such as Aldus PageMaker version 5.0, readily accept a TIFF file that contains an erroneously placed Alpha channel. PageMaker ignores this information channel; you can print a typeset page with the image included, as is. More modest applications, however, such as Microsoft Publisher, cause a system error and boot you clear back to DOS if you try importing a TIF image with a Photoshop Alpha channel embedded in the file.

In any event, make it your personal practice to delete channels and paths from your image file after you're certain that you no longer need them in a copy of an image. At very least, channels add to your printing time. The extra information channel is read to the printer, but there's nothing for it to print.

Should You Do Your Own Color Separations?

Photoshop has the capability to generate color separations from an image. This means that the Cyan, Magenta, Yellow, and Black plates a commercial printer runs on a press can be made directly from laser or imagesetter copies. (But it doesn't mean that *you* necessarily want to do this.)

Besides being the application of choice for artists on both the Mac and PC platforms, Photoshop is a magnificent tool for commercial printing houses to use in their work. Many copies of this program reside in production departments, service bureaus, and advertising agencies because the other half of *creating* an image is *printing* an image. And Photoshop has features to do both.

But color printing is a science and, as such, is best left to professionals. For this reason, we recommend against making use of Photoshop's color pre-press features. Let the people who know best about the medium of *publishing* handle your work. You may go through two or three commercial printers before you settle on one who can express a style or look you want to convey in an image. But making a career of printing dots of ink precisely on a page could easily take you as long as it's *already taken* commercial printers.

A good commercial printer who's wise in the ways of Adobe Photoshop can guide you and your work through the world of process printing. They can show you how to make duotones out of Grayscale Mode images. And only they know best which line-screen angles yield optimal results with the four process plates they run on their presses.

The Most Convenient Routes to Color Printing

This chapter has described the options and requirements for getting a good black-and-white print from both your personal laser printer and a commercial printing press. Our recommendations about leaving your floppy disks in the hands of a trustworthy commercial printer to make your RGB image into a CMYK one on paper come from experience. An artist with an understanding of computers may cross over into several different fields, but the likelihood of immediately understanding an entirely different profession, commercial printing, is slim.

The best, quickest, easiest, and most economical way to make all these virtual images into physical ones you can show around in a portfolio is to take the files to a service bureau. There they can make custom prints and different format chromes (slides) of your work. Chapter 21 is all about what to expect from a service bureau and the rewards you'll find there.

Service bureaus specialize in high-quality, limited-run editions of color images. But if you're constantly in a bind to produce medium-quality color images on the printed page, the grace note to this chapter is on the personal color printer.

Glorious Color from the Personal Printer

A few years ago, a personal color printer was out of the budget and out of the question for most imaging-type individuals. But the demand for presentations and color proofing has driven prices way down to a point that's close to affordable. Although personal color printers don't generate an image nearly as refined as offset or lithographic commercial printing, they do provide a reasonable way to get a sample of your work across town.

Printer manufacturers have come up with several ways to get color images onto paper. The technologies deployed, and what the color printers use for pigment, are as follows: color ink ribbon (dot matrix printers), sprayed ink on the paper (inkjet), heated, colored wax (thermal wax transfer), superheated dyes that are absorbed by special papers (dye sublimation), and the color laser printer. Color printers range in price from $500 for a dot matrix to $20,000 for a color laser printer.

The range in price is significant, and so is the quality of the work these printers can produce. If you are looking for something that approaches photographic quality, expect to pay at least $8,000 for a good dye-sublimation printer. What you get for less money produces anything from an approximation to a parody of your original digital image.

Don't rely on personal color printers to provide *proof* colors for images destined for slide or print-press reproduction. Each type of color printer mentioned earlier uses different kinds of pigments and papers that don't correspond to your monitor, to photographic film, or to print-press ink. And each technology produces a different range, or *gamut*, of color. Blue can easily shift to purple, and yellow to orange, using personal color printers.

At the current time and level of color technology, *personal* color printers can not be recommended as faithful reproducers of photorealistic work. At best, they give you a general overview and feeling for your image if you remember that what you're looking at is rendered with only a fair degree of faithfulness to your digital file.

But *high-end* versions of some of these technologies (in the $20,000 to $250,000 price range) can produce images that range from splendid to final-proof quality. These machines typically are found at your printer or service bureau.

If you want to see what your work really looks like, have a slide made of it. The cost is between $10 and $15. If you need an idea of what it will look like when it's *process-color printed* to a press, take your file to your printer or service bureau and have them make a proof for you. The cost usually ranges from $15 to $50 a page, depending on which machine they use to make the proof.

Printing a Color Image from Photoshop

Most color printers are PostScript, although several smaller models that don't use Adobe's interpreter (relying instead on their own technology to render color) are available for less than $1,000. Although a non-PostScript color printer can't take advantage of some of Photoshop's imaging features, color printing to a personal printer is basically the same as printing from any other Windows application. In fact, if you've used a laser printer before with Photoshop, you probably won't notice many differences in the Print options boxes.

Remember that many of Photoshop's color options refer to color *separations*—four black-and-white halftones from which plates are made to print process color using a commercial press. These options don't apply to a personal color printer.

The first step to printing an image is to open the file you want to print. Photoshop won't let you change any settings for color or black-and-white printing unless an active image window is in the workspace. Similarly, certain options are not available in Photoshop when a color printer is not defined. Therefore, the examples in the next section are informational rather than constructed as an exercise. The VANILLA.TIF image, shown in figure 20.18, is used as an example in this section.

The first step in color printing is to go to Page Setup in the File menu. The Page Setup screen always looks the same, unless your printer shipped with proprietary drivers that pop up a dialog box when you go to print. In Page Setup, you select, from the drop-down list of print drivers, the Specific Printer to do your color printing.

Figure 20.18
An RGB image can be sent directly from Photoshop to a color printer.

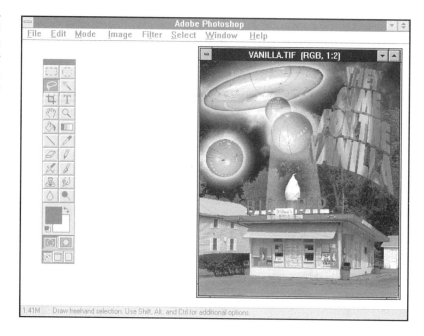

Screens

As you can see from figure 20.19, we selected Use Printer's **D**efault Screen as the Scree**n**s option in Page Setup. Unless you're attempting to achieve a special effect with your color print, or are very familiar with the specs for your machine, this is a good option to leave checked. Personal color printer manufacturers have built the optimal screen angles right into the machine—there's really no need to change them. When you click on this option, the Halftone Screen option goes gray. You cannot change the halftone-screen settings then.

Screen angles for color PostScript printers are set at angles that are oblique to each other, which greatly reduces the chance that the Cyan, Magenta, Yellow, and Black inks will build a moiré pattern into your printed image when they are printed, one on top of the other.

Creating Duotones

Duotones are a convention adopted many years ago to compensate for the reality that the printing inks used commercially don't express the range of grayscale in an original halftone image. A duotone, tritone, and quadtone are grayscale images printed using different colored inks, each ink covering and reinforcing a particular density range in the representation of the original grayscale image. If you were to see a well-done black and medium-gray duotone print in a book, you might not even realize that different inks were used. The gray, in the case of the duotone in the book, was added by the commercial printer from a second screen of the grayscale, whose image displayed more or less contrast than the screen for the black plate.

When inks other than black and gray are used, duotones create wonderfully evocative images. Steeltone images (black and cold blue inks), and sepia tones created by using duotones, have become an art form. And although Photoshop can build the color separations a commercial printer would need to print a duotone, personal color printers can achieve the same effect if you know how to navigate the Photoshop controls for this feature.

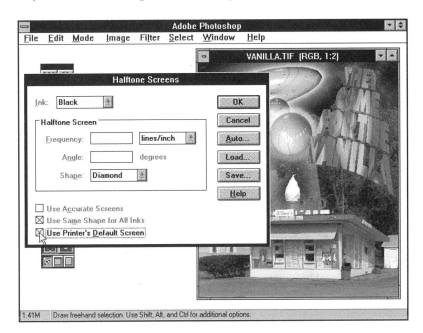

Figure 20.19
Default screen lets your color printer use factory-set angles and frequencies.

Duotones Start with a Grayscale Image

Whether your color printer is PostScript or not determines if you can faithfully render a duotone image. Photoshop saves a duotone image only as a proprietary PSD format, EPS, or RAW image file. To create a duotone, you must first be working with a grayscale image. Then when you print, the Encapsulated PostScript language interprets the duotone qualities of the image, and the graphical information is saved in a single, special Duotone Channel. This EPS information about the duotone image is then passed along to a PostScript printer as specific, color-coded parameters that affect only part of the grayscale image.

Specifying a Type of Duotone

Creating a good-looking duotone from a grayscale image takes a great deal of trial, error, and practice. For this reason, Photoshop includes many sample schemes to apply to a grayscale image. (You learn how to access this Photoshop sample library in the next exercise.) Even if you don't own a color printer, duotones are simply nice for creating something special out of a grayscale image. Imaging work shouldn't be limited to only the tools you own. If you like your duotone image enough, you may want to have it printed commercially, or at a service bureau!

Creating a Duotone Image

Open the VANILLA image from the companion CD	Image you use to create a duotone image.
Choose **M**ode, **G**rayscale, then click on Yes to discard color information	Converts VANILLA.RGB image to grayscale.
Choose **M**ode, **D**uotone	Displays Duotone Options dialog box.
Click on **L**oad	Displays directory structure of your hard drive.
Find the duotones subdirectory under your Photoshop directory	Duotone sample files were installed here when you installed Photoshop.
Click on the PMS subdirectory beneath Duotones	Subdirectory of PANTONE colors you can specify for color inks used to create duotone.
Scroll down to the 349-4.ADO file in the files list, click on it, then click on OK	Selects PANTONE Process Black P and PANTONE process color 349 P as the colors used to make the duotone (see fig. 20.20).
Click on OK	Accepts defaults for this duotone color scheme, then displays Photoshop's workspace.
Choose **F**ile, Sa**v**e As VANILLA.PSD	Saves file in Photoshop's format (one of three formats in which a duotone can be saved).

Figure 20.20
Photoshop installs with many different selections of premade duotone schemes.

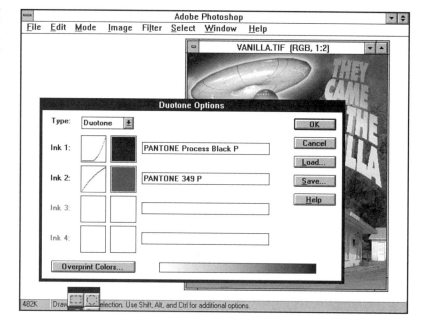

If you followed the last exercise, you should now have an emerald-shaded duotone on your screen. It's striking, eye-pleasing, and is *not* the same as colorizing an image in Photoshop. In fact, a great deal of thought went into building the curves that distribute each color of ink across the tonal range of the grayscale image. These are tried-and-true formulas, but if you'd like to tinker with duotone color distributions of your own, click on the curve box to the left of the Color names before you click on OK. We clicked on the curve next to PANTONE 349 and, as you can see in figure 20.21, the curve for distributing this ink heightens the percentages so that the middle densities of green ink are more pronounced.

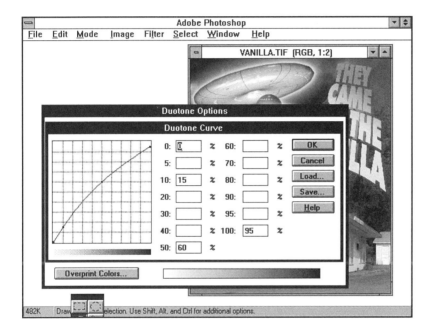

Figure 20.21
The PANTONE color is most visible in the medium tonal range of the printed image.

You can "tune" a duotone curve to produce different effects. But *don't* confuse the duotone curve with Photoshop's Curves command. When you adjust an ink-distribution curve in a duotone, you change the densities of ink across a percentage scale. The Curves command is used to redistribute tonal values in pixels across a brightness scale of 0 to 255. Ink and pixels aren't the same thing. If you're really interested in creating duotone prints, try experimenting with some of Photoshop's sample files of duotone curves before creating your own.

The names for the beautifully designed duotone samples that ship with Photoshop are logically opaque; the names in the duotones subdirectory for duotone, tritone, and quadtone samples are *numbers* that relate to the type color you should see when printing to exacting ink and paper specifications.

continues

If you come across a duotone combination you like, write down the number and the effect because you'll never remember the file name alone!

PANTONE colors are numbered and coded for specific color values as ink is reproduced on coated, varnished stock paper, and uncoated paper. Process colors (CMYK) also are combined to produce other color values. If your assignment calls for precise color matching, you'd do well to invest in a PANTONE color-swatch book, available for about $80 at commercial art supply stores.

Taking a Duotone to Another Application

As mentioned earlier, Photoshop images can be imported to other applications, such as desktop publishing programs. If you own a PostScript color printer, you can print a duotone image from another application that also "speaks" the PANTONE color-naming system.

Aldus PageMaker is used in the next exercise, which explains how to save and export a duotone. Although you may not own PageMaker, if you have another application that uses the PANTONE naming convention, you'd use the same techniques.

Exporting a Duotone

Open the VANILLA.PSD file from your hard disk	Image Sa**v**ed As a duotone in the last exercise. (Skip this step if image is still open in Photoshop's workspace.)
Choose **F**ile, Sa**v**e As	Displays Photoshop's Save As dialog box.
Choose EPS (*.EPS) as Save File as Format **T**ype; name the file VANILLA.EPS	Displays EPS Format dialog box.
Click on the 8-bit IBM-PC Preview radio button, then click on OK	Tells Photoshop to give you an 8-bit, 256-color "thumbnail" image that you can place in another application for position.

An Encapsulated PostScript file is a description for the printer as to how an image should be rendered, or *rasterized*. Unlike other image file formats, EPS images aren't viewable—they are printer instructions. For this reason, a low-resolution bitmap of the duotone file travels along with the EPS printer information file, so that users can position the image in a different application.

Placing a Duotone in a Desktop-Publishing Document

We chose PageMaker as the application that receives the exported VANILLA.EPS image file because PageMaker understands the short PANTONE names contained in the EPS image information. You need to specify Sh**o**rt PANTONE Names before exporting an image that uses a PANTONE color as a part of the image. If you look back to Chapter 4, you'll see that using Sh**o**rt PANTONE Names is an option set in General Preferences (press Ctrl+K). This is the only way to ensure that an application that speaks PANTONE can read the correct color.

If you want to use an application that can't understand the PANTONE naming system as the host for a duotone, you must choose (in the Duotone options box) a name the other application can understand and send to the printer as PostScript information for the color.

This PANTONE 349 P color, for example, is a shade of green. If you typed Green as the name for this color in the Duotones Options box, most other applications would recognize the information in the EPS file and send their interpretation of what green looks like when the application sends your file to the color printer.

You won't get *exactly* the same PANTONE color you specified when you created the duotone in Photoshop, but the duotone *will* print from another, PANTONE-short-name-"unaware" application.

For figure 20.22, we created a PageMaker document that calls for the sort of subject matter VANILLA.EPS suggests. PageMaker will print to a color printer, as well as perform color separations from which a commercial printer can run the press. You lose control over further refinements to an image when you export it to an application that features no image-editing tools, but the printed color image will look just the way it did when you saved it—all within the context of another document. As you can see, PageMaker's color palette, generally used for specifying its own native text and borders, registers the short PANTONE names as the same ones you specified in Photoshop.

Figure 20.22
You can design in Photoshop, using PANTONE colors, and print from other applications that recognize the colors.

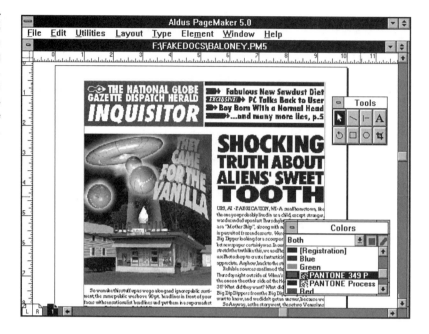

Summary

This chapter covers a lot of ground, describing the measures you can take to print your digital image—at the office, at home, or with a commercial printer. As printing technology evolves, and as you grow more experienced and curious about the printed medium, you'll discover tips, tricks, and truths of your own.

This chapter doesn't pretend to be the complete guide to Photoshop printing. Rather, it is a place to start making your continuing adventures with Photoshop more rewarding. Even a less-than-perfect hard copy of your image is sometimes better than inviting a host of people over to stare at your monitor!

As someone interested in creating computer graphics, you owe it to yourself to learn about every means available to make virtual images into real, physical ones. There's a world outside the computer, filled with people who may not *use* computers. And printing is one way to bring your art to them.

Another way to get a copy of your digital image is to send it to a slide service bureau. These service bureaus are custom shops that can image single orders of your digital work and usually make a color print for you, in case you don't have access to a color printer. But the mainstay of their profession is making color *slides*—slides to use for presentations, slides that photofinishers can use to make color glossies for you. 35mm slides (and larger) that contain *no dots per inch*, like printers do. Just glorious, continuous-tone color!

In the next chapter, you'll get the inside scoop on an industry specifically created to serve the computer-graphics individual. You'll learn about the possibilities and the rewards of making slides from your images.

V

Inking Up and Doing Yourself a Service

Chapter Snapshot

In this chapter, you learn how to:

The Service Bureau

A good service bureau is a great resource for the Photoshop user. The professionals who work at a service bureau specialize in producing wonderful, high-quality output so that you can devote your time to producing great stuff *worthy* of output. Whether it's output to a slide or a custom print, service bureau folks concentrate their efforts on a corner of computer expertise called *imaging*—the art of rendering a digital image to a physical format you can show around in professional circles.

Like most other things in the computer world, more advanced techniques, equipment, and software for imaging become available every day. Knowing the fine points of the imaging equipment a service bureau uses, and how to produce great results, is a craft imaging people continually upgrade, and the personal attention your image file receives at a bureau reflects their devotion to their art. As a *designer* of computer images, you'll want to understand the basic processes of slide and custom print making, so that you know what to ask for and what to expect from a service bureau.

Just as you do with the commercial printing firms mentioned in the last chapter, you interface with another art when you work with a service bureau. The professionals who work there typically don't design, but rather specialize in bringing *your* design to a finished state. Their craft is practiced through tools such as imagesetters and film recorders whose price is beyond most designers' budgets. And service bureau professionals know about the other half of computer design, which is making a byte stream of computer information *physical*, so that *you* don't have to.

Transferring a Photoshop Image to a 35mm Slide

Slides play an important part in the worlds of business and education. They are an extremely effective and portable way to show visual information to a large group of people.

How do you get your Photoshop image onto a 35mm slide? You use a *film recorder.* A film recorder "prints" a digital file to 35mm slide or negative film. After the film has been exposed to your image, it can be processed and handled just like film exposed by a 35mm camera.

To ensure that your slides look every byte as good as they do on your monitor, you have to become more familiar with file formats, data types, aspect ratios, monitor settings, and the size of your file. This chapter shows you how each of these digital issues can affect your work, pleasantly or otherwise.

File Formats and Data Types

Most imaging centers want files saved to either the TIF or Targa format. These are two technologically sophisticated 24-bit, RGB file formats. Because the bureau may prefer one over the other, you should ask which format they prefer before you take them your file. What they definitely *don't* want are image files that contain Alpha channels or paths, which not only bloat a file unnecessarily but also may cause some software to crash. Time is money to a service bureau, and the operators don't need the headache of unnecessary Alpha channels and paths in your files. Save a file with paths and Alpha channels for your own use, but when you make a copy for the bureau, delete them.

When you save a file to take to the service bureau, try to choose a file format that will preserve the color structure you used when you designed the image.

If you created a grayscale image to be finished at the service bureau, definitely save the image as a Grayscale Mode image in Photoshop and give the bureau a grayscale image. Grayscale image files are inherently smaller than the those for the same image saved as RGB TrueColor. Whether you send the image to the bureau by modem, by tape, or by disk, transporting an 8-bit image in an 8-bit file format is always easier, and takes less time to image once it arrives at the service bureau.

If your image is color, send it as RGB—all the glorious colors are available when you print to film, so use them. Send indexed color, 8-bit files only if your image has only the few colors that can be accommodated by the format. If you send a 24-bit TrueColor image to a bureau as an indexed 8-bit file, your colors are rendered as *dithered* ones. You end up with only 256 or fewer

colors to represent your once glorious 16.7 million color image—the print or slide will look awful. Let your monitor be your guide (and check out Chapter 1 for more information on determining the proper data type for an image and Chapter 2 for a look at images that have been color dithered).

Your Monitor's Setup

Both your monitor and a film recorder use an RGB color model. When you save a Photoshop file in a 24-bit RGB file format such as TIFF or Targa, every color used in the file has been described in terms of its red, green, and blue values. The film recorder reads these values to determine how to expose the film. If your monitor is properly calibrated, the colors you see on the monitor will be accurately represented on the slide. If your monitor is *not* properly calibrated, you might get orange instead of gold, and purple where you wanted blue.

The best insurance against this potential problem is to calibrate your monitor as described in Chapter 4. A good double-check to ensure monitor fidelity is to use a PANTONE or other color-matching swatch book. Pick the Custom option on Photoshop's Color Picker dialog box, choose the PANTONE color you want to compare to the physical swatch, then fill an area on your screen with the color. Hold the physical PANTONE swatch (with the same number as the on-screen PANTONE color) up to the monitor to see how well they match. The match will not be perfect—colored light can never equal opaque ink on paper exactly. But if the colors are way off, you need to recalibrate your monitor to match the swatch book.

Keep in mind that colors never match exactly. Every output medium varies in its color-display capability, and how closely colors match between different media depends as much on viewer aesthetics as technology. A monitor, a television set, film, press ink on paper, the *same* ink on *different* paper, and different printing technologies—inkjet, thermal wax, dye sublimation—all display color based on values calibrated for the way they physically express color. Fortunately, *film* can express a wide range of colors. And (if you used a properly calibrated monitor to edit your image) these colors can accurately represent the colors you want in the image.

The Magic 2:3 Ratio Is an Aspect of Your Image File

Aspect ratio is the height-to-width proportion of an image. If you want your image to fill the frame of the 35mm slide, your work must match the 2:3 ratio of the film. If you know before you produce a piece that you'll be sending it to a film recorder, you can plan your composition to a 2:3 (or 3:2) aspect ratio.

One of the things that sends a service bureau up the wall is receiving a file for slide imaging that is *not* in a 2:3 aspect ratio. Although a conscientious service bureau will add a dark background to fill the edges of the slide so that your viewers won't be blinded by the projector's light, this is *not* their *responsibility*. It's yours. And it is never their responsibility to crop an image, unless you specifically instruct them to do so.

Both of these actions mean extra work for the bureau—and you might be charged for their time. But more important than the extra money you might be charged, you'd have relinquished artistic control and responsibility for producing finished artwork that meets your design criteria. It's a shame to use your creative talents to produce good work, only to have it ruined by a bad crop or an unaesthetic border.

You don't have to be a math wizard, or even own a pocket calculator, to ensure that your work has the proper aspect ratio to be imaged as a 35mm slide. Let Photoshop do the math, then use your eye to decide whether to crop or to place a background around the image.

The next exercise shows you how to "trick" Photoshop into doing the math for you:

Determining an Image's Aspect Ratio

Choose **F**ile, **N**ew	Displays New dialog box (see fig. 21.1).
Click on each of the drop-down boxes and click to set the units to inches and pixels/inches	Sets the units of measurement.
Click on the Mode drop-down box and set to RGB Color	Sets the Image Mode for the new window.
In the **W**idth text box, enter **3**; in the H**e**ight box, enter **2**; enter **72** in the Resolution box, then click on OK	Opens new file, with aspect ratio of 2:3, in wordspace.
Choose **F**ile, **O**pen OCT_FEST.TIF from the companion CD	OCT_FEST.TIF is active window in workspace.
Choose **I**mage, **I**mage Size (see fig. 21.2)	Opens Image Size dialog box Change settings to inches (if not that way).
With the **P**roportion box *checked* and the File Size box *unchecked*, enter a value of **3** into the Width text box	Height value automatically changes to 1.808 (image is at a 1.808:3 ratio).
Write (on paper) the Current Width and Height vlaues shown in the upper part of the dialog box (4.967,2.993), and then click on Cancel	Image size remains unchanged.

You pressed Cancel because you *do not* want to change the image size.

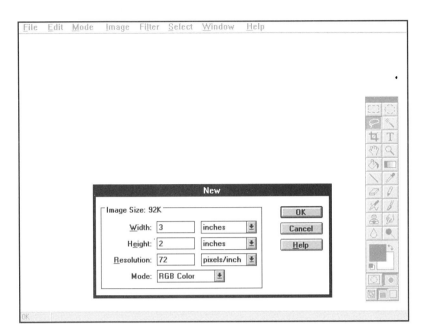

Figure 21.1
Use these settings when you create a file to use as an aspect ratio "calculator."

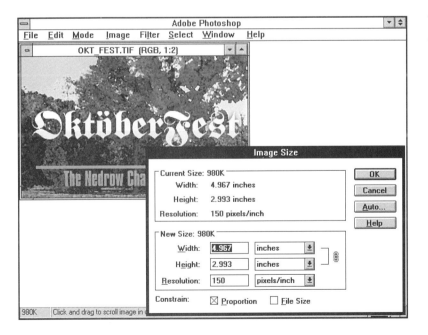

Figure 21.2
The Image Size dialog box, showing OCT_FEST.TIF image's current dimensions.

When the Proportion box is checked, changing one dimension changes the other automatically to a value that retains the image's *current* aspect ratio. By setting the value to 3 in the width box, you can quickly determine whether the image can be scaled to a 2:3 proportion. In this example, the height came up short of 2, which indicates that it is not a 2:3 proportioned image.

If you remove the check from the Proportion box and increase the height to bring it into a 2:3 ratio, you *distort* the image. To bring this image into a 2:3 ratio, you have to crop the image or add to it. But you might not want to crop one of your finished images *or* build more image information around one aspect of the image's borders. A good alternative, which is also image-enhancing, is to increase the size of the background canvas to create a border around the image, bringing the overall image into the proper aspect ratio.

When you do this yourself, you decide what the background color should be and how large the border should be to add artistic value to the slide. You please the service bureau folks, too! No one likes to play art critic, especially when they're not getting paid to do it. In the next exercise, you use your new file—the one you just created with a current aspect ratio of 2:3— to figure out how large to make the new canvas for OCT_FEST.TIF.

Calculating an Aspect Ratio

Click on Untitled-1's title bar	Makes Untitled-1 the active image.
Choose **I**mage, **I**mage Size	Displays Image Size dialog box for Untitled-1.
Enter a value of **5.25** in the **W**idth box; the H**e**ight value changes to 3.5, the dimension that maintains the current 2:3 aspect ratio (see fig. 21.3); write these numbers down, and then choose Cancel	These dimensions will bring OCT_FEST.TIF into a 2:3 ratio.
Click on the OCT_FEST.TIF title bar	Makes OCT_FEST.TIF the active image.
Click on the Eyedropper tool in the toolbox, then click the Eyedropper over the medium-green tree on the left	Sets new color for foreground (see fig. 21.4).
Click on the Inverse Colors icon in the toolbox	Changes foreground to white and background color to green sampled with Eyedropper.
Choose **I**mage, Canvas **S**ize, set measurements to inches, if necessary, then click on center sqaure in Placement field	Places image in center of new canvas.

By default, the canvas color is the current background color defined by the color-selection boxes on the toolbox.

Enter **5.25** in the Width box and **3.5** in the Height box (see fig. 21.5)	The numbers that Untitled-1's Image Size box calculated for you.
Click on OK	The nicely centered image with an attractive color border is in proper ratio for slides (see fig. 21.6).

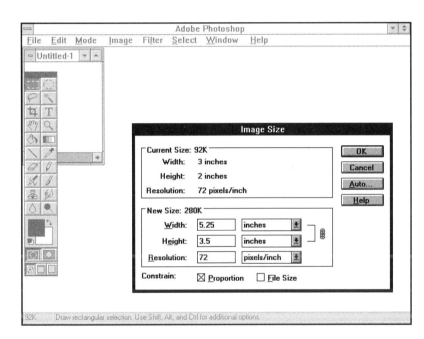

Figure 21.3

When you change the value in the width box, the value for height changes to maintain the current image proportions.

Figure 21.4
Use the
Eyedropper to
select a medium
green for the
image's new
border.

Figure 21.5
Changing the size
of the canvas
brings the image
to the proper
aspect ratio.

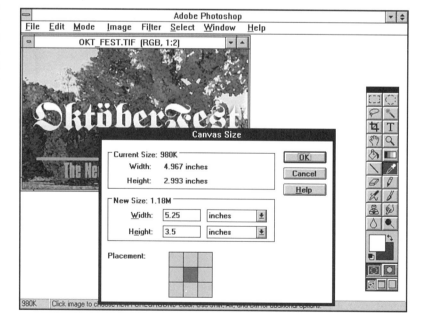

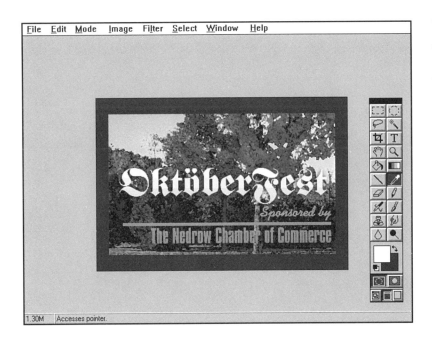

Figure 21.6
OCT_FEST.TIF now has the proper aspect ratio for a slide—and also looks good.

To make this image span the width of the slide, you enter its length (4.967) in Untitled-1's Image Size Width box and get a calculated value of 3.311 for the Height. Setting the OCT_FEST.TIF Canvas size to these measurements puts a border at the top and bottom only (see fig. 21.7). An image's size and the way it's positioned on the canvas are design decisions you make for each image—but the math for the 2:3 slide aspect ratio is always the same.

Changing the Canvas Size of the image changes the image. Be sure to save the bordered image under a different file name, so that you still have a copy of the unbordered image.

If you have a film recorder attached to your machine, and you're imaging your file from Photoshop, you could have Photoshop insert a background color. This option is available by choosing **F**ile, Pa**g**e Setup and then choosing Bac**k**ground. This doesn't change the image—just the way it prints. If you use this option, you can't preview the image to see how it looks before you image the file—which means this method leaves more to chance than adjusting the Canvas size.

When Photoshop inserts background as a printing option from Page Setup, it adds background only to the sides where you are "short." Your image, when printed, would look like figure 21.7. Don't give up your artistic control to save a few steps. Use the Canvas Size command instead.

Figure 21.7
OCT_FEST.TIF
with only a top
and bottom
border produces
a larger image.

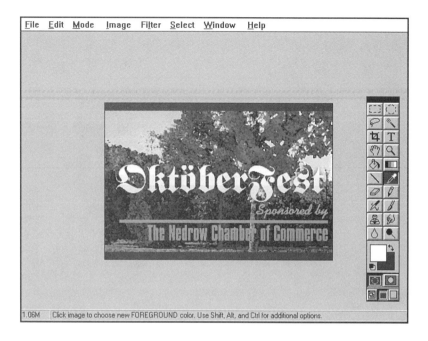

Converting a Portrait Design to a Landscape Slide

Most slides used in business presentations are *landscape* (wider than they are tall) views, in which the 3 aspect represents the design's horizontal dimensions and the 2 represents its vertical ones. A landscape presentation that includes *portrait* slides (which are taller than they are wide) can be disorientating to the audience (and drive a projectionist nuts). When you sit down to design images for slide presentations, stick to the landscape view of your 2:3 aspect ratio.

If you are having your work made into slides or film from which you'll print photos, you don't have to limit your designs to landscape proportions. But you still want to have the image in a 2:3 aspect ratio so that it fills the film frame. Instead of assigning the 2:3 proportion to the height and width, let it represent the width and height of the image.

Most film recorders are set up for landscape imaging, which satisfies most users' needs. Before you save your file to disk to send to the service bureau, you might want to turn your image on its side, to get the whole image in frame and avoid excessive cropping.

Photoshop makes this easy for you to do, albeit the process is not so easy on your system's resources. Rotating images is processor-intensive. It's a Photoshop effect, exactly like a Perspective or Distort command. Before you use the Rotate command, be sure that you've eliminated any unnecessary channels and paths and that no other images or applications are open. To rotate the image from portrait to landscape from the Image menu, choose Rotate and then click on 90CW or 90CCW.

Sending the Right Size File

Determining the proper file size to send to a service bureau for slide making is not as straight-forward a process as calculating resolution for print presses. Printing to paper and film imaging are different processes and different media. Measurements for image files rendered by film recorders are expressed in memory units (kilobytes/megabytes), not in pixels per inch. The ultimate quality of a film recorder's output is based on *how much* information it has to work with.

When service bureaus describe their services, they'll sometimes say that they do 2K or 2,000-line imaging or 4K or 4,000-line imaging. These terms refer to the size of the *pixel grid* the film recorder can render. When a file is imaged at 2K, the "2K" describes a pixel grid that is 2,048 pixels wide by 2,048 pixels high. A 4K image is a pixel grid of 4,096 by 4,096. Because the pixel grid is square, not in a 2:3 ratio, it can accommodate either portrait or landscape images.

Service bureaus usually image in landscape mode only, however; and you should send your files in that dimensional format. Because film recorders image data line-by-line, from top to bottom, there *is* a definite "this end up" to consider when you prepare an image for 35mm film. Rotate the image 90 degrees to make a portrait mode image a landscape mode image.

Image Sizes in Film Recorder Measurements

A 24-bit RGB file that is 2,048 pixels wide by 1,365 pixels high (2:3 ratio), produces an 8M file. A grayscale image the same size is only 2.67M. A 24-bit RGB file imaged to 4K and in a 2:3 ratio would be 4,086 pixels wide by 2,731 pixels high and would occupy 32M, where its grayscale counterpart would only occupy 10.7M.

This doesn't mean that creating a 32M image for a service bureau to image is necessarily a good idea, or even *feasible!* To manipulate a file in Photoshop with any degree of ease, your computer system must have memory three times the size of the file. To produce a 32M file, your PC and the PC at the service bureau would have to have 96M of memory. Most PC motherboards don't *hold* more than 64M of memory. Even if they did, at current RAM prices, you'd have to invest more than $5,000.00 to accommodate this image. At which point, most imaging-type people would start counting up how many boxes of charcoals or Nikons they could buy for this much money.

How Large Is Large Enough?

So how large *should* your file be? There *is* no hard and fast rule. It depends on what you want to do with the slide, how detailed the slide is, and how critical an eye your viewing audience has. Slides have nice juicy colors; when slides are projected, the difference between a "low resolution" slide and a "high resolution" slide is often difficult to see. If you look at both together, side by side, through a loupe, on a good day, in a good mood... you may see a difference.

Most service bureaus are willing to run a test slide or two for you. Experiment with different sizes of files to find the size that suits your needs, your patience, and your pocketbook. Files that are too large to fit on a floppy disk are unwieldy to transport. Time is money to a service bureau. Large files take longer to process—and you are charged for that time.

The fundamental question of how large your image should be boils down to your definition of *acceptable*—a relative term, but it's somewhere between 1.13M and 4.5M.

If your job absolutely depends on a fantastic, "no one could ever criticize you" slide, design your piece for 4.5M. If the slide is for you to keep, for in-house use, or even to be used as part of an information package you send clients, create a copy of your image to a smaller file size. Our personal experience has been that slides created from 1.13M files are quite acceptable. Start at the low end of the range and work your way up to the point that gives you the results you need for your situation. Ask your service bureau to show you slides they've made from files of different sizes so that you get the scope of the meaning of "acceptable."

Misjudging the file size can get you caught between a rock and a hard place. If you start with an image design that's too small, you can't increase the information without interpolating the data and losing some file integrity and quality. On the other hand, if you design to create a large file, say of a house, at a 1:1 scale, you tax your system, your patience, and your wallet. Remember also that moving large files from place to place is not simple. Moving large files to the service bureau involves the same potential problems as moving them to a commercial printer. Chapter 20 has a section that's an "idea guide" for handling large image file transportation.

If you think a design you've created has too small a file size to be successfully made into a slide, *don't* consider increasing it with Photoshop's Image Size commands. When a film recorder gets an image, it does bilinear interpolation of its own; the interpolating you did to increase the file size would be subject to interpolation a second time. One interpolation is more than enough averaging of original image data—let the film recorder handle the size increase when it images your file.

What To Do If Your File Is Too Small

If you already have a piece designed, and it's smaller than you think it should be—image it anyway. You may be pleasantly surprised. Figure 21.8, POOL.TIF, is "small"—only 720K. It's on the companion CD, if you want to look at it in color. The file was created in a computer modeling and rendering program, then retouched a little in Photoshop. It was sent to a service bureau as an RGB TIF and made into a slide. The slide impressed a conference room full of people—and not one stood up and criticized the resolution.

After the meeting, we decided to have some inexpensive 4 by 6 color prints made for the sort of handouts one never expects to get back. We could have taken the file back to the service bureau and had a film negative made, thereby avoiding one generation of processing and the

resulting loss of some image quality. Instead, we checked the slides into the local one-hour photo place, had a negative made from the slide, and made regular, batch-mode color prints from the new negative.

Figure 21.8
POOL.TIF produced a good quality slide from a file that is only 720K.

The *prints* looked fine, too! If POOL.TIF was destined for a museum, or was going to be the source material for producing a magazine cover by traditional means, we probably wouldn't have been so cavalier with this image. But if we'd been more careful with the image, we would never have discovered what the *perceived* quality was for a third generation, 720K digital image. Although the prints did not match the original onscreen colors exactly, they were close enough to convey the image accurately and were suitable for their intended purpose.

Having a 35mm Negative Made

You may want to have your service bureau image your file to 35mm negative film instead of slide film. With a negative, you can have photographic prints made of your image. Or you can give the negative to a printer who is not computer savvy and uses traditional photographic production methods.

The process of making a 35mm negative is almost identical to that of making a 35mm slide. The following sections detail a few differences that you'll want to keep in mind.

File Sizes for Making 35mm Negatives

If you plan to have a large, high-quality photographic print made from the negative, the first consideration you need to address is file size. You'll want to send a larger file than you normally send for a slide. Just as you need a large-format negative to make a really large print in traditional photography, with digital photography, larger files go hand-in-hand with larger prints.

As with a slide, there is no hard and fast rule for what size file makes an "acceptable" print. Kodak states that photofinishers should not make prints larger than 8 by 10 inches from the standard version of a Kodak Photo CD file, which includes an 18M BASE file. We believe that Kodak's definition of what an acceptable print would look like is very conservative and that you will find a print made with a much smaller file to be "acceptable." Again, as with the slides, this is something about which you have to find your own level of comfort, as you find the balance between file size and quality of the output.

Also, if your commercial printer is not a computer "guru," and you plan to give them the negative for traditional prepress production and placement into a printed document, produce your negative from a larger file size.

Whether it's for the printing press or for yourself, tell the service bureau *why* you want a negative made. If the service bureau is aware of the specific purpose for the negative, they can make tiny adjustments to the film recorder's settings and "tweak" the negative so that it is optimized for photographic printing, or print press printing.

Aspect Ratios for 35mm Negatives

The aspect ratio for 35mm *negative* film is the same as for 35mm slide film—a 2:3 ratio. All the techniques and considerations that go into getting a file into the proper aspect ratio for slide-making apply, except one: what you do if your image is not full-frame.

In the exercise on slide preparation earlier in this chapter, you increased the canvas size of an image to a 2:3 proportion, and made that additional canvas a dark color. Dark borders on slides are good because they keep the audience's attention on the image information, and spare viewers from the brilliant light of the projector as it passes through clear areas in the slide. But on prints and negatives, the tradition is to use *white* borders instead of dark ones. White is the border color most people expect on a print. And if the image is to be cropped, white usually makes the "live area"—the image area—easier to crop.

Other Service Bureau Services

In addition to being able to make color slides and negatives of your work, many service bureaus can also make high-quality color prints from your image files. Some of the different kinds of color print options are discussed in Chapter 20.

Computer-driven color output is a field that changes almost daily. New makes, models, and technologies that produce better and better results are constantly being introduced. If you want to make a limited number of color copies of your work to hand out, or for proofs, the service bureau is the place to go.

Make an appointment with your service bureau when you both have some time to talk about what you want and what they can produce for you. Have them show you prints made on different kinds of color output devices. Quality also has its price; you can expect a wide range of costs associated with different types of prints when you shop around. You'll want to be familiar with what a service bureau can produce with its different color printers and match the expense of each kind of print to what you need the print for. Also discuss with the bureau any special page-proportion requirements or file format preferences they may have for each kind of output device.

Most service bureaus can print an image file to T-shirt transfer paper. This stuff is great—you iron the transfer onto a T-shirt and presto—you have an instant, custom promotional or gift item.

Keep your design simple because the colors available aren't very subtle, and intricate detail can get lost. But hey, T-shirts aren't *supposed* to be subtle, and it's just plain fun to wear your own designer T-shirt.

Your "Before You Hit the Door" Service Bureau Checklist

When you choose a service bureau, you are choosing a design partner. These are the people who take your design and move it from the digital world to the physical world. When you choose a service bureau, you need to look for the same kind of qualities you look for in any other partner you choose. You need to be able to trust them, you need to be able to talk to them, and you need to be able to work together to achieve a common goal—producing great output.

Shop Around for the Best Capabilities

It is worth your while to visit *several* service bureaus. Make an appointment first and bring some of your work with you. Ask them to have samples of their work on hand to show you. Then sit down with them and talk to them about:

✔ Your work

✔ The programs you use

✔ What you do with the images you produce

✔ What services you think you'll need from them

✔ What *other* services they have that might be useful to you. Some service bureaus offer typesetting, desktop publishing, and basic design capabilities that might make it easier for you to integrate your image for portfolio or business promotion purposes.

Get To Know a Service Bureau's Preferences

Ask a knowledgeable person at a service bureau (and proceed with tact because this might *not* be the owner or a salesperson!) the following questions:

✔ Whether they have a preferred file format, aspect ratio, and file size for each service they offer

✔ About turn-around time (rush service is always more costly)

✔ Whether they require advance notice if you send them large amounts of work at one time

✔ Last but definitely not least, ask how they prefer to receive large files. A good service bureau has several methods for receiving large files and will advise you what works best for them. Then, together, you can work out what's most convenient for both of you.

The key to good relations and good results with your service bureau is to ask ahead of time. No one likes last minute surprises—they can cause you a world of grief and make you miss your deadlines.

Summary

This chapter covered many details about the service bureaus—the do's and don'ts, the special preparations to go through, and so on. The *rewards* you'll find there, in giving your digital image a physical form, are more than compensated for. There is no way to show readers just how excellent a well-done 35mm slide looks after a film recorder renders your file to this format. And when you slip one of your images into a ho-hum presentation, the looks your work receives are a reward in and of themselves. Simply put, slides of your Photoshop work will blow the audience away!

This book has taken you from the source to the sample, to finally getting your Photoshop work to media that your clients, your boss, your friends, and family can hold in their hands. The next—and final—chapter has nothing to with these other people, file formats, pixels, or even very much to do with Photoshop. Having read the chapters and followed the exercises, you—the artist—have a very natural need to reflect on your knowledge and skills and discover what you've earned by learning. Naturally, we want to give you the next stepping stone.

Chapter Snapshot

In this chapter, you learn how to:

How Good Is Good?

People from all corners of the business world are attracted by the promise that a personal computer can help them improve their craft. And all sorts of people whose profession and interest lies in conveying a message graphically are discovering Adobe Photoshop. But no matter how much you've integrated computers into your work, or what level of skill you've achieved with Photoshop, every once in a while you'll wonder how far you've actually come. You'll question whether the images you've produced—the images that have been digitized, modified, sliced, diced, blended, and otherwise tinkered with as computer information—are conveying their intended message as powerfully as they could.

It's a natural question, and you may find yourself asking it for several different reasons. Your work may not be immediately recognized by the community you live in as legitimate artwork because it was "done by a computer." Or perhaps you've just seen an exhibit of computer art—the work blows your socks off and you feel intimidated. Or you may be experiencing the frustration of adapting to the new medium of computer graphics. When you deal with unfamiliar and often uncooperative hardware, belligerent software, and an operating system that won't go to work when *you* want to—you may question whether any of it is worthwhile.

This chapter is intended as a guide you can turn to for a little "reality check" every once in a while. Artists lose their perspective almost hourly, and it's easy to get drawn into the PC to such a degree that time melts away and you lose track of things like regular meals, friends and family, occasionally your personal hygiene (!), but most important—your perspective.

An artist's perspective—the way you see and express ideas—is a personal thing, and it has nothing to do with Adobe Photoshop. But to use Photoshop or any other tool successfully, you need to reevaluate the quality of your work regularly, and how you spend the time invested in it. As your artistic vision matures, as your level of skill and technique improve, your vision changes. Whether the tools you use to communicate your vision are conventional ones you hold in your hand or digital tools that you guide with a mouse, you need to examine them to discover the best way to use them to express your vision.

This chapter is a combination checklist/point-of-reflection for you to glance back to as you evaluate how working with Photoshop and computer imaging in general has altered your perspective. Instead of giving you formal exercises, this chapter asks you to think about how the various topics covered in this book relate to you and the goals you set for your work. If you followed the exercises in the other chapters, you've acquired new skills and techniques that you might not even be aware of right now. In fact, you're probably better at this computer graphics stuff than you imagine! But how good *is* good?

The Uniqueness of the Photoshop Professional

Although this book covers some of the ways graphic designers and photographers can use Photoshop, *Inside Adobe Photoshop* is not complete coverage of the program. Photoshop is so feature-rich that a complete documentation would fill a library shelf. And the uses for Photoshop go beyond art and photography. Commercial printers use the program to do color separations, and the motion picture industry uses it to create special effects in movies. Wherever a concept needs graphic expression, Photoshop can plug in.

You may never use Photoshop for anything more than retouching part of an image. But even the simplest task, accomplished through Photoshop, lends a uniqueness to both your assignment and your craft.

Color-Correcting Is a Breeze

The authors own not one but several computer-graphics applications, each of which has unique fortés. But Adobe Photoshop addresses the task of color-correcting a photographic image more directly and simply than any of the other programs.

If you work for an advertising agency, a newspaper, or any other place where tons of photos come in every day, the folks you work for will definitely appreciate your ability to "crank out" color-corrected images. Custom-developed and printed photos are rare. About 99 percent of the images that come one's way usually come via the local Fotomat or other bulk-processing place. Bulk-processed prints can't do justice to what the photographer saw because they were not given the individual attention an image needs to make it shine.

Consider how effortlessly you can adjust most of these photos with an **I**mage, **A**djust, Levels command. The Auto range button restores a muddy picture to readability dramatically. In many cases, the only step you need to take to create a presentable image from an unpresentable one may be to use the Auto button.

Variations and Color Balance are two other **I**mage, **A**djust commands that make simple work of removing color casting from a photo. Many people still use indoor film outdoors, and vice versa. This mismatching of the film's color temperature to the photographed environment produces an orange or blue cast to the print. If you skipped over Chapter 6, invest the time to learn how about 30 seconds of work with these two commands can correct an image.

Not all of Photoshop's tools are automatic, as you'll realize after you spend more time with this program. Although Photoshop can be used very effectively in an "assembly line" environment at work, the program's main virtue lies in its features that enable you to refine individual images according to their needs. The point here is that in time, as you gain experience with Photoshop, you'll be able to mass-produce acceptable images quickly—and you will have more time to concentrate on images that need extra work and attention.

I can't think of another software program that you can work with in this way. When you are familiar enough with Photoshop to be able to work on assignments in a seemingly effortless way, other professionals will come to you for answers. They'll be amazed, but you'll know that the *appearance* of effortlessness is achieved through the combination of Photoshop's adaptability to different situations, and your ability to put it to use. Color correcting a ton of pictures is only one area where you can excel, and your excellence will stand out because you've invested some "front end" time exploring the features in Photoshop.

Channels Give You Unprecedented Control

Photoshop imitators have ported the concept of channels into their programs, and for good reason. Alpha channels, as well as a digital image's native channels, give you unprecedented control over modifying an image. You can add a Gradient blend to an Alpha channel, then composite a copy of it in different ways to change the lighting in an image. You can create masks with semitransparent edges to blend a copied image into another seamlessly. To gently alter the camera lens focus of an original photo, you can selectively blur or sharpen a color channel in an RGB image.

Part 3 in this book has numerous techniques for using channels to accomplish different things. Whether you want to embellish an image or simply correct it, channels are one of Photoshop's real strengths. Understanding what channels are and how to use them is essential for an imaging professional. By using channels, you have the opportunity not only to do some exceptional imaging work but also to use a tool creatively. The unique *skill* of knowing how to use a tool creatively is more rare than an unusual software feature.

Selections

Fully understanding the similar (and different) uses for selection areas, floating selections, masks, and channels may take a while. Experience is the key to using selections in Photoshop in a dynamic way. You have to set aside the time to play with a selection area, switch to Quick

Mask mode to refine the selection, copy it to a different channel, press Ctrl+Alt and click and drag the selection so that you're only moving a selection *border,* back again, and one more time! Having this sort of control over what you cut and paste is an exciting experience in and of itself with Photoshop!

It's a great feeling to be able to reposition a bit-mapped image and not have it lock into place unintentionally. When I first started with the program, Photoshop immediately rewarded me by its forgiving nature when it comes to pasting copies of selections. Unlike vector-type images, which consist of discrete objects that always *remain* discrete, bit-mapped image areas tend to cling and fuse together (usually when you don't want them to). In Photoshop, as long as the marquee selection is surrounding the image area, you can do anything you please with it; it remains selected until you composite it into the background image.

Photoshop's floating selections are a designer's dream. With most image editing programs, cutting a selection out of an image leaves a hole in the image. Attempting to repair it can slow down your work. Floating selections, whether you've created them by pasting a copy into the background image or used the **S**elect, **F**loat command, leave the background image intact. Think about it: you can use this feature to save time when you're working with patterns, or when you want to feather or defringe an area that's already in place.

Chapter 15 has a good example of the malleability of images that are saved as selection areas. Building the composite image in that chapter would have been difficult, or impossible, with a program less capable than Photoshop.

Besides uniqueness, Photoshop offers the user simple routes to do complex things. Although it's not a simple program to *master,* the work you can do in it is above average imaging. Don't ever get the idea that the exercises in this book can be accomplished as simply, or even at all, with a different application. Yes, you are doing *the fantastic* with Photoshop! Take a look at what you can accomplish through this book's exercises. Could you do this sort of stuff before you got Photoshop?

An Integrated Workspace

If Photoshop is the only program you own for designing, you already own a wealth of tools in one application. Consider the effects and filters by themselves. Photoshop handles the creation of special-effects imaging masterfully because of its capability to interpolate information. Whenever you stretch, bend, warp, spherize, or otherwise change the dimensional aspect of an image, Photoshop compensates for the gaps between pixels by mathematically averaging what color and type of pixel, or pixels, should fill the gap. *Interpolation* of image data is a science, and Adobe's contribution to refining this aspect of imaging is nothing short of remarkable.

In addition to special effects, Photoshop gives you smooth type-handling capability. Putting type in a digital photo is usually accomplished by exporting the image to a desktop publishing program or other program that specializes in handling text. *Text as art* is becoming more and more popular in graphic design work. With Photoshop, you can treat type as a graphic and

use all of Photoshop's features and filters to distort, emboss, or gradient-fill text—in short, to do anything with lettering that you can do to a photo. Because the Type feature is built into Photoshop, all the special treatments you may have for graphics can be placed in a photographic image without a trace of cutting or pasting.

The effects that Photoshop's patterns and custom brushes create can go head-to-head with artwork produced by vector-based design programs. Until I started using Photoshop, I used to labor for hours on end creating a repeat pattern for an illustration background. Then I got wise to the fact that you can marquee-select an image area with the Rectangular Marquee tool, define the image area as a pattern, then use the Paint Bucket tool to flood-fill any given amount of selected image area. And being able to define an image area as a custom Brushes tip enables the Photoshop user to "paint" with strokes that resemble anything from texture to a design.

Photoshop has enough spectacular features all under one roof to keep an ambitious individual learning for months on end. You will continue to expand your talents in handling the computer graphic, and adopt plenty of other tools to further your art—but you'll probably never find a program that steers your artistic sensibilities as firmly and convincingly into computer graphics as Photoshop.

Putting Your One-Upsmanship into Practice

You begin your career as an imaging person using Adobe Photoshop with an advantage. You have an understanding of how to work with features not found in many other imaging programs—and you should keep this in mind. By understanding and refining your skills through practice, you'll be able to offer a client a product that your competitors *can't* offer. But you should also keep in touch with reality, and real-world needs, because getting caught up in the fantastic Photoshop effects and features is easy to do—and sometimes that's not part of your assignment. Keep an eye on what your work really calls for as you keep a perspective on what your talent can produce.

The exercises in Parts 2 and 3 of the book are designed to give you experience in fixing the most common problems found in images. Although you don't learn to create incredible, surrealistic Photoshop masterpieces with these exercises, they are stepping stones to higher plateaus of computer graphics. In fact, Chapter 19 in Part 4 is a good example of creating high-tech imagery by using techniques covered several times throughout the book, using a few images you might even find commonplace.

The point to remember is that Photoshop is a very "concentrated" application; a little bit of it goes a long way toward completing a paying assignment. Use what you need of the tools and features, and trust your own judgment as to when you've completed a task. Don't *embellish* just because you *can*. If you use the features in Photoshop in combination with your artistic sensibilities, you're farther ahead of your competition than you think. Photoshop's edge is the speed and refinement it lends to an image. Your *own* advantage is your good taste. This is always true, whether the artist uses a computer or not.

Can I Make a Career Out of Photoshop?

Many people come to Photoshop from a classical art background and are presently getting to know the Windows operating environment in *addition* to computer graphics programs. Computer graphics are relatively new to the world of IBM-compatible PCs. The release of Windows 3.0 in 1991 gave PCs the interface needed to do high-quality graphic work. Before then, the IBM-PC seemed incapable of producing graphical work as sumptuous as that produced by the Macintosh, and very few *applications* that met artists' most basic needs had been written for the IBM-PC.

It's reasonable to assume that anyone in the 1980s who wanted to make a serious career out of computer graphics looked elsewhere in the computer world for the hardware and software tools of their trade. Many commercial printers, advertising agencies, and publications presently have in their production departments Macintosh users who've been working with the Mac version of Adobe Photoshop for quite a few years.

Photoshop is new to the IBM-PC community—the Windows version was released in January, 1993, giving PC users a first look at the program that's already widely used in the motion picture and publication fields as a Macintosh program. If your threshold of interest in Photoshop is that of an IBM-PC "hobbyist," you have some fine, exciting experiences in store for many years to come. But if you want to make a *career* of computer graphics, buying Photoshop was your very best first step. And following the exercises in this book (in addition to a lot of "woodshedding") should be your second. Definite career possibilities exist for an artist with experience in computer graphics. And the IBM-PC platform is quickly being acknowledged as a very real platform for the creation of wonderful, professional images.

The Private Road to an Imaging Career

When you reach a level of proficiency with the program, you'll travel one—or possibly two— roads in your Photoshop career. You can work in a production department in a firm that does a lot of photography and publishing. Or if you have the budget, you may decide to hang out your own shingle in the marketplace.

Building a computer graphic design business by yourself also requires building a network of "support services" around it. Unless your last name is Getty, color printers, film recorders, proofing devices, and storage for megabytes of image files can put a serious dent in your wallet. We discussed service bureaus and commercial printers in Chapters 20 and 21, and recommend that you get to know the people who run these businesses. You'll need to depend on their expertise to produce a finished piece from your work. Spend *your* time concentrating on your craft with Photoshop and understanding your customers' need to communicate ideas visually.

The Picture of Your Profession

Corporate annual reports, in-house business newsletters, flyers, slides, presentations, and product brochures are all business staples—whether the business is large or small. You can add your artistic flair to them with Photoshop, and people do pay good money for a handsome product. But they usually *don't* want to engage *you*, *then* a service bureau, *then* a proofing house, then a commercial printer to get their printed piece done. As a computer graphic designer, you need to develop relationships with other professionals—photographers, service bureaus, copywriters, mailing houses, and other business links—that support your contribution and help bring an assignment to completion.

Private Partnerships

People communicate with pictures *and* words. And as an imaging-type person, you may want to strike up a relationship with a wordsmith to create a desktop publishing firm. It's not as involved or as difficult as it may sound. This kind of business also requires having good relationships with production-end contacts.

Aldus PageMaker, QuarkXPress, and several other desktop publishing applications are as feature-rich as Photoshop in their own milieu. They make it easy to place your imaging work in a publication. Like any software application, desktop publishing is complex, and has its own rules and people who devote their careers to it. If you can find an experienced PC user or a Macintosh user who is proficient in desktop publishing, a partnership between you two could blossom into a wide range of work opportunities. Like Photoshop, Quark and PageMaker have their Macintosh equivalents, and any individual who has crossed over to the IBM-PC platform with skills in these programs is likely to contribute a wealth in desktop publishing experience.

Small partnerships and self-employment are steps you can take to making a living from your Photoshop skills. But as more and more businesses decide to do in-house publishing, opportunities also exist in production departments.

Taking Your Skills to a Business

Businesses whose products are based on publishing, communications, and art can definitely benefit from a person with a well-rounded art and computer background. Photoshop skills can give you a critical advantage over another person seeking employment at one of these places. The business you go to may be Macintosh-based or may not own Photoshop, but the techniques you learn with Photoshop are portable. The Mac version of Photoshop is identical to the IBM-PC version, and aside from a few conventions the Mac operating system has that are different from Windows, you can get up to speed quickly using a Macintosh.

Even if a business doesn't own Photoshop (Mac or PC), your experience and understanding of this program can be put to good, productive use at a company. Artists find that when they have a firm grasp of the *concept* of bit-map imaging, the skills and approaches developed with Photoshop can be modified to accommodate other software packages. It's at this point that you become an accomplished designer, with your design tools in the background and your talents up front. This is the key to finding rewarding, satisfying employment as an imaging professional at a business. Then, when you're comfortable after a few months employment there, you can suggest that the company *purchase* Photoshop!

Careers and Applications Are Personal Decisions

How far you take your adventures with Photoshop on a professional level is largely up to your own ambition and the perspective you have on your own life. Photoshop can take you up to the Hollywood stars; many motion picture artists use Photoshop to enhance their artwork. John Knoll, one of several software developers who built Adobe Photoshop, recently won an Oscar for LucasFilms, for Best Special Effects in a motion picture.

And technicians at department stores, who help prepare camera-ready art for newspaper advertisements, also find Photoshop rewarding. Regardless of the profession you decide on, whether it's for yourself or for a company, there will be a direct correlation between the hours you invest in mastering Photoshop and the success with which you earn money from your talents. This is true of any profession.

Expanding Your Artist's Toolbox Beyond Photoshop's

It would be naive to suggest that Photoshop is an end unto itself in your computer graphics experiences. Tons of software programs are available for creating computer graphics on the PC platform. Adobe Photoshop is simply one that's at the *top* of them.

Getting "lost" in a program as fascinating as Photoshop is an incredibly easy thing to do. That's why you should do a reality check regularly and look at the task you have at hand. We've stressed throughout this book that computer graphics are best produced with the right tool for the proper purpose. That's why artists own a *collection* of tools—to help them express themselves more completely.

The Companion CD includes some utilities to augment your creative process with Photoshop. Other utilities you may find useful in combination with Photoshop are available as freeware, shareware, and commercial programs. The Resource section in the back of this book lists names and numbers to contact about other applications that can round out your virtual toolbox.

Plug-ins

Adobe Photoshop for Windows 2.5 ships with plug-in filters written by John Knoll and other Adobe technical folk. Photoshop doesn't excite just graphically minded people. Computer programmers find Photoshop an exciting and hospitable program that accomodates their utilities and filters. Photoshop's capability to integrate, or to "plug in," third-party programs makes it possible to continue adding effects and supplemental features to Photoshop long after you purchase version 2.5.

Plug-in software comes with its own installation instructions to make it work inside the Photoshop workspace. After a third-party plug-in has been properly installed, it acts as though it were part of Photoshop; you can use it on any image. Most plug-ins produce special effects and usually are accessed through the Filters menu. Some plug-ins—designed to add different compression schemes or the capability to work with additional file formats—may appear in the Open, Open As, Save, and Save As dialog boxes.

Because the PC version of Photoshop is so new, many of the plug-ins you see advertised may have been designed as Macintosh-only. Before you buy a plug-in, ask whether it is available for the *Windows* version of Photoshop.

HSC Software's Kai's Power Tools was released in a Windows version in December 1993. Kai's Power Tools are superb special effects filters that produce looks ranging from thermograms to surrealistic rainbows in your images. Macintosh users have been using Kai Kraus's product as a plug-in to Photoshop for quite a while; the effects you'll be able to create in Photoshop for Windows are equally stunning.

Aldus Gallery Effects, Editions 2 and 3 can plug directly into Photoshop. Aldus' Edition 1 hasn't been rewritten to adapt to Adobe's workspace as of this writing, but the other two are Photoshop-compatible. Effects can be applied to an entire image or to a selected portion of an image to produce "painterly" effects with a digital photograph. Gallery Effects are particularly useful when you have a color image that's compositionally boring! Apply Bas Relief, Texturizer, or Glowing Edges to an image to add some visual pizazz!

Fractal Design's Painter will *accept* plug-ins, but Painter itself does not *offer* plug-ins to be used in Photoshop. It's a stroke of reverse-engineering. Photoshop's native plug-ins (Spherize, Crystallize, Wind, and all the rest) can be used from within the Painter workspace. If you buy Painter, you can take advantage of its virtual brushes and canvases (as you saw in Chapter 18) and apply Adobe's plug-in filters to your masterpiece while you "paint"!

As time goes by, additional plug-ins from different manufacturers will become available for Adobe Photoshop for Windows. Photoshop is a mature Macintosh product. As soon as developers realize that Photoshop is destined to become the #1 imaging program for a hundredfold more IBM-PC users, those developers will produce Windows versions of their products as well.

The Drawing Application

Drawing programs, such as Adobe Illustrator, CorelDRAW!, and Micrografx Designer are vector-based graphics programs that should be part of your arsenal of computer graphics tools to use with Photoshop. As discussed in Chapter 1, a vector graphic is resolution-independent.

A vector graphic is composed of mathematical equations that describe the independent objects you draw. Vector drawing programs operate with the precision of a mechanical pencil.

By contrast, a bitmapped or raster graphic, which is the kind Photoshop produces, has no independent objects in its finished file format (TIF, PCX, BMP). Its images are formed by arranging pixels that contain color information in an imaginary grid. The size of that grid determines how much resolution the image has. The way Photoshop treats images more closely resembles using a brush. The program excels at pouring soft, warm, naturalistic colors into an image window.

But sometimes your work on the computer calls for using *both* kinds of graphical images (just as in the world of traditional art, you might use both a pencil and a brush on a single piece). Photoshop understands vector-based information, and how to convert (*rasterize*, or *map*) this information to *bit-mapped* information. You can work in a drawing program, then export a vector drawing for use in your Photoshop creations by using Photoshop's EPS Rasterizer.

CorelDRAW! has been the most successfully marketed vector-type drawing program on the PC platform, and for good reason. Corel's interface (shown in Chapter 19) is designed with the physical-drafting-table professional in mind. Within days of picking up the program, people who are new to computers can create simple, salable artwork with Corel. Adobe Illustrator, Micrografx Designer, and Aldus Freehand also are vector drawing programs, each with its own unique interfaces, strengths, and features.

If you want to use a logo or some twisted or extruded type, or if you need to edit lines and curves with an nth degree of precision for use in Photoshop, you'd want to use a vector drawing program. Again, it's a matter of using the right tool for the right job. Photoshop can import a wide variety of bit-mapped file formats but ships with only two vector file import filters: EPS and Adobe's own AI (Adobe Illustrator). When you select a vector drawing program, be sure that it can export files to a bit-mapped file format or as EPS and AI files. CorelDRAW!, Micrografx Designer, and Aldus Freehand all have good Import/Export features that transfer vector art successfully into Photoshop.

Utilities

Programs that simplify your work in other programs are called *utilities*. Regular use of Photoshop will produce hundreds of megabytes of image files on your hard drive, floppy disk, and back-up tapes for years to come. You'll want to be able to view, index, compress, collate, and standardize not one, but *hundreds* of Photoshop images at a time! This is where PC file-management utilities come into your imaging life. These utilities range from as cheap as freeware to an expensive application that creates a video slide show from your work.

The Fully Equipped Windows Shell

A Windows "shell" is a good starting place in your quest for utilities that make life with Photoshop a breeze. To use Photoshop on the PC platform, you need Microsoft Windows. But

Windows Program Manager, the place where you copy and view programs, directories, and files, leaves much to be desired in ease of use and functionality.

Symantec's Norton Desktop for Windows and Central Point Software's PCTools for Windows are replacements for Windows Program Manager and File Manager. Each suite of tools is actually a collection of much-needed utilities that can assist you in everyday computer "housekeeping" so that you can spend more time with your imaging profession. Both products offer similar features, such as virusscanning, a simplified way of looking at directories and files, viewers for both images and text, file searchers (when you've forgotten what you named your image!), and many other items from a computer user's wish list.

Image Cataloging

Kodak's Shoebox, Corel Mosaic!, and U-Lead's Image Pals all offer cataloguing features for image files. You can print collections of "thumbnails" of images stored on your hard drive. The file formats each product supports vary, but all will view TIF image formats. For all the organizational power the computer has brought to our lives, a printout or two of image files goes a long way in helping you retrieve files you want to edit out of the sea of image files you'll soon own.

An on-screen slide show of your work can provide immediate gratification after long weeks of building a collection of images for a corporate presentation. Chapter 21 discussed the value of a service bureau, but more and more companies are putting together a presentation that's run directly from a monitor or projected onto a wall by using an LCD panel hooked up to a PC.

The Shareware Video Slide Show Utilities

The most basic way to show your "slides" in sequence is to save them as GIF files. GIF files are CompuServe's contribution to the computer Graphics Image Format. A GIF file is highly-compressed until it's read into your system RAM. CompuServe developed the GIF format so that they could offer their subscribers high-quality, indexed, 256-color images to download without the users having to spend a fortune in connect time.

If you use on-line services or local BBSs, you'll find many shareware GIF-file "players." VPIC, CSHOW, and WINGIF all can produce a timed slide show of images saved to the GIF format. VPIC and CSHOW are DOS programs that can display PCX file formats also. If you want to try out one of these inexpensive shareware programs, use Photoshop's Save As command to save copies of your images as GIF files. For PCX shows, first use the **M**odes command to change your RGB image to an 8- or 4-bit Indexed data type. Then use the Save As command to save your image in the PCX file format.

The "try it before you buy it" policy of shareware designers is a great gift to artists. Shareware authors are often prompted to write a utility because they can't find a feature they want in an existing commercial application. These unexpected gems pop up in the least likely places; keep an eye on what's happening in this alternative method of software distribution.

Commercial Slide Show and MultiMedia Programs

You may already own a slide show program and be unaware of it. Many companies include a slide show feature as a sidekick to their main program. But whether it's a part of a program or a stand-alone, showing a collection of bit-mapped slides at a reasonable pace on your PC requires a great deal of system "umph." You can address this problem by packing a fast 486 PC with at least 20M of RAM, and you can use Photoshop's dithering options to convert a copy of an RGB image to Indexed color, which shrinks the image file size and demands less of your PC's resources.

If you want to include your images in a *super* slide show—complete with sound, video clips, and fancy dissolves—you'll want to get a full-featured presentation graphics package such as Microsoft PowerPoint, SPCs Harvard Graphics, Lotus Freelance Graphics, or WordPerfect Presentations. All are mainstream, commercial presentation packages that support at least 256-color images. These packages are more complex and more capable than the shareware programs, and take longer to learn than their simpler siblings.

Full-fledged *multimedia* software, the top tier of show-type products, can be used to produce slide shows, video tapes, and CD-ROM-based shows. Mastering a MultiMedia application takes as much time and effort as mastering Photoshop (and *authoring* programs are *not* inexpensive). If you want to use your Photoshop imaging work as parts of high-quality animation sequences, moving slide shows, self-running demo disks, and sight-sound-motion presentations, you might want to take a look at MacroMedia Author or HSC Interactive.

Full-Featured MultiMedia Applications as "Utilities"

At some point you cross a line where a utility becomes another application. Photoshop can be used to create a graphic whose purpose is to play a minor role in a desktop publishing document. In this sense, Photoshop has "played utility" to a program that didn't have a rich set of graphics tools. Then again, in a rendering and modeling program (discussed in Chapter 19) that lacks sophisticated photo-finishing tools, a design exists as several images until those images come to Photoshop for compositing. Sometimes it's difficult to tell which image "belongs" to a specific application. If the application in which you finish a design counts as "owner," you'll find you own only one application—the rest are Photoshop *utilities*!

Manufacturers have their own definition of what a utility is. Some state that it's a program which depends on the finished product of *another* program, such as a word processing macro. Utilities have to be defined by the individual artist because the artist alone has to evaluate what a program is good *for* as it relates to his or her work. Sometimes a full-featured application has a minor feature you'd like to use as a utility. Buying an entire application to own a single feature is an expensive solution to whatever you're trying to accomplish—but sometimes a necessary one, and definitely worth it.

PIXAR *Typestry* was used throughout this book to create simple, graphical examples for our readers, and yet we used perhaps a tenth of the program's feature set. We used Typestry because we knew how adept Typestry is at creating dimensional text and graphics, and that we could then refine and fine-tune them in Photoshop faster than if we tried to build the same image entirely within Photoshop.

Define a utility, that which helps your Photoshop work, in your own mind. Don't depend on a label on a box.

How Good Can You Get?

We hope you're not disappointed that this chapter didn't have Shift+Click+Drag in every other sentence! We've discussed things that connect with Photoshop, such as other programs, and especially the artist, with the intention of providing you with a little scope and perspective on the rich, satisfying, complex aspects of computer imaging and graphics.

A creative person learns and does so much along the path to achieving a real, true master-piece, that he or she can lose *direction* easily. We've found that pinching yourself at regular intervals, as you pore through pages and pages of how-tos, helps to restore both your circulation and the humanity you bond to a software application in creating art. Technical skill alone isn't going to make you a great Photoshop designer. If getting great at image editing and design work is your heart's desire, you now have the learning tools and the software program on your side. But education and Photoshop alone won't make you as good at computer art as you'd like to be.

Patience, desire, perspective, and open-mindedness are other ingredients that complete the recipe for turning a good imaging-type person into a great one. Talent can be a big contribu-tor to achieving Photoshop greatness. Let's get real; having artistic flair when you sit before a PC for the first time *can* give you an edge. But I've seen many a determined individual with *mediocre* skills, or talent (whatever you want to call trained, reflexive inspiration) *succeed* in business and their personal lives because they had a perspective on the right methods at the right time in their lives to accomplish what they wanted. And I've seen people with phenom-enal, innate artistic abilities fall by the wayside because they had no sense of humility or perspective about a craft they believe they mastered shortly after birth.

You must take responsibility for maintaining your own personal perspective as you determine the right blend of Photoshop, practice, and ingenuity for successfully communicating a thought—yours or someone else's—in a digital, visual fashion.

So how good *is* good? Here are some guidelines:

✔ If you practice diligently with Photoshop and can recognize elements in your work that are eye-pleasing and inspire you to keep on trying, then you are already "good."

✔ If you can share images you created using Photoshop, images you're proud of, and still hang on to the "failures" and not feel embarrassed about them, then you are "great."

✔ If you can balance the yearning to learn more with a continuous sense of achievement, and allow an image to *speak for itself* with an eloquence you've freely given to it, then you are a *success*.

Part VI

Appendixes

APPENDIX

Resource Guide

As you become more familiar with Adobe Photoshop and image editing, you'll become more ambitious and will want to augment your core group of imaging tools. The following is a list of hardware, software, and services you may not find elsewhere in your quest for additional resources. It's part wish list and part "private bag of tricks and secrets." A lot of this information came to us through personal contacts with vendors.

See our acknowledgments for the individuals at companies who directly contributed to this book, through their time and gracious loans of their equipment. We believe that thanking them in writing is nice, but letting people know how to get in *touch* with them is even better!

Design Software

Adobe Systems, Inc.
1585 Charleston Road
PO Box 7900
Mountain View, CA 94039-7900
800-833-6687
Adobe Photoshop, Adobe Illustrator

Aldus Corporation
411 First Avenue South
Seattle, Washington 98104-2871
206-622-5500
Aldus Gallery Effects—Photoshop special effects plug-ins
Aldus PageMaker—premier desktop publishing program

Corel Corporation
1600 Carling Avenue
Ottawa, Ontario, Canada K1Z 8R7
716-423-8200
613-728-8200
CorelDRAW!
Vector graphic-based drawing program, comes with other graphic utilities, and lots and lots of typefaces and clip art

Fractal Design Corporation
101 Madeline Drive, Suite 204
Aptos, CA 95003
408-688-8800
Fractal Design Painter—natural media paint program

HSC Software
1661 Lincoln Blvd., Suite 101
Santa Monica, CA 90404
310-392-8441
Fax: 310-392-6015
Kai's Power Tools—Photoshop special effects plug-in filters
HSC Interactive—multi-media authoring system

HumanCAD Division of Biomechanics Corp. of America
1800 Walt Whitman Road
Melville, NY 11747
516-752-3568
Mannequin—human form modeling program

Macromedia, Inc.
600 Townsend Street
Suite 310W
San Francisco, CA 94103
MacroModel, Author, Action!

Pixar
1001 West Cutting Blvd.
Richmond, CA 94804
510-236-4000
Typestry—3D typographic rendering program

Visual Software
21731 Ventura Blvd.
Woodland Hills, CA 91364
818-593-3750
Renderize for Windows—full-featured 3D rendering program

Hardware

CD-ROM Drives

Procom Technology, Inc.
2181 Dupont Drive
Irvine, CA 92715
800-800-8600
714-852-1000
Makers of the double-speed MCD-DS CD-ROM drive, a multi-session, XA and PhotoCD-compliant drive

Pressure Sensitive Tablets

CalComp
PO Box 3250
Anaheim, Ca 92803
800-932-1212
Fax: 714-821-2714
Makers of pressure-sensitive graphics tablets

Wacom Technology Corp.
501 S.E. Columbia Shores Blvd., Suite 300
Vancouver, WA 98661
800-922-6613
206-750-8882
Fax: 206-750-8924
Makers of pressure-sensitive graphics tablets

Scanners

Logitech, Inc.
6505 Kaiser Drive
Fremont, CA 94555
510-713-4463
Fax: 510-792-8901
FotoMan—black-and-white digital camera
ScanMan Color—easy to use TWAIN-compliant hand scanner

UMAX
3170 Coronado Drive
Santa Clara, CA 95054
800-562-0311
408-982-0771
Fax: 408-892-0776
UMAX U8400 Flatbed Color Scanner

Image Cataloging/Management Software

Eastman Kodak Company
343 State Street
Rochester, NY 14650
800-242-2424 (ext. 53)
Acquire Module for Photoshop, Access for Windows, PhotoEdge Shoebox

U-Lead Systems, Inc.
970 West 190th Street, Suite 520
Torrance, CA 90502
310-523-9393
Fax: 310-523-9399
Image Pals—an excellent image file manager/cataloger, also includes capture and image enhancing utilities

Imaging Centers/Service Bureaus

Graphic Masters, Inc.
John and Susan Niestemski
6883 E. Genesee Street
PO Box 469
Fayetteville, NY 13066
315-445-1800
Aldus Authorized Imaging Center—PC and Mac Imaging, 35mm slides, color prints, scanning, overheads

Slide Systems, Inc.
16 West 19th Street
NY, NY 10011
212-924-8555
Fax: 212-929-9280
E-6 color processing, Cibacopy, overheads, 35mm for Mac and PC

T-Tech Services
888 East Belvidere Road, Suite 124
Grayslake, IL 60030
708-223-0789
PC and Macintosh imagesetting, pre-press services, desktop publishing

Textures

IMAGETECTS™
P.O. Box #4
Saratoga, CA 95071
or
7200 Bollinger Road, Suite 802
San Jose, CA 95129
ImageCELs®—libraries consist of textures and patterns in TIF and other formats. Should you have further questions or requests about any ImageCELs® library or other ImageCELs® products, please contact IMAGETECTS™ by calling 408-252-5487 between 9–5 PST, Monday through Friday. Twenty-four-hour fax number 408-252-7409, ImageCELs® ONLINE 202-686-2373 (Modem settings 8–N–1)

Pixar
1001 West Cutting Blvd.
Richmond, CA 94804
510-236-4000
Pixar One-Twenty-Eight—seamlessly tiling digital textures

Stock Photography Agencies— Pay-per-Use

Kodak Picture Exchange
Eastman Kodak Company
343 State Street
Rochester, NY 14650
Online service features images available from more than 17 professional stock photography agencies
800-579-8737 for enrollment information, services, charges, and to request a free demo disk

Color Image Library
Port to Print
Madison, Wisconsin
On-line commercial stock photography agency with 2500 plus images available
800-236-4887 for enrollment information, services, and charges

International Color Stock Archive
Press Link
Reston, Virginia
On-line news and commercial stock photography agency with 2500 plus images available
703-758-1740 for enrollment information, services, and charges

Stock Photography—Royalty Free

Allegro New Media
387 Passaic Avenue
Fairfield, NJ 07004
201-808-1992
Royalty-free graphic textures and graphic photos on CD-ROMs

Aris Entertainment
310 Washington Boulevard
Marina del Ray, CA 90292
310-821-0234
Fax: 310-821-6463
Royalty-free stock photography on CD-ROMs

Corel Corporation
1600 Carling Avenue
Ottawa, Ontario, Canada K1Z 8R7
716-423-8200
613-728-8200
Corel Professional Photos CD-ROM—royalty-free stock photos

Image Club Graphics, Inc.
729 24th Avenue Southwest
Calgary, Alberta Canada T2G 1P5
800-661-9410
403-262-8008
403-261-7013
CompuServe 72560,2323
America On-Line Image Club—specializes in typefaces, quality clip art, and stock photography;
free catalog often contains Photoshop tips

Jasmine Multimedia Publishing
6746 Valjean Avenue Suite 100
Van Nuys, CA 91406
800-798-7535
818-780-3344
Fax: 818-780-8705
Royalty-free stock photography and video on CD-ROM

PhotoCD

Capitol Filmworks
909 Forest Avenue
Montgomery, AL 36106
800-974-8323
Kodak PhotoCD Masters made from 35mm slides or negatives, film developing, and image 35mm slides
Mac and PC-based

Digix Imaging Center
1 Choke Cherry Lane
Rockville, MD 20850
800-344-4969
301-977-0519
Kodak PhotoCD Masters made from 35mm and Kodak Pro PhotoCD Masters made from large format film
(35mm, 2 1/4-inch, 4 by 5)

Eastman Kodak's PhotoCD Hotline
800-235-6325
Information, literature, and support for Kodak's PhotoCD products and technology
Also can get information on the nearest PhotoCD Master and Pro PhotoCD Master imaging sites

VI

Appendixes

Publications

Publish Magazine
Subscriptions
PO Box 55415
Boulder, CO 80322
800-274-5116
Monthly magazine, by subscription and on newsstands

Utilities

Central Point Software
15220 N.W. Greenbrier Parkway
Beaverton, OR 97006
800-445-2110
Fax: 800-626-2778 (information)
Fax: 503-690-6650 (technical support)
BBS: 503-690-6650
Central Point PC Tools for Windows—complete File Management and Utilities program for Windows, replaces Windows Program and File Managers

Corel Corporation
1600 Carling Avenue
Ottawa, Ontario, Canada K1Z 8R7
716-423-8200
613-728-8200
CorelSCSI!—SCSI devices drivers

JASC, Inc.
10901 Red Circle Drive
Suite 340
Minnetonka, MN 55343 USA
612-930-9171
CIS: 72557,256
Paint Shop Pro—Graphic utility

Helix Software Company
4709 30th Street
Long Island City, NY 11101
718-392-3000 (general information)
718-392-3735 (technical support)
Fax: 718-392-4212
BBS: 718-392-4054
Helix Netroom—memory management program for stand-alone or networked PCs

Nico-Mak
P.O. Box 919
Bristol, CT 06011-0919
70056,241 on CompuServe, to Nico_Mak on BIX, or by sending US Mail
WinZip—file-archiving and file-compression shell that works with PKZIP, ARJ, LHA, ARC, and other formats

PKWARE, Inc.
9025 N. Deerwood Drive
Brown Deer, WI 53223-2437
414-354-8699
Fax: 414-354-8559
BBS: 414-354-8670
PKZIP—file compression and archiving program

Stac Electronics
5993 Avenue Encinas
Carlsbad, CA 92008-9708
619-431-7474 (general information)
BBS: 619-431-5956
Fax: 619-431-8585 (FAXback service)
Stacker—widely used hard disk compression utility that can double your available hard drive space

Symantec Corporation
10201 Torre Avenue
Cupertino, CA 95014-2132
408-253-9600
The Norton Desktop for Windows—complete file management and utilities program for Windows, replaces Windows program and file managers

TOGGLE BOOLEANS
PO Box 4204, Station E
Ottawa, Ontario, Canada, K15 5B2
Compuserve 71534, 3255 @ compuserve.com
Resource Monitor—a nifty utility for checking Windows user and GDI heaps

The Companion CD

You may have noticed something special about this book when you first picked it up. Besides being the first complete reference guide for Adobe Photoshop for Windows, it's also a workbook; the chapters are divided into practical exercises that teach you Photoshop techniques for use in your own work. Hey, you have to start someplace with any new application!

What's on the Companion CD?

To give you hands-on experience with the techniques described throughout this book, a companion CD is tucked into an envelope in the front of this book. This CD contains all the images that you retouch in the chapter exercises, in addition to a lot of shareware utilities and stock digital photography from software manufacturers. Stock photography in digital computer format can be a lifesaver for the budding imaging-type person, and these samplers are meant to give you a taste of what's available from these companies.

Please do not use the images contained in directories—*other* than those images in the EXERCISE subdirectory—for any commercial purposes per our agreement with the manufacturers who allowed us to use them. For further information, restrictions, and special requirements pertaining to the stock photo images, read the accompanying text on the companion CD from your Windows text editor (use Windows Write, Word for Windows, and so on), and check Appendix A, "Resource Guide," as to how to get in touch with the various companies.

How Do You Use the Sucker?

For following along with the exercises in each chapter, we've made it really easy to open the files from the companion CD. All you need to know is the following:

✔ That you have a CD disk drive properly hooked to your system. You must have a CD-ROM drive—external, internal, or over a network—linked to your PC in order to take advantage of the CD enclosed in the front of this book.

✔ How to "navigate" the directory structure of the companion CD. If you're familiar with directory structures in Windows File Manager, the companion CD is set up exactly the same way. If not, we have a "mock" exercise coming up that you can use for a guide.

✔ The directory tree on the companion CD branches from the root into different file categories. The subdirectory you'll be working from to do all the chapter exercises is called EXERCISE. The subdirectories beneath EXERCISE are labeled "CHAP01," for images used in Chapter 1, and so on. The other companion CD subdirectories relate to other software vendors and their products. There are some rules you need to follow, legality-wise, if you decide to access these other CD subdirectories. Check the README.TXTs in each of these subdirectories before wandering too far!

An Exercise Before You Do the Exercises

Inside Adobe Photoshop for Windows is a visual book as well as a hands-on one, so in keeping with this format, the following exercise will show you how to open an exercise file from the companion CD. Whenever you come to a chapter exercise, the first step is usually to open a file from the companion CD. We have the step in an exercise marked:

Open the XXXXXXXX.TIF image from the companion CD

The Xs represent the file name for the particular image you need. Let's do this now:

Opening a Companion CD Image

Take the companion CD out of its envelope, located in the front of this book	You've broken the seal and accepted all responsibilities as expressed by the manufacturers.
Place the CD, face up, into the CD-ROM drive's caddy or in your CD-ROM drive	There are a few CD-ROM drives that don't require a disk caddy. Check your manufacturer's documentation on this step. Loads the media, and your system can now read the information on the companion CD.
Double-click on the Photoshop icon in its Windows Program Manager group	Launches the Photoshop software. You may also do this from **F**ile, **R**un in File Manager, or you may have a Windows "shell" (for example, Norton Desktop) that requires similar procedures to execute, or launch, Photoshop.
When Photoshop's workspace is open on your screen, choose **F**ile, **O**pen (or press Ctrl+O)	Calls up the open menu, as shown in figure B.1.
Click on the down arrow next to Dri**v**es, and select your CD-ROM drive	Allows your system to read the directories for the CD-ROM drive in Photoshop's **D**irectories list.
Click on the EXERCISE subdirectory in the **D**irectories box	Displays the subdirectories of the chapter exercise images beneath the EXERCISE subdirectory, as shown in figure B.2.

continues

VI

Appendixes

continued

Click on CHAP_19 in the **D**irectories list box	Expands the Chapter 19 subdirectory to reveal individual image files contained in it under the File **N**ame box, as shown in figure B.3.
Click on HEART.TIF in the File **N**ame list box, and then click on OK	Selects the HEART.TIF image for use in this mock exercise, and the image file appears in your Photoshop workspace (see fig. B.4).

Figure B.1
Photoshop's Open menu provides a directory list for all your drives.

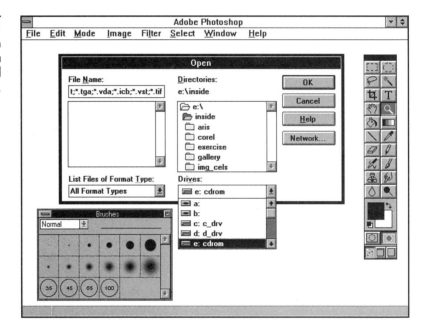

If you followed along, you see how easy it is to get the materials you need to actually follow the steps to doing great imaging work found in this book. All these preceding steps are the "longhand" treatment for the

Open the HEART.TIF image from the companion CD

step found in Chapter 19. On occasion, you'll be given specific instructions to open a saved copy you've been working on when the exercise calls for it, but you'll have specific exercise instruction steps in those cases.

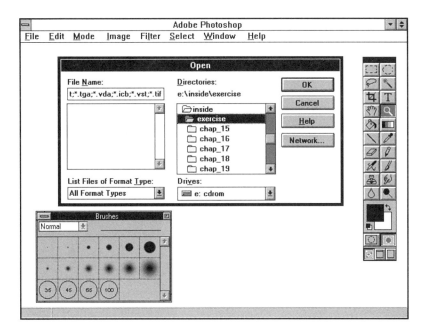

Figure B.2
EXERCISE is a subdirectory containing the chapter exercise images used in this book.

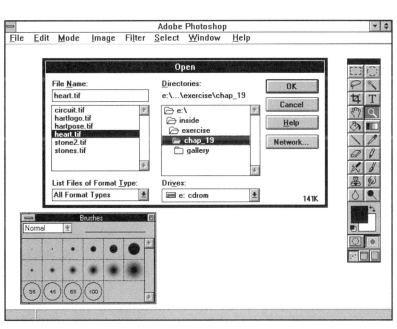

Figure B.3
Individual image files you'll use are located in numbered chapter subdirectories on the companion CD.

Figure B.4
An image file that
you use in our
exercises in

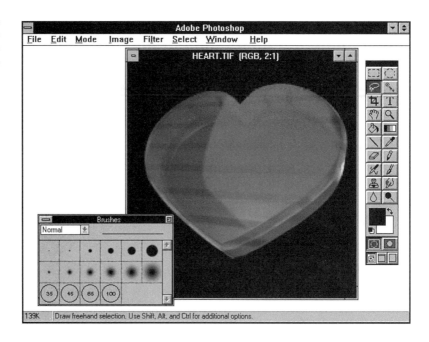

Be aware that this companion CD, like all CD disks, is **C**ompact **D**isk **R**ead-**O**nly **M**emory; you cannot *write* to the companion CD, and all your work must be saved to a writeable type of media, like your hard or floppy disk. This gets confusing sometimes because Photoshop and a lot of other programs give you the option to save to the CD, but then pop up a strange warning like the one in figure B.5.

If you're the ambitious type, you'll accumulate several megabytes of finished exercise images through the course of following along with *Inside Photoshop*. You may want to keep these images organized on your hard disk by creating a subdirectory called MYWORK (or any other inspired eight character name!). After you use **F**ile **S**ave, or **F**ile, Sa**v**e As, you'll be able to retrieve these images, as called for at various points in the exercises, as easily as you can find them on the companion CD.

If you're new to the Windows environment and aren't a "Directory Tree Guru" yet, you may want to learn more about directory structures, copying files, and good hard disk "housekeeping." New Riders Publishing offers *Windows for Non-Nerds* and *Inside Windows 3.1*, which describe in detail how to organize your Windows applications and files. These books are perfect companions for your PC imaging adventures.

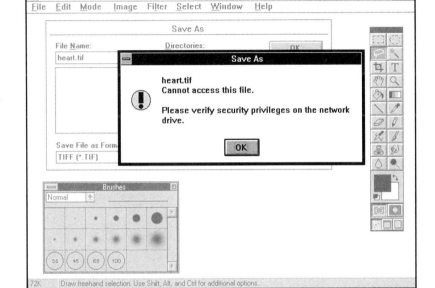

Figure B.5
Photoshop cannot write to our companion CD, or any other CD Read-Only Memory media.

What's In Store

We hope you'll find actually working with images in exercises to be an exciting medium. Most folks find "how to" books rather dry, and New Riders Publishing is happy to provide new users interested in manipulating digital images this companion CD alternative. *Inside Photoshop* brings education to a more intimate level, and you'll find very practical uses in your own imaging work for the techniques, tricks, and tips that it brings to you.

Have fun! That's what imaging is all about!

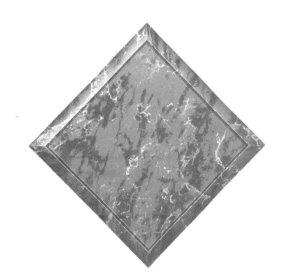

Super Glossary

2.935 times the information in most user guides!

Acquire Command

Located on the File menu, this command gives Photoshop users access to plug-in filters for importing EPS format images saved with JPEG lossey compression technology. Also allows the use of a TWAIN interface to scan an image directly into Photoshop's workspace, and use of a digital camera for directly acquiring digital images.

Adjust Submenu

Submenu of the Image menu. Provides a list of commands that display dialog boxes (Levels, Variations, Brightness/Contrast, Hue/Saturation, and Curves) that are used to perform color and tonal corrections.

Airbrush Tool

A paint application tool that applies an extremely diffused "spray" of foreground color to an active image area. Owners of digitizing tablets can take advantage of the Airbrush pressure option (the slider on the Brushes palette) when working with this tool in Photoshop.

Anchor Point

A component of a path, created with Photoshop's Pen tool (located on the Paths palette). An Anchor point is situated between path segments; it can have direction points that allow the Photoshop user to bend or angle path segments between anchor points. You cannot have a Path without Anchor points. *See Chapter 10 for how to work with Paths and Anchor points.*

Anti-Aliasing

Photoshop's method for smoothing the appearance of bitmap-type image selections, which by their nature, contain "stairsteppy" edges created by square-shaped pixels. Anti-Aliasing places semitransparent edge pixels between other edge pixels, causing the eye to see a gradual fall-off in color at the border of a selection area. The Defringe command (under the Select menu) is often necessary to remove anti-alias pixels from a selection that has been pasted into a background image.

ASCII

Acronym for American Standard Code for Information Interchange. A standard that assigns a unique binary number to each text character and control character.

Aspect Ratio

The proportional relationship of an image's height to width. 35mm film has an aspect ratio of 2:3. If you send Photoshop images to a film recorder to have 35mm slides or film negatives made, image dimensions must also have a 2:3 aspect ratio if the image is to fill the 35mm frame. Chapter 21 shows you how to achieve a 2:3 aspect ratio with a digital image if it does not already have one.

Bézier Drawing

Drawing a path segment by clicking and dragging the Pen tool to create *curved* path segments between Anchor points is called *Bézier drawing* or *Bézier curve drawing.* The method is difficult to master. Most new Photoshop users prefer to simply click on points with the Pen tool to get straight path segments between anchor points, then use the Corner tool to shape them into curved path segments by pulling on direction points. The Pen tool and the Corner tool are both on the Paths palette. *See Chapter 10 for how to work with Bézier drawing, Paths, and Anchor points. See also Anchor points.*

Bit

The smallest measurement of computer information, based on the way electricity is handled in the computer; electricity is either on or off in a data signal, and a bit of information is the placeholder for this physical occurrence. Computer users generally evaluate computer files in terms of bytes (each byte has 8 bits), Ks (kilobytes, or thousands of bytes), and Ms (megabytes, or millions of bytes). You cannot create serious image work with only one bit of information.

Bit Depth

Term used to express color capability of an image format. In Grayscale and Indexed color images, 8 bits of information are assigned to each pixel in the image. Each of the eight bits can be either on or off, which yields 2 to the 8th power, or 256 possible on/off combinations each pixel can express. Each of these combinations can be assigned a color. An RGB color image has a bit-depth of 24. Because each pixel in an RGB image has 24 bits associated with it (three channels, each 8 bits deep), it is capable of expressing 2 to the 24th power, or 16.7 million possible color combinations.

Bitmap

The type of computer graphic image Photoshop works with and produces. Bitmap images are raster images; they are arranged on screen and sent to a printer as lines of color pixels arranged in an imaginary grid. (Vector images are the opposite of bitmap images.) Bitmaps are also called *resolution-dependent images.*

Also, Adobe uses the term bitmap to describe a Photoshop Mode that corresponds to an image with a bit depth of one bit. Each pixel in an image in Bitmap Mode is either off (black) or on (white). Most other programs and a lot of scanner manufacturers refer to this image data type as 1 Bit, black and white, or Line Art.

Black Point

Photoshop evaluates every image according to the brightness of its tonal ranges, measured from 0 to 255 (a total of 256 values). The black point corresponds to the darkest tonal value in the image. Photoshop assigns this tonal value to 0. You can reset the black point in an image by using either the Levels or Curves command, or both commands. Decreasing the black point value in an image gives a picture less contrast, whereas increasing it displays more contrast in the image.

Blur Filters

A submenu of Photoshop's Filters menu, Blur offers a variety of blurring options for softening selected image areas or entire images. Radial, Motion, and Gaussian Blurs can be used to create effects or assist in retouching an image. Techniques for using blurs are discussed in Parts 3 and 4 of this book.

Blur/Sharpen Tool

Tool that enables the user to selectively reduce (Blur) or increase (Sharpen) the tonal (gray component) differences in neighboring pixels by dragging the tool's cursor over an active image area. To switch between the two functions, hold down the Alt key while using the tool to access the inverse tool mode. You can also double-click on the Blur/Sharpen tool button to reset its default to either Blur or Sharpen. *See Chapters 7, 12, and 13 for examples of how and when to use the Blur/Sharpen tool.*

BMP

File extension for a bitmap image format made popular by Microsoft Windows. A BMP image is an Indexed color image; it can be read by systems operating under DOS and Windows. OS/2 uses a special version of this format.

Border Command

When a selection border is created around an area of an image, the Border Command (located in the **S**elect menu) can be used to create a pair of selection borders that are equidistant from the original selection border. This creates a "band," or border, around the original shape. The image area inside the two new selection borders becomes the selected area in the image (and can be modified by applying filters, effects, and painting and editing tools). You can set the width of the border you create.

Brightness

One of the three qualities of color, the other two being Saturation and Hue. Brightness is measured by the amount of light reflected (or passed through) an object. A true, physical subject that reflects light is only *represented* in a computer image, but brightness in a Hue, Saturation, Brightness (HSB) color model plays a very real role in digital image quality. Contrast and gamma are also related to brightness. *Value* is a term used by some other imaging applications instead of Brightness.

Brightness/Contrast Command

Command in the Adjust submenu, used to access slider controls that can be set from –100 to +100. The higher the value, the more brightness or contrast is added to the selected image area.

Brush Options

A dialog box accessed by double-clicking on a brush tip or on a vacant area on the Brushes palette. Brush options include setting the brush tip size (diameter), measured in pixels, the spacing between strokes, and the degree of hardness a tip has. The tip you select from the Brushes palette determines some of the behavior not only of the Paintbrush tool but also of other painting tools such as the Rubber Stamp tool or the Pencil tool. Brushes palette settings also affect such Editing tools as the Smudge tool and the Blur/Sharpen tool.

Brushes Palette

From the Brushes palette you can access controls for specifying the characteristics of the tips of painting and editing tools. Tip size, Brush Options, modes in which you paint and edit, and custom Brushes palettes are all controlled from the Brushes palette. The slider on the Brushes palette controls the degree of opacity at which you apply or remove "paint" with a painting tool, as well as the degree or pressure of an effect when you use an editing tool, such as the Smudge or Dodge/Burn tool. Pressing F5 displays the Brushes palette. *See Chapters 4 and 7 for more information about using custom Brushes palettes and designing custom tips.*

You can control the mode by which a pasted selection area is composited into an image by clicking and dragging on the slider on the Brushes palette, but only when a selection tool (Lasso, Rectangular, and Elliptical Marquee) is currently active.

Calculate Command

Located on the Photoshop Image menu, the Calculate function enables you to perform mathematical calculations based on two different channels in the same image, or on two different images of exactly the same size. Calculate, among other things, can Add, Subtract, or show the differences between two images. It can also create a new image based on the calculations you specify. Particularly useful for modifying selection borders and for copying selection borders from one image to another. *See Chapter 18 for examples of how to use the Calculate functions.*

Calibration

Accessed from the File menu (Preferences, Monitor Setup). Photoshop users should calibrate (standardize) their monitors before producing work that will be sent to a commercial printer or service bureau. Calibrating your monitor adjusts it so that the colors you see and the gamma (brightness) of your monitor more closely match the colors produced by other output devices, such as slide recorders and print presses. Room lighting, choice of paper to print on, and age of the phosphors on a monitor are all contributing factors that must be taken into account when calibrating a monitor. *See Chapters 4 and 21.*

Canvas Size Command

Located on the Image menu. Used to set the canvas size, the height and width dimensions of the virtual "paper" or "canvas" on which an image is created. Decreasing the canvas size of an existing image crops it. Increasing the canvas size adds "canvas" to the image. The size of the existing image does not change; the new canvas exposed around the image is filled with the color specified as background color from the background color selection box on the toolbox. *See Chapter 21.*

Channels

Channels are a digital image *model* used to express color components as well as additional noncolor information components in a digital image file. RGB, 24-bit color images have three channels—Red, Green, and Blue. Photoshop displays a composite channel made from these three channels, called the RGB channel, which gives the user a working view of the whole image.

Users can view one channel at a time in an image, although it is possible to effect changes on several channels simultaneously, by clicking on the pencil icon next to the channel name on the Channels palette. Indexed and Grayscale images have only one channel.

Channels, Alpha

Alpha channels are user-defined channels that contain masks and selection areas (information) within the image file. An alpha channel is an additional information channel, 8-bits in depth. Photoshop users can add up to 16 extra Alpha channels to Indexed, RGB, or Grayscale images. Extra channels in an image dramatically increase the file size of the image.

Clear Command

Accessed from the Edit menu, this command deletes a floating selection and leaves a background image intact. It also reveals background color in an image that contains a nonfloating selection. The Clear command is equivalent to the Delete key on your keyboard.

Clipboard

Part of the Microsoft Windows operating environment that stores many different data types, which are cut and copied to it. Photoshop uses Windows' Clipboard when you copy or cut a selection area. When you choose Export Clipboard from File, General Preferences in Photoshop, the selection areas you copy in a Photoshop session are made available to other applications after you exit a Photoshop session.

Clipping

Clipping occurs when you oversaturate an area. Clipping is usually an unintended, unwanted effect because it creates flat, undifferentiated "blocked in" or "blown out" areas of color. Clipping is displayed in bright neon highlights in the Variations command thumbnails when you color-correct an image. Try to avoid color corrections that cause clipping. *See Chapter 6.*

Clipping Paths

Have nothing to do with Clipping as it occurs in Variations. Clipping Paths are paths you create in an image to export to a drawing program such as Adobe Illustrator. The exported Clipping Path is used in the drawing program as a guide that describes the shape or size of an area in a bitmap Photoshop image. Clipping Paths are vector-type information; they must be rasterized with a PostScript interpreter to be visible. This rasterization is usually an automatic process, in which the user selects a few options from a dialog box before viewing a Clipping Path.

CMYK Color

Cyan, Magenta, Yellow, and Black are the four process colors used to make ink-on-paper prints from a digital image. They are not part of the RGB color model used to view images on a monitor; both the CMYK mode and the color model are used for printing-press production of an image. You may never use CMYK Mode in Photoshop if you don't need digital process color separations made from an RGB image. When you change from RGB to CMYK color, Photoshop must translate color values because, whereas an RGB image has three color information channels, CMYK color is modeled around four. Something of the original data is always lost or changed in the translation.

Color Balance Command

Color Balance is accessed from the Adjust submenu. Use it to change the balance between the primary additive and subtractive colors in an image (Red, Green, Blue being additive; Cyan, Magenta, and Yellow being the subtractive primaries). The adjustments can be made to change the balance of color in an image's shadows areas, midtone areas, and highlight areas. By specifying different color balance settings for an image, you can make dramatic changes to the "feel" of the image. *See Chapter 13.*

Color Modes

Photoshop's Mode menu enables you to determine what image type, or mode, an image should have. Many of the modes relate to the image's bit depth; others relate to the color model used to describe the image. A mode is not a viewing-only scheme. When you specify

continues

Grayscale for an RGB image, color information about the image is literally discarded to create a Grayscale-only image. If you save an RGB image as a Grayscale, the color information in it is lost forever. Native image modes (the type of image you begin with), can be Indexed color, Grayscale, RGB, and several others that relate to commercial printer specifications. Only RGB, Indexed, Grayscale, and Bitmap images can be saved as file format types that can be used with most other software applications. *See Chapter 1.*

Color Picker

Used to choose colors, the color picker is accessed by clicking on the color selection boxes on the toolbox or on the Colors palette. Colors may be selected by clicking and dragging a target point in a model of the color spectrum, or by numerical entries that describe the color according to the various color models (RGB, HSB, CYMK, or LAB). Custom color-matching schemes such as PANTONE or TRUEMATCH can also be specified.

Color Selection Box

Area on Photoshop's toolbox used to specify foreground and background colors. Clicking on the overlapping color swatches displays the Color Picker; foreground or background can be selected from a spectrum or specified numerically according to a variety of color models. The inverse colors icon next to the color selection boxes switches foreground and background color values as they are applied by tools. The default colors icon (to the lower left of the color selection boxes) always restores foreground color to black, background to white.

Colors Palette

Pressing F7 displays the Colors palette in Photoshop's workspace. This palette can hold swatches of user-definable colors for later use and has a scratch pad area for mixing custom colors. You can load various color models, such as RGB, HSB, or LAB, and then click and drag the sliders on this palette to create precise colors.

Command Button

The upper left corner of Photoshop palettes, which offers additional options. Commands such as Close, Save Palette, and Delete are located in the command button drop-down list, just as command options are available in Windows programs from the larger command buttons in the upper-left corner. *See Chapter 16.*

Composite Channel

By default, a color composite of a color image is always what you see. When you use the Channels palette to view the separate channels in an RGB image, the main view (the RGB "channel") is referred to as the composite view of the other three.

Composite Controls

An image area pasted on top of an image background must be composited (blended) into the framework of the underlying pixels. Use Composite Controls, located on the Edit menu, to guide the process. Composite Control settings govern the degree of blending (the Opacity) between the two images, the mode (Normal, Color, Multiply, and so on) used to blend the images, and the range of colors being composited in the floating selection or background image. When a floating selection is on an image background, the same kind of modes for blending the selection into the background can be accessed from the Brushes palette (but using the slider on the Brushes palette doesn't offer the full functionality of the Composite Controls). *See also Brushes Palette.*

Contrast

The amount of tonal difference between the shadows, highlights, and midtones in an image. When sharp differences in these values exist, an image is considered to have high contrast. The Adjust submenu's Levels, Curves, and Contrast/Brightness commands all can be used to change the contrast in an image.

Corner Tool

Located on the Paths palette, this tool gives anchor points direction points. Use it also to set the angle between direction lines. *See Anchor Point.*

Cropping Tool

Tool that enables you to marquee-select an image area to be cropped. After the area has been marquee selected, you place the cursor inside the marquee selection and click. The size of the image is reduced and new borders are established from the marquee selection.

Double-clicking on the Cropping Tool calls up a dialog box where the user can set specific dimensions and a resolution for the cropped area. To reset the Cropping tool to *no* specifications after doing this, clear the entry fields in the dialog box (leave each field blank, do not leave a 0!).

Another way to crop an image is to use the Rectangular Marquee tool in combination with the **E**dit, Crop command.

Curves Command

Accessed from the **A**djust submenu, Curves gives you a graph that represents the tonal scale of an image. You can select points in the graph to accentuate or diminish specific tonal values, or shape the graph into a curve to change the tonal "landscape" of an image. The black and white points in an image can be adjusted here. *See Chapter 6.*

Define Pattern Command

An image area selected by using the Rectangular Marquee tool can be defined as a pattern that can be used by the **E**dit, **F**ill command and the Paint Bucket tool as "paint," or by the Rubber Stamp tool as an area to sample from. *See Chapter 9.*

Defringe Command

Located on the Select menu, Defringe removes edge pixels from a floating selection area, replacing them with pixels that contain colors found in the floating image but not in the fringe area that contains color from the background image. You can specify the number of edge pixels Defringe should remove from a selection (1 or 2 is usually best), which is useful when a selection is Anti-Aliased.

Direction Lines, Points

Properties of Anchor points. Direction lines indicate the flow of Path segments between Anchor points in a Path; direction points are at the end of these direction lines. You can click and drag direction points to change the curve of a Path segment, but only when the Path segment is curved.

Distort Command

Located in the Image, Effects submenu. Places a rectangle around the selection area, enabling you to reshape and reproportion the contents of a selection area by manipulating the rectangle. As the selection area is stretched or changed, Photoshop interpolates "in-between" pixels' values and helps create a smooth transition in areas in which the selection has been distorted. *See Chapter 10.*

Dithering

The arranging of pixels, either in an image or on the monitor, to simulate more colors than are available in a file format or viewing mode. A diffusion dither pattern, displayed by using a PC's 256-color-enabled video driver, provides a soft yet inaccurate view of a 16.7 million color image. *Chapter 2 contains examples of dithered images.*

Dodge/Burn Tool

Editing tool on the toolbox that affects the lightness of the area over which you drag the tool. Dodging an area lightens it, burning an area darkens it. The dual-functionality of this single tool can be set or changed by holding down the Alt key while editing, or by double-clicking the tool to get a dialog box where specifications may be chosen.

Duotone

A patented process for printing a grayscale image using different colored inks to represent different tonal values of the image. (Tritones and Quadtones are variations of the concept.) Photoshop ships with premade samples of density curves of different inks as they'd be used to create a Duotone. The information necessary for the printer to control the placement of the different colored inks is written in the PostScript language. You can view a Duotone on-screen, but you can save the file only in the PSD, EPS, or RAW file formats, which preserve the Duotone printing instructions. *See Chapter 20.*

Effects Submenu

Accessed from the Image menu, this submenu includes the Distort, Skew, Perspective, and Scale options. You can stretch or shrink a selected image area by clicking and dragging on a corner of the Effects boundary box that encloses your selection. To make an effect permanent, click inside the Effects box to confirm your Effects manipulations. A selection area to which you apply an Effect remains a selection until you click outside the marquee selection border. Effects are not the same as the many *special* effects you can add to an image through the Filter menu, and are located in a different menu.

Elliptical Marquee Tool

A selection tool located in Photoshop's toolbox. Use the Alt, Shift, and Ctrl keys in combination with click+diagonal dragging to change the way this tool draws the elliptical selection. Double-clicking on the Elliptical Marquee tool displays an Options box where you can specify a Feathering radius for the tool to use when making selections, or you can set the tool to make only selections with a specific aspect ratio or a specific height and width, measured in pixels.

EPS

The acronym for Encapsulated PostScript, an Adobe Systems invention. EPS image files typically hold object information (vector information) and are small; they contain information about how the image should be rasterized to a printer or a monitor. Vector EPS images are not bitmap-type files, but they become bitmaps when you open an EPS image file in Photoshop. When you open an EPS image in Photoshop, you are asked to specify the size, resolution, and image type to which the EPS file should be rasterized.

EPS files may also be created to hold bitmapped information, as opposed to the more common vector information. These files can be quite large, and are often unecessary because there are so many other native bitmap file formats (like TIFs) that are almost universally supported by applications and operating platforms.

Equalize Command

Located on the Map submenu of the Image menu. Equalizing an image redistributes the brightness values in the image so that the image has an almost even distribution of values across the entire tonal range. Equalizing a dull photo makes it display more contrast, but equalizing an average image may produce an unpleasant effect.

Eraser Tool

Located in Photoshop's toolbox, the Eraser tool removes foreground image areas to reveal background color. Its size is fixed, unlike other painting or editing tools which use the Brushes palette for tip-size adjustments. When you press the Alt key, the Eraser becomes a Magic Eraser and removes the current layer of image to reveal image information about the last-saved version of the image. Beware—double-clicking on this tool erases the *entire* active image window!

Export Command

Amiga HAM, Adobe Illustrator AI file formats, and EPS JPEG images can be made of your bitmap-type work in Photoshop. The Export command is a collection of filters that make a copy of your image that's readable in these other formats.

Eye Icon

Small symbols to the left of the Channel titles on the Channels palette. It toggles on and off like its companion icon, the pencil icon. This symbol enables the user to turn on and shut off channel views of an RGB, Grayscale, or other multichannel document. The use of the switchable channel views by using the eye icon is invaluable when a user wants to edit (create a change) to an Alpha channel, but needs to *view* from a different channel. The eye icon is a toggling function. *See also Pencil Icon.*

Eyedropper Tool

Located in Photoshop's toolbox. This tool is useful for sampling a color in an image so that you can paint with that color. Clicking over an image area with this tool makes the color you've clicked over Photoshop's foreground color. Pressing Alt and clicking over an image area with the Eyedropper sets Photoshop's background color. To access the Eyedropper function while using a painting tool, hold down the Alt key. The Eyedropper may also be toggled to from other commands, like the Levels and Curves commands, and is always used to "pick up" a color or tonal value from within an active image window.

Feather Command

Located on the Select menu. Feathering creates a user-definable area both inside and outside a selection area. When a copy of a selection is placed in another image, Feathering makes transition pixels inside and outside the selection border blend smoothly from one color value to another. *Unlike* Anti-Aliasing, feathering causes visible loss of image detail.

Filling

One of Photoshop's two basic paint applications, filling consists of applying color to an enclosed area. The Fill command, located on the Edit menu and the Paths palette's command-button drop-down list, is used to fill an area enclosed by pixels with a solid color or pattern you have previously defined. The Paint Bucket tool can also fill an enclosed area.

Film Recorder

A device commonly found at a service bureau that takes digital information and displays it line by line on a small monitor (CRT) within the recorder. The light from the CRT exposes the film, and thereby transfers the digital display to the photographic film. This is how you can have your Photoshop images turned into slides or film negatives. *For more information about this process, see Chapter 21.*

Filters

Accessed from the Filter menu, filters are modules that apply special effects such as Blurring or Embossing to an image area. Several filters come with Photoshop; many more are available from third-party manufacturers. Many filters distort areas three-dimensionally, whereas the Effects submenu options (Distort, Perspective, and so on) provide more common two-dimensional effects.

Flip Command

Accessed from the Image menu, this command flips an image area horizontally or vertically. The Flip command essentially does mirroring.

Float Command

Located on the Select menu, Float makes a selection "float" above the background that it was part of before you selected it. What's underneath the floating selection? A copy of that selection area, still in place in the image.

Function Keys

Keys on the keyboard, numbered from F1 to F12. Photoshop has defined some of these keys for you to use as short cuts to access the Photoshop palettes, display Photoshop Help (press F1 for general help or Shift+F1 for context-sensitive help), or rearrange your windows display.

Gamma

The measurement of contrast in the midtones of an image. Images have black points and white points in their *tonal ranges* (the way brightness is measured). Between these two points is a range of brightness (the *midtone range*) that contains valuable visual detail. Gamma adjustment is done by increasing or decreasing only this midtone range. An overly brilliant image, such as a PhotoCD file, has a higher gamma than the PC's optimal 1.8 value. Television sets have a gamma of 2.2, which is why PhotoCD images look better on them without adjustment. Gamma can be controlled in an image through the Levels or Curves commands, which enable you to decide on the overall brightness and contrast a picture displays. Gamma for your monitor, which is *different* than image gamma, is adjusted from the File, Preferences, Monitor setup menu.

Gamut

The possible range of color values in an image. TrueColor, 24-bit images have a gamut of 16.7 million colors. Also the range of color that a color printer or a commercial press can accurately produce. Color printers and presses have a narrower gamut than 24-bit TrueColor images because they can't reproduce as many colors as your eye can see or your monitor can show.

General Preferences

To access this set of options, press Ctrl+K. Enables you to specify the operating parameters and defaults that Photoshop uses. Options include the way interpolation is performed, how an image is dithered when the amount of colors in the image exceeds the capability of the PC's video driver, and whether Photoshop should beep when it finishes an action.

Gradient Tool

Toolbox tool used for applying Gradient fills (either radial or linear) to a selection area of an image. Gradient fills make a gradual, smooth transition between the foreground and background colors you select with the Color Picker, Eyedropper tool, or Colors palette. To access options for applying a Gradient fill, double-click on the Gradient tool button on the toolbox. (In other applications, Gradient fills are called *color ramps* and *Fountain fills*.)

Grayscale Image

An 8-bit image that can hold as many as 256 different tonal densities to make up the image. Grayscales have "color," in that they are different shades of black, but no color other than the various intensities of black in a grayscale can be used. Grayscale is a mode (accessed from the Mode submenu) and an image type, not a file format for images. A Grayscale is considered a separate entity from an Indexed color-image type, even though it contains only 256 unique shades. You must convert a Grayscale image to RGB or another mode before you add color to it or perform some other kinds of actions on it.

Grow Command

Located under the Select menu. Typically used in combination with the Magic Wand tool. After you select a certain range of color pixels in an image with the Magic Wand, use the Grow command to include color pixels adjacent to the original selection also. The Grow command uses the same Tolerance value for selecting color pixels as the Magic Wand tool.

Halftone

A collection of dots arranged in a line to simulate variations in tones found in Grayscale and other continuous-tone images. These lines of halftone dots compose a line screen that, viewed from a distance, respresents a grayscale image by using patterns of black and white visual information. A PostScript printer is capable of generating halftone dot screens. Photoshop can generate custom halftone screens at printing time, and a user can apply a halftone screen to an image when the image is in bit-map mode, which converts image information to black and white only. Some scanners can directly convert a grayscale to halftone. Color halftones are used to print TrueColor images; one halftone screen is used for each of the four process colors.

Hand Tool

Located on the toolbox. You can use this tool instead of clicking on and dragging a scroll bar next to an image window. Double-click on this tool's button on the toolbox to display the active image window as a full view, without the image window's scroll bars.

Header Information

Unreadable by humans, this information is computer code at the beginning of a file that tells the program reading a file what to do with the data the file contains.

HiColor

Type of image that can contain up to 32,768 unique colors (16 bit depth). A HiColor image is not a TrueColor image, which is 24 bits in depth. HiColor was developed as an offering from scanner and video card manufacturers to create color image files that are smaller than TrueColor, yet retain a semblance of real world photographic color. HiColor images are read by Photoshop as being RGB images (5 Red, 6 Green, and 5 Blue bits of channel information) instead of Indexed color, although Photoshop itself does not create HiColor image types. *See also TrueColor.*

Histogram

A mapped representation of the tonal values of all the pixels that make up a selected image. The Levels command offers a histogram of an image before and after you change its brightness mapping. The Histogram command on the Edit menu offers you the *present* mapping of the brightness in an image, in addition to other file information.

HSB Color

A color model used to express the color components of an image. (HSB stands for Hue, Saturation, and Brightness.) This is perhaps the easiest color model to work with and understand in Photoshop. RGB, LAB, and CMYK are other color models used to describe color.

Hue

The essence of a color. Hue is the primary component the human eye recognizes; it is shaded by Saturation and Brightness. Technically, hue is the wavelength of a particular color expressed as light reflected from or passed through a physical object.

Image Format

Images must be saved as files when you finish working with them. A file format is an agreed-upon method for organizing and storing information that describes the image. Different formats can store different amounts of color information; some formats can store additional information, such as paths and Alpha channels. *See also BMP, PCX, PSD, TGA, and TIF.*

Image Size

Expressed as a relationship between an image's dimensions and the number of pixels/inch (image resolution) in which the image is created. Without altering an image in any way, decreasing the image's dimensions increases its resolution.

Image Type

Images are evaluated by bit depth. In Photoshop, a grayscale image has an 8-bit depth and (because of its bit depth) is capable of having 256 shades of color. An RGB image has a 24-bit depth and can have as many as 16.7 million colors in its composition. Image types ultimately are saved to an image-file format. To maintain a faithful copy of your original image, you must match an image type with a suitable image format. *See Chapter 1 for a discussion of Image Types.*

Indexed Color

A type of image, not an image format. Indexed color images use a lookup table (or color palette) to map the color to the image when it is saved or viewed. Indexed color images must be converted to an RGB image type before the full set of Photoshop tools can be used on them. The BMP and PCX file formats are good ones for storing an Indexed color image because the file's header information is small, typically limited to 256 colors.

Info Palette

Accessed by pressing F8. Displays information about the color makeup of pixels under the cursor. It also displays information about the cursor's position on the screen and can report the measurements of a rectangular selection area.

Interpolation

The action Photoshop takes to create smooth transitions in the mapping of bit information (bitmapping) to pixels when a user has stretched or applied another effect to a digital image. Photoshop can use several different mathematical means to calculate and average differences between pixel colors, then assign pixels new values that are adjacent to the border or area to which an Effect has been applied.

Inverse Command

Located on the **S**elect menu, this command reverses the current selection so that it encompasses everything except the original area selected.

Invert Command

Chosen from the **I**mage, **M**ap menus, or by pressing Ctrl+I, this command creates a negative of the selected image area. It is very useful for making masks into selections in Alpha channels. *Not* to be confused with the Inverse command.

JPEG

A file format and a lossey compression scheme developed by the Joint Photographer's Experts Group. Photoshop can save a large RGB image to a *.JPG file extension, retain most of the image's visual information, and compress the file from 5 to 100 times smaller than the size of the original file. *See Lossey. Also see Chapter 2.*

LAB Color

LAB is both a color model and an image type. As a color model, it defines color mathematically. This allows any properly calibrated device that understands the LAB model to faithfully reproduce color. It is also an image type found on the Mode menu. LAB images are 24-bit images with three channels. The L channel contains luminance information, the A channel contains hue information in the green to magenta range, and the B channel contains hue information from blue to yellow. The LAB image type is used by Photoshop as an intermediate type used when converting RGB images to CMYK. Images in the LAB format are especially useful when printing to a color Postscript Level 2 device.

Lasso Tool

A freehand selection tool on the toolbox. With this tool, your selection activity with the mouse is unconstrained, and the selection shape you can define is unlimited. The Alt, Shift, and Ctrl key combinations add options to your selecting work. Double-click on the tool's button to set a Feathering radius and an Anti-Alias option for this tool.

Level Command

Similar in function to the Curves command, it is accessed from the Adjust menu. With this command, you can remap (redistribute) the brightness values in an image by specifying a new black point, white point, and midpoint. The Auto option performs this function quite well to optimize visual detail in an image 90 percent of the time. You can also save a Levels setting and apply the same values to other images by using the Levels dialog box.

Line Tool

Located on the toolbox, this tool is used for drawing lines and editing masks. Arrow heads and line width can be defined for lines by double-clicking on the Line tool button before you draw a line.

Load Settings

A button, as well as a command; found several places in Photoshop. If you've saved a setting in any of the Adjust dialog boxes, click on the Load button in the dialog box to retrieve the

settings. If you want a different set of tips for the Brushes palette, you Load a different set from the command button drop-down list on the palette.

Lossey

Term used to describe an image file-compression scheme in which some of the color information is thrown away when an image is saved. The viewer typically is unaware that lossey compression has been performed on an original image file because the "lost" image data areas are extremely subtle, and mostly unimportant to the human eye. You cannot (and should not) use a lossey compression scheme to save spreadsheets, however!

Lossless

Used to describe a compression scheme in which no data is lost. Typically performed by ARJ, PKZIP, and LZW compression utilities, image or other types of data are copied, and the copy consists of all original data "shorthanded" where redundant segments of code occur. Depending on the complexity of the data, lossless compression schemes can result in a copy of a file that is anywhere from the same size, to a fraction of the original's. Lossless compression typically involves a decompression scheme to make the data readable again, so the file cannot be accessed in real time.

Magic Wand Tool

A tool that selects image areas based on color values, not geometric proportions or properties. To set the Magic Wand's Tolerance (the range) of color pixels it selects, double-click on the tool button.

Marquee Selection

The act of clicking and dragging the cursor diagonally in an image window when a tool is active. You can marquee-select an image area, or you can marquee-zoom into an image. Also refers to a selection with little moving dotted lines or *marquee lines* running around it. Marquee lines or marquee selection borders serve as visual indicators that an area is selected. To turn off the display of the lines and borders without deactivating the selection, choose Hide Edges from the Select menu (or press Ctrl+H).

Masking

Protecting an image area from changes you may apply to the rest of the image. An area outside an active selection border is considered Masked. Photoshop's Quick Mask feature can display a Masked area with an editable color tint when this option is chosen from the Masking Options dialog box by double-clicking the Quick Mask tool button. The advantage of displaying a mask in Quick Mask mode over describing an area as a marquee selection, is that you can edit the selection area with both painting and selection tools.

Masking, Partial

An area in an Alpha channel that is not completely black or white. When a partial mask selection is Loaded (from the Select, Load Selection command), it does not completely select or protect an image area in the RGB composite view, so changes within this area are only partially executed. Partial masks are most commonly created by assigning an Alpha channel to an image, then painting a shade of gray into the channel. A partial mask is not created by marquee-selecting an area then saving it through the Select, Save Selection command; rather, a complete mask is a result of this action.

Partial masks are good for creating subtle shadows in the composite view of an image.

Merging Channels

Command option located on the Channels palette's drop-down list. It fuses channels that have been split into separate files back into one image file. An advanced Photoshop feature; the process involves loss of image quality and therefore should be used infrequently.

Mode

Used to refer to the toolbox functions, Mode can be an editing view, as in Quick Mask or Standard mode, or a Display mode, as in full-screen or scroll-bar mode. When used in reference to **I**mage/Calculate, or Composite Controls, mode refers to the way one image is templated over another to form a blend of the two. Also, the Brushes palette uses the word mode in assigning painting attributes to paint application tools, which are the same (Lighten, Darken, Dissolve, and so on) as the mode options for compositing and/or calculating. More confusing still, a **M**ode menu item describes the color model and color capability of an image (as in Indexed Color, RGB color, Grayscale).

Model

Term used to describe a chart, map, or set of specifications for something that doesn't physically exist. A model then enables you to work with these nonphysical specifications. For example, HSB is a model used to describe color in terms of the relationship between Hue, Saturation, and Brightness. Models represent qualities, but don't necessarily portray them in an accurate, scientific fashion. Working with a model should give you the results you want, however.

Moiré

A visual phenomenon—the result of a pattern laid over a similar pattern at an oblique angle. Right angles (90, 180, 270 degrees) are not oblique; when two patterns are offset at an oblique rotation angle, a visual resonance occurs at irregular intervals when you view the patterns.

Because moiré patterns are to be avoided in four-color process printing, the halftone screens are set at angles mathematically calculated to minimize the moiré pattern effect.

Multichannel Mode

Assigns the channels in color images to unordered ones; that is, the Red, Green, and Blue channels become three numbered, grayscale channels that make up the image. If you accidentally delete a color channel from an RGB image, Photoshop immediately converts the image to Multichannel. Four people on earth understand the practical uses for this mode, and two of them are the Knoll brothers.

Multiple Document Interface

The capability to have more than one image displayed simultaneously on the Photoshop workspace. The acronym commonly seen for this capability is MDI. Many programs do not have this feature.

Opacity

The amount of image that shows through another image before the two are composited together. Opacity controls are located on the Brushes palette and in the Composite Controls dialog box, reached through the Edit menu. Attributing opacity to a pasted-in selection gives the Photoshop user more control over what the dominant elements should be in a composite blend of two images.

Paintbrush Tool

A user-definable tool, with characteristics such as spacing, size, hardness, and angle. Most of these characteristics are set in the Brushes palette.

Paint Bucket Tool

Located on the toolbox, this tool flood-fills an enclosed area with a color or a pattern—both are user-definable. To access the Tolerance setting for the Paint Bucket tool, double-click on the Paint Bucket button. *See Define Pattern, also see Fill.*

Pasting Selections

Photoshop enables you to paste behind, paste into, or paste over a selection area cut or copied from a source into an active document. Pasting produces a floating selection above a background image, which can be placed anywhere in the image. Using the Paste Into or Paste Behind command positions a floating selection in or behind an active selection border in a document. When the pasted piece is deselected, it becomes a part of the area inside the selection border only (Paste Into), or behind the selection border only (Paste Behind).

Paths, Paths Palette

Paths are vector-based "guidelines" the Photoshop user can design into an image. They are visible as they are rasterized to the monitor, but do not print. These vector-based, scaleable segments are connected by anchor points created with the Paths palette Pen tool. The purpose of a Path is not to add an element to the image, but rather to base a selection area on its shape, or to stroke or fill closed path segments with colors or patterns. *See Anchor Point.*

Patterns

Used to describe an image area selected with the Rectangular Marquee tool and applied later by using the Paint Bucket tool, the Rubber Stamp tool, or the **E**dit, **F**ill command. Also describes a collection of Adobe Illustrator (AI format) patterns located in a Photoshop subdirectory. The concept of patterns is to sample one (user-created or supplied by Adobe), use the Define Pattern command to make it an active pattern, then apply the pattern with one of the painting tools. *See Chapter 9.*

PCX File Format

An Indexed color image format originally created by the ZSoft Corporation. The standards for the image format were openly published many years ago, and third-party software manufacturers adopted, refined, and expanded the format. This has led to a state of affairs in which no less than 5 "standards" now exist for the PCX image format, and users are advised to carefully check a host application's capabilities to import a specific "flavor" of PCX file.

Some PCX varieties support 16.7 million colors but are prone to crashing applications that don't understand the complex header information of the image file. The most common variety of PCX image is limited to 256 colors. PCX images are comparatively small in file size, and they are ported to the Macintosh platform fairly effortlessly.

Pen Tool

The tool for rendering Paths. When the Pen tool is selected from the Paths palette, you can click and drag the Pen to create curved path segments between anchor points, or simply click on a progressive number of points to create anchor points that are connected automatically by straight path segments. *See Anchor Point. Also see Chapter 10.*

Pencil Tool

Has nothing to do with the Pen tool. Located on Photoshop's toolbox, the pencil provides hard-edge shapes and lines when the tool is used for coloring an image area. The Pencil is similar to the Paintbrush tool; its Fade-Out option is accessed by double-clicking on its button. To set other Pencil tool characteristics, use the Brushes palette.

Pencil Icon

Has nothing to do with the Pencil tool. This icon is located to the left of a Channel title on the Channels palette. When a user clicks on the Pencil icon, the channel it relates to ceases to be editable, and the pencil disappears from view. Conversely, when the space a Pencil icon would occupy on the Channels palette is clicked on, the Pencil icon reappears, and this particular channel may be edited and changes may be applied to it. *See also Eye Icon.*

Perspective Command

Located on the **I**mage, **E**ffects menu, Perspective enables you to create a three-dimensional effect by two-dimensionally slanting the top, bottom, or sides of a selection toward or away from the viewer. *See also Scale, Skew, and Distort.*

Pixel

The smallest measurement of part of an image, as displayed on a monitor or written as information to a file. The size and shape of a pixel is relative, when measured dimensionally by height and width. The size of a pixel can be measured also by the number of bits of information attached to the pixel (not a relative measurement). If image dimensions are measured in inches and image resolution is measured in pixels per inch, both file size and pixel dimensions will change when you alter image resolution. If image dimensions are measured in pixels, the file size on disk and in memory is determined by the *bit depth* of the pixels; in this case, *pixels per inch* resolution does not affect file size.

PostScript

A trademarked Adobe Systems technology. PostScript allows for smooth rendering of curves during the image printing process. The PostScript descriptor language is responsible for halftone dots as well as on-the-fly typeface rendering with Adobe Type Manager installed on a PC. EPS images cannot be printed to a non-PostScript printer unless the descriptor language that makes up the file has been through an interpreting software, then rasterized so that a non-PostScript printer can understand it.

Similarly, PostScript images don't actually appear on screen. They are nonviewable information files that describe an object rather than depict it. PostScript format images contain a low-resolution graphical header so that users can place the information file in another application's document with a sense of accuracy.

Posterizing

The action of reducing the number of colors in an image to a very small number. Accessed from the **I**mage, **M**ap command, the Posterize option creates a high-contrast image that contains the fixed number of shades you instructed Photoshop to use.

Previewing

In many of the **I**mage, **A**djust dialog boxes, a check mark in the Previews box enables you to see the changes you are making in an image before you click on OK. Previewing works only if you previously checked the **V**ideo LUT Animation option under General Preferences (Ctrl+K) beforehand.

PSD Format

A proprietary Photoshop file format, capable of saving images that are 24-bit in nature, as well as a Duotone image. This is a useful format for imaging individuals to save their work in if an image requires several different Photoshop sessions to complete because the PSD format retains all of a native image's qualities. Very few applications other than Photoshop can make use of a PSD format image, and it is best to save one's work to a more common one, like TIFF, if the image is to port to a different application, or if sent to a service bureau or commercial printer.

Quick Mask/Quick Mask Mode

A mode that enables you to edit a selection area with painting and selection tools. A Quick Mask is temporary; you must choose **S**elect, **S**ave Selection to reuse an area constructed using Quick Mask. You can edit only the mask (not an image) in Quick Mask mode. To find out quickly whether a marquee selection is defining a mask or a selection, click on the Quick Mask button. Quick Mask mode's opposite is Standard mode; the two buttons are next to each other on the toolbox. Double-clicking on the Quick Mask button displays an options dialog box from which you set Mask Options.

Raster

The opposite of vector. Used to describe a class of images composed of colored pixels arranged in an imaginary grid (bitmapped images). EPS images are vector-based, and must be rasterized before printing or viewing. *See Bitmap. Also see Vector Image.*

Rectangular Marquee Tool

Located on the toolbox, this tool produces selections that have right angles. Holding down the Alt, Ctrl, or Shift keys while using this tool modifies its action. Check the status bar for reminders of what the options are. Double-clicking on its button on the toolbox reveals additional options for this tool.

Resolution

The measurement of a bitmap-type image expressed in units per inch. The resolution of scanners is expressed in samples/inch, that of screen images in pixels/inch, and that of printers in dots/inch. Image dimensions are directly affected by resolution, as is image quality.

Revert Command

Changes the present active image back to the way it appeared when you last saved the file. Very useful when you've made a disastrous mistake with your only copy of an image! Also causes you to lose all the work you've done up to the time you choose **F**ile, **R**evert.

RGB Color

The highest-quality color-image type commonly available, an RGB image can define 16.7 million colors for an image. Most of the images on the companion CD are RGB images. Color scanners usually offer only RGB as a color image type. RGB image information is divided into three color channels. RGB images usually are saved in a TIF file format, although TGA is also a good file format for RGB images. An RGB image can also be called a TrueColor image. RGB is also a color model that describes color as being a combination of Red, Green, and Blue components. Monitors use the RGB color model to display color.

Rotate Command

Located in the Image, Effects menu. Features 90-degree rotation, in addition to Arbitrary and Free rotation. With the Arbitrary setting, after you type a whole increment degree value from 1 to 359 in a box, Photoshop automatically rotates the selection by that many degrees. Free rotation enables you to click and drag a rotation box around a selection for greater artistic control. Rotate, like other Photoshop effects and filters, is processor-intensive.

Rubber Stamp Tool

Enables you to take a sample from an area in an image, from a predefined pattern, or from a snapshot of an image, then "clone" the sample into an image area in a brushstroke-like manner. Settings in the Rubber Stamp Options dialog box, accessed by double-clicking on the tool button on the toolbox, determine where the Rubber Stamp gets its sample material and how it uses the sample material.

Rulers

Can be toggled on or off from an active image window's sides by pressing Crtl+R. To set the increments (inches, cm, pixels), choose **F**ile, Pre**f**erences, then Units from the menu bar.

Saturation

The amount of color component in a pixel. A fully saturated pixel displays no gray component (neutral density color). One of the three components in the HSB color model, Saturation is responsible for how "alive" a color value looks. Lack of saturation in a color pixel produces a dull image area that resembles a grayscale image.

Save Selection

From the **S**elect menu, this command saves a selection area to a channel in an active image. Selections contain only 8 bits of visual information (grayscale) and can be used for masking an image area. The Save Selection command automatically numbers selections. Saved selections can be seen, edited, or deleted using controls on the Channels palette.

Scale Command

Like the other **I**mage, **E**ffects commands, Scale enables you to redefine a selection's proportions by clicking on and dragging the corner of an Effects box. Alt, Shift, and Ctrl key combinations add options to the way the Scales command operates.

Selection Border

The edge of a selection, to which the Border, Stroke, Defringe, Feather, and Anti-Aliasing options can be applied. Choosing **S**elect, Hide **E**dges causes the marquee border, which visibly defines a selection border, to become invisible. The inverse of a selection is called a mask.

Selection Tools

The Rectangular Marquee, the Elliptical Marquee, the Lasso, and the Magic Wand are selection tools. The rest of the tools on the toolbox are considered painting and editing tools.

Sharpen Filters

The opposite of the blur filters, sharpen filters increase the contrast between neighboring pixels in an image. The UnSharpen Mask is the most sophisticated sharpen filter, and the one over which the Photoshop user has the most control.

Similar Command

From the **S**elect menu, this command selects nonadjacent pixels in addition to pixels selected earlier with the Magic Wand tool. *See Magic Wand. See also Tolerance.*

Skew Command

Another **I**mage, **E**ffects command, Skew enables you to shift opposite sides of a selection in opposite directions. The Skew command is the desktop publishing equivalent of italicizing a character. It is useful for creating shadows in images.

Smudge Tool

An editing tool located in the toolbox. With no coloring capability of its own, clicking and dragging the Smudge tool in an image area produces an effect similar to pushing wet paint with a finger. The modes on the Brushes palette provide further options that affect the use of the Smudge tool.

Snapshot

An Edit command that loads an extra copy of the active image file into memory so that you can access it indirectly with the Rubber Stamp tool. After you take a Snapshot of an image, you can use the Snapshot as the source from which the Rubber Stamp samples and then clones into the image currently active in the workspace. When you've messed up an image, you can selectively restore it from a Snapshot.

Splitting Channels Command

Accessed from the Channels palette's command-button drop-down list, this command should be used only by professional printing people and imaging experts. The command splits the channels in an RGB or other multichannel image into separate, discrete images. This transforms them and these images cannot be successfully merged back into one image with all the color fidelity of the original.

Stroking

One of Photoshop's two basic paint applications. Strokes are used to create enclosed or open shapes. You can create a Brush stroke with a painting tool, stroke a Path (using the Paths command button option), or stroke a selection (using the Edit command).

System Palette

The Microsoft Windows color model for the Windows environment. Although many programs "hook" into the system palette to create color images, Photoshop offers its own, proprietary Color Picker. You can specify the Windows system palette by selecting it in the **F**ile, Preferences, General Preferences dialog box, but using it deprives you of the many color models Photoshop offers with its Color Picker.

Targa

A high-quality image format used extensively in the television industry. A trademarked technology of the TrueVision Corporation, it is a file format on par in terms of color capability with the Tagged Image File Format (TIFF image). Files saved with the TGA extension may be used only by other applications that "speak" Targa format. An image saved in Targa format has color channels, and may be assigned *one* Alpha channel because the capability of the format is limited to 32 bits. If you save an image with more than one channel and choose 32-bit format, Photoshop will warn you that not all the information can be saved and ask if you want to proceed. If you do, the image becomes unusable by Photoshop or any other application.

Text Tool

Located on the toolbox. When you select the tool and click on an active image space, a dialog box pops up in which you can enter a single character or several lines of type. Upon completion of text entry, click on OK; the text appears as a floating selection in the foreground color specified by the color selection boxes on the toolbar. You can specify font size and type. Font selection is limited to the typefaces, currently active in Windows, that were loaded by Adobe Type Manager (or other Type 1 type managers) or by the TrueType fonts loaded and accessed through Windows' Control Panel. Many other options are available for Text in the Text Tool dialog box.

Threshold Command

Located on the **I**mage, **M**ap menu, Threshold separates all the tonal values in an image into either black or white. You can define the "break point" for exactly which image tonal values go to black or white.

TIFF

The acronym for Tagged Image File Format, originally developed by Aldus Corporation. It is the preferred file format for saving 24-bit, TrueColor RGB images and Grayscales. This format can be read by the Macintosh. An image saved as a TIF file can be manipulated with the complete set of Photoshop tools.

Tolerance

What a user needs to practice when operating under the Microsoft Windows environment. Also, the setting (used with the Paint Bucket, Magic Wand, and other tools) that evaluates the similarity of adjacent, colored pixels in an image, on a scale of 1 to 255. A low Tolerance setting acts upon a narrow range of color differences in pixels adjacent to where you click in an image. A Tolerance setting of 255 includes every pixel in an image, regardless of where you click. Tolerance is set in an options box revealed by double-clicking on a tool. The amount of tolerance that you set depends on the tool being used and what results you want to achieve with the tool. Tolerance is a setting that requires experimenting with on a case-by-case basis.

TrueColor

Also spelled *Truecolor*, and *True Color*. Term used to describe an image in a file format capable of holding 24 bits, or 16.7 million colors. It's derivation comes from the general sentiment that 16.7 million colors is adequate for displaying the true colors found in the real world. It is a descriptive term for an RGB mode image, but it is a popular term, not a technical one, used mostly by manufacturers to indicate the capabilities of a scanner or video card. *See also HiColor.*

TWAIN

Somewhat obscure, whimsical acronym for Toolkit Without An Interesting Name. TWAIN is a source interface that connects a hardware device (usually a scanner) to a Windows application. Every scanner that is TWAIN-compliant ships with software that "handshakes" with TWAIN-aware programs (like Photoshop) and allows the program to host a scanning session directly from the application's workspace. TWAIN interfaces vary from manufacturer to manufacturer, but they are commonly accessed from the File, Acquire menu, so that a user can work, scan, then continue to work from inside a single application. TWAIN is an openly published standard not only for scanners, but also for devices like digital cameras, and future peripherals that manufacturers haven't thought of yet!

Undo Command

Offers users who have made a mistake or changed their minds to "take back" the very last step performed on an image. Ctrl+Z is the shortcut key for Undo. The specific Menu option varies (Edit, Undo...), depending on the last effect or coloring done to an image. The Undo command is useless if you want to "take back" a step executed *several* steps ago.

Unit Preferences

Located on the File, Preferences menu, this dialog box enables you to specify increments for measuring an image. Centimeters, pixels, and inches all may be specified. The specified units are used by the Rulers feature, the Image Size, and Canvas Size commands.

Variations

Accessed from the **I**mage, **A**djust menu, the Variations command displays several thumbnails of an image with different color casts applied to it. For instance, you can specify more Green or less Magenta for an image selection area or the entire image. More and less saturation can be applied in three tonal regions of an image. Variations also displays clipping, the *only* warning that Photoshop ever provides the user before performing a change that causes an image area to exceed 100 percent density, lightness, or color saturation.

Vector Image

A type of computer graphic that is fundamentally different in construction than the bitmapped-type images Photoshop works with. Vector images are resolution-independent, object-oriented constructions, made up of mathematical information relating to degrees of arcs, relative positions and numbers of objects built, line width and color, and closed line fill. These information files carry incredibly precise image information, and because they are not built from an imaginary grid with square dots of color in them (like bitmaps), they require rasterizing in order to see them on a monitor and print them as hard copy. A vector type computer graphic can be saved in an EPS (Encapsulated PostScript) file format.

Window Mode

Three buttons at the very bottom of the toolbox display different views of the active image window. The button on the left (the default) displays an image with scroll bars and a view of Photoshop's workspace, when the image is small enough. The middle button removes an active image's scroll bars. The view is less visually cluttered, but you must then use the Hand tool to view different image areas at higher viewing resolutions. The button on the right removes Photoshop's menu palettes *and* window scroll bars.

(Control+)Z

A lifesaving command you will want to familiarize yourself with. This is the hot key for the **U**ndo command, which undoes your last editing, painting, or effects move, depending on the error.

Zoom Tool

The button marked with a magnifying glass on the toolbox, used for viewing an image at different screen resolutions. You can marquee-zoom, by clicking on the Zoom tool and dragging it diagonally, or press Alt and click on it to magnify your view. Double-clicking on the Zoom tool button displays an active image at a 1:1 resolution. Press Alt and click to zoom out by a resolution factor of 2.

ZZZZZZZ

The expression typically found in a speech balloon of a cartoon character to express Sleeping or Fatigue Mode. Also applicable to readers who may have read this glossary in one fell swoop. Also applicable to the authors and editors at this time.

INDEX

INDEX

INDEX

INDEX

INDEX

INDEX

INDEX

INDEX

INDEX

INDEX

INDEX

INDEX

INDEX

INDEX

INDEX

INDEX

INDEX

INDEX

INDEX

INDEX

INDEX

INDEX

INDEX

INDEX

The Universal Appeal of Adobe Photoshop

Inside Adobe Photoshop version 2.5 for Windows was originally written for IBM-compatible PC users facing a very robust program that Macintosh users have also been facing.

The Dual-Platform Photoshop CD

The attraction to the de facto image editing program continues to expand to other platforms, and New Riders Publishing wants to make the learning experiences contained in this book as widely accessible as possible. To that end, the root of the *Inside Adobe Photoshop Companion CD* is split into partitions almost identical in content. All the raw materials for completing the chapter assignments are identical because JPEG, TIF, EPS, PCD, and PCX formats can be read by both the Mac and IBM PC.

Unfortunately, the shareware programs contained in the PC partition of the CD were written by MS-DOS and Windows people; even if they were converted to the Mac format, they wouldn't run. However, the CD also contains high-quality freeware images (to the tune of 75 MB), and these images are indeed in both PC and Macintosh format.

For Photoshop users from both platforms, accessing the CD is identical, and we hope you'll use it as a resource for fantastic imaging work.

Slightly Different Photoshop Conventions

Adobe Systems paid careful attention when they designed the MS-Windows version of Photoshop to ensure that the program is as "platform transparent" as possible. In other words, a Macintosh user performs the same moves and commands as the Windows Photoshop user, with one or two exceptions.

The keyboards of Macs and PCs aren't mapped identically, but they are certainly close enough for a Macintosh Photoshop-type person to follow the exercises in this book. This might shock some and please others, but the following is the equivalency chart for Macintosh-to-PC commands while in Photoshop 2.5:

Macintosh to PC Keyboard Equivalencies

Macintosh Key	PC Key
Option	Alt
Command	Ctrl

If you're working with a Mac and this book, don't assume your Control key is equivalent to the IBM PC Ctrl key; it's not— Ctrl(PC users) = Command (Mac users).

Now, this is only for Photoshop, but you can see that it's ridiculously easy to cross platforms and work with the images in the exercises. For instance, the following is a set of steps from an exercise in Chapter 16, "PC Photoshop Language":

Press Alt and click on the background area in the LAURIE.TIF image	Samples another color from the image
Release the Alt key, then click on the scratch pad area on the Colors palette	Applies dot of color sampled with the Eyedropper tool

The Macintosh translation is as follows:

Press Option and click on the background area in the LAURIE.TIF image	Samples another color from the image
Release the Option key, then click on the scratch pad area on the Colors palette	Applies dot of color sampled with the Eyedropper tool

That's it!

Oh, and the PC version of PS 2.5 comes with a Custom Brushes Palette, which the Macintosh version calls a Patterns Palette, in case there's any confusion when you get to Chapter 4, "Setting Photoshop's Defaults and Options."

Platform-Independent Experience

The exercises in these chapters were designed with a twofold purpose; to show how effects are created, and to familiarize the reader with commands so they eventually become second-nature. When you can intuitively know which tool or effect to use in Photoshop, you're no longer bound to a specific computer platform. Whether you use a Mac or PC, the proof is in the pixel—great imaging work begins with your own concept. Use *Inside Photoshop* as your guide to learning, then reinforcing the skills you want, and you'll find that there are more similarities than differences when it comes to computer graphics on the top two operating platforms.

"Dollar for Dollar and Pound for Pound,
Pixar One Twenty Eight is the Best."
-Scott Hamlin
Contributing Editor, Corel Magazine

Why is Pixar One Twenty Eight the best collection of photographic textures available on CD-ROM?

Because...
- ...each of the 128 textures was created by a professional photographer and designed specifically for use in production quality digital imaging.
- ...the texture collection incorporates a patented technology which allows the textures to be tiled seamlessly.
- ...seamlessly tiling smaller images offers the quality expected from much larger ones, saving both valuable time and disk space.
- ...each 512x512, 24 bit texture can be tiled to fit any area up to 4000 x 4000, or 300 dpi at 13.3" x 13.3".
- ...the CD includes a handy Photoshop compatible plug-in which allows you to automatically and seamlessly tile a texure into any area.
- ...the textures can be used as backgrounds or as materials for mapping into 3D graphics.
- ...the textures can be used with any application that reads PICT or TIFF files on Mac, Windows or UNIX machines.
- ...the best, most versatile, collection of high-quality photographic textures is available at the incredible price of

$99 for Adobe Photoshop Users!!

Don't Miss this Great Offer - Order Today!

Please mention "Inside Adobe Photoshop for Windows" when ordering.

By phone: call Pixar at **800-888-9856** or 510-236-4000
By fax: fax this form to 510-236-0388
By mail: mail this form to Pixar, 1001 W. Cutting Blvd, Richmond, CA 94804

Name _____

Company _____

Address _____ City _____ State _____ Zip _____

Phone _____

☐ Visa   ☐ Master Card   ☐ Am. Exp.

Card # _____

Signature _____

Exp. Date _____

Item	Retail	Special	Total
Pixar One Twenty Eight CD	$299	$99	
CA residents add sales tax			
Add $7 Shipping - US only			
		TOTAL	

GO AHEAD. PLUG YOURSELF INTO
PRENTICE HALL COMPUTER PUBLISHING.

Introducing the PHCP Forum on CompuServe®

Yes, it's true. Now, you can have CompuServe access to the same professional, friendly folks who have made computers easier for years. On the PHCP Forum, you'll find additional information on the topics covered by every PHCP imprint—including Que, Sams Publishing, New Riders Publishing, Alpha Books, Brady Books, Hayden Books, and Adobe Press. In addition, you'll be able to receive technical support and disk updates for the software produced by Que Software and Paramount Interactive, a division of the Paramount Technology Group. It's a great way to supplement the best information in the business.

WHAT CAN YOU DO ON THE PHCP FORUM?

Play an important role in the publishing process—and make our books better while you make your work easier:

- Leave messages and ask questions about PHCP books and software—you're guaranteed a response within 24 hours

- Download helpful tips and software to help you get the most out of your computer

- Contact authors of your favorite PHCP books through electronic mail

- Present your own book ideas

- Keep up to date on all the latest books available from each of PHCP's exciting imprints

JOIN NOW AND GET A FREE COMPUSERVE STARTER KIT!

To receive your free CompuServe Introductory Membership, call toll-free, **1-800-848-8199** and ask for representative **#597**. The Starter Kit Includes:

- Personal ID number and password

- $15 credit on the system

- Subscription to CompuServe Magazine

HERE'S HOW TO PLUG INTO PHCP:

Once on the CompuServe System, type any of these phrases to access the PHCP Forum:

GO PHCP   **GO BRADY**
GO QUEBOOKS   **GO HAYDEN**
GO SAMS   **GO QUESOFT**
GO NEWRIDERS   **GO PARAMOUNTINTER**
GO ALPHA

Once you're on the CompuServe Information Service, be sure to take advantage of all of CompuServe's resources. CompuServe is home to more than 1,700 products and services—plus it has over 1.5 million members worldwide. You'll find valuable online reference materials, travel and investor services, electronic mail, weather updates, leisure-time games and hassle-free shopping (no jam-packed parking lots or crowded stores).

Seek out the hundreds of other forums that populate CompuServe. Covering diverse topics such as pet care, rock music, cooking, and political issues, you're sure to find others with the sames concerns as you—and expand your knowledge at the same time.

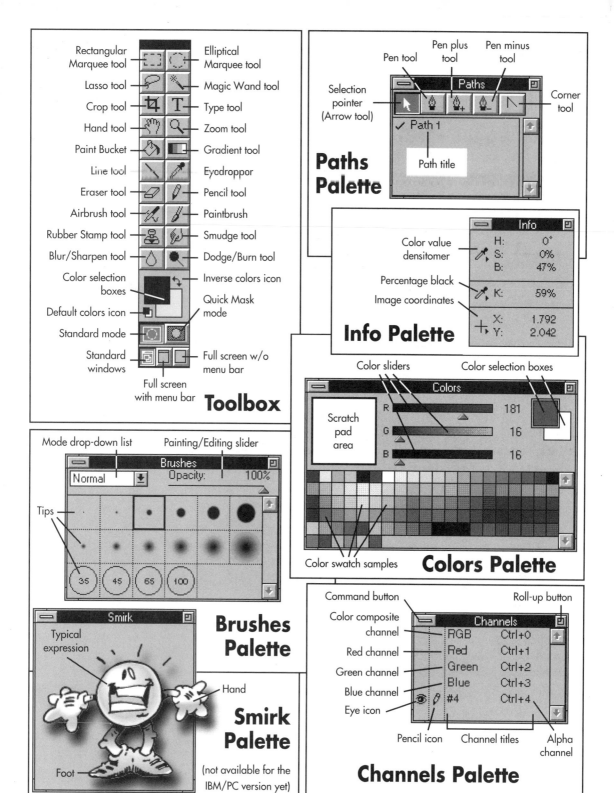

Toolbox

Rectangular Marquee tool	Elliptical Marquee tool
Lasso tool	Magic Wand tool
Crop tool	Type tool
Hand tool	Zoom tool
Paint Bucket	Gradient tool
Line tool	Eyedropper
Eraser tool	Pencil tool
Airbrush tool	Paintbrush
Rubber Stamp tool	Smudge tool
Blur/Sharpen tool	Dodge/Burn tool
Color selection boxes	Inverse colors icon
Default colors icon	Quick Mask mode
Standard mode	
Standard windows	Full screen w/o menu bar
Full screen with menu bar	

Paths Palette

- Selection pointer (Arrow tool)
- Pen tool
- Pen plus tool
- Pen minus tool
- Corner tool
- ✓ Path 1
- Path title

Info Palette

- Color value densitometer
- Percentage black
- Image coordinates

H:	0°
S:	0%
B:	47%
K:	59%
X:	1.792
Y:	2.042

Brushes Palette

- Mode drop-down list
- Painting/Editing slider
- Tips

Normal   Opacity: 100%

35 45 65 100

Colors Palette

- Color sliders
- Color selection boxes
- Scratch pad area
- Color swatch samples

R	181
G	16
B	16

Smirk Palette

- Typical expression
- Hand
- Foot

(not available for the IBM/PC version yet)

Channels Palette

- Command button
- Roll-up button
- Color composite channel
- Red channel
- Green channel
- Blue channel
- Eye icon
- Pencil icon
- Channel titles
- Alpha channel

RGB	Ctrl+0
Red	Ctrl+1
Green	Ctrl+2
Blue	Ctrl+3
#4	Ctrl+4